MANAGING ORGANIZATIONAL CHANGE

Roy McLennan

PRENTICE HALL, ENGLEWOOD CLIFFS, NEW JERSEY 07632

McLennan, Roy.
    Managing organizational change / Roy McLennan.
        p.   cm.
    ISBN 0-13-551508-4 :
    1. Organizational change—Management.   I. Title.
HD58.8.M35 1988
658.4′06—dc19

Editorial/production supervision
  and interior design: Carolyn Kart
Cover design: Joel Mitnick Design
Manufacturing buyer: Ed O'Dougherty

To Felicity, Rebecca, Kate and Peter, for putting up with me writing books.

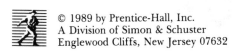 © 1989 by Prentice-Hall, Inc.
A Division of Simon & Schuster
Englewood Cliffs, New Jersey 07632

Printed in the United States of America

10 9 8 7 6 5 4 3 2 1

0-13-551508-4

Prentice-Hall International (UK) Limited, *London*
Prentice-Hall of Australia Pty. Limited, *Sydney*
Prentice-Hall Canada Inc., *Toronto*
Prentice-Hall Hispanoamericana, S.A., *Mexico*
Prentice-Hall of India Private Limited, *New Delhi*
Prentice-Hall of Japan, Inc., *Tokyo*
Simon & Schuster Asia Pte. Ltd., *Singapore*
Editora Prentice-Hall do Brasil, Ltda., *Rio de Janeiro*

CONTENTS

———❖———

PREFACE   xiii

    **A Note on Tavistock Work on Organizational Change,
Roy McLennan**   1

PART ONE: APPROACHES TO MANAGING ORGANIZATIONAL CHANGE

1 THE HISTORY OF MANAGING ORGANIZATIONAL CHANGE

    Introduction   4

EXPERIENCES:

    Maclaurin and MIT (A), Roy McLennan   6

    Maclaurin and MIT (B), Roy McLennan   9

    Maclaurin and MIT (C), Roy McLennan   14

    **Organization Development Begins at Lakeside,
Robert R. Blake & Jane S. Mouton**   19

    The R & D Department, William G. Dyer   21

    The Fairview Company, Edgar H. Schein   23

MODELS & SCHEMES:

    **A Brief History of Organization Development,
Wendell L. French and Cecil H. Bell Jr.**   26

    The Historical Perspective, Michael Foster   34

The Emergence of Humanistic Philosophy in Management
and Organizations, Newton Margulies and
Anthony P. Raia   39

Aspects of the Professional Facilitation of Planned Change,
Eric Trist   42

2 ORGANIZATION MODELS AND INTERVENTION METHOD

Introduction   46

EXPERIENCES:

Organizational Profile Exercise, Rensis Likert   49

Plant Z (A), Robert H. Guest et al.   52

Plant Z (B), Robert H. Guest et al.   58

Hovey & Beard Company, Part 1, Alex Bavelas and
George Strauss   62

The Action Company, Edgar H. Schein   63

MODELS & SCHEMES:

The "Rational" and "Natural-System" Models of
Organizational Analysis, Paul R. Lawrence et al.   65

Two Universal Models, Jay W. Lorsch and Steven Trooboff 68

Culture, Elliott Jaques   76

A Formal Definition of Organization Culture,
Edgar H. Schein   77

Structure vs. Process, Edgar H. Schein   80

A Contingency Model of Consultation, Newton Margulies
and Anthony P. Raia   82

The Role of the Consultant: Content Expert or Process
Facilitator?, Edgar H. Schein   83

Organizational Development and Industrial Democracy,
Eric J. Miller   91

The Relation of the "Pure" and the "Applied" to the
"Professional Model" in the Social Sciences, Council of
the Tavistock Institute of Human Relations   93

The Different Kinds of Knowledge Makers,
F. J. Roethlisberger   95

3 ORGANIZATION DEVELOPMENT, ACTION RESEARCH AND THE INTERVENTION MODEL

Introduction   100

EXPERIENCES:

Investigation of a Change, Roy McLennan   103

Values and Assumptions of Organization Development:
A Questionnaire, Roy McLennan   104

The HLW Department, William G. Dyer   108

Goodyear New Zealand Limited (A), Roy McLennan   110

Matheson Electronics Company, Roy McLennan   120

Atlantis Supermarkets, Roy McLennan   124

MODELS & SCHEMES:

Applied Organization Change in Industry, Harold J. Leavitt   128

Common Approaches to Change, Larry E. Greiner   138

What is Organization Development? Richard Beckhard   141

Action Research and Planned Change, Don Bryant   146

Definition of Action Research, Gerald I. Susman and
Roger D. Evered   148

Action Research, Frank P. Sherwood   151

Action Research as Applied to Organization Development,
Mark A. Frohman, Marshall Sashkin, and
Michael J. Kavanagh   153

Phases in Action-Research OD, Mark A. Frohman et al.   155

The Intervention Model, Roy McLennan   161

Interviewing, Marshall Sashkin and William C. Morris   167

Interviewing, Jack K. Fordyce and Raymond Weil   172

PART TWO: INTERACTION AND INTERVENTION

4 RESISTANCE AND THE PROCESS OF CHANGE

Introduction   175

EXPERIENCES:

**The Tremont Hotel Project: How We Began,
William Foote Whyte and Edith Lenz Hamilton**   177

The Retail Chain, Jack K. Fordyce and Raymond Weil   183

WMBA and Channel 12, William G. Dyer   189

The Washbourne Office, Roy McLennan   192

MODELS & SCHEMES:

The Psychology of Resistance to Change, Don Bryant   193

Resistance to Change, Paul R. Lawrence   196

Dealing With Resistance, Peter Block   199

**The Effect of Group Decision on Subsequent Behavior,
Paul R. Lawrence and John A. Seiler**   205

**Participation in Decision-Making and Work Group
Productivity, Paul R. Lawrence and John A. Seiler**   207

Planned Change Theory, Edgar H. Schein   209

Action Research OD Processes, Mark A. Frohman et al.   213

**The Characteristics of Action Research, Michael Peters
and Viviane Robinson**   216

5 GATHERING DATA: WATCHING, INTERVIEWING, USING GROUPS AND QUESTIONNAIRES

Introduction   220

EXPERIENCES:

Sherlock, Rick Roskin   222

The Industrial Products Division, David A. Nadler   228

Northeastern Hospital, David A. Nadler   229

MODELS & SCHEMES:

An Introducion to Gathering Data, Edgar H. Schein 233

Structured Naturalistic Observation, D. N. T. Perkins, D. A. Nadler and M. D. Hanlon 237

From "Strategy for Watching", Leonard Schatzman and Anselm L. Strauss 242

Interviewing, Edgar H. Schein 250

Active Listening and Questioning, Marshall Sashkin and William C. Morris 251

Sensing: The Group Interview, Jack K. Fordyce and Raymond Weil 255

The Organization Mirror, Jack K. Fordyce and Raymond Weil 259

Questionnaires and Instruments, Jack K. Fordyce and Raymond Weil 263

Feedback, Floyd C. Mann 265

Designing and Conducting Organizational Surveys, Marshall Sashkin 268

6 *THE USE OF GROUPS TO FACILITATE CHANGE*

Introduction 273

EXPERIENCES:

Group Dynamics Simulation Exercise, David A. Kolb, Irwin M. Rubin, and James M. McIntyre 275

Chemical Engineering Consulting Company, Jack K. Fordyce and Raymond Weil 281

Boyd Consumer Goods Company, Edgar H. Schein 289

MODELS & SCHEMES:

Emerging Principles of Achieving Change, Dorwin Cartwright 292

Group Dynamics, David A. Kolb, Irwin M. Rubin, and James M. McIntyre 297

Task Related Factors Influencing Team Effectiveness,
David A. Kolb, Irwin M. Rubin, and James M. McIntyre   308

The Intergroup Team-Building Meeting, Jack K. Fordyce
and Raymond Weil   312

7   OBSERVATION, INTERACTION AND SUBJECTIVITY

Introduction   317

MODELS & SCHEMES:

Participant Observation, Martin Dodge and Robert Bogdan   319

The Nature of Symbolic Interactionism, Herbert Blumer   323

Naturalistic Enquiry, Norman K. Denzin   327

"Inquiry from the Inside" and "Inquiry from the Outside",
Roger Evered and Meryl Reis Louis   331

The Self-Fulfilling Prophecy, Robert K. Merton   337

Objectivity and Subjectivity, Roy McLennan   340

The Baseline Frame of Reference, Roy McLennan   341

Intersubjectivity, Colin Eden et al.   343

PART THREE: PHASES IN THE INTERVENTION PROCESS

8   EARLY IN THE PROCESS

Introduction   348

EXPERIENCES:

The Le Court Cheshire Home, Eric Miller and
Geraldine Gwynne   350

The Multi Company (A), Edgar H. Schein   361

The Etna Production Company, Edgar H. Schein   366

Changing Your Organization, Roy McLennan   367

MODELS & SCHEMES:

The Client's Problem, Roy McLennan   368

Entering into Relationships, Leonard Schatzman and
Anselm L. Strauss   371

The Entry Problem in Consultation, John C. Glidewell   373

Orientation to the Client, Roy McLennan   379

The Internal Consultant, Robert R. Blake and
    Jane S. Mouton   382

Organizational Diagnosis, Marvin R. Weisbord   384

Selecting a Setting and a Method of Work, Edgar H. Schein   392

The Organization Development Contract Revisited,
    Marvin R. Weisbord   395

9   IN THE MIDST OF THE PROCESS

Introduction   404

EXPERIENCES:

The Torenton Mine (A), James F. Gavin   406

The Multi Company (B), Edgar H. Schein   414

Pan Pacific, Roy McLennan   419

MODELS & SCHEMES:

Structuring Activities in Interventions, Wendell L. French
    and Cecil H. Bell Jr.   420

Models of Consulting, Roy McLennan   422

Argyris's Model 1 and Model 11, Edgar H. Schein   423

The Consultant Role, A. K. Rice   425

It Takes a Group to Understand a Group, Roy McLennan   430

Working Notes, A. K. Rice   433

The Action Research Process, Roy McLennan   435

The Dynamics of Dependency, Roy McLennan   439

Choosing the Depth of Organizational Intervention,
    Roger Harrison   443

10   LATER IN THE PROCESS

Introduction   458

EXPERIENCES:

The Multi Company (C), Edgar H. Schein	460
The Torenton Mine (B), James F. Gavin	464
The Torenton Mine (C), James F. Gavin	468
The Torenton Mine (D), James F. Gavin	470
The Apex Manufacturing Company, Edgar H. Schein	472

MODELS & SCHEMES:

Evaluation of Results and Disengagement, Edgar H. Schein	482
Behavior Changes in Successful Organization Development Efforts, Jerry I. Porras and Susan J. Hoffer	487
Intervention and Historical Process, Roy McLennan	493

CONCLUSION: MANAGING ORGANIZATIONAL CHANGE, VALUES AND SCIENCE

Introduction	499

EXPERIENCES:

The Rushton Quality-of-Work-Life Experiment (A), Melvin Blumberg and Charles D. Pringle	502
The Rushton Quality-of-Work-Life Experiment (B), Melvin Blumberg and Charles D. Pringle	506
Preface to an Intervention, Chris Argyris	508

MODELS & SCHEMES:

Traditional Research Design, Melvin Blumberg and Charles D. Pringle	513
The Involved Helper, Chris Argyris	514
Themes for Collaborative Research, Eric Trist	516
Qualitative Research, Iain Mangham	518
The Organizing Myth in the Social Sciences, W. Gordon Lawrence	521

Ethnographic Versus Clinical Perspective, Edgar H. Schein   **524**

Action Science, Chris Argyris   **526**

**Comparisons of Positivist Science and Action Research,
Gerald I. Susman and Roger D. Evered**   **528**

**Action Research as a Corrective to the Deficiencies of
Positivist Science, Gerald I. Susman and
Roger D. Evered**   **529**

**Two Versions of Action Research, Michael Peters and
Viviane Robinson**   **531**

**Towards a Definition of Action Research, Margarete Hult
and Sven-Åke Lennung**   **534**

Values and OD, Clayton P. Alderfer   **544**

Open-Endedness, Eric J. Miller   **547**

Managing Change, Eric J. Miller   **549**

PREFACE

---•◆•---

This book presents a fresh, intensely practical, yet scientifically based approach to managing organizational change. It offers a range of materials that provide the basis for three distinctive but related learning experiences: a field experience–led classroom course for people who want to become managerial or consultant change agents; a purely classroom-based, realistic course to educate graduate and advanced undergraduates in managing organizational change; and a range of workshops and executive development courses to provide managers with insight and skill in managing organizational change.

The book presents, within the covers of a single volume, an effective, systemic means for the manager to develop the knowledge and skill to be able to manage organizational change by becoming a trained change agent. As such, he or she may continue to work as a manager, using his or her expertise in managing change in a particular enterprise, or, alternatively, become a consultant whose skills are available to a range of organizations that need them.

The second and third purposes are to provide the means to enable the manager, and the student of management, to develop a firm grasp of what managing organizational change entails, and to become able to play a constructive role in leading and contributing to enterprise change efforts.

The Need for Managing Change

Why this book on this subject at this time? Given the stupendous variety of changes affecting large and small enterprises all around the globe, and the sheer pace of change, managing organizational change is surely the very essence of what it is to be a manager in the late twentieth and early twenty-first centuries. Knowledge and skill in managing change is as fundamental to the executive as knowledge and skill in managing money, markets, people, productive resources, and corporate strategy. Managing change is every manager's essential business. It is therefore appropriately the focus of substantial training, study, and commitment.

Yet the impact of change agents trained in the human sciences in bringing about constructive enterprise change has so far been modest in the extreme. Economists surely have vastly greater impact in deliberately setting about to change organizations than applied behavioral scientists do. The situation seems to be much as Mao Ze Dong, a different kind of change agent, referred to in his remark to Henry Kissinger: "I have not been able to change the world. I have only been able to change a few places in the vicinity of Beijing." In the field of managing organizational change there is a world to conquer.

On the presumption that business schools do want to develop effective managers, and don't want to go the way of the dinosaurs, thoroughgoing training in managing organizational change must become an essential, necessary, required component of MBA and MS degree programs, and first degree programs as well. The development of knowledge and skill in the effective management of enterprise change must similarly become the basic content of a comprehensive range of workshops for managers, and an essential, proportionately large element in executive development programs. This book provides a kitbag of learning experiences, concepts, and tools that can fuel such efforts.

Managers, Consultants, and Change Agents

An increase in the number of general managers who are skillful in managing organizational change is highly desirable, and a state to which this book is intended to contribute. A significant slice of the book's emphasis focuses on the manager as his or her own change agent. The change agent may or may not, however, be the manager in the enterprise undergoing planned change: he or she may be a consultant from outside. The-manager-as-change-agent is the exception rather than the rule in this book, as in the world to which it relates. There are role-related and pedagogical reasons why this should be the case.

Two gross considerations are of prime importance in successfully managing organizational change: the location of appropriate knowledge and skill in managing change, on the one hand, and the support of some significant member or members of the hierarchy of the enterprise undergoing change, on the other.[1] Successful, effective organizational change involves bringing these components together: change takes place by mobilizing appropriate knowledge and skill via the enterprise's hierarchy.

Very often the knowledge and skill required resides outside the enterprise, in the head and activities of an applied behavioral scientist who works in some business school, institute, or consultancy. In this common case promulgating change consists of introducing the necessary knowledge and skill to the organization by means of the consultant entering it and working with its members. Sometimes—too infrequently for the good of most enterprises—a

---

[1] This book assumes evolutionary, top-down change, rather than revolutionary, bottom-up change.

highly placed person in the enterprise possesses the necessary knowledge and skill, either intuitively or via some business school course or executive program. In this instance there is, broadly speaking, less need to import someone from outside.

The two related roles that arise from these considerations, those of change agent (source of knowledge and skill on managing change) and enterprise powerholder (significant member of the hierarchy), are largely treated separately in this book. This is partly because it is the role of the change agent that is under the spotlight, rather than the related but wider, distinctive role of the manager. Studying organizational change amid the demands, activities, and concerns inherent in the general manager's role radically widens the range of variables to be considered and obscures the role of the change agent. That role can more easily be placed under the spotlight and explored by separating it from the authority/power relationship inherent in organizational leadership.

The book aims at getting at the underlying dynamics and issues any manager or consultant change agent has to face and cope with in developing a proactive approach to enterprise change. Two core, underlying, embracing propositions are at its heart. One of these is about the primacy of experience, the other human interaction process. The book ultimately advances a paradigm concerning the nature of the field of managing organizational change, and how one may learn about it. The paradigm is founded on empiricism and interaction.

THE PRIMACY OF EXPERIENCE

This book proposes a series of live, vicarious experiences to help people learn about enterprise change and its management. Learning proceeds by zeroing in on specific, concrete data about interventions, generated and provided by three sources. One is personal "here-and-now" field experience of intervening, another is "there-and-then" written accounts of interventions, and the third is experience generated by experiential exercises inside the classroom. Field experience, intervention accounts, and experiential exercises function partly as introspective and projective devices, in which the learner confronts his or her personal experiences, assumptions, and values and undergoes training in needed skills. The learner's personal perceptions embodying widespread "truths" about the characteristics of work and life in organizations are contrasted and compared with those of applied behavioral scientists, and the tension between the two is exploited for learning purposes.

The book stresses the usefulness of the trainee change agent taking part in an action research intervention, and provides a tested, practical way of setting up a small-scale, standard, action research field experience in the minimum lead time. This field experience serves as an anchor to the trainee's learning and a powerful stimulus to his or her efforts to master the field of managing change. Several distinctive experiential exercises provide supplementary orientation and practice in the skills implicated in the field experience.

In these ways the book spotlights a particular, data-based, heavily empirical approach to managing organizational change. It accords primacy to working on concrete organizational data of one sort or another, anchoring learning in real-world concerns, only subsequently bringing in those of the scholar or scientist. It is founded on a definite, if rough, learning model, which proposes that concrete, explicit experience—one's own and other people's—best helps the learner grasp what managing organizational change is really all about.

Intervention Accounts

The there-and-then accounts of managing change episodes that appear in the book provide the learner with the opportunity to develop insight into a range of interventions, carried out in different enterprises in different places, times, and circumstances. The accounts have widely varied settings, and are drawn from large and small business and government organizations. There are accounts of interventions in enterprises in consumer goods manufacturing, industrial chemicals, broadcasting, mining, sales, and research and development; in multibranch and multinational companies; in the hotel, retailing, and toy industries; in state government; in a university, a hospital, and a newspaper; and in a total institution. Several of these accounts concern classic interventions, well known in the literature.

Each such account should, ideally, be presented in the words and form that the change agent concerned thought about it—given meanings he or she ascribed to it—as the intervention process unfolds. It is highly desirable that the interventionist write introspectively about how he or she is going about the task as he or she goes along. Such documents enable the learner to compare his or her own reactions, and analyses of the unfolding intervention, to those of the change agent concerned. They help the trainee see things through the interventionist's eyes, to develop an insider's appreciation of managing change. Several of the accounts presented in this book are written from this personal, center-stage point of view of the change agent intimately involved in the change process. The accounts were edited from the experiences of Chris Argyris, Alex Bavelas and George Strauss, Robert R. Blake and Jane S. Mouton, Marvin Blumberg and Charles D. Pringle, William G. Dyer, Jack K. Fordyce and Raymond Weil, James F. Gavin, Robert H. Guest, Paul Hersey and Kenneth H. Blanchard, Eric J. Miller and Geraldine Gwynne, David A. Nadler, Edgar H. Schein, William Foote Whyte, and the author.[2]

The trainee change agent should be encouraged to ask himself or

---

[2] I spent a good deal of time—more years than I care to remember—searching for, editing, and testing published and unpublished intervention accounts that showed possibilities of being the sort outlined here. The mortality rate was high.

herself questions about the data in each intervention account—such questions as what kind of data is it? How accurate is it? To what kinds of distortion is it susceptible? What does it add to what I already know or suspect about intervening? How might I use the data in conjunction with other data I've learned from other interventions? Answers to these questions help the learner put into perspective the data currently being inspected. The trainee sifts through large amounts of information about a number of interventions, then draws tentative inferences, which he or she then subjects to further testing.

Developing Generalizations

The trainee slowly develops and tests, over the life of the managing change course, personal generalizations about effective ways to manage organizational change, which are closely connected with intervention data. Inferences about effectively managing enterprise change are in this way constructed in the light of various intervention experiences. Consideration of the empirical data leads inevitably to the need to generalize, to build models, to seek explanation.

The book espouses the viewpoint that the truth of a proposition is made more probable by the accumulation of confirming evidence. This view is, in essence, founded on inductive logic. Such "analytical induction," as John Van Maanen calls it, is first and last empirical. As Van Maanen suggests

> [It] begins with close-up, detailed observation. The specific and local are sought as a primary data base within which patterns may or may not be found. . . . Generalizations are to be built from the ground up and only tentatively offered on the basis of their ability to fully contain the data in hand.[3]

In this way George C. Homans' dictum, that "no one will go far wrong theoretically who remains in close touch with and seeks to understand a body of concrete phenomena," is treated seriously by this book.[4] Analytical induction is a common pattern in social science research, and is defensible in terms of the empiricist philosophy of the likes of David Hume.

Induction, Deduction, and the Literature

The inductive approach contrasts with the deductive approach, much more familiar to the academician, which proceeds by applying generalizations, derived from previous research, to a particular organization and its context. It may be highly desirable to be able to use deduction in managing enterprise change, especially considering that most of us are much more educated in deduction than induction. This is, however, not possible. The most powerful

[3] John Van Maanen et al., *Varieties of Qualitative Research* (Beverly Hills, Calif.: Sage 1982), p. 16.
[4] *Handbook of Modern Sociology* (Chicago: Rand McNally, 1978), pp. 975–976.

models we have in the field of intervention are of limited scope and applicability. No model of the intervention process exists that is of the stature or power necessary for the purpose.

Field experience, exercises, and intervention accounts anchor trainee learning in real-world concerns. Over time they accumulate and facilitate interest and understanding of attempts to formulate generalizations about managing change methodology. These are, of course, the concerns of the scholar, researcher, and scientist.

Grasp of the dynamics of managing change from intervention data should precede building systematic knowledge of what is at best a semicoherent organization development literature, rather than the other way around. By grappling with what it means to manage organizational change via the systematic approach presented here, the learner is ultimately placed in a position to draw on the diverse organization development and human sciences literature in a well-informed way as the need demands.

Unlike many books in the field of organization development, this one does not attempt to survey the whole field, or treat it as a relatively atheoretical wonderland of semirelated techniques. And instead of simply advocating the usefulness of action research and asserting that such propositions as Kurt Lewin's unfreezing-changing-refreezing model are of central importance, it focuses rather on applying them. In this way it integrates a lot of diverse contributions to organization development, redefines that field, and moves it forward a sizeable step. It shows how a wide, apparently eclectic range of experience, viewpoints, and conceptual schemes mesh together to provide a coherent approach to intervention. *Managing Organizational Change* is thus a stand-alone text, strong on theory as well as practice. It takes to heart Lewin's well-known dictum that "good theory is intensely practical."

Models and Schemes

Many of the brief readings presented in the book are classics, well known to scholars in the field. Most of them present only the nub of the original paper, rather than the reading in its entirety, and are called here models and schemes. A few older, lengthy, classic contributions to the literature are incorporated in the book by means of summaries from other sources. Several models and schemes included originate from the Tavistock Institute of Human Relations, and are much less well known.

As well as drawing on the organization development and action research literature, the book also utilizes certain aspects and fragments of anthropological, sociological, and psychoanalytic origin. It makes use of several social science field research traditions, especially observational methods, unstructured interviewing, field work methods, and history or chronology. The intellectual pedigree of the approach presented here originates from Kurt Lewin, the NTL Institute of Behavioral Science–inspired tradition, survey research, the Chicago School, and the Tavistock Institute. The people whose work has been particularly influential in shaping it are Edgar H. Schein, Eric J. Miller, Herbert Blumer, Wendell L. French, and Fritz J. Roethlisberger.

THE INTERACTION PROCESS APPROACH

The second core, underlying proposition at the heart of this book is that human interaction process is central to managing organizational change. As Schein remarks, "The various functions which make up an organization are always mediated by the interactions of people, so that the organization can never escape its human processes."[5] In order to carry out any planned, concerted change in an enterprise its leaders and members have to interact in some or other way, to generate, assemble, share, and massage data and meanings in order to take action. This is true no matter what the specific organizational issues are. In the context of any and every change episode there are recurrent issues about who talks to whom, when, and where; and about what, why, and with what consequences for further interaction. The currency of life in enterprises, and of intervention into that life, is interaction process. Similarly, interventions start and end in interaction.

Interaction should thus be the central process of concern to those who want to understand and change the organization's direction, adaptation and effectiveness, and the satisfactions of its participants. No enterprise can change without some ongoing interaction process. The corollary proposition is that organizational change is a time-related process, where what comes next is profoundly affected by what came before. What happens later in any intervention is inevitably and fundamentally affected by—a function of—what came before. Indeed, it remains to be seen if the outcomes of attempts to manage enterprise change can be understood at all without an understanding of the sequence of events. What happens in the end can only be understood by looking back in order to discover cause and effect.

Change Agent Skills

The change agent's expertise accordingly consists of knowledge and skill in tapping into the enterprise's interaction processes, in order to discover what members of it do, feel, think, and experience; how they define and act in their unique organizational world. The would-be change agent needs to develop the ability to detect and comprehend the meaning ascribed by members of the enterprise, in order to help them change it. He or she helps them elaborate appropriate interaction processes, to capture and generate data on themselves and the organization, and to utilize that data, most or all of which resides in their heads and experience. The change agent provides and imparts knowledge and skill in how to work with that data.

---

[5] *Process Consultation: Its Role in Organization Development* (Reading, Mass.: Addison-Wesley, 1969), p. 9.

Given the centrality of the interaction process, it follows that a systematic approach based on it should give detailed attention to the varieties of interaction process, which may be used in gathering data in order to promote planned change. The trainee change agent also needs to take part in interaction processes in order to learn about them. Skill and practice in interaction process, as in anything else, go hand-in-hand and are synonymous. Change agent skills and the models, schemes, and rationale of this book may be fused together in the trainee's head and behavior by the underlying focus on the interaction process as the way in which every organization works and changes.

Organizational and National Cultures

As the generic currency of organizational change, interaction is conceptually separate from the specific denominations, clothing, content, and context of any particular intervention. The approach presented in this book is thus acceptant of the proposition that intervention is culture-bound, that what fits the values, mores, interpersonal practices, and decision-making style of one organization does not fit another. Some or other interaction process underlies any organization's culture, and hence that process is essentially acultural. It is thus a universal approach and not ethnocentric in the organizational sense.

The ubiquitous sub-strata of interaction process in relation to any culture operates in an intercultural and intersocietal sense as well. It facilitates the introduction of materials on managing change interaction processes of British origin, largely from the Tavistock Institute of Human Relations, into an essentially American book. The book thus bears a definite transatlantic flavor, and has the advantage of drawing on more than one tradition on managing change. The intent here is to help prospective change agents gain insights and useful schema from both traditions, and pragmatically draw on both in their interventions, as the need arises.

The book's approach is also acultural or universal in the organizational sense that it may be applied equally to intervening in business, government, and voluntary organizations, of whatever size, ownership, design, technology, structure, membership, history, or environment.

BOOK DESIGN

The here-and-now and there-and-then experiences and the models and schemes that make up the book are presented in three cycles or parts. The sequence of chapters and of the book as a whole are set out in an evolutionary, tested design framework. Each presents material arranged around a single or a few related points. Virtually every chapter begins with several experiences, which one way or another state the themes, issues, and problems of the chapter in concrete organizational terms and encourage the course participant to wrestle with them. The accounts and experiential exercises anchor the chapter in real concerns, and facilitate understanding of and interest in successive, progressively more fundamental formulations of how managing change may be handled. In the overall sense the book proceeds from concrete, specific, matter-of-fact practice to scientific principle, from the elementary to the complex, the simple to the abstract.

The *Note on Tavistock Work on Organizational Change* outlines the sources of the materials on Tavistock intervention methods presented at various points in the book.

Part One: Approaches to Managing Organizational Change has two objectives: first, to provide a brief introduction to the approach to managing enterprise change espoused by this book, which will facilitate grasp of its essence; and, second, for those who want it, to facilitate the initiation of a field experience of managing change, based on the standard model advocated here,[6] with all possible speed.

Chapter 1: The History of Managing Organizational Change introduces major issues concerning methods, assumptions, roles, and values in managing change by focusing on the origins and history of intervening in enterprises. The chapter begins with a set of there-and-then experiences of enterprise change. All of these intervention accounts concern the early days of attempts to manage organizational change. The models and schemes are introduced by summaries of historical developments that shaped the field of managing enterprise change: the work of Kurt Lewin, laboratory training, survey feedback, and action research.

Chapter 2: Organization Models and Intervention Methods provides several varied data-rich accounts of interventions. It proceeds partly by comparative method, contrasting personal perceptions of what is commonly accepted as being true about the characteristics of work and life in organizations with those of applied behavioral scientists, and trying to exploit the tension between the two for learning purposes.

Chapter 3: Organization Development, Action Research, and the Intervention Model provides a synoptic view of the essentials of these conceptual schemes and how they relate in interventions. The chapter is intended to facilitate an initial grasp of the essence of the approach to managing organizational change advocated by this book, and to help course participants initiate, under the leadership of their instructor, standard, small-scale, data-gathering and feedback interventions, based on action research, in chosen organizations.

Part Two: Interaction in Interventions consists of a second cycle through the components of intervention, and emphasizes the various kinds of data-gathering encounters between the change agent and members of the client organization: watching, interviewing, utilizing questionnaires and surveys, and using groups. Effective group dynamic practices are the salient counterpart, in the processing of data to effective methods of gathering it in the first place, and are therefore incorporated at this point in the book. In managing

---

[6] See the intervention model and associated experiences, models, and schemes in Chapter 3, pp. 100–72.

organizational change the data gathered, by whatever means, is usually fed back, reviewed, evaluated, and decided and acted on by some kind of group acting on behalf of the organization concerned. This part of the book also provides a set of underlying rationales and overarching conceptual schemes for the approach to managing change adopted here.

Those who are developing their knowledge and expertise of managing enterprise change via the field intervention option suggested will be, during the time they are studying Part Two, in the early stages of their interventions. Many of the issues they are likely to regard as salient tend to relate to data-gathering and feedback practices and methods, hence the placement and content of this section of the book.

The overall aim of *Chapter 4: Resistance and the Process of Change* is to review organizational change from several perspectives, with reference to several models. The chapter has the intended function of drawing attention to the significance and nature of resistance to change and reviewing the necessary processes implicated in enterprise change via neo-Lewinian planned change theory.

Chapter 5: Gathering Data: Watching, Interviewing, Using Groups and Questionnaires explores the alternative means by which data may be gathered in interventions and the considerations and dynamics involved. The experiences concentrate on the questionnaire as a data-gathering mechanism, whereas the models and schemes treat interviewing, questionnaires, and instruments.

The data gathered in an intervention is usually fed back to some executive, representative, or task force group or committee. The group explores the data and make decisions concerning it. Expertise in working with group dynamics is one of the essential engines driving effective planned organizational change, which complements and facilitates utilization of data gathered.

Chapter 6: The Use of Groups to Facilitate Change provides introductory here-and-now training in the use of group dynamics in the course of interventions, and ties that training to there-and-then accounts and analyses of the group dynamics that take place in interventions.

Chapter 7: Observation, Interaction, and Subjectivity departs from the experiences-models-and-schemes format of the earlier chapters and, proceeding at a higher level of abstraction, provides the beginnings of an underlying rationale for the conceptual schemes and applications presented earlier, and the approach of this book. This is the culmination of Part Two of the book.

The final section of the book, **Part Three: Phases in the Intervention Process**, endeavors to spotlight the profound and intimate effect of time on interventions, the temporarily bound sequences of interactions, activities, and events that occur. One purpose here is to permit time-based analyses of interventions over an extended period. Issues about evaluation and termination of interventions, briefly touched on in this part, lead to the final chapter and the book's conclusion.

Chapter 8: Early in the Process provides the introductory episodes of the first of two significant, extended, multipart intervention accounts, each of which chronicles an intervention from its origin to its conclusion. Each account extends over two or three chapters of this part of the book, provides a stream of consultant introspections about what he thought he was doing to help manage enterprise change, and why he did those things. These narrative accounts of interventions encourage the acquisition of retrospective knowledge.

Chapter 9: In the Midst of the Process provides installments detailing the initiation or development of the two intervention stories. The models and schemes in this chapter begin with contributions about the design of activities in interventions, and consider the role of the change agent and consultant. Emphasis is placed on tailor-making any intervention to fit the unique circumstances of the organization concerned, in the light of the range of intervention possibilities available *in situ*, and from experiences and concepts employed elsewhere.

Chapter 10: Later in the Process concentrates on the dynamics that occur in interventions after they mature in client organizations, or have run their course. The chapter presents the final episodes of the two intervention stories introduced in Chapters 8 and 9. The models and schemes review evaluation of managing change efforts and historical process in interventions.

Conclusion: Managing Organizational Change, Values and Science places the practice and process of managing enterprise change in a scientific context, links it to a consideration of values, shows how these may be operationalized in the service or organizations and individuals, and encourages thinking about how best to do research in this field. The handful of there-and-then experiences included has a definite research flavor; they are intended to raise issues about appropriate scientific methodology. The models and schemes are intended to provide a suggestive sketch of the scientific, ethical, and philosophic issues suggested by attempts to manage organizational change.

USING THIS BOOK

Delivering useful learning experiences in managing enterprise change is a difficult business, about as difficult as any found in a business school. An Instructor's Manual, available to adopters, recognizes this difficulty and provides commentaries on the author's practices in using the here-and-now and then-and-there experiences and models and schemes, in various kinds of learning environments. It presents designs for graduate courses, management workshops, and executive development programs. A substantial, detailed study of Tavistock intervention method, previously unpublished, is also included.

The greatest strength of this book is probably as a stand-alone text in a graduate classroom, especially for executive MBAs and the like. The field experience–led classroom-based approach to *Managing Organizational Change* may be adopted by faculty substantially unfamiliar with the contents of this book in two stages. The first stage consists of purely classroom-based teaching of the bulk of the intervention accounts, experiential exercises, and models and schemes presented in the book, in order to build familiarity in working with the basic elements in the approach. Then, the second time around in teaching the course, the faculty member may introduce the additional complexity of the here-and-now field intervention experience.

Learning to manage enterprise change via a field intervention is, realistically speaking, open only to students and managers with significant working experience. It is not intended to suggest here that inexperienced undergraduates should carry out field interventions on the lines advocated. Faculty may, however, fruitfully lead teams of such students in ongoing interventions, and adapt the standard intervention model to handling larger trainee groups.

Graduate and undergraduate courses that approach teaching managing change by presenting typical textbook principles are bound to fail, in this writer's opinion, largely because of the abstraction in the typical textbook's content. Such an approach comes across as dry, dull and boring, the topics disconnected and unrelated to the real world. What is needed is a way for the graduate or advanced undergraduate to learn about real, flesh and blood enterprise change, how it was done in such-and-such a corporation, before getting anywhere near theory. The less one lectures in teaching managing organizational change, the better the course goes, as a reader of an earlier version of this book remarked.

This book cracks the problem of teaching managing change in this way by emphasizing intervention accounts, which confronts the student with realistic, concrete organizational situations, rather than by more or less disembodied concepts. Students enjoy learning about the real world, and relate to this much more easily than to an organization development text. Accounts of interventions also serve to help students develop a kind of vicarious experience of ongoing change in organizations, and provide a partial substitute for work experience. Briefer intervention accounts with focused questions are more effective for this purpose. The Instructor's Manual includes suggested questions. The experiential exercises supplement the intervention accounts, and encourage student-centered discussion.

Executive development workshops on managing change should encourage the manager to work over his or her experiences of enterprise change, which are often deeply felt. They should also exploit the contrasting experiences of the participants for their mutual learning by setting up different kinds of discussion exercises. The Instructor's Manual suggests suitable designs for residential workshops and evening executive programs.

This book has been a long time in coming. The germ of the idea to edit and write it took hold during a sabbatical I spent some years ago at the Tavistock Institute and the Univeristy of Washington. I spent several fruitful months at the Tavistock, interviewing Institute consultants on their intervention methods. Then I moved to Seattle, to Wendell French's department, where I wrote up the Tavistock material, and was approached by Bob Davis of Prentice Hall to write a book on organization development. The more distant sources of the book were my participation in the Practicum in Organization Development at MIT, and my training as a group consultant at the hands of the Tavistock Institute.

This book would not exist without the help of the bright, keen, experienced graduate students who undertook my managing change course. I owe them a debt. Over several years of working on it I came to regard the design of change agent education and training, inside or outside a business school, as the most difficult design problem I have encountered in my career as an organizational behaviorist. The ultimate attraction of synthesizing the book, from my point of view, is probably the sheer difficulty of the task.

Over several years I developed an evolutionary series of resolutions of the problem of how to train the change agent, suited to participants of executive MBA graduate programs in a business school classroom. Interventions based on the approach were carried out by class members in corporations, government departments, and voluntary organizations. Later, as consultant on managing change to the State Services Commission of the New Zealand government, I developed a series of residential executive appreciation workshops, based on the same pool of experiences and concepts. Finally, I developed a series of shorter courses for students and managers, similarly based.

I want to thank Edgar H. Schein, Alfred P. Sloan School of Management, Massachusetts Institute of Technology; Eric J. Miller, Tavistock Institute of Human Relations; Arthur N. Turner, late of the Harvard Business School; and Wendell L. French, University of Washington, for their steady support—and tolerance—of my efforts in developing the approach and materials presented here.

I would like to acknowledge the financial assistance provided by the Internal Research Committee, Victoria University, in funding a research assistant to help me finish the book. The research assistant, Felicity McLennan, did a fine, dedicated, partly paid and partly unpaid job. We became a husband and wife team in the book-generation sense.

Barbro Harris and Margaret Peace, of the Reference Section, Victoria University Library, were always positive, constructive, and downright pleasant in pursuing the multitudinous persons and addresses the book's vast permissions correspondence entailed. Susan Stokes, librarian at the American Embassy in Wellington, was helpful in locating many persons and addresses. Alison Reeves, management editor at Prentice-Hall, was always constructive and positive during the protracted go-stop-go periods when I was writing and editing the book. I am grateful for her steady support. The book is better integrated as the direct outcome of the searching critiques of Prentice-Hall's six business school reviewers. Carolyn Kart, production editor, took the trouble to tell me what was happening with the book, what would happen next, and what I should do about it. This was no mean feat, given the distance between Englewood Cliffs and Wellington.

The many authors and publishers who kindly granted me permission to quote the copyright material appearing in the experiences, models, and schemes deserve my warm thanks. The source of each quotation and the grantor of permission are cited at the appropriate place in the text.

I naturally absolve all the good people who helped in making this book possible from all responsibility for its faults. Blame me.

Roy McLennan
Victoria University of Wellington
18 January 1988

A Note on Tavistock Work on Organizational Change*

Roy McLennan

A good part of the work on organizational change and development carried out by consultants at the Tavistock Institute of Human Relations is and has been, in the words of an established Tavistock consultant, "outside the dominant social science paradigms, 'exiled' from the salient disciplines and schools of social science."[1] "Institutional fantasies," stereotyping in terms of the past,[2] and partial and provincial reviews[3] deepen that sense of exile and isolation, and make it even less likely that change agents at work elsewhere will be inclined to draw upon what the Tavistock tradition has to offer. The descriptions of Tavistock work on organizational change appearing in this book are part of an attempt to terminate that exile. From one point of view they provide valuable insights and conceptualizations concerning an alternative, British approach to intervening in the life of organizations. These will, I hope, provide other change agents with different perspectives on the process of intervening. These outlines of the frames of reference, schema, and methods of Tavistock action researchers can help other interventionists expand their repertoire and methodology of working with client organizations, and hence their effectiveness.

The impetus for presenting these descriptions of what Tavistock Institute consultants think and do originates from a sabbatical of several months I spent as a visitor to the Tavistock, interviewing a number of consultants at some length, usually with the aid of a tape recorder, and studying the literature on the Institute's action research tradition. Those interviewed consisted of Eric Miller, Gordon Lawrence, Isabel Menzies Lyth, Michael Foster, Don Bryant, Elliot Stern, Fiddy Abraham, Tim Dartington, and John Stringer. I also talked to several other Tavistock action researchers more briefly and informally.

I offered an undertaking to each participant, at the beginning of each interview, not to publish anything before circulating a pre-publication draft for correction, revision, and comment. Copies of the draft paper were accordingly

*I should like to acknowledge the generous help of Dr. Eric J. Miller, Tavistock Institute of Human Relations, in carrying out the research project summarized here. I should also like to thank Mr. W. Gordon Lawrence, late of the Tavistock Institute, for his warm support, and the scientific staff of Tavistock for their interest in the project.

[1] W. Gordon Lawrence, 1980, p. 15.

[2] Eric J. Miller, personal letter.

[3] For example, R. K. Brown, "Research and Consultancy in Industrial Enterprises," *Sociology*, 1 (1967).

sent to the consultants interviewed, and their comments seriously taken into account in revising it. Despite these efforts the opinions expressed in the notes printed in this book are, no doubt, ultimately my own. Most of the items presented here are taken from two source papers arising from this revised draft: "Feelings and Emotions in Action Research"[4] and "Action Research Consultancy."[5] As far as practicable the notes proceed by means of direct quotations from the interviews and printed sources, in order to let the Tavistock interventionists speak for themselves. Quotations without superscript numbers refer to interview material.

A limiting caveat is necessary. These notes do not present a "balanced" presentation of the general mode of Tavistock consultancy, but rather describe how a considerable number of present and past Institute consultants commonly think about issues, and handle themselves during the course of an intervention. There is no unitary "Tavistock Approach" to conceptualizing and working as an action research consultant.

REFERENCES

BAIN, A. "Presenting Problems in Social Consultancy: Three Case Histories Concerning the Selection of Managers," *Human Relations,* 29 (1976).

BION, W. R. *Experiences with Groups.* London: Tavistock, 1961.

BROWN, R. K. "Research and Consultancy in Industrial Enterprises," *Sociology,* 1 (1967).

BRYANT, DON. *Work Plus: An Account of an Experiment to Improve the Quality of Worklife in the Cominco Lead Smelter in Trail, B.C.* Vancouver: British Columbia Research Council and Tavistock Institute of Human Relations, 1979.

BRYANT, DON, and PAINTER, BERT. "An Action Research Approach to Organization Design." In *Manpower Planning and Organization Design.* Edited by D. T. Bryant and R. J. Niehaus. New York: Plenum Press, 1978.

COLES, R. B., and BRIDGER, H. "The Consultant and His Roles," *British Journal of Medical Psychology,* 42 (1969).

Council of the Tavistock Institute of Human Relations. *Social Research and a National Policy for Science.* London: Tavistock, 1964.

DE BOARD, ROBERT. *The Psycho-Analysis of Organizations.* London: Tavistock, 1978.

FOSTER, P. M. "An Introduction to the Theory and Practice of Action Research in Work Organizations," *Human Relations,* 25 (1972).

FOSTER, P. M., and LAWRENCE, W. G. *Towards Forms of Education for "New Forms of Work Organization."* London: Tavistock Institute of Human Relations, 1978.

GRAY, S. G. "The Tavistock Institute of Human Relations." In *Fifty Years of the Tavistock Clinic.* Edited by H. V. Dicks. London: Routledge and Kegan Paul, 1970.

HIGGIN, GURTH. "The Tavistock Institute: Work in the Personnel Field," *Personnel Management,* 45 (1963).

JAQUES, E. "Some Principles of Organization of a Social Therapeutic Institution," *Journal of Social Issues,* 3 (1947a).

JAQUES, E. "Social Therapy: Technocracy or Collaboration?" *Journal of Social Issues,* 3 (1947b).

JAQUES, E. *The Changing Culture of a Factory.* London: Tavistock, 1951.

KING, P. M. H. "Task Perception and Interpersonal Relations in Industrial Training: Part II." *Human Relations,* 1 (1948).

KLAUBER, J. "History-taking in the Light of Knowledge of Unconscious Mental Processes." *The Lancet,* July 22, 1961.

KLEIN, LISL. *A Social Scientist in Industry.* London: Croom Helm, 1976.

KLEIN, M. "Our Adult World and Its Roots in Infancy," *Human Relations,* 16 (1963).

[4] "Feelings and Emotions in Action Research: A Tavistock Approach," paper delivered at the Management Educators' Conference, Monash University, Victoria, Australia, August 1980.

[5] "Action Research Consultancy: A Tavistock Approach," *Journal of Enterprise Management,* 3 (1981), 251–260.

LAWRENCE, W. G. *Making Life at Work Have Quality.* London: Tavistock Institute of Human Relations Document No. 2T 281, 1979.

LAWRENCE, W. G. *Some Psychic and Political Dimensions of Work Experiences.* London: Tavistock Institute of Human Relations Document No. 2T 282, 1979.

LAWRENCE, W. G. "A Psycho-analytic Perspective for Understanding Organizational Life." In *OD Practices in Europe.* Edited by R. N. Ottaway. New York: John Wiley, 1980. (typed manuscript).

LAWRENCE, W. G., ed. *Exploring Individual and Organizational Boundaries.* New York: John Wiley, 1979.

LAWRENCE, W. G., and MILLER, E. J. "Epilogue." In *Task and Organization.* Edited by E. J. Miller. New York: John Wiley, 1976.

MENZIES, I. E. P. "A Case Study in the Functioning of Social Systems as a Defense Against Anxiety," *Human Relations,* 13 (1960).

MILLER, E. J. "Demands and Problems of Face-to-Face Work with People." In Open University, A Post-Experience Course, The Handicapped Person in the Community, Units 1–10, Block 3, Part 1. Providing Supporting Services. Milton Keynes: Open University Press, 1975.

MILLER, E. J. "Introductory Essay: Role Perspectives and the Understanding of Organizational Behaviour." In *Task and Organization.* Edited by E. J. Miller. New York: John Wiley, 1976.

MILLER, E. J. "Organizational Development and Industrial Democracy: A Current Case Study." In *Organizational Development in the UK and the USA.* Edited by C. L. Cooper. London: Macmillan, 1977.

MILLER, E. J. "Autonomy, Dependency and Organizational Change." In *Innovation in Patient Care.* Edited by D. Towell and C. Harries. London: Croom Helm, 1979a.

MILLER, E. J. "The Politics of Involvement." Unpublished address to the A. K. Rice Institute, Houston, Texas, 1979b.

MILLER, E. J., and GWYNNE, G. V. *A Life Apart.* London: Tavistock, 1972.

RAPOPORT, R. N. "Three Dilemmas in Action Research," *Human Relations,* 23 (1970).

RICE, A. K. "The Use of Unrecognized Cultural Mechanisms in an Expanding Machine Shop," *Human Relations,* 4 (1951).

RICE, A. K. *The Enterprise and Its Environment.* London: Tavistock, 1963.

RICE, A. K. *Learning for Leadership.* London: Tavistock, 1965.

RICE, A. K. "Individual, Group and Intergroup Processes," *Human Relations,* 22 (1969).

SOFER, C. *The Organization from Within.* London: Tavistock, 1961.

SOFER, C. *Organizations in Theory and Practice.* London: Heinemann, 1972.

STERN, E., and ABRAHAM, F. *The Systems Group: Its Internal and External Relations.* London: Tavistock Institute of Human Relations, Document No. 2T 276, 1979.

SUTHERLAND, J. D., and MENZIES, I. E. "Two Industrial Projects," *Journal of Social Issues,* 3 (1947).

TRIST, ERIC. "The Professional Facilitation of Planned Change in Organizations." In *Reviews, Abstracts, Working Groups: XVII International Congress of Applied Psychology.* Amsterdam: Swets and Zeitlinger, 1968. Reprinted in *Management and Motivation.* V. H. Vroom and E. L. Deci, eds. London: Penguin, 1970.

TRIST, ERIC. "Epilogue and Summary from the Tavistock Perspective." In *Towards a New Philosophy of Management,* P. Hill. London: Gower, 1971.

TRIST, ERIC. "Engaging with Large Scale Systems." In *Experimenting with Organizational Life.* Edited by A. W. Clark. New York: Plenum, 1976.

WILSON, A. T. M. "Some Implications of Medical Practice and Social Case-Work for Action Research," *Journal of Social Issues,* 3 (1947).

WILSON, A. T. M. "Some Aspects of Social Process," *Journal of Social Issues.* Supplement Series No. 5 (1951).

WILSON, A. T. M. "Introduction." In *The Changing Culture of a Factory,* E. Jaques. London: Tavistock, 1951.

1
THE HISTORY OF MANAGING ORGANIZATIONAL CHANGE

———◆———

INTRODUCTION

This chapter introduces major issues concerning methods, assumptions, roles, and values in managing organizational change by focusing on the origins and history of intervening in enterprises. The chapter begins with Maclaurin and MIT, a there-and-then, sequential account of an organization in difficulty. The account is broken into three parts, consisting of the "before," "during," and "after" phases of major change in the life of the organization.

Maclaurin and MIT (A) presents an overview of the organization in a troubled state, and encourages readers to consider what they would do if they were new brooms in that organization. *Maclaurin and MIT (B)* describes the entry of a new chief executive officer, outlines his situation, orientation and methods, and facilitates comparisons between one's own point of view and that of the new chief. *Maclaurin and MIT (C)* follows the organization's successes and failures under his leadership over several years and presents opportunities to trace out causes and effects. The series provides several opportunities to discuss a number of significant issues in the context of managing organizational change, including leadership, goal setting, initiating action, organizational processes, and the mobilization of human resources. In this account the roles of organization leader and change agent cohere in the same person.

Organization Development Begins at Lakeside concerns the introduction of an applied behavioral scientist to a long internship within a large manufacturing plant, and considerations about the initiation and development of that role, in the early days of the field of organization development.

In *The R&D Department* an executive returns from a management training program, and proposes that he meet with his managers for a few days in an off-site meeting to look at a range of issues. Discussion turns as to what that meeting might be like and how effective it might be in changing the organization. *The Fairview Company* outlines the process by which company members interacted with an external change agent to work on a headquarters—field conflict problem, and encourages readers to analyse that process.

Planned organizational change did not spring suddenly out of the woodwork full-blown: trends and developments were taking place in Western societies, economies and organizations that generated attempts to develop proactive approaches to enterprise change. The models and schemes in this chapter attempt various sorts of explanations about what these trends and developments were.

These explanations are introduced by *A Brief History of Organization Development*, a succinct summary of historical developments that shaped the field of managing organizational change: the work of Kurt Lewin, laboratory training, and survey feedback. This is succeeded by *The Historical Perspective*, on the history of action research. This piece outlines Lewin's contributions in some detail and reviews early literature influential in the action research approach to managing change.

The Emergence of Humanistic Philosophy in Management and Organizations emphasizes the related theme that connects the Hawthorne studies, via Maslow's theory of motivation, to the work of Chris Argyris, Douglas McGregor and Rensis Likert, highly influential contributors to the field of managing organizational change.

Aspects of the Professional Facilitation of Planned Change suggests several underlying historical reasons for the attention paid to facilitating organizational change, and the emergence of sociotechnical systems theory as a valuable scheme for thinking about and bringing about change in enterprises.

The historical context of the genesis of managing organizational change is somewhat controversial. It is not properly established who conceived what and why it happened—"the parentage is questionable"—in someone else's felicitous phrase. What do we know of something if we cannot trace it back to its roots? The answer must be not very much. The field of managing change is weak on history, to its detriment. The issue of origins of the field is important and needs to be established with greater certainty.

Maclaurin and MIT (A)*

Roy McLennan

MIT IN 1909

In the first decade of the century MIT was in a state of crisis. The organization was poor, small (about 1,500 students) and struggling. Perhaps even its very survival was at stake. Founded in 1861 on the basis of some land and money granted by the State of Massachusetts, MIT had been established to break away from the traditional pattern of university education in order that "education might be obtained in science but without over-looking letters." The Institute's charter stated that it was founded for "aiding generally by suitable means the advancement, development and practical application of science in connection with arts, manufactures and commerce."

The way forward for an organization pioneering a radically new approach to higher education had been arduous. But in the late 19th century MIT had achieved considerable standing for its prowess in engineering, the keenness and competence of its graduates, its able and enthusiastic faculty, and a dedication to hard work. In the American university tradition it was supported by a small but enthusiastic alumni association of former graduates, organised on a territorial basis.

Like the archetypal small, growing business, however, the Institute had been plagued from the start by a chronic shortage of capital. The shortage of capital itself reflected the limited public acceptance of MIT's concept of higher education. The continuing problem expressed itself in a variety of guises. One form was budget deficits. In 1909, for example, the organization's expenditure exceeded its income by 46%. And even the basis of this unsatisfactory funding—partly from the State of Massachusetts and partly from its alumni—was coming apart at the seams.

MIT's financial malaise was physically reflected in buildings as well as in facilities and academic salaries. The Institute was housed in a widely scattered, motley collection of buildings in inner Boston. Some of the structures had been erected for what had at the time been believed to be temporary use. Some had fallen into disrepair, and were on the verge of being condemned as unsafe. The buildings were underequipped and overcrowded. Student facilities were almost non-existent. Beyond the architectural manifestations of malaise lay the

* SOURCE: Roy McLennan, "The Career of Richard C. Maclaurin: 1—The Early Years" and "2—The Later Years," *Working Papers*, Nos. 783 and 784–85, Alfred P. Sloan School of Management, Massachusetts Institute of Technology, 1975.

6

Institute's inability to provide adequate laboratories and decent salaries for faculty members.

There was also a major failure on the part of the Institute, in a public relations sense, to make the case in the mind of Bostonians that the organization's objectives were worthy of their support. Many Bostonians were "oblivious of the Institute's very existence, or thought of it as a trade school, supported by the state." And in a wider sense MIT was not successfully pursuing its mission of service to society via the application of science to practical problems. American industry, economy and society were, in the first decade of the 20th century, rapidly changing. The Institute's teaching programmes and research activities needed expansion and updating on the basis of present and probable future development. There was a need for organizational leadership to re-interpret MIT's mission in the light of current and future environmental conditions.

As chief executive the MIT president had to work with the MIT corporation, the Institute's governing body, the administration, the faculty, and the alumni association. The corporation had a membership of about 50. For practical day-to-day purposes one president had instituted an executive committee of the corporation, consisting of seven members, chaired by him.

A major attempt had been made in 1904 to solve the organization's problems. This had taken the form of a move inside MIT to make it Harvard University's engineering school, in this way to obtain access to the University's healthier funding. A voluntary takeover of MIT had been proposed inside the Institute. The proposition was presented to the organization by the then chief executive, president Pritchett, almost as a *fait accompli*. It seemed to most faculty and alumni like the first step down a primrose path which would lead to the organization's demise. A protracted and sometimes bitter struggle took place inside the Institute over Pritchett's proposal. The proposal instigated a major conflict. It engendered "pronounced and lasting feelings of distrust in the motives of those who were most active in attempting to bring about the alliance."

In 1905 two expressions of opinion on the merger proposition were recorded. Seventy per cent of the almost 3,000 alumni who responded to a poll were against the merger, as were 89 per cent of senior faculty. Finally a legal decision affecting MIT's ability to negotiate knocked the scheme on the head. Three months later Pritchett resigned.

In these circumstances it was hardly any wonder that the two distinguished academics officially known to have been offered the presidency after Pritchett resigned turned it down. For years many others would not touch it either. MIT had too many problems for its presidency to appeal to leading American scientists and technologists, and filling the post with a competent man was difficult. In the meantime the organization soldiered on under a caretaker arrangement.

The presidential hiatus was finally broken in 1909 by the election of Richard C. Maclaurin to the presidency. Maclaurin, a 39-year-old New Zealand and Cambridge educated mathematician, had had an unusually broad education and professional experience. He had held a chair of mathematics, the Deanship of a law school, and at the time of his selection held the chair of mathematical physics at Columbia University. He had been only months in the United States, was clearly a dark horse in the American academic firmament and had very limited knowledge of American institutions of higher education. But while the MIT selection committee apparently regarded him as being "wholly without administrative experience" he had in fact been chairman of a professorial board and dean of Victoria University College, a tiny New Zealand college, when it was carrying out its initial building programme. He had also studied many aspects of higher education and educational change, and the issues about influence implicated in securing change.

Maclaurin was elected as chief executive in October 1908, and took office the following June.

Maclaurin and MIT (B)*

Roy McLennan

In the interval between his election and taking office Maclaurin gave his attention to studying the Institute intensively, and talking to the organization's faculty and alumni associations. In late 1908 he read and reread an authoritative two volume work concerning MIT's founder, W. B. Rogers. With his book he began what became a careful and systematic study of the origins, history and development of the Institute, its goals, values and mission. He "saturated himself with its spirit and tradition." About the same time he gave a series of addresses to Institute faculty and the regional alumni associations. In these speeches he stressed that

> The experience of most similar institutions in other parts of the world is that a bold policy, a courageous policy of trust in the future is a wise one. To advance rapidly, an institution must not be afraid of its own development. The Institute ... has everything it could want in the shape of great traditions, distinguished and enthusiastic professors and alumni.

In his inaugural address in June 1909 he acknowledged that he was "somewhat a stranger" to his audience. Consequently he felt it appropriate to outline his values about university education. He commented that he believed that the actual discipline a student studied at university was not the most important thing about his education; instead "it is the how rather than the what of study." What mattered in high education was the *process* of learning, rather than the substance or thing learned.

At the subsequent alumni dinner he announced the policy of his administration on two central strategic issues which had hung fire for years: the location of MIT, and relations with Harvard.

He stressed that "the thing to do first is to secure a new site, and on that new site raise a new (Massachusetts Institute of) Technology with all the characteristics of the old." To secure this objective a million dollars would probably be needed. If the cost seemed high people should consider the alternative of doing nothing—the decline of the organization—which was totally unacceptable.

He was equally definite on the second issue: "There will be no more talk of merger with Harvard." But "in the domain of applied science there is

* SOURCE: Roy McLennan, "The Career of Richard C. Maclaurin: 1—The Early Years" and "2—The Later Years," *Working Papers*, nos. 783 and 784–85, Alfred P. Sloan School of Management, Massachusetts Institute of Technology, 1975.

much we can do for our mutual help . . . to make cooperation real and practical, we must be strong enough for independence."

Later in 1909 Maclaurin gave a paper on organizational purpose and university education. He began with a statement about the motivating value of definite organizational objectives: "The Institute would . . . never have achieved what it has," he declared, "if it had not had clear and definite organization goals:

> There has never been any uncertainty or indefiniteness as to what the Institute is aiming at in its scheme of education . . . so many schools and colleges drift around, apparently without compass or rudder, with no definite ideas as to what port they are trying to reach, or how they should go to reach it. . . (MIT) is an institution that, *from the very outset*, has had very definite ideas on these matters.

For the guidance of MIT Rogers, the founder, had

> laid down a few simple but far-reaching principles, which have governed the Institute ever since. The first of these is the *importance of being useful*. There is of course no necessary antithesis between the individual and the social end in education. However, the laying of the emphasis is important, and Rogers laid it unhesitatingly on efficiency in the service of society. . . (Rogers) set forth the *value* and the *dignity* of the *practical* professions for which they (students) were to prepare themselves.

Rogers emphasised, said Maclaurin,

> the value of science in its . . . applications to the practical arts of life, to human comfort, and health, and to social wealth and power. . . . In education he laid greater stress on broad principles and their derivation than on details of fact. . . . The most truly practical education . . . is one founded on a thorough knowledge of scientific laws and principles, and one which unites with habits of close observation and exact reasoning, *a large general cultivation*. (Rogers) understood that when one gets to the root of things in education, the *method* rather than the *subject* is of supreme importance, and his insistence on the value of method in teaching was the cardinal doctrine in his creed and the one that has contributed most to the success of the Institute. . . . What method, then, is the right one? His fundamental idea was not original . . . (and) has been clearly expressed before, but rarely, if ever, adopted . . . as the basis of educational methods and applied systematically. . . . The idea is . . . of *learning by doing*. "How can a man learn to know himself?" asked Goethe. "Never by thinking, but by doing." Add to this the doctrine of Carlyle that "the end of man is an action and not a thought, though it were the noblest," and you have the whole thing in a nutshell.

Maclaurin's first major presidential effort was directed towards securing the immediate financial future of his organization. MIT's annual grant of $25,000 from the State of Massachusetts was due to expire after 1910. The Institute should clearly try to make the strongest possible case for continued state support to tide the organization over its difficult straits. The question was on what grounds to make the case. Should MIT rest its case on the defensive ground of dependency and financial weakness? After intensive discussion between the president, executive committee, corporation, alumni association and faculty, a task force under Maclaurin's chairmanship was formed to tackle the issue in a positive, optimistic and confident way. The approach adopted rested essentially on the proposition that the contribution of the Institute to scientific applications and educating graduates benefited the state: These useful activities justified a generous subsidy.

Unified efforts by the task force and supporters led to a bill being introduced to the state legislature to grant the Institute $100,000 each year for ten years. A variety of systematic efforts were made, converging on the objective of ensuring its successful passage. Members of the alumni association talked privately to legislators. A two day Congress of Massachusetts Institute of Technology was planned, the theme of which was to be the role played by science and technology in the development of industry. The whole conception for a Congress was intended to serve a promotional purpose, to dramatise the value of MIT's activities. The concept had originated in the creative mind of Arthur D. Little, a very active alumnus. These unified and comprehensive efforts met their reward in the face of "somewhat formidable opposition" in securing the $100,000 for ten years. The old grant had been quadrupled. In this way a central and reliable sheet anchor to MIT's funding was established. It constituted Maclaurin's first success as organization leader.

In the conduct of his office Maclaurin showed an abhorrence of presidential affectation and ritual. He dispensed with protective barriers in the form of a barrage of secretaries, and maintained only one. In the beginning the Institute provided him with a young assistant, as was the custom. Maclaurin soon found him superfluous, got rid of him, and did not replace him. He operated with an "open door," which encouraged people to call to consult him about work or personal problems. They found him a patient and non-judgmental listener.

People at MIT soon found Maclaurin to be a sympathetic listener, with a capacity for absorbing their views. He knew when to listen. He spent a long time "listening, observing, pondering, and took no step under impulse." Institute people found him reserved and reticent—even aloof—with his own views and attitudes. His oldest American friend observed that "I do not believe it ever occurred to him that his own personal affairs could possibly be of interest to anybody else. His reserve was absolutely natural, not worn as a defence."

Maclaurin fairly quickly moulded the administrative and liaison arrangements for the presidency into a shape which he found personally comfortable. He took the existing organizational arrangements and fitted them without much change of structure, to his own assumptions and leadership style. It became his practice to hold frequent conferences with the corporation executive committee, which he treated as an inner council of the corporation. In these conferences he never used Robert's Rules or other semi-legalistic parliamentary methods emphasising the control of the chairman. Francis R. Hart, a member, remarked that the president's "manner of presenting matters requiring decision and action by the committee encouraged discussion and suggestion, and rarely led to heated argument." Maclaurin did not expect concurrence with any preselected line of action, but preferred to develop one as the discussion progressed. He rarely expressed his preferences, and then only tentatively, but instead waited for an analysis of the issue to emerge from the discussion. Hart notes, "He was quick to grasp the significance of some new point of view which . . . discussion developed." Maclaurin, Hart found, was "wholly lacking in argumentative obstinacy." Members of the committee "shared with him responsibility for the decisions reached." Hart commented about how the committee developed over time:

> From the beginning he had our respect and we gave him our confidence. As his rare qualities became understood and appreciated, we all came to have for him a deep personal affection and trust. Each of us felt it a privilege to be his personal friend.

Maclaurin fairly rapidly evolved a full time administrative group within MIT, consisting of the Registrar, the Bursar, and the Dean of Students. As the leader of the group Maclaurin showed his liking for working in an informal fashion. The team met more or less daily. It did not adhere to strictly formal definitions of job roles. Maclaurin instead chose one or other of the group to meet special problems as they arose, matching the problem to the man, rather than the role definition. He seemed to know intuitively how to delegate responsibility. When he asked one of them or a group to tackle a particular task he would turn the whole job over to them.

In getting tasks done he encouraged his people to exercise the maximum freedom of action. Close, informal and cooperative effort characterised relations with the office holders of the alumni association in the shared effort to develop the organization. His relations with the Institute's faculty were equally smooth: Over time confidence grew in his steadfast efforts for them and the organization.

Given the corporation, executive, the administrative group and alumni association officers to help him as president, Maclaurin remarked that he was in the position of an English solicitor who said that his sole responsibility was to

> distinguish hard cases from easy and routine ones. The latter I hand over to the office boy, the former to the barristers: I have nothing left to do but collect the fees.

He was suspicious and puzzled at the emphasis of other people on elaborate formal organization. He called this "organization for its own sake," and was averse to business efficiency practices *a la* Scientific Management being applied to university organizations. In a review of a bulletin by Morris L. Cooke, written at the request of a New York newspaper, he enjoyed himself at Cooke's expense:

The report is written from the point of view of the man who is used to report on the efficiency of a glue factory or a soap works. . . .

The most serious objection I see to it (the report) lies in its abuse rather than its legitimate use. I fear that it will tend to increase the administrative machinery of our educational institutions, machinery that is already far too much in evidence. . . . Think for a moment of the effect on men like Newton or Faraday of the "snap and vigour" treatment that Mr. Cooke suggests in his discussion of research. They must make frequent reports on the progress of their research, and constantly justify the expenditure thereon. The Superintendent . . . calls upon Mr. Newton.

Superintendent: Your theory of gravitation is hanging fire unduly. The director insists on a finished report filed in his office by 9 a.m. Monday next, summarised on one page, typewritten, and the main points underlined. Also, a careful estimate of the cost of the research a student hour.

Newton: But there is one difficulty that has been puzzling me for fourteen years, and I am not quite—

Superintendent (with snap and vigour): I guess you had better overcome that difficulty by Monday morning or quit.

Maclaurin and MIT (C)*

Roy McLennan

With the immediate viability of MIT in the existing building complex secure, Maclaurin turned his attention to acquiring a new site for rehousing the entire organisation. He "patiently examined a long list of possible locations and, with expert advice, weighed their several advantages and disadvantages." It was of course necessary to examine which site would be most suitable from the viewpoint of present and future location. Maclaurin and his advisers reached the conclusion that MIT could be relocated on one of several alternative sites in the greater Boston area.

The corporation gave him power to appoint a committee to make the final selection from the handful of alternatives ultimately considered. Instead of opting for a particular one—and there was one he especially favoured—he instead began a set of complex, interdependent negotiations to secure the options on the alternative sites. When the options were secured it became imperative to secure about $1 million quite rapidly in order to realise on them.

He appealed for support to likely sources of educational funds, such as the Rockefeller and Sage Foundations, Andrew Carnegie, a noted "big giver," and T. Coleman du Pont, an MIT graduate. They all turned him down. Du Pont, president of E. L. du Pont de Nemours Powder Company, did say in his letter of refusal, however, that he was prepared to see Maclaurin to discuss the Institute. Maclaurin set out to visit du Pont:

> I described the broad features of our condition and said that we must move to a new site. He asked what sites were under consideration and wanted a brief description of each. The first one I mentioned was 25 acres in area. He said, "Can't you double it?" and I said "Not this particular site." "Well," he said, "I don't like the look of twenty-five acres. It seems to me too small. Almost invariably when a man comes to me to approve plans of a new factory . . . I tell him to double the size of everything and almost invariably I wish afterwards that I had used a larger factor of safety. (Massachusetts Institute of) Technology will occupy a great position in the future and must have room to grow. I don't feel much attracted by twenty-five acres, but I should be interested in fifty." I agreed with this policy, but told him of course that the main obstacle was cost. "What would fifty acres cost?" he asked. I told him "Three quarters of a million," and he said he would contribute half a million.

The rest of the money needed to purchase the site, a property in Cambridge bordering the Charles River basin opposite the heart of Boston, was contributed by members of the corporation and friends of MIT.

* SOURCE: Roy McLennan, "The Career of Richard C. Maclaurin: 1—The Early Years" and "2—The Later Years," *Working Papers*, nos. 783–75 and 784–75, Alfred P. Sloan School of Management, Massachusetts Institute of Technology, 1975.

After securing the site Maclaurin focused his attention on a search for funds to permit the Institute to build on it. Suitable buildings were likely to cost at least $2 million. The maximum contribution which could be expected from MIT's generally youthful, not often rich and not numerous alumni was estimated at $750,000. More than $1 million would thus have to be found elsewhere.

Maclaurin considered that "the obvious policy was to try to get one donation so large as to remove doubts that the whole thing could be done." With this end in view he journeyed to alumni dinners and luncheons in New York, Philadelphia, Pittsburgh, Washington, Chicago and Rochester, among other cities, always on the lookout for a "big giver." He bore the news of the successes over the state grants and the du Pont gift, using optimism and confidence in the future as an approach to fund raising. But he returned to Boston disappointed.

While on the visit to Rochester he took the opportunity of spending a day looking at the principal plant of Eastman Kodak, the photographic manufacturer. George Eastman, the self-made, self-educated chief executive of the company was away, but it did not seem to matter too much. Eastman had the reputation of not being interested in supporting higher education, despite his great wealth. His reputation derived from a gift of $78,000 towards a science building for his local university. Eastman had followed up the gift with the remark that he had made it because the university's president had "let me alone."

But Frank W. Lovejoy, an MIT graduate who was one of the leading managers in Eastman Kodak, put in some spadework to try to cultivate an interest in MIT on the part of Eastman, and suggested that Maclaurin write proposing a meeting. The result was a letter from the president to Eastman, "telling him something of our problems," to which Eastman replied suggesting a date and place. The two men met for dinner at the Hotel Belmont in New York and spent the evening going over the Institute's situation carefully. They considered the estimates concerning the probable costs of the various aspects of the building programme. Eastman, said Maclaurin,

> made it clear that his . . . interest (in MIT) would depend on its problems being attacked in a bold way. . . . He . . . believed that (Massachusetts Institute of) Technology had only to embrace its destiny to rise to a position of transcendent usefulness and his only anxiety . . . lest at any time narrower views should prevail.

When Eastman was about to leave he suddenly asked, "What will it cost to put up the new buildings?" Maclaurin answered that it would cost about $2.5 million. Eastman said "I'll send you a draft." Maclaurin had found his "big giver."

From the first Maclaurin had considered the question of MIT and Harvard University, and what relationship—if any—might be appropriate between them. After much study he became convinced that the interests of

MIT and higher education in general would unquestionably benefit from close cooperation with Harvard in teaching applied science, especially engineering.

He formulated the view that if the resources of the two organizations could be concentrated together in a joint venture the outcome would surely be the finest school of engineering in the world in teaching and research terms, an immeasurable gain to applied science, and a significant contribution to the prosperity of the United States. Close cooperation between MIT and the University would avoid wasteful duplication in expensive engineering and plant and resources, he concluded, while still preserving the autonomy of each.

He found a like-minded colleague in his counterpart at Harvard, president A. Lawrence Lowell. The engineering effort at Harvard was comparatively small and weak. The University had received a large endowment intended to support engineering, and wanted to put the money to work without years of delay. MIT had the people, and Harvard the money. At the beginning of their contacts the two presidents concurred on a process of working towards an agreement about the joint venture, without which negotiations would probably not have taken place at all. All negotiations between the presidents and executives were to remain confidential until agreement was reached. Lengthy negotiations between the two organisations followed. At one point during these Lowell complained about the difficulty of agreeing "upon the distribution of a cake if each of the claimants feels entitled to the whole of it." Maclaurin replied, "It would seem to me that we are discussing the making of a cake rather than its distribution."

The negotiations had begun when MIT was still in a state of financial crisis. As the Institute's financial condition improved Maclaurin stressed and even anticipated its growing strength *vis-a-vis* Harvard, and used it as a lever to influence the outcome of the negotiations. In a letter to Eastman he said he felt that "the readiness of the Harvard authorities to accept (MIT) suggestions . . . was largely due indirectly to the momentum of the Institute that has been gained through your support."

The president's labour drew towards a successful conclusion in 1913. A comprehensive draft agreement was emerging by which Harvard and MIT engineering students would be taught in MIT's buildings by a joint staff of Institute and University professors, bankrolled by Harvard's money. The two chief executives and their committees began to consider ways of consulting their respective governing bodies, faculties, alumni and publics about it, in such a way as to secure a satisfactory income.

For his part as chief executive of MIT Maclaurin believed that consultation with rank-and-file faculty and alumni would jeopardise reaching any workable conclusion. Many or some would, he thought, exhibit provincial and institutional perspectives towards the plans, which could threaten the success of the whole enterprise. For this reason he limited faculty and alumni participation in finalising the agreement. He asked past, present and future presidents of the alumni associaton to study the draft, in confidence, and make suggestions or criticisms of it. Heads of the academic departments affected by the agreement were similarly consulted. A number of such suggestions were incorporated into the final document, and the alumni presidents pronounced themselves satisfied.

Maclaurin was anxious to bring the endowment trustees into the work at this point, so that their views might be canvassed, any adjustments made in the draft agreement, and the final version receive their support. But this matter lay in the hands of the Harvard leadership, who believed it unnecessary. In early 1914 the final version of the agreement was approved by the University and the Institute. In the 1914–15 academic year the joint engineering school opened its doors.

At the close of World War I the trustees of the endowment fund used to finance the operation successfully challenged the Harvard-MIT agreement in the courts. The court's decision meant that the University had to set up its own engineering school in order to draw upon the endowment's funds.

At a corporation meeting in December 1918 it was decided that MIT would in two years need an endowment of at least $7 million to re-establish itself on a sound financial footing. Maclaurin put together a special committee of eight people to pursue this objective, including himself, and asked du Pont to chair it. The committee rapidly set to work. It became obvious by June 1919, however, that the best efforts of the members, including Maclaurin, were making little impression on the large target sum. Maclaurin spent a day with Eastman and "went over the . . . situation carefully." He came back to the Institute bearing the news of a conditional offer from Eastman of $4 million, which could bring in an income of $200,000 per year. Eastman's condition was that MIT raise, by one means or another, a further $3 or $4 million. Maclaurin set the objective at the higher figure. He then gave up his summer vacation to the cause of fund raising. Over and above the Eastman millions he had by the autumn raised a further $1.25 million by these activities. It was evident, however, that only through an organized effort of the alumni on a large scale would the target be reached in keeping with the deadline of 1 July 1920 set by Eastman. A race against the clock began. The corporation, alumni and students were quickly involved in the work. A series of committees and secretariats were set up. It seemed obvious, however, that the money still required to meet Eastman's deadline would not be obtained by gifts alone, even with the help of a major campaign. Some other supplementary scheme was needed.

Maclaurin's administration generalised and systematised concepts from financing schemes already operating on a local, modest scale within MIT to cover the entire organization. A "Technology Plan" was formulated with the objective of providing a clearing house for scientific, technical and industrial problems, giving industrial organizations access to the knowledge, research and consultative skills of Institute members relevant to particular products and processes. The Plan aimed "to bridge the gap between the school and the factory, between the idea and the process." Companies could join the Plan by the payment of an annual fee for five years. For this fee MIT would provide liaison and consultative help from the departments in touch with the client's problems.

The Plan created an administrative Division of Industrial Cooperation and Research within the Institute to put the concept into practice. It was the first systematic scheme "ever worked out by a technical institution for cooperation between a school of pure and applied science and the industries dependent upon this science." The Plan was the first attempt of its kind to do for industry in the United States what the German government had years before done for German industry: to directly associate science with industry, to the mutual benefit of each.

The endowment fund campaign and the efforts to enlist companies under the Plan quickly gathered strength from the dedicated efforts of the president, corporation, alumni and student organizations. By mid-December 1919 $3 million of the $4 million necessary had been secured. On Friday 9 January 1920 the target sum was reached, five months ahead of schedule. Nearly 10,000 donors, alumni and undergraduates had between them contributed $2.9 million. Even the students had contributed at an average of over $50 each. Almost 200 industrial organizations had paid fees totalling $1.2 million under the Technology Plan. But on the very Friday the thumping success of the campaign was announced Maclaurin was ordered to bed. The following Thursday, worn out by his unending efforts for MIT and the country, he died of pneumonia at the age of 49.

The endowment campaign assured to MIT, for the first time since its birth, funds adequate to provide independence and security. Given such funding the Institute was at last in a position to fulfill the mission first proclaimed for it by Rogers, and articulated and operationalized by Maclaurin. In 1920 the Institute had 300 to 400 faculty members and over 3,000 students—double the number of a decade before. When Maclaurin came to the organization in 1909 the total property owned by the Institute was valued at $4 million. At the time of his death, less than eleven years later, the value had risen to over $26 million. By means of the endowment campaign the total sum upon which his organization could depend for income was over $14 million.

Organization Development Begins at Lakeside*

Robert R. Blake and Jane S. Mouton

Quinn Morton, top manager of Lakeside, a big manufacturing plant, came to a behavioral science seminar where I was an instructor. He wasn't in my group so I didn't get to know him personally at the time. Yet, because I took a lot of responsibility for lectures during general sessions, he got to know something about my thinking.

The last Thursday evening after dinner, he and I began talking about the week's learning. He said he was impressed with some of the issues we had focused on because they represented the kinds of dilemmas he was trying to deal with day after day.

As we continued talking, an idea began to take shape. He finally put it into words. He said, "Look, Bob, would you be interested in coming to Lakeside for two or three years to help us put these principles into practice and so increase our effectiveness as an organization? Our goal would be to see how good you can make a company when you really go all out to make it *excellent*."

That was the kind of a challenge that doesn't come to a university professor every day. I was convinced that behavioral science principles had significant implications, not only for increasing productivity, but also for increasing the gratification that people receive from their work. I said, "Quinn, I'd like to think that one over. It's too big a question for a 'yes' or 'no' right off the top of my head. I'd like to talk with my family and my colleagues, and then I'll be back in touch with you by the middle of next week."

I did this, and the Lakeside project came into being. Two stages of development were involved. First, several hundred managerial personnel went to seminars to learn key theories of behavioral science regarding individual, group, and intergroup factors influencing action in problem solving. The idea was that before people could really think constructively in terms of organization excellence they ought to examine and understand fundamental ideas of conflict, teamwork, candor, and so on.

The second stage of the project was for me to move physically into the company with a view to getting the principles that had been learned in the seminars applied to the operational problem-solving life of Lakeside. For about two months I did an initial study of the organization and interviewed many of the people I had gotten to know during the training program. The absence of precedents for this situation marked the beginning of OD.

* SOURCE: Robert R. Blake and Jane S. Mouton, *Diary of an OD Man* (Houston, Tex.: Gulf, 1976), pp. 1–2. Reprinted with permission.

From the very outset, I had specified conditions under which I would join the organization. It was agreed that if I joined, I would in no way involve myself in personnel evaluation. I wanted no part in trying to influence reconstruction of the power system in terms of "which people should be placed in what roles." I had a clear reason, based on systematic behavioral science criteria, for adopting this approach. This was that, to a substantial degree, the problems of an organization are not to be found "inside" people, but are more closely related to organization-wide assumptions as to how people should relate with one another, and to attitudes existing between groups. Therefore, my contribution would be to help people directly in their relationships with one another; to help reform interpersonal attitudes within groups; and to help resolve problems between groups. I also indicated I wanted no company car, office, telephone, or any other symbols that might imply I was occupying a position within Lakeside's organizational format.

I joined the organization under these circumstances. For some time, initially, it was difficult for Quinn to adjust to my presence without forever asking me with whom I was working and on what problems I was engaged. Frequently he quizzed me on these points, but on each occasion I referred him back to our earlier agreement. I said I appreciated his need to monitor my performance, but on the other hand he should appreciate *my* problem of ensuring that the confidences and secrets presently being entrusted to me would continue to be made available. This would be the case only if I maintained the conditions of non-reporting that we had previously agreed upon. Eventually he came to accept this.

By taking this approach, I was able to become active in any part of the organization to which I could attach myself. Wherever I could gain access, I was free to do whatever I wanted. First, I became a member of a special one-day-a-week meeting in the Engineering Department. Then, as labor contract bargaining got underway, I regularly attended the preparatory conferences where the management team members were briefed on the technical points involved in upcoming sessions. I sat in at management's post-bargaining evaluation meetings as well. In all of these situations my only basis for participation was in terms of questioning or commenting upon attitudes, assumptions, and process problems.

The R&D Department*

William G. Dyer

Tom Haymond, manager of the research and development department of the chemicals division of a large manufacturing company, had just returned from a management training program. It had been an intensive five days and he had heard some things about his own management style and strategy that bothered him. Tom knew things were not going all that well in his department. Because of that, he had contacted the training office and asked them to recommend a good management development course—maybe he could get some new ideas that would be helpful. The training office had directed him to a well-known program that had a strong laboratory-training-group focus and Tom made arrangements to attend.

The week's activity had been a real eye-opener for Tom. The seven other people in his group had given him a lot of feedback about the way he tried to handle things in the group, and there were a lot of comments when he described how he ran his department back home. Tom knew he was a hard-driving, results-oriented person; he couldn't stand to see anyone or anything just sitting around. The group members at the conference told him that his insistence that the group get organized and moving had really antagonized them, and some had deliberately tried to block his efforts. One member commented that she would certainly not like to work under Tom, if Tom were the same way back home as he was when the group started. Tom was quite sure he was the same way back home. That's what bothered him.

Tom had talked with his group facilitator before he left and got an agreement that if Tom wanted to do something in his own department, the facilitator would be available to help as an outside resource person.

After returning home from the conference, Tom spent part of several days planning a strategy. Finally he was ready to take action. He called an extended staff meeting for all of the section heads and project directors who reported to him—a group of ten people. At the staff meeting, Tom laid out a series of issues and concerns:

1. He described the conditions in the department that had led him to attend the training course—the number of new developments was down, some key people had recently quit or asked for transfers, in one exit interview the terminating person had placed the reason for leaving on Tom's ineffective management behavior, and the attendance and participation at staff meetings was low.
2. Tom summarized the feedback given him at the management program. He pointed out his concern about the feedback and his fear that his behavior at

* SOURCE: William G. Dyer, *Team Building*. ©1977. Addison-Wesley Publishing Company, Inc., Reading, Mass., pp. 29, 31. Reprinted with permission.

work was similar to that displayed during the conference. He felt that if he were to get feedback from the work group, it would be similar.

3. Tom then pointed out the dilemma for him. On the one hand he wanted to improve the performance level of the R&D department, but, on the other hand, he had some information that indicated he himself might be a contributing factor to low performance. Without clear feedback both from them to him and from him to them, they might not get the basic problems. A plan of action for improving the situation was badly needed.

4. Tom asked for their suggestions. "What can I do and what can you do to help us all work on the problems that I have identified?" There was a long silence. One project head said, "I don't think things are as bad as you paint them Tom. In my book, you're a pretty good manager." (There were nods of agreement and someone said, "Right on!")

Tom replied, "I appreciate your support, but I think we would all have to agree that this department has not been as effective recently as it was two years ago. Something has happened and I'd like to find out what that is and remedy it.

"I would like to make a suggestion. I propose that we spend two or three days away from the office looking intensively at the issues I have raised today. Each person would then come prepared to give his or her own information—what basic problems affect each of us personally on the job, what causes these problems, and what we might do about them. If we put all of our information together, we might come up with some interesting new solutions.

"Also, I would like to recommend bringing in an outside resource person to help us during the two-to-three-day meeting. This person could watch us work and see if anything in my actions or the way we work together might need improving. What do you think?"

The staff began to discuss the proposal at length and, after an intensive wrestling with the issues presented, the group agreed both to go ahead with the meeting (it would start Wednesday evening and finish Friday afternoon) and to bring in an outside resource person.

The Fairview Company*

Edgar H. Schein

It became clear to some members of the central training department of the Fairview Company that one of the company's major difficulties was conflict between the central headquarters and various field units. There were conflicts over how much decentralisation of decision-making authority there should be, over lines of authority, and how much the system actually reflected earlier agreements to decentralise. The company had strong functional directors in the headquarters organisation. As they developed financial and marketing programmes they tended to bypass the formal line organisation, through the executive vice-president and the regional managers, and deal directly with the financial and marketing people in the field.

A number of people in the central training department had become exposed to sensitivity training several years back, had introduced it into their middle and senior management development programmes, and had gained a good deal of sophistication in analysing organisational processes.

There was an annual meeting of all the key executives in the company, including both headquarters and field people, some 15 managers in all. The training group consulted me about the possibility of organising one of these meetings in such a way as to enable the entire group to work on the headquarters-field problem. They felt strongly that something should be tried at the meeting. They were not sure how Jack Bell, the president, or Louis Adler, the vice-president, would respond to what we might plan, since there was no prior history of exposure of the executive group to an outside consultant. However, a number of the regional managers had attended T-groups, and learned something about the potentialities inherent in bringing in a 'behaviourally-oriented consultant.'

A core group, consisting of the training director, two of his staff and an enthusiastic regional manager, met with me for a day to plan a strategy. We decided that in order to successfully confront the organisational problem at the executive meeting, it was necessary that some substantial number of the people who would be at the meeting become involved in the planning and design of it. A planning group was formed, consisting of equal numbers of headquarters and regional managers. The mission of this group was to meet for two days to plan the executive meeting. The plan developed by the group was then to be presented to Jack Bell and Louis Adler for their approval.

During the two-day meeting of the planning group I had to steer the

* SOURCE: Edited by Roy McLennan and abstracted from Edgar H. Schein, *Process Consultation*. ©1969. Addison-Wesley Publishing Company, Inc., Reading, Mass. Reprinted with permission.

members *away* from a traditional format, in which I would be expected to make presentations about headquarters/field type problems for the meeting to discuss. And I also had to take responsibility for the success of the meeting format finally chosen, and find a role for myself which would make this format work.

The plan which emerged from the planning group had the following elements:

1. The annual meeting would be billed as an exploration of organisational problems at the top of the company, towards the end of improving organisational relationships;
2. The meeting would be chaired by me rather than the company president;
3. The meeting's agenda would be developed by a procedure used by Richard Beckhard:

> Each member of the group would be asked to write me a letter, at my home, outlining what he saw to be the major organisational problems facing the company. It would then be my job to put together the information in the letters into major themes and issues. These themes and issues were to be presented by me to the meeting at our first session, and would constitute the agenda for the three day event.

The first purpose in having such letters written was to provide each person with the opportunity to be completely frank, without having to expose himself to the possible wrath of the boss or other members of the meeting. Second, it provided an opportunity to gather data from all the members before the meeting began. Third, it involved each member in helping to set the agenda, a considerable departure from previous meetings, where the agenda had been set by the vice-president. It could be expected, therefore, that all the members would feel more involved in the meeting from the outset.

The letter-writing idea had two problems connected with it. It seemed a little bit gimmicky, and it was difficult to know how the manager who had not as yet met me would react. Would he write a frank letter to a strange professor about rather critical organisational issues? We decided we would have to run the risk of getting no response or poor response. But we could minimise the risk by having the members of the planning group talk to other managers they knew, who would be at the meeting, and make a personal appeal to write a frank letter.

Our conclusions were presented to the president and vice-president, received their enthusiastic approval, and thus became the plan for the meeting. I pointed out to Jack and Louis that they would have to be careful about how they managed their roles. If they reverted too quickly to their power positions, and abandoned the role of helping to diagnose organisational problems, the executive group would retreat into silence and the problem would remain unsolved. I felt that both men understood the risks, were willing to take them, and had the kind of personality which would help them accept the somewhat strange format we had designed for the meeting.

Having agreed to go ahead, it was then decided that Louis would send out the letter explaining the meeting format, and inviting the diagnostic letters. Members of the planning group were to follow up in the districts, to ensure that everyone understood the plan, and the fact that the plan had come from company members themselves (even though I had suggested many of the separate elements). This rather lengthy procedure was essential to obtain the involvement of the managers in a process-oriented meeting. Even though the ideas for it came from the training department and from me, it clearly became a concept which appealed to regional and headquarters managers. Had they not become committed, it would not have been possible to hold such a meeting at all.

I constructed the agenda for the meeting in a way intended to maximise the probability that the managerial group would confront issues of importance to its members. On the first day I presented the major categories of issues which the letters had revealed, and illustrated each issue by paraphrasing from one or more letters. The group thus received feedback, while the identity of the individual who had provided it was protected. The senior people were receptive, willing to listen to the issues, and able to work on them constructively. I noticed that as the members became more comfortable with each other, they were increasingly able to make their own points, and identify themselves openly with the various issues. They less and less leaned on me as the source of input.

A Brief History of Organization Development*

Wendell L. French and Cecil H. Bell, Jr.

Less than two decades ago, organization development emerged from three basic sources: (1) the laboratory training movement, (2) the development of survey research and feedback methodology; and, basic to both of these, (3) the writings, efforts, energy, and impetus of the late Kurt Lewin. In this historical survey we will highlight what we believe to be the significant innovations and contributions that helped to shape OD.

LABORATORY TRAINING MOVEMENT

Laboratory training, unstructured small-group situations in which participants learn from their own interactions and the evolving group dynamics, developed about 1946 from various experiments in the use of discussion groups to achieve changes in behavior in back-home situations. In particular, a workshop held at the State Teachers College at New Britain, Connecticut, in the summer of 1946 marked the emergence of laboratory training. This workshop was sponsored by the Connecticut Interracial Commission and The Research Center for Group Dynamics, then at the Massachusetts Institute of Technology. The leadership team for this action research was Kurt Lewin, Kenneth Benne, Leland Bradford, and Ronald Lippitt. From this project emerged a three-week session during the summer of 1947 at Bethel, Maine, initially financed by the Office of Naval Research and sponsored by the National Education Association and the Research Center for Group Dynamics. The work of that summer was to evolve into the National Training Laboratories for Group Development and contemporary T-Group training.[1]

Over the next decade, as trainers in the laboratory training and group dynamics movement began to work with social systems of more permanency

---

* SOURCE: Wendell L. French and Cecil H. Bell, Jr., "A Brief History of Organization Development," *Journal of Contemporary Business* (Summer 1972), 1–8. Reprinted with permission.

[1] See Leland P. Bradford, Jack R. Gibb, and Kenneth D. Benne, T-Group Theory and Laboratory Method (New York: John Wiley & Sons, 1964), pp. 3, 81–83; Alfred J. Marrow, *The Practical Theorist: The Life and Work of Kurt Lewin* (New York: Basic Books, 1969), pp. 210–14. For additional history, see Leland P. Bradford, "Biography of an Institution," *Journal of Applied Behavioral Science*, April–May–June 1967, pp. 127–43. For reference to the impact of John Dewey and others, see Bradford et al., *T-Group Theory*, especially p. 466.

and complexity than T-groups, they began to experience considerable frustration in the transfer of laboratory behavioral skills and insights of individuals into the solution of problems in organizations. Personal skills learned in the "stranger" T-group setting were very difficult to transfer to complex organizations. However, the training of "teams" from the same organization had emerged early at Bethel and, undoubtedly, was a link to the total organizational focus of Douglas McGregor, Herbert Shepard, Robert Blake, and others.[2]

The late Douglas McGregor, working with Union Carbide beginning about 1957, is considered to be one of the first behavioral scientists to begin to solve the transfer problem and to talk systematically about and to help implement the application of laboratory training skills to a complex organization.[3] In collaboration with McGregor, John Paul Jones, with the support of the Union Carbide's executive vice president and director, Birny Mason, Jr. (later president of the corporation), established a small internal consulting group which, in large part, used behavioral science knowledge in assisting line managers. Jones' organization was later called an "organization development group."[4]

During the same year, Herbert Shepard joined the Employee Relations Department of Esso Standard Oil as a research associate on organization. In 1958 and 1959 he launched experiments in organization development at three major Esso refineries: Bayonne, Baton Rouge, and Bayway. At Bayonne an interview survey and diagnosis were made and discussed with top management, followed by a series of three-day laboratories for all members of management. Paul Buchanan, who had been using a somewhat similar approach in Republic Aviation, collaborated with Shepard at Bayonne and subsequently joined the Esso staff. (Buchanan previously had been employed as a consulting psychologist by the Naval Ordinance Test Station at China Lake, California, where he had engaged the management in a number of activities, including "retreats" in which they worked on interpersonal relations.)[5]

---

[2] We are indebted to Ronald Lippitt for his correspondence, which contributed this historical link and for his assistance in clarifying the paragraph immediately preceding and the one following. According to correspondence with Ronald Lippitt, as early as 1945, Lee Bradford and Ronald Lippitt were conducting "three-level training" at Freedman's Hospital in Washington, D.C., in an effort "to induce interdependent changes in all parts of the same system." Lippitt also reports that Lee Bradford was acting on a basic concept of "multiple entry," which is highly congruent with contemporary OD efforts.

[3] Richard Beckhard, W. Warner Burke, and Fred I. Steele, "The Program for Specialists in Organization Training and Development" (NTL Institute for Applied Behavioral Science, December 1967) (mimeographed paper), p. ii; John Paul Jones, "What's Wrong with Work?" *What's Wong with Work?* (New York: National Association of Manufacturers, 1967), p. 8.

[4] Gilbert Burch, "Union Carbide's Patient Schemers," *Fortune*, December 1965, pp. 147–49. For McGregor's account, see Douglas McGregor, "Team-Building at Union Carbide," *The Professional Manager* (New York: McGraw-Hill, 1967), pp. 106–10.

[5] Much of the historical account in this paragraph and the next three paragraphs is based on correspondence with Herbert Shepard, with some information added from correspondence with Robert Blake. For additional historical information about the activities at Esso, see the essay by Robert Blake and Jane Mouton in this issue.

At Baton Rouge, Robert Blake joined Shepard, and they initiated a series of two-week laboratories attended by all members of "middle" management. At first, an effort was made to combine the case method with laboratory method, but the designs soon emphasized T-groups, organizational exercises, and relevant lectures. One innovation in this training program was an emphasis on intergroup as well as interpersonal relations. Although working on interpersonal problems affecting work performance was clearly an organizational effort, between-group problem solving had even more "organization development" implications in that a broader and more complex segment of the organization was involved.

At Baton Rouge, efforts to involve top management failed, and, as a result, follow-up resources for implementing organization development were not made available. By the time the Bayway program started, two fundamental OD lessons had been learned: (1) the requirement for active involvement in and leadership of the program by top management and (2) the need for on-the-job application.

At Bayway there were two significant innovations. First, Shepard, Blake, and Murray Horwitz utilized the instrumented laboratory which Blake and Jane Mouton had been developing in social psychology classes at the University of Texas (which they later developed into the Managerial Grid approach to organization development).[6] (An essential dimension of the instrumented lab is the use of feedback based on scales and measurements of group and individual behavior during sessions.)[7] Second, at Bayway more resources were devoted to team development, consultation, intergroup conflict resolution, etc., than were devoted to laboratory training of "cousins," i.e., organization members from different departments.

As Robert Blake has stated, "It was learning to *reject* T-group, stranger-type labs that permitted OD to come into focus." As he has further commented, intergroup projects in particular "triggered real OD."[8] As is evident from the Esso and Union Carbide activities, Shepard, Blake, McGregor, and others clearly were trying to build on the insights and learnings of laboratory training toward more linkage with and impact on the problems and dynamics of ongoing organizations.

It is not entirely clear who coined the term, *organization development*, but

---

[6] Correspondence from Robert Blake and Herbert Shepard. For further reference to Murray Horwitz and Paul Buchanan, as well as comments about the innovative contributions of Michael Blansfield, see Herbert A. Shepard, "Explorations in Observant Participation," in Bradford et al., *T-Group Theory*, pp. 382–83.

[7] See Robert Blake and Jane Srygley Mouton, "The Instrumented Training Laboratory," in *Selected Readings Series Five: Issues in Training*, ed. Irving R. Weschler and Edgar M. Schein (Washington, D.C.: National Training Laboratories, 1962), pp. 61–85. In this chapter, Blake and Mouton credit Muzafer and Carolyn Sherif with important contributions to early intergroup experiments. Reference is also made to the contributions of Frank Cassens of Humble Oil and Refinery in the early phases of the Esso Program.

[8] Based on correspondence from Robert Blake to the authors.

in all probablility it was Robert Blake, Herbert Shepard, and Jane Mouton.[9] The phrase *development group* had been used earlier by Blake and Mouton in connection with human relations training at the University of Texas and appeared in their 1956 document "Training for Decision Making in Groups," which was distributed for use in connection with the Baton Rouge experiment.[10] (The same phrase appeared in a Mouton and Blake article first published in the journal, *Group Psychotherapy*, in 1957.)[11] The Baton Rouge T-groups were called "Development Groups"[12] and this terminology, coupled with the insights which were emerging, undoubtedly culminated in the concept of "organization development."

It is of considerable significance that the emergence of organization development efforts in the first two firms to be involved, Union Carbide and Esso, included employee relations—industrial relations people seeing themselves in new roles. At Union Carbide, John Paul Jones, who had come up through industrial relations, now saw himself in the role of a behavioral science consultant to other managers.[13] At Esso, the headquarters human relations research division began to view itself as an internal consulting group, which offers services to field managers, rather than as a research group which develops reports for top management.[14] Thus, in the history of OD, we see both external consultants and internal staff departments departing from traditional roles and collaborating in quite a new approach to organization improvement.

SURVEY RESEARCH AND FEEDBACK METHOD

Of particular importance to the history of organization development is a specialized form of action research which we will call survey research and feedback. This refers to the use of attitude surveys and data feedback in workshop sessions and constitutes the second major thrust in the history of organization development.

The history of this thrust parallels the laboratory training thrust to OD and revolves around the experience staff members at the Research Center for Group Dynamics, founded in 1945 by Kurt Lewin, were gaining over a period

---

[9] Based on correspondence from Robert Blake to the authors.

[10] Based on correspondence from Robert Blake to the authors.

[11] Jane Srygley Mouton and Robert R. Blake, "University Training in Human Relations Skills," *Selected Readings Series Three: Forces in Learning* (Washington, D.C.: National Training Laboratories, 1961), pp. 88–96 (reprinted from *Group Psychotherapy* 10 (1957), pp. 342–45).

[12] Shepard and Blake correspondence.

[13] Burck, "Union Carbide," p. 149.

[14] Harry D. Kolb, "Introduction," *An Action Research Program for Organization Improvement* (Ann Arbor: Foundation for Research on Human Behavior, 1960), p. i. The phrase "organization development" is used several times in this monograph based on a 1959 meeting about the Esso programs written by Kolb et al.

of years in "action research." The Center was first established at the Massachusetts Institute of Technology; subsequently after Lewin's death in 1947, the staff moved to the University of Michigan to join with Michigan's Survey Research Center to form the Institute for Social Research. A few of the key figures involved at MIT in addition to Lewin were Marian Radke, Leon Festinger, Ronald Lippitt, Douglas McGregor, John R. P. French, Jr., Dorwin Cartwright, and Morton Deutsch.[15] Names conspicuous in the work at Michigan in recent years include Floyd Mann and Rensis Likert.

As one example, in 1948 at The Detroit Edison Company, researchers began systematic feedback of data from a companywide employee and management attitude survey.[16] In this project, data from an attitude survey were fed back in participating accounting departments in what Mann calls an "interlocking chain of conferences."[17] Some of the insights which emerged from this process have a very contemporary "OD" ring. To illustrate, in drawing conclusions from the Detroit Edison study, Baumgartel stated:

> The results of this experimental study lend support to the idea that an intensive, group discussion procedure for utilizing the results of an employee questionnaire survey can be an effective tool for introducing positive change in a business organization. It may be that the effectiveness of this method, in comparison to traditional training courses, is that it deals with the system of human relationships as a whole (superior and subordinate can change together) and it deals with each manager, supervisor, and employee in the context of his own job, his own problems, and his own work relationships.[18]

KURT LEWIN

If laboratory training and survey research feedback constitute two main historical origins of organization development, then certainly Kurt Lewin and his work in developing a field theory of social psychology must also be recognized. His passionate interest in applied behavioral science was the main thrust to both laboratory training and survey research. Lewin was a central figure in the origin of both the National Training Laboratories (now NTL Institute for Applied Behavioral Science) and the Research Center for Group

[15] For part of this history, see Marrow, *Practical Theorist*, chap. 19; and *A Quarter Century of Social Research* (Institute for Social Research, 1971).

[16] Floyd C. Mann, "Studying and Creating Change," in *The Planning of Change*, ed. Warren Bennis, Kenneth Benne, and Robert Chin (New York: Holt, Rinehart, & Winston, 1961), pp. 605–13. Another early project which had some overtones of organization development but was not published for many years was the "Tremont Hotel Project." See William Foote Whyte and Edith Lentz Hamilton, *Action Research for Management* (Homewood, Ill.: Richard D. Irwin, 1955), pp. 1–282.

[17] Ibid., p. 609.

[18] Howard Baumgartel, "Using Employee Questionnaire Results for Improving Organizations: The Survey 'Feedback' Experiment," *Kansas Business Review*, December 1959, pp. 2–6.

Dynamics. Although Lewin died only two years after the founding of the Research Center and just before the first formal session of NTL, he had a profound influence on both organizations and the people associated with them—and his influence continues today.[19]

EXTENT OF APPLICATION

Applications emerging from one or both of the two stems above are evident in the organization development efforts which are becoming visible in many countries, including England, Japan, Norway, Canada, Sweden, Australia, and Holland, as well as in the United States. Just a few of the growing number of organizations in North America which have embarked on organization development efforts are Union Carbide and Esso (the first two companies), Hotel Corporation of America, Alcan, National Aeronautics and Space Administration (NASA), Saga Foods, Polaroid, Armour and Company, Texas Instruments, American Airlines, and TRW Systems Group. Applications at TRW Systems Group, a large research and development organization in the aerospace field, commenced in 1961 and may be as extensive and innovative as anywhere in the world.[20] Efforts there have included laboratory training, team building, interface laboratories between departments and between company and customers, and career planning. In England and Europe, illustrative of growing interest in organization development is the involvement of such companies as Imperial Chemical Industries, Ltd., J. Lyons & Company, and the Shell Oil Company. Projects at Imperial Chemical Industries, a large chemical company headquartered in London, have included job enrichment, survey feedback, and team-building approaches.

However, industrial organizations are by no means the only kinds of institutions involved. We know of applications, for example, in public school systems, colleges, social welfare agencies, police departments, governmental departments, churches, and in certain American Indian tribes.

Symptomatic of the widespread application of organization development concepts is the emergence and growth of the OD Network of the NTL Institute for Applied Behavioral Science, which began in 1964 and now has a membership of more than 200. Most members either have major roles in the OD efforts of organizations and/or are scholars in the OD field. An OD Division of the

---

[19] For an excellent and detailed account of Lewin's life and influence, see Marrow, *Practical Theorist*, Parts I–III. This book is rich with events which are important in the history of OD. For example, Marrow mentions a 1944 dinner which Rensis Likert arranged in order for Douglas McGregor and Kurt Lewin to explore the feasibility of a group dynamics center at MIT (p. 164).

[20] See Sheldon A. Davis, "An Organic Problem-Solving Method of Organizational Change," *Journal of Applied Behavioral Science*, November 1, 1967, pp. 3–21. See also the case study of TRW Systems Group in Gene Dalton, Paul Lawrence, and Larry Greiner, eds., *Organizational Change and Development* (Homewood, Ill.: Richard D. Irwin, and Dorsey Press, 1970), pp. 104–43.

American Society of Training and Development started in 1968 and had almost 800 members toward the end of 1970.[21]

It is also significant that in 1971 the Academy of Management, whose members are mostly professors in management and related areas, began a Division of Organization Development within its structure. As of 1972, membership in the division was approximately 240. Another organization, the Division of Industrial and Organizational Psychology of the American Psychological Association, included a workshop on organization development in the annual APA convention; several annual conventions going back to at least 1965 had included papers or symposia on organization development or related topics.[22]

The first doctoral program devoted to training OD specialists was founded by Herbert Shepard in 1960 at the Case Institute of Technology. First called, "The Organizational Behavior Group," this program now is part of the Department of Organization and Administration of Case-Western Reserve. In addition, we know of at least the following additional universities having graduate courses directly bearing on organization development: Harvard, UCLA, Yale, University of Missouri (St. Louis), San Jose State College, University of Southern California, University of Wyoming, Boston University, the George Washington University, Southern Methodist University, the University of Washington, University of North Carolina, Virginia Polytechnic Institute, Ohio University, and MIT

Giving major impetus to this rapid growth in interest and attention had been NTL's Program for Specialists in Organization Training and Development, which is an intensive, month-long session. A major part of this program is devoted to consultation skills. The first such program was held in 1967 in Bethel, Maine, as an outgrowth of an Organization Intern Program which had included some OD training. In subsequent years, programs have been offered in two locations. Other shorter programs are beginning to appear under the sponsorship of the NTL Institute, universities and foundations, and other institutions.

CONCLUDING COMMENTS

In conclusion, what has come to be called "organization development" has a set of identifiable characteristics and techniques that have emerged from the laboratory training movement and from survey feedback technology. The work of the late Kurt Lewin was prominent in the evolution of both of these sources

---

[21] Forrest R. Belcher, "A Report on ASTD's 1970 Accomplishments," *Training and Development Journal*, March 1971.

[22] For example, the following topics were included in the program of the 1964 convention: "Strategies for Organization Improvement: Research and Consultation," "Managerial Grid Organization Development," and "The Impact of Laboratory Training in a Research and Development Environment," *American Psychologist*, July 1965, pp. 549, 562, and 565.

to OD. The phenomenon of employee relations—industrial relations units seeing themselves in new consultancy roles is also a significant part of this history.

The evolution of the OD field proceeds apace. The practitioner-scholars whose essays appear in this issue have had major roles in shaping the field as we know it today, and, based on what we see in their essays, they clearly will have a major impact on the organization development of tomorrow.

The Historical Perspective*

Michael Foster

The history of action research is not characterized by a process of steadily advancing knowledge. On the contrary, the picture is more of fits and starts with developments taking place in different parts of the field. Too often, it seems that the originators are unaware of the work of others and fail to make use of it, which lends weight to the suspicion that action researchers are short on reading. Lewin is generally credited with being the father of the approach. Towards the end of the 1940's and the early 1950's there was an outpouring of reports from the Research Centre for Group Dynamics and the Commission on Community Interrelations[1] in the United States, paralleled by a similar outpouring from the Tavistock Institute of Human Relations in Great Britain. Accounts of these studies appear in early editions of the *Journal of Human Relations* (1947); the *Journal of Social Issues* (1947); Newcombe & Hartley's book, *Readings in social psychology* (1947); and in Cartwright (1952). It will be recalled that these were the days of the great debate between supporters of the Gestalt and Behaviourist schools of psychology. The arguments advanced by Lewin for the merits of action research were Gestaltist in origin. He stressed the limitations of studying complex, real social events in a laboratory, the artificiality of splitting out single behavioural elements from an integrated system, and the advantages of understanding the dynamic nature of change, by studying it under controlled conditions as it takes place. Many psychologists and sociologists became involved with problem-centred research during World War II, and this pragmatic interest was reflected in their desire to develop social science to reach 'the level of the practical usefulness which society needs' (Lewin, 1947a). As a method of change Lewin strongly favoured 'changing group standards' rather than 'individual procedures'. In some circumstances, he advocated separating 'the groups from the larger setting . . . and creating cultural islands'. These ideas are demonstrated in his experiments on changing behaviour in such matters as milk consumption, giving orange juice and cod liver oil to babies, and other family food habits. On collaborating with the client he stressed that: 'any research programme set up within the framework of an organization desiring social action must be guided by the needs of that organization'. And that it was necessary to be aware of 'the importance of the spirit of co-operation for research on group processes' (Lewin, 1947a).

* SOURCE: Michael Foster, "An Introduction to the Theory and Practice of Action Research in Work Organizations," *Human Relations*, 25 1972, 529–533. Reprinted with permission of the Plenum Publishing Corp.

[1] This was an undertaking of the American Jewish Congress. It was launched in 1944. A description of how it came into being is given by Marrow (1967).

He identified several of the roles which the research staff might play. For example:

i. as consultants on methods of action
ii. as evaluation experts
iii. as experimentalists by pre-testing with controls, etc. on proposed administrative policy
iv. as autonomous researchers having earned the sanction to carry on pure research and contribute to long-term policy.

He was very much aware of the problem of values:

> The social scientist . . . has to see realistically the problems of power, which are interwoven with many of the questions he is to study, without his becoming a servant to vested interests . . . The problem of our own values, objectives, and of objectivity are nowhere more interwoven and more important than in action research.

Lewin employed a number of tactics for bringing about change (cf. particularly Newcombe & Hartley, 1947). The more important were:

i. an early identification of the leading parts of the target system (i.e. the gate-keepers)
ii. paying attention to the social context in which the 'gate-keeper' behaviour took place
iii. enhancing individual involvement by problem-posing in a group situation
iv. avoiding 'ego-risk' by posing the problem in terms of the problem for 'the other'
v. providing experts to feed-in information as required (i.e. a process of 'discovery learning')
vi. requiring a public statement by every individual as to future behavioural intentions
vii. indicating to subjects that a check on subsequent behaviour would be made.

A significant aspect of Lewin's background theory of social change is described in the following paragraph:

> . . . it is clear that by a state of no social change we do not refer to a stationary but to a quasi-stationary equilibrium; that is to say a state comparable to that of a river which flows with a given velocity in a given direction during a certain time interval. A social change is comparable to a change in the velocity or direction of that river (1947b).

It follows that strategies of change are viewed by him in terms of reducing or changing the direction of forces within the social system, or of applying forces from without and harnessing them together with those in the system, so as to pull in the desired direction. A further important notion of Lewin's which has not perhaps been fully utilized is the state of 'social habit'

(Lewin, 1947b), a kind of inertia which requires a sufficient input of energy before movement can take place. The implications in action research practice are two-fold: first, that the change agent should have reserves available so as to be able to apply a sufficient critical mass, and second, that he should 'keep his nerve' during the initial period when nothing seems to happen.

Lewin's three-step process of unfreezing, moving and freezing at the new level, is often quoted, but sometimes without the warning that freezing at the new level should be a deliberate planned objective. Merely reaching a new level is no guarantee of its permanency, even in the short term.

On looking back at what Lewin had to say, there is a glimpse of an experimenter/subject relationship which today would be considered manipulative. Values have shifted so that change agents have become more concerned to share with clients their *own* objectives (both *research* and *action*) as well as the ways and means they have in mind for achieving them. This goes a long way towards meeting charges of manipulation, but raises anxieties amongst social scientists about the restriction of research goals, and the contamination of results (see Rapoport, 1970).

Another contribution in the late 1940's was from Chein, Cook & Harding (1948). These authors throw further light on the meaning of action research at that time. They invite us to compare the task of the physical scientist with the action researcher. The action researcher must not only face all the difficulties which confront a researcher in the laboratory, but others. His task does not come to an end when he has made some advance or discovery. For, if the change agent is to complete his task, he must by definition see that 'the results of his labours are applied.' This goal involves him 'with a host of problems to do with human, personal and social resistance to change.' He finds 'special limitations imposed at every level of his work, from the choice of problem areas, the specific formulation of the problem, the selection of procedures, the presentation of his findings, on through to application.'

Bennis (1963) and Bradford *et al.* (1964) remind us that it was also at about this time (1947) that T-groups originated in Bethel under the guidance of Bradford, Benne and Lippitt, who were all influenced by Lewin's concept of change in the group setting. However, the main objective of early laboratory training was personal self-insight and it was not until the early 1950's that the T-group became part of the repertoire of the change agent involved in organizational settings.

The Bethel development was not the only one of its kind. At the same time something similar, but with different antecedents, was taking place in Britain. Rees (1945), a pre-war member of the Tavistock Clinic, had established an inter-disciplinary social psychiatry team in the British Army. One of the members was Bion, a psychiatrist and psychoanalyst, who being under pressure to extend his psychotherapeutic services hit upon the idea of treating patients in groups. Such an approach to treatment, he came to believe, also had special merit for some purposes in that it made it possible to include a social component. His early work appears in Bion & Rickman (1943) as well as in a series of papers in *Human Relations* (1947 to 1951) and later published as a book, Bion (1961). Bion's approach fitted in admirably with those of his colleagues at the Tavistock when he returned with others after the war. They were also 'group minded' and, like those at Bethel, admirers of Lewin. Not surprisingly a similar T-group development took place.

There were great hopes that action research would 'catch on' and yield fundamental insights into the nature of change processes. This has not come about at the speed which the early pioneers had hoped for. Indeed Sanford (1970) recently published an article which he entitled 'Whatever happened to action research?' However, Sanford's paper was perhaps intended to shock us, as reports of action research studies have continued to appear in the literature over the years. These developments have recently been outlined by Rapoport (1970). He traces four streams:

a. *The Tavistock Stream*
   An integrative psychoanalytical, social science approach which centred on the solution of social as distinct from individual problems. 'The main theme was the need to get collaboration from members of an organisation while attempting to help them solve their own problems.'

b. *The Group Dynamics Stream*
   The work of the Center for Group Dynamics emphasized individual and small group processes. It placed less emphasis than the Tavistock Institute on larger scale social systems. In addition, it was more academic and with closer links to experimental psychology.

c. *The Operational Research Stream*
   This is an approach which is practised by members of the Institute for Operational Research at the Tavistock Institute, by Ackoff and Churchman in America, where joint problem-centred field work has been undertaken by operational researchers and social scientists, and where operational researchers have attempted to introduce human factor parameters into their models (see Lawrence, 1966).

d. *The Applied Anthropology Stream*
   This approach is exemplified by the work of the Society for Applied Anthropology who publish the journal, *Human Organisation*. Many of the articles in this journal reveal an action orientation to the study of cultural change.

REFERENCES

BENNIS, W. G. (1963–64). A new role for the behavioural sciences affecting organisational change. *Admin. Science Quarterly* Vol. 8.

BION, W. R. & RICKMAN, J. (1943). Intra-group tensions in therapy. *Lancet* Nov.

BION, W. R. (1961). *Experiences in groups, and other papers*. London: Tavistock Publications.

BRADFORD, L. P., GIBB, J. R. & BENNE, K. D. (1964). *T-group therapy and laboratory method*. New York: Wiley.

CARTWRIGHT, D. (ed.) (1952). *Field theory in social science*. (Papers by K. Lewin.) London: Tavistock Publications.

CHEIN, I., COOK, S. & HARDING, J. (1948). The field of action research. *Amer. Psychol.* Vol. 3.

CHERNS, A. B. (1969). Social research and its diffusion. *Hum. relat.* Vol. 22, No. 3.

JONES, G. (1968). *Planned organisational change: a study of group dynamics*. London: Routledge, Kegan, Paul.

LAWRENCE, J. R. (ed.) (1966). *Operational research and the social sciences*. London: Tavistock Publications.

LEWIN, K. (1947a). Frontiers in group dynamics. 1. Concept, method and reality in social sciences: social equilibria and social change. 2. Channels of group life; social planning and action research. *Hum. relat.* Vol. 1, Nos 1 & 2.

LEWIN, K. (1947b). Group decision and social change. In: Newcombe, T. M. & Hartley, E. L. (eds), *Readings in social psychology*. New York: Holt, Rinehart & Winston.

MARROW, A. J. (1967). *The Practical Theorist: The Life and Work of Kurt Lewin*. New York: Basic Books.

NEWCOMBE, T. M. & HARTLEY, E. L. (eds) (1947). *Readings in social psychology*. New York: Holt, Rinehart & Winston.

RAPOPORT, R. N. (1970). Three dilemmas in action research. *Hum. relat.* Vol. 23, No. 6.

REES, J. R. (1945). *The shaping of psychiatry by war*. New York: Norton.

SANFORD, N. (1970). Whatever happened to action research? *Jour. of Soc. Iss.* Vol. 26, No. 4.

The Emergence of Humanistic Philosophy in Management and Organizations*

Newton Margulies and Anthony P. Raia

The Hawthorne studies of the late twenties and early thirties raised management's awareness of the impact of the human element on organizational performance.[1] "Human relations" became important both as a field of academic study and as subject matter in the training of managers. While the subject of human relations received some attention, it was not until the late fifties that it became something more than an addition to the manager's tool kit. A number of prominent social scientists developed the theoretical foundations that made human relations a management philosophy and approach. Their writings struck at the heart of the value orientations of managers and at the assumptions underlying our organizational models. Their analysis included not only a criticism of current organizational and management practices but also recommended an alternative set of values which were more humanistic in nature. A number of these writings are considered by some to be classics insofar as they contributed in a major way to both the theory and the practice of management. While there were many contributors, we will mention only a few of those whose work provided a springboard for further exploration and experimentation in the field.

Abraham Maslow's theory of motivation became a platform from which organizational analysis, as well as worker motivation, was studied.[2] His concepts of the "need hierarchy," and particularly his notion of self-actualization, became popular with managers who tried to incorporate them into their styles of managing and into their approach to organization. Maslow's theory was understandable, could be easily translated into organizational terms as a way to analyze and formulate approaches to motivation and morale, and had the additional advantage of lending itself to the personalization of the work place. The most significant impact, however, came from the notion of self-actualization. The idea that each individual strives to reach some ideal point of achievement,

* SOURCE: Newton Margulies and Anthony P. Raia, *Conceptual Foundations of Organizational Development* (New York: McGraw-Hill, 1978), pp. 130–132. Reprinted with permission.

[1] F. J. Roethlisberger and W. J. Dickson, *Management and the Worker*. New York: Wiley, 1939.

[2] See A. Maslow, *Motivation and Personality*. New York: Harper, 1954; and A. Eupsychian, *Management: A Journal*. Homewood, Ill.: Irwin-Dorsey, 1965.

to fully realize his or her potential, seemed to strike many a responsive chord. Some organizations tried to build a structure and a set of norms which would permit the workplace to provide self-actualizing opportunities for people in organizations.[3]

Building on Maslow's concepts of organizational models, Chris Argyris further explored the relationship between the needs of individuals and the organizational context within which the individuals work.[4] Argyris argued against much of what was then being attributed to the classical or bureaucratic model of organization and the classical views of the management process. He showed that the notions on which the organizational society was built had inherent contradictions that ran counter to the natural development of human beings.

Further treatment came from Douglas McGregor, who in 1960 wrote *The Human Side of Enterprise*.[5] McGregor, like Argyris, built on Maslow's theory of motivation. Very briefly, McGregor proposed two sets of orientations, or values about management, organization, and the work place. On the one hand, he described a set of values, or propositions, Theory X, that basically represented a negative, nontrusting, economic view of people and organizations. McGregor's idea was that if one built an organization and a management style or theory based upon this view, what was likely to emerge was a highly bureaucratic organization having many rules and many procedures. It would incorporate communication patterns which were essentially downward (and unidirectional) and would encompass a management role which was centered on control. On the other hand, McGregor proposed an alternative set of propositions, or values, Theory Y, which took a positive, trusting, more complete view of people and organizations. Managing under the Theory Y assumptions would require the integration of individual needs and organizational goals. Under these conditions, managers would not need to spend so much time on the control function. In fact, the individuals in the organization would monitor and control their own performance—i.e., exert "self-control." The result would be increased consonance between what individuals wanted from the job environment and what the organization needed to provide for its own survival. It is easy to see the relationship between McGregor's orientation toward management and Maslow's description of environments in which individuals can "self-actualize."

Rensis Likert, building on some of these early notions, noted that the major building blocks of successful organizations need not be individuals, but could in fact be social organisms, such as the work group.[6] From this perspective, the organization is viewed as consisting of many such social organisms which are linked together by managers ("linking pins") who play very special roles in

---

[3] A. H. Kuriloff, "Management by Integration and Self-Control," in P. R. Lawrence and J. A. Seiler (eds), *Organizational Behavior and Administration*. Homewood, Ill.: Irwin-Dorsey, 1965.

[4] C. Argyris, *Personality and Organization*. New York: Harper, 1957.

[5] D. McGregor, *The Human Side of Enterprise*. New York: McGraw-Hill, 1960.

[6] R. Likert, *New Patterns of Management*. New York: McGraw-Hill, 1961.

the work groups of which they are members. Likert's orientation, like those of his contemporaries, was to view the organization as a more humanistic social organism than as a bureaucracy designed to maximize the technical efficiency of human beings.

Taken collectively, these humanistic views reflected a prescriptive (as opposed to descriptive) orientation toward organization change and development.

Aspects of the Professional Facilitation of Planned Change*

Eric Trist

The facilitation of planned organizational change as a process involving collaborative relationships between client systems and social science professionals may now be said to have emerged as a recognized though still precarious activity in human affairs. The action research studies which provide its first models were undertaken during the Second World War independently and against the background of distinct traditions in the U.S. and Britain when conditions of crisis compelled rapid change. Subsequently, work of this kind has made its appearance in most western and in one or two eastern European countries, and in developing countries as different as India and Mexico. After the immediate post-war years came a lull during which the different norms of the academic and practical worlds were separately reasserted; but in manifold ways pressures towards change continued to mount and from the late fifties onwards collaborative activities have grown in frequency while increasing their variety, their depth, their scope and their duration. Their persistence and elaboration over the past quarter of this century suggests that they represent a response, however groping, to a widespread 'felt need' in the contemporary world. This need arises from the continuous presence in the social environment of a more rapid change-rate (stemming from an acceleration of technological innovation and scientific advance) which has created higher orders of complexity and interdependence and a higher level of uncertainty than have previously characterized the human condition. These pose new problems of adaptation for individuals and the organizations through which their relations are regulated and on which they are dependent. New attitudes and values must be found; old organizations require to renew themselves; new organizational forms and behaviours have to be brought into being and tested.

One way of attempting to increase adaptive capability under these conditions is to couple the resources of the social sciences with the competences already available in organizations. One way of effecting this coupling is through establishing a collaborative, action-research type relationship between social scientists outside and independent of the organization and those inside it who represent its various systems and are directly concerned with its affairs. In such a relationship joint responsibility is accepted for bringing about organizational

* SOURCE: Eric Trist, "The Professional Facilitation of Planned Change in Organizations," in *Reviews, Abstracts, Working Groups: XVI International Congress of Applied Psychology* (Amsterdam: Swets and Zeitlinger, 1968), pp. 111–120. Reprinted with permission.

change towards agreed ends identified through a search process to which each party makes his own contribution, though all decisions regarding the actual introduction of any change of whatever character remain strictly with members of the client system. Frequent evaluations must be made both of what is experienced and done so that, on the one hand, a process of social learning can be released in the organization and, on the other, an increase in knowledge be returned to the scientific community.

These last two aspects are of central importance, for even if the available social science resources were the only constraint, the number of organizations able and willing to enter into thorough-going engagements of this type must be limited. Even if not formally researched, every such engagement should be regarded as a research undertaking in the formal sense, from which an attempt should be made to secure a 'multiplier effect'. This effect is beginning to be brought about in a number of ways. For example, both the organizations and the social scientists concerned in such programmes are getting to know each other within and across national boundaries. The overlapping informal sets so composed have the properties of a low register but higher order system capable of influencing neighbouring sets to which their members also belong. There are now also many more people inside organizations with varying degrees of social science competence so that there often exists a third force, an internal as well as an external, resource group, whose presence can accelerate the rate at which change can take place. The character of the organization-changing system is itself changing; it is already far more complex than the model of the single change-agent working with the single organization.

In the United States the mainstream of work concerned with changing organizations derives from the field experiments on various aspects of social change carried out by Kurt Lewin (1951) and his associates during the last years of his life. These led to a field theory formulation of how to bring about social change which has affected areas of work far wider than that with which we are here concerned. It also led through the unexpected effect on the members of an experimental workshop on community relations to the discovery of the T-Group, the innovation of the laboratory method of training, the concept of the cultural island and the establishment of a new type of social science institution—the National Training Laboratories (NTL) (Bradford, Gibb and Benne, 1964.) This development was premised on the need to abstract the individual from his usual organizational setting in order to learn experientially about small group processes and himself in relation to them—in the 'here and now.' In these respects the method proved to have great power, but the effects on their organizations of the abstracted members when they returned were negligible; while the effects of returning on them were often to undo what had been gained. The original model of the strangers' human relations training laboratory was not in itself a method of effecting organizational change. Its transformation into such a method took another ten years to discover.

In Britain the counterpart of the Lewin change experiments was the development in the war-time Army by a group, most of whom had been at the pre-war Tavistock Clinic, of a form of operational field psychiatry—a sort of psychological equivalent of operational research (Rees, 1945). As the tasks undertaken became more complex psychologists, sociologists and anthropologists were added to the team. Interdisciplinary collaboration was achieved in an action frame of reference, and a common set of understandings developed, based on a shared core value—commitment to the social engagement of social science both as a strategy for advancing the base of fundamental knowledge and as a way of enabling the social sciences to contribute to 'the important practical affairs of men.' The value position was the same as Lewin's—though the conceptual background was different—that of a psychoanalytically oriented, interdisciplinary, social psychiatry rather than of a social psychology based on field theory. As, however, the British group became better acquainted with Lewin's work its influence on them was far-reaching. Indeed, some mixture of these two heritages may be detected in most of the work on changing organizations that developed in the early post-war years.

The method developed by the British group depended in the first place on a free search of the military environment to discover points of relevant engagement. The right had then to be earned to have a problem which could not be met by customary military methods referred to the technical team for investigation and diagnosis. The diagnosis would next be discussed with appropriate regimental personnel and a likely remedy jointly worked out. The feasibility and acceptability of this remedy as well as its technical efficacy would be tested in a pilot scheme under protected conditions and technical control. As the pilot proved itself the scheme would become operational, control being handed back to regimental personnel, the technical team 'recreating' to advisory roles or removing their presence entirely except for purposes of monitoring and follow-up. What was learned was how to take the collaborative role in innovating special purpose service organizations with built-in social capability in a large multi-organization of which the social science professionals were themselves members—the army—under conditions of crisis.

The second phase in the theme that now unfolds covers the decade which elapsed between Lewin's death in 1947 and the fusion which took place between the training centred laboratory of NTL and the consulting studies of organizational change demanded in increasing volume towards the end of the fifties by large-scale science-based industries in the United States. . . .

A second trend in work at the Tavistock entailed a shift in the unit of analysis from the social system to the socio-technical system, which in turn required the replacement of a closed by an open system approach (Emery, 1959; Trist and Bamforth, 1951; Trist *et al.*, 1963). The studies in the British coal industry, which provided the first detailed empirical evidence of the superiority of certain forms of work organization over others for the same technological tasks, led to the concept of the joint optimization of the technical and social systems as a goal of organizational change and raised the question of the participation of the social scientists in the design process. An opportunity for such participation arose in collaborative work with the Sarabhai group of companies in India (Rice, 1958, 1963). The opening phase of this project was concerned with the sociotechnical reorganization of an automatic weaving shed where Rice became a member of a spontaneously formed design team which included the workers as well as the management and himself. . . .

In the writer's hypothesis (cf. Emery, 1967; Emery and Trist, 1965), these developments were occasioned by the mounting need of the science-based industries in the world's most advanced economy—in face of higher orders of complexity and environmental uncertainty—to evolve organizational forms, climates and values beyond and different from those of the more customary bureaucratic patterns which were no longer adaptive. These needs account also for the impact of Theory Y as formulated by McGregor (1960) which, by stating the direction of emergent relevant values, indicated the new type of organizational relationships likely to be required. . . .

REFERENCES

BRADFORD, L. P., GIBB, J. R., and BENNE, K. D. (1964), *T-Group Theory and Laboratory Method*, Wiley.

EMERY, F. E. (1959), *Characteristics of Socio-Technical Systems*, Tavistock Publications, no. 527.

EMERY, F. E. (1967), 'The next thirty years: concepts, methods and anticipation,' *Hum. Rel.*, vol. 20, pp. 199–237.

EMERY, F. E., and TRIST, E. L. (1965), 'The causal texture of organizational environments,' *Hum. Rel.*, vol. 18, pp. 21–32.

LEWIN, K. (1951), *Field Theory in Social Science*, with editing by D. Cartwright, Harper.

McGREGOR, D. (1960), *The Human Side of Enterprise*, McGraw-Hill.

REES, J. R. (1945), *The Shaping of Psychiatry by War*, Norton.

RICE, A. K. (1958), *Productivity and Social Organization, The Ahmedabad Experiment*, Tavistock Publications.

RICE, A. K. (1963), *The Enterprise and its Environment*, Tavistock Publications.

TRIST, E. L., and BAMFORTH, K. W. (1951), 'Some social and psychological consequences of the Longwall method of coal-getting,' *Hum. Rel.*, vol. 4, pp. 3–38.

TRIST, E. L., HIGGIN, G. W., MURRAY, H., and POLLOCK, A. B. (1963), *Organizational Choice: Capabilities of Groups at the Coal Face under Changing Technologies*, Tavistock Publications.

2

ORGANIZATION MODELS AND INTERVENTION METHOD

———◆———

INTRODUCTION

This chapter provides a set of experiences, models, and schemes that will facilitate grasping the essence of the approach to managing organizational change advocated by this book. It is also intended to help initiate a field intervention experience based on the approach. The chapter proceeds partly by comparative method, contrasting personal perceptions of what is commonly accepted as being true about the characteristics of work and life in organizations with those of professional behavioral scientists, and tries to exploit the tension between the two for learning purposes.

The *Organizational Profile Exercise,* based on the work of Rensis Likert, compares perceptions of how a familiar organization stacks up on a range of organizational variables with those concerning an ideal organization. There is usually considerable tension between the two. The exercise nourishes the conviction that the organizations we know could be better in several significant respects.

Plant Z (A) and (B) presents detailed "before," "during," and "after" pictures of the change process undergone by a large, semi-independent unit of a substantial, complex enterprise. The enterprise faces deep-seated troubles from foreign competition, when a new manager is appointed. Discussion may fruitfully focus on the sequence of events and outcomes in each part of the change process. The account lends itself to a comparison of managerial leadership of change with the Maclaurin and MIT series presented in Chapter 1. In both accounts the change agent is the leader of his organization: the two roles cohere in the one person.

The classic *Hovey and Beard Company* study is presented here in a multipart prediction form, intended to concentrate on the human process by which part of the company, and the company itself, underwent a sequence of changes. The prediction form is intended to oblige the student, in the interest of maximizing learning, to declare a position, advance and defend it, and compare it with that of the actors in the actual situation before studying the succeeding part.* The idea of planned organizational change as essentially an interaction process of some duration, where what happens next is constrained and affected by what came before, is likely to emerge from discussion.

The Action Company provides a sketch of an organization's culture from the point of view of an external change agent, and gives his impressions about why his efforts to help the company adopt what seemed to be better practices were relatively unsuccessful. Discussion turns on why this was the case.

The models and schemes presented in this chapter consist of several conceptual sets. Some are intended to explicate similarities and differences between various organizations. Others outline alternative approaches to changing enterprises by the use of an outside consultant, and provide a brief consideration of the nature of knowledge and research in the field of planned organization change.

"Rational" and "Natural-System" Models of Organizational Analysis and *Two Universal Models* contrast several ideal types of organizations. People with significant working experience usually have, via that experience, insight into the rational/mechanical/classical model, which helps them develop a firm appreciation of its characteristics in the workplace. This model is extremely important in practice. It remains to be seen if many of today's organizations can be understood without some grasp of behavior based on this model. For many people the concepts presented here put into formal, academic terms what they have experienced in their everyday working life in corporations or other organizations.

The participative model is, by contrast, much less familiar from everyday working life and has instead been founded on the research of such leading behavioral scientists as Kurt Lewin, Douglas McGregor, Rensis Likert, and Chris Argyris. The consequences of the assumptive bases of the participative and rational/mechanical/classical models are compared in a table that will repay close study.

Why does one way of thinking and behaving work for one organization

* The subsequent parts of the study and questions pertaining to each are available in the Instructor's Manual.

but not another? The answer seems to lie in the differences between respective organization cultures. A definition of organization culture, given in a classic, midcentury study of a manufacturing plant, is presented in *Culture*. According to *A Formal Definition of Organization Culture,* culture is the "learned product of group experience." It concerns the pattern of basic assumptions operating unconsciously in organizational life.

Structure vs. Process explores the alternative considerations and paths by which a manager or consultant may help an organization to change. *A Contingency Model of Consultation* summarizes the gross differences between the consultant as a technical expert and as a process facilitator in convenient tabular form. *The Role of the Consultant* explores content versus process issues and provides a searching exploration of the "purchase of expertise," "doctor-patient," and "process" models of consultation. The approach to organizational change this book espouses is close to the latter.

Organizational Development and Industrial Democracy presents salutary, cogent remarks about manipulation and the naïveté of some change agents.

The last two items make position statements about science, research, and the field of managing organizational change, and tend to be more difficult than most readings in the book. *The Relation of the "Pure" and the "Applied"* outlines an influential position about research into organizations, widely adopted by Tavistock consultant/researchers. *The Different Kinds of Knowledge Makers* elegantly outlines the respective, distinctive sorts of contributors and contributions made to the field of organizational behavior. The outline proceeds at an abstract, conceptual level. The subfield of managing organizational change clearly emerges as an area dominated by clinical knowledge and skill.

Organizational Profile Exercise*

Rensis Likert

In this exercise you should think of an organization you are familiar with (perhaps one in which you are currently involved or one you have been part of in the past). Describe that organization by indicating the most accurate statement with respect to each organizational variable. You have a range of twenty points along the scale to describe the relative degree of each item.

After describing this organization you should now think of an *ideal* organization, not a mythological one, but one you think would be most effective. What characteristics do you think you would see in this type of organization? Describe this organization with another color or marking. Then connect the set of points for your actual organization in a vertical profile. Do the same for your ideal organization.

If you are like most people the ideal organization will be a profile to the right of your actual organization. This raises the question of changing organizations to make them more effective and, in turn, more rewarding. You might discuss this topic in groups or in class.

You will notice the System 1–4 headings on the profile sheet. These classifications identify the differences in overall description of the general organization climate. In Likert's model overall responses which fall in the range of each of the four systems are defined as follows: System 1—Exploitive authoritative; System 2—Benevolent authoritative; System 3—Consultative; System 4—Participative Group.

*Source: Adapted from Rensis Likert, *The Human Organization* (New York: McGraw-Hill, 1967). pp. 197–211. Reprinted by permission.

Exhibit 1 Profile of Organization Characteristics

Organizational variables	System 1	System 2	System 3	System 4
Leadership				
1. How much confidence is shown in subordinates?	None	Condescending	Substantial	Complete
2. How free do they feel to talk to superiors about job?	Not at all	Not very	Rather free	Fully free
3. Are subordinates' ideas sought and used, if worthy?	Seldom	Sometimes	Usually	Always
Motivation				
4. Is predominant use made of 1 fear, 2 threats, 3 punishment, 4 rewards, 5 involvement?	1, 2, 3 occasionally 4	4, some 3	4, some 3 and 5	5, 4 based on group
5. Where is responsibility felt for achieving organization's goals?	Mostly at top	Top and middle	Fairly general	At all levels
6. How much cooperative teamwork exists?	None	Little	Some	Great deal
Communication				
7. What is the direction of information flow?	Downward	Mostly downward	Down and up	Down, up and sideways
8. How is downward communication accepted?	With suspicion	Possibly with suspicion	With caution	With a receptive mind
9. How accurate is upward communication?	Often wrong	Censored for the boss	Limited accuracy	Accurate
10. How well do superiors know problems faced by subordinates?	Know little	Some knowledge	Quite well	Very well

(continued)

Exhibit 1 (*continued*)

Decisions	11.	At what level are decisions made?	Mostly at top	Policy at top, some delegation	Broad policy at top, more delegation	Throughout but well integrated
	12.	Are subordinates involved in decisions related to their work?	Not at all	Occasionally consulted	Generally consulted	Fully involved
	13.	What does decision-making process contribute to motivation?	Nothing, often weakens it	Relatively little	Some contribution	Substantial contribution
Goals	14.	How are organizational goals established?	Orders issued	Orders, some comments invited	After discussion, by orders	By group action (except in crisis)
	15.	How much covert resistance to goals is present?	Strong resistance	Moderate resistance	Some resistance at times	Little or none
Control	16.	How concentrated are review and control functions?	Highly at top	Relatively highly at top	Moderate delegation to lower levels	Quite widely shared
	17.	Is there an informal organization resisting the formal one?	Yes	Usually	Sometimes	No—same goals as formal
	18.	What are cost, productivity, and other control data used for?	Policing, punishment	Reward and punishment	Reward, some self-guidance	Self-guidance problem-solving

51

Plant Z (A)*

Robert H. Guest et al.

Plant Z is a unit of a giant American corporation. It machines and assembles a major component of a large consumer product. It is one of several plants in a division of a corporation that operates many dozens of plants throughout the world.

Market conditions were rapidly deteriorating at the beginning of this four-year study, and a new plant manager had been appointed. Plant employment was down to 2,500 hourly and 435 salaried employees, almost half its full capacity of workers. Production costs and quality performance were the poorest in the division. Indeed, the new manager was told that Plant Z would probably be phased out within four years unless it could demonstrate a performance level high enough to merit a new product line. According to anecdotal information, the previous manager's leadership style was not unlike that of Plant Y's Stewart. He "went strictly by the book," using his position power to punish those who didn't "toe the mark and stay in line." He was said to have technical competence, but fear pervaded all levels of the organization.

The new plant manager, Tim Rafferty, had worked previously at Plant Z in a middle-management capacity, having worked his way up from fork-lift driver. He, too, according to a former foreman, "could ream you flat out." In his earlier positions at Plant Z he was respected for his operational knowledge. He admitted that he had been raised in an authoritarian mode which also characterized the life style of the entire plant and corporate hierarchy.

As he put it:

> This corporation is a traditional organization and I've been a traditional manager. I like being the boss and I like giving orders and I like immediate response and no bull. That's been my style for twenty years.

Union-management relations were no better nor worse than in many other plants in the corporation. A brief wildcat strike had been called some years earlier. Many comments similar to a committeeman's "anyone with a tie, we didn't trust," were heard frequently. Whenever changes were made in a worker's job the automatic reaction was "to call a committeeman." At the time Rafferty became manager the workforce had been reduced to those with a minimum of fifteen years' seniority. "They knew how to hassle foremen and play the grievance game."

* SOURCE: Robert H. Guest/Paul Hersey/Kenneth H. Blanchard, *Organizational Change Through Effective Leadership*, 2/E, ©1986, pp. 172–190. Reprinted by permission of Prentice Hall, Inc., Englewood Cliffs, N.J.

Just prior to Tim Rafferty's appointment as plant manager, the corporation and the international union signed an agreement that both would cooperate in a sustained effort to increase the involvement of employees in matters affecting their work—matters that were outside the collective bargaining process. This agreement reflected the concern felt by both parties and was needed to combat the threat of declining markets due to intense foreign competition. Foreign companies had found that improved quality performance and productivity resulted from involving workers in workplace decisions. The generic name for this employee involvement and participation movement became popularly known as Quality of Work Life or QWL.

Tough-minded Tim Rafferty was aware of these new developments. Frustrated by the company's traditional confrontational approach to worker relationships, he saw emerging in the agreement a new management philosophy. More important, he was personally frustrated with his own authoritarian style. Although successful in the past, it was not giving him personal satisfaction. He wondered whether this mode of managing was the way to operate in the future. He knew (and talked about it with his wife) that there existed a great potential for creativity among rank-and-file workers and his staff, if only they were given a chance. The company-union agreement triggered action on his part, and he announced to his staff and union representatives that the old ways of operating "are past and we have to take a new approach."

A month later he called a meeting of his top managers and the powerful and combative union chairman, together with two consultants who had long experience in helping organizations initiate QWL activities. Keeping to guidelines established in the national agreement, he urged that a joint union-management committee lay the groundwork for greater employee participation.

The union chairman, as he himself later admitted, was highly skeptical of the idea even though he was fully aware of the commitment made by his national union officials. Telling the manager and others in the group that he would "wait and see," he did agree to appoint some elected union committeemen to serve on a joint union-management committee. He acknowledged privately that he did not believe the company would change. And, knowing the plant manager from past experience, he was highly skeptical that Rafferty had had a real change of heart. What forced the chairman to go along was that something had to be done to save the plant. His constituents' jobs were foremost in his mind. He had seen plant employment reduced to half, and he knew that Plant Z was targeted for closure if performance did not improve.

In the weeks that followed, the newly created committee took shape; it was made up of six top managers (but not including the plant manager) and six elected shop floor committeemen (not the top bargaining committee). A line manager, who had some previous experience in QWL efforts in another plant, and the union chairman assumed responsibility for co-chairing the coordinating committee.

As the national guidelines had stipulated, the coordinating committee was not allowed to deal with formal contractual matters. They discussed plans for publicizing QWL, for communicating its purpose, and for implementing a structure for action. They asked for volunteers among the hourly ranks to form problem-solving groups. No limits were placed on the problems these groups would address, although the theme of *quality* (not productivity) was stressed. The groups were to choose their own leaders, were granted an hour per week "on company time," and were to be provided with a meeting room in the center of the plant. A letter went to all employees announcing the establishment of the joint committee and spelling out the philosophy of QWL. Top corporate, division, and national union representatives visited the plant to reinforce the importance of QWL and to show the managers and all union officials that QWL had full endorsement at the highest levels. Over a period of six weeks the plant manager held departmental meetings with all hourly employees to inform them of the economic status of the plant, to emphasize the urgent need for improved quality performance, and to express his personal committee to QWL.

Not unrelated to QWL was a decision by manager Rafferty to decentralize the organizational structure. He decided to divide the plant into two separate production areas. Each area manager would be responsible not only for the line supervision of superintendents, general foremen, and foremen but also for representatives from quality control and engineering. The latter two groups had previously reported to their separate staff function managers. The move was made, the plant manager said, because production managers had no direct control over decisions of quality controllers or engineering personnel, decisions that would directly affect the management of line operations. This structural change was to have a profound effect later in facilitating the QWL efforts of the hourly workers' problem-solving groups.

Two months after the establishment of the joint committee, a survey was conducted to determine the impact of the many efforts to communicate the purposes of QWL at Plant Z. Most of the respondents, including supervisors and hourly workers, acknowledged that they had heard something about the program, but many were skeptical. This skepticism was expressed in different ways:

> I don't believe management is going to let guys on the line have any say about plant operations. They have dictated things too long. You can't change a zebra's stripes overnight (a worker with 25 years seniority).
> We have had all kinds of human relations programs come down from the division and corporation. They made a big splash but then fizzled out. The top people didn't practice what they preached (member of the personnel department).
> This sounds like an attempt to do an end run around the union. I know the national agreement says that this QWL thing was approved by the union but we've been fighting with the company too long to believe they mean to cooperate (union district committeeman).

Toward the end of three months the first two problem-solving groups were formed. They were chosen by the joint coordinating committee for several reasons: The hourly workers volunteered, and their foremen expressed interest; they were in two departments in separate areas of the plant; and the union district committeemen for these departments wanted to see QWL get off the ground successfully.

The group structure that emerged set the basic pattern for the more than sixty groups that followed during the next three years. There were seven hourly workers, their foreman, an inspector, and a process engineer. Union representatives sat in on the initial meetings as observers. The management co-chairman of the joint coordinating committee together with the consultants made a brief orientation about the purpose and process of QWL problem-solving. They were to choose their own group leader and select whatever problems they wished to work on as long as they did not concern issues covered in the labor-management contract.

In the first meeting and many that followed the temporary plant QWL coordinator (the management co-chairman of the joint committee) emphasized that the group was not simply to identify problems and then "dump" them on management for solution. Rather, they were granted both the authority and responsibility to come up with concrete solutions. If they needed assistance they could call upon those present who could provide further information—their foreman, the engineer, or the inspection representative. If necessary they could seek further information from anyone in the plant, including superintendents, managers, and the joint coordinating committee itself.

The reaction of the group members to the first few meetings ranged from expressed skepticism to enthusiastic support. Many could not believe that management would pay attention to their ideas. Others were concerned that the orientation had been done by the coordinator who was a member of management and they had yet to get firm endorsement from the union. Both groups "tested" the system by choosing one of their own hourly workers as group leader, not one of their foremen. Most of the problems they identified early were related to working conditions and environmental factors, but they turned soon to specific operating problems that concerned them directly. From their comments it was obvious that they were aware of the precarious condition of the plant, that unless quality performance improved the plant might even close down.

By the fourth month of the QWL "kick-off," other workers in other departments, hearing about the activities of the initial pilot groups, expressed interest in starting groups in their own departments. The joint committee agreed to allow five more groups to be established.

It was at this time that another significant event occurred. A change in plant layout was being considered, involving the elimination of four assembly lines and building two longer lines in their place. The usual approach would have been for the engineers and management experts to develop the blueprints and then have the construction people make the change. Plant manager Rafferty, committed to the idea of worker involvement, told the assembly superintendent and his supervisors to meet with the hourly workers who were to run the new lines and ask for their ideas. The workers made many suggestions which were implemented. The operation started up with few hitches. As the manager of industrial relations put it, "In times past we have always been flooded with grievances and threats from the union when changes like this occurred. We learned a lesson this time which will set a pattern for the future."

Another month passed. Word about QWL was spreading beyond the factory floor. Office workers made it known that they, too, wanted to be involved. Manager Rafferty and his staff recognized that the "total team approach" could exclude no one, not even those without union representation. On their own a group of clerical employees and a supervisor set up its own coordinating committee. They spoke with personnel in the staff and service functions and invited participation. One problem-solving group formed quickly and chose to develop a modernized word processing system for the office. They were self-directing; no supervisor was present. On learning that they were free to take whatever steps were necessary, they called in vendors from leading word processor companies, held hearings, developed cost estimates, and made a formal presentation to top management. The plan was adopted. As one member reflected,

> We clericals were always neglected in this place. We didn't have a union to speak for us. And being women in a male-dominated plant we were taken for granted. Now we have a say. The real shot in the arm came when we heard that we were the first QWL salaried group to form in any plant in the entire corporation.

Within a year several other white-collar groups were functioning; many addressed communication and information procedures linking staff operations with the plant production departments.

As the number of problem-solving groups in the plant continued to expand during the next year, the joint coordinating committee, encouraged by the plant manager, saw the need to find a permanent coordinator to oversee the establishment of more groups and to provide orientation and training. The decision was made to select someone not from personnel or training as was usually the case in the other plants. An enthusiastic young man, well-respected in the comptroller's department, was chosen. He attended a division training program in group dynamics and was advised by the consultants on background issues and future perspectives. He conducted a two-day workshop on problem-solving techniques, attended by representatives of already established problem-solving groups, by staff support personnel, joint committee members, the plant manager, and supervisors in departments where the new groups were to be set up.

In the weeks following the appointment of the full-time QWL coordinator a number of communication activities were generated and led by plant manager Rafferty. At every meeting of his staff and members of middle management, he voiced strong support for QWL. As he put it at one of these meetings:

We have to make sure that the guys out on the floor know that the top people here are supporting them and that we keep stressing the successes of the problem-solving groups we have going. We can put millions into systems and equipment, but only our people right out on the floor can save us.

Rafferty mailed a letter to all employees outlining the general business conditions and plant performance and expressing his complete endorsement of the QWL efforts. The union and management co-chairmen of the joint coordinating committee sent a note to the six on-going problem-solving groups thanking them for their efforts. The letter was posted on all bulletin boards. One of the hourly groups also posted a note urging others to support QWL. The note included phrases such as, "We care, and we know you care. In the present crisis our personal and our company attitudes must change."

Word of Plant Z's progress in promoting QWL went beyond the plant itself. Members of the national joint committee, including a corporate vice-president and the union vice-president over all the company's plants, paid a one-day visit. Among the significant presentations was that of the powerful local union chairman, who had initially expressed skepticism about QWL. He openly admitted to the visitors that "attitudes on the shop floor had improved 90 percent." Two members from the shop floor problem-solving groups gave a straightforward, enthusiastic endorsement of their experience. The visit was covered by the local big city newspaper with large captions and pictures taken during a tour of the departments where the groups were active.

In spite of the surface enthusiasm by some during the first year, there were some problems. Less than 5 percent of the departmental units were directly involved in QWL. Few persons in middle management were participating in any direct way. Also, among the current problem-solving groups, there was some difficulty in stimulating staff support personnel from engineering, quality control and plant maintenance to assist in carrying through recommendations made by the problem-solving groups themselves. The most serious issue facing the QWL coordinator was "credibility." That is, he found in his orientation sessions with new groups a persistent, deep-seated skepticism as to his role. In spite of his statements that the effort was supported by the union, he was looked upon as a "management" man. Plant manager Rafferty, the joint committee and the consultants were fully aware of the problem but were stymied by corporate policy which held that although an hourly worker could be a "facilitator," in QWL he would have to report to the management coordinator. Rafferty, who had already ignored some other administrative directives, quietly passed the word to the joint committee to appoint a full-time union representative as the QWL co-coordinator with equal status. This appointment measurably helped to dissipate the suspicion of large numbers of hourly workers as new groups were formed.

Plant Z (B)*

Robert H. Guest et al.

In the following months 20 new groups were formed. The two coordinators developed an elaborate manual dealing with every aspect of orientation, training, group leadership, guidance and project implementation. Initially the coordinators were critical of the consultants for not providing a complete training "package" and doing the training themselves, inasmuch as they were known to be experts in QWL. The coordinators in time came to realize that if they developed the training themselves they, and the personnel in the plant, would feel a greater sense of ownership.

The rapid growth in the number of problem-solving groups in the first year and a half (forty-three by this time) required an addition to the QWL organizational structure. The two coordinators simply could not handle all the training, guidance, and implementation follow-through.

One production zone had set the example by appointing a utility general foreman as a kind of minicoordinator for all six departments in the zone. This person, trained by the QWL coordinators, took on the responsibility for coordinating the six problem-solving groups in the zone.

Partly because of the success achieved in QWL in this zone and partly to streamline the organization, Tim Rafferty decided to eliminate the level of general foreman throughout the ten production zones of the plant. Each superintendent was assigned a staff person charged with a dual function: to act as a planner for the superintendent, and to serve as a QWL coordinator or "facilitator" for his zone. Not only did union and management plant coordinators conduct a two-day training session for these persons in their new roles, but a full day's session explaining the new arrangement was conducted for all superintendents, foremen, production engineers, quality control supervisors, and all union committeemen. Thus, at the end of two years almost everyone at Plant Z was made aware of the purpose and function of QWL.

It was within the groups that substantial changes could be observed. No longer did one hear that management was dominating their efforts. They were "tasting" success and they sought more solutions. Whereas most groups in their early days tended to work on "creature comfort" problems (lighting, ventilation, etc.), the large majority came to deal directly with production problems. They were well-organized and set priorities. Minutes were taken at each meeting. Members were assigned to gather information and report back

* SOURCE: Robert H. Guest/Paul Hersey/Kenneth H. Blanchard, *Organizational Change Through Effective Leadership*, 2/E, ©1986, pp. 172–190. Reprinted by permission of Prentice Hall, Inc., Englewood Cliffs, N.J.

at the next meeting. Decisions were posted in the departments and copies sent to various persons including members of the joint committee.

As indicated earlier, each group had "support" representatives from staff functions such as quality control and engineering. The engineers were initially skeptical. They thought that hourly workers did not have enough technical background to solve complex problems of tooling, assembly, and the like. They thought they were being asked to "hold hands" with the workers when there were more important things to do. One incident was typical of their change in attitude. A young process engineer, who had openly expressed skepticism about the whole idea, said as he came out of a meeting with his group, "My God, those guys know a hell of a lot more technical stuff than I gave them credit for. They just solved a problem of machine coolants which the engineering department wasn't able to solve in three years."

The work groups increasingly found that they had the "right" to go to any source for information and action. In many instances they worked up a proposal with all the cost estimates for installations requiring substantial sums of money. They made formal presentations to high level managers, to the joint committee and to plant manager Rafferty, himself. Most of the proposals were accepted and implemented.

Two observations are in order. The first is that management refused, despite pressure from division executives, to impose progress measurements on the work groups. The groups were never told by higher authorities to work on a specific problem of concern to management. Neither management nor the joint committee kept records for the expressed purpose of holding the groups accountable for performance. The only discipline imposed by management was on managers and supervisors. The annual formal performance review was expanded to include the degree to which a member of management helped in enhancing the QWL process.

A second point is that in spite of the existence of a formal suggestion system, no group in four years filed a suggestion to receive a monetary reward for improvements made. Judging from comments by the workers and their union representatives, the most common expression was something such as, "Just being involved for the first time in improving operations in our own work areas is its own reward."

Going into the third year Plant Z faced a number of challenges which would put strains on any organization. Based on a decision of the division and corporation, Plant Z was given the responsibility of making a product previously made in another plant many miles distant. This meant the transfer of more than 300 machines and the retooling of many more. Again, largely because of the QWL experience, the transfer and installation was not managed solely by the technical experts. Launch teams of engineers, supervisors, tooling experts, and hourly workers were set up in those areas where the incoming equipment was to be installed. If the set-up and layout was not correct, the hourly workers could refuse to sign the blueprints and process sheets. Rafferty acknowledged that the QWL experience made it possible to give shop floor workers both the authority and responsibility for final sign-off.

Also, during the third year, general business conditions picked up substantially. More than 1,100 hourly workers were recalled or newly hired. This required job posting. "Bumping" caused changes in the makeup of the problem-solving groups. An orientation program was set up for all the incoming workers. This included talks by Rafferty and the top union representatives. Many of these workers expressed interest in becoming part of a problem-solving process. It was discovered that the existing group members, according to one of the coordinators, "did a remarkable job absorbing the new members and getting them up to speed as problem-solvers."

The many changes that were taking place at this time, including the continued expansion in the number of problem-solving groups, put serious strains on the union and management coordinators and on the zone facilitators. There was no time for those responsible for QWL to service all the proposals for change being generated (more than 600 had been implemented or were in the process). Linked to this was another basic organizational problem which had disturbed Rafferty and the joint committee. Middle management and many district union committeemen were still not in the mainstream of the QWL process.

To address both concerns a mini-joint committee for each of the two major production areas was established. Each area subcommittee included the area manager, superintendents from the staff support functions, the QWL coordinators and some union district committeemen. They met bi-weekly and served in a coordinating capacity within their areas, linking themselves to the top plant joint committee. Thus a complete organization for carrying out QWL was put in place which was "parallel" to the formal organization structure. All parties were simultaneously involved in the dual function of performing their daily tasks and of facilitating the QWL process.

In another significant structural change in QWL, the union representation on the top level joint committee was strengthened. The plant bargaining committee itself took the place of the former group of lower level district committeemen. This move signified to the entire local membership that the union had made its strongest commitment to QWL.

Rafferty subsequently carried the team concept further at the highest management levels. He created what might be called the "office of plant manager," which included himself and his three top operating managers. He stated that henceforth all major decisions would be made by the team and not by him alone. (These men were also the management representatives of the joint union-management coordinating committee.) Each of the functional areas under the top management team was set up to manage itself as a team. Rafferty took the unprecedented step of eliminating the positions of plant controller and chief engineer. Thus, over time he had reduced the number of management levels from seven (when he took over) to four. The number of top managers was reduced from fourteen to six. In spite of the increase of more than one thousand hourly employees when business picked up, the number of salaried employees was halved from the year before Rafferty took over.

By the end of four years more than sixty-five shop floor problem-solving groups were functioning representing 90 percent of all production and service departments. In addition, a coordinator for the salaried and white-collar personnel had been selected during an earlier period. Almost a quarter of all such personnel were directly involved in QWL. Unlike the shop floor groups, which had remained essentially the same in structure and function, the white-collar groups included task force groups, participation teams, floor groups (supervisors and engineers) as well as various interdepartmental teams.

What about Plant Z's overall performance in the four years following the succession of the new plant manager and the implementation of QWL?

In what is known as "labor and overhead performance," the plant improved on an average of 7.5 percent each year, the best performance of any of the seven plants in the division. The plant was operating at 80 percent of original design capacity, yet with only 54 percent of the original workforce. The most dramatic change came in quality performance, accurately measured by the number of rejects and repairs and customer complaints. Here Plant Z enjoyed a 60 percent improvement over the period of four years earlier. Not only was this the best performance among all plants in the division but, according to widely shared data, the best in any company in the world (more than 15 companies) making a similar product.

To all members of the Plant Z team the most rewarding fact was that the corporation, which had stated earlier that Plant Z was to be closed, now made it clear that its life was to be extended indefinitely.

Part of the improvement can be explained by the introduction of new technologies, new systems and improvements in design. But in the judgment of the plant manager, the principal cause was the implementation and diffusion of QWL. As he put it simply to a group of visiting executives, managers, and union representatives from other large American companies, "The QWL process is the primary reason for the success of this plant and my people." By this he did not mean the contributions of the hourly problem-solving groups alone, and these were substantial with more than 700 new changes generated by these groups. Rather he meant that the entire spirit of involvement and creativity permeated the organization so there could be dramatic structural changes in the management organization staff, changes that substantially reduced levels and personnel. As Rafferty explained:

> We simply learned how to use our resources better, and it was our own people from top to bottom who were involved in this change process. We still have a long way to go. There are still many dozens of people in here who are not on teams of some form or another. Our joint union-management committee is already at work on plans to radically alter the participation system so that every person in the plant, on a voluntary basis, can become involved.

Hovey and Beard Company*

Alex Bavelas and George Strauss

PART 1

The Hovey and Beard Company manufactured wooden toys of various kinds: wooden animals, pull toys, and the like. One part of the manufacturing process involved spraying paint on the partially assembled toys. This operation was staffed entirely by women.

The toys were cut, sanded, and partially assembled in the wood room. Then they were dipped into shellac, following which they were painted. The toys were predominantly two-colored; a few were made in more than two colors. Each color required an additional trip through the paint room.

For a number of years, production of these toys had been entirely handwork. However, to meet tremendously increased demand, the painting operation had recently been re-engineered so that the eight women who did the painting sat in a line by an endless chain of hooks. These hooks were in continuous motion, past the line of women and into a long horizontal oven. Each woman sat at her own painting booth, so designed as to carry away fumes and to backstop excess paint. The woman would take a toy from the tray beside her, position it in a jig inside the painting cubicle, spray on the color according to a pattern, then release the toy and hang it on the hook passing by. The rate at which the hooks moved had been calculated by the engineers so that each woman, when fully trained, would be able to hang a painted toy on each hook before it passed beyond her reach.

The women working in the paint room were on a group bonus plan. Since the operation was new to them, they were receiving a learning bonus which decreased by regular amounts each month. The learning bonus was scheduled to vanish in six months, by which time it was expected that they would be on their own—that is, able to meet the standard and to earn a group bonus when they exceeded it.

* Source: Alex Bavelas and George Strauss, "Group Dynamics and Intergroup Relations" (under the title "The Hovey and Beard Company"), from *Money and Motivation,* ed. William F. Whyte. Copyright ©1955 by Harper & Row, Publishers, Inc. Reprinted by permission of the publisher.

The Action Company*

Edgar H. Schein

In the Action Company one encounters at the visible level an organization with open office landscape architecture; extreme informality of dress and manners; an absence of status symbols (so that it is hard to decipher who has what status in the organization); a very dynamic environment in the sense of rapid pace, enthusiasm, intensity, energy, and impatience; and, finally, a high level of interpersonal confrontation, argumentativeness, and conflict. One also discovers that people are constantly busy going to meetings of various sorts and expressing considerable ambivalence about committees and meetings. Committees are considered frustrating but necessary, and the level of debate and argument within meetings is intense.

If one goes beyond these surface phenomena and talks to people about what they do and why, one discovers some of their *values*: high regard for individual creativity, an absolute belief in individual accountability, but, at the same time, a strong commitment to obtaining consensus on important matters before moving ahead to a decision. Individuals at all levels in the organization are expected to think for themselves and take what they consider to be the correct course of action, even if it means going against a previous decision. Insubordination is positively valued if the action leads to a better outcome. The language one hears in the company reflects these values in that it glorifies "arguing back," "doing the right thing," and so on.

Inquiries about what the "boss" wants are typically considered irrelevant, giving one the impression that authority is not much respected in the organization. In fact, there are frequent complaints that decisions made at higher levels do not get implemented, that people at lower levels feel they can reverse a decision if their insight tells them to do something different, and that insubordination is rarely if ever punished. When people in higher authority positions are asked why they are not more decisive, why they let groups work things out, they state that they are "not smart enough" to make the decision by themselves. Consequently, they stimulate group debate and argument and create the kind of group atmosphere that I described above.

. . . I was called in to help a management group improve its communication, interpersonal relationships, and decision making. After sitting in on a number of meetings, I observed, among other things, high levels of interrupting, confrontation, and debate; excessive emotionality about proposed courses of action; great frustration over the difficulty of getting a point of view

* SOURCE: Abstracted from Edgar H. Schein and edited by Roy McLennan. *Organizational Culture and Leadership: A Dynamic View* (San Francisco: Jossey-Bass, 1985), pp. 2, 9–11. With permission.

across; and a sense that every member of the group wanted to win all the time. Over a period of several months, I made many suggestions about better listening, less interrupting, more orderly processing of the agenda, the potential negative effects of high emotionality and conflict, and the need to reduce the frustration level. The group members said that the suggestions were helpful, and they modified certain aspects of their procedure, such as lengthening some of their meetings. However, the basic pattern did not change, no matter what kind of intervention I attempted. I could not understand why my efforts to improve the group's problem-solving process were not more successful. . . .

The organization's founding group comes from an engineering back-ground, is intensely practical and pragmatic in its orientation, has built a strong and loyal "family" spirit that makes it possible to confront and have conflict without risk of loss of membership, and clearly believes that "truth" lies not in revealed wisdom or authority but in "what works," both technologically and in the marketplace. The assumption that the individual is the source of ideas but that no one individual is smart enough to evaluate his or her own ideas is at the root of the organization's problem-solving/decision-making model. Thus, creativity is always strongly encouraged, but new ideas have to be sold to all potentially affected parties before they will be blessed by higher authority.

Without understanding these assumptions, one cannot decipher most of the behavior observed, particularly the seeming incongruity between intense individualism and intense commitment to group work and consensus. Similarly, one cannot understand why there is simultaneously intense conflict with authority figures and intense loyalty to the organization without also under-standing the assumption "We are one family who will take care of each other." Finally, without these assumptions one cannot decipher why a group would want a consultant to help it become more effective, yet ignore most of the suggestions on how to be more effective.

I now realize that what the group members meant by "effective" was, within their cultural assumptions, to be better at sorting out the truth. The group was merely a means to an end; the real process going on in the group was a basic, deep search for solutions that one could have confidence in because they stood up. Once I shifted my focus to improving the *decision* process instead of the *group* process, my interventions were more quickly acted on. For example, I began to help more with agenda setting, time management, clarifying some of the debate, summarizing, consensus testing once debate was running dry, and in other ways focusing on the "task process" rather than the "interpersonal process." But the basic confrontive, interruptive style continued because the culture of the group legitimized operating that way, based on the assumption that truth is determined through confrontive debate.

The "Rational" and "Natural-System" Models of Organizational Analysis*

Paul R. Lawrence et al.

Alvin W. Gouldner[1] proposes that a major task confronting organizational analysts is the reconciliation of two major methods for conceiving of how organizations operate. A selection from Gouldner's contribution, which represents the central theme of his argument, follows.[2]

THE RATIONAL MODEL OF ORGANIZATIONAL ANALYSIS

In the rational model, the organization is conceived as an "instrument"—that is, as a rationally conceived means to the realization of expressly announced group goals. Its structures are understood as tools deliberately established for the efficient realization of these group purposes. Organizational behavior is thus viewed as consciously and rationally administered, and changes in organizational patterns are viewed as planned devices to improve the level of efficiency. The rational model assumes that decisions are made on the basis of a rational survey of the situation, utilizing certified knowledge with a deliberate orientation to an expressly codified legal apparatus. The focus is, therefore, on the legally prescribed structures—*i.e.*, the formally "blueprinted" patterns—since these are more largely subject to deliberate inspection and rational manipulation.

This model takes account of departures from rationality but often tends to assume that these departures derive from random mistakes, due to ignorance or error in calculation. Fundamentally, the rational model implies a "mechanical" model, in that it views the organization as a structure of manipulable parts, each of which is separately modifiable with a view to enhancing the efficiency of the whole. Individual organizational elements are seen as subject to successful and planned modification, enactable by deliberate decision. The long-range

* Source: Paul R. Lawrence et al., *Organization Behavior and Administration: Cases, Concepts, and Research Findings* (Homewood, Ill.: Richard D. Irwin, 1961), pp. 756–758. Reprinted with permission.

[1] "Organizational Analysis," in *Sociology Today: Problems and Prospects*, ed. Robert K. Merton, Leonard Broom, and Leonard S. Cottrell, Jr., (New York: Basic Books, 1959).
[2] "Organizational Analysis", pp. 404–407.

development of the organization as a whole is also regarded as subject to planned control and as capable of being brought into increasing conformity with explicitly held plans and goals.

THE NATURAL-SYSTEM MODEL OF ORGANIZATIONAL ANALYSIS

The natural-system model regards the organization as a "natural whole," or system. The realization of the goals of the system as a whole is but one of several important needs to which the organization is oriented. Its component structures are seen as emergent institutions, which can be understood only in relation to the diverse needs of the total system. The organization, according to this model, strives to survive and to maintain its equilibrium, and this striving may persist even after its explicitly held goals have been successfully attained. This strain toward survival may even on occasion lead to the neglect or distortion of the organization's goals. Whatever the plans of their creators, organizations, say the natural-system theorists, become ends in themselves and possess their own distinctive needs which have to be satisfied. Once established, organizations tend to generate new ends which constrain subsequent decisions and limit the manner in which the nominal group goals can be pursued.

Organizational structures are viewed as spontaneously and homeostatically maintained. Changes in organizational patterns are considered the results of cumulative, unplanned, adaptive responses to threats to the equilibrium of the system as a whole. Responses to problems are thought of as taking the form of crescively developed defense mechanisms and as being importantly shaped by shared values which are deeply internalized in the members. The empirical focus is thus directed to the spontaneously emergent and normatively sanctioned structures in the organization.

The focus is not on deviations from rationality but, rather, on disruptions of organizational equilibrium, and particularly on the mechanisms by which equilibrium is homeostatically maintained. When deviations from planned purposes are considered, they are viewed not so much as due to ignorance or error but as arising from constraints imposed by the existent social structure. In given situations, the ignorance of certain participants may not be considered injurious but functional to the maintenance of the system's equilibrium.

The natural-system model is typically based upon an underlying "organismic" model which stresses the interdependence of the component parts. Planned changes are therefore expected to have ramifying consequences for the whole organizational system. When, as frequently happens, these consequences are unanticipated, they are usually seen as divergent from, and not as supportive of, the planner's intentions. Natural-system theorists tend to regard the organization as a whole as organically "growing," with a "natural history" of its own which is planfully modifiable only at great peril, if at all. Long-range organizational development is then regarded as an evolution, conforming to "natural laws" rather than to the planner's designs.

THE TWO MODELS COMPARED

Needless to say, these two models are ideal types in the sense that few modern sociologists studying organizations adopt one to the complete exclusion of the other. Nevertheless, as we have mentioned previously, some sociologists tend to stress one model more than the other.

Each of these models has certain characteristic strengths and weaknesses. The rational model, for example, has the indisputable merit of focusing attention on some of the very patterns which distinguish the modern organization, particularly its rationality. At the same time, however, it tends to neglect the manner in which those patterns which the modern organization shares with "natural" groups may also affect behavior within them. The fact is, of course, that the distinguishing characteristics of a bureaucratic organization are not its only characteristics; systematic attention must also be directed to those features of modern organizations, such as the need for loyalty, which they have in common with other types of groups.

The natural-system model, on the other hand, has the merit of focusing attention on the spontaneous and unplanned (that is, "informal") patterns of belief and interaction that arise even within the rationally planned organization. Often, however, the natural-system model tends to neglect the distinctively rational features of the modern organization.

Two Universal Models*

Jay W. Lorsch and Stevan Trooboff

The classical and participative models of organization closely parallel Gouldner's rational and natural system models. . . .

Gouldner's rational model which views the organization as composed of manipulative parts clearly coincides with the classic model's authors' view of organizational structure. The natural system model is akin to the participative model in that both are cognizant of accounting for the individual's needs within the structure of the organization. However, while Gouldner stresses the interdependence of the organization's component parts and the organization's tendency to maintain its equilibrium as characteristic of the natural system model, the participative model of organization does not mention explicitly these strivings for organizational balance.

In studying the classical and participative models, you might find it helpful to bear in mind the passages from Gouldner. . . .

By better understanding the theoretical contradictions between rational and natural system models, you should be able to develop a better understanding of the classical and participative models.

THE CLASSICAL MODEL OF ORGANIZATION

Despite the fact that the classical model of organization might seem old-fashioned or outdated when compared with some of the behavioral science ideas, it is extremely important, historically and in terms of current practice. Historically, the classical model is deeply entrenched in our culture. Max Weber's writings on the structure of the bureaucracy have a strong parallel to the classical model in terms of the mechanical approach to the problems of organizational design.[1] And the work of Frederick Taylor in subdividing tasks through time and motion studies gave strong impetus to and is based on the "sound principles" of the classical model.[2] Even today many businessmen

* SOURCE: Jay W. Lorsch and Stevan Trooboff, "Two Universal Models," in Jay W. Lorsch and Paul R. Lawrence, *Organization Planning: Cases and Concepts* (Homewood, Ill.: Richard D. Irwin, 1972), pp. 7–16. Reprinted with permission.

[1] A. M. Henderson and Talcott Parsons, eds., *The Theory of Social and Economic Organization* (Glencoe, Ill.: Free Press and Falcon's Wing Press, 1947).

[2] Frederick Winslow Taylor, *Principles of Scientific Management* (New York: Harper & Row, 1947).

adhere to the principles of the classical model in thinking about organizational issues.

The classical model focuses primarily on the relationship between two groups—management and the (production) workers. In discussing these two groups, the classical authors make many assumptions and value judgments about the individuals. For instance, workers are viewed as instruments, solely motivated by economic motives, existing to carry out organizational objectives. Managers, on the other hand, are characterized as rational, omniscient, and possessing outstanding personal qualities such as kindness and fairness. However, despite these qualities, the manager's role defines him as having to be firm with workers.

Because of the model's view of the workers as "economic man," rewards and punishments to the workers should be economic in nature. An astute classical manager would give detailed instructions to his subordinates. Then, according to the model, he must measure or assess exactly what has been done by the workers and if the employee should be rewarded or punished for his performance in executing the task.

The classical authors recognized that the task assigned to the worker would often create an inherent conflict for the employee between his personal goals and those of the organization. Under the model's assumptions, however, the workers are expected to accept the superordinate goals of the organization. The resolution of this conflict and the ensuing acceptance by the worker of the corporate position were to be resolved by fitting the "right" man into the "right" job. This fit was to be defined by personal characteristics such as physical strength, manual dexterity, or specific craft skill. Further, in addition to this fit of the individual and the job skills required for a specific task, heavy formalization of procedures was to minimize the potential conflict by clearly defining what was expected of organization members. This emphasis on formal organization, formal communications, and formal job and task descriptions would keep the worker oriented toward the organization's goals rather than his personal objectives.

Organizational Patterns

The classical organization resembles the pyramid shape displayed in Exhibit 1. At the top point of the structure is the omnipotent manager and the workers. Within this structure, both the chain of command and the channels of communication are vertical. The vertical chain of command stipulates that each person in the organization is to have only one superior or boss, for according to the classicist it is impossible for an organization to adapt itself to the complexities of dual command. Similarly, each member is to have authority delegated to him which is equal to his responsibility. In the channels of communication, information is expected to flow downward in accordance with the authority structure and upward only in relation to the results of task performance.

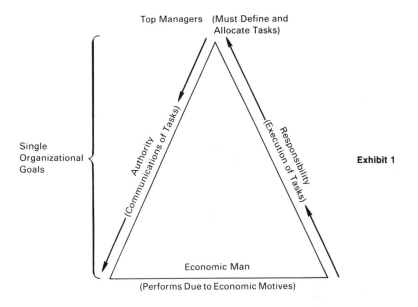

Top Managers (Must Define and Allocate Tasks)

Single Organizational Goals

(Communications of Tasks)

Authority

Responsibility (Execution of Tasks)

Economic Man

(Performs Due to Economic Motives)

Exhibit 1

Organizational States and Processes

Specialization. Within this pyramid structure, specialization is a major tenet of how tasks are to be assigned. The principal goal the classical authors were concerned with, apropos of specialization, was to divide the tasks of the organization so that each individual would have the narrowest task; while, at the same time, the total activities of all individuals would add up to the organization's superordinate goals and objectives. This is so because it was assumed that men differ in capacity and skill and can better their individual performance through specialization, that a man can't learn everything in a lifetime, and that no individual can perform more than one task at a time. Men were therefore assigned specialized tasks of a finite nature within their departments. In turn, the men were expected to become highly skilled at performing that particular task.

Most of the classical modelists discussed this specialization in terms of assigning the specific tasks to functional departments. . . .

Coordination. As highly specialized as this pyramid structure and the individuals within it appear to be, the classical authors' emphasis that the sum of the individual tasks would equal the overall organizational goal indicates their recognition of the need for coordination or integration. Primarily, the integration of the highly specialized efforts towards the singular and centrally determined corporate goal was expected to be achieved because subgoals would add up to the superordinate goal. Any flaws in this approach would be dealt with through the management hierarchy. In other words, individuals in the organization's hierarchy with appropriate authority are expected to delegate tasks in a manner which will turn out to be an integrated effort. If this doesn't work, they are expected to coordinate subordinate efforts.

. . . The classicists primarily relied on this hierarchical pattern for achieving integration. . . .

Conflict Resolution. For the most part, the classical authors ignored the topic of conflict resolution. They believed that the structure they had designed alleviated the possibility of conflict within the organization. The few classical authors who did recognize the need for tools to resolve intraorganizational conflict relied on the philosophy that conflicting ideas or actions should be "pushed up the hierarchical pyramid for a decision." It was the manager's responsibility to arbitrate disputes between hostile subordinates.

Sources of the Classical Model

The classical model is descriptive of the early organizational structures with which we are all familiar—the church, the military, and the railroads. We can easily picture the military organization as a pyramid with the commander in chief at the top and the structure spreading out below down through the majors, lieutenants, noncommissioned officers, and finally privates. Each individual reports to one other individual on his execution of a specifically designed task. And, the cumulative total of these tasks should add up to the mission of the entire military organization.

Descriptions of the classical model can be found in the works of Fayol (1916), Koontz and O'Donnell (1950s), Newman (1963), Gulick and Urwick (1937), and Mooney.[3] While there are a number of variations in their thinking about the model, depending on their own experience and the time during which they were writing, the views expressed in this short note were mostly universal as concern all organizations. That is, while there might be minor variations from these principles, they were to be rigorously adhered to in all organizations regardless of task, location, and, to a large extent, size. In essence, applying these principles to the design of organizations facing any and all conditions would lead to effective permanence of the organization.

THE PARTICIPATIVE MODEL

Whereas the classical model of organization is largely derived from an analysis of the early experience of practitioners, the participative model is derived from the work of behavioral scientists. The participative model is one which many

[3] Henri Fayol, *General and Industrial Management* (London: Pitman, 1916, 1949. C. Storrs, translator, Harold Koontz and Cyril O'Donnell, *Principles of Management* (New York: McGraw-Hill Book Co., Inc., 1968); William Henry Newman, *Administrative Action* (Englewood Cliffs, N.J.: Prentice-Hall, Inc., 1963); Gulick and Urwick, *Papers on the Science of Administration* (Columbia University, 1937); James D. Mooney, *The Principles of Organization.*

students tend to think of as McGregor's "Theory Y".[4] While the model's assumptions about individuals are closely akin to McGregor's thinking about people, the model has assumptions and implications which are more far-reaching than Theory Y. . . .

The Individual

According to the participative authors, the individual in the organization is engaged in a multidimensional process of development. Within this dynamic developmental process, the individual is seen as moving through the process of maturity. As he matures, this individual's needs, goals, and desires tend to move in a specific direction. The individual seeks to be in a position of relative independence in which he has some level of self-determination about his future. He begins to seek deeper, more constant, and increasingly complex interests with which to be challenged. And, he also seeks a greater depth to his behavioral interaction within the organization.

At the same time the individual is experiencing these personal changes, his process of thinking about the organization and his position within the organization begin to change. His time perspective begins to become more long range in thinking about his goals and growth in the organization. In the future, he is concerned about having an equal or superordinate position with respect to his peers.

In other words, the maturity process described above is one in which the individual is seeking self-actualization. The individual wants control over himself. He is developing a sense of integrity and feeling of self-worth.

Organizational States and Processes

According to the participative theorists, the overall objective of the organization is to achieve a satisfactory integration between the needs and desires of the members of the organization and the persons functionally related to it such as consumers, shareholders, and suppliers.

It is assumed that management can make full use of the potential capacities of its human resources only when each person in the organization is a member of one or more effectively functioning work groups, thus participating in the overall organizational effort. Further, it is required that these groups have a high degree of group loyalty, effective skills, and high performance goals.

These groups are to be linked together into an overall organization by means of people who hold overlapping group membership. Exhibit 2 depicts what this overlapping organization looks like. The individual who is represented by an "X" in the exhibit is referred to as the "linking pin."[5]

[4] Douglas M. McGregor, *The Human Side of Enterprise* (New York: McGraw-Hill Book Co., Inc., 1960).

[5] A term coined by R. Likert, *New Patterns of Management* (New York: McGraw-Hill Book Co., Inc., 1961).

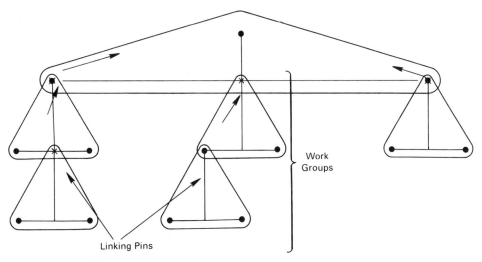

Exhibit 2   An Introduction to Organizational Models (the linking-pin organization)

Under the participative modelists' assumptions, the linking pin is a key figure in the organization. He provides a means of transmitting information and influence throughout the organization to achieve integration. Formalized groups such as ad hoc committees and staff groups or meetings across two levels of the organization are designed to augment interaction and the flow of communication and information throughout the organization.

Interaction within the System

The participative organization modelists make a number of assumptions about interaction within the system both at the level of the individual and in light of the entire organizational system.

At the individual level, integration of the individual into the entire organizational system is described by the principle of supportive relationships. This principle states that organizational interaction should be conducted so that individuals will view their interactions as supportive. That is, that in all interactions and in all relationships within the organization, the individual in light of his background, values, and expectations will feel these interactions build and maintain his sense of personal worth and importance.

The participative modelists believe that high managerial goals are a precondition to high subordinate goals. And that in order for the subordinates to accept these goals without resentment, the supportive relationships described above should exist. Further, they believe the maximum participation in decision-making and supportive behavior, defined by the model, help establish these high goals and produce a high level of commitment to the goals' achievement.

Supportive behavior and group decision making, according to the participative model, contribute to good communications and coordination within the framework of overlapping groups. The best-performing organizations, according to this model, are those which motivate the individual to cooperate, not compete. In achieving this cooperation, the group leader is accountable and must accept final responsibility for the group performance. However, in spite of the leader's responsibility for group performance, he must consider accepting group decisions with which he does not concur if he feels he could adversely affect group loyalty by not following the group's decisions.

Organizational Change

The participative model of organization views change as a total system codification rather than an atomistic alteration. That is, if a manager wishes to create a change in the participative organization, he can not merely change one small piece of the organization but he has to prepare the entire organization, since under the model's linking pin design the entire organization would be affected.

Consequently, according to the participative designers, change should start by altering the most influential causal variables affecting what you want to change. Then, there should be systematic plans prepared to modify all other affected parts of the organization in carefully coordinated steps.

Conflict Management

The change method described above would involve each individual in the change process, securing each person's commitment to the proposed change, and therefore minimizing the potential for any conflict. In fact, under the model's assumptions, all conflict is managed by the participation of the individuals in joint decision-making processes such as the change process. During the decision-making period, ideas may be challenged. But once this group makes a decision, be it a meeting of four or five or the collective "group" of an entire organization, the participative theorists see everyone as committed to the decision since they helped reach that determination. And if conflict does arise, the participative modelists believe that individuals who trust each other and are seeking to cooperate with one another will be able to resolve this conflict.

Sources of Data

While the participative model is closely linked to the thinking of later researchers like McGregor and Argyris, and to a greater extent on the work of Rensis Likert and his colleagues at the University of Michigan, the deepest roots of the participative model are in the work of Kurt Lewin.[6] While there

---

[6] McGregor, *Human Side of Enterprise;* Chris Argyris, *Personality and Organization* (New York: Harper & Row, 1957); Kurt Lewin, *Resolving Social Conflicts* (New York: Harper & Row, 1948).

are some differences in the various researchers' points of view, they all find common ground in their universal application of the model. That is, irrespective of time, size, location, or nature of business, they all feel that the participative model is the way in which an organization should and can be most effectively designed.

The conclusion is based on the researchers' studies of organizations which have shown that in the highest performing organization, many of the kinds of behavior defined and described by the participative modelists are present.

Although it is impossible to review all the research on the participative model, Exhibit 3 is a flowchart of the general pattern of research findings.

Exhibit 3 An Introduction to Organizational Models

IF A MANAGER HAS:		
Well-organized plan of operation High performance goals High technical competence (managers or staff assistants)		
AND IF THE MANAGER MANAGES VIA:		
Causal Variables	Direct hierarchical pressure for results including the usual contexts and other practices of the traditional systems	Principle of supportive relationships, group methods of supervision, and other principles of systems
HIS ORGANIZATION WILL DISPLAY:		
Intervening Variables	Less group loyalty Lower performance goals Greater conflict and less cooperation Less technical assistance to peers Greater feeling of unreasonable pressure Less favorable attitudes toward manager Lower motivation to produce	Greater group loyalty Higher performance goals Greater cooperation More technical assistance to peers Less feeling of unreasonable pressure More favorable attitudes toward manager Higher motivation to produce
AND HIS ORGANIZATION WILL ATTAIN:		
End-Result Variables	Lower sales volume Higher sales cost Lower quality of business sold Lower earnings by salesmen	Higher sales volume Lower sales cost Higher quality of business sold Higher earnings by salesmen
N.B. The same principle applies to other than sales organizations.		

Taken from Rensis Likert, *The Human Organization* (New York: McGraw-Hill Book Co., Inc., 1967), p. 76.

Culture*

Elliott Jaques

The culture of the factory is its customary and traditional way of thinking and of doing things, which is shared to a greater or lesser degree by all its members, and which new members must learn, and at least partially accept, in order to be accepted into service in the firm. Culture in this sense covers a wide range of behaviour: the methods of production; job skills and technical knowledge; attitudes towards discipline and punishment; the customs and habits of managerial behaviour; the objectives of the concern; its way of doing business; the methods of payment; the values placed on different types of work; beliefs in democratic living and joint consultation; and the less conscious conventions and taboos. Culture is part of second nature to those who have been with the firm for some time. Ignorance of culture marks out the newcomers, while maladjusted members are recognized as those who reject or are otherwise unable to use the culture of the firm. In short, the making of relationships requires the taking up of roles within a social structure; the quality of these relationships is governed by the extent to which the individuals concerned have each absorbed the culture of the organization so as to be able to operate within the same general code. The culture of the factory consists of the means or techniques which lie at the disposal of the individual for handling his relationships, and on which he depends for making his way among, and with, other members and groups.

* SOURCE: Elliott Jaques, *The Changing Culture of a Factory* (London: Tavistock Publications, in collaboration with Routledge and Kegan Paul, 1951), p. 251. Reprinted with permission.

A Formal Definition
of Organization Culture*

Edgar H. Schein

. . . The term "culture" should be reserved for the deeper level of *basic assumptions* and *beliefs* that are shared by members of an organization, that operate unconsciously, and that define in a basic "taken-for-granted" fashion an organization's view of itself and its environment. These assumptions and beliefs are *learned* responses to a group's problems of *survival* in its external environment and its problems of *internal integration*. They come to be taken for granted because they solve those problems repeatedly and reliably. This deeper level of assumptions is to be distinguished from the "artifacts" and "values" that are manifestations or surface levels of the culture but not the essence of the culture.

But this definition immediately brings us to a problem. What do we mean by the word "group" or "organization," which, by implication, is the locale of a given culture?

Organizations are not easy to define in time and space. They are themselves open systems in constant interaction with their many environments, and they consist of many subgroups, occupational units, hierarchical layers, and geographically dispersed segments. If we are to locate a given organization's culture, where do we look, and how general a concept are we looking for?

Culture should be viewed as a property of an independently defined stable social unit. That is, if one can demonstrate that a given set of people have shared a significant number of important experiences in the process of solving external and internal problems, one can assume that such common experiences have led them, over time, to a shared view of the world around them and their place in it. There has to have been enough shared experience to have led to a shared view, and this shared view has to have worked for long enough to have come to be taken for granted and to have dropped out of awareness. Culture, in this sense, is a *learned product of group experience* and is, therefore, to be found only where there is a definable group with a significant history.

Whether or not a given company has a single culture in addition to various subcultures then becomes an empirical question to be answered by locating stable groups within that company and determining what their shared experience has been, as well as determining the shared experiences of the members of the total organization. One may well find that there are several cultures operating within the larger social unit called the company or the

* SOURCE: Edgar H. Schein, *Organizational Culture and Leadership: A Dynamic View* (San Francisco: Jossey-Bass, 1985), pp. 6–9, 11. With permission.

organization: a managerial culture, various occupationally based cultures in functional units, group cultures based on geographical proximity, worker cultures based on shared hierarchical experiences, and so on. The organization as a whole may be found to have an overall culture if that whole organization has a significant shared history, but we cannot assume the existence of such a culture ahead of time.

This concept of culture is rooted more in theories of group dynamics and group growth than in anthropological theories of how large cultures evolve. When we study organizations, we do not have to decipher a completely strange language or set of customs and mores. Rather, our problem is to distinguish—within a broader host culture—the unique features of a particular social unit in which we are interested. This social unit often will have a history that can be deciphered, and the key actors in the formation of that culture can often be studied, so that we are not limited, as the anthropologist is often limited, by the lack of historical data.

Because we are looking at evolving social units within a larger host culture, we also can take advantage of learning theories and develop a dynamic concept of organizational culture. Culture is learned, evolves with new experiences, and can be changed if one understands the dynamics of the learning process. If one is concerned about managing or changing culture, one must look to what we know about the learning and unlearning of complex beliefs and assumptions that underlie social behavior.

The word "culture" can be applied to any size of social unit that has had the opportunity to learn and stabilize its view of itself and the environment around it—its basic assumptions. At the broadest level, we have *civilizations* and refer to Western or Eastern cultures; at the next level down, we have *countries* with sufficient ethnic commonality that we speak of American culture or Mexican culture. But we recognize immediately that within a country we also have various *ethnic groups* to which we attribute different cultures. Even more specific is the level of *occupation, profession*, or *occupational community*. If such groups can be defined as stable units with a shared history of experience, they will have developed their own cultures. Finally, we get to the level of analysis that is the focus of this book—*organizations*. Within organizations we will find subunits that can be referred to as *groups*, and such groups may develop group cultures.

To summarize, at any of these structural levels, I will mean by "culture": *a pattern of basic assumptions—invented, discovered, or developed by a given group as it learns to cope with its problems of external adaptation and internal integration—that has worked well enough to be considered valid and, therefore, to be taught to new members as the correct way to perceive, think, and feel in relation to those problems.*

Because such assumptions have worked repeatedly, they are likely to be taken for granted and to have dropped out of awareness. Note that the definition does not include overt behavior patterns. I believe that overt behavior is always determined both by the cultural predisposition (the assumptions, perceptions, thoughts, and feelings that are patterned) and by the situational contingencies that arise from the external environment. Behavioral regularities could thus be as much a reflection of the environment as of the culture and should, therefore, not be a prime basis for *defining* the culture. Or, to put it another way, when we observe behavior regularities, we do not know whether we are dealing with a cultural artifact or not. Only after we have discovered the deeper layers that I am defining as the culture can we specify what is and what is not an artifact that reflects the culture.

REFERENCES

DYER, W. G., JR. "Culture in Organizations: A Case Study and Analysis." Unpublished paper, Sloan School of Management, MIT, 1982.

LOUIS, M. R. "Organizations as Culture Bearing Milieux." In L. R. Pondy and others, Eds., *Organizational Symbolism*. Greenwich, Conn.: JAI Press, 1983.

SCHEIN, E. H. "Does Japanese Management Style Have a Message for American Managers?" *Sloan Management Review*, 1981a, *23*, 55–68.

SCHEIN, E. H. "The Role of the Founder in Creating Organizational Culture." *Organizational Dynamics*, Summer 1983, 13–28.

SCHEIN, E. H. "Coming to a New Awareness of Organizational Culture." *Sloan Management Review*, 1984, *25*, 3–16.

Structure vs. Process*

Edgar H. Schein

Early studies of organization were dominated by the "scientific management" school of thought leading to an almost exclusive preoccupation with the "structural" or static elements of organization: What is the correct division of labor? Who should have which responsibilities? Should the production department report directly to the president or through a product organization involving other functions? What is the right span of control? How many levels should there be in the hierarchy? and so on. This concern for organizational statics is understandable and appropriate because organizations are open systems which exist in an uncertain environment. In order to survive as organizations they must conserve stability in the face of recurring disintegrative pressures from the environment. Just as total societies develop a social structure, laws, traditions, and culture as a way of stabilizing themselves, so organizations develop and must conserve their structures and culture.

The appeal of the structural approach can readily be seen in the field of consultation. Management consulting firms are often brought in to examine the existing management *structure* and to recommend alternate forms which are presumed to be more effective for achieving organizational goals.[1] If the recommendations are acted upon, reporting relations are likely to be changed, departments are likely to be phased out or moved, and other similar drastic alterations made. The personalities of individual managers are taken into account in the diagnostic process, but these also tend to be viewed structurally as static factors to be considered in designing the new structure.

The problem with this approach is not that it is wrong but that it is incomplete. The network of positions and roles which define the formal organizational structure is occupied by people, and those people in varying degrees put their own personalities into getting their job done. The effect of this is not only that each role occupant has a certain style of doing his work, but that he has certain patterns of relating to other people in the organization. These patterns become structured, and out of such patterns arise traditions which govern the way members of the organization relate to each other.

Such traditions cannot be inferred or deciphered from knowing only the formal organizational relations; it is therefore doubtful that they can be changed by changing only the formal structure. I believe that the consultant must also examine the *processes* which occur between people as a way of

* SOURCE: Edgar H. Schein, *Process Consultation.* ©1969. Addison-Wesley Publishing Company, Inc., Reading, Mass., pp. 10–11. Reprinted with permission.

[1] DANIEL, D. R. "Reorganizing for Results" *Harvard Business Review*, 1966, *44*, 96–104.

understanding the informal relationships, the traditions, and the culture which surrounds the structure.

To put the issue another way, the roles which people occupy partly determine how they will behave. It is important to have the right structure of roles for effective organizational performance, but at the same time, people's personalities, perceptions, and experiences also determine how they will behave in their roles and how they will relate to others.

Only if these relationships among the role occupants are working smoothly can organizational effectiveness be ensured. If the consultant is interested in organization improvement, he must therefore study the processes which occur between people and groups.

A Contingency Model of Consultation*

Newton Margulies
and Anthony P. Raia

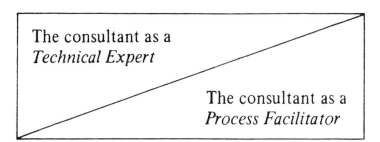

The consultant as a
Technical Expert

The consultant as a
Process Facilitator

ENGINEERING OR PURCHASE MODELS

1. The client's statement of the problem is either accepted at face value or verified by the consultant on the basis of his or her technical expertise relative to the problem.
2. Little time is spent on developing the consultant-client relationship. The connection is generally short-term and problem-oriented.
3. The solution, or prescription, to the problem is generally developed by the consultant and implemented by the client.
4. The consultant brings technical expertise to bear on the client's problem(s).
5. The consultant is primarily concerned with increasing the client's knowledge and skill relative to the stated problem(s).
6. In general, the consultant does it for and to the client.

CLINICAL OR PROCESS MODELS

1. The client's statement of the problem is treated as information. The problem is verified *jointly* by both the client and the consultant.
2. The consultant-client relationship is viewed as an essential ingredient in the process and considerable attention is given to its development.
3. The major focus of the consultant is to help the client to discover and implement appropriate solutions for himself or herself.
4. The consultant is an expert in how to diagnose and facilitate organizational processes.
5. The consultant is primarily concerned with improving the client's diagnostic and problem-solving skills.
6. In general, the consultant helps the client to do it for and to himself or herself.

* SOURCE: Newton Margulies and Anthony P. Raia, *Conceptual Foundations of Organizational Development* (New York: McGraw-Hill, 1978), p. 113. Reprinted with permission.

The Role of the Consultant: Content Expert or Process Facilitator?*

Edgar H. Schein

One of the persistent dilemmas that faces any consultant, helper, therapist, or manager is how to be helpful in a situation in which there is a choice between telling others what to do, being a content expert, or facilitating through various interventions a better problem-solving process that permits those same others to solve the problem for themselves (Schein 1969). In this article, I would like to spell out in greater detail some of the assumptions that underlie different models of consultation, and indicate the kinds of interventions that are most suitable in the process model.

The expert model of consultation has basically two versions: (a) *purchase* of specific information or expertise as in the case of hiring a consultant to do a market survey, or (b) *doctor-patient* as in the case of hiring a consultant to come into an organization to do a diagnosis and suggest various remedies for whatever ailments are found. The difference between these two models is in the degree to which the client retains control and wants only specific solutions or information. The consultant is hired because of specific skills in eliciting that information or specific knowledge to solve a given problem. The client decides what to do with the information, if anything. In the doctor-patient model the client abdicates some degree of control by admitting that he or she does not know what is wrong, giving the consultant broad powers to come into the organization to do a diagnosis (often the client does not even realize that some of the diagnostic techniques themselves may disturb or change the organization), and implicitly commits himself or herself to accepting some kind of prescription or remedial course of action.

The process consultation model also has two versions: (a) *catalyst* model where the consultant does not know the solution but has skills in helping a client to figure out his or her own solution, and (b) *facilitator* model where the consultant may have ideas and possible solutions of his or her own but for various reasons decides that a better solution and better implementation of that solution will result if he or she withholds his or her own content suggestions and, instead, consciously concentrates on helping the group or client system to

* Source: Edgar H. Schein, "The Role of the Consultant: Content Expert or Process Facilitator?" *Personnel and Guidance Journal*, 56 (1978), 339–343. Copyright AACD. Reprinted with permission. No further reproduction authorized without further permission of AACD.

solve their own problem. This last version of process consultation frequently applies in managerial situations where the manager decides to "help" a subordinate or group to achieve their own solution by creating a good decision-making process rather than making the decision personally. Occasionally managers also find themselves playing the catalyst role in complex problem-solving situations because they genuinely do not know the solutions yet are accountable for reaching some solutions within a given period of time.

CONTENT VS. PROCESS

Any human problem-solving activity can be analyzed both at the level of content and process. If we are to understand clearly the role of the consultant vis-a-vis content or process, we must first have a clear idea of what we really mean by these two underlying concepts. At its simplest, content refers to the actual task to be performed or problem to be solved, while process refers to the *way* in which the problem is attacked, defined, worked on, and ultimately solved. Content is what the typical secretary of a group would keep records on during the meeting—the agenda, the ideas that were presented, the solutions that were offered, the decisions that were reached, and the future agendas that were settled on. In contrast, if one were to observe the process of this same meeting, one might record the communication patterns (who spoke to whom, who spoke how often, who interrupted, who shouted, who asked questions, who made assertions) quite independent of the actual content of what each person said. Similarly, one might track leadership behavior in terms of initiating activity, pushing toward consensus, summarizing, and testing feelings. Or one might catalogue all of the decisions made in the group in terms of whether they were reached autocratically, by some means of minority rule, by majority rule, by consensus, or by unanimous agreement. Process observations can be made, regardless of what the group is talking about, because they focus on the problem-solving activity per se rather than the intellectual content of the problem. . . .

In actual practice one will find, of course, that there are subtle connections between the content of what is being worked on and the process by which the work is being done. Sometimes the process mirrors the content but more often the content is a subtle reflection of underlying feelings and thus mirrors the process. For example, in training groups it was a common experience to have the group choose as its "topic" something that was related to its underlying process, e.g., the group might choose to discuss leadership as an agenda item when it was in fact hung up on a severe leadership struggle among several members. Process *issues* are usually reflections of underlying emotional currents in the person or group which reflect unconscious or denied assumptions, norms, and feelings. To help an individual or a group to confront process issues can be seen as a process of "surfacing," making something unspoken or unconscious available for examination, review, and analysis. Whether or not one chooses to confront such issues depends upon the consultant's diagnosis of how much the process issues are getting in the way of effective problem solving or goal attainment. I will deal with this question in greater detail later in the paper, but wish to point out for now that, though content and process are very different and can be observed totally independently of each other if one chooses to do so, they are in fact subtly interrelated and one of the consultant's toughest decisions is when and how to focus on that interaction.

THREE MODELS OF CONSULTATION
AND THEIR UNDERLYING ASSUMPTIONS

The initiative for seeking help and involving a consultant is always with the client. Most clients are at the outset *content* centered. They cannot achieve some important goal, they cannot solve a particular problem, they cannot get a particular set of information, or they lack a necessary skill to fix something which does not work, so they turn to a helper.

Model 1: Purchase of Expertise. The core characteristic of this model is that the client has made up his or her mind on what the problem is, what kinds of help are needed, and to whom to go for this help. The client expects expert help and expects to pay for it but not to get involved in the process of consultation itself. The extreme pure model is the television repairman or auto mechanic. When something doesn't work, we want it fixed. Other examples might be the purchase of a market research survey, the hiring of a consultant to develop a computer program for a given problem, or the hiring of a lawyer to determine whether a given course of action will run into difficulty or not. The essence of the message from the client to the consultant is "here is the problem, bring me back an answer and tell me how much it will cost." Psychologically, the essence of this relationship is that the client gives away the problem temporarily to the helper, which permits the client to relax, secure in the knowledge that an expert has taken it on and will come up with a solution. This model is, almost by definition, totally *content* oriented.

In order for this model to work successfully, the following assumptions have to be met, however,

1. *That the client has made a correct diagnosis of his or her own problem.* If I have misdiagnosed my problem the consultant will typically *not* feel obligated in this model to help me rediagnose to discover what is really the problem. That is not part of the consultant's contract unless I make it so, in which case I shift into one of the other two models to be presented below.

2. *That the client has correctly identified the consultant's capabilities to solve the problem.* If I go to the wrong expert and get a poor solution, that is my problem as the client. Furthermore, in my discussions with the consultant I have to be aware that the consultant is perfectly within his or her rights to attempt to "sell" me, and that I have no excuse if the service proves to be less expert than I expected. The burden is on the client to evaluate the expertise.

3. *That the client has correctly communicated the problem.* If I fail to make it clear to the consultant what problem I am really trying to solve, there is a good chance that I will end up paying for services or information that will not be relevant. The process often breaks down here because clients do not check whether consultants have "heard" correctly what the client's problem is before they charge off to solve it. Many market surveys end up being useless and many counseling sessions end up being nonhelpful because the client sought "advice" but did not fully and clearly get across what the problem really was, and the consultant in this model is under no obligation to check out whether the initial problem statement is in fact accurate or not.

4. *That the client has thought through and accepted the potential consequences of the help that will be received.* How often have we gone to a service repairman and then resented paying the bill when we are told that our equipment was beyond repair and should be replaced altogether? How ready are we to pay attention to the results of the market survey once we have launched it, or, more commonly, how ready are companies to deal with the results of opinion and attitude surveys that get into morale questions if the results do not fit their prior assumptions? Consultants who operate by the purchase of expertise models have learned over and over again that clients become angry and disillusioned if the expert information they are given does not fit in with their prior expectations.

In summary, this model of consultation is appropriate when clients have diagnosed their needs correctly, have correctly identified consultant capabilities, have done a good job of communicating what problem they are actually trying to solve, and have thought through the consequences of the help they have sought. As can be seen, this model is "client intensive," in that it puts a tremendous load on the client to do things correctly if the problem is to be solved. If problems are complex and difficult to diagnose, it is highly likely that this model will not prove helpful.

If the client recognizes that the diagnostic process itself is a problem, that something is not working but it is not clear what kind of help is needed, the client will adopt one of the next two models—doctor-patient or process consultant.

Model 2: Doctor-Patient. The core of this model is that the client experiences some symptoms that something is wrong but does not have a clue as to how to go about figuring out what is wrong or how to fix it. The diagnostic process itself is delegated completely to the consultant along with the obligation to come up with a remedy. The client becomes totally dependent upon the consultant until such time as the consultant makes a prescription, unless the consultant engages the client in becoming more active on his or her own behalf. As we will see, to the extent that the consultant does that, he or she is moving toward the process model. Several implicit assumptions are the key to whether or not the doctor-patient model will in fact provide help to the client.

1. *That the client has correctly interpreted the symptoms and the sick "area."* I cannot get help from an orthopedic surgeon if my pains are of hysterical origin. This is why it is often important to go first to a general practitioner who

functions partially as a process consultant before engaging in a "pure" doctor-patient relationship. In the organizational area we see many examples where companies conclude that they are hurting in the financial area, bring in a financially oriented consulting firm, work up new financial strategies, and then find a year or so later that things are no better than they were. No one discovered that the problem did not lie in finance, or organization, or product strategy or sales promotion, or whatever. It is very easy for clients and consultants to get caught up in a mutually reinforcing incorrect diagnosis if they move too rapidly into a doctor-patient mode of operating. Charlatans or just plain bad doctors are consultants who play on the client's dependence and purvey prescriptions that fit the doctor's area of expertise rather than the client's problem area.

2. *That the client can trust the diagnostic information that is provided by the consultant.* One of the biggest problems in this model is that the client has no way of evaluating whether or not the consultant's conclusions that the problem is X, is in fact a correct diagnosis. Often the consultant is deliberately obscure, technical, or otherwise esoteric in order to impress the client and to insure that further services will be purchased. There is nothing in the contract that obligates the "doctor" to worry about the client's degree of understanding of the diagnosis or its consequences except professional norms. In medicine these norms are reasonably clear and are enforced through collegial and professional associations. In the field of consulting such norms are much less clear and there are few practical ways of enforcing them because more of the client/consultant contact is hidden from view.

3. *That the "sick" person or group will reveal the correct information necessary to arrive at a diagnosis and cure, i.e., will trust the doctor enough to "level" with him or her.* In my own experience in working with groups there are two sources of distortion that make diagnosis difficult: (a) the person or group identified as "sick" or in need of help is resentful about that very identification and handles the resentment by denying or just plain "clamming up"; or (b) the person or group thus identified is so relieved to finally get some much-needed attention that they unburden themselves of all the accumulated grievances of the past, thus making it very difficult to put what is said into any kind of reasonable perspective. Consequently, when a client asks me to visit a group in which "there is a problem" I tend to resist that request until I have a much clearer idea of what is going on in that group from the initial client's perspective. The issue here, as in model 1, is whether or not the consultant is willing to take the problem on his or her own shoulders and allow the client to become even temporarily dependent. Such dependence, if allowed, may undermine the reaching of an accurate diagnosis.

4. *That the client has thought through the consequences, i.e., is willing to accept and implement whatever prescription is given.* It is a comforting feeling to give away one's problem and to be dependent upon a helper, but it is not always comfortable to be told at a later time what one will have to do to "cure" the problem. The consultant comes in, makes the diagnosis, and then recommends a "reorganization." This solution may be entirely correct in the abstract but

may not fit some prior assumptions that the client had made about the future or some values that are held by key managers, or may conflict with some other "facts" about the culture of the organization that may never have been revealed to the consultant. If the client is then upset about the prescription or having wasted money on something that he or she considers not implementable, the blame is on the client for having entered into the doctor-patient model without accepting all of its consequences. Of course, if the consultant cares about implementation, he or she will anticipate this problem and avoid getting into the pure doctor role in the first place.

5. *That the patient/client will be able to remain healthy after the doctor/consultant leaves.* If this model of consultation is to be useful, it must be applied in those areas where one can reasonably assume problem-solving capacity on the part of the client. If the problem is likely to recur because the client has not really learned how to solve problems of this sort, the dependency on the doctor/ consultant simply remains and the client then must decide whether or not such continued dependency is or is not appropriate. But there is nothing in the model itself that ensures increased problem-solving skills on the part of the client.

In summary, the doctor-patient model of consultation highlights the dependence of the client on the consultant both for diagnosis and prescription and thus puts a great burden on the client to correctly identify sick areas, accurately communicate symptoms, and think through the consequences of being given a prescription. Contrary to medicine, the field of consultation does not provide the client with the same safeguards against charlatans, and hence puts a greater burden on the client to protect himself or herself from unnecessary or inappropriate help.

If the consultant or helper is dedicated to producing change, to implementing solutions, and to increasing the overall "health" of the client through improving the client's own problem-solving skills, some version of the process consultation model must be applied.

Model 3: Process consultation. The core of this model is the assumption that for many kinds of problems that clients face, the *only* way to locate a workable solution, one that the client will accept and implement, is to involve the client in the diagnosis of the problem and the generating of that solution. The focus shifts from the content of the problem to the process by which problems are solved, and the consultant offers "process expertise" in how to help and how to solve problems, not expertise on the particular content of the client's problem. The consultant does not take the problem onto his or her own shoulders in this model. The "monkey always remains on the client's back," but the consultant offers to become jointly involved with the client in figuring out what is the problem, why it is a problem, why it is a problem right now, and what might be done about it. This consulting model is not a panacea appropriate to all problems and all situations. It also rests on some specific assumptions that have to be met if the model is to be viewed as the appropriate way to work with a client.

1. *That the nature of the problem is such that the client not only needs help in making an initial diagnosis but would benefit from participation in the process of making that diagnosis.* In my experience most problems that are nontechnical, that involve one or more other persons, that have group or organizational components, that involve values, attitudes, assumptions, and cultural elements, and which involve the client's own feelings fall into this category. Behind this assumption lies the further assumption that the information that is relevant to the diagnosis is fairly deeply imbedded in the client system and would not be easily elicited by an outsider functioning in a consulting role, but might be accessible if the client and consultant are working together both to elicit and interpret the information. Equally important is the assumption that the client would improve his or her problem solving *capacity* for future problem solving by learning through involvement with the consultant how to think about diagnosis, how to gather information, how to interpret it and how to draw conclusions about possible remedies. The consultant's skill lies in the process of helping—knowing what questions to ask, what to look for, how to stimulate alternate ways of thinking about problems, how to separate facts from feelings, how to involve others in thinking things through for themselves. All of these are skills that the client should improve.

2. *That the client has constructive intent and some problem-solving ability.* If the client is determined to be dependent or destructive, or if the client totally lacks problem-solving skills, this model obviously is inapplicable, as indeed might be any form of consultation. But the process model is clearly more vulnerable to the manipulative or destructive client, and hence the consultant must determine early in the relationship how much constructive intent is present and be prepared to terminate the relationship if it is not present.

3. *That the client is ultimately the only one who knows what form of solution or intervention will work in his or her situation.* Because of the degree to which the relevant information about values, assumptions, and attitudes is likely to be hidden in the client system it is essential to let the client generate the solution. Nine times out of ten when I have given "advice" I have been immediately told some new fact that made that solution irrelevant or unworkable. Instead of being angry with the client for resisting the advice, consultants should recognize that advice may have been inappropriate in the first place and that the client should have been helped to solve the problem. One way of doing this is to offer alternatives instead of advice and encourage the client to generate additional alternatives.

4. *That if the client selects and implements his or her own solution, the client's problem-solving skills for future problems will increase.* As was said at the outset of this section, one of the crucial elements of this model is the assumption that the goal of the consultation process is improved overall problem-solving skill on the part of the client, not only immediate problem solution. If there is no prospect of such skill improvement, the doctor-patient or expert models may be appropriate and less expensive.

A theoretical principle that underlies this model is that all human systems, whether individuals, groups, or organizations, are imperfect, have strengths and weaknesses, and can perpetually improve and grow. If this assumption or principle is accepted, it follows that any human system will benefit from increased capacity to diagnose and improve itself. It then becomes the ultimate function of the process consultant to help the client to perceive, understand, and act upon the process and content events that occur in his or her environment in order to improve the functioning of that client.

The philosophy of improvement does not imply that the consultant imposes his or her model of health on the client, but rather, accepts the goals and targets of that client system. If the consultant feels that those goals and targets are inappropriate, the consultant must be prepared to confront the issue, negotiate, and, if necessary, terminate the relationship. But the process consultant cannot at any time take over the client's problems, specify the client's goals, or in any other way allow client dependence. It is essential in this model for the client to perceive himself or herself as owning the problem and being in charge of finding the solution, with the consultant's help. And help is here defined as focusing on the process of problem solving rather than the content of the problem itself.

REFERENCE

SCHEIN, EDGAR H. *Process Consultation* (Reading, Mass.: Addison-Wesley, 1969).

Organizational Development and Industrial Democracy*

Eric J. Miller

Neither 'organizational development' nor 'industrial democracy' has a single, widely accepted definition, though both terms are very much in vogue. In Britain, the Government recently set up the Bullock Committee to make recommendations on mechanisms for a narrowly defined version of industrial democracy: the appointment of trade union members to boards of directors. But the term also has a wide extension, which includes, at one end of the spectrum, devices for employee participation (another term that is heavily used and quite imprecise) in managerial decision-making at shop-floor, factory and company levels, and, at the other end of the spectrum, notions of worker control, through collectives, co-operatives and other organizational forms. Associated with these different meanings, are, often, divergent ideologies and strong emotions. Much the same applies to 'organizational development'. Inherent in every definition is an explicit or implicit view of man, of organizations and of the nature of the relationship between them—which includes assumptions about the nature of authority. Goals range from the idealistic, such as egalitarianism, to the pragmatic, such as improving efficiency. Interventions made by OD practitioners may be consistent with stated goals, but quite often they are more consistent with different, unstated and perhaps unintended goals. Commonly, for example, OD is concerned to temper the instrumental view of employees as components in an organizational machine with the more liberal notion that employees are human individuals with drives, attitudes and emotions which the organization must allow space for and, indeed, put to positive use. In the process, however, OD may become unwittingly involved in the rather different task of displaying that bosses are human too— and, perhaps, suppressing evidence to the contrary. Understandably, this leads OD to be viewed with suspicion by those who interpret the boss—employee relationship in class terms and perceive an irreconcilable conflict of interests between the two groupings in capitalist societies: from this standpoint OD is a cunning palliative. Suspicions of manipulation are sometimes justified by the avowed intentions of OD practitioners and not just by inadvertent side-effects of pursuing more creditable goals. Thus I have met those who see OD as something to be applied on behalf of their clients, top management, to the rest

* SOURCE: Eric J. Miller, "Organizational Development and Industrial Democracy: A Current Case-Study," in *Organizational Development in the UK and USA: A Joint Evaluation*, ed. Cary L. Cooper (London: Macmillan, 1977), pp. 31–33. Reprinted with permission.

of the organization—top management itself being exempt from the process. Among these practitioners are some for whom this is a calculated exemption, on the principle of not biting the hand that feeds you. Others, astonishingly, have not even considered that there might be alternative stances.

Plainly, therefore, the terms 'industrial democracy' and 'organizational development' can be used to denote only a broad area of work and concerns. They are open to widely differing interpretations, some of which are political interpretations. In fact consultancy in this area cannot but be a political activity, at least insofar as it promotes some values and not others. Professional status, despite the claims often made for it, does not place the practitioner beyond the realm of values. Even in medicine, where the myth of purity and disinterest dies hard, values intrude in crude and subtle ways. The doctor who decides to give one patient better treatment than another is thereby engaging in a political act—regardless of whether his motives are economic or humanitarian. Less obviously, the decision to treat both patients equally, on the premise that all lives are equally important, is also a political decision, since it implements one particular set of values. If even the treatment of individuals has political connotations, in the 'treatment' of organizations they are patently much more significant. Hence my contention that the responsible professional has to try to make explicit the values that, consciously and perhaps less consciously, bear upon his role. Although we are intellectually aware of the problem, social scientists in general do not pay enough attention to the way in which values enter into the selection of conceptual frameworks and measuring instruments. It is not only the consultant who is in the game of political intervention. As I hinted earlier, frameworks and instruments that appear to be objective and scientific nevertheless favour certain interpretations of 'reality' and preclude others. The 'pure' research worker too is affecting the organization he is studying simply by being selective—unavoidably so—in the people he addresses and in the assumed roles in which they are addressed: he is not neutral. As Heisenberg pointed out, a sub-atomic physicist can demonstrate that electrons have wave-like properties; but another, taking another perspective and using different measuring instruments, can show that electrons behave as particles. Out of the range of properties of a situation, we see those that we are predisposed to look for. Hence we have an obligation to try to specify our predispositions.

The Relation of the "Pure" and the "Applied" to the "Professional Model" in the Social Sciences*

Council of the Tavistock Institute of Human Relations

1. The relation between the 'pure' and the 'applied' is different in the case of the social sciences as compared with the natural sciences. This difference crucially affects the conditions that the social sciences require for their development and needs to be understood if such development is to take place.

2. In the natural sciences, the fundamental data are reached by abstracting the phenomena to be studied from their natural contexts and submitting them to basic research through experimental manipulation in a laboratory. It is only some time later that possible applications may be thought of, and it is only then that a second process of applied research is set under way. The social scientist can use these methods only to a limited extent. On the whole he has to reach his fundamental data (people, institutions, etc.) in their natural state, and his problem is how to reach them in that state. His means of gaining access is through a professional relationship which gives him privileged conditions. The professional relationship is a first analogue of the laboratory for the social sciences. Unless he wins conditions privileged in this way, the social scientist cannot find out anything that the layman cannot find out equally well, and he can earn these privileges only by proving his competence in supplying some kind of service. In a sense, therefore, the social scientist begins in practice, however imperfect scientifically, and works back to theory and the more systematic research which may test this, and then back again to improved practice. Though this way of working is well understood in the case of medicine, it is not so well understood, even among social scientists, that the same type of model applies to a very wide range of social science activities. The model may in fact be called the 'professional model'.

3. Yet it is often contended that the social sciences should first proceed in isolation, and then one day, when they have advanced far enough in their basic work, they will become capable of developing practical applications. It is

* SOURCE: Council of the Tavistock Institute of Human Relations, *Social Research and a National Policy for Science* (London: Tavistock Publications, 1964), pp. 27–28. Reprinted with permission.

further contended that this first stage will be carried through by a few brilliant minds (as it was in the natural sciences) and that, until this stage is over and practical utilization of firmly established knowledge becomes possible, little is to be expected. It follows that for the time being light support only is warranted. Nothing could be more misleading than this viewpoint, which treats the relation between the pure and the applied in the social sciences as comparable with that in the natural sciences, ignores the distinctiveness of the professional model, and fails to see its special relevance to the social sciences.

4. Another advantage of following the professional as compared with the pure-applied model is that it allows the problems studied to be determined to a greater extent by the needs of the individuals, groups, or communities concerned than by the social scientist himself. This is not, of course, to say that presenting symptoms are accepted at their face value or that the client's prescription is obediently followed. The professional role implies interpretation and redefinition. It does, however, imply a considerable degree of 'field determination'.

5. Such an approach, it is submitted, is proper when a science (and this is the case in many areas of the social sciences) has not yet advanced to the point where there is a large body of fully attested empirical knowledge related to generally accepted theories. For if at this stage the problem is determined too exclusively by the scientist himself, the hypotheses to be tested will tend to be doctrines rather than true theories, or, as a reaction against this, investigation will become artificially restricted to what can be measured exactly. One may expect both too much formal conceptualization of a shallow kind and too much secondary manipulation of meagre primary data.

6. There is, of course, a great difference between simply acting as a consultant and acting as a researcher in a role where professional as well as scientific responsibility is accepted. In the first case there is no commitment to the advancement of scientific knowledge, either on the part of the consultant or on the part of those for whom the inquiry is being made. In the second case this commitment is fundamental and must be explicitly accepted by both sides. It is this that makes the relationship truly collaborative. Though far from all social science research needs to follow such an approach it is unlikely that the study of change processes, and of dynamic problems more generally, can be extended without it. . . .

The Different Kinds
of Knowledge Makers*

Fritz J. Roethlisberger

---

1. Foremost are the conceptual logicians who are interested in defining their concepts and relating them to each other in some logically consistent conceptual system. They are the concept makers and concept systematizers, sometimes called (in spite of George Homans' cries of outrage) theory builders. Although the conceptual logicians have a useful contribution to make (after all, the phenomena have to be classified and their properties specified), the trouble arises when they try to logicize their conceptual schemes of investigation into conceptual systems of explanation. Because of this misapprehension these conceptual logicians or system makers tend to become dictionary makers, logic choppers, and word manipulators who create futile verbal arguments. Each contradiction of findings only produces more words, definitions, and terminologies. My impression is that contributions of the conceptual logicians dominate the literature. Although their contributions are valuable, my impression is that the behavioral sciences suffer from an overabundance of them.

2. Entirely different from these conceptual logicians or magicians—in fact, almost at the opposite pole—are the clinicians, who are interested in matters of practice. They prefer staying close to particular concrete situations and tend to shy away from sweeping generalizations. Their contributions are insightful and perceptive. Their habitat is the field, not a laboratory or computer center. They are more comfortable inside a work group or sensitivity training group than inside the covers of a book. In debate with an expert conceptual logician, they may be reduced to putty, for their ideas are often not distinct or clear. But when matters of judgment are involved, they may make the conceptual logician look naive. They often call the conceptual scheme they bring to their fieldwork a theory. This is all right, so long as they do not think it is a theory of explanation for the phenomena they are investigating and trying to understand. The clinicians are often good initial discoverers, practitioners, and understanders, but they are usually not so hot in verifying or explaining the clinical uniformities they discover or the insights they have.

3. Indeed, the clinicians often leave verification and explanation to the correlation seekers and testers. The latter use questionnaires and survey methods to find out how some variable does or does not correlate with some other variable, such as productivity with satisfaction. They indulge little in

* SOURCE: From Fritz J. Roethlisberger, *The Elusive Phenomena* (Boston: Division of Research, Harvard Business School, 1977), pp. 388–393. Reprinted by permission.

theory, but sometimes they think that their correlations in and of themselves explain something. They are masters of transforming soft data into hard data by means of simple measuring scales and statistical devices. But no matter how hard they try, they cannot equate a correlation with an explanation. The literature, it seems to me, is littered with such unexplained correlations.

In the early days of my reading seminar the clinicians and the correlation seekers were having a running battle about the utility of field work versus questionnaire data. Ten years later they were having a love feast. They needed each other desperately to hold their own against the new knowledge makers that were coming into the field.

4. The new knowledge makers include the hypothesis seekers and testers. They are concerned with the discovery and verification of causal hypotheses. They use rigorous methods of measurement, sophisticated statistical procedures for the analysis of data, and broad experimental designs. These are truly the methodologists, the hard-boiled and realistic men of science. They have little use for the insights of clinicians or for the nonoperational definitions of conceptual logicians. Their goal is to be operational; for them only what can be made operational is real. Their skills are technical and exacting. They live in a world of their own. When they talk about matters of application and practice—which is not often—they sound naive.

They are the high priests of independent and dependent variables. They often treat the independent variable as the cause of the dependent one and in this sense claim they have explained it. In a loose sense of explanation this is true.

5. Strictly speaking, however, explanation is in the hands of the general-proposition makers. They search for general propositions from which the simple uniformities found at the empirical level can be derived under specified conditions. They are not analyzers, but synthesizers, and they synthesize propositions, not concepts. For them a scientific proposition states the empirical and not the logical relation between two concepts. For them a concept describes a property of nature, not of logic. Once concepts are empirically related into propositions, however, then the propositions so stated (not the concepts) can be arranged in a deductive system, and this system constitutes a scientific explanation.

The skill of the general-proposition maker is to show how a variety of empirical generalizations follow logically from a small number of general propositions under certain conditions. In his search for general propositions, the general-proposition maker is willing to use the empirical findings of practical experience as well as those obtained by clinical investigation or by more rigorous and sophisticated methods of research. He is just as willing to take the findings of practical experience, such as "You scratch my back and I'll scratch yours," or "The wheel that squeaks the loudest is the one that gets the grease," or "Nothing succeeds like success," as he is to accept such unexplained uniformities as "The size of the nuclear family is an inverse function of position in the stratification system."

Because a general proposition is reached by intuition and invention, its discovery is a leap of creativity and imagination. When it has been achieved, the full-grown knowledge tree is in existence. There is always room at the top, of course, for a yet more general proposition to explain the ones that have already been stated. The knowledge tree looks very different when it is viewed from the bottom up than it does from the top down. Going from the bottom up involves sweat, tears, toil, a great deal of imagination, and little deductive logic. However, one goes from the top to the lower levels by pure logic. So the tree, when looked at from the bottom up, is indeed less elegant than when looked at from the top down.

6. During the 1960s a new kind of knowledge maker and knowledge user appeared on the scene. These were the model makers or model builders. They built their mathematical models not only for attaining descriptive knowledge about phenomena, but also as normative knowledge to be applied to the phenomena. As they use their models (often not too clearly) in both senses and because I do not want to get hung up on this descriptive-normative issue now, I will confine what I say here to model builders who use their models for empirical discovery rather than for solving practical problems.

There is a similarity between the use of models for empirical discovery and what Henderson refers to as a conceptual scheme. Both are used for empirical investigation. There is also a big difference. Whereas a new conceptual scheme comes forth once in a generation or so, these new model makers, like the automobile manufacturers, put out a new model each year. Nay, I am doing them an injustice. About the time when I stopped teaching my seminar in 1967, the production of models rose sharply. It seemed that a new one appeared each day. Rumor had it that "a model a day keeps the doctor away." At this time I had difficulty in distinguishing model makers from the conceptual logicians and magicians I cited earlier.

The model maker also bears some resemblance to the general-proposition maker in the sense that the products of both the mathematical model and the general proposition are highly creative inductive leaps of the imagination to which empirical meanings can be given. But the general-proposition makers (at least the ones I know), once they have conceived their inventions, deliver their children slowly, one at a time, by simple deductive logic alone. The model makers turn out their progeny in much larger quantities and at a much faster rate by means of black boxes called computers.

PRODUCTS AND FINDINGS OF THE KNOWLEDGE ENTERPRISE

Thus far, I have represented the knowledge enterprise in terms of developmental levels or stages, of which I have distinguished three principal ones: skill, clinical, and analytical or scientific. I have argued that the passage from a lower to a higher stage requires some new ingredient. The first attempts to study a class of phenomena start with knowledge of acquaintance and skill in dealing with the phenomena. Going from skill to the clinical level requires a conceptual scheme and elementary methods of observation and interviewing. Going from the clinical to the analytical level requires concepts and definitions that refer more precisely to the properties of the phenomena and the relations among them. It also requires some elementary methods of measurement.

Within the analytical level I distinguish three sublevels: elementary concepts, empirical propositions, and general propositions. Going from elementary concepts to empirical-propositional statements requires operational definitions and rigorous methods of measurement. From empirical propositions to general-propositional statements requires a creative leap of an esthetic kind, by which it can be shown that statements about a great variety of different matters can be derived under certain conditions from a small number of simple, general statements. Once a general-propositional statement has been achieved as part of a deductive system, empirical propositions can be stated in a form that gives them the appearance of having been arrived at deductively. This appearance can be misleading, for empirical propositions often result from observation or other ways of building theories before a general proposition has been conceived. Indeed, many empirical propositions remain just such, without contributing to the leap of imagination that leads to the creation of the kind of explanatory system that is the goal of scientific statement.

Each level of knowledge has its own kinds of products and findings. Knowledge of acquaintance at the level of skill results in simple how-to-do-it statements of aphorisms about the phenomena. The products at the clinical level are descriptive cases about the phenomena or statements of clinical uniformities or syndromes in the phenomena. The products at the level of elementary concepts are statements such as x is the function of y; x is dependent on y; x has a consequence for y; or x correlates with y. The products at the level of empirical propositions are statements to the effect that x varies with y in such and such a fashion under certain given conditions (e.g., Boyle's law). At the level of general propositions, the products are sets of statements that include general propositions from which, under certain stated conditions, empirical propositions can be deduced (e.g., Newton's laws of motion). At this level, scientific theory and explanation have been achieved. I have summarized these views in the accompanying table.

If a knowledge seeker is satisfied with the state of knowledge at which he is working, there is nothing which requires him to proceed to the next higher level of the knowledge enterprise. If he nevertheless proceeds to the next stage, he has to abide by the rules of the game at that level. Each knowledge seeker may become enamored with the tools and methods of his level, so long as he does not think these tools alone will get him over the hump to the next level. If he does not realize that by themselves they are not enough, he becomes "hung up" at the lower level. There is no more serious mistake than for a knowledge seeker who is at one level of the knowledge enterprise to think that he is at another; that is, he should not think he is applying a scientific theory before he has achieved one. If he does, he is not only kidding himself; he is also confusing others. It is equally serious when a knowledge maker becomes overcommitted to the tools of one level and takes a polemical stance with regard to their value in explaining the phenomena. The following are some examples of this mistake: the clinician who plasters descriptions of situations with diagnostic concepts and thinks that he is thereby explaining them; the conceptual logician who thinks that he is explaining phenomena by tying his concepts into neat logical bundles; the correlation seeker who thinks his significant correlations explain something; the causal hypothesis seeker who thinks he has the tools for getting hold of propositions that will explain themselves by stating what the causes of the phenomena really are; the general-proposition maker who is so enamored with scientific explanations that he ceases to understand the phenomena with which he deals.

The Knowledge Enterprise*

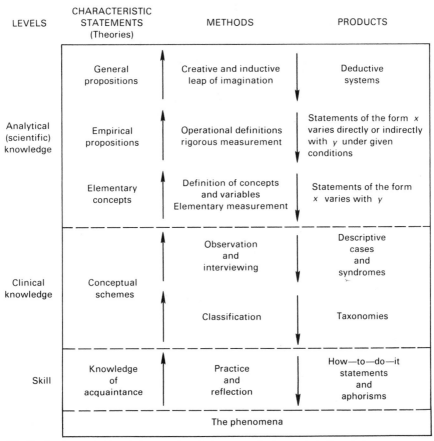

LEVELS	CHARACTERISTIC STATEMENTS (Theories)	METHODS	PRODUCTS
Analytical (scientific) knowledge	General propositions	Creative and inductive leap of imagination	Deductive systems
	Empirical propositions	Operational definitions rigorous measurement	Statements of the form x varies directly or indirectly with y under given conditions
	Elementary concepts	Definition of concepts and variables Elementary measurement	Statements of the form x varies with y
Clinical knowledge	Conceptual schemes	Observation and interviewing	Descriptive cases and syndromes
		Classification	Taxonomies
Skill	Knowledge of acquaintance	Practice and reflection	How—to—do—it statements and aphorisms
	The phenomena		

* For the development of knowledge, read from the bottom up; for the practice of knowledge, read from the top down.

3

ORGANIZATION DEVELOPMENT, ACTION RESEARCH, AND THE INTERVENTION MODEL

————◆————

INTRODUCTION

This chapter is intended to help faculty and students initiate small-scale interventions in chosen organizations, on the lines of the standard model advocated in this book. It is also intended to provide an overview of intervention for a wider range of readers. To achieve these aims, it focuses on the essentials of organization development and action research and how the two relate in interventions. The chapter presents introspective and projective experiential exercises, intended to crystallize and make explicit certain assumptions and values, as well as to provide specific training in needed skills. These experiences are complemented by a systematic, related set of readings.

Investigation of a Change is an exercise intended to help the participant surface his or her introspections about a personally experienced organizational change episode, to make them available for examination and comparison with those of others.

Organization development is a portmanteaux, people-centered approach to organizational change. The would-be change agent needs to grasp securely what organization development is—to internalize a working definition—in order to be able to read, understand, and draw upon the varied literature written under that banner. *Values and Assumptions of Organization Development* is an instrument intended to enable course participants make explicit comparisons between their own positions and those commonly held by organization development practitioners. Such comparisons, and discussion of them, help the novice penetrate below the bland external surface of a multi-faceted concept. This instrument forms a useful pair with Richard Beckhard's well-established definition of organization development, which appears in the models and schemes section of this chapter.

The HLW Department presents a brief account of the origins and arrangements made for a team development intervention, which invites discussion about how far the action proposed constitutes organization development as usually understood, and whether it will be successful.

Goodyear New Zealand Limited (A) consists of an account of the use of the standard intervention model this book advocates to provide change agent field training, to gather and feed back data concerning the attitudes, behavior, and performance of people working in a small corner of a large international company. The account explores several aspects of the use of the intervention model and is intended to be useful in fostering trainee change agent insight.*

Matheson Electronics Company and *Atlantis Supermarkets* are role plays intended to foster skill acquisition in the context of the intervention model. The former exercise is intended to help develop insight and skills to handle the initiation or entry stage of the intervention; the latter to provide practice in carrying out data-gathering interviews. Both call on interviewing skills discussed in the models and schemes section of this chapter.

The models and schemes section begins with the wide focus of *Applied Organization Change in Industry*, a celebrated review of alternative ways of initiating change. The "people" methods reviewed focus squarely on the role of human processes in organizational change. *Common Approaches to Change* arrays the strategies often used to introduce change along a power distribution continuum. This typology provides a simple, useful way of thinking about and categorizing change episodes, including the personal experiences brought to light in the Investigation of a Change exercise. *What Is Organization Development?*—one of the most systematic, frequently quoted and useful definitions of OD—has withstood the test of time well.

Several successive readings build up an initial picture of what action research—a more difficult if less diffuse concept than organization development—is. A concentrated, economical overview is provided in *Action Research and Planned Change*. *Definition of Action Research* shows it as a cyclical process. *Action Research* contrasts the high degree of client control over action research

---

* A brief analysis of the intervention and reflections on the use of the intervention model are presented in *Goodyear New Zealand Limited (B)*, *Goodyear New Zealand Limited (C)* and *Goodyear New Zealand Limited (D)* which appear in the Instructor's Manual.

with the high degree of investigator control under traditional social science research.

Action research is a complex set of ideas and practices at the heart of managing organizational change, worthy of study, thought, and application on several counts. This book proposes initial models and schemes about action research in this chapter and advances additional schemes in Chapters 4 and 9. The concluding chapter considers action research as presenting a useful, defensible, scientific rationale for the field of managing organizational change.

The relationship of organization development to action research is addressed by a pair of related readings, drawn from a common source. In *Action Research as Applied to Organization Development*, the two concepts are compared in a table that highlights common and distinctive characteristics of each. *Phases in Action Research OD* outlines the time-based sequence of an intervention from its inception to its conclusion. These readings bear the hallmarks of being written by experienced change agents.

The *Intervention Model* outlines the standard data-gathering and feedback action research model this book advocates for training change agents, and provides a commentary on its use and development. Given the time it takes to carry out even a minimum scale intervention, the instructor should require students to begin drafting their intervention proposals the moment the course begins. The interventions should be firmed up and launched as rapidly as possible. In the first few weeks of the course the there-and-then experiences and models and schemes studied and discussed should be targeted toward ensuring the viability of these field efforts. The Instructor's Manual suggests teaching sequences to help accomplish this.

The last two readings, on *Interviewing*, focus on the practical objective of how best, in the context of the intervention model, to use the interview to gather data. The first item draws on the Survey Research Center's extensive expertise; the second pointedly outlines the advantages and shortcomings of interviews from the perspective of experienced consultants. See Chapter 5 for additional models and schemes about interviewing as a data-gathering device.

Investigation of a Change*

Roy McLennan

INTRODUCTION

This exercise is intended to help you improve your grasp, insight and under-standing concerning the human processes by which changes are made by organisations.

METHOD

Think of a specific change carried out in a particular organisation you are familiar with. It is ideal if you are familiar with first hand experience of the change. Try to find a change which is recent enough to be fresh in your memory. The change need not be earth shattering or organisation-wide. A change affecting a single group is quite sufficient for the purpose of the exercise.

Your task is (a) to think about the information you have on the change, especially the human processes by which it was made, i.e., who did what with and/or to whom, and when, in the course of the change; and (b) to analyse the information thoroughly. Pay particular attention to:

i. Causes and perceptions: What were the causes of the change? Who/what precipitated it? Who perceived what problem?
ii. Problem solving and decision making process: In what way was the change decided on and implemented? Who decided on it? Who was involved? How/Why?
iii. Outcome: Did the attempted change work? Was the change accepted, resisted or rejected by the people affected by it? How did they react/behave?

Prepare a careful, systematic description of the change, for verbal presentation to other people, in terms of causes, human processes and outcomes. You should try to explain why the change attained the level of success or failure it did.

* SOURCE: Copyright © Roy McLennan 1983.

VALUES AND ASSUMPTIONS OF ORGANIZATION DEVELOPMENT: A QUESTIONNAIRE*

Roy McLennan

This instrument is intended to provide an opportunity to arrive at an indication of how far you share the values and assumptions implicated in Organization Development. It consists of a set of propositions. You are asked to respond to each of the propositions by circling any ONE of the possible answers: Agree; Neither Agree nor Disagree (i.e. neutral or indifferent); Disagree

1. In the vast majority of organizations, people learn from their experience that their attempts to make constructive contributions are not rewarded, and may even be penalised.

    DISAGREE   NEITHER AGREE NOR DISAGREE   AGREE

2. The best way of obtaining solutions to most organizational problems involving attitudes and motivation is for the people involved to alter their relationships.

    DISAGREE   NEITHER AGREE NOR DISAGREE   AGREE

3. Emotions are best handled in work organizations by repressing them—feelings are taboo on the job.

    DISAGREE   NEITHER AGREE NOR DISAGREE   AGREE

4. What goes on in an individual's work group or team has great significance for the individual's feelings of satisfaction and competence.

    DISAGREE   NEITHER AGREE NOR DISAGREE   AGREE

5. Most managerial and administrative groups, teams and committees lack problem-solving skills.

    DISAGREE   NEITHER AGREE NOR DISAGREE   AGREE

* SOURCE: Adapted from Roy McLennan, ed., *Participation and Change in the New Zealand Workplace* (Wellington, New Zealand: Fourth Estate, 1978). The propositions are based on Wendell L. French and Cecil H. Bell, *Organization Development* (Englewood Cliffs, NJ.: Prentice-Hall, 1978, 1984).

6. Improvement in the effectiveness of departments, sections or units in most organizations requires fuller participation on the part of their members.

	NEITHER AGREE	
DISAGREE	NOR DISAGREE	AGREE

7. In order for a group or team to optimise its effectiveness, the formal leader cannot perform all its leadership functions.

	NEITHER AGREE	
DISAGREE	NOR DISAGREE	AGREE

8. Conflict or competition between either individuals or groups, in which one comes out the winner and the other the loser, is in the long run not an effective approach to solving organizational problems.

	NEITHER AGREE	
DISAGREE	NOR DISAGREE	AGREE

9. What happens in one section, unit, part or sub-system of an organization will affect and be influenced by other parts of the organization.

	NEITHER AGREE	
DISAGREE	NOR DISAGREE	AGREE

10. In order for an organization to benefit from an Organization Development programme, its members must value collaborative effort.

	NEITHER AGREE	
DISAGREE	NOR DISAGREE	AGREE

11. When provided with a working environment which supports and challenges them, most people will strive to grow and acquire new knowledge, skills and abilities.

	NEITHER AGREE	
DISAGREE	NOR DISAGREE	AGREE

12. The level of trust, support and co-operation existing between people in most groups and organizations is much higher than is either necessary or desirable.

	NEITHER AGREE	
DISAGREE	NOR DISAGREE	AGREE

13. Most managers and administrators need to augment the authority given to them by their positions by developing skills in responding to their subordinates and their needs.

	NEITHER AGREE	
DISAGREE	NOR DISAGREE	AGREE

14. It makes most sense to conceive of organizations as consisting of a network of individuals, rather than a network of groups or teams.

	NEITHER AGREE	
DISAGREE	NOR DISAGREE	AGREE

15. Most people can help their work group or team solve problems.

	NEITHER AGREE	
DISAGREE	NOR DISAGREE	AGREE

16. How a manager behaves in relation to his subordinates is strongly influenced by how his superior behaves in relation to him.

DISAGREE   NEITHER AGREE NOR DISAGREE   AGREE

17. Some values must be held in common between protagonists in an organizational conflict if conflict-reducing and problem-solving techniques are to be useful.

DISAGREE   NEITHER AGREE NOR DISAGREE   AGREE

18. Organization Development practitioners are concerned both with the personal growth of people in organizations and increasing organizational effectiveness.

DISAGREE   NEITHER AGREE NOR DISAGREE   AGREE

19. The ordinary organization member inherently prefers to avoid responsibility, has little ambition, and wants security above all.

DISAGREE   NEITHER AGREE NOR DISAGREE   AGREE

20. Most organizations will become more effective if they become more responsive to the needs of their members.

DISAGREE   NEITHER AGREE NOR DISAGREE   AGREE

21. Understanding people's feelings, and skill in working with feelings, opens up avenues for improved organizational performance.

DISAGREE   NEITHER AGREE NOR DISAGREE   AGREE

22. Most people want to be accepted by and interact co-operatively with their work group.

DISAGREE   NEITHER AGREE NOR DISAGREE   AGREE

23. A leader may be recognised by the deference paid to him by his subordinates.

DISAGREE   NEITHER AGREE NOR DISAGREE   AGREE

24. Organization Development strategies will be unsuccessful in organizations where members place high value on anarchy, hate, violence or destruction.

DISAGREE   NEITHER AGREE NOR DISAGREE   AGREE

25. The average organization member has an inherent dislike of work and will avoid it if he can.

DISAGREE   NEITHER AGREE NOR DISAGREE   AGREE

26. Suppressed feeling or emotions adversely affect problem-solving, personal growth and job satisfaction.

DISAGREE   NEITHER AGREE NOR DISAGREE   AGREE

27. One of the most relevant and powerful influences on most people in organizations is the work group or team they are in.

DISAGREE   NEITHER AGREE NOR DISAGREE   AGREE

28. Leadership skills may be acquired by most people, regardless of their particular inborn traits or abilities.

DISAGREE   NEITHER AGREE NOR DISAGREE   AGREE

29. A major avenue towards increasing organizational effectiveness is through creating conditions under which members can make greater contributions to organization goals.

DISAGREE   NEITHER AGREE NOR DISAGREE   AGREE

30. The development of skill in handling expressions of feelings requires learning, which can most fruitfully take place in the work group or team.

DISAGREE   NEITHER AGREE NOR DISAGREE   AGREE

31. Organizations can be usefully characterised as consisting of an overlapping set of groups or teams, with each group's superior serving as the link or anchor man for his team.

DISAGREE   NEITHER AGREE NOR DISAGREE   AGREE

32. Most people desire to make, and are capable of making, a higher level of contribution to the attainment of organization goals than most organizational environments will permit.

DISAGREE   NEITHER AGREE NOR DISAGREE   AGREE

33. The extensive use of teams and committees in most organizations usually results in a good bit of wasted time.

DISAGREE   NEITHER AGREE NOR DISAGREE   AGREE

The HLW Department*

William G. Dyer

The HLW department is an agency of a state government. It has a central office in the capital city and a series of district offices throughout the state. The agency employs about 500 people and is headed by an executive director who has twelve different department heads reporting to her. Through the years, the agency has been seen by other similar agencies and by the people in the department as doing an effective job in spite of difficult circumstances.

The decision regarding some type of training or development was faced initially by the training and development officer and his assistant. They were reviewing their training budget and were very much aware that approximately $5,000 of unexpended funds remained in the year's budget with less than six months to go. They also knew the training budget might be cut if unused funds were returned to the general fund, and that questions would be raised about the effectiveness of the training department if funds that were allocated, presumably against a preplanned program, were not used.

The two training and development staff people considered several alternatives. First, they rejected the returning of unspent funds. This left them with the alternative of spending the funds. But what type of expenditure would make sense and make a contribution to the department? The assistant commented, "I recently read a good article on organization development. In my opinion, we need some OD work done in our agency."

The training director replied, "That sounds good to me, but how do you get OD started in an organization?"

"From what I read, one of the best ways is to do some team building."

"What's that?" asked the director.

"My understanding is that people who have to work together should learn how to communicate and to solve their problems so they stay solved," said the assistant. "And that sounds to me like something our executive committee [the executive director and the twelve department heads] could really use."

"You can say that again," responded the training director. "But how can we sell that group on a team-building program?"

The assistant thought for a moment. "I think they would go for this program if we could get a good outside consultant to come in and conduct the program for the executive committee. An outside person would be a strong selling point to the committee."

*SOURCE: William G. Dyer, *Team Building*, © 1977, Addison-Wesley Publishing Company, Inc., Reading, Massachusetts. Pp 27 thru 29. Reprinted with permission.

"Agreed," said the T.D. "Let's see if we can line up a good outside person. You get a reprint of that article on OD and we'll circulate that to the executive committee. If we can get the consultant and can set up a time and place for the team—development program that suits everyone, I think we will be in business."

For the next few weeks the training director and his assistant were extremely busy. They contacted several people who were recommended as effective leaders of team—development programs. At least two would be available during the most likely times. The OD article was circulated to all relevant people and a meeting was set up with the executive director. They reviewed the plans with the director.

Her response was favorable. "It all looks pretty good. I think we should go ahead. My own schedule is very tight and I may not be able to stay the whole time, but I can be there to start it out and then I may have to duck out to attend some meetings in Washington. If you have a good outside person, I'm sure the whole thing will move along."

"That's my feeling," said the training director. "A good consultant will make a big difference."

So the plans were developed. A consultant was hired who had impressive credentials and his resume was circulated to the committee. An attractive resort was scheduled for three days. The consultant indicated that he would like to interview people for a couple of days prior to the program and that was agreed on. The executive director raised the team—development issue with the committee. Several people commented that they were "awfully busy," but the executive director was able to overcome these objections by pointing out that "certainly no one could disagree that it was critically important that this group become as effective a team as possible." With that, the motion to move ahead with the team—development program was unanimously approved.

Goodyear New Zealand Limited (A)*

Roy McLennan

Despite sustained effort by executives and managers over a year or two, by late 1977 Goodyear New Zealand's share of the national tyre market seemed to be under threat. Executives were aware of declining total sales in the industry, caused by the longer-lasting radial tyre and the general downturn affecting the economy. They thought the adaptation of the company's field sales staff to these changing conditions was poor, and their attitudes to Head Office initiatives intended to make these adaptations increasingly negative. In a renewed effort to solve these continuing problems the company approached the Department of Business Administration, Victoria University, to ask that a confidential survey of the attitudes of the company's field staff be carried out.

THE COMPANY

In 1977 approximately 200 people worked in Goodyear New Zealand, about 170 based on various sales locations and retread plants in the North and South Islands, and some 30 at the company's Head Office at Seaview, Lower Hutt. The apex of Goodyear's hierarchy consisted of an Executive Committee of three members, who led the managers and staff of Head Office. District Managers were the direct superiors of the managers in the company's retail stores, and intermediary between the stores and Head Office. Each District Manager was formally responsible for all company business in the given geographical area. Diagram 1 presents an organisation chart of the company in mid-1977.

FIRST STEPS

I responded to Goodyear's approach to the Department of Business Administration, and in due course visited the company and met Messrs. Patrick

*Source: Edited from Roy McLennan, "Intervening in Goodyear New Zealand Limited," *New Zealand Journal of Business*, 5 (1983), 18–41.

This account was written largely from tape recordings, documents, and notes generated in the course of the intervention reported here, and is the revised version of a paper given at the New Zealand Administrative Staff College in 1983. I want to thank Tony Loorparg for his help in carrying out the intervention, and Rex Howe, former chief executive of Goodyear New Zealand Limited, for his permission to publish material concerning the Goodyear Company. The opinions expressed here are those of the author, not necessarily those held by Loorparg, Howe, or the Goodyear Company.

SCHEMATIC ORGANIZATION CHART MID—1977

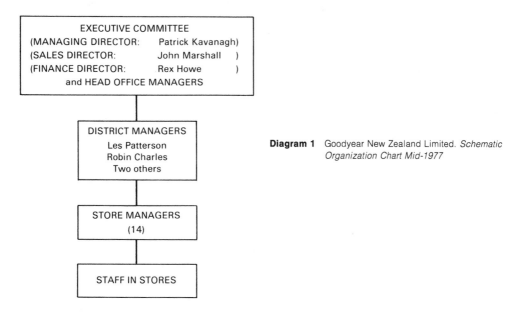

Diagram 1 Goodyear New Zealand Limited. *Schematic Organization Chart Mid-1977*

Kavanagh, John Marshall and Rex Howe, members of the Executive Committee, and Robin Charles, a District Manager, who along with Les Patterson, another District Manager, had been instrumental in the move to approach the university. Charles had, earlier in his career, been awarded a Diploma in Management Studies by a London Polytechnic. Patterson was heavily involved in the New Zealand Institute of Management, and had for some time been an Institute tutor. He was highly regarded in the company for his managerial knowledge and skill, and was heir designate to Marshall as Sales Director.

After several detailed discussions the agreed aim of an initial, modest, tentative intervention was 'to tap the positive and negative attitudes (of field sales staff) . . . to the company and their work,' on this basis to 'seek means to improve involvement and teamwork in the stores,' improve market share and cooperation with management and Head Office 'in the interests of profitability and general company performance.' To pursue these ends I would carry out wide-ranging, exploratory, confidential interviews of Sales Director Marshall and the four District Managers, as a first attempt to meet the agreed aims.[1] After the interviews I was to draw up a summary of the District Managers' views and meet again, together with Marshall, to consider the summary and plan action recommendations arising from it. Marshall, the District Managers and the consultant would then report their recommendations back to the Executive Committee. Among their recommendations were expected to be

---

[1] It was later decided to include Frank Smith, the Retail Store Marketing Manager, in effect Marshall's immediate Head Office sales subordinate, among the interviewees.

some concerning appropriate stores as sites for developing the intervention further. To help with the intervention I recruited Tony Loorparg, an officer working in the Personnel Branch of the Ministry of Defence. Loorparg had completed a master's degree at Victoria University.

In September 1978 the intervention was held in a suite of the St. George Hotel in Wellington. Those who took part consisted of Marshall, Smith, and three of the company's four District Managers. Patterson, the Auckland District Manager, cancelled his attendance at the last moment. After the interviews had been completed, analysed and summarised on wall charts, the consultants took Marshall through them. Then the managers met in a workshop session to explore what they had to say, led by their superior.

The first half of the workshop was devoted to elucidating the District Managers' views about 'how things are in the company at present.' It became clear to all that they regarded their relationship with Head Office as unsatisfactory, owing to continual pressure in the form of a barrage of instructions, admonishments and criticisms. The keynote words describing their views of themselves in their role were 'uncertainty', 'lack of clarity' and 'inadequacy'. They believed themselves by-passed by both Head Office and Store Managers. They thought it difficult to pursue both wholesale and retail sales from the same stores, that Store Managers had a hard time in achieving Head Office's sales goals and, in any case, were insufficiently motivated to do so. There were staffing difficulties in the stores. At the mid-day end of the exploratory discussion Marshall delivered a bombshell. He announced that the reason why Patterson had not come to the workshop was that he had decided to resign from the company.

After lunch the action planning phase of the workshop began, with Loorparg helping the managers prioritise items in the feedback summary in terms of possible action. It soon became very evident that the item accorded the highest priority was the position brought about by Patterson's resignation. This and the general consensus of opinion that the District Manager role was not functioning effectively became the dominant issues in the workshop, and most evidently had to be resolved if any useful action planning of any sort was to emerge.

After extended discussion between the managers, with little consultant input, they agreed that Marshall should put several proposals to the Executive Committee on their behalf: that the company should have three rather than four District Managers, and consequently that the present geographical areas of responsibility should be widened. They concurred that the District Manager was too much involved in mundane activities, and often spent a great deal of time resolving minor administrative problems. To relieve them of much of the time-consuming activities concerned with the supervision, training and investigation of field control procedures, two assistants should be appointed, located in Head Office. Finally, Marshall was to seek a Head Office commitment not to by-pass District Managers, to allow them to influence the quarterly meetings, to look to their education and training, and investigate and act on salary and bonus matters.

ACTION AFTER THE ST. GEORGE INTERVENTION

Marshall immediately and enthusiastically took up these recommendations with the Executive Committee, who had awaited the workshop's outcome with considerable interest. It was quickly agreed that the company should have three District Managers. The scheme pertaining to administrative support of District Managers was also agreed and actioned over the following weeks, and the two assistants appointed. The Committee stated that 'An overall effort will be made to improve communication (Head Office-field) with as much as practicable being passed through the District Managers.' At the three Head Office-District Manager meetings to be held each year, 'presentations will be less formal, preferably prepared in writing, in advance, and circularised to all attendees. In this way certain matters can be thought about prior to District Meetings and discussed more sensibly at the actual meeting.' Smith assumed important responsibilities for training, which was given a new emphasis. In October Howe, the Finance Director, began a major review of company salaries, right across the board. The bonus scheme was revised by Marshall.

In October the Executive Committee and the consultants met to review the St. George intervention. General satisfaction was expressed, and they decided to proceed directly to a second intervention, using the same model, this time focusing on a District Manager and the Store Managers in his district. The executives considered that such an exercise was likely to be more fruitful, in exploring and acting on the attitudes of field staff, than an intervention inside a store: the attitudes of Store Managers were, they believed, of central significance in company sales performance.

They also concluded that the intervention process as a whole should proceed one step at a time, and that each step should be assimilated before attempting another. The possibility of mounting interventions in the other two districts should accordingly be left for the time being, along with ideas of similar exercises at store and Head Office levels. An intervention based on Head Office executives and managers would, they consider, be the likely successor and culmination to the Store Managers' exercise.

The Committee and consultants decided to hold the intervention in the company's Central District, which was managed from Wellington by Charles. This District stretched from New Plymouth in the north-west and Gisborne in the north-east to Wellington in the south, and consisted of seven stores. The objectives of the intervention were similar to the previous exercise: to improve liaison, team work and cooperation inside the District, and between the District and Head Office, in the interests of restoring market share and improving company performance. The wider view was to apply the lessons learned from the intervention to all three company districts.

THE CENTRAL DISTRICT INTERVENTION

The intervention took place at the Solway Hotel, Masterton, over several days in November. All seven Central District Store Managers took part in it, together with Charles and the consultants. A great amount of data was provided by the Store Managers in the interviews, which were analysed and summarised by the consultants, and fed back to the District Manager before the group workshop took place.

The Store Managers thought that company objectives were unclear and felt confused about them. They considered themselves the object of Head Office pressure, overcontrol, ambivalence, criticism and impersonality. Head Office 'overemphasises figures,' they said, and 'describes people as "units".' They affirmed the importance of the District Manager role to them and the company. They felt their own status as Store Managers was demeaned by the kind of vehicle they drove, a utility with company markings. This was a sore point having a long history in the company. They felt the company did not advertise sufficiently. They also thought the company operated to minimum staff levels at low pay, which caused all sorts of difficulties.

The Store Managers sought company action by posing a series of requests to the Executive Committee, intended to reduce the pressures they experienced from Head Office, to encourage their District Manager to be of greater assistance to them, to revise the conception and formal title of their own role, to promote sales by local advertising, and to revise the salary and wage structure throughout the company.

RESPONSE TO THE CENTRAL DISTRICT INTERVENTION

The outcomes of the Solway workshop were awaited with keen anticipation by members of the executive committee. The various recommendations were presented to the Committee by Charles and the consultants, reviewed in a lengthy meeting, a host of decisions made on the spot and others after further study. The Committee later confirmed on paper that a statement on corporate objectives and details of the background reasoning behind them would be presented to Store Managers at the next quarterly District Meeting. An overall effort would be made to improve communication between Head Office and the field, with as much as practicable being passed through the District Managers. District Managers were asked to make more time available for coaching and counselling on visits to stores.

The present title 'Retail Store Manager' was scrapped in favour of 'Manager—Goodyear Tyre Service' (GTS Manager), and the stores were to be referred to in future as 'Branches'. It was stated that a comprehensive revision of salaries, led by Howe, the Finance Director, was proceeding. As GTS managers' utilities came up for replacement some station wagons were to be purchased, at the discretion of Head Office management. An allocation of advertising funds was to be made to each Store Manager, to be used at his discretion—on condition of the District Manager's approval. The Committee stated its readiness to consider appointing Retail Trainees for the purpose of relieving Store managers, and undertook to study the matter in 1979.

The Solway intervention amply confirmed the view, which had gathered weight amongst executives and managers since the St. George exercise, that the key to many issues lay not in the field but in Head Office, and that a similar intervention should be mounted at that office. This would constitute the culmination of the company's efforts in changing the attitudes and behaviour of staff. Early in the New Year the Executive Committee and the consultants accordingly met to plan the Head Office intervention. The executives were clear that they themselves and all managers at Head Office should take part in the exercise. The focus was to be mainly on Head Office-field relations, but there was some feeling that internal Head Office relations also affected dealings with field staff, and should similarly be viewed in the context of company performance and job satisfaction.

Some weeks before the intervention was scheduled to take place a general management meeting was held at Head Office. The Executive Committee intended to test the usefulness of such a means of exploring and resolving several issues and concerns highlighted by the St. George and Solway interventions. The participants consisted of the Sales and Finance Directors and the incumbents of managerial roles. Scheduled to occupy half an hour as a beginning, it lasted for an entire morning and was generally regarded as highly successful.

THE HEAD OFFICE INTERVENTION

The consultants began by carrying out detailed exploratory interviews with the members of the Executive Committee, to inform themselves as closely as possible on the views of the company's leaders. Then in a one week period the consultants interviewed the eight Head Office managers. All interviews were held in the company's Head Office building, and arrangements were made to preserve privacy and prevent interruptions by callers or telephones. As in the earlier interventions all the participants spoke frankly and freely to the consultants. A number said they warmly welcomed the exercise, having heard of the previous interventions carried out.

When the feedback summary was written up by the consultants the Executive Committee met for a half day to explore the vast quantity of observations presented in the feedback summary, and to decide who among them would lead the various parts of the feedback/action planning workshop.

The workshop took place in a suite at the Travel Lodge in Wellington in May. It became amply clear that Head Office managers believed that the company's field sales people had a limited commitment to their work, and lacked proper motivation: they did not share the Head Office 'disease' that 'things have got to be done,' and had an 'eight to five' orientation, and were not self-starters. They acknowledged the existence of internal Head Office problems of fuzzy job roles, titles and chains of command, leading sometimes to overlapping responsibilities. Information processing left a good deal to be desired. Head Office managers tended to adopt a pessimistic leadership style. The impending retirement of Kavanagh, the MD, created unclear career development horizons for several managers. Head Office lacked an adequate lunch/social room, and was too far from the shops for the female staff.

The Travel Lodge intervention generated a number of recommendations, most of which, it was agreed, required clearer definition and action on the part of a variety of committee groups, operating on the principle of mutual influence rather than hierarchy. The action plans paid attention to problems of clarifying the individual manager's job duties and the company's hierarchy, and defining a series of meetings to integrate effort inside Head Office, and between Head Office and the field. Managers were, drawing on the consultants' knowledge, to carry out a programme of self-diagnosis and discussion of their management styles. Training needs were to be attacked systematically.

In June the consultants visited the Executive Committee at Head Office. Progress had been made on a number of action items. Copies of the first version of the new salary administration document, prepared by Howe after a sustained effort over several months, had been given to those responsible for salaries. In the light of the problems surfaced about the Head Office location and amenities the Committee had decided to move Head Office to an urban office block in Lower Hutt, which offered 35 percent more space, social space, and shopping facilities for female staff.[2] Half the work of centralising the two overlapping filing systems had been completed; the remainder awaited the move to the new location. Mitchell, the Administration Manager, was on the day the consultants visited holding his first staff meeting for rank and file Head Office employees. The weekend management meeting, planned to be held in Masterton, had been shelved, however, pending progress on several items. Annual appraisals were about to be carried out on all company managers' performances. The consultant supplied the requested copies of leadership style questionnaires and readings for the managers to complete and discuss.

THE NORTHERN AND SOUTHERN DISTRICTS

During the consultants' visit it was agreed that they should design interventions for the Northern and Southern Districts in the company, to extend the benefits

---

[2] The company's lease on the existing Head Office property was due to expire on 31 July.

of the Central District intervention, as agreed earlier. The objectives of the interventions were broadly the same as previously. But two features differed from those mounted earlier: the use of a questionnaire to gather information, and the use of one rather than two consultants wherever possible and practicable. These measures were agreed to save consultant time and cost.

The consultants used their experience of the Solway exercise and the other interventions to design the questionnaire. It was then utilised in the Northern District. All eight Branch Managers in the District responded in detail to the questionnaire. As planned, Loorparg carried through the analysis of responses on behalf of the consultants.

At the feedback/action planning workshop, held at a motel in Hamilton in late November, the Branch Managers said they would have preferred to have been interviewed, rather than to have filled out a questionnaire. They evinced some uncertainty about the company's sales mission, and said they often found sales targets impossible to achieve. There was insufficient support, 'compared with what our competitors are doing.' While they felt that Head Office did not consult them enough on their information needs, and was at times slow at answering requests to supply information, they also said that contacts with Executive Committee members were usually productive, and that the Branch Operating Manual (a new Head Office creation) proved very useful. They noted the need for emergency back-up staffing in branches, problems in the salary and pay area, and underlined that they looked forward to the culmination of Howe's salary exercise. They asked why only some Branch managers were getting station wagons. They said that training was needed in many aspects of Branch management and staff jobs. Several shortcomings earlier noted by their Central District counterparts were not mentioned.

The workshop recommended that to meet acknowledged problems of supply of product the company should have its own production plant, and should also investigate retread production and marketing. They felt there was a need for greater liaison within Head Office in advance of communication with branches. An Assistant District Manager was needed in the District. Branch Managers should have more say about pay, recruiting, staffing and rebates. Finally, they said the company needed a Training Officer.

On 30 November Loorparg and the Northern District Manager met the Executive Committee at Head Office to consider the intervention's recommendations and outcomes. A decision concerning the planned twin intervention, earlier planned to take place in the Southern District, was postponed. Direct consultant involvement in the Goodyear Company ended at this point.

THE CHIEF EXECUTIVE'S EVALUATION

About two years later I presented Howe, the then incumbent chief executive of Goodyear New Zealand and the former Finance Director, with a draft paper on the intervention, asked for permission to publish it, and visited the company to gather his comments on it. Howe made several points. He felt the concept of using two administrative assistants at Head Office to back up the District Managers, invented at the St. George, had stood the test of time, and was the best administrative structure for the purpose.

He remarked that, 'The first intervention highlighted the fact that we did have a major problem': some managers and staff were seriously underpaid. Others suffered from anomalies or the failure of their superiors to utilise the company's salary scales to the best advantage. 'We went to the point of doing our own (salary) surveys from director level to sales rep.' In the first year he visited eight separate companies, as well as using the results of the Greenwood Survey, a six monthly exercise the company subscribed to. As a result, 'We made some major adjustments in salaries. In the second year we visited half-a-dozen companies, as well as (again) using Greenwood, and again made major adjustments to salaries.' He carried out a third survey in 1980 and concluded, 'We just don't have a problem now.'

Before the intervention, he said, 'There was obviously a problem of communication within Head Office, (from) individual to individual.' There is now a monthly general management meeting at Head Office, and a quarterly meeting of all central office staff. All Head Office executives and managers are included in the former, and district managers as well when they are around. After an initial problem of over-dominance of discussion by executive committee members, a rotating chairman and secretary have become the established and successful practice. All members can put items on the agenda, which is physically circulated around head office by Howe's secretary. During the meeting the executive or manager concerned gives a rundown of forthcoming action or events. Meetings run for as little as half an hour to as much as two or even three hours, as circumstances demand, but typically last for about an hour, terminating with morning tea.

He feels it is 'a very good forum for information flow, ideas and understanding of other people's problems.' During a recent meeting it was suggested that his confidential reports on company performance and outlook be extended to all head office staff. Beginning with the recent quarterly staff meeting, 'I told them a lot of figures and information which before were very confidential. . . . I respect their confidence and they respect mine.'

The company's advertising expenditure is now four or five times as much as in 1978. 'We wanted to be on television (have a company ad on TV) purely as a morale booster, apart from anything else.' Recently Smith, the Sales Director, was undecided about which of two competing advertising proposals, submitted by different advertisting agencies, to choose for 1982. With Howe's encouragement he invited head office managers and staff, and the managements of two handy branch offices, to give their opinions. These opinions were pretty unequivocal and were adopted. This kind of approach, he said, 'Comes out of this type of exercise.'

Before the intervention, he remarked, 'The people side of it—we just ignored it. . . . The people who were included in that exercise (are) constantly referring back to it, and using it as a guide for what they do now. . . . I could write so many papers on so many exercises I've done as a consequence of the intervention!' In summary, he said, 'We had major communication problems from Head Office management to the field and within Head Office. We did three exercises which proved this. We took some steps and we think today we have a better organisation for it. . . . We are stronger today than we have been for a long, long time.' Finally, Howe and I acknowledged that the intervention had begun as a purely confidential, private arrangement between the company and the consultants, in an attempt to solve particular problems, with no thought of carrying out research or publishing the findings. It had become a substantially successful endeavour, however, and, he hoped, of use to other companies and managers, as well as Goodyear, hence he was prepared to authorise publication.

Matheson Electronics Company*

Roy McLennan

This role play is intended to help you understand how it feels to be a manager faced with a worrying, deep-seated company difficulty, and a consultant trying to set up some systematic, useful action to help the manager and the company do something constructive about the difficulty. It is also an opportunity to develop skill in working as a consultant with senior managers. The exercise focuses on the initial phase of setting up an intervention.

You will be asked to study the Role Note of one of the people involved in the role play. Do not read the Role Notes of the other people. Read the introduction and your assigned Role Note carefully a few times, jotting down notes about it. Think about your Role to try to get the feel of what it is like to be that person in that situation. Try to develop your own interpretation of how the person in that position would behave. Let your feelings develop as they would if you actually were the person described in your Role Note. During the role play do not read your Role Note. If issues arise which are not covered in the Note, improvise as best you can to meet the developing situation.

INTRODUCTION

Over some years the Matheson Electronics Company has successfully developed a profitable niche in the market for specialised electronic devices of several kinds. But during the last couple of years sales and profits have fallen away seriously. Company managers have worked on the problem in various ways for many months, but to no avail. Indeed, things have become worse, as the company's latest sales and financial reports confirm.

The company's personnel manager thinks the causes of the problem probably lie in the 'people' area, and has approached a consultant skilled in action research about it. They know each other quite well. After some discussion they made an appointment to see the company's chief executive to propose carrying out an exploratory intervention. The meeting between the personnel manager, the consultant and the chief executive is about to take place in the chief executive's office.

* SOURCE: © Copyright Roy McLennan, 1986, Version 4.

ROLE FOR THE CONSULTANT

You were recently approached by the personnel manager of Matheson Electronics about a predicament the company faces, who remarked that during the last few years the company's sales and profits have declined seriously. The company's managers have worked on the problem from several angles for many months, the manager remarked, but to no avail: things have instead become worse. The causes of the company's difficulties are of course not known, but there is less than perfect team work between managers, and some do not seem to be on top of their jobs. In an attempt to halt the decline the personnel manager wants you, as a consultant on human problems, to explore the advisability of carrying out an intervention in the company.

The two of you agreed that the first thing to do, in any intervention you might carry out, is to seek inside information about what is going on in the company from key managers. You think you could usefully interview all six of the company's top managers, including the chief executive, analyse the data generated, and provide feedback to all of them in an off-site workshop. Action planning of an appropriate sort should follow.

The personnel manager has set up an appointment for you to meet the company's chief executive. When you meet you expect to outline your intervention plan, explore the chief's point of view about it, and decide whether to proceed.

You and the personnel manager have just arrived outside the chief executive's office, and are waiting to be invited inside.

ROLE FOR THE CHIEF EXECUTIVE

You have been chief executive of Matheson Electronics for several years, and took over from the company's founder and chief executive, Tom Matheson. Tom was a tough, hard, self-made engineer, who led the company autocratically. In the last couple of years you've watched helplessly as sales and profits have steadily slipped away. You've tried all sorts of measures, but you can't seem to make much progress in stopping the rot, let alone reversing the trends, whatever their causes.

You think that some of the company's managers are young, well-trained and capable, but are often a little arrogant and difficult to work with. Some of the others are older, came up the 'experience' way, from the shopfloor and the office, and remain to be convinced about the value of such modern notions as 'discounted cash flow', 'market segmentation' and 'job satisfaction'. All of them are inclined to be individualists and leave a good deal to be desired in the team-play sense.

The company's personnel manager has recommended that the company undergo an intervention, in an attempt to get at the problem and solve it. You think the idea of having a 'people' type consultant run some sort of tape measure over the company's senior managers is worth trying. Attempting something new is better than continuing with the existing efforts to do something about the sales-profits decline which, after all, have already failed repeatedly.

But you also feel a little apprehensive as to what this consultant might want to enquire into. What will he or she do in looking into the problem? You also want to satisfy yourself that confidentiality will be maintained, and a decent veil of discretion drawn over the company's secrets.

The personnel manager has arranged a time for you to meet the consultant, to discuss the idea of an intervention and decide whether to proceed. They have both just arrived for their appointment, and are waiting outside your office.

ROLE FOR THE PERSONNEL MANAGER

You've thought long and hard about the possible causes of the worrying decline in the company's sales and profits, and the continuing failure of management's attempts to halt it. You've reached the conclusion that poor team work between the company's top managers is probably among the prime causes of the decline. And some of the company's managers are probably not on top of their jobs—especially the older ones—because they've lived for so long under the shadow of the previous chief executive, a dominating boss who called all the shots. The company's use and development of its human resources is in general pretty primitive, you feel, and could fruitfully be looked into.

You have accordingly approached a consultant who would be prepared to carry out an intervention in the company. You chose this particular person because you know each other via Management Association meetings, are aware of the consultant's good reputation, and you get on well together. You have agreed with the consultant's tentative suggestion that a basic data collection-feedback-action planning intervention cycle, involving the company's top managers, could well be a good way to begin to tap into the problem. You've set up a meeting between the consultant, the company's chief executive and yourself to explore the idea and, you hope, come to the decision to proceed. Some such intervention is very necessary, you're sure, for the health of the company.

You and the consultant are waiting outside the chief executive's office.

Atlantis Supermarkets*

Roy McLennan

INTRODUCTION

During the last few years the market share of Atlantis Supermarkets, a company which operates a number of supermarkets in several cities and towns, has slowly but steadily declined. Company managers have tried to reverse the trend by taking various actions, but have not succeeded. As the latest attempt to do something about the problem, last month's Executive Committee meeting approved the proposal that outside consultants carry out a behavioural science–based intervention. It will take the form of an exercise in which the company's top managers will be interviewed one-on-one by either of the two consultants working on the intervention. The data gathered in this way will be summarized and fed back at an off-site workshop. Interviews of two of the company's leading executives are about to take place. First one consultant will interview the Marketing Manager, then the other will interview the Comptroller. Each interview will take place in the respective manager's office.

* SOURCE: © Copyright Roy McLennan, 1987, version 3.

ROLE FOR CONSULTANTS

Your consultancy firm, Action Research Associates (ARA), was recently approached by Atlantis Supermarkets to look into the long-term decline in the company's market share. Under the terms of the agreed proposal you'll carry out free-ranging, informal, one-on-one interviews with all eight of the company's top managers, analyse the information generated, and provide feedback of your findings to all of them in an off-site workshop. The meaning of the data will be explored and appropriate action considered.

From several discussions with the company's personnel manager and chief executive, when you were jointly putting the proposal together, your vague hunches are that the company is following rather than leading industry practice, tends to be unimaginative in buying and mechandising, and applies modern approaches to its human resources in only patchy ways.

You are now about to carry out your first interviews in the intervention. You think you'll probably start by explaining very briefly to each manager what the intervention is about, his or her role in it, and the sort of help you are asking for. You'll state that you regard the remarks each makes as confidential, and will be fed back in such a way as to preserve their anonymity. Then you'll ask them to tell you about themselves, to explain what they do in their job, who they do it with, and what they like and dislike about it. Then you'll go on to ask how they got into their present job, where they see themselves as going, what they think is going right in Atlantis at present, and what's going wrong. Finally, you'll ask what might be done about it all.

While you have your questions ready you want each manager you interview to have every opportunity to say whatever they like, in whatever order they like. You know they have to do most of the talking if the interview is to be a success.

You are outside the manager's office, waiting to be invited in to begin the interview.

ROLE FOR MARKETING MANAGER

You've been Marketing Manager at Atlantis Supermarkets for over a year, and were appointed from outside the company. You initially saw the job as a creative opportunity to develop a challenging, sophisticated marketing strategy, which would revive the company's sagging market share. You haven't got very far down that track, however, partly because every manager in the company tends to run his department as his own exclusive domain, and doesn't expect to be influenced by colleagues like you. Hence it's difficult to bring your marketing expertise to bear. You seldom meet other Atlantis managers except in response to specific, short-term problems of which there have been a lot lately. Some of the older managers in the place have worked their way up from the bottom, not undergone any significant management education experience, are stuck in their ways, and are frankly plain ignorant about a good deal of modern thinking about the practice of management.

You know from last month's Executive Committee meeting that behavioural science–based consultants have been appointed to look into the company's worrying performance and that one of them will call on each senior manager for a depth interview. Maybe some modern management help is at hand!

One of the consultants is waiting outside your office for that interview right now.

ROLE FOR THE COMPTROLLER

You have been in charge of the accounting function at Atlantis Supermarkets for some years, and worked your way up in the company to this position. For many quarters now you have been well aware that the performance of the company has been increasingly poor in terms of market share, and you are worried about it. You know the company is not doing well, and have hunches that unenterprising buying and stodgy sales and advertising people might be the culprits. The buyers always seem to be breezing around in expensive new company cars. If only they worked in such a dedicated way as the accounts department people do! Some of the younger managers talk constantly in highfaluting jargon which you think does not mean much.

You know from the last Executive Committee meeting that behavioural science–based consultants have been approached to look into the company's perturbing market share and that one of them will call on each senior manager for an informal but thorough interview. You hope they'll have a proper appreciation of the fundamental contribution of the accounting function to the success of the company. Maybe they'll look into the buying and sales departments and wield a hatchet to good effect! More likely they'll talk in some impractical jargon which won't get Atlantis anywhere.

One of the consultants is waiting outside your office for the interview right now.

Applied Organization Change in Industry: Structural, Technical and Human Approaches*

Harold J. Leavitt

This is a mapping chapter. It is part of a search for perspective on complex organizations, in this instance, through consideration of several classes of efforts to change ongoing organizations. Approaches to change provide a kind of sharp caricature of underlying beliefs and prejudices about the important dimensions of organizations. Thereby, perhaps, they provide some insights into areas of real or apparent difference among perspectives on organization theory.

To classify several major approaches to change, I have found it useful, first, to view organizations as multivariate systems, in which at least four interacting variables loom especially large: the variables of task, structure, technology and actors (usually people) (Figure 1).

Roughly speaking, task refers to organizational *raisons d'être*—manufacturing, servicing, etc., including the large numbers of different, but operationally meaningful, subtasks which may exist in complex organizations.

By actors I mean mostly people, but with the qualification that acts usually executed by people need not remain exclusively in the human domain.

By technology I mean technical tools—problem-solving inventions like work measurement, computers or drill presses. Note that I include both machines and programs in this category, but with some uncertainty about the line between structure and technology.

Finally, by structure I mean systems of communication, systems of authority (or other roles) and systems of work flow.

These four are highly interdependent, so that change in any one will most probably result in compensatory (or retaliatory) change in others. In discussing organizational change, therefore, I shall assume that it is one or more of these variables that we seek to change. Sometimes we may aim to change one of these as an end in itself, sometimes as a mechanism for effecting some changes in one or more of the others.

Thus, for example, structural change towards, say, decentralization should change the performance of certain organizational tasks (indeed, even

* SOURCE: Abridged from Harold J. Leavitt, "Applied Organization Change in Industry: Structural, Technical and Human Approaches," in *New Perspectives in Organizational Research*, ed. W. W. Cooper, H. J. Leavitt, and M. W. Shelly (New York: John Wiley, 1964), pp. 55–71. Reprinted with permission from Carnegie Mellon University.

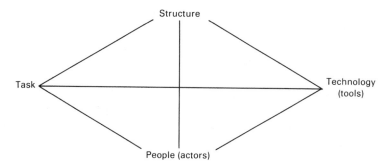

Figure 1

the selection of tasks), the technology that is brought to bear (e.g. changes in accounting procedures), and the nature, numbers, and/or motivation and attitudes of people in the organization. Any of these changes could presumably be consciously intended; or they could occur as unforeseen and often troublesome outcomes of efforts to change only one or two of the variables.

We can turn now to our central focus of, namely, a categorization and evaluation of several approaches to organizational change—approaches that differ markedly in their degree of emphasis and their ordering of these four variables.

Clearly most efforts to effect change, whether they take off from people, technology, structure or task, soon must deal with the others. Human relators must invent technical devices for implementing their ideas, and they must evaluate alternative structures, classing some as consonant and some as dissonant with their views of the world. Structuralists must take stands on the kinds of human interaction that are supportive of their position, and the kinds that threaten to undermine it, etc.

Although I differentiate structural from technical from human approaches to organizational tasks, the differentiation is in points of origin, relative weightings and underlying conceptions and values, not in the exclusion of all other variables.

This categorization must be further complicated by the fact that the objectives of the several approaches to organizational change are not uniform. All of them do share a considerable interest in improved solutions to tasks. But while some of the technical approaches focus almost exclusively on task solutions, that is, on the *quality* of decisions, some of the people approaches are at least as interested in performance of task subsequent to decisions. Although improved task solution serves as a common goal for all of these approaches, several carry other associated objectives that weigh almost as heavily in the eyes of their proponents. Thus some of the early structural approaches were almost as concerned with maintaining a power *status quo* as with improving task performance, and some of the current people approaches are at least as interested in providing organizations that fulfil human needs as they are in efficacious performance of tasks.

The several approaches are still further complicated by variations in the causal chains by which they are supposed to bring about their intended changes. Some of the structural approaches, for example, are not aimed directly at task but at people as mediating intervening variables. In these approaches, one changes structure to change people to improve task performance. Similarly, some of the people approaches seek to change people in order to change structure and tools, to change task performance, and also to make life more fulfilling for people. We can turn now to the several varieties of efforts themselves.

THE STRUCTURAL APPROACHES

Applied efforts to change organizations by changing structure seem to fall into four classes. First, structural change has been the major mechanism of the 'classical' organization theorist. Out of the deductive, logical, largely military-based thinking of early non-empirical organization theory, there evolved the whole set of now familiar 'principles' for optimizing organizational performance by optimizing structure. These are deductive approaches carrying out their analyses from task backwards to appropriate divisions of labor and appropriate systems of authority. These early structural approaches almost always mediated their activities through people to task. One improves task performance by clarifying and defining the jobs of people and setting up appropriate relationships among these jobs.

In retrospect, most of us think of these early approaches as abstractions, formal and legalistic, and poorly anchored in empirical data. They were also almost incredibly naïve in their assumptions about human behavior. In fact, almost the only assumptions that were made were legalistic and moralistic ones: that people, having contracted to work, would then carry out the terms of their contract; that people assigned responsibility would necessarily accept that responsibility; that people when informed of the organization's goals would strive wholeheartedly to achieve those goals.

In one variation or another, such structural approaches are still widely applied. It is still commonplace for consultants or organization planning departments to try to solve organizational problems by redefining areas of responsibility and authority, enforcing the chain of command, and so on.

A second widespread approach to structural change, allied to the first, somewhat more modern and sophisticated and somewhat narrower, too, is the idea of decentralization. The idea of changing organizations by decentralizing their structure was probably more an invention of the accounting profession than anyone else, though it has been widely endorsed by structuralists and by human relators too. Almost nobody is against it.

Decentralization affects the performance of tasks partially through its intervening effects on people. By creating profit centers one presumably increases the motivation and goal-oriented behavior of local managers. One also adds flexibility so that variations in technology appropriate to the different tasks of different decentralized units now become more possible; so do subvariations in structure and local variations in the use of people. Decentralization can be thought of as a mechanism for changing organizations at a meta level, providing local autonomy for further change. Thus, within limits, decentralized units may further change themselves through the use of any one of the many alternatives available, and perhaps for this reason no group has questioned it, at least until the last couple of years.

Recently, two other structural approaches have shown up, but they have not yet reached a widespread level of application. One of them is best represented by Chapple and Sayles (7). Theirs is a form of social engineering aimed at task, but via people. They seek to modify the behavior of people in order to improve task performance, but they do it by modifying structure, in this case, the flow of work. Out of the tradition of applied anthropology, they argue that planning of work flows and groupings of specialities will directly affect the morale, behavior and output of employees. One of the failings of earlier structural models, in their view, is that the design of work was almost entirely determined by task and technical variables, and failed to take account of human social variables. They provide illustrative cases to show that appropriate redesigning of work, in a social engineering sense, affects both human attitudes and output.

I cannot overlook in this discussion of structure the implications of a second approach—the research on communication networks (10). I know of no *direct* applications of this laboratory research to the real world, though it has had some indirect influence on structural planning. In that research, variations in communication nets affect both routine and novel task performance rather significantly. The results suggest that appropriate communication structures might vary considerably within a complex organization, depending upon the type of task that any sub-unit of the organization undertakes. Thus for highly programmed repetitive tasks, highly centralized communications structures seem to operate most efficiently, but with some human costs. For more novel, ill-structured tasks, more wide-open communication nets with larger numbers of channels and less differentiation among members seem to work more effectively.

TECHNOLOGICAL APPROACHES TO ORGANIZATIONAL CHANGE

My first entry in this technological category is Taylor's *Scientific Management* (24). Its birth date was around 1910, its father, Frederick W. Taylor.

Like the early structural approaches, scientific management was to a great extent ahuman, perhaps even inhuman. For in creating the separate planning specialist, it removed planning from its old location—the head of the doer of work. Many observers, both contemporary and subsequent, saw this phase of scientific management as downright demeaning of mankind.

But despite the flurry of congressional investigations and active counterattack by Taylor's contemporaries, scientific management grew and prospered, and radically changed structure, people and the ways jobs got done.

Scientific management receded into a relatively stable and undramatic background in the late 1930s and 1940s and has never made a real comeback in its original form. But the technological approaches were by no means dead. The development of operations research and the more or less contemporaneous invention and exploitation of computers have more than revived them.

I submit that operational operations-research methods for organizational problem solving can be reasonably placed in the same category with scientific management. They have both developed a body of technical methods for solving work problems. They both are usually *external* in their approach, essentially separating the planning of problem-solving programs from the routine acting out of solutions. Operations research, too, is quickly developing in its operational form, a new class of hot-shot staff specialists, in many ways analogous to the earlier staff efficiency man. What is *clearly* different, of course, is the nature of the techniques, although there may be larger differences that are not yet so clear.

The operations-research and information-processing techniques are turning out to be, if not more general, at least applicable to large classes of tasks that scientific management could not touch (Schultz and Whisler, 22). Now armed with linear programming methods, one can approach a task like media selection in an advertising agency, though it would have been nonsense to time-study it.

But note the over-all similarity: change the setting of the movie from Bethlehem, Pa., to Madison Avenue, the time from 1910 to 1962; the costuming from overalls to gray flannel suits; and the tasks from simple muscular labor to complex judgemental decisions. Turn worried laborer Schmidt into worried media executive Jones. Then replace Taylor with Charnes and Cooper and supplant the stopwatch with the computer. It is the same old theme either way—the conflict between technology and humanity.

A distinction needs to be drawn, of course, between operational operations-research and other computer-based, information-processing approaches, although they are often closely allied. 'Management Science' hopefully will mean more than highly operational applications of specific techniques, and organizations are also being changed by simulation techniques and by heuristic, problem-solving methods. Their impact has not yet been felt in anything like full force; but tasks, people and structures are already being rather radically modified by them.

Without delving further into the substance of these more recent technological approaches, it may be worth pointing up one other characteristic that they share with many of their predecessors—a kind of faith in the ultimate victory of *better* problem solutions over less good ones. This faith is often perceived by people-oriented practitioners of change as sheer naïveté about the nature of man. They ascribe it to a pre-Freudian fixation on rationality; to a failure to realize that human acceptance of ideas is the real carrier of change; and that emotional human resistance is the real roadblock. They can point, in evidence, to a monotonously long list of cases in which technological innovations, methods changes or operations-research techniques have fallen short because they ignored the human side of the enterprise. It is not the logically better solutions that get adopted, this argument runs, but the more humanly acceptable, more feasible ones. Unless the new technologist wises up, he may end up a miserable social isolate, like his predecessor, the unhappy industrial engineer.

Often this argument fits the facts. Operations-research people can be incredibly naïve in their insensitivity to human feelings. But in another, more gracious sense, one can say that the technological approaches have simply taken a more macroscopic, longer view of the world than the people approaches.

The technological approaches seem not only to predict the victory of cleaner, more logical, and more parsimonious solutions but also to *value* them. Failure of human beings to search for or use more efficient solutions is a sign, from this perspective, of human weakness and inadequacy. People must be teased or educated into greater logic, greater rationality. Resistance to better solutions is proof only of the poverty of our educational system; certainly it is not in any way an indication that 'optimal' solutions are less than optimal.

THE PEOPLE APPROACHES

The people approaches try to change the organizational world by changing the behavior of actors in the organization. By changing people, it is argued, one can cause the creative invention of new tools, or one can cause modifications in structure (especially power structure). By one or another of these means, changing people will cause changes in solutions to tasks and performance of tasks as well as changes in human growth and fulfilment.

In surveying the people approaches, one is immediately struck by the fact that the literature dealing directly with organizational change is almost all people-oriented. Just in the last four or five years, for example, several volumes specifically concerned with organizational change have been published. All of them are people-type books (see 3, 9, 11, 13, 15).

This tendency to focus on the process of change itself constitutes one of the major distinguishing features of the people approaches. The technological and structural approaches tend to focus on problem-solving, sliding past the microprocesses by which new problem-solving techniques are generated and adopted.

Historically, the people approaches have moved through at least two phases: the first was essentially manipulative, responsive to the primitive and seductive question, 'How can we get people to do what we want them to do?'

Carnegie's *How to Win Friends and Influence People* (6) was first published in 1936, a few years ahead of most of what we now regard as psychological work in the same area. Like the social scientists that followed, Carnegie's model for change focused on the relationship between changer and changee, pointing out that changes in feelings and attitudes were prerequisites to voluntary changes in overt behavior.

Though social scientists have tended to reject it out of hand, current research on influence processes suggests that the Carnegie model is not technically foolish at all, although we have disavowed it as manipulative, slick and of questionable honesty.

However, Carnegie-like interest in face-to-face influence has finally become a respectable area of social scientific research. Several works of Hovland *et al.* (12) on influence and persuasion provide experimental support for the efficacy of certain behavioral techniques of influence over others.

But if we move over into the traditionally more 'legitimate' spheres of social science, we find that much of the work after the Second World War on 'overcoming resistance to change' was still responsive to the same manipulative question. Consider, for example, the now classic work by Kurt Lewin (23) and his associates on changing food habits, or the later industrial work by Coch and French (8). In both cases, A sets out to bring about a predetermined change in the behavior of B. Lewin sets out to cause housewives to purchase and consume more variety meats—a selling problem. Coch and French set out to gain acceptance of a preplanned methods change by hourly workers in a factory. In both cases the methodology included large elements of indirection with less than full information available to the changees.

But whereas Dale Carnegie built warm personal relationships and then bargained with them, neither Lewin nor Coch and French are centrally concerned about intimate relationships between changer and changee. Their concern is much more with warming up the interrelationships among changees.

Thus 32 percent of Lewin's test housewives exposed to a group-decision method served new variety meats, as against only 3 percent of the women exposed to lectures. Lewin accounts for these results by calling upon two concepts: 'involvement' and 'group pressure'. Lectures leave their audiences passive and unpressed by the group, whereas discussions are both active and pressing. Similarly, Coch and French, causing the girls in a pajama factory to accept a methods change, emphasize *group* methods, seeing resistance to change as partially a function of individual frustration, and partially of strong group-generated forces. Their methodology, therefore, is to provide opportunities for need satisfaction and quietly to corner the group forces and redirect them towards the desired change.

One might say that these early studies wrestled rather effectively with questions of affect and involvement, but ducked a key variable—power.

It was to be expected, then, that the next moves in the development of people approaches would be towards working out the power variable. It was obvious, too, that the direction would be towards power equalization rather than towards power differentiation. The theoretical underpinnings, the prevalent values and the initial research results all pointed that way.

But though this is what happened, it happened in a complicated and mostly implicit way. Most of the push has come from work on individuals and small groups, and has then been largely extrapolated to organizations. Client-centered therapy (Rogers, 21) and applied group dynamics (Miles, 19) have been prime movers. In both of those cases, theory and technique explicitly aimed at allocating at least equal power to the changee(s), a fact of considerable importance in later develoment of dicta for organizational change.

At the group level, a comparable development was occurring, namely, the development of the T- (for training) group (or sensitivity training or development group). The T-group is the core tool of programs aimed at teaching people how to lead and change groups. It has also become a core tool for effecting organizational change. T-group leaders try to bring about changes in their groups by taking extremely permissive, extremely non-authoritarian, sometimes utterly non-participative roles, thus encouraging group members not only to solve their own problems but also to define them. The T-group leader becomes, in the language of the profession, a 'resource person', not consciously trying to cause a substantive set of changes but only changes in group processes, which would then, in turn, generate substantive changes.

Though the T-group is a tool, a piece of technology, an invention, I include it in the people rather than the tool approaches, for it evolved out of those approaches as a mechanism specifically designed for effecting change in people.

In contrast to earlier group discussion tools the T-group deals with the power variable directly. Its objective is to transfer more power to the client of the group.

But these are both non-organizational situations. For the therapist, the relationship with the individual client bounds the world. For the T-group trainer, the group is the world. They can both deal more easily with the power variable than change agents working in a time-constrained and work-flow-constrained organizational setting.

At the organizational level, things therefore are a little more vague. The direction is there, in the form of movement towards power equalization, but roadblocks are many and maps are somewhat sketchy and undetailed. McGregor's (18) development of participative Theory Y to replace authoritarian Theory X is a case in point. McGregor's whole conception of Theory Y very clearly implies a shift from an all powerful superior dealing with impotent subordinates to something much more like a balance of power.

Bennis, Benne and Chin (3) specifically set out power equalization (PE) as one of the distinguishing features of the deliberate collaborative process they define as planned change: 'A power distribution in which the client and change agent have equal, or almost equal, opportunities to influence' is part of their definition.

In any case, power equalization has become a key idea in the prevalent people approaches, a first step in the theoretical causal chain leading towards organizational change. It has served as an initial subgoal, a necessary predecessor to creative change in structure, technology, task solving and task implementation. Although the distances are not marked, there is no unclarity about direction—a more egalitarian power distribution is better.

It is worth pointing out that the techniques for causing redistribution of power in these models are themselves power-equalization techniques— techniques like counseling and T-group training. Thus both Lippitt, Watson and Westley (15) and Bennis, Benne and Chin (3) lay great emphasis on the need for collaboration between changer and changee in order for change to take place. But it is understandable that neither those writers nor most other workers in power equalization seriously investigate the possibility that power may be redistributed unilaterally or authoritatively (e.g. by the creation of profit centers in a large business firm or by coercion).

If we examine some of the major variables of organizational behavior, we will see rather quickly that the power-equalization approaches yield outcomes that are very different from those produced by the structural or technological approaches.

Thus in the PE models, *communication* is something to be maximized. The more channels the better, the less filtering the better, the more feedback the better. All these because power will be more equally distributed, validity of information greater, and commitment to organizational goals more intense.

Contrast these views with the earlier structural models which argued for clear but limited communication lines, never to be circumvented, and which disallowed the transmission of affective and therefore task-irrelevant information. They stand in sharp contrast, too, to some current technical views which search for optimal information flows that may be far less than maximum flows.

The PE models also focus much of their attention on issues of *group pressure, cohesiveness* and *conformity*. The more cohesiveness the better, for cohesiveness causes commitment. The broader the group standards, the better. The more supportive the group, the freer the individual to express his individuality.

Consider next the *decision-making* variable. Decision making, from the perspective of power equalization, is viewed not from a cognitive perspective, nor substantively, but as a problem in achieving committed agreement. The much discussed issues are commitment and consensual validation, and means for lowering and spreading decision-making opportunities.

Contrast this with the technical emphasis on working out optimal decision rules, and with the structuralist's emphasis on locating precise decision points and assigning decision-making responsibility always to individuals.

REFERENCES

ASCH, S. E. *Social Psychology*, Prentice-Hall, 1952.

BENDIX, R. *Work and Authority in Industry*, Wiley, 1956.

BENNIS, W. G., K. D. BENNE and R. CHIN eds. *The Planning of Change*, Holt, Rinehart & Winston, 1961.

BENNIS, W. G. and H. A. SHEPARD 'A theory of group development,' in W. G. Bennis, K. D. Benne and Chin, R. (eds.), *The Planning of Change*, Holt, Rinehart & Winston, 1961.

ASCH, S. E. 'Issues in the study of social influences on judgment,' in I. A. Berg and B. Bass (eds.), *Conformity and Deviation*, Harper, 1961.

CARNEGIE, D. *How to Win Friends and Influence People*, Simon & Schuster, 1936.

CHAPPLE, E. D. and L. R. SAYLES *The Measure of Management*, Macmillan, 1961.

COCH, L. and J. R. P. FRENCH 'Overcoming resistance to change,' *Hum. Rel.*, vol. 1 (1948), pp. 512–32.

GINSBERG, E. and E. REILLY *Effecting Change in Large Organizations*, Columbia U.P., 1957.

GLANZER, M. and R. GLASER 'Techniques for the study of group structure and behavior,' *Psychol. Bull.*, vol. 58 (1961), pp. 1–27.

GUEST, R. H. *Organizational Change: The Effect of Successful Leadership*, Dorsey, 1962.

HOVLAND, C., I. JANIS and H. KELLY *Communication and Persuasion*, Yale U.P., 1953.

LAWRENCE, P. R. *The Changing of Organizational Behavior Patterns*, Harvard University Business School, Division of Research, 1958.

LIKERT, R. *New Patterns of Management*, McGraw-Hill, 1961. [See Readings 14 and 23.]

LIPPITT, R., J. WATSON and B. WESTLEY *The Dynamics of Planned Change*, Harcourt, Brace, 1958.

MARCH, J. G. (ed.), *Handbook of Organizations*, Rand McNally, 1964.

MARTIN, N. H. and J. R. SIMMS 'The problem of power,' in W. L. Warner and N. H. Martin (eds.), *Industrial Man*, Harper, 1959.

McGREGOR, D. *The Human Side of Enterprise*, McGraw-Hill, 1960.

MILES, M. B. *Learning to Work in Groups*, Bureau of Publications, Teachers College, Columbia University, 1959.

ROETHLISBERGER, F. J. and W. J. DICKSON, *Management and the Worker*, Harvard U.P., 1939.

ROGERS, C. R. *Counseling and Psychotherapy*, Houghton Mifflin, 1942.

SHULTZ, G. P. and T. L. WHISLER (eds.), *Management Organization and the Computer*, Free Press, 1960.

LEWIN, K. 'Group decision and social change,' in G. E. Swanson, T. Newcombe, and E. Hartley (eds.), *Readings in Social Psychology*, Holt, 2nd edn. 1952.

TAYLOR, F. W. *Scientific Management*, Harper, 1947.

Common Approaches to Change*

Larry E. Greiner

In looking at the various major approaches being used to *introduce* organization change, one is immediately struck by their position along a "power distribution" continuum. At one extreme are those which rely on *unilateral* authority. More toward the middle of the continuum are the *shared* approaches. Finally, at the opposite extreme are the *delegated* approaches.

UNILATERAL ACTION

At this extreme on the power distribution continuum, the organization change is implemented through an emphasis on the authority of a man's hierarchical position in the company. Here, the definition and solution to the problem at hand tend to be specified by the upper echelons and directed downward through formal and impersonal control mechanisms. The use of unilateral authority to introduce organization change appears in three forms.

By Decree. This is probably the most commonly used approach, having its roots in centuries of practice within military and government bureaucracies and taking its authority from the formal position of the person introducing the change. It is essentially a "one-way" announcement that is directed downward to the lower levels in the organization. The spirit of the communication reads something like "today we are this way—tomorrow we must be that way."

In its concrete form it may appear as a memorandum, lecture, policy statement, or verbal command. The general nature of the decree approach is impersonal, formal, and task-oriented. It assumes that people are highly rational and best motivated by authoritative directions. Its expectation is that people will comply in their outward behavior and that this compliance will lead to more effective results.

By Replacement. Often resorted to when the decree approach fails, this involves the replacement of key persons. It is based on the assumption that

* Source: Larry E. Greiner, "Patterns of Organization Change," in *Organizational Change and Development*, ed. Gene W. Dalton, Paul R. Lawrence, and Larry E. Greiner (Homewood, Ill.: Richard D. Irwin, 1970), pp. 215–218. Reprinted with permission.

Author's note: This article is part of a larger study on organizational development, involving my colleagues Louis B. Barnes and D. Paul Leitch, which is supported by the Division of Research, Harvard Business School.

organization problems tend to reside in a few strategically located individuals, and that replacing these people will bring about sweeping and basic changes. As in the decree form, this change is usually initiated at the top and directed downward by a high authority figure. At the same time, however, it tends to be somewhat more personal, since particular individuals are singled out for replacement. Nevertheless, it retains much of the formality and explicit concern for task accomplishment that is common to the decree approach. Similarly, it holds no false optimism about the ability of individuals to change their own behavior without clear outside direction.

By Structure. This old familiar change approach is currently receiving much reevaluation by behavioral scientists. In its earlier form, it involved a highly rational approach to the design of formal organization and to the layout of technology. The basic assumption here was that people behaved in close agreement with the structure and technology governing them. However, it tended to have serious drawbacks, since what seemed logical on paper was not necessarily logical for human goals.

Recently attempts have been made to alter the organizational structure in line with what is becoming known about both the logics and nonlogics of human behavior, such as engineering the job to fit the man, on the one hand, or adjusting formal authority to match informal authority, on the other hand. These attempts, however, still rely heavily on mechanisms for change that tend to be relatively formal, impersonal, and located outside the individual. At the same time, however, because of greater concern for the effects of structure on people, they can probably be characterized as more personal, subtle, and less directive than either the decree or replacement approaches.

SHARING OF POWER

More toward the middle of the power distribution continuum, as noted earlier, are the shared approaches, where authority is still present and used, yet there is also interaction and sharing of power. This approach to change is utilized in two forms.

By Group Decision Making. Here the problems still tend to be defined unilaterally from above, but lower level groups are usually left free to develop alternative solutions and to choose among them. The main assumption tends to be that individuals develop more commitment to action when they have a voice in the decisions that affect them. The net result is that power is shared between bosses and subordinates, though there is a division of labor between those who define the problems and those who develop the solutions.

By Group Problem Solving. This form emphasizes both the definition and the solution of problems within the context of group discussion. Here power is shared throughout the decision process, but, unlike group decision making, there is an added opportunity for lower level subordinates to define the problem. The assumption underlying this approach is not only that people gain greater commitment from being exposed to a wider decision-making role, but also that they have significant knowledge to contribute to the definition of the problem.

DELEGATED AUTHORITY

At the other extreme from unilateral authority are found the delegated approaches, where almost complete responsibility for defining and acting on problems is turned over to the subordinates. These also appear in two forms.

By Case Discussion. This method focuses more on the acquisition of knowledge and skills than on the solution of specific problems at hand. An authority figure, usually a teacher or boss, uses his power only to guide a general discussion of information describing a problem situation, such as a case or a report of research results. The "teacher" refrains from imposing his own analysis or solutions on the group. Instead, he encourages individual members to arrive at their own insights, and they are left to use them as they see fit. The implicit assumption here is that individuals, through the medium of discussion about concrete situations, will develop general problem-solving skills to aid them in carrying out subsequent individual and organization changes.

By T Group Sessions. . . . Usually, they are confined to top management, with the hope that beneficial "spill-over" will result for the rest of the organization. The primary emphasis of the T group tends to be on increasing an individual's self-awareness and sensitivity to group social processes. Compared to the previously discussed approaches, the T group places much less emphasis on the discussion and solution of task-related problems. Instead, the data for discussion are typically the interpersonal actions of individuals in the group; no specific task is assigned to the group.

The basic assumption underlying this approach is that exposure to a structureless situation will release unconscious emotional energies within individuals, which, in turn, will lead to self-analysis, insight, and behavioral change. The authority figure in the group, usually a professional trainer, avoids asserting his own authority in structuring the group. Instead, he often attempts to become an accepted and influential member of the group. Thus, in comparison to the other approaches, much more authority is turned over to the group, from which position it is expected to chart its own course of change in an atmosphere of great informality and highly personal exchanges.

What Is Organization
Development?*

Richard Beckhard

Definition. Organization development is an effort (1) *planned*, (2) *organization-wide*, and (3) *managed* from the *top*, to (4) increase *organization effectiveness* and *health* through (5) *planned interventions* in the organization's "processes," using *behavioral-science* knowledge.

1. It is a *planned change* effort.

An OD program involves a systematic diagnosis of the organization, the development of a strategic plan for improvement, and the mobilization of resources to carry out the effort.

2. It involves the total "*system.*"

An organization development effort is related to a total organization change such as a change in the culture or the reward systems or the total managerial strategy. There may be tactical efforts which work with subparts of the organization but the "system" to be changed is a total, relatively autonomous organization. This is not necessarily a total corporation, or an entire government, but refers to a system which is relatively free to determine its own plans and future within very *general* constraints from the environment.

3. *It is managed from the top.*

In an organization development effort, the top management of the system has a personal investment in the program and its outcomes. They actively participate in the *management* of the effort. This does not mean they must participate in the same *activities* as others, but it does mean that they must have both knowledge and *commitment* to the goals of the program and must actively support the methods used to achieve the goals.

4. It is designed to *increase organization effectiveness* and *health.*

To understand the goals of organization development, it is necessary to have some picture of what an "ideal" effective, healthy organization would look like. What would be its characteristics? Numbers of writers and practitioners in the field have proposed definitions which, although they differ in detail, indicate a strong consensus of what a healthy operating organization is. Let me

* SOURCE: Richard Beckhard, *Organization Development*. © 1969. Addison-Wesley Publishing Company, Inc., Reading, Mass., pp. 9–14. Reprinted with permission.

start with my own definition. An effective organization is one in which:

a. The total organization, the significant subparts, and individuals, manage their work against *goals* and *plans* for achievement of these goals.
b. Form follows function (the problem, or task, or project, determines how the human resources are organized).
c. Decisions are made by and near the sources of information regardless of where these sources are located on the organization chart.
d. The reward system is such that managers and supervisors are rewarded (and punished) comparably for:
    Short-term profit or production performance.
    Growth and development of their subordinates.
    Creating a viable working group.
e. Communication laterally and vertically is *relatively* undistorted. People are generally open and confronting. They share all the relevant facts including feelings.
f. There is a minimum amount of inappropriate win/lose activities between individuals and groups. Constant effort exists at all levels to treat conflict, and conflict situations, as *problems* subject to problem-solving methods.
g. There is high "conflict" (clash of ideas) about tasks and projects, and relatively little energy spent in clashing over *interpersonal* difficulties because they have been generally worked through.
h. The organization and its parts see themselves as interacting with each other *and* with a *larger* environment. The organization is an "open system."
i. There is a shared value, and management strategy to support it, of trying to help each person (or unit) in the organization maintain his (or its) integrity and uniqueness in an interdependent environment.
j. The organization and its members operate in an "action-research" way. General practice is to build in *feedback mechanisms* so that individuals and groups can learn from their own experience.

Another definition is found in John Gardner's set of rules for an effective organization. He describes an effective organization as one which is *self-renewing* and then lists the rules:

The *first rule* is that the organization must have an effective program for the recruitment and development of talent.
The *second rule* for the organization capable of continuous renewal is that it must be a hospitable environment for the individual.
The *third rule* is that the organization must have built-in provisions for self-criticism.
The *fourth rule* is that there must be fluidity in the internal structure.
The *fifth rule* is that the organization must have some means of combating the process by which men become prisoners of their procedures.

Edgar Schein defines organization effectiveness in relation to what he calls "the adaptive coping cycle," that is, an organization that can effectively adapt and cope with the changes in its environment. Specifically, he says:

> The sequence of activities or processes which begins with some change in the internal or external environment and ends with a more adaptive, dynamic equilibrium for dealing with the change, is the organization's "adaptive coping cycle." If we identify the various stages or processes of this cycle, we shall also be able to identify the points where organizations typically may fail to cope adequately and where, therefore, consultants and researchers have been able in a variety of ways to help increase organization effectiveness.

The organization conditions necessary for effective coping, according to Schein, are:

> The ability to take in and communicate information reliably and validly.
> Internal flexibility and creativity to make the changes which are demanded by the information obtained (including structural flexibility).
> Integration and commitment to the goals of the organization from which comes the willingness to change.
> An internal climate of support and freedom from threat, since being threatened undermines good communication, reduces flexibility, and stimulates self-protection rather than concern for the total system.

Miles et al. (1966) define the healthy organization in three broad areas—those concerned with task accomplishment, those concerned with internal integration, and those involving mutual adaptation of the organization and its environment. The following dimensional conditions are listed for each area:

> In the task-accomplishment area, a healthy organization would be one with (1) reasonably clear, accepted, achievable and appropriate goals; (2) relatively understood communications flow; (3) optimal power equalization.
> In the area of internal integration, a healthy organization would be one with (4) resource utilization and individuals' *good fit* between personal disposition and role demands; (5) a reasonable degree of cohesiveness and "organization identity," clear and attractive enough so that persons feel actively connected to it; (6) high morale. In order to have growth and active changefulness, a healthy organization would be one with innovativeness, autonomy, adaptation, and problem-solving adequacy.

Lou Morse, in his recent thesis on organization development, writes that:

> The commonality of goals are cooperative group relations, consensus, integration, and commitment to the goals of the organization (task accomplishment), creativity, authentic behavior, freedom from threat, full utilization of a person's capabilities, and organizational flexibility.

5. Organization development achieves its goals through *planned interventions* using behavioral science knowledge.

A strategy is developed of intervening or moving into the existing organization and helping it, in effect, "stop the music," examine its present ways of work, norms, and values, and look at alternative ways of working, or relating, or rewarding. . . . The interventions used draw on the knowledge and technology of the behavioral sciences about such processes as individual motivation, power, communications, perception, cultural norms, problem-solving, goal-setting, interpersonal relationships, intergroup relationships, and conflict management.

SOME OPERATIONAL GOALS
IN AN ORGANIZATION-DEVELOPMENT EFFORT

To move toward the kind of organization conditions described in the above definitions, OD efforts usually have some of the following operational goals:

1. To develop a self-renewing, *viable system* that can organize in a variety of ways depending on tasks. This means systematic efforts to change and loosen up the way the organization operates, so that it organizes differently depending on the nature of the task. There is movement toward a concept of "form follows function," rather than that *tasks* must *fit* into existing structures.

2. To optimize the effectiveness of both the stable (the basic organization chart) and the temporary systems (the many projects, committees, etc., through which much of the organization's work is accomplished) by built-in, *continuous improvement mechanisms*. This means the introduction of procedures for analyzing work tasks and resource distribution, and for building in continuous "feedback" regarding the way a system or subsystem is operating.

3. To move toward *high collaboration* and *low competition* between inter-dependent units. One of the major obstacles to effective organizations is the amount of dysfunctional energy spent in inappropriate competition—energy that is not, therefore, available for the accomplishment of tasks. If all of the energy that is used by, let's say, manufacturing people disliking or wanting to "get those sales people," or vice versa, were available to improve organization output, productivity would increase tremendously.

4. To create conditions where conflict is brought out and managed. One of the fundamental problems in unhealthy (or less than healthy) organizations is the amount of energy that is dysfunctionally used trying to work around, or avoid, or cover up, conflicts which are inevitable in a complex organization. The goal is to move the organization towards seeing conflict as an inevitable condition and as problems that need to be *worked* before adequate decisions can be made.

5. To reach the point where decisions are made on the basis of information source rather than organizational role. This means the need to move toward a *norm* of the *authority of knowledge* as well as the authority of role.

It does not only mean that decisions should be moved down in the organization; it means that the organization manager should determine which is the best source of information (or combination of sources of information) to work a particular problem, and it is there that the decision making should be located.

REFERENCES

GARDNER, J. W. *How to Prevent Organizational Dry Rot, Harper's Magazine*, October 1965.

MILES, M. B. *et al. Data Feedback and Organization Change in a School System.* (Paper given at a meeting of the American Sociological Association, August 27, 1966.

MORSE, L. H. *Task–Centered Organization Development* (Masters thesis, Sloan School of Management, MIT, June 1968.

SCHEIN, E. H. *Organizational Psychology* (Englewood Cliffs, N.J.: Prentice-Hall 1965).

Action Research
and Planned Change*

Don Bryant

In contrast to traditional approaches based on theories of work organisation, the action research approach takes as its starting point the current problems 'on site' as defined by the members of the organisation themselves. It is an approach to problem solving that has a dual commitment: both to find *and* to implement solutions to problems. The first principle of action research can be stated as 'no research without action; no action without research'. The term 'action research' was first used by Kurt Lewin[1], one of a number of social scientists who led action research studies during World War II.

Action research is essentially a *process* of social change, rather than a set of techniques or a body of knowledge to be applied to particular problems. There are, however, certain basic characteristics:

- it is a *group* process that involves the *participation* of all parties (or at least their representatives) as members of an action research team;
- it is based on a *collaborative relationship* between the interested parties in the organisation and independent resource people who do not function as conventional 'experts' but rather contribute advice on methods on scientific experimentation and group processes;
- it requires a *consensus* amongst the interested parties before attempting the implementation of any experimental changes (say in the design of work);
- it requires the *involvement of the participants in monitoring and evaluating* the effects of any change, with the provision that the situation can be returned to its original state, if the change produces undesired results;
- it assumes that *organisational life is a shared experience* in which people are interdependent for their survival and success and that the commitment of action research resource people is to the organisation as a whole and not to any one sectional interest group (whether this be management, supervision, union or workforce);
- it assumes that, at the individual level, *most people can change* and, under the right conditions, will change, if they want to.

In addition to these basic characteristics, a number of other principles is specifically taken into account: many of these concepts have been derived

---

* SOURCE: Don Bryant, "The Psychology of Resistance to Change," *Management Services* (March 1979), 10–11. Reprinted with permission.

[1] Lewin, K. "Action Research and Minority Problems," *Journal of Social Issues*, 2, 1947, 34–46.

from the creativeness of workers and management in earlier action research studies.

One implicit value of the action research approach is the aspiration to improve the quality of life, whether this be in the work-place or in the community. The aim is to develop strength and cohesion within the organisation (as opposed to the 'efficiency' goal of an engineering approach).

Trist,[2] in reviewing the links between action research and adaptive planning, comments:

> ... The need is to develop a capability, not a product. This strengthening capability has to exist simultaneously at the individual, organisational, and societal levels.
>
> But such a capability cannot be acquired except by those who are willing to look into what they are doing and to regard this in some measure as experimental rather than based on proven fact or incapable of investigation. People with this attitude will expect that what they set out to do will contain error and require modification; they will believe it is worthwhile, indeed essential, to become aware of the implicit assumptions and hypotheses they are making, and to put these to the test by whatever means at hand.

[2] Trist, E. L.   "Action Research and Adaptive Planning," in *Experimenting with Organizational Life: The Action Research Approach*, ed. A. W. Clark (New York: Plenum Press, 1976), p. 223.

Definition of Action Research*

Gerald I. Susman
and Roger D. Evered

Rapoport's (1970: 499) definition of action research is, perhaps, the most frequently quoted in contemporary literature on the subject:

> Action research aims to contribute both to the practical concerns of people in an immediate problematic situation and to the goals of social science by joint collaboration within a mutually acceptable ethical framework.

To the aims of contributing to the practical concerns of people and to the goals of social science, we add a third aim, to develop the self-help competencies of people facing problems.

Foster (1972) suggested that the two aims of action research in the Rapoport definition be sought through the process of changing the problem situation itself. The small face-to-face group is the primary medium through which the problem situation may be changed, as well as in which the interests and ethics of the various parties to this process may be developed "within a mutually acceptable ethical framework." An infra-structure of ad hoc and permanent face-to-face groups is generally developed within a client system to conduct action research. A client system is the social system in which the members face problems to be solved by action research. It may be one of the face-to-face groups, an organization, a network of organizations (Trist et al. 1977), or a community.

While Rapoport's definition of action research focuses on aim, action research can also be viewed as a cyclical process with five phases: diagnosing, action planning, action taking, evaluating, and specifying learning. The infrastructure within the client system and the action researcher maintain and regulate some or all of these five phases jointly (Figure).

We consider all five phases to be necessary for a comprehensive definition of action research. However, action research projects may differ in the number of phases which are carried out in collaboration between action researcher and the client system. Chein, Cook, and Harding (1948) use the term "diagnostic action research" when the researcher is involved only in collecting data for diagnosis and feeding the data back to the client system. Chein, Cook, and Harding use the term "empirical action research" when the

---

* SOURCE: Gerald I. Susman and Roger D. Evered, "An Assessment of the Scientific Merits of Action Research," *Administrative Science Quarterly*, 23 (December 1978), 587–589. Reprinted with permission.

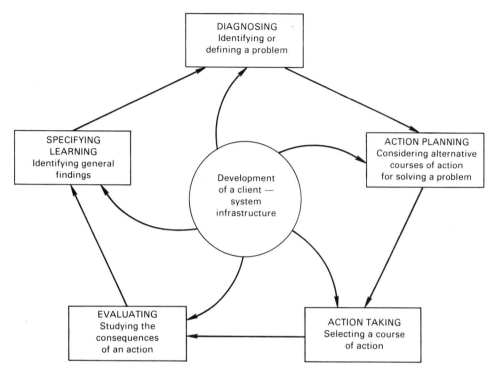

Figure The cyclical process of action research.

researcher only evaluates the actions undertaken by the client system and feeds data back to it. They use the term "participant action research" when diagnosing and action planning are carried out in collaboration between researcher and client system. Finally, they use the term "experimental action research" when researcher and client system collaborate in all or nearly all phases to set up an experiment for taking an action and evaluating its consequences.

In addition to the number of phases that can be carried out in collaboration between action researchers and the client system, contemporary applications of action research can use different techniques for data collection especially in the diagnosing and evaluating phases. Action researchers with a background in psychology tend to prefer questionnaires for such purposes, e.g., those affiliated with the Institute for Social Research at the University of Michigan (Mann, 1957; Seashore and Bowers, 1964; Nadler, 1977), while action researchers with a background in applied anthropology, psychoanalysis or sociotechnical systems tend to prefer direct observation and/or in-depth interviewing (Jaques, 1951; Rice, 1958; Whyte and Hamilton, 1964; Duckles, Duckles, and Maccoby, 1977; Trist, Susman, and Brown, 1977). Action researchers with any of these backgrounds may also retrieve data from the records, memos, and reports that the client system routinely produces.

REFERENCES

CHEIN, ISADOR, STUART W. COOK, and JOHN HARDING 1948. "The field of action research," *American Psychologist*, 3: 43–50.

DUCKLES, MARGARET M., ROBERT DUCKLES, and MICHAEL MACCOBY 1977. "The process of change at Bolivar." *The Journal of Applied Behavioral Science*, 13: 387–399.

FOSTER, MICHAEL 1972. "The theory and practice of action research in work organizations." *Human Relations*, 25: 529–556.

JAQUES, ELLIOTT 1951. *The Changing Culture of a Factory*. London: Tavistock.

MANN, FLOYD C. 1957. "Studying and creating change: a means to understanding social organization." In Conrad M. Arensberg (ed.), *Research in Industrial Human Relations: A Critical Appraisal*: 146–167. New York: Harper.

NADLER, DAVID A. 1977. *Feedback and Organization Development: Using Data-Based Methods*. Reading, MA: Addison-Wesley.

RAPOPORT, ROBERT N. 1970. "Three dilemmas of action research." *Human Relations*, 23, 499–513.

RICE, A. K. 1958. *Productivity and Social Organization: The Ahmedabad Experiment*. London: Tavistock.

SEASHORE, STANLEY, and DAVID G. BOWERS 1964. *Changing the Structure and the Functioning of an Organization*. Ann Arbor: Survey Research Center.

TRIST, ERIC L., GERALD I. SUSMAN, and GRANT R. BROWN 1977. "An experiment in autonomous working in an American underground coal mine." *Human Relations*, 30: 201–236.

WHYTE, WILLIAM FOOTE, and EDITH L. HAMILTON 1964. *Action Research for Management*. Homewood, Il: Irwin, Dorsey.

Action Research*

Frank P. Sherwood

What is the essential idea of action research? How does it differ from our more traditional research modes?

First, it might be well to reflect on the way in which much research in the social sciences (I do not refer here to the physical or natural sciences) is oriented and organized. Most importantly, the problem to be studied is identified by the researcher, and, quite frequently, the problem is framed in such a way as to take advantage of data already assembled in a library, various agency documents, or a computer. Finally, it is a lonely pursuit, by design, to insure the objectivity of the effort. What is then produced is a document assumed to have value in itself. It is not expected to force action and change. It is a one-time sweep, episodic at best. Since it occurs generally outside the system and permits relatively little involvement by the parties to the problem, the research does not contribute to the capacity of an organization to learn and to develop.

It would appear that action research has been conceived as a polar opposite to these traditional orientations, most observable in three fundamental ways:

- As the name implies, it is action-oriented, indeed action-forcing. There is a clear problem orientation, not just of intellectual dimension, but of social and administrative consequence.
- It operates on a real-time basis. The research is present-oriented; and throughout its conduct, it is to be expected that new data will be generated. It would be unthinkable to conceive of an action research project in which the data were "on the shelf" at its inception.
- It is involving, which suggests that the relationship goes both ways: emphasis tends to be placed on the involvement of the administrator and the client in the research, but it also has come to be recognized that the research is similarly involved in the action. By undertaking research that is real-time and action-oriented, the researcher himself is no longer the passive observer. His objectivity and professional integrity must be found within himself, not in the role he occupies.

The observance of these conditions provides a collective dimension to the learning process. Where, in the traditional system, the learning is largely restricted to the researcher and dependent on his motivations for any broader dissemination, action research by its nature is collaborative. Because it does go

* SOURCE: Frank P. Sherwood, "Action Research," *Administration and Society*, 8 (1976), 176–178. Reprinted with permission of Sage Publications, Inc.

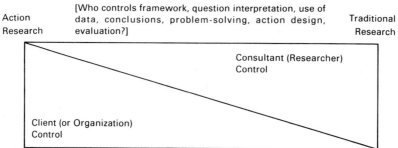

NOTE: Such OD approaches as survey feedback, the Blake OD phases, team-building, and others may be arrayed along a continuum between a position of complete consultant dominance to one of complete client control. This model has been suggested by James F. Wolf as a means of conceptualizing the factor of control in the elements in action research.

Figure 1: Research Participants: A Continuum

beyond the individual, action research has the potential to contribute significantly to organization learning—about which we know very little and practice even less.

Action-Research as Applied to Organization Development*

Mark A. Frohman,
Marshall Sashkin,
and Michael J. Kavanagh

Action-research OD is one of a variety of OD approaches. In general, OD involves the application of behavioral science knowledge in organizations, through client-consultant collaboration, for the purpose of creating effective and lasting changes in the system (i.e., adaptive responses to organizational problems). While there is some overlap between our descriptions of action-research and OD, there are also some elements present in one but not the other, Table 1 summarizes these similarities and differences.

Let us now see how the approaches . . . might be united, or how action-research can be tied to an OD approach. The action-research approach as applied to OD involves data collection interventions by an OD practitioner in collaboration with the client. Thus, working together, they can obtain useful information which will enable them to jointly: develop and implement action plans for change in the client system; evaluate the effects and effectiveness of these action plans; and based on these evaluations, create and implement further action plans. The ultimate aims of the changes are increased organizational effectiveness and the development of internal organizational resources for creating adaptive, problem-solving change. The total process is based on the interlocking, interdependent, and interactive processes of research (data collection and evaluation) and action (directed intervention and implementation of change).

* SOURCE: Mark A. Frohman, Marshall Sashkin, and Michael J. Kavanagh, "Action-Research as Applied to Organization Development," *Organization and Administrative Sciences*, 7 (Spring/Summer 1976). With kind permission of Dr. Anant Negandhi.

Table 1   Comparison of Descriptive Factors in Action-Research and in Organization Development

ORGANIZATION DEVELOPMENT	*BOTH*	*ACTION-RESEARCH*
May involve data-based diagnosis of organization problems.	Involve the planned application of behavioral science knowledge based on consultant-client collaboration.	Emphasizes data-based diagnosis of system problems.
Is aimed at producing effective and lasting system change.	Involve the use of groups.	Is aimed at solving system problems as a means of improving problem solving skills of the client.
Often involves application of a preplanned "package" of actions.	Recognize that any action with respect to a client system is an intervention and may have some effect on the client system.	Rarely involves application of a preplanned "package"; specific actions generally are developed on the basis of specific problems.
May involve training the client in the application of effective processes of change.		Emphasizes training the client in effective problem solving skills and processes.
May or may not include evaluation of results—effects and effectiveness of efforts—in concrete terms.		Generally involves evaluation of results as a basis for further diagnosis of problems, action-planning, and action implementation.
Often does not result in new behavioral science knowledge.		Usually does result in new behavioral science knowledge.

Phases in Action-Research OD*

Mark A. Frohman,
Marshall Sashkin,
and Michael J. Kavanagh

We have described action-research as a cyclical-sequential model, proceeding through several phrases of research and action. These phases are briefly listed and defined, in the context of OD practice, in Table 1. In some respects, our phrases are similar to other models (e.g., Lippitt, Watson, and Westley, 1958). We will discuss each phase in some detail.

Scouting. As Lippit, Watson, and Westley (1958) note, the change agent, consultant, or OD practitioner generally has an implicit "descriptive-analytic theory," a frame of reference (or bias) which he uses to arrange and interpret information about the organization, and which has implications regarding the interventions he will choose to make in the client system. It is important that the OD practitioner consciously understands his own analytic framework, and equally important that the elements of the framework which are of significance to the client be made explicit to the client. Thus, the practitioner-client relationship is collaborative from the beginning. The practitioner exposes his assumptions, biases, and values and receives feedback from the client about how the above factors fit or fail to fit the frame of understanding of the client system members. The concept of scouting is drawn from a model developed by Kolb and Frohman (1970). In the scouting phase, the OD practitioner develops an initial "fix" on the significant characteristics and problems of the client system. He then makes an initial application of his "descriptive-analytic theory" to organize and understand these facts. The general information of interest to the OD practitioner at this point includes various characteristics of the client system (e.g., product or service, structure, size, technology, demographic characteristics of organization members, types of customers, external environmental relationships, prior OD experience) and descriptions of the problem(s) initially perceived by the client. Obtaining these data constitutes the major work of the scouting phase. Such data will play a major role in the client and consultant mutually deciding whether they will enter into a formal relationship and, if so, at what point in the organization the entry will be made.

Entry. The process of establishing a collaborative and open OD practitioner-client relationship and clearly defining the expectations of the parties

* SOURCE: Mark A. Frohman, Marshall Sashkin, and Michael J. Kavanagh, "Action-Research as Applied to Organization Development," *Organization and Administrative Sciences,* 7 (Spring/Summer 1976). With the kind permission of Dr. Anant Negandhi.

Table 1 Summary of Phases in Action-Research

ACTION-RESEARCH PHASE	EMPHASIS	AIM
Scouting	Research	Arriving at a decision of whether or not to enter.
Entry	Action	Establishing a collaborative relationship, initial problem exploration, and selecting data collection/feedback methods.
Data collection	Research	Developing measures of organization variables and processes.
Data feedback	Action	Returning data to the client system for discussion and diagnosis.
Diagnosis	Research	Understanding the state of the system and problems.
Action planning	Action	Developing specific action plans— including determining who will implement the plans and how the effects will be evaluated.
Action implementation	Action	Implementing specific change plans.
Evaluation	Research	Determining effects and effectiveness of action implementation, leading to further efforts or to termination.

(Frohman, 1968) is the major focus of the entry phase. The major emphases at this point are establishing the credibility of the OD practitioner and making certain that those in power positions in the client system openly sanction the OD activity. The lack of such open sanction is a nearly certain guarantee that the OD effort will fail (Clark, 1972). In such an event, any OD actions which occur are likely to be carried out in a nonsystemic manner.

Data Collection. The "prediagnostic" examination of problems during scouting and entry is collaborative in nature and useful for exploring the implications of collecting data about the client system and the problems it faces. Note that such prediagnosis during the first two phases is primarily the product of the OD practitioner. The third phase, data collection, involves client system members to a greater extent—first, in selecting a method and deciding how it will be used, and second, in the actual collection of information (which will inevitably involve client system members via interviews, questionnaire responses, and observations of their behavior, or some combination of these methods). . . .

The first three phases are focused primarily on research activities but, nonetheless, involve certain action interventions which may have some impact on the client system. Some research data, which will be reviewed (Frohman and Waters, 1969), suggest that entry and data collection in and of themselves have little, if any, impact on the client system. These early phases are within the broader phase of social-system change that Lewin (1947) called "unfreezing," or developing a need for change and establishing a client-consultant change relationshp (Lippitt, Watson, and Westley, 1958). These are necessary (but not sufficient) conditions for effective organizational change.

Data Feedback. If diagnosis of problems and action planning are to be collaborative activities (as prescribed by the action-research model), the OD practitioner must fully share with the client the data which are gathered. There are a variety of options for accomplishing this, which we will not detail here. Most, however, involve some form of group or work-team meeting. It is during the data feedback phase that interventions may have some real impact on the client system (Bowers, 1971b; Frohman, 1970), although such effects do not seem to be of major significance.

Feedback provides the client with information about the client system, information which is useful in determining the strengths and weaknesses of that system. Therefore, this fourth phase, data feedback, is intimately tied with the next phase, diagnosis. It is quite artificial to treat them separately; however, there are two reasons for doing so. First, the feedback of data to the client is the first activity of the OD practitioner which is *primarily an action intervention* in the client system, as opposed to the phases described earlier and the next phase, which primarily involve research activities (Brown, 1972). Second, we want to describe the action-research OD process as clearly as possible, and this separation may aid the reader in following and understanding the nature and logic of the model. In practice, data feedback and diagnosis often occur at the same time.

The artificiality of the clear-cut separation of phases is further highlighted by considering the interdependent and interactive nature of the phases. Data collection and data feedback are obviously interdependent; one must collect data if one is to share those data with the client. The phases are also interactive; hence, the feedback targets will, in part, determine the types of data to be collected, while the data obtained will, in part, determine the best presentation or feedback methods.

Diagnosis. The focus of the process shifts back to research as the client system members and the OD practitioner jointly use the data to define and explore organizational problems and strengths. This diagnostic process is very different from the general meaning of "diagnosis." The medical-clinical model defines diagnosis as an activity by the consultant (or physician), who is solely responsible for the specific diagnostic conclusions. In action-research OD, diagnosis is a joint activity of the consultant and the client (Sashkin, 1973). Note that this collaborative diagnosis is no less data based than the traditional form—it is the collaborative nature of the process that is critically different.

An adequate diagnostic process will lead directly to implications for the actions needed to resolve the problems. However, a conclusion that further data are needed for accurate diagnosis is quite possible, in which case the action-research process will "recycle" to the data collection phase. Finally, this research phase of diagnosis is directly and interactively linked to the subsequent action phase (action planning), just as the research phase of data collection is closely linked to the following action-oriented phase (data feedback).

Action Planning. This and the next phase shift the focus of the action-research OD model back to action. The involvement of the client is increased during this phase in that the client participates in planning change activities. At this point, the role of the OD practitioner becomes one of a process helper and a trainer, rather than a consultant-expert. If the OD practitioner solves the client's problems as an "expert," an effective change might take place; but the client will learn little of the skills or processes involved in dealing with problems in the organization—a major goal of many OD programs. Thus, it is at this point that the OD practitioner's aim of developing internal problem-solving skills and resources becomes operationalized.

In accomplishing this aim, the OD practitioner walks a tightrope: he must help in the presentation (feedback), interpretation (diagnosis), and exploration (action planning) of specific data, but he must avoid being cast in the role of expert problem solver. Specific action plans must be created by the client with the assistance of the OD practitioner, not presented to the client by the expert-consultant.

Action Implementation.   This and the preceding two phases fall within the broader phase of social-system change that Lewin (1947) called "moving." By altering certain social forces and removing or introducing others, the social system may be moved toward a new state or "quasi-stationary equilibrium," in Lewin's terms.

The action implementation phase involves the most actively directed OD efforts. One cannot, however, be very specific as to the actual content of the changes. This is because the content of the action implementation phase, the specific actions taken and changes made, depends on the situation and the nature of the problems diagnosed. Thus, the variety of possible action steps is wide in range. Some OD practitioners have produced catalogs of action interventions which can serve as useful reference sources (Fordyce and Weil, 1971; Pfeiffer and Jones, 1970, 1971, 1972a, 1972b); however, the specific plan chosen must be based on situational determinants. Regardless of the content chosen, the primary concern here is with the process of implementation. In this process, the model again specifies active collaboration between client and OD practitioner.

The actions taken may depend greatly on the skills and resources of the OD practitioner, or may be developed almost entirely by the client. Essentially, this means that the professional action-oriented resources of the OD practitioner are not ignored; but the decision to use the change agent in specific ways is reached jointly—by the client *and* the consultant. Thus the OD practitioner may develop and implement a team-training laboratory for certain groups in the client system. A decision to do so, however, would be based on *collaborative* diagnostic and action-planning activities; such action would not be taken on the basis of a consultant recommendation, but rather on the basis of mutual problem exploration, need definition, and examination of various alternative actions. An example of an action implementation carried out primarily by the client would be the decision to institute weekly cross-department coordination and problem-solving meetings. The consultant might offer assistance in conducting such meetings, but the primary action would be accomplished by the client. The decision to implement this specific action would have been made in the same way as the earlier example—through a process of client-consultant collaboration.

The development of action plans requires attention to two major factors. The first is that the action plan must contain an adequately detailed description of what is to be done, who is to do what part, and when. The second factor, too often omitted in OD practice, is that there must be *continual monitoring* of the effects of the action intervention. This must be done throughout the action-research OD process, and most particularly with regard to the specific problem-solving actions planned and implemented in this and the preceding phases of the process. Thus, the model ends with a direct link back to research—the evaluation phase.

Evaluation. The action plan should specify, in detail, evaluation procedures to be implemented during and following the preceding phase. All too often consultants and OD practitioners seem satisfied with little more than guesses as to the effects and effectiveness of actions in and on the client system. But thorough evaluation is an absolute necessity, for both the consultant and the client, for several reasons. First, a data-based evaluation will indicate to the consultant whether the specific change efforts have been successful. Second, the same data will be needed by the client system as a basis for further diagnosis and action planning (recycling). Third, the empirical data will help the client and the OD practitioner determine when it is appropriate that their relationship be ended. And finally, only a well-designed evaluation phase can determine whether and when the primary, overall goal of the OD effort has been achieved: the development of internal client system resources with skills for creating effective, adaptive, problem-solving change in the future.

"Refreezing" (Lewin, 1947) has been one term used to describe this primary goal. Unfortunately, it carries the connotation of a fixed, unchanging, and unchangeable end state. Moreover, Lewin's use of the term was in reference to the attainment and continuation of specific changes, rather than to the development of increased and more effective adaptability on the part of the client system. Frohman's (1970) term, "integration," seems more appropriate but lacks descriptive detail. Lippitt, Watson, and Westley's (1958) term, "stabilization and generalization of change," is more descriptive but omits the focus on evaluation and recycling. An extension of this term to "stabilization of specific, effective changes and generalization of the action-research OD process" seems to best describe the desirable end-state of action-research OD.

REFERENCES

Bowers, D. G. "Development Techniques and Organizational Climate: An Evaluation of the Comparative Importance of Two Potential Forces for Organizational Change." *Technical Report to the U.S. Office of Naval Research.* Ann Arbor, Mich.: Center for Research on Utilization of Scientific Knowledge, Institute for Social Research, University of Michigan, 1971. (b)

Brown, L. D. "'Research Action': Organizational Feedback, Understanding, and Change," *Journal of Applied Behavioral Science,* 1972, *8,* 697–712.

Clark, A. W. "Sanction: A Critical Element in Action Research," *Journal of Applied Behavioral Science,* 1972, *8,* 713–731.

FORDYCE, J. K., and WEIL, R. *Managing with People.* Reading, Mass.: Addison-Wesley, 1971.

FROHMAN, M. A. "Conceptualizing a Helping Relationship." Mimeographed paper. Ann Arbor, Mich.: Center for Research on Utilization of Scientific Knowledge, Institute for Social Research, University of Michigan, 1968.

FROHMAN, M. A. "An Empirical Study of a Model and Strategies for Planned Organizational Change." Unpublished doctoral dissertation, Ann Arbor, Mich.: University of Michigan, 1970.

FROHMAN, M. A., and WATERS, C. A. "Building Internal Resources for Organizational Development." Paper presented before the staff of the Institute for Social Research. University of Michigan, Ann Arbor, Michigan, November 1969.

KOLB, D. A., and FROHMAN, A. L. "An Organization Development Approach to Consulting," *Sloan Management Review,* 1970, *12,* 51–65.

LEWIN, K. "Frontiers in Group Dynamics," *Human Relations,* 1947, *1,* 5–42.

LIPPITT, R., WATSON, J., and WESTLEY, B. *The Dynamics of Planned Change.* New York: Harcourt, Brace & World, 1958.

PFEIFFER, J. W., and JONES, J. E. *A Handbook of Structured Experiences for Human Relations Training.* vol. 2. Iowa City: University Associates Press, 1970.

PFEIFFER, J. W., and JONES, J. E. *A Handbook of Structured Experiences for Human Relations Training.* vol. 3. Iowa City: University Associates Press, 1971.

PFEIFFER, J. W., and JONES, J. E. *A Handbook of Structured Experiences for Human Relations Training.* rev. ed., vol. 1. Iowa City: University Associates Press, 1972. (a)

PFEIFFER, J. W., and JONES, J. E. *The 1972 Annual Handbook for Group Facilitators.* Iowa City: University Associates Press, 1972. (b)

SASHKIN, M., MORRIS, W. C., and HORST, L. "A Comparison of Social and Organizational Change Models: Information Flow and Data Use Processes," *Psychological Review,* 1973, 8c, 510–526.

The Intervention Model

Roy McLennan

Some years ago I began developing an organizational problem-solving model for training my experience-rich graduate management students to intervene in organizations to generate planned change. The model arose from two prime sources. The first, driving source was the evolving trial and error experiences of the graduate students in carrying out their field interventions. The other was an evolving admixture of the kinds of action research advocated and practiced by Kurt Lewin and his followers, Norman R. F. Maier's problem-solving model, E. H. Schein's process consultation, procedures developed by the Survey Research Center, University of Michigan, and more generally human science–based consultant practice in the United States and Britain.

I conceive of the intervention model we developed as a general-purpose process for tackling an organizational issue, problem, or opportunity by an integrated data-gathering, group-enhancing and decision-making exercise. The organizational sites we have used in these interventions over several years include multinational and local companies; laboratory and technical service organizations; government departments, such as defense, education, justice, and foreign affairs; city government; libraries; public hospitals; and various national and voluntary organizations, such as institutes for engineers, youth, administrators, and the arts.[1] This article proceeds by presenting a sketch of the model, followed by a commentary on its use and development, in the belief that it will prove useful to others in the business of training change agents.[2]

THE MODEL

The help of an independent outsider (the trainee change agent or consultant, hereafter referred to as the change agent) is required to operationalize the model. An internal change agent often plays a role in it, but the remarks below refer to the outsider. The model is outlined here as a series of required actions to be taken in temporal sequence, as in a recipe for baking a cake:

[1] The first published accounts of interventions in this tradition, based on the earliest versions of the model, appear in McLennan (1978). Later interventions by McGill, Robertson and McLennan, and McDonald appear in McLennan and Smith (1979). Many accounts of other interventions have not been published.

[2] In my opinion the model also provides a powerful, general-purpose methodology for launching planned change in organizations.

1. The change agent locates an appropriate organizational family group of a manager or superior and his or her immediate or direct subordinates, in terms of an organizational problem or issue (point of entry).

2. The change agent confidentially interviews the manager about his or her objectives, ideas, and concerns about the chosen problem or issue and outlines and explains the action steps in the intervention model (client and change agent orientation to the problem).

3. The change agent carries out confidential interviews of each member of the family group.

4. The change agent makes an analysis of interview data and prepares a substantial summary of the data on charts or transparencies. The summary presents data originating from subordinates only, not from their superior or change agent. Individual confidences are preserved by the change agent, who attempts to lay bare issues, behaviors, and interpretations.

5. The manager and the change agent work through the summary together, in order to prepare the former to lead his or her subordinates through it, so maintaining the existing organizational hierarchy. In this way the manager obtains an initial, detailed understanding of the summated interview data.

6. The manager leads an off-site workshop with his or her family group, devoted to working through the summary together, exploring the meaning and import of the data in it, assisted by the change agent. The key task is data exploration. Decision making and action taking are specifically excluded. The change agent adopts a supportive role to the manager and group.

7. The manager leads the family group members in reviewing the summary and discussion in the light of possible action, assisted by the change agent. They draw up a list of agreed action points and responsibilities for pursuing them, which are allocated to individual members and subgroups.

8. Copies of the summary are distributed to all participants.

9. The manager, group members, and change agent fix a date to review follow-up on the action points.

10. The change agent gathers indications of the effectiveness of the intervention.

Several general intentions and tendencies of the model are worthy of mention:

1. It tends to improve the organization member's work motivation by encouraging use of his or her expertise, experience, and constructive suggestions by opening up or improving channels of upward influence with the member's boss, and strengthening lateral influence between the member and his or her peers.

2. It tends to make available to the family group as a whole substantial data from all its members and to facilitate their use of the information in order to make decisions.

3. It tends to increase the upward influence of subordinates on their superior, improves "we" feeling and teamwork, and also seems to enhance the downward influence of the manager on his or her group members.

4. The model combines diagnosis, data collection, and action and tends to pull these conceptually separate but action-related aspects of intervening together quite strongly, hence facilitating action.

COMMENTARY ON THE MODEL

Why this model rather than some other? Early experience, adopting a "let many flowers bloom" approach, allowing any kind of intervention to be initiated by any graduate student, resulted in what seemed to me to be unnecessary delays in setting up the interventions. Time is of the essence: If you don't succeed in getting them set up quickly in a course, then there will be insufficient time remaining for trainees to carry out the series of steps implicated in the model before the course ends. And allowing any kind of intervention to be initiated by any student clearly increased the confusion among students as to what they were supposed to be doing.

In the interests of getting the field experience going as soon as humanly possible after the course starts the idea of students carrying out a more or less standard data gathering-feedback intervention, based on a clearly articulated model, seemed a good idea. This conclusion was student-led, reached over several successive courses, rather than initiated by me as the faculty member in charge. It was driven by student need for help in establishing the field intervention I insisted they carry out. They talked to me of their difficulties in setting up their interventions, and I responded with assorted tools and ideas drawn from the literature. Between us we gradually built up the model over several years. In retrospect we were observing the spirit of George C. Homans' dictum that "No one will go far wrong theoretically who remains in close touch with and seeks to understand a body of concrete phenomena."[3]

My experience is that some clear-cut set of action steps, such as those provided in the above recipe, are necessary. The trainee change agents are at the beginning of their study and practice of managing organizational change and have no pool of appropriate practices or concepts to draw on in mounting their interventions.

My basic tactic in the first two or three classes in the course became to set things up as rapidly as possible, so that the student knows immediately what field work is required of him or her, and is strongly encouraged to set up an intervention with as much speed as possible. I announce the field experience as a course requirement in the first class meeting and that it forms an important slice of the course grade. I stress that the student's first task is to find potential intervention opportunities in organizations they are working in, have worked in, or are otherwise familiar with.[4] I require each of them to come to the second class prepared to talk about the possible intervention sites he or she knows about, to study the intervention model and associated reading. I follow this up by pressing them to generate their intervention proposals and to present them

---

[3] *Handbook of Modern Sociology*, (Chicago: Rand McNally, 1978), pp. 975–976.

[4] Sometimes I have an appropriate client or two waiting in the wings. While I try to service these requests for help as best I can, I prefer that the students become involved in finding clients, rather than relating to ready-made ones, and regard their active involvement in the intervention process this brings as valuable.

in the ensuing class session. Copies of previous proposals are assigned as examples for study and class discussion. Parts of the next few class sessions are devoted to reviewing and actioning their emerging proposals.

Many report back to the class that they know of one or two conceivable intervention sites into which they might be able to effect entry. Given the firm operating rule I proclaim, that for clear learning reasons no one should intervene alone, rather always in the company of another person, this usually yields a choice of site, which may be explored for goodness of fit with our training needs, ease of entry, learning potential, degree of cooperation, and the like. We discuss the sites and begin setting up teams of two or three persons. The consequent task is an assignment requiring prospective teams to present a one- or two-page proposal setting out basic details of their intended intervention. The proposal must answer the classic questions of what, where, who, when, why, and how. They usually require one or two redraftings, largely because students typically don't answer the "how" or intervention process question adequately at the first attempt. I approve the proposal when I am satisfied that it makes sense and is feasible.

During this early phase in a managing organizational change course, it is often necessary to consult prospective teams, and turn around intervention proposals at short notice. The action cannot await a weekly class. Such demand feeding decreases markedly after the first week or two, when the proposals are approved and field work is going ahead. My experience is that negotiating entry inevitably takes a little time.

Everything else in the managing organizational change course takes a back seat in class time while student interventions are being launched. But while students are busy developing their proposals, accounts of interventions, exercises, models, and schemes are assigned for class preparation. I use the experiences in Chapter 2, together with the associated models and schemes, to establish initial understandings about what organizational consultation is, the process idea, and to link the participants' work experience to notions about organizations. I follow these by drawing on Chapter 1, which provides some historical background on organizational change, and several instructive accounts of interventions. These Chapter 1 items are not too time consuming at the point when the students are pursuing the prime task of setting up their interventions.

We do not always discuss in depth in the classroom the materials drawn from Chapters 1 and 2. Whatever the specific exercises and readings formally assigned for these initial class sessions, the informal agenda will nearly always be the salient, urgent, pressing problems and issues the trainee interventionists are currently experiencing in trying to set up their field work. They are highly energized to seek solutions to these problems. It is much better to recognize and assume this, in the design of classes and assignments, than to act as if the students should be expected to carry a full graduate course study load in addition. The first item on my classroom agenda, I have learned, must always be to try to relate to and meet the students' field work needs.

Two different kinds of entry conditions gradually emerged from the initial experiences in elaborating the model. One was what could be termed the *need* syndrome, the other *obligation* syndrome. In the *need* syndrome the graduate students obtain entry to an organizational site where one or more high status members of the client system genuinely feel they need help with some issue, difficulty, or problem. In the *obligation* syndrome one or more high status members of the client system oblige the graduate student team, and possibly the business school, by allowing their organization to be an intervention site, without any real thought of benefit arising to the organization.[5]

Several of the interventions carried out by my graduate students were established under this obligation umbrella, and tended to suffer from the disadvantage of merely being tolerated by the organizational hosts. Such interventions lack client motivation and urgency and, while in my view undoubtedly valuable for learning purposes, have a fundamentally different dynamic and offer a different experience to the need sort. It is a diagnostic problem for the instructor to determine which, among the various prospective client sites apparently available to an intervention team, genuinely need the kind of help that can be delivered in the brief duration that the intervention will run. Interventions that began life under the obligation syndrome often change their spots into the need syndrome. I am persuaded that really first-rate immersion training in intervening necessitates client need.

For a couple of years we experimented informally with some kind of "successor" intervention, following on from the model. These experiments took place in the context of courses lasting the entire academic year, or in a successor, advanced semester-long course that followed on the first. The additional field experience consisted of either setting up from scratch another, unique intervention, based on whatever design seemed best fitted to the client's situation, or repeating the standard intervention model's formula in a different part of the same organization or in a different organization. We found in practice that a unique successor intervention took a good deal of trainee change agent energy and time to conceive and execute. My conclusion is that, from a training payoff point of view, both unique and standard successor interventions yield diminishing returns. I believe that it is unnecessary, from the point of view of trainee skill-knowledge acquisition, to continue with any further kind of intervention after the steps involved in the basic, standard intervention model cycle have been completed.

The Instructor's Manual provides actual examples of intervention proposals submitted by my trainee change agents and accounts of specific intervention arrangements and considerations in some detail. *Goodyear New Zealand (A)*, (Chapter Three Experience No. 4) and *Goodyear New Zealand (B)* and *(C)*, in the Instructor's Manual, provide a description of the successive exploration of the model in the context of an intervention in a small company.

---

[5] The need and obligation syndromes have clear links to the concepts in E. H. Schein's "Ethnographic versus Clinical Perspective" (see Conclusion).

REFERENCES

Foster, M. "An Introduction to the Theory and Practice of Action Research in Work Organizations," *Human Relations*, 25 (1972), 529–556.

Lewin, K. "Action Research and Minority Problems," *Journal of Social Issues*, 2 (1946), 1–23.

Likert, R. *The Human Organization*. New York: McGraw-Hill Book Co., 1967.

McLennan, R., ed. *Participation and Change in the New Zealand Workplace*. Wellington, New Zealand: Fourth Estate, 1978.

McLennan, R., and G. McDonald "Changing Behaviour in a Coercive Organization," in *People in Organizations: Studies in Australia and New Zealand*, ed. R. McLennan and D. Smith. Wellington, New Zealand: Victoria University, 1979.

McLennan, R., and D. Smith, eds. *People in Organizations: Studies in Australia and New Zealand*. Wellington, New Zealand: Victoria University, 1979.

Maier, N. R. F. *Industrial and Organizational Psychology*. New York: Houghton Mifflin, 1973.

Mann, F. C. "Studying and Creating Change," in *The Planning of Change*, ed. W. Bennis, et al. New York: Holt, Rinehart & Winston, 1961.

McGill, I. "An Intervention in a City Library," in *People in Organizations: Studies in Australia and New Zealand*, ed. R. McLennan and D. Smith. Wellington, New Zealand: Victoria University, 1979.

Neff, F. W. "Survey Research: A Tool for Problem Diagnosis and Improvement in Organizations," in *Applied Sociology*, ed. A. W. Gouldner and S. M. Miller. New York: Free Press, 1966.

Robertson, W. "Organization Development in the Health Care Field—A Pilot Intervention in a City Hospital," in *People in Organizations: Studies in Australia and New Zealand*, ed. R. McLennan and D. Smith. Wellington, New Zealand: Victoria University, 1979.

Schein, E. H. *Process Consultation*. Reading, Mass.: Addison-Wesley, 1969.

Interviewing*

Marshall Sashkin
and William C. Morris

Generally speaking, every interview situation consists of two significant factors. First, *the interviewer must establish a degree of rapport* with the interviewee, attempting to make the interviewee feel comfortable. The interviewer should present himself as openly as possible, explaining the reasons for the interview, what he hopes to accomplish, what the information will be used for, and that the interview will be confidential. Second, *the interviewee should do most of the talking*. Although this principle holds for almost any interview situation, and seems obvious, it is surprising how often an interviewer will take up more "air time" than the interviewee.

BUILDING THE INTERVIEWING RELATIONSHIP[1]

On first thought one might believe it is simple to go and ask another person questions about various topics. By their very nature human beings communicate with those around them—with family, friends, co-workers, casual acquaintances, sales clerks, and so on. We all learn early to participate in the question-and-answer process, and it would appear that this constant training would simply facilitate the job of the interviewer.

Communication is not simple, however, and communication in interviewing is complicated by the personalities of the people involved. It has been found that respondents react more readily to their relationships with the interviewer than to the content of the questions they are asked. In other words, respondents may remember more about the interviewer and about how the interview was conducted than they do about the topics covered in the interview. This shows how important it is for the interviewer to be an understanding person capable of accepting what the respondent says without judging or rejecting the respondent. Thus, the first step in the interviewing process involves setting up a friendly relationship with the respondent and getting him to cooperate in giving the needed information—that is, it involves establishing rapport.

* SOURCE: Marshall Sashkin and William C. Morris, *Organizational Behavior: Concepts and Experiences* (Reston, Va.: Reston, 1984), pp. 39–42.

[1] Reprinted in abridged and modified form from Survey Research Center (1969, Chap. 3). Used by special permission.

Increasing Respondent's Receptiveness.

Three factors help to improve the respondent's receptiveness:

1. *The respondent needs to feel that his acquaintance with the interviewer will be pleasant and satisfying.*
2. *The respondent needs to see the interview as important and worthwhile.*
   The extent to which an interviewer might have to explain the survey will vary considerably from person to person. In some interviews a respondent knows what is expected of him; that is the case, for example, in a job interview or in an interview with a doctor. That is not the case in most survey research interviews.
3. *Barriers to the interview in the respondent's mind need to be overcome.*
   Usually the respondent will be polite enough to let the interviewer talk. The interviewer must use this time to advantage, and must be alert to doubts the respondent may feel, even if the respondent does not express them vocally.
      The interviewer's own state of mind is often reflected in the respondent's reaction to the request for an interview. If the interviewer's approach is uncertain or uneasy, if the interviewer cannot answer the questions the respondent asks and appears unknowing about the work and its purposes, this feeling is communicated to the respondent, who will react accordingly. The interviewer must approach the introduction with sensitivity to the respondent's needs and goals. Thus, to conduct a successful interview one must develop rapport with the respondent.

Characteristics of a Successful Interviewing Relationship

The characteristics of a successful interviewing relationship can be described in the following terms:

Warmth and responsiveness on the part of the interviewer. The respondent needs to feel the interviewer is genuinely interested in him, and accepts him as a person.

A permissive atmosphere in which the respondent feels completely free to express any feeling or viewpoint. The interviewer's attitude should be one of complete acceptance and understanding of the respondent's statements.

Freedom from any kind of pressure or coercion. The interviewer should not at any time state ideas, reactions, or preferences, and should remain completely objective.

In this kind of atmosphere, the respondent obtains satisfaction in "opening up" without argument or hurry. The respondent feels that his ideas are acceptable to the interviewer. It is the feeling of "Here is that rare thing—a person to whom I can really talk." Nothing that the respondent says is too trivial for the attention of the interviewer. *Through his relationship with the interviewer, the respondent not only feels free to talk, but is actually stimulated to do so.*

ASKING QUESTIONS

Unless the interview is conducted for purely exploratory purposes, the interviewer should have a specific list of questions to ask of all interviewees in the same way and in the same order. Often, an interview is little more than a verbal questionnaire. The advantages over a written questionnaire are that questions can be followed up in depth during an interview, and that the interviewer can try to make sure that the respondent understands the questions fully and does not accidentally give an inaccurate response. This type of structured interview may involve either a fixed set of response options (for example, "Do you feel very certain, certain, somewhat certain, not very certain, or not at all certain?"), or may leave the response open (for example, "How do you feel about that?"). Whether the questions have closed or open-ended responses, they should be carefully structured—clearly worded and presented in a precisely consistent way. Preparing such questions requires skill and is not at all easy, although some excellent books (such as Oppenheim, 1966) can provide help as can books of questionnaires that offer examples of interview questions. Usually, the interviewer memorizes the questions, and brings along brief notes to jog his memory. Furthermore, both closed and open-ended questions can be used as take-off points for in-depth probing of the respondent's thoughts, feelings, opinions, and so on. To do this, the interviewer must be able to stimulate discussion through effective probing.

STIMULATING DISCUSSION BY PROBING[2]

One of the most challenging and important aspects of the interviewer's work is probing. The quality of the interview depends a great deal on the interviewer's ability to probe meaningfully and successfully.

What Is Probing?

Probing is the technique used by the interviewer to stimulate discussion and obtain more information. A question has been asked and an answer given. For any number of reasons, the answer may be inadequate and may require the interviewer to seek more information to meet the survey objectives. Probing is the art of getting this additional information.

Probes have two major functions:

1. Probes motivate the respondent to communicate more fully by enlarging or clarifying.

---

[2] Reprinted in abridged and modified form from the Survey Research Center (1969). Used by special permission.

2. Probes focus the discussion on the specific content of the interview, eliminating unnecessary information.

Kinds of Probes

Several different neutral techniques that should appear as a natural and casual part of normal conversation may be used to stimulate a fuller, clearer response.

- *A brief assertion of understanding and interest.* By saying such things as "uh-huh" or "I see" or "Yes" or "That's interesting," the interviewer can stimulate the other person to talk further.
- *An expectant pause.* The simplest way to convey to a respondent that you know he has begun to answer the question, but that you feel he has more to say, is to be silent. The pause—often accompanied by an expectant look or a nod of the head—allows the respondent to gather his thoughts. Silence is sometimes truly "golden" in that it elicits more useful information.
  One word of caution. The interviewer must be sensitive to each respondent when using this technique. A pause will not stimulate respondents to further discussion if they are truly out of ideas. Instead of the "pregnant pause," you could have an "embarrassed silence."
- *Repeating the question.* When the respondent does not seem to understand the question, when he misinterprets it, when he seems unable to make up his mind, or when he strays from the subject, it is often useful to repeat the question just as it is written in the questionnaire. Many respondents, on hearing it for a second time, will realize what kind of answer is needed.
- *Repeating the respondent's reply.* Simply repeating, in your own words, what the respondent has said as soon as he has stopped talking is often an excellent probe. Hearing his idea repeated often, he may be further stimulated into thought.
- *A neutral question or comment.* Neutral questions or comments are frequently used to obtain clearer and fuller responses. Some examples are:
  "Could you tell me more about your thinking on that?"
  "Why do you think that is so?"
  "Could you tell me why you feel that way?"
  "Anything else?"
  Such questions indicate the interviewer is interested and they make a direct bid for more information.
- *Asking for further clarification.* In probing, a useful technique for the interviewer now and then is to appear slightly bewildered by the respondent's answer, and to intimate in the probe that he might have failed to understand. (For example: "I'm not quite sure I know what you mean by that—could you tell me a little more?") This technique can arouse the respondent's desire to cooperate with a human being trying to do a good job.

Probing Methods Should Be Neutral

Remember that we have described probing as the technique that motivates the respondent to communicate more fully and that focuses the discussion on specific topics. Both of these things must be done without introducing bias.

The potential for bias is great in the use of probes. Under the pressure of the interviewing situation, the interviewer may quite unintentionally imply that some responses are more acceptable than others, or may hint that a respondent might wish to consider or include this or that in giving his responses.

CONCLUDING THE INTERVIEW

When all questions have been asked, responses recorded, and follow-up probing has exhausted the topics covered, it is time to end the interview. The interviewer should make certain that, at some time during the interview, the respondent has been assured of anonymity. Further, any questions or unclear points in the respondent's mind should be answered or cleared up. It may be appropriate for the interviewer to briefly summarize what the respondent has said, and the respondent should definitely be asked if there is anything else he might like to tell the interviewer. Finally, the respondent should receive a sincere "thanks" for taking the time to help with the study. In sum, when the interview is over, the respondent should feel that the time was well spent and that the interview was worthwhile, and he or she should have a sense of completion or closure.

INTERVIEWING: SUMMARY

Effective interviewing depends on careful planning and on the interviewer's skills. Skill is needed at the beginning of the interview to establish rapport and build the relationship with the interviewee. In the body of the interview, skills at probing are needed to get at deeper or hidden thoughts and feelings. Skills are also needed at the end of the interview to leave the respondent with a positive experience. The effectiveness of the interview depends on skillful handling of the three major phases:

- *Building Rapport.* During this phase, the interviewer gives an introduction; explains the purpose of the interview; becomes comfortable in the interaction; assures the respondent of confidentiality (when and if appropriate).
- *Questioning and Probing.* Here the interviewer presents questions in a standard, carefully planned manner; and follows up on specific questions as appropriate.
- *Leaving the Respondent.* At this point the interviewer ties up all loose ends and achieves closure, leaving the respondent satisfied.

Interviewing*

Jack K. Fordyce
and Raymond Weil

Before a team-building or similar meeting, it is common practice to interview the participants. The interviewer is generally a Third Party. The purpose of the interview is to explore ways in which the group can be more effective. The interviews uncover both positive and negative opinions and sentiments about a wide range of subjects—for example, clarity of individual and group goals, impact of the manager's style, and personal concerns that have never been aired.

The questions should help the interviewee to express whatever is on his or her mind about life in the organization. Examples of general opening questions:

"How are things going around here?"
"What changes would you like to see?"
"How do you think this organization could be more effective? What do you feel it does best? Does poorly?"

The interviewer may also ask about management:

"How would you describe the management style of X? How do you think he or she could be more effective?"

Questions may also be asked about relationships within the organization:

"Whom do you like to work with most? Least?"
"Who is most influential in your organization?"
"Are you kept informed of what goes on?"

And about relationships with other organizations:

"When there are problems with other organizations, what can you do about them?"
"Can you give examples of unresolved issues with other organizations?"
"Do you think you could give them advice that would help them do a better job?"

* SOURCE: Jack K. Fordyce and Raymond Weil, *Managing with People*, 2nd ed. © 1979. Addison-Wesley Publishing Company, Inc., Reading, Mass., pp. 145–147. Reprinted with permission.

Information from the interviews is fed back to the total group, usually at the beginning of the meeting.

USES

Interviewing is a way to get private views and feelings out on the table. The information collected often furnishes the principal basis for the meeting agenda.

BENEFITS

The interview is an excellent way to probe for the problems and opportunities of the organization. Interviewing has the virtue of facilitating private expression. A sensitive interviewer can also invite ideas and emotions that the subject has not previously formulated in any conscious way. Interviewing also furnishes an occasion to develop trust between the Third Party and members of the organization; such trust is valuable in later work.

LIMITATIONS

A good interview often takes one to two hours. For a large organization, interviewing can therefore consume a lot of time.

Skillful interviewing runs the risk of turning up more information of a personal and perhaps threatening nature than the group is ready to deal with. When confronted with the interview findings, the group may close up, reject the information, and attack the interviewers.

If the interviewer is clumsy, or is not trusted as impartial, interviewing may worsen matters. Under these circumstances, it is best to gather information by open group process.

There should be an understanding between the interviewer, the manager, and members of the team as to how the information will be used, especially with respect to protecting the privacy of sources. Normally, interviewees are promised that the information will be presented anonymously. The interviewer must keep that promise.

The information can be presented verbatim or thematically. The former has greater impact but does not protect privacy as well, and some data may be too hot for the group to handle. Thematically presented material has the opposite virtues: it's cooler, protects privacy better, has a softer impact. It is usually easily summarized, and hence easier to grasp.

One variation in reporting is to present themes and to back them up with supporting verbatim quotes.

If the findings are highly critical of the manager or another member of the group, it is advisable for the interviewer to disclose enough of the information to the manager in advance of the group meeting so that he or she will not feel ambushed.

Interviews may be carried out on an individual or subgroup basis, the latter having the obvious advantage of saving time. Interviewing of subgroups does not confer the same advantages of privacy and sensitivity, but the information disclosed tends to be of a character that the group is ready and willing to deal with. Moreover, the person who volunteers data in a subgroup interview normally feels committed to confirm it in a larger meeting.

A way to disseminate the interview findings is to type and distribute copies to all members of the group. Summary statements and corroborative information can then be posted on chart pads.

4

RESISTANCE AND THE PROCESS OF CHANGE

———— ◆ ————

INTRODUCTION

The overall aim of this chapter is to review the process of organizational change from several perspectives and with reference to several models. The chapter has in part the function of drawing attention to the continuing importance of resistance to change.

The Tremont Hotel Project: How We Began offers an outline of the considerations a consulting team took into account and the arrangements made when the team began an attempt to create positive organizational change. Discussion of their experiences encourages the novice change agent to realize that others also have had to start from first principles as they struggle to mount an effective intervention.

The Retail Chain describes the evolutionary process by which, over a period of several months, an enterprise endeavored to transform its bottom line. The experience may be fruitfully studied together with Memo I, which casts light on central aspects of the issues concerned.*

WMBA and Channel 12 provides an account of a systematic attempt to improve the lagging performance of a small organization, by widely used contemporary methods intended to bring about constructive organizational change while minimizing resistance. The description provides a compact and useful discussion vehicle, which encourages insight and grasp of everyday, sound practice in managing organizational change.

* Memo I appears as an exhibit in the Apex Manufacturing Company in Chapter 10, p. 469–478.

The Washbourne Office concerns the decline in performance of a branch sales office. It calls for the course participant to design an interaction process around relevant considerations in order to reverse the decline. Lively, illuminating discussion of different designs is likely.

The models and schemes presented in the chapter commence with two brief outlines of resistance to change. *The Psychology of Resistance to Change* summarizes the broad causes of resistance, only one of which is addressed in this book: the way in which change is introduced. *Resistance to Change,* an excerpt from a well-established paper, contrasts two ways in which change may be introduced, one that tends to initiate and encourage resistance and another that tends to foster teamwork and readiness for further change. *Dealing with Resistance* concerns the specific steps a change agent can take to help a client cope with resistance in a constructive way and help him or her solve the organizational problem at issue. The method consists of coping with the resistance by not tackling it head-on.

Two brief summaries of celebrated, historic pieces of research follow. The first, *The Effect of Group Decision on Subsequent Behavior,* relates the Kurt Lewin–inspired experiments during World War II on various methods of influencing people in order to change their behavior. The second, *Participation in Decision Making and Work Group Productivity,* outlines the outcomes of a classic research project founded on the hypothesis that participation in planning and carrying out change make a significant difference to people's acceptance of the change.

Planned Change Theory fits resistance to change into a special case within the larger pattern of the necessary processes implicated in organizational change. Building on the seminal work of Kurt Lewin, this "Lewin-Schein" model specifies a set of assumptions under which change may take place and another, equally important set, under which change will not take place. It suggests mechanisms to clothe Lewin's well-known three-stage trichotomy: unfreezing–changing–refreezing. The Lewin-Schein model is one of the most fundamental conceptual schemes underpinning effective practice in managing organizational change, and will repay close study.

The last two items consider the definition and characteristics of action research in the context of the process of promulgating organizational change, and deepen themes introduced in Chapter 3. *Action-Research OD Processes* stresses that the real strength of action research lies in "its emphasis on the processes involved in the client-consultant relationship" and describes the processes involved. *The Characteristics of Action Research* outlines the concept both as a methodology and as a social science theory, on the basis of a survey of the espousals of 11 action researchers. It leads towards considerations about science and managing change in the third and final cluster of readings on action research in the concluding chapter.

The Tremont Hotel Project: How We Began*

William Foote Whyte
and Edith Lenz Hamilton

The Tremont Hotel project had its inception, fittingly enough, in the Hotel Tremont. It occurred toward the end of my year-long study of human relations in the restaurant industry, financed and sponsored by the National Restaurant Association. As part of the process of letting Association members know that something was going on, I was invited to give talks at regional meetings in several cities. One such talk I gave at the Hotel Tremont, and Mr. Smith, vice-president and general manager of that hotel, was present in the audience.

He told me later that the notion that relations among people could be subjected to study was a completely new idea to him; apparently he was fascinated with it. He persuaded me to stay over an additional day in the city to present my talk to a meeting of the hotel management organization.

Mr. Smith then consulted me about the position of Tremont personnel manager, which was then vacant. Could I recommend a man, trained along the lines of my own work, who would become his next personnel manager? I inquired regarding his recent experiences with men in that position and learned that he had had three men on the job in little more than a year. Apparently it was a rather hazardous job. I told Mr. Smith that I could not in good conscience recommend the job to any student of mine, but I was prepared to make a counterproposal. If he would accept—and finance—an action-research program under my general direction, I thought I would be able to recommend to him a good potential personnel manager and also to provide a field research worker. He thought it over, and, in a subsequent meeting, we worked out the arrangements.

It was in this way that Meredith Wiley came to be personnel manager of the Tremont Hotel. Edith Lentz assumed the role of field research worker. Miss Lentz was to be responsible only to me, but we arranged that she work closely with Wiley and that he have access to all her notes on interviews and observations, just as I did. No one else in the hotel was to see these notes, no matter how curious or how important he might be.

I was to spend one day a month at the Tremont discussing progress with Miss Lentz and Mr. Wiley, consulting with Mr. Smith, and talking with

* SOURCE: William Foote Whyte and Edith Lenz Hamilton, *Action Research for Management* (Homewood, Ill.: Richard D. Irwin, 1964), pp. 5–13. Reprinted with permission.

other management people either in meetings or individually. Miss Lentz was to spend two days a month at the University of Chicago going over progress and plans with me.

Though the Tremont Hotel put up the money, Miss Lentz received her paycheck from the University of Chicago. Wiley was directly on the payroll of the hotel, responsible to Mr. Smith, with a mandate to develop a new approach to the Tremont personnel program. While I had no direct control over Wiley and had to take care that Mr. Smith and I did not find ourselves pulling in opposite directions, Wiley, Miss Lentz, and I firmly intended to work as closely together as we could in developing this action-research program. In fact, we recognized that unless we could so work together no such program would develop.

As I look back upon this beginning, I am rather awed by the nerve we had in undertaking the project at all. Now that I am a good deal older and perhaps a little wiser, I wonder whether I would dare to take on an enterprise so uncertain in outcome when I was equally uncertain in advance as to how I should proceed.

Consider this picture for the three main participants: At the beginning of the project, I was 31 years old and had had field research experience in only two industrial settings, the petroleum industry and the restaurant industry. I knew nothing about hotels—except that they had restaurants in them. I had never applied human relations research findings to anything. In my short experience, I had seen no more than one personnel man in action.

Meredith Wiley was then 25, and he was moving into a position where he would outrank many men much older than he. He had studied personnel administration—among other things—but he had had no experience in personnel work, let alone as a director of personnel. Nor did he know anything about hotels.

Edith Lentz came to the project with a background of a number of years of factory experience obtained before she resumed work for her college degree. She had worked with me on the restaurant industry study, beginning as a part-time waitress who kept a work diary and later moving on to a regular research position. While she was then far from the professional she has since become, her experience in field research was probably closer to the responsibilities of her new job than was the case for either Wiley or me.

From the standpoint of Wiley, Lentz, and Whyte, the Tremont Hotel project was in part an adventure story. We began with only a vague idea of what we were doing and learned as we went along. Uncertain as we were, particularly in the early stages, we had to give the hotel staff the impression that we knew what we were doing. While we were trying to find out for ourselves what we were doing, we had to keep up our own spirits on the many occasions when we were puzzled and discouraged.

I have stressed our lack of previous experience in the type of project we were now about to undertake. However, it should not be assumed that we went in completely unarmed, hoping to make our way on a catch-as-catch-can basis. We were armed with certain skills, and we went in with certain reasonably well-founded assumptions as to the problems with which we would have to deal and with certain general strategies of action.

For the purposes of this report, I should present a memorandum, written *before* the project began, telling in general what we might expect to find and, at least in very general terms, what we proposed to do about these problems. Unfortunately, no such memorandum was ever written. We are thus faced with the task of reconstructing our beginning state of mind and trying to keep it from being contaminated by what we learned in the course of the project and in the succeeding years.

While the accuracy of such a retrospective statement cannot be guaranteed, by examining some of the things we learned in the restaurant study which immediately preceded the Tremont project (together with the literature of research familiar to us at the time) we can make some reasonable assumptions as to what we knew in 1945 (before Tremont) and as to the skills we possessed.

The restaurant experience was particularly relevant, since the hotel contained three large restaurants and a soda fountain, and two thirds of the hotel's income was then coming from food and drinks. We could then begin in familiar restaurant territory, without feeling that we were ducking important problem areas.

Judging from our restaurant experiences, and from what we had heard about Mr. Smith, we assumed that the hotel would be managed by rather high-pressure, top-down supervision, with little effective communication coming from the bottom up. Since we had been impressed with the importance of work-flow relations in the restaurant (customer-waitress-service pantry-kitchen, for example), we assumed that the hotel would have an even more complex and sensitive network of lateral relationships and that this area would provide many severe friction points. Our project would involve examining the hierarchy of authority and the networks of lateral relationships and devising a strategy for working on both sets of relationships together in some systematic way.

We assumed that executives at high levels in the organization would have inadequate knowledge and distorted ideas regarding problems existing at the work level. This would come about partly because demands on the executive's time would make it difficult for him to give much attention to any single problem at the work level. Another prime source of distortion we expected to find was in the pattern of communication up and down the hierarchy. Given the existing top-down pressures, we could expect each man to tailor his reports to his boss in terms of his perception of what the boss wanted to hear and in terms of what the subordinate thought would be useful to himself to say. In earlier research, I had found some really fantastic notions about work level problems lodged in the heads of presumably able and certainly well-paid executives. These notions seemed a natural product of the refraction that took place as a story moved up step by step from the bottom to the higher levels.

With direct access to the lower levels of the organization, I had no doubt that concerning human problems, we could gather information that was otherwise inaccessible to men at higher levels. I did not expect that this information would come easily to us. As had been the case in other studies in my experience, I expected that our activities would be met by widespread suspicion and anxiety and that few people would be willing to talk freely with Miss Lentz or Mr. Wiley in the early stages. I believed that they could accept resistance and even hostility as a normal response to strange people and strange new activities and live with those reactions until they were able to work their way through them.

This is, in fact, what happens when a skilled interviewer enters an organization for research purposes. At first people respond to him with superficial generalities, and he takes care not to press them with questions that would require them to commit themselves on sensitive issues. He may tell people that his first task is to understand the jobs in a department and how they fit together. His first questions can be answered entirely in technical terms, but the informant may go on, if he wishes, to volunteer comments about the supervisor, the union, and other sensitive matters. The interviewer counts on building up a certain frequency of interaction with potential informants so that, as they get used to having him around, they begin to test him out with feelings they want to express but hesitate to discuss freely.

If relations in the organization are reasonably harmonious and little tension is felt, informants are likely to open up with little hesitation. If the level of tension and conflict is high, the resistance to the interviewer will at first be high also. On the other hand, the higher the tension, the more important it will be to organization members to be able to talk to someone about their problems. If we played our parts correctly, eventually the dam would break and people would begin to confide in us.

I was therefore confident that we could get the data that were out of reach of the executives. I was also confident that we could analyze the data to better effect than could someone who had not been trained in our field of study. In part, I was counting on a theoretical framework, which, rudimentary though it was, helped us to know what to look for and how to analyze what we found. This is not the place to present that framework, but it may be helpful to point out three of the major ways in which we expected that our approach would differ from that of the executives and supervisors in the hotel.

1. *Moral judgment or explanation?* Based on our experience with other management people, we expected the hotelmen to look at human problems in moral terms. If something went wrong, their question would be: who is to blame? Instead, we would be seeking to explain human events, to discover the pattern in them.

2. *The individual and the group.* In a society which places a great emphasis upon individualism, we expected the hotelmen to seek their explanations of problems through examining the personality and character of particular individuals. While events would sometimes force them to recognize social forces influencing the individual, somehow these forces would be considered illegitimate. They wanted each man to respond to the job situation in terms of his abilities and moral fiber. While we necessarily gathered much of our information

through interviewing individuals, we recognized that many of the human problems we would study could more profitably be viewed as group phenomena. That is, the individuals were not reacting to the job in social isolation. The individuals had their place in a social system. Since we often found individuals occupying the same organizational position reacting similarly, we had a pattern of behavior to observe and explain. Not that it is unimportant to seek to understand individuals. . . . Here I am simply noting our initial assumption that a group approach would be more explanatory than would an analysis in terms of individual psychology.

3. *Cause and effect or mutual dependence?* I had noted within management a common tendency to think in rather simple cause-effect terms, at least in the field of human problems. If something went wrong, "the cause" had to be found, and causes tended to be sought right in the immediate situation. As a corollary to this, a given management action was expected to have an effect only in the immediate situation in which the action was taken. We had found management people constantly being surprised at the unintended consequences of their actions. This surprise grew out of their failure to recognize that they were dealing with a social system, made up of mutually dependent parts. Here mutual dependence means that a change introduced at one point in the system will give rise to changes in other parts of the system. The executive will therefore find it useful to abandon search for "the cause," and to broaden his vision so as to see his actions and those of others as fitting into the pattern of a social system of mutually dependent parts.

If we could get the information and make sense out of it, could we transmit it in a useful fashion? If people were to talk freely with us, we had to guarantee them that what they said would be confidential—and we had to keep that promise. This meant that the information we presented had to be general enough to protect our confidences and yet revealing enough to be helpful to management. Here we knew what we were aiming for, but we had to work out the specific techniques in practice.

What actions would we take or recommend in order to solve the problems we were to find? In detail, that of course depended upon what we found, but we had some general strategies in mind.

To ease downward pressure and to stimulate upward communication, we had great faith in group meetings. We assumed that if the supervisor would call his subordinates together on a regular basis—perhaps once a week—to discuss the problems of the department with them, this could have a constructive effect upon both morale and efficiency. If the meetings were conducted skillfully by the supervisor, the subordinates would have a feeling of catharsis through getting their problems off their chests. While this could be of some importance in itself, particularly in a high tension situation, we recognized that the good effects of opening the upward channel of communication would soon disappear if they were not accompanied by changes in the initiation of activities. We did not believe, as it was then so often said; that good human relations were simply a matter of good communications or of "making the workers feel they are participating." As subordinates participated in these discussions, they would raise complaints and make suggestions. If the supervisor took no action on these complaints and suggestions, the discussions would soon lose their cathartic effects, and the meetings would do management more harm than good. On the other hand, if the supervisor responded to these complaints and suggestions on a reasonably regular basis, changing his own behavior and the organization of activities in his department, then a real change in management would have taken place. Thus the supervisor would be building a problem-solving organization, and the subordinates would feel a real sense of participation in the department.

We knew in a general way how the supervisor should act in order to achieve these results. We were going to have to learn how to get the process started and how to help the supervisor perform in this new leadership role.

We expected also that much of Wiley's efforts toward change would be channeled into consultation with individual supervisors and executives. Here we were not counting on Wiley to tell people what to do. We had great faith—too much faith, as later events disclosed—in the power of the interview. We assumed that if Wiley began by interviewing the supervisor or executive on his problems, this process would have two constructive results. First, the informant would get things off his chest. We felt he would need this catharsis as much as the workers did, and this effect would strengthen his ties with Wiley. Second, the process of being interviewed would help him to clarify his ideas about the human problems of his department. Here Wiley would not be simply a passive listener. His questions would point to aspects of the problem the supervisor might have overlooked.

We did not rule out advice giving altogether. At times we expected that such action would be necessary and desirable. But our aim was to strengthen people in solving their own problems, so Mr. Wiley was to try to help people work through to their own solutions rather than give them his solution.

How would we exercise our power in the organization? We never fully answered that question in advance. We recognized that we necessarily carried great potential influence. Our aim was to change the organization through having people voluntarily decide that the new ways were better. We were not at all sure how this would work out in practice.

As to our relations with the structure of the organization, we had our strategy worked out in these general terms: I would be primarily responsible at first for interpreting the project to Smith and for consulting with him and the other key executives. Wiley would, we hoped, develop relationships such that he could work on problems at all levels of the organization. When the problem in question occurred at a low level, Wiley would try to help the immediate supervisor to solve it instead of reporting the problem to the top. Smith would only receive reports on problems when lower level officials had begun to make progress on them. We expected that this strategy would help us to win the cooperation of the first-line supervisors and of middle managers. But would it satisfy Smith, who was inclined to want to know everything and to get quick results?

The Retail Chain*

Jack K. Fordyce
and Raymond Weil

SITUATION

The district manager (DM) of a retail chain wants to increase profits substantially.

About half the time of the DM and staff is devoted to store inspections and the necessary travel between stores. These are intended to be helpful to the store managers. We don't know *their* opinion of the visits.

He sees the behavior of his staff, mostly merchandising specialists, as an obstacle and wants to change their mode of operating. *They* want strong control over the store managers and the resolute backing of the DM. *He* believes the store managers—he was once one himself—need greater autonomy and that the staff should accomplish more on their own before coming back to him with new demands for enforcement. The staff appears to him to be frustrated. Perhaps they think he's weak.

The DM has made a highly private assessment of the forces that aid and those that hinder him. He chooses the staff's method of operating as the key variable. His diagnosis of the situation is based on his own observation. . . .

The DM has attended a headquarters team-building meeting and wants one for himself and his staff.

Meeting of the DM with Third Party (2 hours)
The DM describes his profit objectives and his diagnosis of the problem to the Third Party. They agree to consult the staff about a team-building meeting.

Meeting of the DM, Third Party, and District Staff at a Regular Staff Meeting (1 hour)
The staff agrees to the team-building meeting.

Information Gathering (1 hour per interview)
The Third Party interviews staff members individually about the changes they want, and how they and the DM function as a team.

* SOURCE: Jack K. Fordyce and Raymond Weil, *Managing with People,* 2nd ed. © 1979. Addison-Wesley Publishing Company, Inc., Reading, Mass., pp. 29–38. Reprinted with permission.

Team-Building Meeting with DM and Staff (2½ days)

The DM invites the staff to air their complaints. They do, and there are three: (1) the DM won't back their directives to store managers, (2) he won't close down unprofitable stores, and (3) he won't fire incompetent store managers in spite of the staff's repeated recommendations. In short, in their view, he *is* a weak and indecisive leader! After considerable discussion, the DM now consents to some of their recommendations. On others they compromise. The DM now feeds back to the staff *his* dissatisfaction with their way of operating.

Following more work on their desires and relationships, the team develops a "turned-on" feeling. The staff members now want to include the store managers in their team.

The DM formally announces an ambitious profit goal.

The announcement of a specific dollar goal at this point serves as a major stimulus to the group. However, at this point the goal is still a dream.

. . . early in the meeting, the members frequently (and truculently) insist that their only reason for being is *profit*. By the end of the meeting there is a shift in emphasis: profit is a measure of themselves as a team.

They begin to plan ways to link the people instrumental to the change. They now have higher standards for the closeness of these linkages (relationships).

After much analysis and debate, they agree to the DM's goal and draw up a list of the steps needed to reach it. Three of these are particularly significant:

- Recognizing that achievement of this goal requires the same commitment from the store managers as *they* now feel, as well as close teamwork between them, they recommend that the DM conduct a similar meeting with store managers, followed by a joint meeting of store managers and staff.
- They realize that they have been acting as policemen to the stores, a role they now want to cast off. They want to change the nature of their store inspections to allow for more healthy give-and-take between the store managers and themselves.
- They introduce an innovation. They will invite a representative group of store managers to take part in developing this year's standards of performance for store managers.

Visits of the Third Party to Several Ensuing Biweekly Meetings of the DM and Staff (1 day each)

The Third Party consults with the group on its progress. In each case there are fresh difficulties; unforeseen factors have appeared and new issues have arisen between them that they did not openly confront. Some feel that the manager or certain staff members are backsliding on commitments. These problems are finally confronted and resolved.

. . . After several experiences, the group members learn in their hearts what they already knew in their heads: that no one can change characteristic behavior without repeated reinforcement, that neither the DM nor any other single person alone can carry the responsibility for meeting all the commitments made. Each has to assume responsibility for helping the others stay honest.

Meeting Between DM, the Staff, Four Store Managers, and the Third Party (1½ days)

This is the meeting on standards of performance recommended by the staff at their team-building meeting.

This meeting also serves as a means of bridging to the store manager group. The store managers invited were all outspoken people and highly respected by their peers. They jointly decide in the meeting that the store managers should not act as "shills" within their own group, but should feel free to discuss any aspect of the meeting according to their own judgment. . . .

The four store managers are briefed on the earlier meeting and the new profit goal. They debate the new goal.

The store managers agree that, to achieve the goal, standards of performance must be given more weight, and the relationship between the staff and the store managers must change.

The goal grows more real as personal risks intensify. In turn, this focuses attention on the need for improved ways of helping one another.

The store managers seriously question the usefulness of store inspections; the DM agrees to improve them, but not to reduce frequency.

The DM still does not feel free to "let go."

Team-Building Meeting with the DM, Store Managers, and Third Party (2½ days)

The DM sets the stage for this meeting by inviting the store managers to get their problems off their chests, including the problems with *him,* and by stating that they are there to tear apart their whole pattern of working and put it back together again in a better way. All his earlier decisions are subject to question, and he is prepared to fight the battle higher up if necessary.

By this time, the manager clearly realizes that he is and wants to be involved in a major change process. In his own way, he states clearly the process of change in a human system; a period of unfreezing the old system, exploring and deciding on new ways, and refreezing.

As he and the group unlock from the old system, their horizons broaden, and they experience a feeling of increased power to determine their own destiny. They will tangle with headquarters, if necessary!

As in the staff team-building meeting, when issues and feelings are ventilated, the group experiences a sense of unity.

. . . Without exception, all of the store managers reveal themselves as strongly motivated to do a better job, although many of them previously felt themselves hobbled by a need to protect themselves from the staff. They had been harassed by police and judged by judges, whereas what they had needed was people who could help them. Now, when they see the real possibility of remaking their business world into one of their own choice, they are understandably excited.

They explore ways in which there could be more help in merchandising methods from the staff, other store managers, or experienced department managers (within each store).

They are starting to design the new world.

Their solution to the problem with the staff (the hottest issue) is to make the staff *jointly* responsible with them for the effectiveness of merchandising in their stores. Only the DM is the policeman; his principal means of control will be a quarterly review of store managers' performance against their annual standards.

The DM isn't ready to reply to either this recommendation or the one on store inspections, but carries them over until the intergroup meeting between the store managers and the staff.

The DM learns that he is in a period of exploration in which withholding decisions does not signify indecisiveness. On the other hand, he still needs to make his views known, with the understanding that they are tentative. The give-and-take has made the group members confident enough that he can speak freely without inhibiting them.

The DM makes a five-state tour during which he meets individually with each store manager to negotiate the store manager's performance standards for the year. The staff no longer takes part in setting standards for store managers.

The increase in trust makes these negotiations more realistic.

Intergroup Team-Building Meeting Between the Staff and the Store Managers, with the DM and Third Party (2½ days)

Each group presents the other with its complaints.

The store managers present their solution:

- The staff should have less close relations with the DM and instead should associate with the store managers, taking equal rights and responsibilities.

This recommendation has earth-shaking implications. For the staff it means a departure from the organization chart box at the DM's level, with an implication of loss of status and power. But the staff is now disenchanted with that role. They see themselves having more real influence by working *with* the store managers, with no distinction in rank. For the store managers, this recommendation means trusting the staff enough to give them complete access to their stores. For both of them, it means being willing to fight out issues between them. For the DM, it means apparent isolation. The staff can no longer serve as his intelligence agents or help him make decisions about store managers. But he trusts their commitment to work responsibly. The strengthened personal bonds mitigate his feeling of isolation.

- The store managers, in like manner, will work jointly with their department (e.g., sporting goods) managers in the stores.

After a good deal of probing and soul-searching, this concept is approved and bought by all, including the DM.

In round-robin nose-to-nose confrontations, working in small groups, store managers and staff members disclose what they like and don't like about their past relations and how they want to frame a new contract.

They are further strengthening relations and starting to work out details.

The DM agrees that there will be *no more routine inspections,* and that when inspections are necessary, the inspecting group may include other store managers but will *not* include the staff (since they would now also be implicated in any cases of poor performance). In future, the purpose of inspection will be to solve problems, not to trap "delinquents."

A new trust and the new ways of working reduce the DM's dependence on these traditional controls so that he can let go. This means bucking the system, because regular inspections are company standard practice. The DM had already paved the way for this by keeping the vice-president informed of what he was doing. . . .

They agree that store managers may at any time request a task force of their choice to help them, including other store managers and store department managers.

The culture is changing from isolation, defensiveness, and destructive competition to one of open competition with collaboration, which the participants now see as to their mutual benefit and personal satisfaction.

They decide that their quarterly performance reviews with the DM should be conducted *in the total group,* so they can learn from one another, help one another, and maintain group discipline! These same meetings will also be used to formulate critiques of their progress as a team. They decide to *invite the vice-president* to these meetings!

Here is testimony to their increased level of confidence! This is a creative and highly important decision. It accomplishes two things, both basic to change by OD methods. First, the total group assumes responsibility for the change and its management. Group collaboration and discipline replaces inefficient management controls. Second, a mechanism for periodic "*critiquing*" is built in. In OD, periodic group "critiquing" is a basic method for maintaining forward thrust and adjusting the direction of thrust.

Situation as of Today

The basic change in the situation occurred in about four months. In effect, the change in relationships makes it possible to shift a large amount of energy and talent from policing, attack and defense, and plain idleness to mutual help. Management energy now flows in the same direction.

... This organization in four months has moved a long way from ill health toward good health. A number of threads, common to OD change efforts, run through this process.

One significant characteristic of the management team after these events is that it has developed a fair amount of sophistication about how it got there and what it has to do to keep going. The members of the team have developed a code to warn one another of backsliding. Backsliding means:

- Not confronting issues.
- Not listening to one another.
- Not living up to commitments.
- Trying to do things *to,* rather than *with,* one another.

The manager of such a change needs, above all else, courage and persistence. He needs the strength to listen to accounts of his real and imagined defects without counterattacking, to risk experimenting with ways of "running the railroad" that are not generally understood and accepted, and to deal with his boss or other power figures when the need arises. He needs persistence, in the face of competing demands for resources and his time, to carry through the change process and make it stick. It takes a lot of energy and it costs money to execute a major change.

WMBA and Channel 12*

William G. Dyer

When the staff of a broadcast system composed of radio station WMBA and TV channel 12 began a major organization improvement effort, it was the result of several months of thinking and planning. Bruce Chamberlain, the station manager, had been extremely conscious of a loss of revenues, harder times in selling TV and radio spots, and evidence of a drop-off in listening and viewing publics. There were indications that the radio and TV groups were at odds with each other, program materials were not as creative as they used to be, and the sales staff seemed to be dragging its collective feet.

Bruce reviewed these conditions with the managers who reported to him. The total station staff fluctuated between forty and sixty people, depending on the season and work load, and was divided into the major groupings of radio, TV, production, sales, personnel, finances, and smaller special groups in FM radio, special effects and projects, and public service. A managers' meeting was held each week and Chamberlain had suggested that the whole station needed to review its overall activities to see how all phases of their operations could improve. Bruce had contacted a nearby university and found a professor knowledgeable in organization development methods who had met with him and outlined a series of alternatives. Since the station management group annually got together for a kind of retreat for business and social reasons, Bruce felt that this time could be better used to seriously review their entire organization, do some more effective planning and coordination, and iron out some of the interface problems.

This proposal was discussed at length in the managers' meeting and finally agreed to. The dates were set, location agreed on, a decision was made to hire an outside resource person, and a committee was set up to make all detailed arrangements.

The outside person met with the managers at a later meeting and outlined the purpose of such a two-day program. The managers suggested issues they would like addressed, the consultant reviewed several possible design arrangements, and it was agreed that the committee assigned (which included Chamberlain) would work with the consultant in making final program plans. Notice of the meeting was shared with all station personnel, and those who were to participate received both a verbal and written invitation. They were asked to come prepared to review the total functioning of the broadcast system and to spend time giving their suggestions for improving the entire system.

The initial session began on Wednesday evening and the program was

* SOURCE: William G. Dyer, *Team Building.* © 1977. Addison-Wesley Publishing Company, Inc., Reading, Mass., pp. 64–67. Reprinted with permission.

to end at 3:00 P.M. on Friday. Following dinner, the Wednesday evening session began at 7:30. Chamberlain first outlined the need for the session as he saw it and noted some problems he hoped to address. The consultant was introduced and her role clarified—she would handle some parts of the program, present some lecture inputs, direct some activities, and be a process observer. The group was then asked to break into four subgroups, with four or five people in each group. Eighteen people had been invited to this session. This group included the key management, supervisory, and administration people who all worked quite closely together.

The subgroups were asked to think about the overall broadcasting system and to come up with an animal, vehicle, general image, or any combination of things that would best describe the organization as they saw it.

In the groups there was a lot of laughter as people came up with wild ideas. After a half hour, each group shared its images with the rest. The images that everyone agreed were most appropriate were:

    a. The organization was like a combination dog—a pointer-setter-terrier. It would point at flaws or problems; it would sit down and wait for someone to do something; and it would yelp like a terrier if anyone did anything out of the ordinary.

    b. The organization was like a kaleidoscope. Lots of beautiful images were created, but with just a slight turn of anything the image would change. Nothing was very stable or constant, but the picture always looked good to an outside observer.

Individuals were asked to do some private planning that evening and work in the small groups again in the morning. The topics: What do we do that makes us feel we have the image we think we have? What are our biggest problems as an organization? What do we need to do to alter our image and deal with our problem areas?

The next morning the small groups met for nearly two hours. When the groups came together and combined their data, the list of issues was sobering. The major concerns were: (1) too much time was spent trying to please the board of directors and not enough attention was being paid to the public; (2) each area was fighting with others, trying to "build a kingdom" rather than sharing ideas and information; (3) staff meetings were bull sessions rather than productive working periods; (4) people were trying to pad budgets and expenses; (5) those who had to serve TV, radio, and FM in special staff capacities were not clear as to priorities, time commitments, or assignments; (6) there was a tendency to put blame for problems on someone else—nobody ever admitted any problems in one's own area; (7) a major goal was to try to look good on paper—have everything in order without being concerned about quality performance.

The total group arranged the seven major problem areas into a priority list of work items. The group was now reformed into four new work groups and each group was given a problem to manage. These new groups were carefully formed to make sure that a cross-section of people from all departments was included in each unit. Each group was asked to take the problem assigned and come up with the following: (1) What specific actions should be taken to deal with the problem area? (2) Who should be responsible for the actions (give specific names)? (3) Who should be responsible for supervising or managing the actions? (4) When should the actions start and end? (5) What would be the date for the first report of results? (6) What rewards or penalties should be expected for success or failure to take action?

The groups worked hard at their tasks and late in the day they all came together to get the first group report. There was a serious discussion about the proposals made. People had to agree to assignments, deadlines, and the rewards and penalties. The consultant (who had been a roving observer and facilitator to the small groups) actively helped the group to look at the way it arrived at its final decisions. In addition, some problems in factions blocking each other, reactions to Chamberlain, and low commitment had to be worked out. But the group plugged away at the task until a final set of actions, to which all agreed, had been developed for every problem area.

By Friday afternoon the staff was tired, but very satisfied. They had a complete list of action assignments with deadlines and dates for reporting progress. More importantly, they had experienced the satisfaction of honestly facing their real problems for the first time and felt successful in being able to work together in arriving at solutions that made sense to them. Many commented that this was the best work session they had ever had, and there was a sense of confidence that they could handle future problems more easily.

The Washbourne Office*

Roy McLennan

You are an established manager in the Hutcheson Company and work in the company's head office, which is located in Thorndon, a major city. One morning, Bill McNamara, your boss, calls you in and says the performance of the company's Washbourne sales office has fallen off and is causing concern to senior company executives. He wants you to look into it.

Bill explains that there has been a marked downturn in Washbourne's sales, while the company's other sales offices have maintained satisfactory performances. Analysis of the figures shows that this decline has taken place gradually over a period of about two years, during which time the Washbourne area has experienced trading conditions similar to the rest of the country. Washbourne usually contributes a significant proportion of the company's total sales. The Washbourne office consists of a manager, six salespeople, and two secretary/clerks. It is located over 250 miles (400 kilometers) away from head office. Bill agrees that everyone at Washbourne is well trained and experienced in sales work, and thinks the causes of the problem probably lie in deficiencies in their motivation, team work, morale, leadership, decision making, or other "people" causes, rather than in any economic, financial, or market considerations. He says it is important to the company to rebuild Washbourne's performance.

You can have a free hand in tackling the problem, he confirms, and you should regard it as a priority matter in terms of the time you spend on it. He says he knows it will take a while to turn the office's performance around, but it must be done.

How would you tackle the problem? Write a one or two page plan outlining how you would proceed, and the considerations you would take into account. Compare your plan with those of others.

The Psychology of Resistance to Change*

Don Bryant

INTRODUCTION

All of us at one time or another have had the experience that, despite the planning, hard work and careful thought we've put into a new scheme, people won't go along with it. This is often a source of bitter disappointment or even bewilderment to us when we find that our brilliant ideas and logical analysis are just simply rejected: even a begrudging acceptance on the part of those for whom the change is intended to benefit can be upsetting for those of us who earn our living as change agents. In a way, it is better to be told that your plan stinks than to meet the kind of half-baked attitude that implies 'I'll give it a fair chance before throwing it out!'

Change, however, is more than an intellectual process; it is a psychological process as well. Unless the change being proposed strengthens in a visible and unambiguous way the psychological security of the people affected, it will be resisted. Most of us, being human, feel our security threatened from time to time. The extent to which we feel secure is mainly dependent on our cumulative experiences since birth. These feelings tend to be deeply ingrained and we are not, for the most part, entirely conscious of them.

SEVEN FACTORS THAT INFLUENCE ATTITUDES

As change agents, we need to have an understanding of these deeply-ingrained feelings about change and security. One writer[1] has suggested that there are at least seven factors that interact to determine how an individual might feel about a change that affects him:

- basic predisposition to change (derived from birth experiences, early feeding and weaning, toilet training, sibling rivalries, etc)
- personal sense of security (dependent on individual personality and current circumstances such as financial and marital status, etc)
- prevailing cultural beliefs (relating to a particular country, or community, class, trade or even work groups)
- extent of trust and loyalty (resulting from past and present relationships with management, union and work groups)

---

* SOURCE: Don Bryant, "The Psychology of Resistance to Change," *Management Services* (March 1979), pp. 9–10. Reprinted with permission.

- objective historic events (including the nature of after-effects of past changes, natural and regional patterns of unemployment, labour mobility, government interventions, etc)
- specific apprehensions and expectations about the particular change (relating the individual to the content and method of the change, to the work group and to the organization as a whole)

Each situation and each individual tend to be unique and hence it is difficult to predict how a particular change will be regarded by those affected. In any case, it would be wrong to suppose that human beings will always resist change, despite the deep-seated and universal nature of the fears. Indeed, as Peter Drucker has asserted, there is no being in heaven or earth greedier for new things:

> '. . . But there has to be conditions for man's psychological readiness to change. The change must appear rational to him; man always presents to himself as rational even his most irrational, most erratic changes. It must appear as an improvement. And it must not be so rapid or so great as to obliterate the psychological landmarks which make a man feel at home: his understanding of his work, his relations to his fellow-workers, his concepts of skill, prestige and social standing in certain jobs. . . .' (Quoted by Judson in[1] p. 87).

Of all of the factors that influence an individual's attitude towards a change, the manner of change is the one most under the control of the change agent, manager, consultant, or whoever is introducing the change. Some general principles of reducing resistance to change[2] are briefly considered under three types of heading: who brings the change?; what kind of change?; and how is it best done?

WHO BRINGS THE CHANGE?

Resistance will be less:

- if managers, supervisors, union leaders and other key people involved in the oganization feel that a programme of planned change is their own—not one devised and operated by outsiders;
- the way in which the change is introduced.
- if any programme started clearly has the whole-hearted support from the top people with the groups concerned.

WHAT KIND OF CHANGE?

Resistance will be less:

- if participants in any project see the change as reducing rather than increasing their current burdens;

- if the project accords with values and ideals which have long been acknowledged by the participants;
- if the programme offers the kind of new experience that interests participants;
- if participants feel that their autonomy and security is not threatened.

PROCEDURES IN INSTITUTING CHANGE?

Resistance will be reduced:

- if participants have joined in diagnostic efforts leading them to agree on what the basic problem is and to feel its importance;
- if the project is adopted by consensus following group discussion;
- if the parties involved can see both sides of the question and recognise valid objections and take steps to relieve unnecessary fears;
- if it is recognised that innovations are likely to be misunderstood and misinterpreted, and if provision is made for feedback of views on the project and any further clarification;
- if participants can begin to develop acceptance of each other and so experience support, trust and confidence in their relations with one another;
- if the project is kept open to revision and reconsideration if experience indicates that a change in direction or emphasis would be desirable.

These and other procedures for instituting planned change can be regarded as a *process* (i.e., the 'how' of the change as distinct from the 'what' or *content* of the change).

REFERENCES

Judson, Arnold S. *A Manager's Guide to Making Changes.* London: Wiley, 1966.

Bryant, D., G. Mars, and P. Mitchell "Solving Manpower Problems in Hotels and Restaurants: A Case Study Approach," *Tavistock Institute of Human Relations Document No. 2T75,* 1978.

Resistance to Change*†

Paul R. Lawrence

Recently, while making some research observations in a factory manufacturing electronic products, a colleague and I had an opportunity to observe a number of incidents that for us threw new light on this matter of resistance to change.[1] One incident was particularly illuminating:

We were observing the work of one of the industrial engineers and a production operator who had been assigned to work with the engineer on assembling and testing an experimental product that the engineer was developing. The engineer and the operator were in almost constant daily contact in their work. It was a common occurrence for the engineer to suggest an idea for some modification in a part of the new product; he would then discuss his idea with the operator and ask her to try out the change to see how it worked. It was also a common occurrence for the operator to get an idea as she assembled parts and to pass this idea on to the engineer, who would then consider it and, on occasion, ask the operator to try out the idea and see if it proved useful.

A typical exchange between these two people might run somewhat as follows:

ENGINEER: I got to thinking last night about that difficulty we've been having on assembling the x part in the last few days. It occurred to me that we might get around that trouble if we washed the part in a cleaning solution just prior to assembling it.

OPERATOR: Well, that sounds to me like it's worth trying.

ENGINEER: I'll get you some of the right kind of cleaning solution, and why don't you try doing that with about 50 parts and keep track of what happens.

OPERATOR: Sure, I'll keep track of it and let you know how it works.

With this episode in mind, let us take a look at a second episode involving the same production operator. One day we noticed another engineer

* SOURCE: Reprinted with permission of the *Harvard Business Review*. Excerpt and exhibit from "How to Deal with Resistance to Change," by Paul R. Lawrence, May/June 1954. Copyright © 1954 by the President and Fellows of Harvard College; all rights reserved.

† Excerpts from the article "How to Deal with Resistance to Change," *Harvard Business Review*, May–June, 1954. Reprinted by permission.

[1] For a complete report of the study, see Harriet O. Ronken and Paul R. Lawrence, *Administering Changes: A Case Study of Human Relations in a Factory* (Boston: Division of Research, Harvard Business School, 1952).

approaching the production operator. We knew that this particular engineer had had no previous contact with the production operator. He had been asked to take a look at one specific problem on the new product because of his special technical qualifications. He had decided to make a change in one of the parts of the product to eliminate the problem, and he had prepared some of these parts using his new method. Here is what happened:

> He walked up to the production operator with the new parts in his hand and indicated to her by a gesture that he wanted her to try assembling some units using his new part. The operator picked up one of the parts and proceeded to assemble it. We noticed that she did not handle the part with her usual care. After she had assembled the product, she tested it and it failed to pass inspection. She turned to the new engineer and, with a triumphant air, said, "It doesn't work."
>
> The new engineer indicated that she should try another part. She did so, and again it did not work. She then proceeded to assemble units using all of the new parts that were available. She handled each of them in an unusually rough manner. None of them worked. Again she turned to the engineer and said that the new parts did not work.
>
> The engineer left, and later the operator, with evident satisfaction, commented to the original industrial engineer that the new engineer's idea was just no good.

SOCIAL CHANGE

What can we learn from these episodes? To begin, it will be useful for our purposes to think of change as having both a technical and a social aspect. The *technical* aspect of the change is the making of a measurable modification in the physical routines of the job. The *social* aspect of the change refers to the way those affected by it think it will alter their established relationships in the organization.

We can clarify this distinction by referring to the two foregoing episodes. In both of them, the technical aspects of the changes introduced were virtually identical: the operator was asked to use a slightly changed part in assembling the finished product. By contrast, the social aspects of the changes were quite different.

In the first episode, the interaction between the industrial engineer and the operator tended to sustain the give-and-take kind of relationship that these two people were accustomed to. The operator was used to being treated as a person with some valuable skills and knowledge and some sense of responsibility about her work; when the engineer approached her with his idea, she felt she was being dealt with in the usual way. But, in the second episode, the new engineer was introducing not only a technical change but also a change in the operator's customary way of relating herself to others in the organization. By his brusque manner and by his lack of any explanation, he led the operator to fear that her usual work relationships were being changed. And she just did not like the new way she was being treated.

The results of these two episodes were quite different also. In the first episode there were no symptoms of resistance to change, a very good chance that the experimental change would determine fairly whether a cleaning solution would improve product quality, and a willingness on the part of the operator to accept future changes when the industrial engineer suggested them. In the second episode, however, there were signs of resistance to change (the operator's careless handling of parts and her satisfaction in their failure to work), failure to prove whether the modified part was an improvement or not, and indications that the operator would resist any further changes by the engineer. We might summarize the two contrasting patterns of human behavior in the two episodes in graphic form; see Exhibit 1.

It is apparent from these two patterns that the variable that determines the result is the *social* aspect of the change. In other words, the operator did not resist the technical change as such but rather the accompanying change in her human relationships.

Exhibit 1 Two contrasting patterns of human behavior

	CHANGE		
	Technical Aspect	*Social Aspect*	*Results*
Episode 1	Clean part prior to assembly	Sustaining the customary work relationship of operator	1. No resistance 2. Useful technical result 3. Readiness for more change
Episode 2	Use new part in assembly	Threatening the customary work relationship of operator	1. Signs of resistance 2. No useful technical result 3. Lack of readiness for more change

Dealing with Resistance*

Peter Block

People use the phrase "overcoming resistance" as though resistance or defensiveness were an adversary to be wrestled to the ground and subdued. "Overcoming resistance" would have you use data and logical arguments to win the point and convince the client. There is no way you can talk clients out of their resistance, because resistance is an emotional process. Behind the resistance are certain feelings. You cannot talk people out of how they are feeling.

There are specific steps a consultant can take to help a client get past the resistance and get on with solving the problem. The basic strategy is to help the resistance to blow itself out, like a storm, and not to fight the resistance head-on.

Feelings pass and change when they get expressed directly. The skill for the consultant is to ask clients to put directly into words what the client is experiencing. To ask the client to be authentic. The most effective way to encourage the client to be authentic is for the consultant to also behave authentically. That's all there is to it.

This way of dealing with resistance—by not fighting it head-on—has a Zen quality to it. If you fight the resistance and feel you have to conquer it, all you will do is intensify the resistance. If a client is objecting to your methodology (and has been doing it for more than ten minutes) and you keep defending the method, citing references, and recounting other experiences, the client is going to get even more frustrated. The client is likely to become even more committed to finding holes in your method than he was when the discussion started. The alternative to defending your method is to ask the client more about his concerns and try to get to why your methodology is so important. Getting the client to talk more about his concerns is helping the storm to pass. Defending methodology is keeping the storm alive. . . .

This is the way to deal with resistance—to encourage full expression of the concern so that they pass. Fighting resistance, trying to overcome it with arguments and data, doesn't work as well. Remember that resistance is the *indirect* expression of client reservations. The goal is to help the line manager begin stating the reservations directly, and stop the subterfuge. When the client's concerns are stated directly, the consultant knows what the real issues are and can respond effectively.

There are three specific steps for handling resistance.

* SOURCE: Peter Block, *Flawless Consulting: A Guide to Getting Your Expertise Used* (Austin, Tex.: Learning Concepts, 1981), pp. 131–138. Reprinted with permission.

Step 1: Identify in your own mind what form the resistance is taking. The skill is to pick up the cues from the manager and then, in your head, to put some words on what you see happening.

Step 2: State, in a neutral, nonpunishing way, the form the resistance is taking. This is called "naming the resistance." The skill is to find the neutral language.

Step 3: Be quiet. Let the line manager respond to your statement about the resistance.

People who are technically trained in such disciplines as computer science, engineering, or accounting often find it difficult to recognize the early signs of resistance. Technical training so focuses your attention on facts, figures, data, and the rational level, that you are not accustomed to closely paying attention to the interpersonal, emotional level of conversations. Developing skill in dealing with resistance requires knowing what form the resistance is taking, but the first step is simply to notice what is happening.

Here are some ways to pick up the cues.

Pay attention to the nonverbal messages from the client. Suppose the client is:

Constantly moving away from you
Tied up in knots like a pretzel
Pointing a finger and clenching the other fist
Shaking his head each time you speak
Bent over toward you like a servant

Take any of these signs that the client is feeling uneasy about this project and is most likely being resistant.

Looking at nonverbal behavior is a good way to pick up the cues of resistance.

Another way to know that you are encountering resistance is to use your own body as a thermometer. When you start feeling uneasy in a discussion with the client, it may be an early sign that resistance is on its way. Certainly when you find yourself getting bored or irritated, take it as evidence that the client is resisting. When a discussion is confronting real issues directly, it is not boring or irritating. When you notice yourself yawning or suppressing some negative feelings, take it as a cue. These reactions of yours act as red flags, attention-getting devices. They are messages that you should begin to put words on the form of resistance you are encountering.

A sure cue for resistance is when you hear the same idea explained to you for the third time. Or when you hear yourself answering the same question for the third time. Repetition of ideas and questions is resistance because expressing the idea or answering the question the first time did not get the job done. There must be some underlying concern that is surfacing indirectly through the repetition.

You also hear certain phrases which tell you that the client is not feeling understood.

> You have to understand that . . .
> Let me explain something to you.
> I want to make sure this isn't an academic exercise.

These phrases are very aggressive in a subtle way. They express some frustration and treat the consultant like a serious mistake was about to be made, but somehow this statement from the client is supposed to save us.

There are probably certain phrases you hear a lot that signal difficulty. Take the time to make a list of them now, and update your list as you grow more skilled in picking up the cues of resistance.

When you become aware of resistance, the next step is to put it into words. Name it. It is best to use neutral, everyday language. The skill is to describe the form of the resistance in a way that encourages the client to make a more direct statement of the reservation he or she is experiencing. Here are some examples of resistance and neutral language describing the form of resistance.

WHEN THE RESISTANCE TAKES THIS FORM	NAME IT BY MAKING THIS STATEMENT
Client's avoiding responsibility for the problem or the solution	You don't see yourself as part of the problem.
Flooding you with detail	You are giving me more detail than I need. How would you describe it in a short statement?
One-word answers	You are giving me very short answers. Could you say more?
Changing the subject	The subject keeps shifting. Could we stay focused on one area at a time?
Compliance	You seem willing to do anything I suggest. I can't tell what your real feelings are.
Silence	You are very quiet. I don't know how to read your silence.
Press for solutions	It's too early for solutions. I'm still trying to find out . . .
Attack	You are really questioning a lot of what I do. You seem angry about something.

The easiest way is to look for everyday language to describe the resistance. Someone in a workshop once suggested that it is easier to name the resistance if you think of what you would say to a close friend or spouse, and say that to the client. The sentiment in this suggestion that is helpful is to keep the statement very simple and direct.

Here are some other forms of resistance. Try naming each resistance in a neutral, nonaggressive way.

Questions of methodology
Intellectualizing and spinning great theories
Confusion and vagueness
Low energy, inattention

How did you do? Here are some examples of naming statements you might make to these forms of resistance.

Methodology: You are asking a lot of questions about my methods. Do you have any doubts about the credibility of the results?

Intellectualizing: Each time we get close to deciding what to do, you go back to developing theories to understand what is happening.

Confusion: You seem very confused about what we are discussing. Are you confused about the problem or just not sure what to do about it?

Low energy, inattention: You look like you have other things on your mind, and have low energy for this project.

In a high percentage of cases, clients will respond with a more direct statement of what they are feeling about a project. Sometimes naming the resistance won't work. It may be that there is nothing you can do about it.

If naming the resistance isn't helping, an option is to put into words how *you* are feeling about the discussion. When you meet resistance, it is uncomfortable, frustrating. Sometimes it makes you feel stupid, irrelevant or unimportant. Try stating this to the client with statements like these.

I feel very frustrated by this discussion.
It seems my comments are treated as though they are irrelevant or unimportant.

Sometimes the client will stop short and ask you why you feel that way, and this might get you to a direct discussion of the problem. Expressing your feelings can be riskier at times than just naming the client's resistance. The client may not care how you are feeling, and say, "So, you are feeling uncomfortable. What has that got to do with getting this equipment working?" But stating your own feelings is being authentic and acts to encourage a like response from the client, which is what you are after.

After naming the resistance, there is a tendency for the consultant to keep talking.

To an unmotivated client:
You seem to have very little motivation to go ahead with this project. Let me tell you four reasons why I think this project is important and you should feel differently . . .

The first sentence is good—a neutral naming of the concern. By continuing to talk, though, the consultant is taking the client off the hook and making it easy for the client to *not* take responsibility for his or her actions.

We keep talking to reduce the tension we feel when we confront the client. Don't keep talking. Live with the tension. Make the statement about resistance and remain silent.

A client's behavior is not a reflection on you.

Many of us have a habit of analyzing what we did wrong. In a recent workshop, I asked a group of engineers to make a list of what they did well as consultants and what they did poorly as consultants. They were all able to quickly list eight to ten things they did poorly or had problems with. The lists of positive qualities averaged two items, and took twice as long to make! This passion for self-criticism is very common and gets in the way of keeping the resistance focused on the client where it belongs.

If you must take the client's reactions personally, the rule is to do it after six o'clock in the evening—on your own time. Spend the whole night at it and involve your friends. But don't take resistance personally when you are with the client. If you have, in fact, done a poor job, and the client tells you, you have to own up to it and shape up your act. This doesn't happen often— and it's not resistance from the client, it is a mistake by the consultant.

Remember that client defenses are not to be denied. In fact, they need clear expression. If suppressed, they just pop up later and more dangerously. The key is how you respond to the defenses.

A couple of points to summarize.

> Don't take it personally. Despite the words used, the resistance is not designed to discredit your competence.
>
> Defenses and resistance are a sign that you have touched something important and valuable. The fact is now simply coming out in a difficult form.
>
> Most questions are statements in disguise. Try to get behind the question, to get the statement articulated.
>
> This takes the burden off you to answer a phantom question.

Dealing with resistance is harder than actually doing data collection and much harder than coming up with good interventions. The meat of the consultation is dealing with resistance.

The majority of questions you get about methodology and the project are just expressions of the discomfort and defensiveness the client is feeling. It is important, however, to respond to the substance of the questions as best you can.

One ground rule is to give *two good faith responses* to every question you are asked. If you are asked about methodology and your summary, or how you designed the questionnaire, answer each question twice. The third time the same question is asked, interpret it as a form of resistance and do not respond to the content of the question. Instead, realize that clients who ask the same question over and over are in effect expressing their caution about committing to the process and owning up to their own problems. The third time the same question is asked, the only rational response is to make the statement that perhaps what the client is feeling is some reluctance to commit to the problem or the process.

After two good faith responses, deal with the problems of commitment and taking responsibility—don't deal with resistance as though it were merely a problem of procedure or method. Make the two good faith responses, then treat the questions as resistance.

The Effect of Group Decision on Subsequent Behavior*

Paul R. Lawrence
and John A. Seiler

EXPERIMENTS ON CHANGING FOOD HABITS

During World War II the government was interested in encouraging the consumption of certain nourishing foods for which there was relatively low demand. The Food Habits Committee of the National Research Council sponsored a series of experiments to determine the most effective methods of persuading consumers to change their family diet. These experiments have been widely cited as showing the superiority of group discussion to lectures or individual persuasion as a method of influencing behavior. Decisions to use certain foods were more likely to be followed by those who reached a "group decision" than by those exposed to other influence techniques.[1]

In the first experiment, three groups of Red Cross volunteers (13 to 17 members) were given a persuasive lecture on the advantages of serving beef hearts, sweetbreads, and kidneys, as well as advice on how to overcome resistance to such foods. Three similar groups participated in a discussion led by an experienced group worker; in general, the same points were brought out as had been covered by the lecture. Both discussion and lecture groups were asked how many had previously served any of these meats and, at the end of the meeting, to indicate by a show of hands whether they were now willing to serve one of them during the following week. Discussion group members were also told that they would later be asked whether they had made any change in their family diets, whereas those who attended the lectures were not given this information. The follow-up (after one week) disclosed that 32 per cent of the discussion group members, compared with only 3 per cent of those who heard the lecture, had served one of the meats which they had never served before.

In a subsequent experiment the groups consisted of six to nine housewives who were neighbors but not accustomed to meeting together. This time the same person conducted both lectures and discussions. She was not

* SOURCE: Paul R. Lawrence and John A. Seiler, *Organizational Behavior and Administration* (Homewood, Ill.: Richard D. Irwin, 1965), pp. 933–934. With permission.

[1] Kurt Lewin, "Studies in Group Decision," in D. Cartwright and A. Zander (eds.), *Group Dynamics* (Evanston, Ill.: Row Peterson Co., 1953), pp. 287–301; and "Group Decision and Social Change," in Newcombe and Hartley (eds.), *Readings in Social Psychology* (1947), pp. 330–44.

highly trained as a discussion leader. The desired change was an increased consumption of fresh and evaporated milk. Between 15 and 30 per cent of those who attended lectures reported an increase in their family's milk consumption after two and four weeks, whereas from 45 to 50 per cent of the group decision housewives reported a similar change. The results were almost the same after four weeks as after two weeks, although at the two-week follow-up, neither population was told that a later check would be made.

In a third experiment, group decision was found more effective than *individual* instruction in persuading mothers to feed their newly born babies cod liver oil and orange juice. When a nutritionist gave each mother 20–25 minutes of individual instruction, approximately 20 per cent of the mothers followed the nutritionist's advice on cod liver oil and 40 per cent on orange juice after two weeks, and 55 per cent of them followed it on both foods after four weeks. However, when groups of six mothers reached a decision (after instruction and discussion), some 45 per cent of them followed this decision in regard to cod liver oil and 85 per cent in regard to orange juice after two weeks. After four weeks the corresponding percentages had increased to 88 per cent and 100 per cent.

Taken as a whole, this series of experiments showed that while there was more resistance to some changes in food habits than to others, such changes were much more likely when a group discussed and decided to make the change than when the arguments in favor of the change were presented by lecture or individual instruction. The principal reason seemed to be the greater involvement aroused by the group decision method.

Participation in Decision Making and Work Group Productivity*

Paul Lawrence and John Seiler

An experiment was conducted in a clothing factory to test the effects of participative methods of introducing job changes on productivity.[1] In this factory, job changes occurred frequently and nearly always were accompanied by a sharp drop in productivity. The researchers set up four experimental groups to test their hypothesis that participation in planning and carrying out the change would make a significant difference in people's acceptance of the change. In each of these four groups the proposed change modified the established work procedure to about the same degree; all the groups were paid on a modified piece-rate method.

Group 1, the control or "no participation" group, went through the usual factory routine. The production department modified the job, and a new piece rate was set. The small group of operators was called into a meeting, where they were told that competition necessitated a job change. The change was explained in detail, as was the new piece rate. Questions were answered, and the group was then directed to resume work using the new method.

Group 2, the "participation through representation" group, was handled differently. Before any changes took place, a group meeting was held, and the need for a change was presented as dramatically as possible. Management then presented a plan to set up the new methods and new piece rate. This plan was essentially the same as the usual one except that a few representatives of the group were elected to help management work out the new method and the new rate.

Groups 3 and 4, the "total participation" groups, were both handled in the same way. All the operators met with management, and the need for cost reduction was presented. A general agreement was reached that some savings could be effected. The groups then discussed how existing work methods could be improved and unnecessary operations eliminated. When the new work methods were agreed on, all the operators were trained in the new methods, and all were observed by the time-study men for purposes of establishing a new piece rate on the job.

* SOURCE: Paul R. Lawrence and John A. Seiler, *Organizational Behavior and Administration: Cases, Concepts, and Research Findings* (Homewood, Ill.: Richard D. Irwin, 1965), pp. 931–932. Reprinted with permission.

[1] Lester Coch and J. R. P. French, Jr., "Overcoming Resistance to Change," *Human Relations*, Vol. I, No. 4 (1948). Reprinted in D. Cartwright and A. Zander (eds.), *Group Dynamics* (Evanston, Ill.: Row Peterson Co., 1953), pp. 257–79.

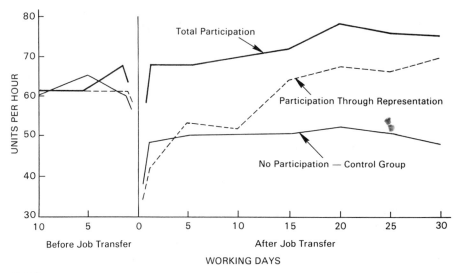

Exhibit 1

Exhibit 1 presents the productivity data for the groups.

In addition to these results, the researchers reported that in Group 1, "resistance developed almost immediately after the change. Marked expressions of aggression against management occurred, such as conflict with the methods engineer, . . . hostility toward the supervisor, deliberate restriction of production, and lack of cooperation with the supervisor. There were 17% quits in the first 40 days. Grievances were filed about piece rates; but when the rate was checked, it was found to be a little 'loose.'" In contrast, in Groups 3 and 4, there were no signs of hostility toward the staff or toward the supervisors, and there were no "quits" during the experimental period.

Planned Change Theory*

Edgar H. Schein

In order to plan effective interventions one needs some kind of comprehensive change theory which explains how to initiate change, how to manage the total change process, and how to stabilize desired change outcomes. The problem of initiating change is especially salient because of the common observation that people resist change, even when the goals are apparently highly desirable. There are many theories of change reflecting a spectrum from revolution to evolution (Hornstein, Bunker, Burke, Gindes, & Lewicki, 1971; Bennis et al., 1969). For purposes of understanding how planned change occurs in groups and organizations of the kind we have discussed here, it is most useful to start with the model first proposed by Lewin (1952) and Lippitt and his collaborators (1958) in their analysis of planned change. Schein subsequently elaborated this model and used it to try to understand various phenomena, ranging from the coercive persuasion of prisoners of war to the kinds of change that occur in educational or developmental settings (Schein, Schneier, & Barker, 1961; Schein, 1961; Schein & Bennis, 1965; Schein, 1972). Several assumptions underlie this model:

1. Any change process involves not only learning something new, but *unlearning* something that is already present and possibly well integrated into the personality and social relationships of the individual.
2. No change will occur unless there is motivation to change, and if such motivation to change is not already present, the induction of that motivation is often the most difficult part of the change process.
3. Organizational changes such as new structures, processes, reward systems, and so on occur only through individual changes in key members of the organization; hence organizational change is always mediated through individual changes.
4. Most adult change involves attitudes, values, and self-images, and the unlearning of present responses in these areas is initially *inherently* painful and threatening.
5. Change is a multistage cycle similar to the adaptive coping cycle previously reviewed, and all stages must be negotiated somehow or other before a stable change can be said to have taken place.

STAGE 1: UNFREEZING—THE CREATION OF MOTIVATION TO CHANGE

The creation of motivation to change is a complex process that involves three specific mechanisms, all of which must be operating in order for the individual to feel "motivated" to unlearn present behavior or attitudes:

* SOURCE: Edgar H. Schein, *Organizational Psychology*, 3rd ed. © 1980, pp. 243–247. Reprinted by permission of Prentice-Hall, Inc., Englewood Cliffs, N.J.

Mechanism 1: Present behavior or attitudes must actually be *disconfirmed,* or must fail to be confirmed over a period of time. In other words, the individual discovers that his or her assumptions about the world are not validated or that some behavior does not lead to expected outcomes and may even lead to undesirable outcomes. Such disconfirmation can arise from any of a wide variety of sources and is the primary source of pain or discomfort that initiates a change process. If everything is working fine there is no discomfort and hence no motivation to change. The most serious ethical questions surrounding the intervention process have to do with the question of when it is legitimate to *induce* discomfort by providing the person with information that will be discomforting. If others have done the disconfirming and the person then comes to the consultant for help, there is obviously less of an ethical issue.

Mechanism 2: The disconfirmation must set up sufficient *guilt* or *anxiety* to motivate a change. If the discomfort is at a low level, it is easily dealt with by denial or by avoidance of the disconfirming source. However, if the person realizes that he or she has really failed to live up to some important value or ideal (guilt) or is in danger of being overwhelmed by inner feelings or may miss some important rewards he or she is seeking (anxiety), then the discomfort becomes a real motivator. However, the person may still seek to use defenses to avoid the pain of change.

Mechanism 3: The creation of *psychological safety,* either by reducing barriers to change or by reducing the threat inherent in the recognition of past failures, is the critical third ingredient. The role of change agent here is to make the person feel secure and capable of changing without reducing the power or validity of the disconfirming information. No matter how much pressure is brought to bear on a person to change, no change will occur until that person feels it is safe to give up the old responses and to enter the uncertainty of learning something new. Probably the single most difficult aspect of initiating change is the balancing of painful disconfirming messages with reassurance that change is possible and can be embarked upon with some sense of personal safety. Once the person has accepted the disconfirming message and has become motivated to change because he or she feels it is safe to change, some new learning can take place.

STAGE 2: CHANGING—DEVELOPING NEW ATTITUDES AND BEHAVIORS ON THE BASIS OF NEW INFORMATION AND COGNITIVE REDEFINITION

The effect of creating a motivation to change is to open the person up to new sources of information and new concepts or new ways of looking at old information (cognitive redefinition). This process occurs through one of two mechanisms:

Mechanism 1: Identification with a role model, mentor, friend, or some other person and learning to see things from that other person's point of view.

One of the most powerful ways of learning a new point of view or concept or attitude is to see it in operation in another person and to use that person as a role model for one's own new attitudes or behavior. Change agents sometimes become the target of identification which is why it is so important that the consultant's behavior be totally congruent with the new attitudes or behaviors to be learned. However, identification can also be a very limiting way of learning in that it focuses the person too much on a single source of information.

Mechanism 2: Scanning the environment for information specifically relevant to one's particular problem and the selection of information from multiple sources is more difficult but often produces more valid change. What we learn from a role model may not fit our particular personality. What we learn by scanning fits by definition, since we only use relevant information and remain in control of what we use.

It should be noted that change is a cognitive process which is facilitated by the obtaining of new information and concepts. But the person will not pay attention to that information or try to learn new concepts unless there is real motivation to change. Thus, many change programs err in moving directly to stage 2 without first testing whether they can in fact tap any motivation to change. If motivation is not there, the change program must move to the more difficult emotional level of attempting to create circumstances which will induce motivation.

STAGE 3: RE-FREEZING—STABILIZING THE CHANGES

It is often found that programs designed to induce attitudinal changes do have observable effects during the training period but do not last once the person is back in a normal routine. The problem usually is that the new things learned either did not fit into the person's total personality or are in varying degrees out of line with what his or her significant relationships will tolerate. The manager learns a new attitude toward subordinates but the manager's own boss and subordinates are really more comfortable with the old attitudes, so they immediately begin to disconfirm the new attitudes and thus initiate a new cycle of change back toward the original state. Thus, to ensure the stability of any change requires specific attention to the integration of the new responses.

Mechanism 1: The person should have an opportunity of testing whether the new attitudes or behaviors really *fit his or her self-concept,* are congruent with other parts of the personality, and can be integrated comfortably. It should be noted that one advantage of scanning over identification as a change mechanism is that from the start the person is more likely to select only those responses which fit him or her. The consultant or change agent should be cautious about pronouncing initial change as stable, especially if it is based on identification or imitation.

Mechanism 2: The person should have an opportunity to test whether *significant others will accept and confirm* the new attitudes and behavior patterns;

alternatively, the change program should be targeted at sets of people or groups who will be able to reinforce the new behaviors in each other. The second approach is one of the reasons why team training in organizations may be more powerful than individual training: It ensures that behavior patterns learned and reinforced in concert will become part of each member's behavioral repertoire. This kind of change may require a good deal more give-and-take and thus may be initially slower but it will last longer.

Within this framework, the consultant or change agent has to employ various tactics to ensure that each stage and/or mechanism will be properly negotiated. If the target is organizational change, not merely individual change, further models are needed to determine with whom to begin a change process—how powerful is a certain individual, how well linked to others in the organization, how ready to change? The complexity of organizational change derives not only from the difficulty of estimating the probability of a specific change in *individual* attitudes but from the complexity of *orchestrating change in various individuals* to produce an organizational outcome.

REFERENCES

BENNIS, W. G., K. D. BENNE, and R. CHIN, *The Planning of Change,* 2nd ed., New York: Holt, Rinehart and Winston, 1969.

HORNSTEIN, H. A., B. B. BUNKER, W. W. BURKE, M. GINDES, and R. J. LEWICKI, *Social Intervention,* New York: Free Press, 1971.

LEWIN, K. Group Decision and Social Change. In G. E. Swanson, T. N. Newcombe, & E. L. Hartley (eds.), *Readings in Social Psychology,* Rev. ed. New York: Holt, 1952.

LIPPITT, R., J. WATSON, and B. WESTLEY, *The Dy-namics of Planned Change.* New York: Harcourt, Brace, 1958.

SCHEIN, E. H.   Management Development as a Process of Influence. *Industrial Management Review,* 1961, *2,* 59–77.

SCHEIN, E. H.   *Professional Education: Some New Directions.* New York: McGraw-Hill, 1972.

SCHEIN, E. H., and W. G. BENNIS *Personal and Organizational Change Through Group Methods.* New York: Wiley, 1965.

SCHEIN, E. H., I. SCHNEIER, and C. H. BARKER, *Coercive Persuasion.* New York: Norton, 1961.

Action-Research OD Processes*

Mark A. Frohman,
Marshall Sashkin,
and Michael J. Kavanagh

The real strength of the action-research OD approach is its emphasis on the processes involved in the client-consultant relationship. Thus, the identification of critical processes characteristic of action-research OD is perhaps more important than a comparison or integration of the elements of the two approaches. . . .

There are five processes or methods of operation basic to and continuous throughout the application of the action-research model. These are not tied to a specific time or phase, but all five share a common element—a *problem-solving orientation*. Even though the processes can be identified clearly and discussed independently, it is obvious that in practice they do not operate independently. The commonality of problem orientation binds them to one another. Each process will be briefly defined, but no order or priority is implied by the listing.

Client-Consultant Collaboration. The previous descriptions of the phases consistently emphasized the process of collaboration between client and consultant in each phase and in all activities. This process is most critical in diagnosis and action planning, where older models prescribed decision making primarily by the consultant. Of course, this is where the OD practitioner may most easily fall into the trap of becoming the expert problem solver on content issues, rather than the process trainer. The OD practitioner, through this close client collaboration, aims not only to help the client solve immediate problems but, more significantly, to help the client learn a generally useful problem-solving process. To some extent, the OD practitioner is a model for the client. Acceptance of his behavior as desirable to model is facilitated by collaboration between the two parties. In other words, effective internalization of modeled behavior (Kelman, 1958) depends upon a base of referent power (French and Raven, 1959), which is developed and enhanced through the collaborative relationship.

. . . [t]he collaborative process is also crucially important in establishing client system involvement in the OD effort. While involvement is necessary to attain the overall aims of the OD effort, it is also required to successfully accomplish many of the specific activities of each phase. For example, the OD

* SOURCE: Mark A. Frohman, Marshall Sashkin, and Michael J. Kavanagh, "Action-Research as Applied to Organization Development," *Organization and Administrative Sciences*, (Spring/Summer 1976). pp. 129–161. With the kind permission of Dr. Anant Negandhi.

effort must respond to relevant demands and characteristics of the client system. This requires collecting accurate and adequately detailed data about the client system, an activity greatly facilitated by client involvement.

Client Learning for Internal Resource Development. By helping the client understand the action-research OD approach, the OD practitioner becomes a trainer. Through this training, the client learns to use the action-research OD model and develops the internal skills for effective use of the model on a continuing basis. Client learning is an important process element in each phase of the model. To a large extent, the OD practitioner trains by *modeling,* although other learning approaches are also likely to be involved (conceptual instruction, guided skill practices, etc.). In the broadest sense, the client system learns to use the action-research OD approach by *doing;* this is an experiential learning process. It is important to note that this client-learning process has its major emphasis on problem solving and is not merely an academic exercise or an attempt to make "sensitivity trainers" of the organization's membership.

Monitoring and Evaluation. Action-research is data based, which means that "tracking"—empirical monitoring and evaluation of the effort—is continuous throughout, not just limited to the evaluation phase. The particular problems and objectives generated as a result of the client-consultant collaboration provide the focus for the monitoring and evaluation. In terms of client learning, this continuous evaluation provides data-based feedback, a requirement for effective learning. Furthermore, this evaluation demonstrates to the client, in specific, concrete terms, the value (or lack of value) of the OD effort or any specific portion of the program. The monitoring and evaluation function is useful for the consultant as well, for through it he learns more about the action-research OD process and its application and generates information which may be added to the bank of professional knowledge (academic and applied).

Interaction and Link between Research and Action . . . [t]here is an interdependence and interaction among the various phases of the action-research OD process. This reflects the fact that the model, by genesis oriented toward solving problems in the client system (Collier, 1945), is based on the reciprocal interlinking of research and action interventions. This makes explanation of the model difficult, particularly in separating the phases and processes for definition and discussion. Scientific methods of data gathering and analysis are tied to reality with the persistent questions, "What does this information mean, and what implications does it have in terms of *actions?*" The interventions of the OD practitioner may be seen as primarily research or primarily action oriented; however, the effects of research as action are not ignored (Brown, 1972), and actions invariably contain a research element in the design for evaluating their effects.

Flexibility. Finally, the action-research OD approach is characterized throughout by a high degree of flexibility, of ready modifiability. This process is obviously related to the prior two processes and is aimed at resolving one of the deficiencies of many OD efforts. . . . For example, recycling is one aspect of flexibility. Data gathering may yield information which implies a need to return to the client in order to modify the feedback plan, or to obtain further data which will better fit the initial feedback model. The feedback process may result in a request for futher or different data analysis or presentation. Diagnostic discussion may identify a need for more or other data, or for further feedback using the same or a different feedback model. It should be clear that recycling can occur at any point in the process, thus requiring a high degree of flexibility in the application of the model.

Flexibility also means that the range of research methods and action interventions open to the OD practitioner is essentially unlimited. Survey, interview, and observational research methods are all among the options; none is automatically excluded or prescribed. In a similar manner, many different actions are possible—so many, in fact, that it is not feasible to itemize here even those which are part of the OD practitioner's standard repertoire. We might note, however, that actions could even involve the application of a specific OD program, such as Grid OD (Blake and Mouton, 1968), sensitivity training (Bradford, Gibb, and Benne, 1964), or management by objectives. Again, the "problem-centeredness" of the model, applied to the organization as a dynamic entity, requires flexibility in its application.

REFERENCES

BLAKE, R. R., and MOUTON, J. S. *Achieving Corporate Excellence through Grid Organization Development.* Houston: Gulf, 1968.

BRADFORD, L. P.; GIBB, J. R.; and BENNE, K. D. *T-Group Theory and Laboratory Method.* New York: Wiley, 1964.

BROWN, L. D. "'Research Action': Organizational Feedback, Understanding, and Change," *Journal of Applied Behavioral Science,* 1972, *8,* 697–712.

COLLIER, J. "United States Indian Administration as a Laboratory of Ethnic Relations," *Social Research,* 1945, *12,* 275–276.

FRENCH, J. R. P., and RAVEN, B. "The Bases of Social Power" in Dorwin Cartwright, ed., *Studies in Social Power* (Ann Arbor: Institute for Social Research, University of Michigan, 1959, 150–167.

KELMAN, H. C. "Compliance, Identification, and Internalization: Three Processes of Attitude Change," *Journal of Conflict Resolution,* 1958, *2,* 51–60.

The Characteristics of Action Research*

Michael Peters
and Viviane Robinson

The following survey is based on the espousals of 11 action researchers, including Lewin. Although our selection of those who have employed the action research approach is not exhaustive, our final choice reflects two main concerns: to provide a selection that represents a range of different fields of social research, and to include only those authors who have attempted to specify, refine, or develop the approach. We excluded those who merely appealed to Lewin or who employed the label "action research" only to sanction their methodology.

Of the 15 different characteristics of action research revealed by the survey (Table 1), one-third showed high agreement among the authors while fewer than one-third were idiosyncratic. The agreement focuses on the involvement-in-change characteristics (Table 1, a–d) and tends to reflect the primary and widespread acceptance of action research as a research methodology or strategy.

A smaller group of exponents not only sees action research as a particular methodology, but links it to a particular interpretation or theory of social science (Argyris, 1980; Elliot, 1978; Kemmis, 1981). This latter group tends to make claims for the potentially paradigmatic status of action research. We shall deal with these two sorts of claims separately.

ACTION RESEARCH AS METHODOLOGY

Those surveyed emphasize that action research starts with a social or practical problem rather than a theoretical question (Kemmis, 1981; Ketterer et al., 1980). While most authors agree that problem formulation and definition provide a specific stage in the research process, Smith (1977) points out that the assumptions underlying a problem orientation may themselves be open to criticism, for the identification of a problem may be highly contentious whenever several interest groups become involved. Most authors stress that the action researcher develops applicable knowledge in the problematic social situation.

* Source: Michael Peters and Viviane Robinson, "The Origins and Status of Action Research," *Journal of Applied Behavioral Science*, 20, 2 (1984), pp. 118–120. Reprinted with permission.

Table 1 Characteristics of Action Research: A Consensual Summary

	GENERAL												IDIOSYNCRATIC		
	(a) Problem-focused	(b) Action-oriented	(c) Organic process (i.e. "cyclical")	(d) Collaborative/ participatory	(e) Ethically based	(f) Experimental	(g) Scientific	(h) Naturalistic	(i) Normative	(j) Re-educative	(k) Emancipatory	(l) Stresses group dynamic	(m) Concretely critical	(n) Low a priori precision with high accuracy	(o) Unconstrained dialogue
Argyris (1980)	[√]*	√**	[√]	[√]	[√]	[√]	√	√	√	√	√			√	
Corey (1953)	√	√	√	√			√								
Cunningham (1976)	√	[√]	√	√					[√]	[√]		√			
Elliot (1978)	√	√		√	√				√		√				√
Foster (1972)	√	[√]	√	√	√										
French & Bell (1973)	[√]	√	√	√	[√]	√	[√]				√				
Kemmis (1981)	√	√	√	√	[√]	[√]	[√]	[√]	[√]	[√]	√		√		
Ketterer et al. (1980)	√	[√]		√			√								
Rapoport (1970)	√	[√]		√		√	√		√						
Smith (1977)	[√]	[√]	[√]	√	√	√	√			√	[√]	√			
Lewin (1948)	√										[√]	√			

* A check mark in brackets [√] indicates that the author has mentioned this characteristic, but has not highlighted it.

** A check mark indicates that the author has explicitly highlighted this characteristic.

Those surveyed do not see knowledge production and implementation as separate research phases. Overall agreement exists that action research is collaborative and that this characteristic helps to distinguish the approach from other forms of social research. Various degrees and styles of collaboration are suggested, from the consultancy model (Argyris, 1980) to a consciousness-raising variation that precludes the involvement of an independent researcher (Kemmis, 1981). Collaboration, we are told, must take place within a mutually acceptable ethical framework governing the collection, use, and release of data.

While some stress the fundamental importance of action research as an iterative or cyclical process of fact finding, planning, strategic action, and evaluation (Cunningham, 1976; Kemmis, 1981; French & Bell, 1973), others give this characteristic no or scant attention (Foster, 1972; Ketterer et al., 1980; Rapoport, 1970).

ACTION RESEARCH AS A THEORY OF SOCIAL SCIENCE

Of the contemporary authors surveyed, only three have seriously ventured to unpack the presuppositions on which action research is thought to rest (Argyris, 1980; Elliot, 1978; Kemmis, 1981). In each case the author has attempted to link the action research mode of inquiry to a particular interpretation of social science. All three share certain Lewinian emphases. First, they each reject positivist approaches to social reality and embrace instead a belief in the importance of the participants' values, beliefs, and intentions. Second, they emphasize a re-educative or self-critical approach to social problems and practices that they feel arise from and are embedded in a social context. Third, they share a concern for marking out action research as an emancipatory form of social research. This seems to imply that as human beings become active in constructing social reality, they can also act to change it for the better.

Within the broad lines of this commonality, some variation exists. Thus, Elliot (1978) recommends a case-study approach and a naturalistic mode of explanation involving concrete descriptions validated in a process of unconstrained dialogue with those whose actions are to be explained, rather than formal statements of causal laws or statistical correlations. Kemmis (1981) also seems to support a reason-giving or interpretist account of human action rather than a causal one. Argyris (1980), in contrast, emphasizes that "action science," along with "normal science," values "public disconfirmability, order, causality, and elegance" (p. 121) and can produce testable generalizations that can contribute to social theory. He develops an account of "personal causation" in which "meanings and intentions are the causal springs of individually designed social action" (p. 50). Furthermore, for Argyris, "action science" differs from "normal science" in that the former produces generalizations that combine "low *a priori* precision with high accuracy." Such generalizations are not as specific and precise as those in normal science, but they attempt to specify the "wholeness" of a problem by capturing "a pattern of variables whose validity is tested by seeing the degree to which actors can use the model to produce accuracy (or to be effective) under on-line constraints" (pp. 131–132). In normal science, one can achieve precision and validity only at the expense of genuine applicability under on-line conditions.

Of the three authors who have gone beyond methodological questions and attempted to make clear what an action research perspective involves, Argyris (1980) most clearly follows the Lewinian model with his emphasis on testable generalizations embodying causal statements. Kemmis (1981) and Elliot (1978), however, have tended to associate action research with a naturalistic type of explanation that is less likely to produce generalizable conclusions.

REFERENCES

ARGYRIS, C. *Inner contradictions of rigorous research.* New York: Academic Press, 1980.

COREY, S. M. *Action Research to Improve School Practices.* New York: Teachers College, Columbia University, 1953.

CUNNINGHAM, B. Action research: Towards a procedural model. *Human Relations,* 1976, *29,* 215–357.

DAVIDSON, D. Actions, reasons and causes. *Journal of Philosophy,* 1963, *60,* 685–700.

ELLIOT, J. What is action research in schools? *Journal of Curriculum Studies,* 1978, *10,* 355–357.

FOSTER, M. An introduction to the theory and practice of action research in work organizations. *Human Relations,* 1972, *25,* 529–556.

FRENCH, W., & BELL, C. *Organizational development.* Englewood Cliffs, N.J.: Prentice-Hall, 1973.

HANSON, N. *Patterns of discovery.* Cambridge: Cambridge University Press, 1958.

KEMMIS, S. Research approaches and methods: Action research. In D. Anderson & C. Blakers (Eds.), *Transition from school: An exploration of research and policy.* Canberra: Australian National University Press, 1981.

KETTERER, R., PRICE, R., & POLITSER, R. The action research paradigm. In R. Price & P. Politser (Eds.), *Evaluation and action in the social environment.* New York: Academic Press, 1980.

LEWIN, K. *Resolving Social Conflicts.* New York: Harper and Bros, 1948.

RAPOPORT, R. Three dilemmas in action research. *Human Relations,* 1970, *23,* 488–513.

SMITH, D. The action research approach to planned change. In R. McLennan (Ed.), *Research on Organizations: Methods, and Data.* Victoria University of Wellington, Wellington, New Zealand, 1977.

5

GATHERING DATA:
Watching, Interviewing,
Using Groups
and Questionnaires

———◀●▶———

INTRODUCTION

Grasping others' meanings is not simply an intellectual process but a deeper form of experiential learning.

—Robert M. Emerson*

This chapter explores the alternative means by which data may be gathered in interventions and the considerations and dynamics involved. After an exercise on watching as a means of gathering data, the experiences presented focus on the use of questionnaires.†

They begin with *Sherlock*, an experience intended to sharpen visual and verbal observational skills, two methods of gathering data, and connect observations with implicit and explicit frames of reference. A suggested procedure for this exercise is provided in the Instructor's Manual.

Two accounts of interventions follow, where questionnaires were the basic data-gathering device used in an attempt to promote change. In *The Industrial Products Division*, things went wrong with a manager's attempt to improve the morale of his work force. Discussion turns on what role he and

---

* *Contemporary Field Research.* (Boston: Little, Brown, 1983), p. 15.

† (Several experiences on interviewing as a data-gathering device are provided in Chapter 3.)

the consultant had in this failure, and what they might have attempted instead. *Northeastern Hospital* concerns an ambitious intervention by a university team. Discussion may usefully focus on the issue of the stage at which the intervention went sour and why. Was there anything the consultants failed to do that could have made the intervention more effective?

The models and schemes in this chapter begin with *An Introduction to Gathering Data*, a crisp overview of data-gathering methods, which also offers useful comment on how to think about the impact of interviewing as a data-gathering device. The author elsewhere reminds us that:

> one cannot completely separate the stages of data-gathering and intervention. Both occur simultaneously: how one gathers data constitutes an intervention, and the kind of intervention one chooses will reveal new data derived from the reaction to the intervention. The separation of these two processes is, therefore, basically a matter of point of view or frame of reference.‡

Structured Naturalistic Observation presents a straightforward guide to making observations in organizations, at the heart of which is a particular procedure for recording observations. It provides a useful scheme to practice analyzing observations in the *Sherlock* exercise. *From "Strategy for Watching,"* written from the point of view of sociologists with wide experience in research into organizations, outlines considerations about first impressions, presenting properties of organizational situations, and the interactive effects of watching on the observer and the observed.

The next two items build on the earlier discussions of interviewing in Chapter 3. *Interviewing* commends the usefulness of the practice of interviewing members of client systems in a chronological way. *Active Listening and Questioning* provides succinct comment on methods that can assist the change agent to exploit the data-gathering possibilities of the subject-centered interview.

Two cogent summaries on the use of group data-gathering methods follow. *Sensing: The Group Interview* is about the appropriate use of an as yet poorly explored method of data collection. There are obviously time and money advantages available from the use of group interviews in comparison with the individual interview. A second group data-gathering device, described in *The Organization Mirror*, is a valuable method of gathering data from groups on the boundary or interface of the organization with its environment, which has important implications for organizational effectiveness and adaptation.

The next four items concentrate on the use of the questionnaire as a data-gathering mechanism in promoting positive organizational change. *Questionnaires and Instruments* provides a brief overview of this whole area. *Feedback* presents an excerpt from classic research on using questionnaire data to promote organizational change. The chapter concludes with a sage paper on *Designing and Conducting Organizational Surveys*, the core device at the heart of questionnaire-based change strategies.

‡ Edgar H. Schein, *Process Consultation*. (Reading, Mass.: Addison-Wesley, 1969), p. 102.

Sherlock*

Rick Roskin

SHERLOCK ROOM DESCRIPTION SHEET

You have just arrived at the ABC company for an exploratory discussion with the president. You met the president a few weeks ago, during an executive development program. Your conversations during the program led to the president inviting you to visit the ABC company, for an exploratory discussion about how you might help the company overcome a particular problem.

You arrived on time and were met by the president's secretary, who apologized and said that there would be a delay. The president was unexpectedly called into an important conference and will be there for at least fifteen minutes more. In the meantime, the secretary has informed you that you are welcome to wait in the president's private office.

You enter the private office. You know that you will be alone here for at least fifteen minutes. You look around the room, naturally curious about the person you may be working for. . . .

The president's office is carpeted in a short shag in blending colors of olive green, brown, and orange. You sit in one of the two orange club chairs to the left of the doorway. Between the chairs is a low wooden table on which there is an empty green glass ashtray. Next to the ashtray are two books of matches; one is from a Playboy Club and the other is from a local restaurant. On the wall behind you is a picture of an old sailing ship in blues and browns. A rubber plant set in a brown and green woven basket sits against the side wall next to the other chair.

Across from where you are sitting is a large wooden desk, with a black leather desk chair. A framed advertisement for the company hangs on the wall behind the desk, and below that sits a closed briefcase. The black wastebasket next to the wall by the desk chair is full of papers.

You can see most of the objects on the desk. A matching pen-and-pencil stand and a letter opener sit at the front of the desk. To one side of them is a calculator, and next to that is a brass desk lamp. In front of the lamp is a double metal photograph frame with photographs in it. One is of a . . . woman in her thirties with a young boy about eight years old. The other photograph is of a Dalmation dog in a grassy field. In front of the frame is a stack of green file folders. On the desk in front of the desk chair are a few sheets of paper and a felt-tipped pen.

---

* SOURCE: Reprinted from: J. William Pfeiffer and John E. Jones, (Eds.), *A Handbook of Structured Experiences for Human Relations Training*, Vol. VI, San Diego, CA: University Associates, Inc., 1977. Used with permission.

On the other side of the desk is a yellow stoneware mug. In front of it are a leather tabbed book and a legal-sized yellow pad. The book looks as if it is either an address book or an appointment calendar. Beside the yellow pad lies a pile of unopened mail—envelopes of many sizes. And partly on top of the pile and in back of it are half-folded newspapers: the *Wall Street Journal* and the *New York Times*.

Behind the desk and to one side is a credenza on which seven books are lined up. They are *Roget's Thesaurus*, the *Random House Dictionary, Basic Principles of Management, Marketing for Today, Intergroup and Minority Relations, People at Work, You Are What You Eat*, and last year's *World Almanac.* On the far end of the credenza sits a bronze statue; it appears to be of a man sitting with his legs folded in a Yoga position, but it is slightly abstract. In the corner next to the credenza is a philodendron sitting in a brown basket.

There is a window on the far wall, and you get up and go over to look out. Directly in front of the window is a sofa covered in an orange, olive green, and beige print. Two woven throw pillows in brown and beige lie against the arms of the sofa. The draperies at the window behind the sofa are a light beige woven material with an olive green stripe. The view from the window is pleasant: a few tidy shops bordering a small park.

Your gaze turns to the square wooden table next to the sofa. Magazines are scattered in front of a brown ceramic lamp with a beige shade. The magazines are varied: two recent editions of *Time,* and one copy each of *Sports Illustrated, The New Yorker, Psychology Today*, and *Ebony.* Next to the table is the philodendron.

As you turn to walk back to your chair, you notice that the papers on the desk in front of the chair are your resume and that your statement of your sex has been circled with the felt-tipped pen. Since the president may return at any moment, you sit in the orange chair to wait.

Sherlock Room Diagram

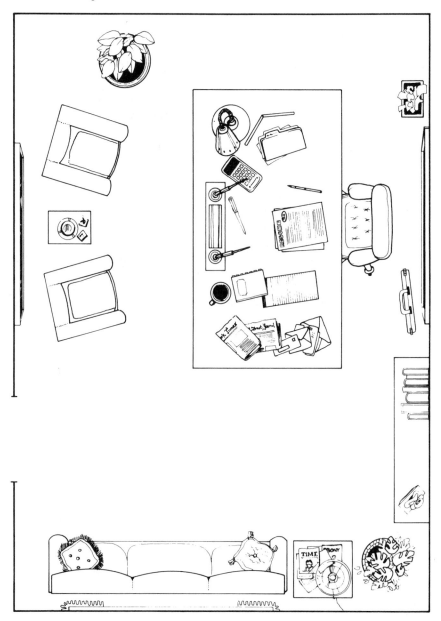

Sherlock Inference Sheet I

Read the Sherlock Room Description Sheet and study the room diagram carefully. Then complete the Sherlock Inference Sheet I as follows:

1. In the left-hand column (Observation) note data from your reading that you think are important clues about the kind of person who occupies the room.
2. In the middle column (Knowledge) note any experiences that you may have had that influence your observation.
3. In the right-hand column (Inference) note whatever conclusions you reach as a result of your observations.

OBSERVATION	KNOWLEDGE	INFERENCE
Raw Data	Experiences that Influence Your Observation	Resultant Perception

Sherlock Inference Sheet II

Most inferences we make about a situation seem to tie together, to make sense. However, if we examine them carefully, there are often some that do not seem to "fit the picture." In forming conclusions, we will find it necessary to identify these aspects. They may indicate that the situation is not as obvious as it seems or that we are on the wrong track, or they may merely be inconsistencies—some of which may be explained later and some of which just happen to exist.

On this sheet, list the consistent inferences you have made in the top section and the inconsistent ones in the bottom section.

CONSISTENT

INCONSISTENT

Discussion Questions

- How do prejudices, assumptions, and self-concepts affect observation?
- How do we resolve inconsistencies in observations, either in our own observations or between our observations and those of others?
- How do we put together a whole image by examining various bits and pieces of data?
- Is it possible to be purely objective in observation? Why?

The Industrial Products Division*

David A. Nadler

Not long ago, the manager of the industrial products division of a manufacturing firm became concerned about what he called "problems of morale" in his organization. Having heard that many organizations use employee surveys as a way of discovering what bothers people, he decided that it might be worthwhile for him to use a questionnaire in his organization. He located a consultant who had previously worked with employee surveys. The manager described the "problems of morale" to the consultant and, after some discussion, the consultant was hired to conduct a survey in the organization.

The consultant decided to use a standardized survey that he had used in many different organizations. He sent copies of the survey and a letter from the division manager to all employees. The employees were to fill out the questionnaire and return it to the consultant. Many employees did not return the questionnaire; however, the consultant felt that a return rate of 50% was good for a mail survey. The consultant had the data from the survey keypunched and run through a computer so that he could analyze the results. He then provided the manager with a large number of descriptive tables and graphs and a short written report which included the consultant's recommendations.

The manager studied the data and the report. All the survey seemed to show was that employees in the lower-level jobs of the organization were dissatisfied; they didn't seem to like their jobs, their supervisors, or their pay. The manager was angry and puzzled. He already knew that these employees were dissatisfied, so that wasn't any news. The survey information presented some interesting points, but he did not know how to use the data. Meanwhile, he heard from members of his staff that since the survey had been administered morale had seemed to drop even lower.

The manager concluded that the survey had not told him anything new. He commented to one of his staff that "Surveys only tell you what you already know. We *know* that there are problems here. What use is there to bringing up those problems over and over again?"

After giving the use of employee surveys some thought, the manager concluded that surveys don't really provide any new insights. In fact, they may even get employees "stirred up" and thinking about problems that they might have been unaware of before. He hoped that any problems caused by the survey would ultimately settle down and decided never to do anything that foolish again.

* SOURCE: David A. Nadler, *Feedback and Organization Development.* © 1977. Addison-Wesley Publishing Company, Inc., Reading, Mass., pp. 3–4. Reprinted with permission.

Northeastern Hospital*

David A. Nadler

Northeastern Hospital is a moderate-sized institution located on the outskirts of a major city. It is a specialized chronic disease and rehabilitation hospital which only admits patients who fall into one of these two categories. Patients with chronic diseases account for about two-thirds of the total number admitted and require long-term care, especially nursing care. Many of these patients have terminal illnesses. Patients requiring rehabilitation are mainly individuals who have suffered from accidents or injuries; following immediate emergency treatment or surgery they are admitted to Northeastern to undergo an intensive program of rehabilitation, guided by physicians, physical therapists, and occupational therapists. The hospital has approximately 300 beds and a total staff of about 600. Northeastern Hospital is affiliated with a religious organization, which is a major source of its financial support.

A few years ago, the top management of Northeastern became concerned about a number of organizational and personnel problems within the hospital. The hospital administrator, Dennis Rettew,[1] was concerned about high levels of employee turnover and absenteeism, an inability to recruit personnel for the nursing staff, poor communications, low levels of morale, and increasing talk of union activity. Rettew was particularly concerned about problems in the nursing service.

During one summer, Rettew began discussions with a consultant affiliated with a nearby university about some of the problems as he saw them. Together they explored the possibility of a consulting relationship. Finally they agreed that the consultant should put together a team of three individuals, also affiliated with the university, to serve as a consulting group for the hospital. This group, which soon became known as the "university team," was to conduct an intensive diagnostic study of the hospital as an organization. This diagnostic work would serve as the basis for additional activities to improve the functioning of the hospital.

In September the university team met with the hospital's executive committee, a group made up of individuals who reported directly to the administrator, including the medical director, the director of nursing, the manager of finance, etc. The university team described their goal of helping the hospital obtain an accurate picture of itself as a human organization so that

* SOURCE: David A. Nadler, *Feedback and Organization Development*, © 1977. Addison-Wesley Publishing Company, Inc., Reading, Mass., pp. 29–34. Reprinted with permission.

[1] Names in this case have been changed to protect confidentiality of those involved.

improvements could be made. The consultants discussed their strategy for diagnosis and feedback of the data.

In the first stage they proposed holding orientation meetings with each hospital work group. One or two members of the team would meet with a work group (for example, a nursing shift on a ward) to introduce themselves, describe the goals of the project, describe the data-collection activities that would occur, and answer any questions that individuals might have.

The second stage would involve data collection. It was proposed that a sample of employees be interviewed in depth, that all employees be given a short questionnaire, that the team have access to hospital records, and that team members be allowed to observe people at work, both on the job and at meetings.

The third stage involved feedback. The consultant team discussed its intention to prepare a written report based on an analysis of the data collected. They also proposed that all employees who participated receive feedback about the results of the study. After some discussion, the executive committee approved the plan. Although some members stated that "this type of study won't tell us anything we don't already know," most agreed that such a project could do little harm and might even be helpful.

In October, the university team began its work. Each team member spent about 15 hours a week at the hospital. As a first step, orientation meetings were held with all work groups. The team members stressed to employees that all data collected would be kept confidential, but that a written report describing the results and making recommendations would be produced after the data had been collected and analyzed. Employees responded well to the team, and many actually seemed anxious to tell team members about problems they had been encountering.

By November, the interviews were started. Rettew had provided the team with an office in the hospital from which to work, and the team began conducting two-hour interviews with a randomly sampled group of employees, representing all levels and departments of the hospital. Approximately 100 people were interviewed. After each interview, the team member who interviewed each employee visited the employee at his or her job location and spent two hours observing the person at work.

In December a standardized questionnaire, which included 30 statements about working in the hospital, was administered. For each statement the employee was to mark one of five possible responses indicating how often the activity described in the statement *actually* occurred. For example, one statement was "supervisors listen to people as well as direct them." For this statement, each employee was to indicate whether this happened *always, frequently, occasionally, seldom,* or *never*. The employee also marked another set of responses for the same statement, this time indicating how often this activity *should* occur.

Data collection continued through January and February, concentrating on direct observation of behavior and analysis of hospital records. Employees were observed at work and at important group meetings. The director of the university team also met weekly with Rettew to report on progress and to obtain help in scheduling additional data-collection activities.

As the team began to put the data together, they identified a number of major problems in the organization. One set of problems was related to top management and the functioning of the executive committee. Members of the executive committee seemed to be confused about their roles and the degree of decision-making authority they had. Many shared the perception that all of the important decisions were made (prior to meetings) by Rettew. Many also perceived that major decisions were made behind closed doors, and that Rettew often made "side deals" with different individuals, promising them special favors or rewards in return for support at the committee meetings. People at this level felt manipulated, confused, and dissatisfied.

Major problems also existed in the nursing service. The director of nursing seemed to be patterning her managerial style after that of Rettew. The nursing staff felt particularly dissatisfied. Nursing supervisors and head nurses felt that they had no authority, while staff nurses complained about a lack of direction and openness by the nursing administration. The structure of the organization was unclear. Nurses were unsure of what their jobs were, whom they should report to, and how decisions were made.

Based on these and other findings, the team put together a 26-page feedback report containing 11 tables and charts which illustrated some of the findings. This report described how the data were collected, and the major patterns observed in the data. It also presented conclusions and recommendations for changes in the hospital. The team chose not to directly address the issue of Rettew's managerial style in the written report, but did make suggestions for changes in the way decisions were made as well as suggestions for the clarification of top managers' roles. The report did, however, include a detailed discussion of problems in the nursing area.

Copies of the report were submitted to Rettew and the executive committee. The team spent several hours working with the group, discussing the findings and the implications of the report and the recommendations made. During these meetings, some committee members reacted positively to the report, while others, such as the director of nursing, became more and more anxious as the discussions continued. During one of the last meetings, the director of nursing walked into the meeting with a thick book on hospital administration under her arm and began attacking the consultant team, claiming that all of their knowledge about organizations was not really applicable to hospitals, because hospitals are different from other kinds of organizations.

A final issue to be discussed with the executive committee was that of feedback. The consultants assumed that copies of their report would be made available to all members of the organization. However, members of the executive committee felt differently. They perceived that the original agreement to give everyone feedback never was intended to guarantee *written* feedback to everyone. Several of the committee members felt that the report could be a "bombshell" and that to make the findings of the report public would create unrest and actually provide ammunition for those employees in nursing who were agitating for a union. Despite the protests of the consultants, the committee refused to allow copies of the report to be distributed to anyone outside of the executive committee. Meetings would be held at which the report could be read aloud, but no copies of the report or the attached charts and tables would be distributed.

In the meantime, the hospital employees were showing an increased interest in the project and were beginning to discuss the long-awaited consultants' report. They awaited the feedback with great anticipation, hoping that the study would bring to the surface many important problems that could then be solved.

In April, a series of feedback meetings were held in the hospital. The executive committee insisted on scheduling the meetings because of the implications of having large numbers of employees away from their jobs at one time. Six different meetings, each including 60 to 100 people from different work units, were held. The consultants read the report to each group, presenting charts and graphs using overhead projections; they then entertained questions and discussion from each group. Members of the executive committee were present (at the rear of the room) for all meetings.

During the first few meetings there was a great deal of discussion, and many questions were asked about why the report was not distributed and what would happen after the meetings. The executive committee members responded, saying that the executive committee would consider the report and its recommendations and would take appropriate action. As the meetings progressed, participation decreased. A rumor developed that people who spoke up at the meetings would "pay for it" later, once the consultants had left. The final meetings were characterized by a lack of employee participation—few questions and little discussion—and discouragement on the part of employees.

The executive committee, in its final meeting with the consultants, thanked them for doing a thorough job and assured them that their recommendations would be seriously considered.

Six months later one of the consultants encountered a group of nurses from Northeastern Hospital on their day off. Upon inquiring about the project, the consultant found that nothing concrete had happened after the university team left and that a number of the more vocal nurses in the service had since left the hospital for other jobs.

An Introduction to Gathering Data*

Edgar H. Schein

We will next discuss data-gathering as a separate stage, but I must emphasize most strongly the point that data-gathering and intervention occur simultaneously throughout the entire consultative process. Every decision to observe something, or to ask a question, or to meet with someone constitutes an intervention into the ongoing organizational process. The consultant cannot, therefore, avoid or escape taking the responsibility for the kind of data-gathering method he uses. If the method is not congruent with his overall values, and if it does not meet the standards for an acceptable intervention, it should not be used.

The point is worth belaboring because all of the traditional consultation models, as well as the models of how to do research on organizations, make the glib assumption that one gathers data prior to intervening; that one observes, interviews, and surveys, *then* makes a diagnosis, and *then* suggests interventions or remedial steps.

From the point of view of P-C this is an inaccurate and dangerous assumption. It is inaccurate because one can clearly demonstrate that the process of being studied influences the parties being studied. If I interview someone about his organization, the very questions I ask give the respondent ideas he never had before. The very process of formulating his own answers gives him points of view which he may never have thought of before. The assumption is also dangerous because the various respondents who have been interviewed, surveyed, or studied may, by virtue of this common experience, band together and decide on their own what kind of action they would like to see. While the researcher-consultant is off analyzing his data, the respondents are busy changing the organization or generating demands which their boss may be quite unprepared for.

What then is the correct assumption, and what are its implications? The correct assumption is that *every act on the part of the process consultant constitutes an intervention*, even the initial act of deciding to work with the organization. The very fact of having asked for help and having had someone accept some responsibility for helping, changes the perceptions and attitudes of some members of the organization. The process consultant cannot ignore these

* SOURCE: Edgar H. Schein, *Process Consultation.* © 1969. Addison-Wesley Publishing Company, Inc., Reading, Mass., pp. 97–101. Reprinted with permission.

changes. He must anticipate them and learn to make them work toward the ultimate goals defined.

The main implication of this latter assumption is that the process consultant must think through everything he does in terms of its probable impact on the organization. He must assume that all of his behavior is an intervention of one sort or another. Finally, he must use data-gathering methods which, at the same time, will constitute valid and useful interventions.

METHODS OF DATA GATHERING

Basically the consultant has only three different methods by which he can gather data:

1. direct observation;
2. individual or group interviews;
3. questionnaires or some other survey instrument to be filled out.

I have already indicated that the third method is too impersonal and too much at variance with P-C assumptions to be useful in the early stages of a P-C project. It may become useful if the number of people to be surveyed is rather large and if the managers with whom the consultant is working fully understand the implications involved in taking a survey.

For early data-gathering the choice is then reduced to observation and/or interview. In my own experience I have found that a combination of these techniques is optimal. I need a certain amount of observation in order to know what kinds of issues should be brought up in interviews, but I need some preliminary interviews in order to know whom and what to observe.

These criteria usually lead to a top-down kind of strategy. I start with the data provided by the contact client. The exploratory meeting is usually an opportunity to gather data in a group-interview setting.

. . . [T]he next step is often an interview of one or more of the *senior* people who will be involved in the project. Their consent must be obtained to do any observation of them in interaction with their group. Regular group members are usually interviewed only after one or two meetings during which I have observed what kinds of issues are being discussed and what kinds of problems exist within the group.

Once a relationship has been formed with some key group in the organization, new projects develop which involve new settings, but the *methods* of gathering data in the new settings are essentially the same. For example, one of the managers of the original group may feel that he would like to know how the members of his own staff group feel about the organization and the work setting. He and I may then plan a series of interviews of his subordinates, leading to a series of feedback meetings. This procedure will not be initiated, however, until the manager has obtained the support and consent of his subordinates and until they too feel that I can be trusted. If it is not convenient for me to meet all of them and/or observe their meetings, a relatively greater burden falls on the manager to persuade his subordinates to participate; but the project cannot proceed until the subordinates genuinely agree.

In this connection, an important criterion for extending a data-gathering method is that the manager who would like to use it should himself have participated in an earlier project. If the manager has been interviewed by me and has heard what kind of feedback I give after a series of interviews, he is in a much better position to decide whether or not such a technique would be useful in his group, and is better equipped to explain to his subordinates what the procedure will be like.

No data-gathering method is right or wrong in the abstract. Whether or not it is appropriate and useful can be judged only from earlier observations and interviews. In a way the entire P-C project must always be viewed as an unfolding series of events where subsequent events can only be predicted from earlier events. The project should be planned in a general way, but the issues that come up in groups are hard to predict, and some of the most important ones are those for which the least planning was done.

What should be the content of interviews or surveys? . . . What does he look for when he is interviewing and/or what kinds of questions does he build into a questionnaire? The answer is that it depends very much on the nature of the problem which is initially presented to the consultant and on his early observations.

The common theme in all of these data-gathering approaches is a concern with organizational relationships and perceptions of organizational processes. The specific questions vary, but the general area is the same. The other common thread is a concern with organizational effectiveness. I always attempt to determine what kinds of things are helping to make the person, group, or unit more effective, and what kinds of things are undermining or hindering effectiveness. My assumption would be that both sets of factors are always present in any organization.

Having identified the kinds of content areas which I explore in interviews, I would like to close the loop to the earlier discussion of the kind of interventions I make when I interview somebody. For example, in the interview itself, my own method of asking questions and the content of what I ask will project a certain image of me. If I want to establish a collaborative, helping relationship with the person being interviewed, I must behave in a manner congruent with such a relationship. This means I cannot play the role of the psychologist who asks obscure questions upon which I then will place "secret" interpretations. My questions have to be understandable, relevant, meaningful, and open. The respondent should be able to interpret his own answers. There should be no trick questions, hidden meanings, obscure interpretations, or the like.

The content of the questions should be self-evidently relevant. If I am concerned about improving organizational effectiveness, then I should ask about it. If I am concerned with improvement, I should ask about those things that are going well, in addition to those which are going poorly.

The questions can push the respondent into areas he might not ordinarily think to mention, provided they are relevant and provided the consultant senses a willingness on the part of the respondent to enter into those areas. For example, in all of the cases mentioned, I asked quite probing questions about how the decision was made to use a consultant, the attitudes expressed by members toward my coming in, what they thought are my particular qualifications for the job, where there might be tension over having a consultant in, and so on. As I mentioned earlier, if the contact client is unwilling to deal with these areas openly in the early discussions, I am likely to be cautious about becoming involved. Once I am working within the organization, unwillingness to deal with areas such as these would be interpreted by me as caution on the respondent's part, and it would be up to me to try to determine what the reasons for the caution were.

The kind of question one asks also puts new ideas into the head of the respondent. For example, I often ask what kind of career planning a person has engaged in with others in the organization. The answer often is "none," but a secondary answer which comes up later in the interview is often "I wonder why no one has sat down with me to talk about my career," or "maybe I should go have a talk with my boss about my future in the company." If I ask a person to describe the network of others with whom he must deal in order to get his job done, he often realizes for the first time what this network is like and why he has problems of keeping up with his job. In other words, the interview can be a powerful tool of influence and education, and the process consultant must consider when and how to use it for influence purposes.

In summary, there are basically three kinds of data-gathering methods: observation, interview, and questionnaire. Because any one of the methods is some kind of intervention into organizational process, the consultant must choose a method which will be most congruent with the values underlying P-C and with the general goals of the P-C project. The way he gathers data and the kinds of question he asks gives the consultant an opportunity to intervene constructively.

Structured Naturalistic Observation*

D. N. T. Perkins, D. A. Nadler
and M. D. Hanlon

Perkins et al. (1981) developed a guide for making observations in natural settings—in factories and offices, as well as in smaller group settings. . . .

THE GENERAL OBSERVATION FORM

Structured naturalistic observation assumes a relatively skilled observer who is familiar with concepts and patterns of organizational behavior. The observer is not highly limited in terms of *what* to observe, but a specific structure is provided for *communicating* what has been observed. This structure is necessary if the observational record is to be made up of comparable data in a retrievable form.

The issue here is how to structure the communication of what has been observed. Typically, if one were to observe a series of activities involving people and report what was seen, the report would include various kinds of information. It is likely that it would mention specific activities or behaviors that occurred. These would be tangible and discrete occurrences, and it would be possible to verify whether or not they did occur as described, especially if several observers were present or if the sequence were videotaped. On the other hand, the report would probably be more than a listing of tangible events. It might include attempts by the observer to make sense of what was seen, to identify patterns, to determine causes and effects, and so on. Of course, these would be speculative. The observational record also might reflect the feelings that the observer had while watching the activity or behavior. If, for example, the observer found one of the people being observed to be personally distasteful, it could influence how that person's behavior is described or explained. The observer, therefore, communicates some perceptions of tangible events, some interpretations of what those events mean, and some feelings he or she experienced during the period of observation. The problem is that these are frequently interwoven, and it is difficult to evaluate the different types of information.

The core of the observation method is the general observation form

* SOURCE: J. E. Jones & J. W. Pfeiffer (eds.). *The 1981 Annual Handbook for Group Facilitators.* San Diego, CA: University Associates, 1981. Used with permission.

(see Figure 1), which includes five categories for recording observations as well as space for various identifying and coding information. The first category is *overview of the event*, a relatively brief summary of the major activities, behaviors, occurrences, etc., that happened during the observation period. Although usually fairly short, it includes enough information so that someone analyzing a series of observations could decide whether to read further or to go on to another recorded observation. Thus, this overview is functionally similar to a table of contents.

The second category is *detailed observations*. This section is the central component of the observation instrument and is intended to provide the first level of information (perceptions). It is a detailed record of what occurred during the observation period and usually is in chronological order. Here it is important to limit the information to that which is factual, i.e., tangible, discrete events that could be verified by other observers or by visual record. It is important to avoid interpretation or causal attribution in this section. The ultimate test of the adequacy of the data in this section might be to ask the observer if he or she would be willing to show the section to the individuals being observed for purposes of verification. If the detailed observations are free of interpretation or observer affect, the information could—in theory— be shown to those involved and verified without concern about misinterpretation.

The third section of the observation form is for *interpretations*. Here the observer is called on to make statements that attempt to make sense of the specific activities and behaviors that have been observed. These are, in fact, propositions or hypotheses that cannot be verified immediately but that can guide future data collection by observation as well as data collection by other methods. Interpretations might include attempts to identify patterns of behavior, attributions concerning the causes of behavior or the factors that motivate the behavior, speculation about the nature and meaning of events, and so on. Ideally, interpretations should be propositions, that is, they should be tentative, and, thus, testable. They might therefore be recorded as questions or hypotheses.

The fourth section, *observer feelings*, concerns the personal reactions of the observer to the events that have been observed. They are the observer's specific affective reactions to what is going on. These reactions tend to influence how choices are made about what behavior to observe and how interpretations are developed. Two purposes are achieved by making these feelings explicit. First, the observer may become more aware of the feelings he or she has and thus more able to correct for their potential bias. Second, others who are using the observational record can consider the observer's feelings in qualifying the data.

The final category is *attachments*. Frequently the observer has access to supporting documents or other information relevant to the behavior or activity being observed. The range of possible attachments is large, and could include meeting agendas, critical memos, correspondence, membership lists, other observational instruments used during the event, handouts from meetings,

Location _____   Circumstances _____

Observer _____   Event _____

Date & Time _____   Things being observed _____

_____

Title:_____

Overview of the event:

Detailed observations:

Interpretations:

Observer's feelings:

Figure 1: A general observation form.

maps, floor plans, or sketches. These should be physically attached to the observation to which they are relevant.

The observer might write a tentative outline, or overview before the activity and then make detailed notes during the period of observation. Separate sheets would be used to record interpretations and observer feelings during the observation itself, with these sheets becoming the last pages of the observation report. Observers often have found it useful to type up the observations as soon as possible after the actual observation period, and the information is then put into the order specified on the form. For an observation of one or two hours, the written observation form could be from five to ten typewritten pages.

CODING AND IDENTIFICATION OF OBSERVATIONS

A major problem in the use of observational data is analysis. If data are to be used for analytic purposes, they need to be identified (labeled and coded) on the general information form so that they can be retrieved and so that specific observations can be related to variables in a conceptual or analytic framework. This approach is best used when some conceptual framework is employed to guide the observations; however, it can be used with an inductive approach in which categories and variables for observation are developed from the data during the course of the study.

A variety of identification and coding data are possible. First, each observation is given a descriptive *title*. This title, while brief, should include enough information so that the observation is easily identified. For example, an observation might be entitled, "Fourth Meeting of the Executive Committee, NPH Project," with the date indicated elsewhere.

Within each setting, it is possible to observe a number of different *events*. Events are major classes of behavior or activity that occur in the setting. For example, an observation of the weekly management team of the plant might be comprised of events that occur frequently, such as weekly staff meetings or monthly performance reviews. In most cases, there will be observations of events that do not fit into any pattern, and these typically are labeled "on-going behavior."

The detailed observations and interpretations noted on the general observation form also can be coded in another way. This third level of coding involves labeling the observations in terms of the variables to which the behaviors or activities observed are relevant. For example, the monthly staff meetings of the top-management group might be coded for "leadership style" or for "conflict resolution" or for "decision making." Variables for coding can be obtained from different sources. In some cases a specific list of variables derived from a conceptual or theoretical framework might be used. In other cases, classes of variables might be developed as the observation proceeds. For example, specific themes that emerge repeatedly in observations might be identified and then used to code existing, subsequent, and prior observations.

When combined with the basic identification (title, site, observer, and date/time), this three-level scheme (setting, event, and other variables) enables full identification and retrieval of observations. Each observation thus becomes a unique piece of information within the larger data set.

REFERENCE

PERKINS, D. N. T., NADLER, D. A., and HANLON, M. D. (1981). A method for structured naturalistic observation of organizational behavior. In J. E. Jones and J. W. Pfeiffer (Eds.), *The 1981 annual handbook for group facilitators*. San Diego, Calif.: University Associates.

From "Strategy for Watching"*

Leonard Schatzman
and Anselm L. Strauss

FIRST IMPRESSIONS

Our discussions of watching will be rather arbitrarily and artificially separated from listening, because each has some unique aspects bearing upon the gathering of data. Yet, we know that watching and listening are closely linked; the researcher is using all his senses simultaneously and also thinking (analyzing). In the field, the "input" of experience is exceedingly high, and however selectively it may be received through a sensory system, there is an internal interchange and a reflective transformation of these experiences. Awareness of this experiential input is particularly apparent to the researcher in the first hours of observation; hence he will take advantage of his initial sensitivities because he knows that within a short time they may be significantly lost to familiarity and to adjustment quite as they have long since been lost to persons indigenous to the places that he visits. First observations—indeed, merely "sensings," of sights, sounds, smells, touch and even of taste—form a special class of experience. Although at first these experiences may be little more than impressions—a product derived as much from the observer as from the observed—they often have considerable value for later description and analysis.

The researcher's awareness of and capitalization on his sensitivity is perhaps his most valued resource and tool for discovery. Let us look at four related components of sensitivity. First, people who work at anything for relatively long periods lose sensitivity to common, recurrent experiences and tend to thrust them into the background, if for no other reason than that they get in the way of whatever else they are immediately sensitive to. This is why any outsider (researcher or other) has some advantage in the observation and analysis of events and structures; he can see properties "lost" to insiders, relate them to still other properties, and thereby discover something of value to theory or to his hosts.

Second, far from depending upon only the first moments of "culture shock" for his descriptive and analytic stimulation, *the researcher strives to maintain a continuing "de novo" sensitivity and appreciation of all events.* Ironically, his very effort to become selective runs counter to this principle. Yet, generally a loss in sensitivity, such as boredom, represents a failure of active relations between

* SOURCE: Leonard Schatzman and Anselm L. Strauss, *Field Research: Strategies for a Natural Sociology.* © 1973, pp. 52–64. Reprinted by permission of Prentice-Hall, Inc., Englewood Cliffs, N.J.

the observer and the observed; hence the researcher seeks to make capital of even the most ordinary and repetitive events, either to wrest something new from them or to use them to test an idea. It helps also to be visiting or staying at more than one sub-site simultaneously, for this sharpens contrast and tends to make the researcher wonder more about the seemingly familiar.

Third, *the researcher is particularly sensitive to his own interpreted experience.* Even the most subtle of his own surprises—whether of delight or disappointment, but especially of incomprehensibility—is a sign that some expectation or hypothesis of his has been altered or even shattered. He asks himself "why," and pursues the import of his own response through active inquiry. This also is how the researcher maintains his necessary state of wonder and excitement even though his substantive materials may seem most mundane.

Fourth, *the researcher also does his best to capitalize on whatever sensitivities may be yielded by his past experiences,* of whatever kind. While these experiences (transposed too liberally or literally to the current scene) may lead him astray, initially they can be a rich source of sensitivities whose validity can later be checked upon. At first those sensitivities only have the status of hypotheses, but possibly fruitful ones. To entirely repress past experiences and their associated observational consequences is neither possible nor useful for the researcher.

GROUNDS FOR WATCHING

Presenting Properties

These last comments especially lead to a new problem: to what will the researcher attend, and how does he decide which of his new and varied observations and experiences might or should constitute his data? Both practically and technically, no observation or experience becomes a datum until it can be put to use as background or context, as a discovered property or feature of a scene, or as a detail which helps clarify or define a class of events. At first, because the researcher will not know how he will eventually code or sort out his many observations, he will probably record considerably more than he will ever use directly. He knows, more intuitively than by design, that many events observed early will "achieve" meaning at a later time. For this reason, and because at this stage he wants to do more "sponging up" (of sights and sounds) than "spewing out" (of interpretations), his observations are governed appreciably by events that naturally present themselves. He attends to people: their numbers, dress, general deportment, and humor. He attends to physical setting: equipment, space, wall posters, and even noise levels. He attends to events or activities: work, play, the vigor of engagement, arguments and discussions, how many work alone or in teams. All these and more are noted, with many of their qualitative and quantitative attributes. . . .

. . . [O]ur model researcher . . . is quite content . . . to experience the ambience of the scene. He has great patience, as well as a tolerance for ambiguity and for his own immediate ignorance. Far from acting like a scientist and telling himself he is one, he is genuinely busy being a learner—indeed, a novice—and perhaps a participant. . . . [T]he researcher may . . . concern himself simply with decisions on whether to stand, sit, or move about for a better look-see. . . . Also, he is taking the measure of emerging properties which will affect his subsequent operations: Are the people shy or afraid? How closely can he station himself to an activity? How actively or penetratingly, at this time, can he raise questions about what he sees? Thus, the selectivity of his perceptions is grounded in different perspectives and methodological needs, and from time to time he shifts these grounds with considerable control. . . . [W]e are at a loss here in describing how any researcher may sequence his observation. For fear that readers may try to seize upon *our* reference to sequencing and thus deduce a pattern—and probably spoil their own native senses of timing and sequencing—we shall simply list some of the many grounds for observation, not attempting to establish a logical sequence for their use.

In addition to the most existential grounds (presenting properties) for observational selection, others command attention: representativeness, perspective, framework, listening, theoretical leads, and verification.

Representativeness is embodied in the plans for sampling which the researcher has already made. This ground provides not only a general basis for observational selection but a defense against input-flooding, whimsical observation, or fruitless and unwitting bias. . . .

Perspective is a relatively difficult concept to deal with; many researchers often fail to make a clear distinction between it and theoretical framework. Taken by itself—that is, without the often used prefix "theoretical"—it opens to us an almost limitless land of "angles," for perspective refers to an *angle of observation*. Like it or not, man is condemned to viewing from one (or more) perspectives or angles, as reality is infinitely complex and no observer can see it all. In "truth," all observation then takes on a biased hue. For the field researcher, the mattter of bias is accepted; his concern is directed at the fruitfulness of observation from any given angle. Given intelligence and skill adequate to the task, he will frequently shift from one angle of observation to another, and assess their relative value to his work. Thus, his observations, though biased, are certainly witting (understood and controlled), and often fruitful of results for his research.

The difficulty in defining perspective is compounded by the fact that several perspectives can be used simultaneously: the perspective of a stated sub-unit or any single actor, of the leadership or the entire organization, and so on. Then, there are perspectives inherent in the observer that probably relate closely to his personal view of man and human life as tragic, humorous, ridiculous, pathetic, and the like. These too will undoubtedly influence not only what he will attend to, but how he will conceptualize. Also, the researcher can look at his activities artistically, scientifically, or "philosophically," and these break down into sub-perspectives. Within the scientific perspective further shifts can be made; he can observe as an economist, political scientist, or anthropologist. What he sees from each of these will significantly vary from the others. Sometimes it helps—especially if events seem too ordinary or situations grow too rapidly familiar—deliberately to adopt one or another of such perspectives as noted above.

Framework. When one adds the concept "theoretical" to that of perspective, he has added another element of control that is rooted in a general theory or network of mutually supporting theories. A set of interrelated concepts is thereby provided that constitutes an additional perspective and provides a framework for conceptual entrée. A relatively encompassing structure of concepts helps organize experience and provides many research questions. From our own theoretical framework, we cannot imagine any noteworthy observations occurring without a minimal set of social science categories.... Such concepts do not necessarily predispose the observer to the direct use or test of any given theory; rather, they provide only some initial order for observing activities that might otherwise seem chaotic. Hopefully, these categories will, in time, move into the background as they are supplemented, or preferably supplanted, by grounded concepts more descriptive and analytic of the activities actually observed.

Just a few comments are necessary to show the relation between *listening* and watching. Even the most astute watching, by itself, will yield limited and often questionable results, particularly because of the complexity and unfamiliarity of the new site, and the limited time available for watching. No observer can escape the necessity of applying categories which identify and give meaning to whatever he is observing. Without verbal indicators from others, he must supply them for himself. Even were he well read on the subject under study, unless his categories were grounded in situations practically identical to those under observation, he is likely to be in trouble. Of course, he might be satisfied with a very superficial order of description; but even then he would probably not enjoy an adequate test of his description. He would tend to project his own "feelings" about the situation into his description and to impute inadquate or even incorrect motives to the people whom he has observed.

Also, watching by itself is quite uneconomical in the expenditure of time when compared to listening; probably this is why there are so many field interviews studies of human situations and few, if any, done by watching alone. Yet, once verbal indicators are given to the observer, particularly by persons who normally act in the given situation, the gain from watching after even a few remarks is considerable. For example, the native actor provides a corrective to designation and meaning: "But the nurse is not just playing cards with the patient, she is making contact, establishing trust, and forming a meaningful relationship with the patient." Another example, this one bearing upon an observation missed: "But we do take into account the patient's physical health; each is given an examination at the time of admission." Such verbal comments provide names for things, indicate relationships between them, reveal sequences and presumed causal or logical connections, and provide meaningful context.

They tell the observer where and when to look, what precisely to look for; and generally make his observations more astute. Sophistication enables the observer to ask more intelligent and incisive questions, and his observation gains accordingly.

Theoretical Leads

When the researcher enters the field, he harbors, wittingly or not, many expectations, conjectures, and hypotheses which provide him with thought and directives on what to look for and to ask about. He has had a good start if he is at all aware of some of these hypotheses. But soon, many of these are disposed of, either because they prove false or lose significance. Simultaneously the researcher is developing new hypotheses, as he identifies the properties of the scene and attempts to relate them variously to each other; he begins, thereby, to develop propositions about what he sees and hears. These propositions, however tentative, constitute sets of hypotheses which function as leads to still other observations—not necessarily "new" ones, but possibly repeats from another perspective—since he is now asking different sorts of questions. Likewise, he is now looking for, or at, things that he had missed just previously, for without the new lead he simply did not see something that is now important to him. However the researcher may deal with these leads, as commands or enticements, he has to take them into account and reorder at least some of his watching operations. This is what observation in the context of discovery is all about.

The need for *verification* and its effect upon watching operations ought to be quite obvious. In the back of his mind, if not in the forefront, the researcher is concerned with the validity of his observations. . . .

WATCHING AS ACTIVE PRESENCE

The presence of a stranger, particularly an observer, in a natural human situation introduces some measure of disturbance in the scene. . . . [A] disturbance occasioned by the presence of the observer need not be seen in a negative light; the "disturbance" may (and often does) prove catalytic by way of revealing aspects of organizational life not easily discovered otherwise. No disturbance— not even an error of deportment—is catastrophic or useless unless it is so bad that the researcher is forced to abandon his research at the site. What this suggests is that the researcher's presence, and the variety of activity options available to him, can be immensely strategic when intelligently controlled, paced, and processed.

. . . . [W]e shall simply list some options according to a logical progression of the researcher's involvement in the observed situation.

Watching From Outside

First, the field researcher remains physically outside the situation. . . . But observing without being observed is virtually impossible to manage in natural social settings. The need to sit in on relatively private discussions, and to ask questions, precludes this tactic as a reasonable option.

Passive Presence

Second, the field researcher is present in the situation but decides to observe passively. He does not enter into interaction with participants and avoids as much as possible obtruding himself into the event. For example, he may sit in the corner of a room and not enter into conversation. The flow of events is not appreciably influenced by his activity (although his sheer physical presence may do so). This is an acceptable option, particularly in the early stages of research, also for short spans of time when witnessing events which particularly preoccupy the hosts, or indicate special symbolic importance to them. . . . But this option poses some dangers: the spectre of a relatively impassive observer whether or not taking notes, barely showing appropriate affect or active curiosity, and offering few if any cues as to what he is "really up to," can be very disturbing to the hosts. This option cannot be carried on indefinitely and universally for all situations. For their own comfort, even in the first periods of observation, the hosts will attempt to involve the observer; to induce him to reveal his true interests and particularly, his person. They want to be observed by a partly known person, not by a stranger.

Limited Interaction

Third, the researcher engages in minimal, clarifying interaction. In this type of situation, the observer does not set himself apart from the participants. His interventions in the flow of interaction are confined mainly to seeking clarification and the meaning of ongoing events. He does not attempt to direct interaction into channels of his own choosing. This type of activity has two distinct advantages: it gets at meaning, and it meets the expectations of the hosts insofar as the researcher is not only an observer, but is revealed as personable and interested; through his comments or questions his apparent agenda is indicated. The agenda is understandable and appears appropriate; therefore, the observer can be thought of as at least "kind of" a member of the group. This allows them quickly to minimize, even temporarily forget his presence, and thus return the situation nearly to "normal." The option is especially useful when the researcher is wary of intruding his person too obviously, when people are just too busy, or where there is danger to someone in his intruding. (For instance, observations made during surgical operations— in a study of medical students, interns and residents—necessarily had to be made, especially at first, with careful attention to placing oneself where one could not possibly get in the way of the staff. Only later, with more experience in this busy and sometimes tense setting, and with much more trust on the part of the staff, was the researcher invited to "step right up and watch," even ask questions, by the chief surgeon.)

Active Control

Fourth, the researcher actively controls interaction along lines designed to provide particular information bearing upon the research. The archetype of this option is the formal interview. As applied to an ongoing situation, the researcher engages in active conversation, not only posing general questions but provocative or challenging ones. There are many meetings and other forms of encounter which can, for a time, or in part, be "usurped" to meet the researcher's need for understanding, beyond what may be revealed on the level of cliché and platitude. The researcher is judiciously directive, albeit warm and positive. If well controlled, this level of participant observation is very stimulating for researcher and hosts alike; for without fear or threat present, an intellectual colleagueship is in formation. . . .

THE OBSERVER IS OBSERVED

Insofar as the researcher is present and active, he himself is subject to observation, and this observation can be expected to affect his work. We have more in mind than deportment in its narrow sense. Deportment can be correct, but yet quite inappropriate: as noted earlier the researcher can sit quietly throughout an entire meeting while the group performs its tasks, yet be so impassive—that is, without vocal or facial expression—as to be disconcerting to the group. Moreover, such behavior would fail to generate data, as well as significantly alter a natural scene. Good deportment alone is not enough. Indeed, for action to be appropriate it must also be functional to the research effort. This last point calls for elaboration, at the risk of breaking the main line of discussion.

The researcher as an observed person provides a seeming paradox. His presence changes the scene, but any failure by him to act appropriately also changes the scene. The question is, What is the real scene which is threatened with change? Who can tell? Granted, in a common-sense way, the observer does not *want* to disturb whatever he would want to see occur naturally, yet "occurrence" is a central property of process, and all the "variables" in a situation are *occurrences in process*, not "things" that would otherwise be there unless disturbed. The field researcher knows experientially that the scenes he is observing are not in all features exactly like others he has observed. More important, he knows that over time they naturally change. He can assume they would have changed without his presence. The paradoxical issue of change and not changed represents a philosophical problem that, perhaps, cannot be genuinely solved, and certainly should preoccupy neither us nor our model fieldworker.

The latter, then, has no other recourse than to act as a field researcher might be expected to act. . . . Taking care not to overact (and we must leave a definition of this to the reader), the researcher asks questions, raises issues, even provides humor occasionally, and takes notes openly on proper occasions. In short, he not only acts the observer, but acts humanly. Within this context, he takes the roles of the others towards himself and from this, as well as from his understanding of his research requirements, organizes his actions. It follows that the researcher's actions, while socially appropriate, also are operationally catalytic and tactical. . . . The data that are obtained through the observer's judicious but active intervention might not actually be readily available to perception and conception were he *not* actively there. For example, the careers or the ideologies of the hosts are not demonstrably there without his being there; they are created or revealed in and through the interaction of the hosts with the observer.

Interviewing*

Edgar H. Schein

David Rioch ... was a brilliant clinician who believed that the way you should pursue science was through very good taxonomic research. He went out and looked at things. He also was very good at interviewing. ... He said if you really want to find out something from a person, don't ask him about it. Get him to talk chronologically and you will soon find out what you want to know. I have always used that principle in data gathering. If you ask people to tell you historically where they are, they soon tell you about their values, their aims, and their goals. If you asked them directly, "What are your values?" they would block; even if they wanted to tell you, they really couldn't because the brain isn't organized that way. ... Their thoughts are organized chronologically; if you don't tap into them that way, the person doesn't remember or becomes blocked in unanticipated ways.

* SOURCE: Excerpt from "Marshall Sashkin Interviews Edgar Schein, Organizational Psychologist," *Group and Organization Studies*, 4 (December 1979), 400–417.

Active Listening and Questioning*

Marshall Sashkin
and William C. Morris

Listening is usually considered a passive state in which you are the "receptacle" of information and your job is merely to try to concentrate on the message and understand it. Actually, effective listening is active, not passive, and requires skill and practice. To understand and learn effective listening skills, we must break them down into their smallest components.

The first "chunk" of listening skill is called *attending*. This consists of postural, visual, and nonverbal indicators that show you are really paying attention to the other person. Three specific behavioral skill elements are characteristic of attending. First is physical body *posture*, such as leaning forward in an open, accepting, neutral position (such as arms *un*crossed). When sitting "bolt upright" in a chair, legs and arms crossed, one displays the exact opposite of attending. The second behavioral element involves *eye contact*. When you look away from the person who is talking, you are not displaying attending behavior. This doesn't mean you should "stare down" the other person, just that you must regularly let your eyes make contact. Finally, some vocal (but nonverbal) expressions *encourage* the other person to keep talking—things like a nod of your head, a smile, or saying, "Um-hmm." These expressions show the other person that you want to hear more. We all know how to be attentive, but we are often lazy or sloppy about doing so. It is helpful to remind yourself to apply attending skills, and even to practice them occasionally.

The second group of skill elements can be called *active listening*, which is much less common than attending. Active listening includes three subskills. The first, simple *repetition*, is used only to clarify what you did not hear—the signal—or are not sure you heard correctly. This is as far as most people go with listening skill, and it is not adequate. The second element involves *paraphrasing*, or repeating in your own words what the other person said. This lets you determine whether or not you correctly interpreted the meaning of what the other person said. Correct paraphrasing requires more active involvement in the listening process than simple repetition, but it is a skill that is relatively easy to learn. The third and most difficult skill element is *listening for feelings* and restating the feeling that the other person has expressed. This skill

* SOURCE: Marshall Sashkin and William C. Morris, *Organizational Behavior: Concepts and Experiences* (Reston, Va.: Reston, © 1984), pp. 140–142. Reprinted by permission of Prentice-Hall, Inc., Englewood Cliffs, N.J.

is difficult to develop for two reasons: first, you must restate the other person's feelings in your own words, not just repeat the term the other person used; and second, you must often figure out just what the other person's feeling is. Sometimes this is obvious, as it is, for example, when someone is very angry and yelling or is very sad and crying. Often, however, our feelings are more subtle and less overt parts of the message. Moreover, you must figure out how to restate the feeling without appearing to be negative or hostile, and this may take some tact. The other person might become very offended if you said, "You seem to feel very jealous of Paul now that he got the promotion and you didn't." If you are accurate, the other person might be even more offended! A better way to state this person's feeling would be, "You feel pretty disappointed at losing that promotion to Paul." This would be better, even if it is a little less accurate than had you labeled the feeling as envy or jealousy.

Paraphrasing combined with listening for feelings is at the heart of active listening. This is the only way to make certain that one person has correctly understood what another person meant. Consider: John says, "The Greenway project is *way* overdue!" What does he mean? Does he mean, "We're in trouble and I'm upset!"? Does he mean, "The project leader is in for trouble!"? Or does he mean, "Our schedule is all fouled up and that upsets me!"? To find out, you might say, "You feel concerned that we are so far off our scheduled project deadlines." Or, you might say, "You seem distressed that we haven't gotten out Greenway on time." These or a wide range of other active listening responses would be equally effective; all serve the same purpose: letting the other person know what you heard and checking for accuracy. John might respond, "Right!" Or, he might say, "No, it's not the overall schedule, it's this client who will probably raise hell with division management!" In one sense it doesn't really matter, because whatever John's response is, you will now know for certain what he really meant.

Of course, your response could have been, "What do you mean by that, John?" John might then respond with a clarification—but his clarification might still leave *you* in the dark! How often has that happened to you? Alternatively, John might say, "Didn't I just *say* that we're way overdue!?" By rephrasing the content and feeling stated in John's message, you show that you are trying to listen for understanding, that you are willing to go halfway with the other person to try to really hear what was said. That is why this is called active listening, because the listener becomes an active participant in the communication process instead of assuming the typical passive role.

A conversation composed only of active listening responses would be very dull. In fact, it would probably be hard to keep such a conversation going for very long, since the parties would quickly begin to repeat what each other had said and felt over and over again. Active listening is useful for specific purposes, not for general conversation. The major purpose is to provide a special kind of feedback, so that the sender knows for sure that the message was heard correctly. Another reason for using active listening is to get the other person to "open up" so that a problem or issue can be explored in depth.

People are more likely to be open when they see that you are trying actively to understand them, without being a judge. Still another use for active listening is to let the other person hear and think over what he is really saying. Sometimes we are surprised by our own comments, when we actually listen to what we said!

The logical follow-up to active listening would be questions, comments, or feedback. Active listening facilitates the communication process, but it is not itself a *model* of this process.

QUESTIONING

Although "everyone" basically knows how to ask questions, *effective* questioning that helps the communication process along is a skill that must be learned and practiced. In the formal interview, questioning is even more than a skill; it can be an art. For our purposes, however, it is enough to be able to understand the different levels of questions, from completely open to completely closed, and to be able to ask a question at whatever level seems appropriate.

Far too many questions are of the completely closed type: "Do you like chocolate ice cream?" Such questions allow only two answers, yes or no (a third possibility is the nonanswer, "I don't know" or "I'm not sure"). In other words, we do not generally use the entire *range* of question types available to us, nor do we stop to decide what type of a question is appropriate in a given situation. At the opposite extreme is the completely open question: "Can you tell me about that?" "What do you think?" This is probably the second most common type of question. Very often it imposes too little structure on the other person's response, which is not really any better for gaining information than the overstructuredness of the completely closed question.

The several intermediate levels of question structure are much more useful than either of the above extremes because they focus the response but do not limit it so much that the important information will be missed. The simplest way of making a question more effective is to limit it to a specific topic or issue: "Tell me about the quality of communication in this company." Going a step further, you can limit the response—without being overly restrictive—by saying, "Give me a couple of examples of good and poor communication that you personally recall, things that may have happened during the past few months." You can become more structured by further defining the topic: "Can you give me some examples that deal with superior-subordinate communication?" If you do want a general categorical answer to a question, there is still no need to limit yourself to just two categories (yes or no). That is, you can ask for an answer that refers to a finer set of categories: "Regarding the quality of communication in this company, if a '1' were completely ineffective and a '5' were to represent perfect communication, how would you rate communication in this company?"

One special type of question is called a "probe." Probes are very short open questions, gestures, or even silences that indicate an interest in "digging deeper" into a particular topic or issue. Examples would be a "quizzical" facial expression (eyebrows raised and eyes wide open), or a brief question like "Then what?" or "How did you deal with that?" Sometimes the best probe is silence. All too often we talk just to fill an uncomfortable silence. It is usually helpful to just wait for the other person to speak, to "pause and probe," even if this feels strange, for the other person will usually feel just as uncomfortable with the silence. By waiting for him to speak, you will get more information than if you just asked another question. Sometimes a pause-probe will elicit information that a person would not give in response to a direct question.

Learning to ask effective questions is not really difficult, but it does take thought and practice. The result is likely to be an increase in the quality of information you get, and that information is more likely to meet your needs than the information from either the yes-no or the completely open types of questions.

Sensing: The Group Interview*

Jack K. Fordyce
and Raymond Weil

Sensing is an organized method by which a manager can learn about the issues, concerns, needs, and resources of persons in any suborganization with which he or she has limited personal contact. It takes the form of an unstructured group interview and is usually tape-recorded. The recording may be then used to educate others.

EXAMPLE

The general manager of an organization which employs 2000 wants to make an annual report to employees highly pertinent to their interests. To discover what subjects most concern them, the personnel manager schedules a series of meetings with a sampling of employees.

The personnel manager schedules four meetings, each two hours in length and each with a different group of 12 employees. To aid the general manager get a "feel" for people in all parts of the organization, the personnel manager selects the attendees as follows:

> Group I—Nonsupervisory, shop and service, and technical and office employees.
> Group II—Professional employees and staff specialists.
> Group III—Supervisors.
> Group IV—A diagonal cross section (i.e., one person from each organizational level; no one of the persons selected reports to any other).

Before scheduling the meetings, the personnel manager contacts the supervisor of each prospective participant. He or she explains the purpose of the meeting and the intention that no direct actions will ensue which might affect the supervisor or people who report to the supervisor.

Each meeting begins with a statement from the personnel manager who says that the general manager will arrive in half an hour. The personnel manager explains the general manager's purpose for the meeting and the hope that the conversation will be open and informal. The personnel manager suggests: "Suppose you board an airplane to Europe and you happen to find yourself sitting next to the general manager. What would you say?" The

---

* SOURCE: Jack K. Fordyce and Raymond Weil, *Managing with People*, 2nd ed. © 1979. Addison-Wesley Publishing Company, Inc., Reading, Mass., pp. 147–150. Reprinted with permission.

personnel manager also tells the group that, unless they object, to ease the burden of notetaking, the meeting will be tape-recorded. The general manager may also later use the tape as an aid to memory or to present illustrative excerpts to the division's top staff. If any member of the group prefers, the recorder will be promptly turned off now or at any time during the conversation.

During the meeting, the general manager spends most of the time listening, sometimes asking clarifying questions. The general manager also expresses his or her own thoughts and intentions regarding the various topics introduced.

ANOTHER EXAMPLE

A manager has been hearing from outsiders that recently hired engineers in the organization are dissatisfied. To better understand the nature of their complaints, the manager asks the personnel manager to arrange sensing sessions with several groups of engineers and a group of engineering supervisors.

ANOTHER EXAMPLE

A Third Party uses the Sensing procedure to make a quick assessment of the health of a company. He or she meets with four representative small groups from different parts of the organization, asking each group to discuss what is going well in the company and what needs to be changed. To avoid inhibiting the discussion, the Third Party does not record it but periodically stops the conversation and, in front of the group, dictates into the tape recorder a digest of what they have said. Then, with the recorder still running, he or she asks if they have been heard correctly and records their response. In a day's time, a 15-minute tape can summarize the four discussions. This tape is given to the top management group of the company.

If the consultant were collecting information for a teambuilding meeting, he or she might use a different question, such as: "The General Manager and the Divison Directors are going to hold an offsite meeting to work on improving their performance as a management team. What issues do you think they should take up?"

USES

To collect information as part of a general diagnosis of the organization. . . .

To learn the desires and agonies of a group that seems to be dissatisfied.

To learn how organization objectives are understood by diverse people within an organization.

To test a proposed course of action for its effect on various groups of people.

To collect information for a team-building meeting.

BENEFITS

The interaction of the group often produces rich information and ideas.

More economical than individual interviews.

May provide a quick glimpse of what's going on.

Allows for communication of impressions and feelings as well as opinions and ideas.

Provides a check on conventional and more formal communication channels.

Admits the rumble of humanity into the ivory tower.

Tapes from sensing sessions communicate more vividly to later listeners than secondhand transmission, written reports, or questionnaires.

LIMITATIONS

Won't work well unless the relations at various levels in the organization are basically trusting.

Is not as statistically rigorous or as economical as a questionnaire.

May be suspected as "snooping."

Success of the meeting is highly dependent on the manager's ability to listen effectively and on a willingness to engage with the members of the group in a personal way.

The meeting may fail to get at the attendees' real concerns because for one reason or another they are not willing to reveal them.

Operating Hints

Make sure that all intermediate supervisors understand the objectives and possible outcomes of the meeting so that they will not feel "spied upon." Be clear and explicit about the objectives of the meeting and what is to become of the information.

Notetaking may interfere with easy, informal discussion while the tape recorder is less likely to. But tape-record the session only if the group is willing. Be explicit about how the tape will be used and make a commitment to control its use.

Don't try to use sensing as a substitute for maintaining effective communication channels throughout the organization, or to "get the boss's message across," or to reprimand or judge.

Allow about two hours (enough time for a comfortable discussion).

Provide some warm-up time with a Third Party, especially for people who have never seen the big boss.

Convene the session in a comfortable setting and one that is not strange or intimidating to the group. (Don't meet in the boss's office.)

Establish a single and limited objective for a given sensing session. Don't try to cover too much at once. Start the meeting in an open-ended way. This will permit individuals to express their viewpoints (e.g., "How does it feel to work around here?" or "I'm interested in how things are going," rather than, "Do you like the company benefits plan?").

If the manager doing the sensing is a poor listener, include a Third Party who, by prearrangement, can intervene if the manager seems to be blocking the group's efforts to express itself.

Don't do a lot of sensing unless the groups sensed can see positive results coming from it. Overuse of sensing can be as bad as overuse of questionnaires. Sensing may be conducted by persons other than a key manager; for example, by a Third Party or someone from the personnel department.

The Organization Mirror*

Jack K. Fordyce
and Raymond Weil

An Organization Mirror is a particular kind of meeting that allows an organizational unit to collect feedback from a number of key organizations to which it relates (e.g., customers, suppliers, users of services within the larger organization). The meeting closes with a list of specific tasks for improvement of operations, products, or services.

EXAMPLE

A seven-member central staff group has been laboring to improve its effectiveness for about a year. Yet the group still experiences friction or indifference from the line groups it is supposed to aid.

To the Organization Mirror, the staff group invites two guests from each of the line groups. Just before the meeting, the Third Party interviews all participants, singly or in groups with the goal of preparing the participants for the meeting, learning something about the size of the problem as they see it, and collecting information on the issues for presentation early in the meeting.

The staff director begins by outlining the objectives for the meeting and the planned activities of the day and then posts a schedule of activity, as follows:

MEETING SCHEDULE

8:30– 9:00	Introduction by staff director
9:00– 9:30	Review of interview data by Third Party
9:30–10:15	Outsiders Fishbowl ... to discuss and interpret the data (insiders listen and take notes)
10:15–11:00	Insiders Fishbowl to discuss what they heard outsiders say and identify issues needing clarification
11:00–12:00	General discussion to summarize what has happened thus far (ground rule: don't start working problems)
12:00– 1:00	Break for lunch

* SOURCE: Jack K. Fordyce and Raymond Weil, *Managing with People*, 2nd ed. © 1979. Addison-Wesley Publishing Company, Inc., Reading, Mass., pp. 110–114.

1:00– 1:30	Four task subgroups, each comprising both outsiders and insiders, identify the five most important changes needed to improve the effectiveness of the organization
1:30– 2:00	Reports from subgroups
2:00– 2:30	Total group synthesizes lists
2:30– 4:30	The four task subgroups develop a plan and specific action items for change
4:30– 5:00	Meeting summary—each task group reports plans, action items, persons responsible, and reporting dates
5:00– 5:30	Staff director concludes meeting by reviewing day's work and assigning remaining action items

After the meeting, the Third Party conversed briefly with about half of the participants. The following are some typical reactions to the meeting:

OUTSIDERS:

"I think they finally heard what we've been trying to tell them."

"I believe they will get out of their offices now and see what kind of pressure we're under on the line."

"I was encouraged by the way they paid attention to our comments. I don't know if I could have listened to that kind of stuff."

"I have a better sense of all they have to put up with. I'll be a little more responsive in the future."

INSIDERS:

"I was surprised at the number of good things they had to say about us."

"We sure have a lot of work to do!"

USES

When an organization has progressed in teambuilding, a natural next step is to improve relations with important outside groups.

Particularly useful for staff service groups.

When an organization is being bypassed.

When things seem too good.

When the product isn't being bought.

When a group receives no information (or conflicting information) about its performance.

When a group receives undeserved criticism.

When ability to perform is impaired by other groups.

When interface problems embrace a number of other groups.

BENEFITS

Provides feedback simultaneously from a number of sources in a systematic way.

Permits setting of priorities and planning to improve both the organization image and effectiveness.

Often converts critics to helpers.

Converts bellyaching to constructive action.

LIMITATIONS

A complex and demanding procedure that entails some risk of negative outcome.

Typically requires much effort in follow-through.

The process requires careful planning, management, and commitment.

Takes more than a couple of hours.

Needs a skilled Third Party.

Operating Hints

Allow enough time (1 or 2 days). Plan the meeting carefully and cleanly divide the time into segments. As the meeting progresses, permit some latitude for schedule changes, but don't allow planned segments to blur.

The inside and outside groups should be about the same size. The total group should not exceed 20. Select the outsiders carefully. They should be people who are influential and respected in their organizations, who may have some insight into your problems, who are willing to spend the time, who are constructive and articulate but not argumentative. Outsiders should come from groups with whom you do a lot of business.

Encourage both positive and negative feedback. Avoid working troublesome individual relationships. Postpone this for another time.

Record results of all meeting segments on chart pads. Post clearly identified action items for all to see. Don't use this type of meeting only to collect feedback, but do go through the entire cycle of joint planning and execution of changes. It is the latter part that cements relationships.

Commit yourself to a time and method for reporting progress to everyone. Consider inviting the outsiders back at a later time to evaluate progress and give assistance.

Procedure for the Organization Mirror

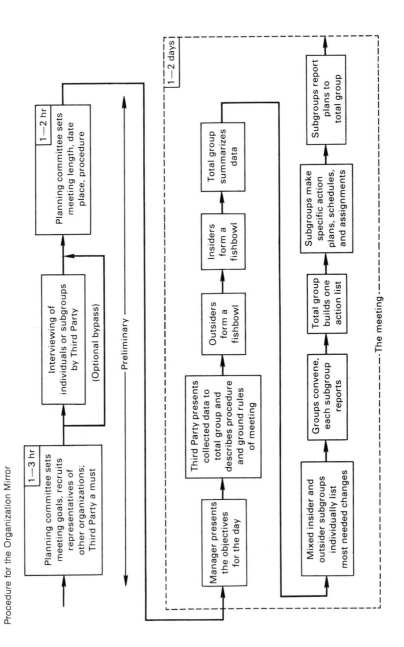

Questionnaires and Instruments*

Jack K. Fordyce
and Raymond Weil

Questionnaires are an old standby for detecting opinion and sentiment. We send out questionnaires to customers, production workers, the professional staff, constituents, television and movie viewers, lower levels of management, people who sojourn at motels and ride in planes, and others.

Unfortunately, traditional questionnaires have often been disappointing as a means of bringing about significant change within organizations. They do not create the kind of personal involvement and discussion that is so valuable in changing hearts and minds. The information garnered by questionnaires tends to be canned, anonymous, ambiguous, and detached—cool data rather than hot. The replies may be interesting but they lack punch. It is too easy to hold them at arm's length, put them off until another day, or take token action. And the questionnaire asks the person only what *we* want to know, not what he or she thinks we should know. You might say a filled-out questionnaire amounts to half a conversation. The employee opinion questionnaire is regarded by many as a device that some managements used to avoid coming to grips with strong opinions and sentiments.

Nevertheless, to our mind the questionnaire can be useful when it is developed jointly by the manager and representatives of the population to be canvassed.

The *instrument* as used in organization development is similar to the questionnaire, with the important addition that it is constructed around a theory of management in such manner as to help the respondent understand the theory and rate himself or herself or the organization in terms of that theory. Thus in "Grid Organization Development," the manager answers questions which help to place himself or herself in the grid model of management styles. Others in the group rate the manager too. In this manner, instruments are a means by which a group can collect information from itself about itself. This information then provides the starting point for feedback and confrontation within the group.

USES

As a primary vehicle for learning in one complete system of organization development (Grid Organization Development).

* SOURCE: Jack K. Fordyce and Raymond Weil, *Managing with People.* © 1979. Addison-Wesley Publishing Company, Inc., Reading, Mass., pp. 143–145. Reprinted with permission.

To collect information as part of a specific, planned strategy of change, preferably jointly managed.

Instruments may be used by a group to collect information quickly about itself, as part of a diagnostic or team-building meeting. In this use, the instrument is the same as Polling except that the instrument is predesigned and may incorporate criteria for evaluation.

BENEFITS

Questionnaires and instruments are economical means for gathering information from a large population.

They lend themselves readily to legitimate statistical use.

Instruments are valuable for self-confrontation, for learning, and as stepping stones to interpersonal confrontations.

You can more readily afford to spend time and money on the quality of the questionnaires or instruments because the unit cost is low.

There is wide acceptance of these methods.

They reduce reliance on expert third parties.

Anonymity may bring to light previously undisclosed strong sentiment.

LIMITATIONS

Questionnaires and instruments produce findings which seem canned, a quality which is mitigated if they are used, as in Grid Organization Development, as a stepping stone to confrontation. The hazard is that the parties involved may merely imitate the motions of engaging with one another—shadowbox, so to speak.

One becomes too readily dependent on the questionnaire, pressing upon it (and thrusting away from oneself) a load it can't carry: direct human communication.

OPERATING HINTS

Unless the objective is purely personal learning, be sure the questionnaire or instrument leads to real engagement among people. Make sure that those involved are really hearing one another well enough—both heart-to-heart and head-to-head—so that their communication may have consequences in constructive action.

Feedback*

Floyd C. Mann

**FEEDBACK: CHANGING PATTERNS OF RELATIONSHIPS
BETWEEN SUPERIORS AND SUBORDINATES BY USING
SURVEY FINDINGS**

Long-range interest in the actual varying of significant variables in organizations has necessitated that members of the Human Relations Program of the Institute for Social Research, University of Michigan, not only study existing programs for training and changing people in organizations, but that we *develop* new techniques for changing relationships, and that we learn how to *measure* the effects of such changes within organizations. As a result, we have invested a good deal of professional effort in exploring the effectiveness of different procedures for changing attitudes, perceptions, and relationships among individuals in complex hierarchies without changing the personnel of the units. The latter is an important qualification, for we have found that the changes in subordinates' perceptions and attitudes which follow a change in supervisory personnel are frequently of a much larger order than those generated by training or other procedures for changing the attitudes or behavior of incumbents.

Exploratory and Developmental Phase

One procedure which we developed and subsequently found to be effective in changing perceptions and relationships within organizations has been called "feedback." This change process evolved over a period of years as we tried to learn how to report findings from human relations research into organizations so that they would be understood and used in day-to-day operations. Work began on this process in 1948 following a company-wide study of employee and management attitudes and opinions. Over a period of two years, three different sets of data were fed back: (1) information on the attitudes and perceptions of 8000 nonsupervisory employees toward their work, promotion opportunities, supervision, fellow employees, etc.; (2) first- and second-line supervisor's feelings about the various aspects of their jobs and supervisory beliefs; and (3) information from intermediate and top levels of management about their supervisory philosophies, roles in policy formation,

* SOURCE: Floyd C. Mann, "Studying and Creating Change" Research in Industrial Human Relations, Industrial Relations Research Association, Publication No. 17, 1957, pp. 146–67.

problems of organizational integration, etc. We had several aims in this exploratory phase: (1) to develop through first-hand experience an understanding of the problems of producing change; (2) to improve relationships; (3) to identify factors which affected the extent of the change; and (4) to develop working hypotheses for later, more directed research.

The process which finally appeared to maximize the acceptance and utilization of survey and research findings can be described structurally as an interlocking chain of conferences. It began with a report of the major findings of the survey to the president and his senior officers, and then progressed slowly down through the hierarchical levels along functional lines to where supervisors and their employees were discussing the data. These meetings were structured in terms of organizational "families"[1] or units—each superior and his immediate subordinates considering the survey data together. The data presented to each group were those pertaining to their own group or for those subunits for which members of the organizational unit were responsible.

Members of each group were asked to help interpret the data and then decide what further analyses of the data should be made to aid them in formulating plans for constructive administrative actions. They also planned the introduction of the findings to the next level. The meetings were typically led by the line officer responsible for the coordination of the subunits at a particular level. Usually, a member of the Survey Research Center and the company's personnel staff assisted the line officer in preparing for these meetings, but attended the meetings only as resource people who could be called upon for information about the feasibility of additional analyses.

These meetings took place in the office of the line supervisor whose organizational unit was meeting, or in the department's own small conference room. All of the survey findings relative to each group were given to the leader and the members of his organizational unit; they decided what to consider first, how fast to work through each topic, and when they had gone as far as they could and needed to involve the next echelon in the process.

This feedback change procedure was developed in an organization where a great amount of effort had aready been invested in the training of management and supervisors. During the war the company had participated in the various J-programs sponsored by the War Manpower Commission, and more important, during the several years we were experimentally developing the feedback process, Dr. Norman R. F. Maier was working with all levels of management to improve their understanding of human relations and supervision.[2] The supervisors with whom we were working to increase their understanding of their own organizational units therefore had a great deal of training in the application of psychological principles to management.

---

[1] F. Mann and J. Dent, "The Supervisor: Member of Two Organizational Families," *Harvard Business Review*, XXXII (November–December 1954), pp. 103–112.

[2] For a thorough description of this training, see N. R. F. Maier, *Principles of Human Relations* (New York: Wiley, 1952).

Our observations of the feedback procedure as it developed suggested that it was a powerful process for creating and supporting changes within an organization.[3] However, there was no quantitative proof of this, for our work up to this point had been exploratory and developmental.

---

[3] F. Mann and R. Likert, "The Need for Research on Communicating Research Results," *Human Organization*, XI (Winter 1952), pp. 15–19.

Designing and Conducting Organizational Surveys*

Marshall Sashkin

Everyone is familiar with the results of some survey, but how those results are obtained usually is a mystery known only to the experts—whoever they are. Actually, the development of a survey instrument is primarily a matter of care, common sense, and skill developed through practice (and based on the ability to write coherently). No set of instructions can be a substitute for basic aptitudes or practice, but the following guidelines can tell a beginning surveyor how to take care, what common sense is, and where to invest efforts that amount to practice.

Step 1: Define the Objectives. What precisely is the survey trying to find out? Can the data be obtained in some way other than a survey? If not, the objectives should be defined as precisely as possible, in writing, and should be limited to those that are really important. If there are more than four or five basic issues, the survey probably will be too long and the people who are asked to fill out the questionnaire will not respond.

Step 2: Identify the Population to Be Studied. The population is everyone from whom the surveyor would need to have a response in order to completely and correctly answer the basic questions. Studying managers' attitudes about worker participation is very different from studying the same attitudes of managers in a specific organization. The populations are quite different. It is important to be precise in defining the population to be used. Although this does not mean that a list should be made of everyone in the specific population, this is the time to consider how the survey instrument will be physically brought to the people in the respondent population. For example, will the members of a group be assembled in one place? Or will the questionnaire be mailed to them at their homes or business addresses?

Step 3: Select the Survey Sample. Ideally, one would like to conduct a census, a survey that includes everyone in the population of interest. Obviously, this is not possible if we are talking about "all managers." Usually one must settle for a sample of the population, preferably a sample that will provide the same results as if all managers had actually responded. Less obviously, a consultant working with a particular client organization may also be faced with

* Source: Reprinted from: John E. Jones and J. William Pfeiffer, (Eds.), *The 1981 Annual Handbook for Group Facilitation*, San Diego, CA: University Associates, Inc., 1981. Used with permission.

an unrealistic task if, for example, there are 783 managers in the entire company. With limited resources, an individual consultant may find it impossible to obtain and analyze that much data. Typically, one conducts a census-type survey only when the population is relatively small or when the need for total participation is extremely great.

Sampling techniques have been developed and refined extensively over the past forty years or so, but the nonexpert can generally get by with two concepts: randomness and stratification. Normally, every person in the population should have an equal chance of being picked to be in the sample. This can be accomplished by random selection.

Step 4: Construct the Questionnaire. In order to develop a concise questionnaire, one must have some skill in writing and must also be able to endure the tedium of rewriting the questions (or items) over and over again until they are as nearly perfect as possible. A typical questionnaire has at least four basic parts: the cover letter; the items; the scales; and the codes. Each of these must be prepared with maximum care in order to achieve optimum results. Each also requires skill, and such skill is attained only with much practice.

The *cover letter* should be clearly and simply written, and should not contain jargon or technical words. It should speak to the respondent on at least three issues: (a) why the survey is being conducted; (b) what the benefit of the survey might be, especially with respect to the respondent; and (c) the guaranteed anonymity and security of responses.

The *items* are, of course, the heart of the survey instrument, but writing the questionnaire items is surely the most tedious aspect of survey design. It is also the most important aspect. One begins with the objectives (defined in Step 1) and attempts to translate them into specific questions. Often one can receive much guidance from the efforts of others, since the topic to be examined has probably been studied before. Sometimes, one can borrow items appropriate to fairly specific needs and use them with only minor modifications. Some well-developed research questionnaires can be used or adapted freely; in other cases one must obtain written permission from the author or buy the instruments from a distributor. Obviously, one must be careful to maintain professional ethics in the use of questionnaires and questionnaire items authored by others.

The construction of effective items depends on common-sense writing skills: avoid leading questions, try to phrase items objectively, use common rather than obscure terms, and strive for brevity and clarity. In the long run, only practice can provide the skills needed to write questionnaire items that will be readily understood.

Scaling need not be overly technical. The most commonly used scale is called a "Likert scale," after the man who developed it, Rensis Likert (1932), the former director of the Institute for Social Research at the University of Michigan and head of the Survey Research Center. A Likert scale typically has five or seven multiple-choice alternatives, such as the following:

To what extent are you satisfied with your job?

1 _____	2 _____	3 _____	4 _____	5 _____
To a very great extent	To a great extent	To a moderate extent	To a little extent	To a very little extent

There is no one best set of scale labels. Among labels commonly used are "agree-disagree," "how much," "how often," "to what degree," and "how important."

Research shows that the "right" number of points on a scale is usually between five and nine. This is the "comfortable" range of discrimination, for most people.

Finally, we come to the matter of *coding* responses. To prepare to analyze the data, one must construct a "code book," which consists of a copy of the questionnaire that has been marked to indicate how to score each item and how to deal with "problem responses."

Step 5: Pretest the Questionnaire. No matter how well developed the survey instrument is, some problems will still have to be identified and corrected. This is the function of the pretest. A small number of instruments are typed up. Volunteers then respond to the items on the questionnaire as though they were members of the sample population. In fact, some of these pretesters should be members of the population from which respondents are to be drawn. Immediately after completing the instrument, each of these volunteers is interviewed so that flaws or errors on the form can be identified. Even if the sample of volunteers is limited to two or three, a pretest is crucial. It is almost certain that some errors will be identified.

Step 6: Prepare the Final Draft. After errors identified through pretesting are corrected, problems are resolved, and an attractive, clean, final copy is prepared for reproduction, the survey form must be checked carefully; to remedy errors from here on will probably be too costly. Even if some data are discarded, that, too, is a costly cure.

Step 7: Administer the Questionnaire. Ideally, one would administer the questionnaire to everyone in the sample at the same time, perhaps in one large group meeting. Usually, this is impossible. Even the next-best situation, having several group administration sessions, is not always feasible. Quite often it is necessary to distribute questionnaires to individual respondents who complete and return them either by hand, intracompany mail, or U.S. mail. Although this can serve to increase privacy and anonymity for respondents, it also leads to decreased return rates. When such a voluntary return procedure cannot be avoided, the surveyor must do everything possible to boost the return rate. There are at least four ways to do this:

- Emphasize the importance of the study, its usefulness and potential benefits.
- Make clear the confidentiality and privacy of individual responses.
- Invest as much time and effort as possible in personal contact with potential respondents.
- Make the instructions as clear and simple as possible.

Step 8: Code the Responses. Accounting ledgers can be used as tally sheets for raw data, and forms designed for this purpose are also available. The latter forms are particularly useful when the data are to be analyzed by a computer (which is certainly the easiest way to analyze the data). This step is very important because minor errors can have serious impact. A few of the survey questionnaires always should be checked at random to see if there are errors in coding.

Step 9: Tabulate the Results. The aim here is to present the data so that people can understand the results of the survey and make interpretations from this information. Simple tabulations of responses for each item in the form of percentages (not just raw numbers) generally will suffice. Percentages can be filled in on a copy of the questionnarie where the check marks would go. Many results may be ignored later, but it is important to begin by tabulating everything.

The next step is cross-tabulation for items that have some important relation to one another. For example, to determine whether older workers are less satisfied than younger workers, one would cross-tabulate age by satisfaction.

Obviously, there must be a reason for setting up cross-tabulations. If the data are to be analyzed by computer, it is quick and inexpensive to cross-tabulate everything by everything, but then one must wade through mounds of printout. So even when the calculations are easy, it is worth spending some time to decide what, if any, variables should be cross-tabulated.

It is important to prepare data that might be used to help identify problems in the group or organization under study.

Step 10: Prepare the Report. Before preparing a final report, one must pull together all thoughts about the survey in a brief overview or summary paper. The aim is to organize these ideas and the data, not to communicate results. On the basis of this summary paper, the needs of the organization, and the circumstances of the survey consultation, one can then proceed with a formal, final report.

The summary paper should begin with about a page of description, highlighting what the data show and referring to the tables constructed in the previous step.

The final report will be based on the summary, but should be tailored to the circumstances. For example, if it is clear that management is quite uninterested in doing anything with the results of the survey and would be threatened by a negative tone, it probably would be wise to prepare a brief, bland report that plays down the negative aspects of the survey results. Unless there is reason to believe that some good would come of full exposure, there is little to be gained by "stirring things up" just for the sake of doing so. If, on the other hand, management is seriously interested in doing something with the results of the survey, the final report should be presented in a more usable form. That exact form will, however, still depend on circumstances. If the data are to be used to work on problems with small groups involved at all levels, the report should avoid inferences and conclusions; should contain data grouped by unit, department, or division; and should be clear to a nonexpert. If top managers are to work on the data to derive action plans, then more summary details, charts, and recommendations are usually desirable. The guidelines for preparing the final report are: (a) consider who will use it, and (b) consider the purpose for which it will be used. The surveyor should prepare a report that (a) will not, in itself, do harm to the people or organization studied, (b) is targeted to the users, and (c) is in an appropriately usable form.

SUMMARY: DESIGNING AND CONDUCTING QUESTIONNAIRE SURVEYS

We have discussed, in a ten-step model, professional, technical, and common-sense guidelines for planning and conducting paper-and-pencil questionnaire surveys of groups and organizations. The steps are abbreviated and incomplete, however, because the practical details involved cannot be covered in a few pages. More important, the skills needed to effectively design and conduct organizational surveys cannot be learned by reading but can be developed only by practice, correction, and more practice. The ten steps are:

Step 1:   Define the objectives
Step 2:   Identify the population to be studied
Step 3:   Select the survey sample
Step 4:   Construct the questionnaire
Step 5:   Pretest the questionnaire
Step 6:   Prepare the final draft
Step 7:   Administer the questionnaire
Step 8:   Code the responses
Step 9:   Tabulate the results
Step 10:   Prepare the report

6

THE USE OF GROUPS TO FACILITATE CHANGE

INTRODUCTION

Explanation of the structure of social groups depends upon interaction.
—Barry Glassner*

Expertise in working with group dynamics is one of the essential, basic engines driving effective planned organizational change, which complements and facilitates exploitation of the data gathered by whatever means. The data gathered is usually fed back to some executive, representative, or task force group or committee to explore and to make decisions concerning it. This chapter is intended to provide introductory here-and-now training in the use of group dynamics in the course of interventions, and to tie that training to there-and-then understanding of the group dynamics that occur in accounts of managing change.

The experiences open with *Group Dynamics Simulation Exercise*, a concentrated, high-quality, standard experiential exercise, which usually generates a substantial quantity of observations of a wide range of behaviors commonly exhibited in and by groups and makes them available for skill development. The idea of process emerges as important in group dynamics, just as it is in the life course of an intervention. This exercise can serve only as a beginning in working with group dynamics, however, and needs substantial follow-up. Regular practice in observing the intervention classroom group and feeding back, discussing, and evaluating the observations so gained may be

* *Essential Interactionism* (London: Routledge & Kegan Paul, 1980), p. 8.

fruitfully initiated at this point.† Over time, the would-be change agent should develop a personal scheme for making and feeding back observations of group behavior in the course of interventions with which he or she feels comfortable.‡

The *Chemical Engineering Consulting Company* presents a graphic account of the systematic, skilled application of group dynamics knowledge and skill in a team-building intervention. Discussion of it may usefully probe why it is that the intervention seems so successful. The *Boyd Consumer Goods Company* shows a leading group dynamicist at work, trying over a period of time to help an organization improve the effectiveness of its weekly executive meeting. It is worth pondering about what this account tells us about the application of group knowledge and skill to client enterprises.

The chapter's models and schemes are introduced by *Emerging Principles of Achieving Change*, an excerpt from a classic, strategic contribution to the conceptualization of the role of group dynamics in change. The article outlines several principles concerning the group as a medium of change and as a target of change. The considerations suggested seem to be as cogent today as when they were first written.

Group Dynamics provides substantial, concentrated summaries of well-known schemes for observing and acting in groups. This reading complements *Group Dynamics Simulation Exercise. Task-Related Factors Influencing Team Effectiveness* draws attention to goals, roles, procedures, and feelings—issues of prime significance in the effective use of groups in managing change. *The Intergroup Team-Building Meeting* is concerned with dynamics *between* groups that need to improve the way they work together. It outlines a procedure for setting up an intergroup meeting to do something about damaging group differences that arise from the division of labor and distinctive organizational subcultures.

---

† Several methods for doing so are presented in the Instructor's Manual.

‡ It is beyond the scope of this book to provide a major group training experience. The would-be change agent should seek experiential training in groups elsewhere, based on the traditions of, for example, the NTL Institute of Applied Behavioral Science or the Tavistock Institute of Human Relations.

Group Dynamics Simulation Exercise*

David A. Kolb, Irwin M. Rubin, and James M. McIntyre

(Time Allotted: 1 Hour)

The purpose of the following exercise is to sharpen skills both in observing how a group goes about solving a task (diagnosing process) and in participating in the task. An effective group member is one who can function well at both of these levels—this person is a *participant-observer*. This unit has four major elements:

1. One-half of a group will be involved in a decision-making exercise (participants) while the other half (observers) attempts to develop a better understanding of the group process.
2. Observers will provide individual feedback to their participant partner.
3. Observers and participants switch roles.
4. All discuss the exercise.

> *Step 1.* The entire class should form into pairs (plus one trio if necessary).
>
> *Step 2.* One-half of each pair will participate in the first round of the decision-making exercises. These people should seat themselves in a small circle. Their partners will be observers for the first round. Observers should seat themselves around the outside of the decision-making group so as to be able to observe their partners.

Note: If the class is very large, two separate simulations should be created.

> *Step 3.* The inner group will have 20 minutes to complete a given task, which will involve coming to a consensus decision (see task A, page 000). Observers should view the group's process in general and their partner's behavior in particular using the Observer Rating Form on page 000. Observers should remain silent.
>
> *Step 4.* Observers meet and give feedback to their participant partner using the observations recorded on the Observer Rating Form as a beginning. (10 minutes)

* SOURCE: David A. Kolb, Irwin M. Rubin, and James M. McIntyre, *Organizational Psychology: An Experiential Approach to Organizational Behavior*, 4th ed., pp. 134–142, © 1984. Reprinted by permission of Prentice-Hall, Inc., Englewood Cliffs, N.J.

Groups should then switch positions and repeat steps 3 and 4 except that the second decision-making group begins with task B, pages 000–000.

B.   Discussion of Group Dynamics Simulation
(Time Allotted: 40 to 60 Minutes)

> *Step 1.*   The discussion of this exercise is probably best conducted within two equal subgroups of the total class. Each subgroup should be made up of several of the originally formed pairs of participant-observers. (30 minutes)

The following points should help to guide this discussion:

a. What task-oriented, maintenance-oriented behaviors seemed most frequently used? Least frequently used?
b. In what ways, if any, did the group's work suffer because certain task/maintenance functions were underutilized?
c. How did "friendly helpers," "tough battlers," and "logical thinkers" interact with and influence each other? What impact did these styles have on group functioning?
d. Tasks A and B were designed to be different along a dimension of potential personal involvement and value implications; for example, task B often engages significant personal values.
   1. Did certain task-oriented, maintenance-oriented, and self-oriented behaviors arise more frequently around task A versus task B? With what consequence?
   2. What kinds of task-oriented, maintenance-oriented behaviors are particularly critical in highly charged task situations? In more neutral situations?
e. The second group to move into the inner circle often exhibits some form of intergroup competition ("They never finished and/or did a poor job. Let's do better!") Did any such competition develop? If so, how did it influence the group's process?

> *Step 2.*   This final discussion is still another live example of a group trying to accomplish a task. To what extent during the discussion in step 1, have you been able to function as both a participant and an observer—to what extent has this group concerned itself with process issues that might have arisen as the group discussed the earlier exercise? Discuss your process over the last 20 minutes. (10 minutes)

TASK A

1.   The group should develop a consensus ranking of the following items in terms of their importance for improving the effectiveness of organizations. Place number 1 by the most important item, number 2 by the next most important item, and so on to 10, which represents the least important consideration. Make your rankings in terms of organizations in general.

_____ Create conditions where employees can participate in making decisions that vitally affect them.

_____ Develop early retirement programs to weed out people in the older age categories who are nonproductive.

_____ Give craft, technical, or social skill training to improve skills at all levels.

_____ Expand personal contact between top management and the rest of the organization.

_____ Fill jobs on qualifications rather than by seniority.

_____ Improve incentive system for nonsupervisory personnel.

_____ Institute regular replacement hiring program.

_____ Discharge all poor performance personnel, including supervisors.

_____ Stress feedback in communication programs.

_____ Put key categories of employees on merit salary.

Note: If the first decision-making group finishes task 1 before its time is up, it should begin same process with task 2.

2.   The group should develop a consensus ranking of the following items in terms of their importance in selecting a middle manager, like department head, who is effective in making and carrying out decisions. Place number 1 by the most important item, number 2 by the next most important item, and so on to 10, which represents the least important consideration.

_____ Able to grasp the structure of the organization quickly and to use it effectively.

_____ Able to give clear-cut instructions.

_____ Keeps all parties who are concerned with a decision fully informed on progress and final actions taken.

_____ Able to change own conclusions when they prove to be wrong.

_____ Goes about decision making by developing a range of alternatives before coming to a final verdict.

_____ Able to grasp instructions and to act appropriately in terms of them.

_____ Capable of making fast decision under time and other pressures.

_____ Able to delegate effectively.

_____ Capable of seeing appropriate relations among a variety of items.

_____ Able to resist shaping an opinion before all the facts are in.

TASK B

Here you will find two situations described involving a difficult personal choice. The group should develop a consensus choice for situation 1. If the group finishes situation 1 before its 30 minutes have elapsed, it should move on to situation 2.

Situation 1

Mr. A., a 45-year-old concert pianist with two children in high school, has recently been informed by his physician that he has a partially plugged artery (sclerosis) in his right arm. The condition causes continuous and severe pain, but he is able to carry on his career with no reduction in skill. The physician informs Mr. A. that there is a new surgical operation, which, if successful, would completely relieve the condition. If the operation failed, his hand would be left useless, and it would be impossible for him to go on with his work as a pianist.

Imagine that your group is Mr. A. Several probabilities or odds that the operation will prove successful follow. *Check the lowest probability that your group would consider acceptable for the operation to be performed.*

___ The chances are 0 in 10 that the operation will be a success (i.e., the operation is certain to be a failure).

___ The chances are 1 in 10 that the operation will be a success.

___ The chances are 2 in 10 that the operation will be a success.

___ The chances are 3 in 10 that the operation will be a success.

___ The chances are 4 in 10 that the operation will be a success.

___ The chances are 5 in 10 that the operation will be a success.

___ The chances are 6 in 10 that the operation will be a success.

___ The chances are 7 in 10 that the operation will be a success.

___ The chances are 8 in 10 that the operation will be a success.

___ The chances are 9 in 10 that the operation will be a success.

___ The chances are 10 in 10 that the operation will be a success (i.e., the operation is certain to be a success).

Situation 2

Mr. and Mrs. H., a childless couple, have been attempting to have a child for a number of years. Mrs. H. is now pregnant, but a complication has arisen. The doctor has advised Mr. and Mrs. H. that if the pregnancy is allowed to progress, Mrs. H.'s life will be in danger. If further complications do develop, the doctor will not be able to save the child and may not be able to save Mrs. H. If the pregnancy is terminated at this time, it will be impossible for Mrs. H. to become pregnant again.

Imagine that your group is advising Mr. and Mrs. H. Several probabilities that *no* further complications will occur during Mrs. H.'s pregnancy follow. *Check the lowest probability of the occurrence of no additional complications that your group would consider acceptable for Mr. and Mrs. H. to allow the pregnancy to progress.*

_____ The chances are 0 in 10 that further complication *will not* arise (i.e., it is certain that further complications *will* arise).

_____ The chances are 1 in 10 that further complications will *not* arise.

_____ The chances are 2 in 10 that further complications will *not* arise.

_____ The chances are 3 in 10 that further complications will *not* arise.

_____ The chances are 4 in 10 that further complications will *not* arise.

_____ The chances are 5 in 10 that further complications will *not* arise.

_____ The chances are 6 in 10 that further complications will *not* arise.

_____ The chances are 7 in 10 that further complications will *not* arise.

_____ The chances are 8 in 10 that further complications will *not* arise.

_____ The chances are 9 in 10 that further complications will *not* arise.

_____ The chances are 10 in 10 that further complications will *not* arise (i.e., it is certain that further complications *will not* arise).

Observer Rating Form

EXAMPLES OF: PROCESS DIMENSION/CATEGORY	IMPACT ON GROUP FUNCTIONING
1. Task-oriented behaviors	
2. Maintenance-oriented behaviors	
3. Self-oriented behaviors	
4. Group norms observed	
5. Communication patterns	
6. Decision-making patterns	

Chemical Engineering Consulting Company*

Jack K. Fordyce
and Raymond Weil

SITUATION

Ben was the founder and president of a firm of consulting chemical engineers consisting of about 120 people, including a home office in the midwest and four regional offices. The company had expanded steadily until about two years before. But now the firm's future prospects seemed flat and Ben was troubled. The reason for the organization's drop in vitality, Ben believed, was that the four regional managers were acting more and more independently of the home office and of him. None of them was pursuing new business prospects in a vigorous and concerted way—this in spite of agreements they had made at annual planning meetings to pool fiscal and technical resources in pursuit of larger opportunities. But as each year wore on, the plans seemed to be forgotten. Instead, each regional office went its own way, sharing neither funds nor opportunities, and recruiting its own technical specialists. Feeling increasingly isolated and less in control of the company, Ben sought to hire an assistant from outside the company. He wanted someone to take on part of his routine management responsibilities so that he would be free to orchestrate new business activity for the home and regional offices. He was seeking new blood and also someone to talk to—perhaps to relieve some of the loneliness at the top. He thought he had found an ideal person to fill the position, but at the last moment the prospect declined the offer in favor of another opportunity. Ben was dejected.

The annual meeting was a month off and the taste in Ben's mouth was of wormwood. He had established an informal working atmosphere that had persisted for the life of the company. There never seemed any real friction among his managers and everyone appeared friendly and cooperative. Yet, listening carefully to his managers and reading between the lines of their reports, he became convinced that the home and regional offices had grown even further apart in the past year. They were becoming five separate camps. Since he was convinced that success depended on their working in concert, he foresaw serious failure only a few years off. He wanted to lead his company but he didn't know what to do next.

* SOURCE: Jack K. Fordyce and Raymond Weil, *Managing with People*, 2nd ed. © 1979. Addison-Wesley Publishing Company, Inc., Reading, Mass., pp. 70–88.

Ben had heard about team building and decided to try it. He engaged Louise, an OD consultant, as Third Party to assist him in planning the meeting.

Information Gathering (1 hour per interview). The Third Party interviewed all the attendees of the annual meeting. She saw the four regional managers the day before at the meeting place.

From Louise's point of view, the situation that Ben had presented seemed fairly typical. She thought that it was likely that Ben was at the source of the problems he was attributing to others. After interviewing the managers, she concluded that relations among them were indeed cordial, as Ben had said. In the privacy of the interviews, however, she learned of various subjects that the managers had discussed rarely with one another and never with Ben. She concluded that most of the managers were indeed amicably protecting their own interests and going their own way. Thus it was clear why their joint business planning had come to little. But even if her diagnosis was accurate, she believed that it would be of small value to disclose it to her client. What was needed was for the management group to make its own diagnosis in the forthcoming meeting. To do that effectively, they must get past politeness. They must deal collectively with some of the observations they had made privately to her. If they could do that much, Louise believed, then their chance of becoming an effective team would improve. Thus her goals in entering the team-building meeting were to promote frank discussion of buried issues and so lead the team to a self-diagnosis of its strengths and failings.

In a final chat with Ben on the eve of the meeting, Louise advised him that, as the most powerful person present, he would have to take leadership in setting the tone of the meeting. He must make plain that he himself would expect criticism—in fact he must invite it. Only in this way could they hope for honest discussion. Ben swallowed—and agreed.

Team-building Meeting (2½ days). Everyone came to the meeting room early for coffee and light banter. Louise perceived the tone of the group as suspicious, but also curious about the meeting to come. The attendees were:

Ben—the president

Louise—the Third Party consultant

Home Office staff, consisting of:

> *Phil*—the Director of Applied Technology. A quiet man, Phil had been with the company almost since its inception. He was a widely known and respected chemical engineer, and the company's reputation was in good part based on his technical innovations. He headed a small staff of specialists to support the regional offices. He was responsible for exploring new technical areas and developing them into business opportunities.

> *Oscar*—the Comptroller. Oscar was 30 and had been with the firm four years. In a company run by engineers, he felt that financial management was not given its proper importance.

Mike—the Director of Administrative Services. Mike was 60 and a veteran of the company. He was somewhat passive about his role.

Regional Managers, who were:

George, who had helped Ben found the company, and was his closest friend. Now looking toward retirement, he had become an elder statesman who kept his own counsel. He valued his own privacy and respected that of others.

Angelo, independent, hard-driving, and outspoken. He had been the most successful at working with clients, and at generating profitable new business.

Les, a man of abundant common sense. He was more willing to trust others than most. He performed his duties in a calm and responsible manner, and his people liked working for him.

Brad, who was a brilliant man, considered tops in his specialty. He seemed cold and businesslike.

Ben opened by saying that he wanted the meeting to be a critique of how they were doing as a management team, and that he had invited Louise to help them with that process. For the critique to be useful, he observed, all team members would have to speak their minds openly. Therefore he bade them to be frank with him. "I want to know what you think about the way I've run this place, good *and* bad."

Then Ben revealed his worries about the future of the company. The group appeared somewhat embarrassed and defensive. He spoke of increasing disunity and failure to execute plans they had made. He ended by saying, "I want us to act as a team, because I've come to realize that we're stuck if we don't."

Louise studied the faces in the room as Ben's words hung heavily in the air. The faces were inexpressive. She felt uncomfortable and knew they were uneasy too.

She was about to step into the silence. She might have asked each person to jot down what he wanted to happen at this meeting and what he wanted not to happen. In this way, she'd be asking them to take some responsibility for the course of the meeting. Before Louise could speak, however, she heard Angelo's blunt voice.

"I guess we're all supposed to let our hair down in this seance, but I don't see us doing it. I don't think we trust each other that much."

Mike, an older man, broke in, "I don't know what you mean, Angelo. I trust everyone here."

"All right, Mike," Angelo shot back, "Let's see how frank you can be in your critique of the way Ben's been running this place."

Mike responded weakly, "If I have an issue with someone, I tell them as I go along."

No one seemed convinced. Mike was always smoothing things over.

Part of Louise's job was to help the group become more explicit in their communications and to keep issues from becoming diffused into generalities. She had noted that Angelo said, "I don't think *we* can trust *each other* that much." The "we" and "each other" were such generalities. A clearer statement would have been, "I don't trust your reactions, Ben, if I say something you don't like to hear. I do trust you, Les, and we've discussed all these things before." Louise could have highlighted the generalities and pushed Angelo to be more specific. Instead, she chose a structured routine in order to allow the group more time to warm up.

Louise said, "Let's form two groups—the staff in one and the regional managers in the other. Then I'd like each group to draw up a list of the issues they think should be discussed at this meeting. Take 20 minutes. Then post the lists on the wall at the front of the room."

She gave each group large sheets of paper and felt-tipped pens.

When the groups were engaged, Louise shared with Ben impressions of what had transpired so far, and she explained the procedure they were now using.

When the two groups had finished their lists, Louise asked them to make up yet another list. "On this list, write the issues that you believe other people have with you—with you as a group, or with you individually. And Ben, why don't you draw up a list, too?"

They laughed at the reversal. "I can't think of any issue you fellows could have with a nice guy like me," said Les. But the method intrigued them.

When they were done, each group posted its first list. As they saw their names, or the names of programs with which they were identified, boldly cited on the wall as issues for discussion the feelings of tension in the room rose. The last item on the regional managers' list was "Ben's Management Style."

There was a lengthy silence.

Next they posted their second lists. Tension gave way to amusement at the similarities between the sets of lists. Here were the issues that divided them. They knew them well. But they had not previously discussed them together. More precisely, they had not talked to the person most affected, or had done so only in banter.

Finally, Ben taped his list on the wall. There was only item on it: "Ben's Management Style."

Oscar, the Comptroller, was the youngest and newest of the group. While he was the least secure, he was also the most determined. He said, "You district managers wrote the accounting and reporting systems down as an issue. At least, when you refer to it as red tape I guess you mean it's an issue. And on our list, Item 6 says that your lack of cooperation over accounting and reporting is an issue. That's my item. I'd like to talk about it."

In the past, Oscar had been easy to ignore. But now they listened, and they debated for almost an hour.

Ben allowed Oscar to carry his own burden in the discussion, after which Ben spoke up for what *he* needed as president. Effectively, he supported

Oscar's position. Then, after a long silence, the elder statesman, George, turned to Oscar. "Oscar," he said, "you done good!" Oscar remarked later in the meeting that this was the first time he had felt like a member of the team.

Several hours were devoted to other items on the lists. Louise noticed that the group had been choosing relatively safe topics and doing well with them, but were beginning to get fatigued and bored. They should be ready for something tougher, she thought.

She was about to suggest a short break when, glancing around the room, she saw George eyeing Ben as though he wanted to speak to him. Louise guessed what he wanted to say, that it needed to be said, and that George, as Ben's oldest friend present, was the right one to say it. "What's on your mind, George?" she asked.

George glanced quickly at Louise and then back at Ben, "Well," he said, "I think I owe you an apology, Ben. I consider us to be friends, and yet for several years I've watched you lose credibility in this organization and I've said nothing to you about it."

Despite himself, Ben was shocked and looked it.

George continued: "You tell everyone what you want done, but you don't follow through. You *say* the new business plan is vital, then you jump up in a meeting and introduce a brand new top priority. But you don't put the resources behind it, and you spend your time on entirely different things. People watch what you do, not what you say. We're losing discipline . . . we're drifting."

Ben was stunned. They watched his face flush and waited for him to erupt. But his response came coldly: "We are supposed to be an organization staffed with mature managers and engineers. Once we decide to do something, I see no reason why I should have to lead everyone by the hand. Perhaps if you gentlemen were doing your jobs, I wouldn't have a credibility problem, if indeed *I* am the one with a problem of credibility."

Now Mike's anxious, placating voice was heard again. "Ben has a good point. If we were all doing our jobs and not laying it on him, there might not be a credibility problem."

There was an uneasy silence. No one seemed willing to proceed.

Ignoring Mike's comment, Louise turned to the irate executive. "Ben, what do you think George was trying to do?"

For Louise, this was a critical point in the meeting. The boss had been confronted and had responded with a powerful blow. People were starting to back down, and what had so far been gained was in danger of being lost; if openness didn't pay off, they might well retreat to the old communications norms.

But Ben had subsided and was now worrying about the effect of his attack. "George was trying to be helpful," he answered. "He really was."

"Very well," said Louise, "I think so too. Would you like to know how the others in the group feel about your credibility?" Ben looked around the room. "Yes," he said. "*Do* I have a credibility problem?" Almost all the heads nodded back at him.

"Les," said George, "we've talked about it. Maybe you can put it better than I did." He knew Les was respected and trusted for his fairness and common sense.

"OK," Les spoke calmly, "I'll call it as I see it, and maybe I'm beginning to see what we can do about it. I don't agree with Mike that if we all did our jobs, there wouldn't be any credibility problem. Ben, you have a lot of ideas and enthusiasm. It's one of the things that's built this company, but it makes problems too. And you're volatile. You get upset about something and you want to fix it right away. . . ."

Ben nodded. He knew those things about himself.

". . . so that the idea or problem that's your top priority one week gets lost in other priorities by the next week. We can't give top priority to everything, and I, at least, wind up making assumptions about what's really important to you, Ben. I think one way I can help is to start checking out some of those assumptions. Like, for instance, one thing I want to know from you, Ben, is just how serious you *are* about the annual business plan."

Now Louise went to the wall where she had posted a large sheet of blank paper. On it she wrote "Communications Skills," and underneath: (1) Check assumptions. (2) I want X from Y.

"Of course I'm serious about the business plan," replied Ben in exasperation.

"That's not what I asked, Ben. I know you're serious. I asked *how* serious, because it seems to me that if you were very serious you would have been doing some things differently."

Ben reflected, "I'd like to think that one over before answering."

"Suppose we take a break," said Louise, "and when we come back, start with the annual plan." They agreed.

"But before we do, I have some unfinished business with you, Mike, " said Louise. She was aware that Mike had looked sad since she had cut him off. He had seemed further depressed when George disagreed with him point-blank. "When George told Ben that he has been losing credibility, you tried to help Ben. You agreed with him that the rest of you might not be living up to your responsibilities. I cut you off because I thought it would be better for Ben to understand what George was trying to get across."

Ben agreed. "You were trying to get me off the hook, Mike. Maybe I liked it at the moment, but it isn't what we . . . what I need now. I know I do tend to act the way Les described, but I didn't know it mattered that much. I want to talk more about it before this meeting is over."

Mike seemed bewildered. This was contrary to everything he had learned in *his* school of experience.

"Put it this way, Mike," said Louise. "At least in this meeting, can we talk to each other without chicken soup? You know, that term—chicken soup—comes from the proverbial Jewish mother who doles out chicken soup for all ailments and all problems. Chicken soup tastes good, but it's also a way of smoothing over problems instead of facing them."

Louise sensed the group's understanding and support on this point. She added to the "Communications Skills" list a third point, (3) No chicken soup.

"OK, Mike, old buddy," said the normally cold, businesslike Brad, "you and me are going to have to take a vow of no more chicken soup, right?"

"Right," said Mike, grateful for the friendly hand.

Louise knew that because she had highlighted the chicken soup issue, Mike now felt group pressure to change life-long ways of avoiding conflict. That pressure might be helpful to Mike. On the other hand, his apparent ready agreement might have been simply another appeasement. Louise knew that it was less important for Mike to agree about chicken soup than to feel free to disagree. Louise decided to air this issue before the end of the meeting, without putting Mike on the spot.

The group had warmed to its task and it was given a good start by Ben, who had by now concluded that Les' allegations were true. If the annual business plan had indeed been as important to him as he had been saying, he would surely have put more muscle behind it. He had been as guilty of indifference as the regional managers whom he had been accusing. He had also concluded, however, that as a company they had let as much time slip by as they could safely afford, and he was now ready to make a larger personal commitment of his time and energy to the company's top priorities.

At this point Phil, the Director of Applied Technology, spoke up. Since he was responsible for developing new technical areas into business opportunities, he had imagined fingers pointing in his direction at various times during the meeting. Phil had never enjoyed business development, and now he proposed that the function be set up as a separate job, reporting directly to Ben. He further suggested that Angelo take the job, since he was the most vigorous promoter.

That sounded right to everyone, including Ben, and they agreed that Angelo would take the job for two years, with the support of a steering committee made up of his fellow regional managers and Phil.

Ben was particularly delighted at the outcome. The regional managers, who had been going their separate ways, had now become jointly responsible for results. This was discussed openly.

"You know," Ben said, "I no longer feel the need for an assistant."

"What assistant?" asked George.

The room fell suddenly silent. Ben saw their astonished looks, and then he told them in detail how and why he had almost hired an assistant.

"Big white chief speak with forked tongue," said Mike. "You *wantum* team; you *no* wantum team?" Everyone laughed, including Ben. It was no longer an issue.

Louise now asked the group to critique the meeting thus far; what they liked, what they didn't like, and what remained to be done. The responses were largely positive, and a few small agenda items were brought up. Louise suggested a way of handling these, and also a way to check for remaining bits of "unfinished business."

She asked them to take a piece of paper and write on it the names of all the others in this group. "Then ask yourself three questions about your relationship with each person: 'What do I want from him?', 'What *don't* I want from him?', and 'What can I give him?' Make notes. Then, if it seems that you have any unfinished business with anyone, please tell him directly."

Phil was finally willing to take up with the regional managers the issue that had been bothering him for months. "I want you four to make more use of our services and stop hiring specialists yourselves."

The others were willing to discuss this issue with Phil. As they conversed, the picture became clear: the regional managers had high respect for Phil and for most of his senior people; however, some of the less experienced specialists were not getting enough supervision from Phil and they were not working closely with the regional managers they were supposed to be supporting. Within an hour an agreement had been worked out, including commitment from the regional managers that if things worked well in the next six months, they would put some of their specialists under Phil's direct supervision.

Then the discussion turned sharply, and became an exchange of positive feedback.

By and large they were very pleased with the support they had received from one another, both in the office and during the meeting, and they said so, individually and specifically. When they were done, Louise continued the winding-up process by inviting them to review all the papers on the wall with her. She reviewed the "Communications Skills" list, which now had twelve items. . . . She noted which skills she felt they were practicing well and which they were still weak in.

She went over the running record of the meeting, especially the "Agreements," "Decisions," and "Action Items," and together they cleared up remaining ambiguities.

Then Louise called for a final critique of the meeting. Les summarized the responses: "We were a pretty good team when we came here, but we're a better one now, and I think we're going to get more action."

As the meeting dispersed, Louise compared notes with Ben. Although he realized that they had not solved every one of the company's problems and there were surely be some backsliding from commitments made, nevertheless he now felt more optimistic about his company's future.

Boyd Consumer Goods Company*

Edgar H. Schein

In the Boyd Consumer Goods Company, the contact client was a member of the personnel department who had known of my interests for some time, had had other contacts with professors at the Sloan School (M.I.T.), and was interested in finding a consultant to help the newly appointed president manage the transition from "traditional" to more "modern" techniques of management in his organization.

. . . [T]he exploratory meeting was relatively perfunctory because I had already met the president at a management-development session run by the company some months earlier at which I was the speaker. The meeting consisted of the personnel vice-president, the president, and myself, and moved rapidly toward the next stage of actually defining the contract, the goals, and the setting in which to work. . . . The initial exploration led to a favorable response on both my part and that of the contact client.

. . . At the exploratory meeting with the president, Bill, I inquired whether there was some regular meeting which he held with his immediate subordinates. There was such a group which met weekly and it was agreed that I would sit in on it. Bill explained to the group that he had asked me to sit in to help the group function more effectively and then asked me to explain how I saw my own role. I described process consultation and the kinds of things I would be looking for; stated that I would not be very active, but preferred the group just to work along as it normally would; and that I would make comments as I saw opportunities to be helpful. It was decided that after a few meetings I would interview each member of the seven-man group individually.

The climate of the Boyd group was . . . formal; there was . . . reliance on Bill to run the meeting, and . . . ambiguity about the feelings of the members for each other.

. . . . [W]hen I began to interview group members . . . I concentrated . . . on what kind of job each member had, with whom he had to work in the performance of that job, what kinds of problems existed in any of these relationships, what organizational factors aided or hindered effective job performance, what the company climate was like, and so on.

. . . I found that the key Boyd group was strangling itself with formality

* SOURCE: edited by Roy McLennan and abstracted from Edgar H. Schein, *Process Consultation.* ©1969. Addison-Wesley Publishing Company, Inc., Reading, Mass. pp. 80, 83, 92–3, 100, 108–110. Reprinted with permission.

and trivia. Agendas were long and detailed, meetings were highly formal, and members were responsible for reporting to the group on various operational issues on a carefully planned monthly schedule. If anyone tried to make comments on a report, he was quickly reminded that he knew less about the topic than the reporter. Consequently most of the talk during meetings was of a reporting, attack, or defense variety. Little open-ended problem-solving took place. Most members looked (and acted) passive and bored. When interviewed, they confirmed that they felt this way during meetings; yet, surprisingly, they tended to defend their meetings as necessary.

My own feeling was that the members were caught up in their own traditions. They had always run meetings this way; hence they felt that boredom and lack of involvement were the "normal" subjective feelings for participants in a meeting. Those who felt a little more frustrated and rebellious did not know what methods to follow for livelier, more productive meetings. Hence there were widespread feelings of apathy, resignation, and frustration.

I tried a whole series of interventions over a period of several months, most of them unsuccessful from my point of view. First, I asked the group to review its own agenda and share feelings about it. Some members revealed feelings of frustration but still staunchly defended the agenda pattern as necessary. Second, I tried to help the group to differentiate policy from operational decisions. It seemed to me that whenever they tried to discuss policy, operational problems would intervene and preempt a major portion of the time. I also felt that the group tended to hold too limited a concept of policy. The group verbally agreed with me, but failed to change its pattern of operation in any substantial way. Third, I tried being directly confrontive about the apathy and frustration which I saw in the members. The group accepted my confrontation like "good soldiers," defended itself a little bit, told me I had been very helpful, and then resumed its discussions in the old pattern.

A partial breakthrough came some months later. The president of the company had in the meantime attended a sensitivity-training lab and had come back with a somewhat greater enthusiasm for group-process work. He realized that the group could be more productive and recognized the need to make it so. We agreed to devote some time to discussion of what the group's agenda and pattern of operations should be. In the meantime, another event had taken place: the company had reorganized, putting responsibility for many of the day-to-day operational problems clearly on the shoulders of certain key individuals. In order to make the reorganization work, it was decided not to have as much group time devoted to reporting out and monitoring members' work areas.

When the group met to discuss its own future, some of the same depression which I had previously observed was still in evidence. After about twenty minutes of general discussion, I said in a rather exasperated tone that I never saw this group have any *fun*. What would it take to make people want to come to the meeting because the meeting would be *fun*? This comment released a burst of laughter, as if some kind of inner dam had burst. The group had really been operating on the assumption that work could *not* be fun, and was just silently taking its painful medicine.

Once this issue had been brought out into the open, members agreed that meetings could be more fun. In the subsequent discussion, members delineated several key requirements for better meetings: a climate of greater acceptance in the group which would permit members to share ideas, plans, and problems with each other, without feeling that they would be attacked by other members; more concentration on sharing information and problems, and less concentration on trying to make decisions in the group; and more effective use of group time by better agenda control.

The group spent an hour or more discussing how it might operate in the future, and, more importantly, agreed on the use of a process-analysis session at the end of each meeting, to review whether or not it was hitting its own targets. It was decided that one member of the group should be the process recorder and give feedback to the group at the end of the session. This decision was especially good since the members needed practice in observing group process. Shortly afterwards, my participation in the meetings was curtailed by other commitments, but recently I had an opportunity to discuss the group's progress with the president, and he feels that the meetings have improved, that the climate is more open, and that the process-observer role has been very helpful to the group in monitoring its own functioning.

This case illustrates for me the trial-and-error nature of intervention. I could not really have predicted which of my various efforts to loosen the group up would work. Indeed, if there had not been related changes such as the reorganization and the president's experience at the training laboratory, none of my efforts might have worked. Merely helping the group to identify its process does not automatically produce a change in that process, even if the group is quite frustrated and knows a change is needed.

Emerging Principles of Achieving Change*

Dorwin Cartwright

.... What principles of achieving change in people can we see emerging? To begin with the most general proposition, we may state that the behavior, attitudes, beliefs, and values of the individual are all firmly grounded in the groups to which he belongs. How aggressive or cooperative a person is, how much self-respect and self-confidence he has, how energetic and productive his work is, what he aspires to, what he believes to be true and good, whom he loves or hates, and what beliefs, and prejudices he holds—all these characteristics are highly determined by the individual's group memberships. In a real sense, they are properties of groups and of the relationships between people. Whether they change or resist change will, therefore, be greatly influenced by the nature of these groups. Attempts to change them must be concerned with the dynamics of groups.

In examining more specifically how groups enter into the process of change, we find it useful to view groups in at least three different ways. In the first view, the group is seen as a source of influence over its members. Efforts to change behavior can be supported or blocked by pressures on members stemming from the group. To make constructive use of these pressures the group must be used *as a medium of change.* In the second view, the group itself becomes the *target of change.* To change the behavior of individuals it may be necessary to change the standards of the group, its style of leadership, its emotional atmosphere, or its stratification into cliques and hierarchies. Even though the goal may be to change the behavior of *individuals*, the target of change becomes the group. In the third view, it is recognized that many changes of behavior can be brought about only by the organized efforts of groups *as agents of change.* A committee to combat intolerance, a labor union, an employers association, a citizens group to increase the pay of teachers—any action group will be more or less effective depending upon the way it is organized, the satisfactions it provides to its members, the degree to which its goals are clear, and a host of other properties of the group.

An adequate social technology of change, then, requires at the very least a scientific understanding of groups viewed in each of these ways. We shall consider here only the first two aspects of the problem: the group as a medium of change and as a target of change.

* Source: Dorwin Cartwright, "Achieving Change in People: Some Applications of Group Dynamics Theory," *Human Relations,* 4 (1951), pp. 387–391. Reprinted with permission of Plenum Publishing Corporation.

THE GROUP AS A MEDIUM OF CHANGE

> *Principle No. 1.* If the group is to be used effectively as a medium of change, those people who are to be changed and those who are to exert influence for change must have a strong sense of belonging to the same group.

Kurt Lewin described this principle well: "The normal gap between teacher and student, doctor and patient, social workers and public, can . . . be a real obstacle to acceptance of the advocated conduct." In other words, in spite of whatever status differences there might be between them, the teacher and the student have to feel as members of one group in matters involving their sense of values. The chances for reeducation seem to be increased whenever a strong we-feeling is created. Recent experiments by Preston and Heintz have demonstrated greater changes of opinions among members of discussion groups operating with participatory leadership than among those with supervisory leadership. The implications of this principle for classroom teaching are far-reaching. The same may be said of supervision in the factory, army, or hospital.

> *Principle No. 2.* The more attractive the group is to its members the greater is the influence that the group can exert on its members.

This principle has been extensively documented by Festinger and his co-workers. They have been able to show in a variety of settings that in more cohesive groups there is a greater readiness of members to attempt to influence others, a greater readiness to be influenced by others, and stronger pressures toward conformity when conformity is a relevant matter for the group. Important for the practitioner wanting to make use of this principle is, of course, the question of how to increase the attractiveness of groups. This is a question with many answers. Suffice it to say that a group is more attractive the more it satisfies the needs of its members. We have been able to demonstrate experimentally an increase in group cohesiveness by increasing the liking of members for each other as persons, by increasing the perceived importance of the group goal, and by increasing the prestige of the group among other groups. Experienced group workers could add many other ways to this list.

> *Principle No. 3.* In attempts to change attitudes, values, or behavior, the more relevant they are to the basis of attraction to the group, the greater will be the influence that the group can exert upon them.

I believe this principle gives a clue to some otherwise puzzling phenomena. How does it happen that a group, like a labor union, seems to be able to exert such strong discipline over its members in some matters (let us say in dealings with management), while it seems unable to exert nearly the same influence in other matters (let us say in political action)? If we examine why it is that members are attracted to the group, I believe we will find that a particular reason for belonging seems more related to some of the group's activities than to others. If a man joins a union mainly to keep his job and to improve his working conditions, he may be largely uninfluenced by the union's attempt to modify his attitudes toward national and international affairs. Groups differ tremendously in the range of matters that are relevant to them and hence over which they have influence. Much of the inefficiency of adult education could be reduced if more attention were paid to the need that influence attempts be appropriate to the groups in which they are made.

> *Principle No. 4.* The greater the prestige of a group member in the eyes of the other members, the greater the influence he can exert.

Polansky, Lippitt, and Redl have demonstrated this principle with great care and methodological ingenuity in a series of studies in children's summer camps. From a practical point of view it must be emphasized that the things giving prestige to a member may not be those characteristics most prized by the official management of the group. The most prestige-carrying member of a Sunday school class may not possess the characteristics most similar to the minister of the church. The teacher's pet may be a poor source of influence within a class. This principle is the basis for the common observation that the official leader and the actual leader of a group are often not the same individual.

> *Principle No. 5.* Efforts to change individuals or subparts of a group which, if successful, would have the result of making them deviate from the norms of the group will encounter strong resistance.

During the past few years a great deal of evidence has been accumulated showing the tremendous pressures which groups can exert upon members to conform to the group's norms. The price of deviation in most groups is rejection or even expulsion. If the member really wants to belong and be accepted, he cannot withstand this type of pressure. It is for this reason that efforts to change people by taking them from the group and giving them special training so often have disappointing results. This principle also accounts for the finding that people thus trained sometimes display increased tension, aggressiveness toward the group, or a tendency to form cults or cliques with others who have shared their training.

These five principles concerning the group as a medium of change would appear to have readiest application to groups created for the purpose of producing changes in people. They provide certain specifications for building effective training or therapy groups. They also point, however, to a difficulty in producing change in people in that they show how resistant an individual is to changing in any way contrary to group pressures and expectations. In order to achieve many kinds of changes in people, therefore, it is necessary to deal with the group as a target of change.

THE GROUP AS A TARGET OF CHANGE

> *Principle No. 6.* Strong pressure for changes in the group can be established by creating a shared perception by members of the need for change, thus making the source of pressure for change lie within the group.

Marrow and French report a dramatic case study which illustrates this principle quite well. A manufacturing concern had a policy against hiring women over 30 because it was believed that they were slower, more difficult to train, and more likely to be absent. The staff psychologist was able to present to management evidence that this belief was clearly unwarranted at least within their own company. The psychologist's facts, however, were rejected and ignored as a basis for action because they violated accepted beliefs. It was claimed that they went against the direct experience of the foremen. Then the psychologist hit upon a plan for achieving change which differed drastically from the usual one of argument, persuasion, and pressure. He proposed that management conduct its own analysis of the situation. With his help management collected all the facts which they believed were relevant to the problem. When the results were in they were now their own facts rather than those of some "outside" expert. Policy was immediately changed without further resistance. The important point here is that facts are not enough. The facts must be the accepted property of the group if they are to become an effective basis for change. There seems to be all the difference in the world in changes actually carried out between those cases in which a consulting firm is hired to do a study and present a report and those in which technical experts are asked to collaborate with the group in doing its own study.

> *Principle No. 7.* Information relating to the need for changes, plans for change, and consequences of change must be shared by all relevant people in the group.

Another way of stating this principle is to say that change of a group ordinarily requires the opening of communication channels. Newcomb has shown how one of the first consequences of mistrust and hostility is the avoidance of communicating openly and freely about the things producing the tension. If you look closely at a pathological group (that is, one that has trouble making decisions or effecting coordinated efforts of its members), you will certainly find strong restraints in that group against communicating vital information among its members. Until these restraints are removed there can be little hope for any real and lasting changes in the group's functioning. In passing it should be pointed out that the removal of barriers to communication will ordinarily be accompanied by a sudden increase in the communication of hostility. The group may appear to be falling apart, and it will certainly be a painful experience to many of the members. This pain and the fear that things are getting out of hand often stop the process of change once begun.

Principle No. 8. Changes in one part of a group produce strain in other related parts which can be reduced only by eliminating the change or by bringing about read-adjustments in the related parts.

It is a common practice to undertake improvements in group functioning by providing training programs for certain classes of people in the organization. A training program for foremen, for nurses, for teachers, or for group workers is established. If the content of the training is relevant for organizational change, it must of necessity deal with the relationships these people have with other subgroups. If nurses in a hospital change their behavior significantly, it will affect their relations both with the patients and with the doctors. It is unrealistic to assume that both these groups will remain indifferent to any significant changes in this respect. In hierarchical structures this process is most clear. Lippitt has proposed on the basis of research and experience that in such organizations attempts at change should always involve three levels, one being the major target of change and the other two being the one above and the one below.

REFERENCES

CARTWRIGHT, D. "Some Principles of Mass Persuasion: Selected Findings of Research on the Sale of United States War Bonds." *Human Relations* 2 (1949), pp. 253–67.

CARTWRIGHT, D. *The Research Center for Group Dynamics: A Report of Five Years' Activities and a View of Future Needs.* Ann Arbor, Mich.: Institute for Social Research, 1950.

COCH, L., and FRENCH, J. R. P., JR. "Overcoming Resistance to Change." *Human Relations* 1 (1948), pp. 512–32.

FESTINGER, L., et al. *Theory and Experiment in Social Communication.* Collected papers. Ann Arbor, Mich.: Institute for Social Research, 1950.

LEWIN, K. *Resolving Social Conflicts.* New York: Harper & Row, 1948.

LEWIN, K. *Field Theory in Social Science.* New York: Harper & Row, 1951, pp. 229–36.

LEWIN, K.; R. LIPPITT; and R. K. WHITE. "Patterns of Aggressive Behavior in Experimentally Created 'Social Climates'." *Journal of Social Psychology* 10 (1939), pp. 271–99.

LIPPITT, R. *Training in Community Relations.* New York: Harper & Row, 1949.

MARROW, A. J., and J. R. P. FRENCH, JR. "Changing a Stereotype in Industry." *Journal of Social Issues* 1, no. 3 (1945), pp. 33–7.

NEWCOMB, T. M. "Autistic Hostility and Social Reality." *Human Relations* 1 (1947), pp. 69–86.

POLANSKY, N.; R. LIPPITT; and F. REDL. "An Investigation of Behavioral Contagion in Groups." *Human Relations* 3 (1950), pp. 319–48.

PRESTON, M. G., and R. K. HEINTZ. "Effects of Participatory versus Supervisory Leadership on Group Judgment." *Journal of Abnormal and Social Psychology* 44 (1949), pp. 345–55.

Group Dynamics*

David A. Kolb, Irwin M. Rubin, and James M. McIntyre

INTRODUCTION

"A camel is a horse put together by a committee." "Groupthink." These two clichés are often applied to group decision making. Most people believe that working in groups is inevitably less efficient, more time consuming, and very frustrating and that it creates conformity in thinking. Many of these deeply held beliefs are simply unsubstantiated or found to be less generally true than was originally believed. Stoner's work,[1] for example, on the riskiness of group versus individual decisions is a case in point. Although the reasons are not yet fully understood[2] it is clear that, contrary to popular belief, under certain conditions groups make more *risky* decisions than do individuals.

All of us have participated in groups of various sorts, family, gang, team, work group, and the like, but rarely have we taken the time to observe what was going on in the group or why the members were behaving in the way they were.[3] In thinking about groups, few people realize that in any group there are at least two classes of issues operating at any given point. One is the reason for the group's existence in the first place (e.g., to solve a particular problem). These are called *content* or *task issues*. A second, and equally important, set of issues concerns elements of how the group is going about achieving its formal task. These are called *process issues*.[4]

---

* SOURCE: David A. Kolb, Irwin M. Rubin, and James M. McIntyre, *Organizational Psychology: An Experiential Approach to Organizational Behavior*, 4th ed. pp. 128–134, 143–144. ©1984. Reprinted by permission of Prentice-Hall, Inc., Englewood Cliffs, N.J.

[1] James A. F. Stoner, "Risky and Cautious Shifts in Group Decisions: The Influence of Widely Held Values," Working Paper, Sloan School of Management, Massachusetts Institute of Technology, October 1967.

[2] Roger Brown, "Group Dynamics," in *Social Psychology* (New York: Free Press, 1967).

[3] The literature on group dynamics has grown to enormous proportions. See D. Cartwright and A. Zander, eds., *Group Dynamics—Research and Theory*, 3rd ed. (New York: Harper & Row, Publishers, 1968), and B. E. Collins and H. Guetzkow, *A Social Psychology of Group Processes for Decision-Making* (New York: John Wiley & Sons, Inc., 1964).

[4] For a discussion of the differences between content and process issues, see Edgar H. Schein, *Process Consultation: Its Role in Organizational Development* (Reading, Mass.: Addison-Wesley Publishing Co., Inc., 1969).

Content versus Process

When we observe what a group is talking about, we are focusing on the *content*. When we try to observe how the group is handling its communication (i.e., who talks how much or who talks to whom), we are focusing on group *process*. The content of the conversation is often a good clue as to what process issue may be on people's minds when they find it difficult to confront the issue directly. It often seems that groups spend considerable time talking about things that, on the surface, have nothing to do with the task at hand. Discussing the worthlessness of their previous PTA meetings may mean that members are not satisfied with the performance of their present group. The assumption is that it is less threatening to talk about how we feel about PTA meetings (there-and-then) than it is to talk about our feelings about these (here-and-now) meetings.

Communication

One of the easiest aspects of group process to observe is the pattern of communication:

1. Who talks? for how long? how often?
2. Whom do people look at when they talk?
   a. Individuals, possibly potential supporters
   b. The group
   c. Nobody
3. Who talks after whom, or who interrupts whom?
4. What style of communication is used (assertions, questions, tone of voice, gesture, etc.)?

The kind of observations we make gives us clues to other important things that may be going on in the group, such as who leads whom and who influences whom.

Decision-Making Procedures[5]

Whether we are aware of it or not, groups are making decisions all the time, some of them consciously and in reference to the major tasks at hand, some of them without much awareness and in reference to group procedures or standards of operation. It is important to observe how decisions are made in a group, to assess the appropriateness of the decision to the matter being

---

[5] Much of the following material has appeared in a variety of places and is a standard input into many training programs, such as those conducted by the National Training Laboratory. This particular material was abridged, with permission of the author, from an unpublished paper by Edgar H. Schein, "What to Observe in Groups." The Collins and Guetzkow book, *A Social Psychology of Group Processes for Decision-Making*, is also very relevant here.

decided on and to assess whether the consequences of given methods are really what the group members bargained for.

Group decisions are notoriously hard to undo.[6] When someone says, "Well, we decided to do it, didn't we?" any budding opposition is quickly immobilized. We can undo the decision only if we reconstruct and understand how we made it and test whether this method was appropriate or not.

Some methods by which groups make decisions are the following:[7]

1. The *plop:* "I think we should appoint a chairperson." . . . Silence.
2. The *self-authorized agenda:* "I think we should introduce ourselves. My name is Jane Allen. . .".
3. The *handclasp:* Person A: "I wonder if it would be helpful to introduce ourselves?" Person B: "I think it would; my name is Pete Jones."
4. The *minority decision:* "Does anyone object?" or "We all agree."
5. *Majority–minority voting.*
6. *Polling:* "Let's see where everyone stands. What do you think?"
7. *Consensus testing:* Genuine exploration to test for opposition and to determine whether opposition feels strongly enough to refuse to implement decision; not necessarily unanimity but essential agreement by all. Consensus does *not* involve psuedo- "listening" ("Let's hear Joe out") and then doing what we were going to do in the first place ("OK, now that everyone has had a chance to talk, let's go ahead with the original decision").

Task, Maintenance, and Self-oriented Behavior[8]

Behavior in the group can be viewed in terms of what its purpose or function seems to be. When a member says something, is the intent primarily to get the group task accomplished (task) or to improve or patch up some relationship among members (maintenance), or is the behavior primarily meeting a personal need or goal without regard to the group's problems (self-oriented)?

As the group grows and members' needs become integrated with group goals, there will be less self-oriented behavior and more task or maintenance behavior. Types of behavior relevant to the group's fulfillment of its *task* are the following:

1. *Initiating.* For any group to function, some person(s) must be willing to take some initiative. These can be seemingly trivial statements such as "Let's build an agenda" or "It's time we moved on to the next item," but without them, little task-related activity would occur in a group. People would either sit in silence and/or side conversations would develop.

[6] Literature on group conformity is relevant to this point. For a summary, see E. L. Walker and R. W. Heyns, *An Anatomy for Conformity* (Englewood Cliffs, N.J.: Prentice-Hall, Inc., 1962).

[7] This typology was developed by Robert R. Blake.

[8] K. D. Benne and P. Sheats, "Functional Roles of Group Members," *Journal of Social Issues,* Vol. 2 (1948), pp. 42–47.

2,3. *Seeking or giving information or openness.* The clear and efficient flow of information, facts, and opinions is essential to any task accomplishment. Giving-type statements—"I have some information that may be relevant" or "My own opinion in this matter is . . ."—are important to ensure decisions based on full information. Information-seeking statements not only help the seeker but the entire group.

4. *Clarifying and elaborating.* Many useful inputs into group work get lost if this task-related behavior is missing. "Let me give an example that will clarify the point just made" and "Let me elaborate and build upon that idea" are examples of positive behaviors in this regard. They communicate a listening and collaborative stance.

5. *Summarizing.* At various points during a group's work, it is very helpful if someone takes a moment to summarize the group's discussion. This gives the entire group an opportunity to pause for a moment, step back, see how far they have come, where they are, and how much farther they must go to complete their work.

6. *Consensus testing.* Many times a group's work must result in a consensus decision.[9] At various points in the meeting, the statement "Have we made a decision on that point?" can be very helpful. Even if the group is not yet ready to commit itself to a decision, it serves to remind everyone that a decision needs to be made and, as such, it adds positive work tension into the group.

Following are types of behavior relevant to the group's remaining in good working order, with a good climate for task work and good relationships that permit maximum use of member resources—namely, *group maintenance:*

1. *Gatekeeping.* Gatekeeping is an essential maintenance function in a group. Without it, information gets lost, multiple conversations develop, and less assertive people get cut off and drop out of the meeting. "Let's give Joe a chance to finish his thought" and "If people would talk one at a time, I'd find it easier to listen and add to our discussion" are examples in this regard.

2. *Encouraging.* Encouraging also ensures that all the potentially relevant information the group needs is shared, listened to, and considered. "I know you haven't had a chance to work it through in your mind, but keep thinking out loud and we'll try to help." "Before we close this off, Mary, do you have anything to add?"

3. *Harmonizing and compromising.* These two functions are very important but tricky because their overuse or inappropriate use can serve to reduce a group's effectiveness. If smoothing over issues (harmonizing) and each party's giving in a bit (compromise) serve to mask important underlying issues, creative solutions to problems will be fewer in number and commitment to decisions taken will be reduced.

4. *Standard setting and testing.* This category of behavior acts as a kind of overall maintenance function. Its focus is how well the group's needs for task-oriented behavior and maintenance-oriented behaviors are being met. All groups will reach a point where "something is going wrong" or "something doesn't feel right." At such points, effective groups stop the music, test their own process,

---

[9] Not all decisions can/should be made by group consensus. For more details on this issue, see Chapter 12, *Leadership and Decision Making,* and Victor H. Vroom and P. Yetton, *Leadership and Decision Making* (Pittsburgh, Pa.: University of Pittsburgh Press, 1973).

and set new standards where they are required. "I'm losing track of the conversation. If other people are willing, maybe it would help if someone could summarize the last 10 minutes."

For a group to be effective, both task-oriented behavior and maintenance-oriented behavior is needed.

Emotional Issues: Causes of Self-oriented Emotional Behavior[10]

The processes described so far deal with the group's attempt to work and the work-facilitating functions of task and maintenance. But there are many forces active in groups that disturb work, that represent a kind of emotional underground or undercurrent in the stream of group life. These underlying emotional issues produce a variety of self-oriented behaviors that interfere with or are destructive to effective group functioning. They cannot be ignored or wished away, however. Rather, they must be recognized, their causes must be understood, and as the group develops, conditions must be created that permit these same emotional energies to be channeled in the direction of group effort. What are these issues or basic causes?

1. The problem of identity: Who am I here? How am I to present myself to others? What role should I play in the group?
2. The problem of control and power: Who has the power in the situation? How much power, control, and influence do I have in the situation? How much do I need?
3. The problem of goals: Which of my needs and goals can this group fulfill? Can any of my needs be met here? To which of the group's goals can I attach myself?
4. The problem of acceptance and intimacy: Am I accepted by the others? Do I accept them? Do they like me? Do I like them? How close to others do I want to become?

Self-oriented behaviors tend to be more prevalent in a group at certain points in the group's life. Early in the life of a new group one can expect to see many examples of self-oriented behaviors. Members are new to one another and a certain amount of "feeling out" is to be expected. Sometimes this takes place in after-hours social situations—"Why don't we get together after work for a drink?" On a less intense scale, the same phenomenon can be observed at the start of a group meeting with an old, established group. Side conversations and social chatter characterize the first few minutes while people catch up on where they have been since the last meeting.

A third point in a group's life when self-oriented behaviors can be observed is when a newcomer joins an already established group. It is not unlike the dynamics that develop when a new sibling arrives in a family.

---

[10] This section is based on Schein's *Process Consultation*.

Everyone else may be sincerely happy with the newcomer ("We really need her resources"); nonetheless, this is now a "new" group. The old equilibrium has been changed and a new one must take its place.

None of the foregoing sounds particularly like an undercurrent, an emotional underground, that could be potentially destructive to effective group functioning. While all these issues can be observed in a group, their potential destructiveness is highest at that time when the group most needs to be maximally effective—under stress. In that sense, they are akin to regressive individual behaviors: in times of stress, individuals will regress to an earlier stage of development. Different individuals handle their anxiety in different ways, thus generating many different kinds of reactions in groups.

Following are types of emotional behavior that result from tension and from the attempt to resolve underlying problems:[11]

1. Tough emotions: anger, hostility, self-assertiveness
   a. Fighting with others
   b. Punishing others
   c. Controlling others
   d. Counterdependency
2. Tender emotions: love, sympathy, desire to help, need for affiliation with others
   a. Supporting and helping others
   b. Depending on others
   c. Pairing up or affiliating with others
3. Denial of all emotion
   a. Withdrawing from others
   b. Falling back on logic or reason

Individuals have different styles of reducing tension and expressing emotion. Three "pure types" have been identified:

1. The "friendly helper" orientation: acceptance of tender emotions, denial of tough emotions—"Let's not fight, let's help each other"; can give and receive affection but cannot tolerate hostility and fight.
2. The "tough battler" orientation: acceptance of tough emotions and denial of tender emotions—"Let's fight it out"; can deal with hostility but not with love, support, and affiliation.
3. The "logical thinker" orientation: denial of all emotion—"Let's reason this thing out"; cannot deal with tender or tough emotions; hence shuts eyes and ears to much going on around him.

But:

Friendly Helpers will achieve their world of warmth and intimacy *only* by allowing conflicts and differences to be raised and resolved. They find that they can become close with people *only* if they can accept what is dissimilar as well as what is similar in their behavior.

---

[11] For another view of emotional behavior in groups, see William C. Schutz, "Interpersonal Underworld," *Harvard Business Review,* Vol. 36, No. 4 (July–August 1958), pp. 123–125.

Tough Battlers will achieve their world of toughness and conflict *only* if they can create a climate of warmth and trust in which these will be allowed to develop.

Logical Thinkers will achieve their world of understanding and logic *only* if they can accept that their feelings and the feelings of others (both tough and tender) are also facts and contribute importantly toward our ability to understand interpersonal situations (see Table 5-1).

These three, as described, are clearly pure types; the average person has some elements of each. What varies is emphasis or the most characteristic style. The three styles can be depicted as corners of an equilateral triangle:

Group Norms

There is one final issue that must be addressed with respect to group functioning—group norms. A norm in a group is like an individual habit. It is an unwritten, often implicit, rule that defines what attitudes and behaviors constitute being a "good" group member versus a "bad" group member.

All groups create norms as they develop and mature. In and of themselves, norms are neither good nor bad. The important point is whether or not the norms that do exist support the group's work or act to reduce effectiveness.

Let us examine an example. Many groups operate under the norm: "You argue rigorously with everyone's ideas and proposals . . . except the boss's!" In addition to the norm, the group also develops, often in very subtle ways, reward and punishment mechanisms to keep violators of the norm in line, for example, the "Dutch uncle" talk after the meeting that starts off: "Let me tell you something for your own benefit." Now, if the boss's ideas are always better than anyone else's, this norm probably saves the group time and energy. If this were not true it is not hard to see how the group's work can begin to suffer (both in terms of quality and individual commitment).

There is one instance in which a norm always had a bad effect, however. This is when the unspoken rule says, "In this group, no one ever dares to question or suggest that we examine our norms." With respect to the mainte-nance behaviors discussed earlier, there is an absence of standard setting and

Table 5-1   Three Bests of All Possible Worlds

1. FRIENDLY HELPER	2. TOUGH BATTLER	3. LOGICAL THINKER
A world of mutual love, affection, tenderness, sympathy	A world of conflict, fight, power, assertiveness	A world of understanding, logic, systems, knowledge
Task-Maintenance Behavior		
Harmonizing	Initiating	Gathering information
Compromising	Coordinating	Clarifying ideas and words
Gatekeeping by concern	Pressing for results	Systematizing
Encouraging	Pressing for consensus	Procedures
Expressing warmth	Exploring differences	Evaluating the logic of proposals
	Gatekeeping by command	
Constructs Used in Evaluating Others		
Who is warm and who is hostile?	Who is strong and who is weak?	Who is bright and who is stupid?
Who helps and who hurts others?	Who is winning and who is losing?	Who is accurate and who is inaccurate?
		Who thinks clearly and who is fuzzy?
Methods of Influence		
Appeasing	Giving orders	Appealing to rules and regulations
Appealing to pity	Offering challenges	Appealing to logic
	Threatening	Referring to "facts" and overwhelming knowledge
Personal Threats		
That he or she will not be loved	That he or she will lose his or her ability to fight (power)	That his or her world is not ordered
That he or she will be overwhelmed by feelings of hostility	That he or she will become "soft" and "sentimental"	That he or she will be overwhelmed by love or hate

testing and an implied punishment for anyone who engages in such behavior. Such a "Catch 22" norm is unlikely to facilitate an effectively functioning group.

SUMMARY

As society becomes more complex and we continue to make major advances in our technological capability, more and more of organizational life will revolve around a team or group structure. The "information explosion" will guarantee that no one person can expect to have all the facts necessary to make many decisions. "Temporary systems," in which a group of people join for a short-term task and then disperse to form new and different task groups to tackle other problems will become more prevalent.[12] Groups play an important part in organizational life today, and every indication points toward increased importance in the future.

The distinction made in this exercise among task issues, maintenance issues, and self-oriented issues can be important in understanding how groups function. Most of us assume that if a group of people is called together to perform a task, nothing but the task is important or relevant. This assumption rests upon the belief that it is not only feasible but essential that we separate our emotional self (needs, wants, motives) from our intellectual, rational, problem-solving self. This is impossible. When people enter a group situation, they bring their total selves, the emotional as well as the intellectual. In fact, certain aspects of our emotional selves will become more salient because we are in a group situation. Attempts to bury, wish away, or ignore the interpersonal aspects of group interaction is much like sweeping dirt under the rug—sooner or later the pile gets big enough that someone will trip over it.

In some ways, the appointment of a chairperson or moderator reflects recognition of the fact that groups do not always "stay on the track." While this is often useful, there are two potential problems with this approach. First, seldom do the group members spend any time discussing why they are "off the track." More often the chairperson will say something like "We're getting off the main track, let's get back to it!" and that's all that happens. It is extremely important to realize that if people are having difficulty staying on the track, there are reasons for the behavior and simply saying "Let's get back to it" does nothing to eliminate the basic causes. Worse than that, this kind of behavior ("Let's quit wasting time and get to the task") may further accelerate the underlying reasons for lack of involvement and may make the situation worse.

Second, there is no inherent reason that only one person in a group should have the responsibility for worrying about how the group is progressing. Everyone can and should share this responsibility. To delegate this function or role to one individual is in some situations a highly inefficient utilization of resources. People can learn to be effective participant-observers at one and the same time. In such a group, *anyone* who feels that something is not right can and should raise the issue for the total group to examine. Anyone who observes a need for a particular kind of task or maintenance behavior can help the group. In a well-functioning group (working on something other than a routine programmable task), an observer looking in from the outside might not be able to pick out the formal leadership. The "leadership function" could pass around according to the group's need at a particular point.

It is important, in other words, to distinguish between leaders as persons

---

[12] M. B. Miles, "On Temporary Systems," in M. B. Miles, ed., *Innovation in Education* (New York: Teachers College, Columbia University Press, 1964), pp. 84–112. See also Warren G. Bennis and Philip E. Slater, *The Temporary Society* (New York: Harper & Row, Publishers, 1968).

and leadership as a function. To provide a summary or gatekeeping when these are needed by the group is to engage in an important act of leadership. To see the need and fail to respond can be viewed as a failure to fulfill one's membership responsibilities as well. A group is in some ways just like a machine. For a machine to continue to produce a high-quality product, it must continually be maintained. The maintenance function in a group is equally important, for, again, people bring their whole selves to a group, not just that part of themselves having to do with the task.

It is often argued that "We don't have the time to worry about people's feelings or to discuss how the group is working." Sometimes this is perfectly true, and under severe task pressure a different kind of process is necessary and legitimate. People can accept this, however, if they know from past experience that this situation is temporary. More often, however, lack of time is used as a defense mechanism to avoid the discussion completely. Furthermore, if a group really is under severe time pressure continually, some time ought to be spent examining the effectiveness of the group's planning procedures.

A group that ignores individual members' needs and its own process may well find that it meets several times to make the same set of decisions. The reason for this is that the effectiveness of many decisions is based on two factors[13]—logical soundness and the level of psychological commitment among the members to the decision made. These two dimensions are not independent; in fact, some people who are uncommitted (often because of process issues) may withhold, on a logical basis, information necessary to make the soundest decision. In any event, the best decision (on a task or logical level) forged at the expense of individual commitment is indeed not a very good decision at all.

Finally, what can be done to learn to use self-oriented emotional resources more appropriately? As a first step, it is important to accept our own feelings and to realize that everyone has both tender and tough emotions. Within American culture at least, managers (and particularly males) are expected to be tough, hard, aggressive, and the like. Any sign of "tender emotions" (warmth, affection) is taken to be a sign of weakness. But if we can accept the fact that feelings are a part of an individual's and therefore a group's reality, we can begin to explore ways of dealing with these realities rather than trying to clear them away. Given the opportunity to experiment with and get feedback on our emotional behavior (and a climate that supports such behavior), we can become more aware of when it is appropriate to be tough, tender, or neither.

The point here is that it is foolhardy to assume that simply because a group of people assembles to perform a task, it will somehow automatically

---

[13] This dichotomy of a decision's quality is analogous to issues raised during the discussion of the concept of psychological contract in the introduction of Chapter 1, *Organizational Socialization.* In that case, the dichotomy was the decision to join versus the decision to participate. See also Chapter 12, *Leadership and Decision Making,* for more detail on effective decision-making styles.

know how to work together effectively.[14] A comparison between the behavior of a football team and the behavior of a management team highlights the essence of this paradox. The football team spends untold hours practicing teamwork in preparation for the 60 minutes each week that its members' performance as a team really counts. In contrast, most management teams do not spend 60 minutes per week practicing teamwork in spite of the fact that for 40 or more hours every week their behavior as a team really counts.

---

[14] One such process for learning how to work more effectively in groups is called broadly "laboratory training." For a full discussion of this and related educational techniques, see Edgar H. Schein and Warren G. Bennis, *Personal and Organizational Change Through Group Methods: The Laboratory Approach* (New York: John Wiley & Sons, Inc., 1965).

Task-Related Factors Influencing Team Effectiveness—The GRPI Model*

David A. Kolb, Irwin M. Rubin, and James M. McIntyre

There are four categories of work or task-related issues with which all teams must deal successfully if they are to operate effectively: goal issues, role issues, procedural issues, and interpersonal issues.

A. GOAL ISSUES (WHAT IS THE TEAM TRYING TO ACCOMPLISH?)

To be an effectively functioning team, individual members must have a shared, agreed-upon common definition of the team's mission—its reason for existence as a team. Goal priority conflicts must be understood and be clearly resolved. In the absence of these conditions, it would not be surprising to find people working very hard but pulling in different directions.

To many people, these seem like trivial issues. "Of course we all agree," they will say quickly. Seldom, however, does this agreement develop naturally, nor is it an easy task. Part of the difficulty stems from the fact that most managers really wear two hats. They are both the leaders of one team (their subordinates) and a member of a second team (that of their boss). Each of these "two" teams has different, although, it is hoped, related, goals and objectives.

B. ROLE ISSUES (WHO SHOULD BE DOING WHAT TO HELP THIS TEAM REACH ITS GOALS?)

Formal, written job descriptions can, at best, be counted upon to cope only partially with role problems. To use a sports analogy, they can tell you only whether you are a center or a forward but cannot specify how you should

* SOURCE: David A. Kolb, Irwin M. Rubin, and James M. McIntyre, *Organizational Psychology: An Experiential Approach to Organizational Behavior,* 4th ed., pp. 182–183, 189. ©1984. Reprinted by permission of Prentice-Hall, Inc., Englewood Cliffs, N.J.

Much of the conceptual material discussed in this unit is adapted from work done by Plovnick, Fry and Rubin. See "New Developments in O.D. Technology: Programmed Team Development" by Mark Plovnick, Ronald Fry, and Irwin Rubin, *Training and Development Journal,* April 1975.

behave on a day-to-day basis. The way you function as a center (if that were your formal role) varies with (1) the qualities of those on your team playing forward, (2) the nature of the opposition, (3) the score of the game, and so on.

One particular source of role problems on a team is ambiguity. People are simply not clear about what they expect of one another, and often they are hesitant to ask for clarity ("If I ask someone what they expect of me, they will think I don't know my job!").

Beyond the problem of ambiguity, three forms of role conflict are frequently observed. Self–other conflicts arise because what someone else expects of me does not fit my expectation of myself. Two or more other team members can have expectations of me which, although they are unambiguous, are incompatible, thereby creating an other–other conflict. Finally, the sum total of everyone's expectations can result in an overload conflict—there just are not enough hours in the day to fulfill all the expectations.

C. PROCEDURAL ISSUES (HOW SHOULD WE FUNCTION?)

Within the procedural area is a host of "how to" kinds of issues: How will decisions be made? How will conflicts be resolved? How will information be shared? What kinds of meetings will we have? When? What norms do we need to reinforce or extinguish?

Team meetings, as a microcosm of team functioning, are notoriously ineffective for reasons related to procedure. Some people sit in the meeting waiting for the boss's decision; others share opinions as if they were being consulted; others argue assertively for one or another proposal as if a consensus decision-making procedure were in operation; and still others are just plain confused or bored.

D. INTERPERSONAL ISSUES (FEELINGS PEOPLE HAVE TOWARD EACH OTHER)

One hears many references, particularly in poorly functioning teams, to "personality clashes," "bad chemistry," and the like. The negative consequences of poor feelings between team members are not hard to recognize. When the team is meeting, all may look smooth on the surface, but under the table or at the water cooler, hostile barbs fill the air. The extent to which people trust, support, respect, and feel comfortable with one another can certainly influence the effectiveness of teamwork.

Summary

The introduction of the GRPI model expands our understanding of the complex dynamics of team functioning. They can be viewed as content issues with which any work team must deal if they are to function effectively.

The process dimensions discussed in an earlier chapter . . .run through each of the GRPI issues. Task-oriented and maintenance-oriented behaviors are important to a team and will influence *how* the team deals with the need to clarify goals, define roles, and so on. Either one—process *or* content—in the absence of the other creates an incomplete picture.

Two important assumptions that underlie the GRPI framework need to be emphasized. First is the issue of symptoms versus causes. Interpersonal issues are treated, within the GRPI framework, more as symptoms of poor team performance rather than as causes of poor team performance. Unresolved goal conflicts or role conflicts will, for example, often pop us as "personality clashes" or examples of "bad chemistry."

Second, the GRPI framework is a hierarchical model. The issues are listed and described in a recommended sequence. Rationally speaking, issues of roles (who should be doing what?) cannot be successfully resolved until such time as the "what" (goals) issue has been resolved. Similarly, effectively designing team procedures (how?) requires resolution of who and what. Many a team meeting, for example, could be enhanced if a few moments were taken at the start of the meeting to go through at least the GRP sequence.

Finally, although many of the obstacles to effective team functioning lie within the team's boundary, few teams can operate in a completely autonomous fashion. As you probably experienced in this class simulation, while the executive committee was a team, it had to interface with five other teams (the various departments). Each of these departmental teams was related to and influenced by their interactions with the other four departments. Any single team, therefore, is influenced by its wider organizational environment, and the board has an added set of interface problems with the extraorganizational environment. These complex issues of intergroup (interteam) relationships, and the relationship between an organization and its environments, are the subject of the following chapter.

Observer Rating Form

In the spaces provided, write down *behavioral* examples of these kinds of issues that you observed that helped or hindered the accomplishment of the task.	Next to your observations, write down any *consequences* you saw. What was the result of the behavior in terms of the team's ability to get its work done?
G. Things to do with goals	
R. Things to do with roles	
P. Things to do with procedures (i.e., decision making) or group process	
I. Things to do with personality or interpersonal communications	

The Intergroup Team-building Meeting*

Jack K. Fordyce
and Raymond Weil

Peace (noun)—In international affairs, a period of cheating between two periods of fighting.

Ambrose Bierce

Two groups meet to improve their working relationships. The purpose of the meeting is to reach a state of mutual understanding that fosters cooperation and cuts down on isolation, competition, and strife. The process involves:

- A deliberate effort to surface concealed resentment and mistrust (garbage).
- An attempt to distinguish fact from fancy.
- A search for ways in which the two groups can serve each other better in achieving common goals.
- A determination to be explicitly helpful.

A typical procedure for the meeting follows. As in the case of the Family Group Team-building Meeting . . . the procedure is public in the sense that all cards are laid on the table, and all participants are informed of what is in the offing and are encouraged to speak their piece at any stage.

Step 1: Setting the objectives of the meeting. The scope and objectives of the meeting are set by a planning committee. The committee consists, at a minimum, of the managers of the respective groups and a Third Party. The committee meets to:

- Disclose its impressions of current relationships between the two groups.
- Decide what additional information is needed before the groups come together, and how it will be collected.
- Outline the procedure to be followed during the meeting and the follow-up work.
- Decide who should attend, and the time, length, and place of the meeting.

Step 2: Collecting information for the meeting (Optional) . . . .

* SOURCE: Jack K. Fordyce and Raymond Weil, *Managing with People*. 2nd ed. ©1979. Addison-Wesley Publishing Company, Inc., Reading, Mass., pp. 123–129. Reprinted with permission.

Step 3: Conducting the meeting itself. The objectives and procedure of the meeting are made clear. The information collected in Step 2 (optional) is now presented to the whole meeting on chart pads.

Each group meets separately to prepare three lists:

- Positive feedback list: things the group values in the way it has worked with the other group.
- "Bug" list: things the group dislikes.
- Empathy list: a prediction of what the other group has on its lists.

The groups now come together, having first chosen someone to present each group's lists. During this period, the Third Party discourages any discussion not directed specifically to clarification of the other group's point of view. Then the total group prepares a working agenda and sets priorities.

Subgroups are formed to work each item of the agenda and to report back to the total group. It is important that both organizations be represented on each subgroup. One or more of the subgroups may be asked to Fishbowl . . . in the presence of the total group, after which the audience critiques the Fishbowl members for their skill and willingness in helping one another.

The subgroups report back to the total group, which then formulates a list of action items that it commits itself to perform. The action items are assigned and scheduled.

The group adjourns for refreshments.

> *An empty stomach is hostile to every form of joviality.*
>
> *Norman Douglas*

Step 4: Follow-up. . . . After the meeting, follow-up activity must ensure that the agreed-upon action items have been performed and that the level of open communication arrived at in the meeting is maintained.

USES

A specific remedy for parochialism, the medicine is extremely beneficial whenever working relations with another organization seem simply too hard and you wish to ease the pain by performing the other group's functions within your own organization. Relieves finger-pointing fever.

When properly administered and with adequate after-care, the treatment is free of injurious side effects.

Use may be safely prescribed for the classic maladies that affect relations between:

- Staff and line.
- Headquarters and field.
- Supplier and customer.

- Engineering and manufacturing.
- Specialist group A and specialist group B.
- Your tribe and mine.

BENEFITS

Your organization was probably designed to function in collaboration with other groups. The intergroup meeting is a way to restore interdependent activity to design specifications.

The method is cheaper than squirming around or trying to blast through all the roadblocks that seem to spring up spontaneously in the communication channels between working groups.

The method helps to disburden an overloaded chain of command. In a complex modern organization, the top manager hasn't time to settle all the feuds and squabbles that go on underneath.

As a tonic, it stimulates health and vigor in intergroup working relations.

LIMITATIONS

While the medicine is specific, it is not magical. Intergroup relations can be resistant to change and may require continuing attention to detail. The intergroup meeting, however, is an excellent way to set the stage for further cooperation. But watch out for backsliding.

Groups often resist the treatment. It's hard for many groups to comprehend just how poor their relations are. ("Organizations and people are just naturally this way.")

There's also a fear that the cure may be worse than the disease. ("We're so used to war, peace could kill us.")

OPERATING HINTS

Candor: The managers must set the standard for candor. They will be tested by the other participants.

Responsibility: The managers must accept lead responsibility for the meeting. They must first understand what they're getting into.

Attendance: Invite the people who can solve the problem you agree to solve.

Caution: Don't go into an intergroup meeting if you haven't solved serious internal problems; these will contaminate the process of working with another group. Perhaps a Family Group Team-building Meeting . . . is in order first.

Length: One-half day to two days, more if necessary. The group members must feel they have gone "over the top" in meeting the meeting's objectives.

Meeting Place: Anywhere the groups will not be disturbed.

Group Size: From 4 to about 30.

Meeting Scope: Should be restricted to those things the attendees can do something about. Either invite the right people or limit the scope and the expectations.

Discipline: Follow the planned procedures and schedule. Change only upon careful deliberation and for good reason. Confront anyone who slips away from the spirit and/or agreed-upon procedures.

Cultural Differences: In meetings between groups from different kinds of organizations, such as a supplier and customer, look for (and bring out into the open) basic differences in work cultures and roles that may create "noise" in their communications. For example, in some organizations people are freer to speak out and act independently than in others. Allow more time for meetings between groups from different types of organizations.

Emphasis: During the meeting, search for ways in which the groups can help each other. Subgrouping with mixed membership is one way of doing this. Highlighting collaborative ideas or specific offers of help is another.

Follow-through. . . . After the meeting, follow-through is the key to success. Here are some specific suggestions for follow-up intergroup meetings:

- Schedule a shorter, follow-up meeting four to six weeks after the first meeting.
- Keep the subgroups that were established at the meeting functioning until their job is really done and the results put into practice. Continue to use ad hoc mixed-membership subgroups as needed.
- Invite a representative of the other group to meetings in which there is a joint interest.

Procedure for the Intergroup Team-building Meeting

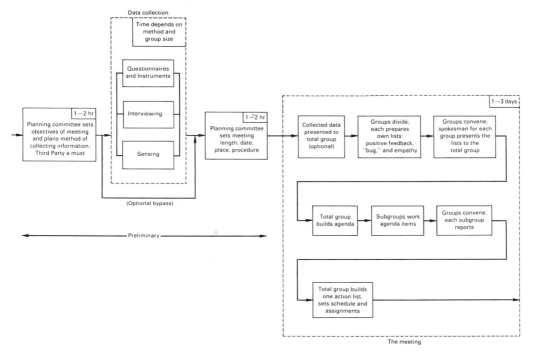

RELATED APPLICATIONS

This format can be used for the first phase of a merger meeting. In this case, the lists prepared by the groups should cover:

What they like about the merger.

What they are concerned about.

Their prediction of the other group's lists.

The second phase should be like the Family Group Team-building Meeting . . . with the total group working in concert around its new joint goals and organization.

At the beginning of the meeting, the manager needs to be specific as to which decisions are firm, and which decisions are open to deliberation by the group.

7

OBSERVATION, INTERACTION, AND SUBJECTIVITY

INTRODUCTION

> What *is known can never be grasped independently of* how *it is known.*
> —Robert M. Emerson*

This chapter is the culmination of Part Two of this book, "Interaction in Interventions," in the conceptual sense. It departs from the experiences-and-models-and-schemes format of the earlier chapters and, proceeding at a higher level of abstraction, provides the beginnings of an underlying, largely social-scientific rationale for the conceptual schemes and applications presented earlier, and the broad approach of this book.

The first item, *Participant Observation,* succinctly explores issues and methods about observation as a field research methodology. Written by experienced field researchers, it penetrates central issues implicated in interactional data-getting methods used in the course of intervening in enterprises. It describes useful practices in gathering observations, and links them to "symbolic interactionism," an appropriate frame of reference for viewing and explaining the statics and dynamics of human behavior in organizations. One of the major contentions of this book is that symbolic interactionism provides a fruitful theoretical base for thinking and acting in managing organizational change.

The Nature of Symbolic Interactionism, written by a leading writer on the subject, asserts that "human beings act towards things on the basis of the

---

* *Contemporary Field Research* (Boston: Little, Brown, 1983), p. 16.

meanings that the things have for them," and that these meanings are products of interaction between people. *Naturalistic Enquiry* summarizes the position of symbolic interactionists and ties it to "naturalistic" methods that penetrate everyday interaction in organizations, via research strategies of participant observation, interviewing, and historical comparative techniques. The paper contrasts quantitative methods and data with qualitative methods and data, *objectivism* and *subjectivism,* the latter implying close involvement between change agents and members of the client system in order to carry out valid research.

"Inquiry from the Inside" and "Inquiry from the Outside" is concerned with "the degree of physical and psychological immersion of the researcher" in the organization—the extent of his or her involvement in and commitment to the enterprise. One posture consists of "becoming a part of the organization and studying it *from the inside,* being there; the other by studying it *from the outside."* The former posture is adopted by this book.

The Self-Fulfilling Prophecy entertainingly makes W. I. Thomas's profound point that "if men define situations as real, they are real in their consequences," so developing an explicit consideration of the subjectivity of data gatherers interacting with organization members in interventions. The next pair of items continues the theme of exploring the role of subjectivity in intervening in enterprises. They are the first in the book to draw on the author's interview-based exploration of the Tavistock Institute of Human Relation's tradition in the field of managing organizational change.† The first, *Objectivity and Subjectivity,* concerns subjectivity and the interventionist; the second, *The Baseline Frame of Reference,* outlines some of the ways Tavistock consultants conceptualize and cope with subjective states.

The final item, *Intersubjectivity,* reviews the idea of pooling particular individual organization members' subjective states, and concludes that "the need to take account of intersubjectivity seems overwhelming." In the light of these considerations, intervention consists, at bottom, of organization members exploring, negotiating, and renegotiating their subjective states through various modes of interaction and action.

The theme of this chapter ultimately leads towards the conclusion of this book, "Managing Organizational Change, Values, and Science," where emphasis is placed on the construction of a logical, defensible, usable social-scientific base for thinking about and carrying out interventions in organizations, and building new knowledge about effective interventions as well.

---

† See *Note on Tavistock Work on Organizational Change,* pp. 1–3, for an explanation about the source material used.

Participant Observation*

Martin Dodge
and Robert Bogdan

THE SYMBOLIC INTERACTION PERSPECTIVE

Symbolic interaction as a way of looking at behavior was largely conceptualized and expressed through the work of philosopher George Herbert Mead,[1] elaborated upon in such writings as those of Herbert Blumer.[2]

This model holds that social interaction proceeds on two levels, the first being nonsymbolic and represented by simple, direct responses to actions or messages. The second level, however, explains more complex human behavior. On this level, called symbolic interaction, an individual interprets and defines another's actions, words, or gestures, and then bases his actions upon those definitions.

The theory suggests that to understand the workings of a group or organization (such as the school classroom), we must also understand how they (those in these social units) define their world.

.... a group is a collection of individuals continuously in the process of forming definitions of objects and events around them so that they may determine how they should behave within that group. When more and more definitions become common among group members, individuals become part of established patterns of group behavior. ... [P]atterns of group behavior are open to change at any time members' definitions cease to be confirmed.

Different groups define different things in different ways. Thus "objectivity" and "truth" are subjectively conferred upon an object or action. Where, for instance, the educational technologist will define a 16mm projector as a device to be used by the teacher to show instructional films relevant to her educational objectives, the teacher may define it as an object to use to entertain her students when she has run out of work for them to do. Or, placed within a culturally primitive societal group, the projector might be defined as a religious icon to be worshiped (until the A-V man arrives bringing with him, perhaps, new perceptions and possibly causing some redefinition).

The imaginations people have of each other, themselves, and every aspect of their world are the solid facts of society. In looking at his world, man is subjective. He selectively perceives, interprets, and places meaning upon his world and then acts accordingly. The solid facts of society are these perceptions,

* SOURCE: Martin Dodge and Robert Bogdan, "Participant Observation: A Promising Research Approach for Educational Technology," *Phi Delta Kappan,* 56 (1974), 67–69. Reprinted with permission.

definitions, interpretations, and meanings. If the researcher in pursuit of truths ignores these facts, through imposing his own definitions on what he assumes the research settings to be, he is thereby ignoring valuable data.

PARTICIPANT OBSERVATION

Participant observation is a research methodology in which the researcher collects data in the field through close contact with subjects within settings in which they normally spend their time. Data, in the form of field notes, are unobtrusively and systematically collected, coded, and analyzed.

While the methodology is put to valuable use in generating theories and in describing organizational forms so that we may better understand them, it can also be used to draw hypotheses from the data as they are collected, hypotheses which can be proved or disproved as observations continue over a prolonged period of time.

The researcher begins by writing down all his preconceived notions as to what will be "discovered" in the field. This is one of the many procedures employed to allow the researcher to confront his own biases and thereby control them. After gaining entrance to the setting, he becomes a marginal, temporary actor within the setting, making himself known as a researcher but "living" the situation along with the actors he is studying. He employs various techniques which maximize the possibility of being perceived by all his subjects as a neutral figure, having no special alliances with any one subject in the situation and having no relationship outside the situation which might hurt them. Being able to establish rapport characterized by trust and a free and open exchange of information is crucial. Various ways of checking the relationship and thus the data are employed.

The observer engages his subjects in casual conversation, joins in activities with them, and shares their concerns and accomplishments. In this way, he obtains their perspectives and discovers how they define objects and events around them. The participant observer thereby gets a wholistic view of the setting under study, gaining an understanding of the complexities of social life by immersing himself within it.

In the ideal, the observer contaminates the setting to an insignificant degree, but he realizes his possible effect and conducts himself accordingly, looking for clues that indicate his success or failure at reaching the ideal. The trained, practiced observer will establish a degree of rapport with his subjects such that he will become an unobtrusive part of the scene. Part of making himself unobtrusive is the avoidance of recording data within sight of the observer's subjects.

Nevertheless, he does keep systematic, complete, accurate, and detailed field notes, and he does this by making himself, as much as possible, an objective recording device. At the close of an observation period, out of the view of his subjects, he immediately records into a set of field notes every significant thing he has seen, heard, smelled, thought, felt, etc., during that period. These notes often are 20 pages in length for an hour's observation.

. . . . the field notes are liberally sprinkled with direct quotes from subjects under study, for conversations and the subjects' own words provide important insights into how they define their world. Second, if the researcher has any subjective comments to make, he separates them from the rest of the data, labels them "Observer's Comments" (O.C.), and puts them in parentheses. The observer also states within his notes any biases he feels he may be holding during the given observational period. He should take action to attempt to control biases; if he cannot control them, he must at least state them in his final report.

While memorizing copious amounts of data may seem (and is!) hard work, it is by no means impossible, given the requisite training, concentration, and experience of the observer—plus a concerted effort to do it. (In fact, for some researchers, the truly grueling part of the job is not the mental recording process but the four or five hours spent at the typewriter transferring data onto paper following a few hours of observation.)

As certain ideas, behaviors, and definitions begin to appear and reappear in the data, the researcher interested in generating hypotheses from the data may narrow his attention to these things. . . .

Investigation of hypotheses may amount to holding them up to the action being observed in the field for comparison and fit, introducing leading questions to subjects to get them talking about areas related to the hypotheses, or examining field notes to determine how much data exists to support or refute them.

During analysis of his data, the researcher groups the data into categories. Sentences and paragraphs are then coded and grouped into these categories. If, during analysis, certain ideas do not seem clear enough to the researcher, he may choose to return to the setting to get clarification, or he may even return to collect more data on topics that appear important.

In this brief presentation, we have completely skipped over a number of concerns which, in themselves, are treated at great length in the literature on participant observation; e.g., controlling observer bias, integrating the method with other methodologies (such as nonstructured interviewing), the ethics of publishing data which might prove embarrassing to the subjects of the study, maintaining confidentiality, etc. The interested reader is invited to study such works as those of Bogdan, McCall and Simmons, and Becker (see footnotes) for greater elaboration on these and other points.

The point we wish to reemphasize in concluding is simply that symbolic interaction is a useful perspective and participant observation a useful methodology for the researcher studying many important questions. . . .

Symbolic interaction is a viable theoretical approach toward getting at the answers, while participant observation is an extremely useful methodology for rooting them out of the research setting.

REFERENCES

BECKER, HOWARD, *Sociological Work* (Chicago: Aldine, 1970).

BLUMER, HERBERT, *Symbolic Interactionism* (Englewood Cliffs, N.J.: Prentice-Hall, 1969).

BOGDAN, ROBERT, *Participant Observation in Organizational Settings* (Syracuse, N.Y.: Syracuse University Press, 1972).

McCALL, GEORGE, and J. L. SIMMONS (eds.), *Issues in Participant Observation* (Reading, Mass.: Addison-Wesley, 1969).

MEAD, GEORGE H., *Mind, Self and Society* (Chicago: University of Chicago Press, 1934).

The Nature of Symbolic Interactionism*

Herbert Blumer

Symbolic interactionism rests in the last analysis on three simple premises. The first premise is that human beings act toward things on the basis of the meanings that the things have for them. Such things include everything that the human being may note in his world—physical objects, such as trees or chairs; other human beings, such as a mother or a store clerk; categories of human beings, such as friends or enemies; institutions, as a school or a government; guiding ideals, such as individual independence or honesty; activities of others, such as their commands or requests; and such situations as an individual encounters in his daily life. The second premise is that the meaning of such things is derived from, or arises out of, the social interaction that one has with one's fellows. The third premise is that these meanings are handled in, and modified through, an interpretative process used by the person in dealing with the things he encounters. I wish to discuss briefly each of these three fundamental premises.

It would seem that few scholars would see anything wrong with the first premise—that human beings act toward things on the basis of the meanings which these things have for them. Yet, oddly enough, this simple view is ignored or played down in practically all of the thought and work in contemporary social science and psychological science. Meaning is either taken for granted and thus pushed aside as unimportant or it is regarded as a mere neutral link between the factors responsible for human behavior and this behavior as the product of such factors. We can see this clearly in the predominant posture of psychological and social science today. Common to both of these fields is the tendency to treat human behavior as the product of various factors that play upon human beings; concern is with the behavior and with the factors regarded as producing them. Thus, psychologists turn to such factors as stimuli, attitudes, conscious or unconscious motives, various kinds of psychological inputs, perception and cognition, and various features of personal organization to account for given forms or instances of human conduct. In a similar fashion sociologists rely on such factors as social position, status demands, social roles, cultural prescriptions, norms and values, social pressures, and group affiliation to provide such explanations. In both such typical psychological and sociological explanations the meanings of things for the human beings who

* SOURCE: Herbert Blumer, *Symbolic Interactionism: Perspective and Method*, pp. 2–6. ©1969. Reprinted by permission of Prentice-Hall, Inc., Englewood Cliffs, N.J.

are acting are either bypassed or swallowed up in the factors used to account for their behavior. If one declares that the given kinds of behavior are the result of the particular factors regarded as producing them, there is no need to concern oneself with the meaning of the things toward which human beings act; one merely identifies the initiating factors and the resulting behavior. Or one may, if pressed, seek to accommodate the element of meaning by lodging it in the initiating factors or by regarding it as a neutral link intervening between the initiating factors and the behavior they are alleged to produce. In the first of these latter cases the meaning disappears by being merged into the initiating or causative factors; in the second case meaning becomes a mere transmission link that can be ignored in favor of the initating factors.

The position of symbolic interactionism, in contrast, is that the meanings that things have for human beings are central in their own right. To ignore the meaning of the things toward which people act is seen as falsifying the behavior under study. To bypass the meaning in favor of factors alleged to produce the behavior is seen as a grievous neglect of the role of meaning in the formation of behavior.

The simple premise that human beings act toward things on the basis of the meaning of such things is much too simple in itself to differentiate symbolic interactionism—there are several other approaches that share this premise. A major line of difference between them and symbolic interactionism is set by the second premise, which refers to the source of meaning. There are two well-known traditional ways of accounting for the origin of meaning. One of them is to regard meaning as being intrinsic to the thing that has it, as being a natural part of the objective makeup of the thing. Thus, a chair is clearly a chair in itself, a cow a cow, a cloud a cloud, a rebellion a rebellion, and so forth. Being inherent in the thing that has it, meaning needs merely to be disengaged by observing the objective thing that has the meaning. The meaning emanates, so to speak, from the thing and as such there is no process involved in its formation; all that is necessary is to recognize the meaning that is there in the thing. It should be immediately apparent that this view reflects the traditional position of "realism" in philosophy—a position that is widely held and deeply entrenched in the social and psychological sciences. The other major traditional view regards "meaning" as a psychical accretion brought to the thing by the person for whom the thing has meaning. This psychical accretion is treated as being an expression of constituent elements of the person's psyche, mind, or psychological organization. The constituent elements are such things as sensations, feelings, ideas, memories, motives, and attitudes. The meaning of a thing is but the expression of the given psychological elements that are brought into play in connection with the perception of the thing; thus one seeks to explain the meaning of a thing by isolating the particular psychological elements that produce the meaning. One sees this in the somewhat ancient and classical psychological practice of analyzing the meaning of an object by identifying the sensations that enter into perception of that object; or in the contemporary practice of tracing the meaning of a thing, such as let us say prostitution, to the attitude of the person who views it. This lodging of the meaning of things in psychological elements limits the processes of the formation of meaning to whatever processes are involved in arousing and bringing together the given psychological elements that produce the meaning. Such processes are psychological in nature, and include perception, cognition, repression, transfer of feelings, and association of ideas.

Symbolic interactionism views meaning as having a different source than those held by the two dominant views just considered. It does not regard meaning as emanating from the intrinsic makeup of the thing that has meaning, nor does it see meaning as arising through a coalescence of psychological elements in the person. Instead, it sees meaning as arising in the process of interaction between people. The meaning of a thing for a person grows out of the ways in which other persons act toward the person with regard to the thing. Their actions operate to define the thing for the person. Thus, symbolic interactionism sees meanings as social products, as creations that are formed in and through the defining activities of people as they interact. This point of view gives symbolic interactionism a very distinctive position, with profound implications that will be discussed later.

The third premise mentioned above further differentiates symbolic interactionism. While the meaning of things is formed in the context of social interaction and is derived by the person from that interaction, it is a mistake to think that the use of meaning by a person is but an application of the meaning so derived. This mistake seriously mars the work of many scholars who otherwise follow the symbolic interactionist approach. They fail to see that the use of meanings by a person in his action involves an interpretative process. In this respect they are similar to the adherents of the two dominant views spoken of above—to those who lodge meaning in the objective makeup of the thing that has it and those who regard it as an expression of psychological elements. All three are alike in viewing the use of meaning by the human being in his action as being no more than an arousing and application of already established meanings. As such, all three fail to see that the use of meanings by the actor occurs through a *process of interpretation*. This process has two distinct steps. First, the actor indicates to himself the things toward which he is acting; he has to point out to himself the things that have meaning. The making of such indications is an internalized social process in that the actor is interacting with himself. This interaction with himself is something other than an interplay of psychological elements; it is an instance of the person engaging in a process of communication with himself. Second, by virtue of this process of communicating with himself, interpretation becomes a matter of handling meanings. The actor selects, checks, suspends, regroups, and transforms the meanings in the light of the situation in which he is placed and the direction of his action. Accordingly, interpretation should not be regarded as a mere automatic application of established meanings but as a formative process in which meanings are used and revised as instruments for the guidance and formation of action. It is necessary to see that meanings play their part in action through a process of self-interaction.

It is not my purpose to discuss at this point the merits of the three views that lodge meaning respectively in the thing, in the psyche, and in social action, nor to elaborate on the contention that meanings are handled flexibly by the actor in the course of forming his action. Instead, I wish merely to note that by being based on these three premises, symbolic interaction is necessarily led to develop an analytical scheme of human society and human conduct that is quite distinctive.

Naturalistic Enquiry*

Norman K. Denzin

. . . The symbolic interactionists (who tract their perspective from the works of James, Dewey, Mead, Cooley, Simmel, Park, Blumer, Strauss, Becker, Thomas, Goffman, and others) assume that human societies are negotiated, emergent productions. They furthermore propose that human beings have the capability to engage in self-directed, linguistically grounded reflections and that this reflective ability enables people to enter into the organization of their own lines of action. Once joined, these individual lines of behavior form interactional patterns. It is these interactional paatterns which must be understood if the character and makeup of social structure is to be grasped.

The naturalistic mode of inquiry flows directly from this view of social process and social structure. The research methods of the sociologist must yield a penetration of everyday worlds of interaction. A fundamental goal of the naturalistic method is to develop theories which explain the feelings, emotions, definitions, attitudes, and actual behaviors of those observed. The special and idiomatic languages of those studied must be understood. Their self-images and identities, the meanings they assign to social objects, the social situations they enter into, and the social relationships they form must all be described, analyzed, and fitted within a theoretical framework which reflects the everyday realities of the participants. Central to such a method are the research strategies . . . participant observation, unobtrusive methods, historical-comparative techniques, interviews, grounded theory construction, and triangulation (the combination of research methods). These strategies do not readily produce classifiable, *quantitative* data; the data produced are *qualitative* in nature. Rather than producing statistical analyses, these methods produce pictures, images, and descriptions of ongoing social interaction.

The method of naturalistic inquiry has not been well articulated in the social and psychological sciences; nor has its logic, which dates from the works of Darwin in the nineteenth century, been well understood. Instead, the naturalistic method has typically been denigrated as "soft science," as premature scientific inquiry (Lundberg, 1929); as humanism in disguise of journalism (Odum and Jocher, 1929); and as nonscientific, nonproductive activity (Giddings, 1901; Blumer, 1969; Glaser and Strauss, 1967; Becker, 1970; Blalock, 1971).

. . . Symbolic interactionism and the naturalistic method of inquiry contradict the dominant paradigm of both the current and the historical sociological community. The discipline is and has been overwhelmingly *quan-*

* Source: From N. K. Denzin, *Sociological Methods: A Sourcebook.* © N. K. Denzin, Department of Sociology, University of Illinois, Urbana, Ill., 1978.

titative in orientation. (See Giddings, 1896, 1901; Bernard, 1934; Lundberg, 1929; Rice, 1931; Goode and Hatt, 1952; Blalock, 1971.) The quantitative paradigm derives from the nineteenth-century writings of Comte, Ward, and Spencer. Their conceptualization assumes that all sciences are quantitative, cumulative, and statistical in nature. The unity of all science, their work supposes, consists of its method and not of its substance. Early American sociologists, including Clark, Sumner, Giddings, Ross, Vincent, Small, and Ward, articulated a quantitative view of social structure, social process, and research methodology. The model of causal analysis used by these early sociologists rests upon the work of J. S. Mill, the nineteenth-century British philosopher of science. This model stresses the effects of independent variables upon dependent variables in strictly structured experimental situations (see Chapin, 1920; Giddings, 1901). Durkheim's (1904) work, in turn, provides a quasi-comparative, historical, and experimental method of social research.

The quantitative, and behavioristic, sociologists soon assumed control over the mainstream of the discipline. This brand of sociology was antisymbolic interactionist. It was "scientific" in its formulations of research design, and it tended not to use the qualitative approaches which are hallmarks of the interactionist tradition—participant observation, life histories, or other naturalistic approaches to theory development. The quantitative and qualitative schools rest their philosophies of science upon antithetical principles. Quantitative sociology rests upon what may be termed the *principle of objectivism.* This principle holds that the closer one comes to one's subject matter, the less objective one can be in the comprehension of the behaviors studied. A distance between the investigator and the objects of investigation must therefore be maintained. Most typically this is accomplished through the use of a structured interview format or through the analysis of census data. Symbolic interactionists consider this principle to be a fallacy and base their philosophy of science upon the *principle of subjectivism.* Concurrent with the naturalistic method, this principle argues that one *must* become closely involved with those persons, situations, and social groups for which one's theory is intended to account. Without such an involvement, interactionists contend, a distorted account will invariably be presented.

TWO MODELS OF SCIENCE

The models of sociological-scientific conduct, which stand in opposition to one another, can now be set forth. The naturalistic method calls for the close-up inspection of ongoing human group life. The quantitative method calls for a more distanced, objective, standardized, classifiable mode of investigation. One's stance toward these two alternatives rests upon divergent views of empirical science.

The quantitative method reverses the demand characteristic effects of the empirical world. This orientation assumes a world of causal analysis that rests upon clearly definable independent, contingent, intervening, and dependent variables. Rather than asking how well its category system represents the empirical world, this methodology demands that the empirical world submit to preconceived methods, techniques, and modes of inquiry. Rather than attempting to mirror empirical phenomena, this method accepts only those phenomena which will reflect themselves through responses to attitude scales, social indicators, and census categories. The resulting picture of the world, symbolic interactionists would affirm, is inherently a distorted image.

The naturalistic mode of inquiry, on the other hand, assumes a different model of causal analysis. . . .

Herbert Blumer, working from the symbolic interactionist perspective, takes the position that the cardinal feature of any science must be its grounding in the empirical world. The ultimate test of the scientist's actions is the ability to reveal, to describe, and to explain the empirical world. Blumer, too, discusses the method and logic of naturalism. He criticizes the formalized, scientific mode of inquiry now so highly favored in the social and psychological sciences. He casts doubt upon the utility of a scientific method that relies upon hypothesis testing, operational definitions, mathematical techniques, elegant logical models, and variable analysis. For the naturalist, the research act involves an ongoing process of exploration and inspection of the empirical realm under examination.

Exploration involves a very free and relatively unstructured set of observational activities. Scientists will admit any data that are ethically allowable and will employ any methods—be they surveys, experiments, interviews, or even introspection—that reveal aspects of the problem under study. A critical attitude will characterize sociologists' activities in this phase. They will be searching for negative cases which refute their emerging understandings of the situation at hand. They will examine the research problem from multiple theoretical perspectives. They will critically evaluate their own theoretical perspective, and they will be conscious of their relationships to those being studied. As new knowledge, or information, ceases to be produced, the researcher moves to the inspection phase of research.

Inspection involves the location of major analytic concepts and elements relevant to the problem at hand. These concepts, loosely sensitizing as opposed to being rigorously operationalized, are lodged in the scientist's actual observations of the behaviors, thoughts, and relationships of those studied. Like detectives, naturalists attempt to unravel a sequence of social interactions; they wish to account for how such interactions were produced. Once an explanation is forged that melds all the observations, inspection is complete.

REFERENCES

BECKER, HOWARD S., 1970, *Sociological Work,* Chicago: Aldine.

BERNARD, L. L. (ed.), 1934. *The Fields and Methods of*

Sociology, New York: Ray Long & Richard R. Smith.

BLALOCK, HUBERT M., 1971. "Aggregation and

Measurement Error," *Social Forces,* vol. 50 (December), pp. 151–165.

BLUMER, HERBERT, 1969. *Symbolic Interactionism: Perspective and Method,* Englewood Cliffs, N.J.: Prentice-Hall.

CHAPIN, F. S., 1920. *Field Work and Social Research,* New York: Century.

DURKHEIM, EMILE, 1904. *Les Règles de la Méthode Sociologique,* Paris: Felix Alean.

GIDDINGS, FRANKLIN H., 1896. *Principles of Sociology,* New York: Macmillan.

———, 1901. *Inductive Sociology,* New York: Macmillan.

GLASER, BARNEY G., and ANSELM L. STRAUSS, 1967. *The Discovery of Grounded Theory,* Chicago: Aldine.

GOODE, WILLIAM J., and PAUL K. HATT, 1952. *Methods in Social Research,* New York: McGraw-Hill.

LUNDBERG, GEORGE A., 1929. *Social Research,* New York: Longmans, Green.

ODUM, H. W. (ed.), 1927. *American Masters of Social Science,* New York: Holt.

———, and KATHARINE JOCHER, 1929. *An Introduction to Social Research,* New York: Henry Holt.

PEARSON, KARL, 1911. *The Grammar of Science,* 3d ed., London: Adam and Charles Black.

RICE, STUART A. (ed.), 1931. *Methods in Social Science,* Chicago: University of Chicago Press.

"Inquiry from the Inside" and "Inquiry from the Outside"*

Roger Evered and Meryl Reis Louis

.... In this article we will deal with two fundamental images (or paradigms) of scientific inquiry rather than with the variety of methods and techniques within either image. . . .

Inquiry and valid knowledge are fostered by coping activities, which differ from those of traditional from-the-outside science. Knowledge about organizations and management is continuously being articulated by managers (i.e., participants in organizational life). The essential difference between coping/ sense making/survival on the one hand and inquiry/research/science on the other hand is essentially this: the latter requires the coping organizational actors to be willing to tell as best they can what they know and how they came to know it—and to submit it to critical discussion. In addition, the knowledge discovered through coping is directly relevant to the purposes of the organizational actors. Inquiry does not necessarily require that any formal "scientific method" be followed.

The distinctions we are making between coping and inquiry in relation to insider versus outsider are presented in Figure 1. At the right side of the figure a spectrum of possible researcher roles is presented. We surmise that the critical aspect of this continuum is the degree of immersion of the researcher in the organization—that is, the extent of experiential involvement in and existential commitment to the organization. Operationally, it may translate into the extent of physical involvement in the setting. . . .

TWO MODES OF INQUIRY

Inquiry from the inside and inquiry from the outside can both serve research purposes, but in different ways and with different effects. When would either be used? We address this question by contrasting the two modes on a number of analytic dimensions, summarized in Figure 2.

We begin by comparing the *researcher's role and relationship to the setting*

* SOURCE: Roger Evered and Meryl Reis Louis, "Alternative Perspectives in the Organizational Sciences: "Inquiry from the Inside" and "Inquiry from the Outside," *Academy of Management Review*, 6 (1981), 385–395. Reprinted by permission of Roger Evered and Meryl Reis Louis.

331

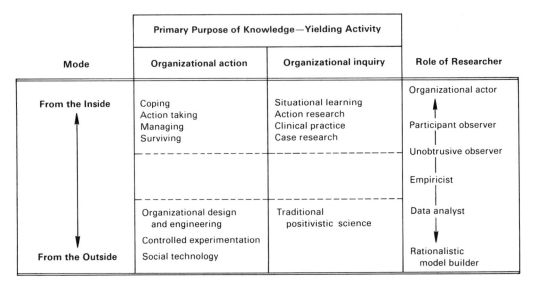

Figure 1: Alternative Modes of Inquiry

under the two modes of inquiry, and by identifying the epistemological and *validity assumptions* underlying the choice of role and relationship. Knowledge and understanding of an organizational situation can be acquired in two ways: (1) by studying, *from the outside*, data generated by the organization (and other organizations deemed to be similar in certain respects), and (2) by becoming a part of the organization and studying it *from the inside*. We can come to "know" the Ford Motor Company or Texas Instruments by examining annual reports,

Figure 2: Differences Between the Two Modes of Inquiry

Dimension of Difference	MODE OF INQUIRY	
	From the Outside	**From the Inside**
Researcher's relationship to setting	Detachment, neutrality ⟷	"Being there," immersion
Validation basis	Measurement and logic ⟷	Experiential
Researcher's role	Onlooker ⟷	Actor
Source of categories	A priori ⟷	Interactively emergent
Aim of inquiry	Universality and generalizability ⟷	Situational relevance
Type of knowledge acquired	Universal, nomothetic: theoria ⟷	Particular, idiographic: praxis
Nature of data and meaning	Factual, context free ⟷	Interpreted, contextually embedded

employment statistics, union announcements, questionnaire results, or observational records; or, alternatively, by functioning within these organizations for a period of time (or talking with those who do).

Inquiry from the outside is characterized by the researcher's detachment from the organizational setting under study. The detachment derives, in part, from the assumption that the thing under study is separate from, unrelated to, independent of, and unaffected by the researcher. Astronomy provides an ideal illustration. The objects of interest are measured with instruments, the data are analyzed to determine if logical patterns seem to exist, and rational theories are constructed to integrate, explain, and perhaps predict a multitude of facts. Knowledge is validated by methodical procedure and logic. Underlying the detachment of the researcher inquiring from the outside are critical epistemological assumptions: the researcher is guided by belief in an *external* reality constituted of *facts* that are *structured* in a law-like manner. This is what Habermas [1973] . . . has referred to as the "objectivist illusion."

In contrast, inquiry from the inside carries with it the assumption that the researcher can best come to know the reality of an organization by *being there*: by becoming immersed in the stream of events and activities, by becoming part of the phenomena of study. "Being there" is essentially what Heidegger [1962] means by his term *Dasein*. Knowledge is validated experientially. Underlying the immersion of a researcher inquiring from the inside is a very different set of epistemological assumptions from those of inquiry from the outside. Fundamental to it is the belief that knowledge comes from human *experience*, which is inherently continuous and *nonlogical*, and which may be *symbolically representable*. It is close to what Polanyi [1964] has termed "personal knowledge." The danger here is normally considered to be that the findings could be distorted and contaminated by the values and purposes of the researcher. This bias has been referred to by Russell [1945] as the "fallacy of subjectivism."

The researcher's role in inquiry from the outside can best be characterized as that of an onlooker. The researcher may use a telescope, microscope, or any other instrument; the essential feature is looking in from the outside at a selected piece of the world. At the extreme is the pure rationalist, sometimes referred to as a speculator, who needs to collect no data from the world to carry out the task of theorizing.

In inquiry from the inside, the researcher becomes an actor in real situations. The researcher must attend to the total situation and integrate information from all directions simultaneously. The relevant world is the field surrounding the individual actor/researcher.

Another difference between the two modes of inquiry is the *source of the analytical categories* around which data are organized. In a typical piece of outside research, the investigator preselects a set of categories that will guide the inquiry. Hypotheses are phrased in terms of these categories, and only those data pertaining to them are collected. The life in the organizational microcosm under study is viewed through the lens of a limited number of categories, such as centralization and formalization, or commitment and job involvement. At the extreme, this may lead to a form of perceptual "screening," so that the researcher sees only what is being sought.

The a priori categories may have been derived from personal idiosyncrasy, from theoretical formulation, or may have emerged in previous from-the-inside research. In the case of inside research, there are no intentionally prescribed categories to constrain the researcher. Instead, important features emerge through the individual's experience in and of the situation, as figure against ground in a perceptual field. Features are noticed and identified through an interpretive, iterative process whereby data and categories emerge simultaneously with successive experience. The process represents an experiential exploration. . . .

A further difference is the *aim of inquiry*. The aim of inquiry from the outside is to generalize from the particular to construct a set of theoretical statements that are universally applicable. The aim is to develop understanding of classes of organizational phenomena, rather than to focus on particular instances in particular settings. Inquiry from the inside, in contrast, is directed toward the historically unique situation, what Lewin [1951] called that "full reality of the whole, here-and-now individual situation." The situationally relevant products of inside research serve both practical and theoretical purposes. They can provide guides for action in the immediate situation and inputs in developing hypotheses to guide inquiry from the outside.

The different modes of inquiry are also associated with different *types of knowledge*. The aim of situational relevancy pursued in inside research is served by knowledge of the particular organization under study. This knowledge of the particular is a necessary, but not sufficient, condition for praxis. By *praxis*, we mean a knowledge of how to act appropriately in a variety of particular situations. The aim of generalizability sought by outside research is served by the development of universal knowledge. . . . Praxis . . . focuses on the particular; it is knowledge that is infused with human organization and human interest, as represented in the situation under study. . . .

While both modes of inquiry are concerned with understanding everyday happenings in organizations, they differ sharply in what they consider to be *data* and the level at which they consider issues of *meaning*. In inquiry from the inside, the aim of understanding particular situations necessitates that researchers make direct experiential contact with the organization under study. Understanding the events, activities, and utterances in a specific situation requires a rich appreciation of the overall organizational context. Context refers to the complex fabric of local culture, people, resources, purposes, earlier events, and future expectations that constitute the time-and-space background of the immediate and particular situation. Facts have no meaning in isolation from the setting. Meaning is developed from the point of view of the organizational participant. Inside research yields knowledge that is keyed to the organization member's definition of the situation. . . . Researchers involve themselves directly in the setting under study in order to appreciate organizational phenomena in light of the context in which they occur and from the participants' points of view.

In inquiry from the outside, the aim of developing universal principles of organizational life necessitates stripping away the idiosyncrasies of the particular organization(s) studied to reveal what is generally applicable to all organizations. The separation of the universal from the particular is accomplished through several processes. With the aid of sampling, aggregation, and other analytic techniques, the uniqueness of individual organizations is randomized, controlled for, and otherwise "washed," revealing the kernel of presumed common truths. The validity of such efforts rests on the comparability of measurements across observations, settings, and times, as well as the completeness with which the observational procedures and situations are documented. Hence, the concern with instrumentation, specification, and precision.

Outside research is designed to be detached from, and independent of, a specific situation under study in a particular organization. The researcher determines the frequencies of, and associations among, events with respect to a set of hypothesized categories and relationships. Meaning is assigned to events on the basis of a priori analytic categories and explicit researcher-free procedures. Interpretations of the researcher are viewed as inherently confounding. The spectrum of organizational life is filtered through the researcher's preset categories; elements related to the categories are selected, coded as data, and simultaneously given meaning by the categories. As a result, data are considered factual when they have the same meaning across situations and settings. That is, they are context-free. . . .

The key feature of our description of from-the-inside inquiry is the physical (and therefore experiential) immersion of the researcher within the organizational setting under study. We believe the critical feature that characterizes the various inquiry paradigms is the degree of physical *and* psychological immersion of the researcher, and that other distinctions commonly discussed derive from this. . . .

Research from the outside systematically overlooks critical features that often render the results epistemologically valueless. Such features include the definition of human *action* in specific settings, the actor's particular *definition of his situation* (world, field), the *human interest* (motives, purposes) of the organizational actor, and the *historical context* of the situation. Such shortcomings can be overcome by inquiry from the inside.

Inquiry from the inside, however, may appear to be so fuzzy that its findings often have dubious precision, rigor, or credibility. But, in turn, these shortcomings can be overcome by inquiry from the outside.

Organizational inquiry is currently characterized by two broad approaches. One is methodologically precise, but often irrelevant to the reality of organizations; the other is crucially relevant, but often too vague to be communicated to or believed by others. We need to find ways to improve the relevancy of the one, and to improve the precision of the other. It follows that we need to identify and refer to exemplars of good research—research that is both methodologically precise and grounded in real-world phenomena.

REFERENCES

HABERMAS, J. *Knowledge and human interest.* Boston: Beacon, 1971.

HEIDEGGER, M. *Being and time.* New York: Harper, 1962.

LEWIN, K. *Field theory in social science.* New York: Harper. 1951.

POLANYI, M. *Personal knowledge.* New York: Harper, 1964.

RUSSELL, B. *A history of Western philosophy.* New York: Simon, 1945.

The Self-Fulfilling Prophecy*

Robert K. Merton

In a series of works seldom consulted outside the academic fraternity, W. I. Thomas, the dean of American sociologists, set forth a theorem basic to the social sciences: "If men define situations as real, they are real in their consequences." Were the Thomas theorem and its implications more widely known more men would understand more of the workings of our society. Though it lacks the sweep and precision of a Newtonian theorem, it possesses the same gift to relevance, being instructively applicable to many, if indeed not most, social processes.

THE THOMAS THEOREM

"If men define situations as real, they are real in their consequences," wrote Professor Thomas. The suspicion that he was driving at a crucial point becomes all the more insistent when we note that essentially the same theorem had been repeatedly set forth by disciplined and observant minds long before Thomas.

When we find such otherwise discrepant minds as the redoubtable Bishop Bossuet in his passionate seventeenth-century defense of Catholic orthodoxy, the ironic Mandeville in his eighteenth-century allegory honeycombed with observations on the paradoxes of human society, the irascible genius Marx in his revision of Hegel's theory of historical change, the seminal Freud in works which have perhaps gone further than any others of his day toward modifying man's outlook on man, and the erudite, dogmatic, and occasionally sound Yale professor, William Graham Sumner, who lives on as the Karl Marx of the middle classes—when we find this mixed company (and I select from a longer if less distinguished list) agreeing on the truth and the pertinence of what is substantially the Thomas theorem, we may conclude that perhaps it is worth our attention as well.

To what, then, are Thomas and Bossuet, Mandeville, Marx, Freud and Sumner directing our attention?

The first part of the theorem provides an unceasing reminder that men respond not only to the objective features of a situation, but also, and at times primarily, to the meaning this situation has for them. And once they have assigned some meaning to the situation, their consequent behavior and some of the consequences of that behavior are determined by the ascribed meaning.

But this is still rather abstract, and abstractions have a way of becoming unintelligible if they are not occasionally tied to concrete data. What is a case in point?

A SOCIOLOGICAL PARABLE

It is the year 1932. The Last National Bank is a flourishing institution. A large part of its resources is liquid without being watered. Cartwright Millingville has ample reason to be proud of the banking institution over which he presides. Until Black Wednesday. As he enters his bank, he notices that business is unusually brisk. A little odd, that, since the men at the A.M.O.K. steel plant and the K.O.M.A. mattress factory are not usually paid until Saturday. Yet here are two dozen men, obviously from the factories, queued up in front of the tellers' cages. As he turns into his private office, the president muses rather compassionately: "Hope they haven't been laid off in midweek. They should be in the shop at this hour."

But speculations of this sort have never made for a thriving bank, and Millingville turns to the pile of documents upon his desk. His precise signature is affixed to fewer than a score of papers when he is disturbed by the absence of something familiar and the intrusion of something alien. The low discreet hum of bank business has given way to a strange and annoying stridency of many voices. A situation has been defined as real. And that is the beginning of what ends as Black Wednesday—the last Wednesday, it might be noted, of the Last National Bank.

Cartwright Millingville had never heard of the Thomas theorem. But he had no difficulty in recognizing its workings. He knew that, despite the comparative liquidity of the bank's assets, a rumor of insolvency, once believed by enough depositors, would result in the insolvency of the bank. And by the close of Black Wednesday—and Blacker Thursday—when the long lines of anxious depositors, each frantically seeking to salvage his own, grew to longer lines of even more anxious depositors, it turned out that he was right.

The stable financial structure of the bank had depended upon one set of definitions on the situation: belief in the validity of the interlocking system of economic promises men live by. Once depositors had defined the situation otherwise, once they questioned the possibility of having these promises fulfilled, the consequences of this unreal definition were real enough.

A familiar type-case this, and one doesn't need the Thomas theorem to understand how it happened—not, at least, if one is old enough to have voted for Franklin Roosevelt in 1932. But with the aid of the theorem the tragic history of Millingville's bank can perhaps be converted into a sociological parable which may help us understand not only what happened to hundreds of banks in the '30's but also what happens to the relations between Negro and white, between Protestant and Catholic and Jew in these days.

The parable tells us that public definitions of a situation (prophecies or predictions) become an integral part of the situation and thus affect subsequent developments. This is peculiar to human affairs. It is not found in the world of nature, untouched by human hands. Predictions of the return of Halley's comet do not influence its orbit. But the rumored insolvency of Millingville's bank did affect the actual outcome. The prophecy of collapse led to its own fulfillment.

Objectivity and Subjectivity*

Roy McLennan

The professional model ... implicates a problem of the action researcher's objectivity/subjectivity: "The problem of becoming personally involved with one's respondents ... is inherent in our method of working" (Miller and Gwynne, p. 7). The consultant tends to become caught up in the client organization and gradually loses his objectivity (Byrant, Dartington): "If he [the consultant] cares [about his clients] and identifies himself with them, then his observations will, of necessity, be prejudiced and less detached than is desirable for scientific assessment ... my clients and their families became my close friends" (Rice, p. 9). In the very process of becoming effective as an action researcher the consultant impairs his objectivity, in ways which would make a laboratory-based psychologist blush. The more apparently rigorous use of experimental methods in the social sciences, however, imported from the physical sciences, also leave much to be desired in the way of objectivity: "Even in the 'hard' physical sciences it is nowadays accepted that observations are influenced by the observer" (Miller, 1975: p. 82). The consultant's projections and the like also influence what is 'observed', i.e. what he makes of what is there (Menzies Lyth). For these and other reasons, "objectivity in human relationships is as attainable as the crock of gold at the end of the rainbow" (Miller, 1975: p. 82). The conclusion is clear: "We disavow the possibility of an objective approach to social research" (Miller and Gwynne, p. 6). But "non-objectivity" does not invalidate the conclusions reached in action research projects based on the professional model: a kind of bounded objectivity may be attained. In the end such objectivity as can be attained is "essentially the clarification of one's own subjectivity" (Lawrence and Miller, p. 365).

REFERENCES

MILLER, E. J., Demands and Problems of Face-to-Face Work with People. In Open University, A Post-Experience Course, The Handicapped Person in the Community, Units 1–10, Block 3, Part 1, Providing Supporting Services (Milton Keynes: Open University Press, 1975).

BRYANT, D., Work Plus: An Account of an Experiment to Improve the Quality of Worklife in the Cominco Lead Smelter in Trail, B.C. (Vancouver: British Columbia Research Council and Tavistock Institute of Human Relations, 1979).

RICE, A. K., The Enterprise and Its Environment (London: Tavistock, 1963).

MILLER, E. J. and GWYNNE, G. V., A Life Apart (London: Tavistock, 1972).

LAWRENCE, W. G. and MILLER, E. J., Epilogue, Task and Organization, E. J. Miller (Ed.) (New York: Wiley, 1976).

* SOURCE: Roy McLennan, "Action Research Consultancy: A Tavistock Approach," *Journal of Enterprise Management*, 3 (1981), 251–252.

The Baseline Frame of Reference*

Roy McLennan

Many action research interventions carried out by Institute members are loosely based on a widely shared frame of reference. This framework or conceptual scheme originates from psycho-analysis, specifically a British psychoanalytic school in which Melanie Klein's "object relations theory" is the most profoundly significant and Wilfred Bion's account of group dynamics is in some sense an application and expansion to groups and organizations. In terms of these concepts the individual is conceived as a "system taking in sensory data from the outside environment, processing them in some way and then communicating with others.... This is done both in conscious and unconscious fashions" (Lawrence).

At the core of the psycho-analytic framework is "the transference", the conception that the patient or client re-enacts, in relation to the psycho-analyst or consultant, feelings and attitudes experienced in other relationships, some contemporary, some from very early in life. The patient or client is inclined to make pleasant experiences part of himself (introjection). He splits off undesirable aspects of himself and projects these into others (projection). He also acts out his feelings towards one person in his relationships with another (displacement and transference). Just as the classic psycho-analyst, armed with couch, pad and pencil, uses projections into him as primary data on what is going on in a patient in order to help him, so the psycho-analytically oriented action researcher uses the projections of client system members into him as primary data for the elucidation of what is going on in the organization. The various forms of the transference in the client-consultant relationship are thus used as a means of illuminating and working on dynamics within the client system. And the basic explanation of organizational action is taken to consist of "consolidated individual behaviors resulting from the inter-connection of individual projection processes" (de Board, p. 117). Psycho-analysis thus provides "an important role model for Tavistock staff working ... with groups and organizations," as well as a central conceptual framework (Miller, 1977: p. 34).

Arising from this frame of reference, consultancy is "akin to midwifery in that it encourages the discovery of repressed, unconscious meanings and allows for these to be born into the world of the conscious" (Lawrence, p. 14). Much of the work of the action researcher with members of a client system is "to enable them to get in touch with their conscious and unconscious feelings and bring them to the surface" (Lawrence, p. 14). In order to possess the skill

* SOURCE: Reprinted with permission from Roy McLennan, "Action Research Consultancy: A Tavistock Approach," *Journal of Enterprise Management*, 3, pp. 251–252. (1981) Pergamon Journals Ltd.

to carry this out the consultant needs to

> ... differentiate, as methodically as possible, between what he is introjecting from the client and what he may be projecting himself. The world of feelings and meanings, if it is to be explored, requires that the initial explorer be as aware as possible of his own subjective inner world and ... be committed to its continued exploration (Lawrence, p. 14).

REFERENCES

BION, W. R., *Experiences with Groups* (London: Tavistock, 1961).

deBOARD, R., *The Psycho-Analysis of Organizations* (London: Tavistock, 1978).

KLEIN M., Our Adult World and its Roots in Infancy, *Human Relations* 16 (1963), No. 4.

LAWRENCE, W. G., A Psycho-analytic Perspective for Understanding Organization Life, *OD Practices in Europe*, R. N. Ottaway (Ed.) (New York: Wiley, 1980).

MILLER, E. J., Demands and Problems of Face-to-Face Work with People. In Open University, A Post-Experience Course, The Handicapped Person in the Community, Units 1–10, Block 3, Part 1, Providing Supporting Services (Milton Keynes: Open University Press, 1975).

MILLER, E. J., Organizational Development and Industrial Democracy: A Current Case Study, *Organizational Development in the UK and the USA*, C. L. Cooper (Ed.) (London: Macmillan, 1977).

Intersubjectivity*

Colin Eden, Sue Jones,
David Sims, and Tim Smithin

Over the past few years the authors of this paper have been attempting to pay attention to intersubjectivity within groups in organisations, and understanding its importance for effective problem-finding and problem-solving in teams.

It is our belief that many systems research, operational research and management science projects have concentrated on "objective", usually quantitative data, at the expense of losing their clients' interest and commitment.

It is our feeling that neglect of the issues raised by the notion of intersubjectivity leads to results in research and consultancy which do not take sufficient account of individual perceptions or definitions of situations and lead, consequently, to "solutions" which no one likes because they relate to problems which no one owns (Eden and Sims, 1977).

As a result of our involvement in a variety of different projects in the field of housing policy, probation, publishing, health care, printing and community relations, all of which have been conducted with a commitment to intersubjectivity, we shall comment upon the problems and paradoxes of our methodological perspective.

The need to take account of intersubjectivity seems overwhelming. Our work is concerned with taking account of intersubjectivity in policy analysis and evaluation. It is orientated to the construction of models that will be owned by our clients because they recognise as legitimate, and explicitly take account of, the subjective and particular knowledge of individuals within organisations. They also explicitly take account of the interaction of shared and individual knowledge as a group comes to define an intersubjective group issue.

In this work we have sought to demonstrate the way in which issues are individually construed by persons, so that different persons will all experience different issues according to their own perceptions, interests and duties (Armstrong and Eden, 1979; Eden and Sims, 1977; Sims, 1978, 1979). Some of our studies emphasise the individual nature of the reality within which problems are constructed. Others (for example Eden and Jones, 1980) concentrate on the way in which a group of people can build and rebuild issues for themselves. We take an essentially phenomenological stance on the nature of experience and the foundations of knowledge. We consider that experience is, at root, confrontation with phenomena rather than "facts" or "laws." All

* SOURCE: Colin Eden, Sue Jones, David Sims, and Tim Smithin, "The Intersubjectivity of Issues and Issues of Intersubjectivity," *Journal of Management Studies*, 18 (1981), 37–47. Reprinted with permission.

knowledge is therefore in one sense purely subjective or personal knowledge as Polyani (1958) describes it. As Vickers implies, issues belong to people; an issue is not the "objective" characteristic of some objective sequence of events, to be discovered by a consultant and proferred by his superior expert knowledge as the "real" issue.

The theoretical and conceptual commitment to the notion of the intersubjectivity of knowledge, which guides our work with teams, is conceptually derived from phenomenology (see for example, Bittner, 1973), the sociology of "defining situations," and the work of cognitive psychologists such as Kelly (1955) and Neisser (1976). Here man the person is seen as *constructing* his or her individual reality according to the psychological frameworks he or she had evolved to make sense of and act in his or her world, rather than *perceiving* some objective reality. In particular we find helpful the succinct aphorism of Thomas and Thomas (1928) where if "men define situations as real they are real in their consequences." As Ball (1972) has said "what Thomas is basically arguing here . . . is that . . . in order to understand social conduct we must look . . . to the meanings of situations and the situated meanings within them as they are phenomenologically experienced by the actors located within them." As we stated above this is not to suggest that meanings and realities are not shared. We see a dialectic between the individuality of reality and reality as a "social construction" (see particularly Berger and Luckmann, 1966), in which meanings are "socially sustained" and experienced "as social facts" (Silverman, 1970), and it is this dialectic which gives rise to the complicated notion of intersubjectivity.

The client's subjective or "assumptive" world (Young, 1977) is represented by a cognitive map. The map consists of concepts, idiomatically expressed in the client's own phrasing, linked by arrows representing a casual link between the concepts of the form "Concept A has consequences for or can be explained by Concept B".

Our experience as well as our conceptual orientation leads us to believe that the issues perceived by individuals are inevitably characterised by important idiosyncratic beliefs and values, concerns about the internal politics of the organisation, and the relationships with other team members. Some, if not all of these are likely to be crucial to choices perceived and made.

INTERSUBJECTIVITY IN TEAMS

When considering the working of teams in organisations it seems important and indeed commonsensical that such working involves the interaction and negotiation of shared *and* idiosyncratic understandings. A team is continually involved in some process of negotiating reality amongst its members. Much of this negotiation, however, is likely to remain implicit, as in most social interaction. Members of teams are rarely given the facility, explicitly or systematically, to explore different as well as similar perspectives.

The usefulness of the notion of intersubjectivity, for us, is based on conceptual necessity. Regardless of the philosophical bases of the following two positions, we find the notion that individuals are separate and alone, each inhabiting their own subjective reality to be, in its extreme form, almost as unhelpful as the opposing notion that the world is a place of facts which can be proved or disproved, and about which we can all be expected to agree. For ourselves, we find that it is best to conceive the world as being individually constructed, with each person's reality being separate and distinctive, and yet with that reality not being so far detached from other persons' realities as to be incomprehensible to them. Usually we find that persons believe their separate realities not to be so far unrelated to one another that they cannot talk, debate, argue, negotiate across those separate and different realities. Indeed, there are some points at which different persons' realities resemble each other so closely that we can speak *as if* they were matters of objective fact.

Organisational situations are particularly well characterised by the notion of intersubjectivity. Characteristically in an organisation, members will have a considerable cultural, organisational and social commonality among them, which would enable two persons from that organisation who had never met before to communicate with one another with much greater confidence than would, for example, an American airline pilot and a Papuan headhunter, who had never met before. At the same time, the different professional backgrounds, political and religious beliefs, values, interests and so on of organisational members mean that their understandings of the world are not so similar that they can be regarded as equivalent. If they were so, then meetings could never have any significance of decision-making, but only for communication, and even the most cynical opponent of committee life would be unlikely to make that claim. For these reasons we consider that intersubjectivity is an important notion for understanding organisational worlds, because it captures a characteristic experience for members of organisations. We acknowledge that notions of consensus, shared goals and shared knowledge do exist, and that many teams do reach a genuine consensus and "team view." We feel that team communication reflects intersubjectivity, meaning that individual subjects communicate with other individual subjects. A group can dialogue with each other and with themselves, to construct an evolving intersubjective definition of the situation. It is likely to contain a significant number of contradictory beliefs, deriving from the different perceptions of the team members, as well as concepts that may have virtually identical verbal tags, the meanings of which, however, as elaborated through their conceptual and belief context, may be significantly different (Eden, 1978).

The construction of an inter-subjective model involves combining the individual models into one overall model, or more particularly, those parts of the individual models that the team members are prepared to reveal to others. Usually the very process of exploring an issue is sufficient to change the nature of the issue, often in such a way that the devising of incisive or ameliorative sets of actions becomes unnecessary or irrelevant.

It is perhaps worth noting that we do not assign strength or importance to particular beliefs, and this is helpful for our work on intersubjectivity. When a team member begins to look at the subjective understanding of an issue of another team member, the role of a facilitator to this process (Sims and Jones, 1980; Sims et al, 1979) is to help the person not too quickly to assign weights to belief of others, but rather to consider them and to toy with them, until he or she has formed an appreciation of how the other came by and held his or her subjective belief, and what that belief means within his or her world. This we consider to be the very essence of how the consideration of intersubjectivity can be useful to team members.

Team processes emphasize listening to other team members, reflection on issues, and careful exploration of individual views, imply a purpose and method of team work which is in contrast to the way many teams reportedly operate in organisations, government and voluntary groups. Managers are sometimes encouraged to have as few meetings as possible and to get on with the "real work." Similarly group chairpersons are often anxious "to do the business efficiently." Our feeling, which has been heightened by recent exercises on intersubjective issues, is that work which ignores individual perspectives can lead to an "efficient" but spurious activity, since many team members are not committed to the activity, and the decisions have not benefited from the range of experience available within the team.

If we were seeking some concept which conveniently encapsulates what we are paying attention to, in devising ways of assisting teams, it would be to find ways of assisting the formal process of *listening*. By this we mean the listening by a consultant to members of a team; by members of a team to each other; and by members of a team to *themselves*. What is consciously and carefully listened to are the theories, attitudes, worries, values and political concerns that members of the team have about the nature, causes and consequences of the current situation, and any picture of some preferred situation that they may have. We believe that listening must also involve the provision of a tool that allows members of a team to hold on to the *complexity* of the different bodies of wisdom and desires of the team, and allows that complexity to be managed and negotiated.

REFERENCES

Armstrong, A. and Eden, C. (1979). 'An exploration of occupational role: an exercise in team development'. *Personnel Review, 8,* 1, 20–23.

Ball, D. W. (1972). ' "Definition of the situation": some theoretical and methodological consequences of taking W. I. Thomas seriously'. *Journal for the Theory of Social Behaviour, 2,* 61–82.

Berger, P. L. and Luckmann, T. (1966). *The Social Construction of Reality.* New York: Doubleday.

Bittner, E. (1973). 'Objectivity and realism in sociology'. In Psathas, E. (Ed.), *Phenomenological Sociology: Issues and Applications.* New York: Wiley.

Eden, C. (1978). 'Operational research and organization development'. *Human Relations, 31,* 657–74.

Eden, C. and Jones, S. (1980). 'Publish or perish—a case study'. *Journal of the O.R. Society, 31,* 131–9.

Eden, C. and Sims, D. (1977). 'Problem definition between consultant and client'. Working Paper,

Centre for the Study of Organizational Change and Development, University of Bath.

KELLY, G. A. (1955). *The Psychology of Personal Constructs*. New York: Norton.

NEISSER, U. (1976). *Cognition and Reality*, San Francisco: Freeman.

POLYANI, M. (1958). *Personal Knowledge*. London: Routledge and Kegan Paul.

SILVERMAN, D. (1970). *The Theory of Organisations*. London: Heinemann.

SIMS, D. (1978). *Problem Construction in Teams*. Doctoral thesis, University of Bath.

SIMS, D. (1979). 'A framework for understanding the definition and formulation of problems in teams'. *Human Relations, 32*, 909–21.

SIMS, D., EDEN, C. and JONES, S. (1979). 'Facilitating problem definition in teams'. Paper presented to 3rd European Congress on Operational Research, Amsterdam, April. (Forthcoming in *European Journal of Operational Research*)

SIMS, D. and JONES, S. (1980). 'Making problem definition explicit in teams'. Working paper, Centre for the Study of Organizational Change and Development, University of Bath.

THOMAS, W. I. and THOMAS, D. S. (1928). *The Child in America: Behavior Problems and Progress*. New York: Knopf.

YOUNG, K. (1977). 'Values in the policy process'. *Policy and Politics, 5*, 1–22.

8
EARLY IN THE
PROCESS

<hr>

INTRODUCTION

*Here and elsewhere we shall not obtain the best insight into things until we actually see them growing from the beginning.**

—Aristotle

The experiences related in this chapter begin with *The Le Court Cheshire Home*, which outlines the development of an intervention from the first contact between the client and the external change agent, and provides a vivid stream of consultant introspections about what they thought they were doing and thinking. The intervention promised a scientific as well as a practical payoff, and raises notty questions as to who was the client.

The chapter introduces the first part of a substantial, four-episode account of an intervention, which chronicles an organizational change from its origin to its conclusion, and extends over the three chapters of this part of the book. *The Multi Company (A)* outlines the initial involvement of the change agent in the organization, with the brief of helping to stimulate innovation in the company, his reactions to what company managers thought about, and how they behaved during the early phase of his association with them.

The *Etna Production Company* consists of a brief account of an approach by company managers to a prospective change agent, which he found unsatisfactory, and therefore decided to terminate further contact with the organization concerned. It directs attention to considerations about circumstances under which a consultant should or should not consider entering or ending his or her

* Quoted in Fremont E. Kast & James E. Rosenzweig, *Organization and Management: A Systems and Contingency Approach,* Fourth Edition, McGraw-Hill, New York, 1985, p. 54.

association with a particular client organization. The option does not lie solely in the hands of managers.

Changing Your Organization suggests a schema for the established, experienced manager to follow in planning and designing an intervention process intended to bring about change in his or her organization.

The models and schemes in this chapter open with four contributions essentially about the initiation of client—consultant relations. *The Client's Problem* summarizes what several Tavistock consultants think about client organizations, at the time they are first approached as prospective change agents. Whatever the "real" problem, it is overlaid and surrounded by an array of emotions.

Entering into Relationships discusses the problem of entrée into an organization and the tactics used to effect it, from the point of view of experienced sociological field researchers. *The Entry Problem in Consultation,* an early attempt to define the problem faced by a client and a change agent when they enter into a working relationship, is helpful in thinking about the issue. It concludes with a pointedly wry sketch of the kind of situation sometimes encountered by an entering consultant.

Orientation to the Client summarizes how Tavistock interventionists often act towards members of the client system, and why they do so. *The Internal Consultant* outlines the respective advantages and disadvantages of an internal consultant vis-à-vis an external consultant, and the grounds for cooperation between the two.

Organizational Diagnosis present's an incisive, sensible set of guidelines to guide the change agent's thinking in his or her early work in the client organization. Several complementary benchmarks are provided in *Selecting a Setting and a Method of Work. The Organization Development Contract Revisited* discusses issues implicated in the intervention contract, in an interaction process fashion congruent with the perspective of this book. A clear statement emerges about what the salient issues are and what the change agent may do about them.

The Le Court Cheshire Home*

Eric Miller and Geraldine Gwynne, Tavistock Institute

THE FIRST CONTACT

Our involvement began in January 1962 with a letter typed on the paper of *The Cheshire Smile: The Quarterly Magazine of the Cheshire Homes,* and gave the address as: Le Court, Liss, Hants. Printed on the right-hand side of the letter-heading was a drawing of a megalocephalic smiling cat, sitting in a wheelchair:

'Dear Dr Miller,
    Mrs R . . . suggested I should send you a copy of this article I have written for the spring issue of the Cheshire Smile.
    If you are interested in it, we wondered whether you would be able to come down and discuss the subject. The Editor . . . has for some years been keen on the idea of using the Homes as therapeutic group communities, since they seem ideally suited to it in many ways. . . .'

The article was entitled 'Oiling the wheels' and plainly had been written by someone informed in the fields of social and individual psychology. It pointed out that Cheshire Homes provided 'a nearly-normal life for people too disabled to manage independently' and that community life could be most rewarding. But the 'strains and hazards of group association' also posed difficulty. It went on to make a convincing case for securing the services of trained social workers 'to help people in adjusting to their disabilities and to each other.' In conclusion: 'When such great strides are being made in group dynamics and social psychology it seems a pity to neglect the opportunity of oiling the wheels of the machinery of this new venture in community living.'
    A second letter filled in more details. Some three years previously, it said, a group of residents at Le Court had tried to get a social worker in a research role. An approach had been made at that stage to the Tavistock Institute, but nothing had come of it. The late Sir Ernest Gowers, then chairman of Le Court's Management Committee, had tried to get something done through the London School of Economics; but 'there was no one with enough interest and enthusiasm to carry it through.' The letter went on to say that the reading of a book by Elliott Jaques, *The changing culture of a factory,* had suggested that the Tavistock Institute could 'be of immense help.' The invitation to visit Le

* SOURCE: E. J. Miller and G. V. Gwynne, *A Life Apart* (London: Tavistock Publications, 1972), pp. 16–31. Reprinted with permission.

Court was reiterated and the concluding sentences of the letter further baited the hook:

> 'It is a particularly crucial time just now as our Matron is leaving to get married and the Secretary is also leaving. Both have been with us for more than four years, so there will be a period of readjustment in which we could do with help and which might also be an opportunity for change. Also the Residents' Welfare Committee will be changing at the end of the month, and for various reasons there is likely to be a period of transition in its affairs.'

The reply to this letter was not overly enthusiastic:

> '. . . My colleagues and I . . . are working under considerable pressure . . . and I do not foresee the likelihood of our having a research worker available. . . . May I suggest that if you are going to be in London, you come in for a discussion. . . .'

The response was forthright:

> '. . . We should very much like to come and see you. . . . As we are all in wheelchairs perhaps it would be as well if only Mr S and I came. It would be quite an undertaking, since Mr S's chair is a long one, and I think we should have to arrange for two cars. . . .'

And this evoked a much more conciliatory answer:

> '. . . I recognize how inconsiderate I must have seemed in suggesting that you come to see me in London. I am afraid I didn't realize it would be such a difficult undertaking. . . . Could I suggest as an alternative that I visit you at Liss. . . ?'

—and the visit duly took place in the spring of 1962. . . .

Of course the problems of such residential communities are socially important and technically interesting; but a great many other problems always seem to have priority. That the disabled should themselves be talking about their needs in terms of group dynamics and therapeutic communities (and using these terms not just as catch-phrases but as concepts) was not really to be believed. Conventional prejudices—so insidious that we are scarcely aware of them—had made it obvious to assume that the letter-writer was something to do with the management of the home, or perhaps a well-read, public-spirited citizen living in the neighbourhood. Consequently, the discovery that this was actually an inmate caused shock and guilt; and the last letter offered reparation by return of post. But such reparation does not betoken unalloyed love and empathy for the disabled: there may well remain—and the evidence of introspection suggests that there persisted for a long time in this case—an underlying sense of having been caught, together with a corresponding wariness about being drawn further in.

That first visit to the Le Court Cheshire Home was disturbing. 'A long, low, fairly modern building, it lay in a large estate with a commanding view over an unpopulated Sussex landscape.' A beautiful setting—but, as one was quickly told, 'You can't converse with the cows.' Meeting the residents sharpened one's ambivalence. There were about forty, almost all severely crippled. It seemed impossible that one would ever be able to cross the barrier of deformity and disfigurement to communicate with the people beyond it; and one could feel that society was not unmotivated in isolating this community as far away as possible from 'normal' neighbours. Yet there was a strong opposing pull, a compound of guilt, compassion, and empathy, and this was reinforced by the recognition that if one could shift one's focus and see across the barrier one was meeting some highly intelligent and insightful individuals.

Certainly, what the residents spoke about on that first visit was not the capacities they lacked, but the difficulties of making the fullest use of those capacities that remained to them. They were conscious that the dependence which in some areas of their lives was complete and inevitable spilled over into other areas where it was not. Institutional life reinforced their dependence in a way that deprived them of the rights and obligations of other adults to make quite ordinary decisions about their own lives—even such apparently trivial decisions as when to go to the bathroom. Correspondingly, the imminent change of staff was especially disturbing. It could so easily lead to the introduction of new routines, which would disrupt the fabric of habitual expectations of everyday life, and of different values, which might more subtly strip the residents of the hard-won elements of personal autonomy to which they clung.

Problems of this kind—and these are only examples—could not but capture our attention. The Tavistock Institute describes itself as being concerned with advancing the social sciences in the service of practical affairs of man. Here was an area that promised both a theoretical and a practical pay-off. Although there was some reality in saying that we were 'working under considerable pressure,' time was nevertheless somehow found to discuss and think about the issues involved. One theme that interested us, for example, was that in contrast to most institutions with a human 'throughput'—airlines, hospitals, colleges—where inmates are transient and staff relatively permanent, in institutions for the disabled and chronic sick the position is reversed; yet it was the staff—the transients—who still had the determining influence on the culture of the establishment. A colleague, Robin Higgins, published a paper about this in *New Society*. . . . We read what we could of the relevant literature; we began to meet other people who in one way or another were involved in the field; and we kept in touch with our original correspondent.

From this source we were subjected to an unrelenting pressure, overt and covert, to get us to undertake practical research. That we were ambivalent about this demand is shown by the contrast between our expressions of concern and our slowness to act. Finance for research is hard to come by and it takes considerable time and effort to formulate a convincing research proposal; but there is little doubt that our delay in trying to find the money reflected underlying hesitations about what we would be letting ourselves in for.

Not until August 1965, three and a half years after the first contact, did we make an approach to a foundation. Although this failed, the Ministry of Health became interested and at the end of March 1966 confirmed that it would meet the cost of the pilot study we had proposed.

THE AIM OF THE PILOT STUDY

Our area of interest has already begun to be made explicit in the preceding pages. An initiative had arisen in one home; but the problems posed were plainly relevant to the many other institutions that provide long-term—usually life-long—residential care for those who, because of chronic illness, physical handicap, or both, cannot look after themselves or be looked after in their own homes. Progress in providing residential care has been uneven and there are still many who need it for whom it is not available. One often hears, for instance, of young chronic sick patients with active minds languishing among senile neighbours in the geriatric wards of general hospitals. But it appeared to us that we were moving into a new phase, in which the basic problems of providing shelter and physical care were at least in sight of solution. For some inmates these benefits were enough in themselves and something for which to be unequivocally grateful. After painful experiences of isolation and insecurity they could now be dependent, without further anxiety or ambition, in a dependable environment. For others, however, once their basic physical needs were satisfied, new problems of a psychosocial nature were beginning to arise.

It has long been recognized by sociologists that institutional life in itself tends to stunt and distort the personal development of inmates. Institutionalization, with its symptoms of apathy and withdrawal, is now almost recognized as an illness in its own right. But it is easier to diagnose than to prevent or cure. The group of residents at Le Court were concerned about this phenomenon not merely for themselves but for many less fortunate inmates elsewhere, who were less articulate about their condition. What could be done about it? Every type of residential institution, of course, has its crop of horror stories about sadistic staff. . . .

The presenting problem for us, however, was not deliberate sadism, which, though appalling, seems rare,[1] but the well-intentioned managements and staff whose behaviour nevertheless appeared to compound the negative effects of institutionalization rather than alleviate them. Very infrequently one heard of the reverse; how and why this happened was obscure.

What we proposed, therefore, and the Ministry of Health accepted, was a pilot study which would have two components. These were, in general

---

[1] It must be stated that many inmates would contest this. For example: 'You always get sadistic people going into institutional work, whether it be prisons or homes, . . . where they're in a position of power, and whether they have an opportunity to exercise their sadism depends largely on the climate in the institution. . . . The bigger the institution, the more likely it is that a great deal of sadism goes unrecorded. . . .'

terms, to identify more precisely what was involved in providing residential care for incurables, and to discover possible ways through which appropriate changes could be brought about.

So far as the former component was concerned, the kind of data we wanted could not be secured by a survey of a large sample of institutions. Normal survey techniques are well suited to collecting uncontroversial factual information and, if carefully used, data on opinions and attitudes. What we particularly wanted to examine was the interplay between attitudes and behaviour. The opinion I profess in answering a questionnaire may be quite inconsistent with the attitude implicit in what I actually do. We therefore elected to sacrifice the representativeness of a larger sample in the interest of concentrating in greater depth on half a dozen institutions. We wanted to find out what problems were being encountered in different kinds of setting and the different ways in which they were being tackled (or left untouched or even unnoticed).

The second component was essentially action research. We planned to find one or two institutions in which changes were being carried out or contemplated and to work with the people concerned in dealing with the processes of implementation. This approach has several merits. In the first place, changes, or attempts at change, often reveal facets of a social system that, though critical, are not normally visible. Second, the institutions selected could provide real-life laboratories in which, with the consent of those involved, hypotheses emerging from the research could be tested. Third, the experience gained from taking part in these specific change processes might be communicated in a way that could be used by others who wanted to initiate changes elsewhere.

FIELDWORK AND ATTENDANT PROBLEMS

We started by using open-ended interviewing techniques. Focusing usually on the life-history of the individual we tried to elicit the issues that were of primary importance to him. We gained additional data by observing the day-to-day activities (and inactivity) of inmates, by attendance at meetings, and by scrutiny of records. People in managerial and staff roles, as well as some voluntary workers, were interviewed in addition to inmates. . . . As a result of this early experience we were able to develop an open-ended questionnaire for use in subsequent interviews with inmates, and another for use with staff. Once these had been formulated they also provided a basis for re-interviewing some of the earlier respondents from whom certain information had not been obtained.

A second and no less important reason for avoiding concentrated periods of fieldwork in one institution was the strain involved. We are referring particularly to the strain on the interviewer. This is not to discount the strain on some of the respondents, who quickly became tired: thus interviews had to be spread over two or even three separate sessions. Speech defects sometimes made the discussion very protracted. Occasionally they were so gross that the words were incomprehensible to the unattuned outsider and a fellow-inmate had to be drafted as an interpreter. A few inmates had no speech at all and we had to rely on securing information about them from other sources. Conditions like this were difficult for the interviewer too; but even more difficult was the content of the interviews . . . the moving stories we listened to, of the depression we absorbed, and of the problem of preventing our emotions from swamping our wits. Spacing the interviews and interspersing them with other work helped in this respect, although it could not solve the problem.

We believed that it was particularly important to acquire and maintain a balanced outlook if we were to be effective. . . . In practice, it was only during this phase that we learned how difficult it was to use our reason without denying the validity of our feelings and vice versa.

THE SETTING FOR ACTION RESEARCH

It was in May 1966 that the Management Committee of Le Court agreed to our using that institution as the centre for the action-research phase of the project. By that time we knew, or thought we knew, a good deal about Le Court, which had been passing through a particularly turbulent phase in the preceding four years.

Le Court was the first of the Cheshire Homes, of which there are now some fifty in the British Isles and many more abroad. It owed its beginnings in 1948 to Group Captain Leonard Cheshire, V.C., who had become a national figure in the Second World War as a courageous bomber pilot and in 1945 was Britain's official observer when the second atomic bomb was dropped on Japan. . . . He left the RAF determined to devote his life to more constructive causes. After failing in one experiment in community living he found himself almost by accident personally caring for a man who was in the terminal stages of cancer and for whom hospitals could do no more. Soon he discovered others in a similar plight. It became his objective (later embodied in Le Court's constitution):

> 'To provide . . . for the care, treatment and maintenance of the young chronic sick and permanently disabled of both sexes irrespective of creed.'

Le Court was to cater in particular for those who

> 'are willing to work insofar as their capacity permits and should be of such intelligence and ability as to benefit from the special facilities and atmosphere of Le Court. . . . Persons suffering from infectious diseases or TB and persons of unsound mind shall not be eligible.'

It was also to be a home rather than a hospital,

'. . . the patients being encouraged to take whatever part they can in the day-to-day running of the home.'

In the early years Cheshire was heavily dependent on the goodwill of local people. They made gifts of furniture and bedding; they helped with the repairs to the dilapidated building; they washed and mended clothes and they also helped to nurse the patients. The practice of involving local volunteers in the work of Le Court and other Cheshire Homes has continued ever since. Those patients who were able to do so assisted with the household chores.

A principle established during this early phase was that a Cheshire Home is a home for life. Inmates were to have security of tenure so long as the home itself survived. By 1954 the survival of Le Court was assured. With the help of a large grant from the Carnegie United Kingdom Trust, a new purpose-built home was in use. There was a cadre of trained nursing staff. The Cheshire Foundation was by this time in existence and through it Cheshire was establishing new homes in other parts of the country. Responsibility for the management of Le Court was formally delegated by the trustees of the Foundation to a local Management Committee which had been set up in 1950.

Given this more stable basis the home began to develop in new ways. The term 'patients' implies passivity and it is no accident that during the next phase the inmates insisted on being called 'residents,' for their activity both in Le Court and outside was substantial. Internally they began to take on some of the jobs that had previously been the responsibility of staff. By 1959, for example, they were running a workshop; those who were proficient in one craft trained newcomers. They were also operating a shop on the premises and arranging their own outings.

Externally they were taking on an increasing amount of public relations and fund-raising work. They formed a film unit to record and publicize their own experiences of disability and their use of technical aids to overcome it as far as possible. Films of this nature were used for fund-raising and teaching purposes and also gave (to quote the title of one film) 'Living proof' of what could be achieved by the disabled. An organization called Holidays for the Disabled, which currently arranges an annual holiday for several hundred handicapped people all over the country, was started by a Le Court resident in 1961. This same resident started the first support group in 1958. An active Residents' Welfare Committee founded the Le Court Association in 1963.[2] This was a particularly interesting venture because it demonstrated that residents were taking the initiative in recruiting supporters in the county and also because in 1963 the Executive Committee of the Association was the one official body where representatives of management, residents, and outside people could meet together.

[2] Support groups contribute to the amenities of the home by raising money for specific projects. Each group is represented on the Le Court Association which acts as a coordinating body between the groups and Le Court.

Residents at this time were well aware of the benefits of living at Le Court. Le Court provided (to quote from an article by one of them):

> 'surroundings where people previously regarding themselves as unwanted clinical material or social outcasts can learn to reach towards full living and often attain horizons of personal and social achievement that would have been impossible had they never become disabled.'

As was shown, however, by the approach to us in 1962, they were also becoming aware that living in a community presented problems with which they did not find it easy to come to terms. In particular, they were anxious about the precariousness of such autonomy as they had managed to win for themselves. They recognized that they were lucky to have so much more freedom and opportunity for achievement than the inmates of most other institutions and at the same time they were afraid that given a change of staff many of their privileges might be arbitrarily curtailed.

These fears proved to be well-founded. That year (1962) saw the departure of a matron who had been at Le Court for five years. During her stay she had come to accept the special needs of an institution of this kind which contrasted so markedly with the hospital régimes to which she had previously been accustomed. In her own words:

> 'I have seen the need—it has been pretty well forced on me at times—to drop more and more of the defence mechanisms, the armoury, the inhibitions acquired during seventeen years of conventional nursing.'

In the eyes of the new matron, wedded to conventional nursing, the régime of Le Court was not merely liberal; it was anarchic. This view appears to have been shared by the full-time warden and by some members of the Management Committee. As a first step towards the restoration of discipline she and the warden imposed certain restrictions, principally on bedtimes and television viewing. Residents protested vehemently. They were perhaps protesting not so much against the rules themselves as against the arbitrary way in which they had been imposed, and more generally because they saw their fragile status as adults being eroded and their helplessness and dependence once again being underlined. Thus the question of the rules became a highly charged ideological issue. One was either for individual freedom or against it, for the residents or against them: there was no middle ground. Even though we ourselves were only remotely connected with Le Court at that stage we nevertheless found ourselves emotionally on the side of the residents. Physically they were totally dependent on the very staff members who were taking away their freedom. It was a situation in which mutual paranoia could be expected to escalate.

Within the home, residents' protests were disregarded and the warden then discontinued the practice of joint consultation with the Residents' Welfare Committee—a procedure that had been in existence for two years. Next, the issues were referred to the Management Committee. Residents proceeded to lobby committee members and friends in the neighbourhood who might be sympathetic to their cause. Management Committee, however, though internally split, backed the administration in threatening to remove first one then several residents at least temporarily to other Cheshire Homes. An appeal was then made to Group Captain Cheshire. He reassured residents that a Cheshire Home was a home for life and promised them security of tenure. At the same time he offered to find a house for those residents who wanted to take over total responsibility for managing a home of their own. At least a third of the residents were interested in such a venture. Lack of funds ultimately made it impossible, but even before this some residents were questioning the advisability of the project, partly because they regarded it as an alternative means of expelling the so-called trouble-makers and partly too because total responsibility was not what they were seeking. They hoped rather to create a cooperative community with caring staff who shared the residents' ideals.

'The troubles' continued for about a year. The new matron, finding her position untenable, left, and efforts to find a replacement were unsuccessful. Eventually the immediate fears of the residents were allayed by the appointment as matron of a sister who had been nursing at Le Court for ten years. During this time she had always been sympathetic to residents' demands for self-determination. Several residents had urged her to apply for the matron's post and were extremely anxious that she should get appointed, and she also had some support among staff, though the Management Committee was at first reluctant. At all events it was clear that she would not arouse the kinds of difficulty that her immediate predecessor had precipitated. Indeed, throughout the three years during which she held the post residents had no cause to complain that they were not consulted.

Perhaps what was not recognized in 1963 was the effect that the new matron's change in role was likely to have on her relationship with residents. In 1962 she had actively campaigned on their behalf and identified herself with residents rather than with staff. The position of matron required somewhat different qualities. Sensitivity to and awareness of residents' needs was a necessary qualification, but over-identification with them could well be a handicap. Staff also had needs, especially in a work situation of this kind which involved personal stress. The nursing and domestic staff had to be led and their standards maintained. Once she occupied an administrative post the new matron must have found her position extremely difficult: her personal satisfaction derived from work with residents; her role, on the other hand, required that she took into account the needs both of staff and of residents and reconciled any conflicts between these that might arise. Her 'capture' by the residents did not leave her free to fill the role of matron and eventually she came under attack for failure in leading her staff. A potentially difficult relationship existed too between the matron and the warden, who had been on opposite sides of the fence during 'the troubles.' Both warden and matron had the difficult task of trying to operate on the boundary of the institution but over the years the warden had tended to move 'outside' while the matron was over-involved 'inside'.

Thus, although the symptoms of the crisis were alleviated by this appointment, it might be seen as buying peace from the residents at the cost of undermining the role of matron. For a more lasting resolution it was necessary to find mechanisms that would allow the residents to feel secure without making the 'boundary' positions of warden and matron so difficult to sustain.

The appointment of a new chairman of Management Committee in February 1965 marked the beginning of a period when such mechanisms were actively being sought and tried out. The new chairman, a barrister, came to Le Court with no prior knowledge either of the home itself or of the Cheshire Foundation (of which he was simultaneously appointed a trustee). Soon after his appointment he inaugurated meetings between representatives of Management Committee, staff, and residents to consider staff and resident representation on the Management Committee. The case for their representation on, or at least attendance at, Management Committee seemed to him, as a newcomer, overwhelming. A few members of the Committee said that they had held this view for some time but had been unable to get it accepted. As a trustee, the new chairman was in a more influential position. As a result of these joint discussions a recommendation was made to the trustees who agreed that residents and staff should each elect two representatives to sit on Management Committee for an experimental two-year period beginning in October 1965. It was hoped that this would break down the distrust which had existed for some time between residents and the Committee and between residents and staff and would also increase staff participation in the affairs of Le Court. Fuller knowledge of decisions taken and the reasons for taking them was expected to avoid misunderstandings arising from rumours and from the passing of inaccurate or incomplete information. In fact, these representatives were not to become full members of Management Committee. Proceedings of the Committee were divided into two parts: Part II was devoted to issues affecting individual staff members and residents, when their personal backgrounds, financial position, and questions of discipline were subject to discussion; representatives received papers for and attended Part I only.

Apart from these important internal developments this was a phase in which the trustees of the Cheshire Foundation became much more active in relation to Le Court and made certain far-reaching decisions. The first move had come in November 1964 when Group Captain Cheshire announced to the Management Committee and to representatives of the residents that the trustees hoped to site the headquarters of the Foundation's Service Corps and its training school at Le Court. This was a new organization set up to recruit and train the staff for all the Foundation's homes. He proposed that it should be administered by the local Management Committee. Plans were also advanced for locating a post-polio respiratory unit for ten people at Le Court. A ballot was held at which the great majority of residents expressed their approval of the scheme. It was subsequently found that there was no particular demand for this facility, and a heavy-nursing unit to cater for a maximum of fifteen people (who might include some post-polio respiratory cases) was substituted. This latter development became a cause of considerable concern to residents who felt that they had been presented with a *fait accompli* which would dramatically change their home and which they were powerless to resist.

By the end of 1965 a new constitution was in effect which formalized the greater involvement of the trustees. It stipulated that up to a quarter of the Management Committee should be nominated by the trustees, and the home was designated 'The Cheshire Foundation Home'. It was to become 'the centre where the trustees can experiment with new ideas' and as far as possible it was to be 'the model of what the Foundation is trying to achieve'. Le Court was the first Cheshire Home and over the years had prided itself, quite justifiably, on being an experiment in social living in which residents' initiative had played a great part. Consequently, it was an obvious symbol of what the Foundation was trying to achieve. What gradually became clear, however, was that its adoption by the trustees meant a reduction in the autonomy of the Management Committee and of the home generally. Thus in some ways the very adoption by the trustees of Le Court as a model was liable to destroy or at least reduce those creative aspects which had made it outstanding.

The Multi Company (A)*

Edgar H. Schein

Initial Involvement in Multi: First Annual Meeting. My involvement with Multi began over five years ago with a major "educational intervention" for the top-management group at its annual worldwide meeting. The manager of management development had heard me speak at an open seminar and suggested to his boss, Ted Richards, the chairman of the executive committee (the group accountable for the company's performance), that my material on career dynamics might be worth sharing with Multi's senior management. . . . Richards wanted to combine work on company problems with some stimulating input for the group, broadly in the area of leadership and creativity. He saw that the company was moving into a more turbulent economic, political, and technological environment that would require new kinds of responses.

The company had apparently seen the need to stimulate creativity for some years and had conducted a variety of seminars on the creative process. At the annual meetings, outsiders had been invited to speak, but in previous years they had concentrated more on marketing and technical issues. My two days of lecturing were to be focused on leadership and creativity in the context of individual career development.

Both the topic of *creativity* and the approach of *lecturing* to the group are completely congruent with Multi's assumptions that (1) creativity is important in science and (2) knowledge is acquired through a scientific process and then communicated through experts in a didactic way. . . .

. . . [I]n Multi everything was planned to the smallest level of detail. The seminar administrator, a former line manager who had moved into executive training, met with me for many hours some months prior to the seminar to plan for the materials to be used, the exercise to be designed to involve the participants, the schedule, and so on. In this process I observed how carefully Multi managers planned for every detail of an activity that they were responsible for. I had to provide a plan that showed virtually minute by minute what would happen during the two days, and the company was clearly willing to commit all the time and energy it might take to design as nearly "perfect" a meeting as possible.

Not only was Multi's high degree of commitment to structure revealed in this process, but, in retrospect, it also revealed how basic the assumption was about managerial turf. The seminar administrator had clear responsibility for the conduct of the meeting, though he was two levels below the participants.

---

* SOURCE: Abstracted from Edgar H. Schein and edited by Roy McLennan from *Organizational Culture and Leadership: A Dynamic View* (San Francisco: Jossey-Bass, 1985), pp. 244–269. Reprinted with permission.

He had formed a review committee for purposes of checking the seminar plan and obtaining prior involvement. This committee included Richards, the chairman of the executive committee, but the group gave considerable freedom to the administrator to make final decisions on seminar format. Thus . . . the culture was displaying itself in the manner in which I encountered the organization, but I did not know this at the time.

The participants at the Multi annual meeting were the chairman of the board, Richards' boss, several board members who showed up as visitors, the nine-person executive committee, all the senior functional and divisional managers, and the most important country managers, totaling forty-five in number. This group met annually for five days or less, depending on specific agenda to be covered.

Though I did not know it at the time, the meeting served a major integrative and communication function in that it legitimized during the meeting what culturally did not happen in day-to-day operations—a high level of open and lateral communication. It also reflected the hierarchical emphasis, however, in that this sharing across units took place in public under the scrutiny of the executive committee and board members. Moreover, there was still a strong tendency to be deferent toward others and to share ideas only when information was specifically asked for. The meeting also provided an opportunity for senior management to get a major message across quickly to the entire organization and, as we will see, to involve the entire organization in crisis management when that was needed.

Impact of First Annual Meeting. The major effects of the two days as I now reconstruct these events were as follows:

1. The group obtained new insights and information about creativity and innovation, especially the insight that innovation occurs within a variety of careers and organizational settings and should not be confused with the pure creative process that scientists are engaged in. . . . The assumption had crept in that only scientists are creative, so those managers who had left their technical identities behind long ago were reassured by my message that managerial role innovations in all the functions of the business were much needed in a healthy organization. This legitimized a great many activities as "creative" that had previously not been perceived as such and liberated some problem-solving energy by linking innovation to day-to-day problem solving. This insight would not have been dramatic but for the fact that the group was so embedded in assumptions about science and the creative process within science.

2. The group obtained new insights from the discussion of career anchors, which emphasized the variety of careers and the different things people are looking for in their careers. . . . The effect was to unfreeze some of the monolithic notions about careers and the role of scientific backgrounds in careers. In an informal dinner, the chairman of the board gave a humorous talk about his own career, which further legitimized the notion of individual differences in careers.

3. The group got to know me and my style as a responsive process

consultant through several spontaneous interventions that I made during the two days. For example, after I had observed the group's limited view of the creative process, based on a science model, I decided to highlight the difference between "creativity" and "role innovation" . . . . (Incidentally, I still had to clear my proposed deviations from the original format with the seminar administrator and the review committee.)

During the informal times at meals and in the evening, my spontaneous responses were geared to getting out of the expert role. I had observed that group members put me into an expert authority role, reflected in the frequent use of my title, "Professor," and in the kinds of general questions posed to me about what was known in my "field" and what I thought of certain approaches to management. I found myself evading answers to these questions, turning the topics back to what was going on in Multi, and reacting to specific inquiries with examples of alternatives rather than broad generalizations. For example, if I was asked what companies were doing today in the field of participative management, I would give examples and highlight the diversity of what I observed rather than generalizing as I was expected to do. I had the sense in this process that I was disappointing some of the managers with whom I was speaking, because I did not fit the stereotype of the scientist who is willing to summarize the state of knowledge in a field. On the other hand, my willingness to delve into the problems of Multi appealed to some managers, and they accepted my self-definition as a process rather than an expert consultant. . . .

My participation in the meeting ended when my two days were finished, but plans were made to institute in broader segments of the company two of the activities that had been illustrated in the seminar and were described in detail in my book *Career Dynamics,* which had been given to all participants. . . . Specifically, Richards and the executive committee decided to ask all senior managers to do the "job/role-planning exercise," which involves rethinking one's own job in the context of how it has changed and will continue to change as one projects ahead five years and analyzes the environment around the job. Richards also encouraged more managers to do the "career anchor interview exercise" as an input to the annual management development process and authorized the development of an adaptation of the original questionnaire for use specifically in the company. This exercise involves the reconstruction of all the major career steps in order to identify the pattern of reasons for each step. The purpose is to locate the "anchor"—those things that the person would not give up if forced to make a choice. I was asked to work with the headquarters management development group to help to implement these two activities by spending roughly ten to fifteen days during the subsequent year as a consultant. My clients were to be the management development manager and Richards, and the broad mission was to increase the ability of the company to innovate in all areas.

First Year's Work: Getting Acquainted. I visited the company several times during the year, each time for two to three days. During these visits I learned more about the management development system, met some of the members of the executive committee, and gradually got involved in what *I* considered my most important activity, the planning of the next annual meeting. From my point of view, if innovation was to take hold, the relatively more open climate of the annual meeting was the most important thing to take advantage of. My goal was to be accepted as a *process* consultant to the entire meeting, not as an educator coming in with wisdom for one or two days.

I found that the notion that I could help "on line" was quite foreign to most of the managers. . . . Initially I thought that the reactions of Multi's managers were simply based on misunderstanding. It was only with repeated experiences of not being invited to working meetings . . . of always being put into an expert role, and of always having to plan my visits in great detail that I realized I was up against something which could be genuinely defined as "cultural."

The perception of Multi managers of what consultants do and how they work reflected their more general assumptions about what managers do and how they work. For example, on several occasions I noticed that managers whom I had met on previous visits looked past me and ignored me when I encountered them in the public lobby or the executive dining room. As I later learned, to be seen with a consultant meant that one had problems and needed help—a position that managers in Multi strongly avoided. Why, then, could I be accepted at all in the system? Because I could be seen as an academic expert telling management development managers how to improve the total function, or I could lecture to management and thereby bring new concepts to them. This formulation of my role fitted Multi's cultural model.

The point is important because my request to attend the next annual meeting in a process consultant role was, unbeknownst to me, strongly countercultural. But Richards was intrigued, and his own innovativeness swayed other members of the planning committee. We compromised on the notion that I would give some lectures on relevant topics based on the events I observed at the meeting, thus legitimizing my attendance. My role as a consultant was further legitimized by my being cast as a scientist who had to be given an opportunity to get to know top management better, so that I could be more helpful in the future. Richards and other senior managers had a specific view of what the total group needed and were prepared to introduce an outsider in the consultant role to facilitate this process. I believe that they wanted to unfreeze the group to get it more receptive to the crisis message they were preparing to deliver. An outsider with new ideas was seen as helpful both as a source of feedback to the group and as an expert on the change process that was about to be launched. Another "outsider," a professor of policy and strategy who also occupied a position on the board of Multi, was invited as well. Our attendance at the meeting was related to a decision made by Richards and the executive committee: that at the annual meeting a major review of company performance, division by division, would be undertaken. Such a review, they believed, would bring out the need for change and innovation and thereby reverse a slide into unprofitability that had been going on but was not clearly recognized or accepted. They also planned to introduce a program of change called the Redirection Project. This business problem had been developing over several years but had not yet been identified as a crisis to be collectively shared with senior management worldwide.

The major divisions of the company, whose headquarters were in the same city as the corporate headquarters, were the primary profit centers. These divisions knew what their individual situations were but seemed unaware of the impact of dropping profit levels in many areas on the company as a whole. Only the executive committee had the total picture. This situation could easily arise because of the low amount of lateral communication, permitting the manager of a division that was losing money to rationalize that his loss was easily compensated for by other divisions and that "things would soon improve." The culture encouraged each manager to worry only about his own piece of the organization, not to take a broad corporate view. Although communications that had gone out to the divisions over the year had suggested a total company problem, no one seemed to take it very seriously. Therefore, much of the annual meeting was to be devoted to "selling" the idea that there was a total company problem, and helping managers in small-group meetings to accept and deal with those problems. Given these goals, the planning committee saw the point of having me help in the design of the meeting and to plan lectures as needed on how to initiate and manage various change projects. In other words, the economic and market environment was creating a financial crisis, top management decided it was time to deal with it, and the consultation process became one piece of management's more general process of launching the Redirection Project.

The Etna Production Company*

Edgar H. Schein

Conrad Robins, Director of Personnel of the Etna Production Company, called to ask me to meet with him and his key personnel group, to evaluate a new performance appraisal programme they were planning to launch across the whole company. The meeting we arranged lasted a day, during which company representatives outlined the proposed programme. I questioned a number of points in the programme which seemed internally inconsistent, and found Conrad becoming obviously defensive. From the way in which he reacted to questions and criticisms, it became clear that he was not willing to re-examine any part of the programme. The farther we went into the discussion the clearer it became that he was completely committed to his programme, and was seeking only reassurance from me: he did not really want an evaluation. I therefore terminated the consulting relationship at the end of the day.

---

* SOURCE: Edited by Roy McLennan and abstracted from Edgar H. Schein, *Process Consultation.* © 1969. Addison-Wesley Publishing Company, Inc., Reading, Mass. Reprinted with permission.

Changing Your Organization*

Roy McLennan

1. Write an outline of a specific change you want to implement in the organization you work for.

The outline should be between a few paragraphs and a page or two in length.

In writing your outline consider the following questions:

- Who needs to take what action, with whom, to achieve the desired outcome?
- Who should or will be involved or affected by the change?
- What problems or difficulties do you anticipate might arise? How may they be overcome?

2. Read and explain your outline to several other people. When you have finished give them the opportunity to explain their reactions to it.

* SOURCE: Copyright © Roy McLennan. Version 2, 1987.

The Client's Problem*

Roy McLennan

Tavistock consultants conclude that leaders and members of organizations and institutions generally prefer to resolve their problems without the help of outside agencies. They are unwilling to seek professional help, or seek such help only as a last resort (e.g. Wilson, 1947:p. 15). In a positive sense this attitude may be expressed as a drive towards organizational autonomy, away from investing any sort of reliance or dependency on the intervention of outsiders. In a more negative sense Institute action researchers consider that there is a reluctance to share insider, private data on the organization, which could be viewed as dirty linen by outsiders. There is the fear that the organization might be thought not to 'measure up' against some yardstick an action researcher will apply. There is the fear that a change in the internal power structure will follow consultant intervention in the organization's affairs. For these and other reasons there is 'always an initial reluctance to the engagement of any sort of outside specialist . . . his employment constitutes an admission that there are imperfections in the organization and that those who man it are unable to remedy these on their own. . . . It is feared that he [the consultant] will judge the leaders of the group by 'professional' standards rather than by those of everyday organizational life, that he will expect too much from them, will expose their deficiencies by direct statement or by demonstrating his own standards of competence' (Sofer, 1961:p. 121–122).

Wilson talks of the manager's 'unwillingness to accept the blow to self-esteem which comes with the recognition of the need for help'. He also remarks on 'the anxiety aroused in executives by the need to seek . . . help', and the 'uncertainty and the inevitable underlying anxiety about the intrusive social scientist' (Wilson, 1947:p. 16, 26). Bryant offers an illuminating parallel: 'In the medical analogy, patients seldom come to the doctor unless they are in pain, or at least in some kind of difficulty. Similarly in organizational settings, the social scientist is rarely called in until the problems have begun to cause some distress' (Bryant, 1979:p. 5). He also comments on the emotional state of the executive who calls him in: 'I have found that the person in the operating manager's role nearly always regards the presence of an outside consultant with some degree of ambivalence—a mixture of welcoming the possibility of fresh insights bringing about improvements and of resenting it at the same time' (Bryant, 1979:p. 14). As a consultant he often 'has the feeling that the problem

---

* SOURCE: Excerpt from "Feelings and Emotions in Action Research: A Tavistock Approach," paper delivered at the Management Educators' Conference, Monash University, Australia, August 1980.

had been left to fester a long time before anything was done. Clients have often said to me things like 'Of course we should have had you in here two years ago, before all this started to get out of hand!' (Bryant, 1979:p. 5).

'If the members of an organization ask me to discuss some problem with them', says Rice, 'I assume that they have done so because they have not been able to find a satisfactory solution for themselves. Implicit in my being called in, therefore, is their acceptance, consciously or unconsciously, of failure' (Rice, 1963:p. 5). Wilson makes remarks about the mental state of the executive in this failure situation: 'As each executive finds his normal methods of dealing with a problem inadequate for the situation, the tendency is to bring into play various neurotic mechanisms. These may consist of denial or evasion of the existence of the problem, misinterpretation of its nature, or the attempt to use authoritarian methods of control, all of these not infrequently make matters worse. Therefore, when the time arrives to consider seeking help, the basic situation is greatly complicated by the development of . . . a neurotic super-structure on top of the original problem' (Wilson, 1947:p. 23).

The action researcher thus begins work in an organizational situation where key members of the client system are in a markedly emotional state, experiencing such feelings as loss of self-esteem or power, ambivalence, denial, evasion, pain, distress, incompetence, guilt and failure. Whatever the 'real' problem, it is overlaid and surrounded by a range or array of emotions.

It follows from these consultant views of the client that the difficulty or issue posed by the client is viewed by the consultant as the symptomatic, presenting, overt or manifest problem or agenda, which he accepts as a starting point to the consultation. 'From the client's viewpoint', says Bryant, 'the presenting problem may be very real: it is 'where it hurts'; and it is what the client is paying for to have put right. The presenting problem may not however be the best place to start head-on in any project, and although the initiative and 'sense of problem' is nearly always with the client, the consultant may have to negotiate a shift of focus as the diagnosis proceeds.' At the same time, 'The consultant has . . . to 'earn the right' to be in the organization by working with the presenting problem as defined by the people in it, before he is allowed to penetrate the system at all' (Bryant, 1979:p. 6). Bain thinks that the presenting problem 'can be used as the vehicle for other needs' (Bain, 1976:p. 643). De Board suggests that the presenting issue is 'a problem that can be openly expressed as socially acceptable' (de Board, 1978:p. 121, based on Menzies, 1960). The researcher assumes that the presenting problem masks or overlays a deeper, underlying, covert problem or agenda at a latent level. 'One of the difficulties of collaborating in the solution of industrial problems', says Sutherland and Menzies, for example, 'is that the problem for which help is sought is so frequently only a symptom, an outer manifestation, of more deeply rooted difficulties' (Sutherland and Menzies, 1947:p. 51). The presenting problem might be due to hidden causes of which the overt problem is only a symptom. The problem is invested with emotional processes unrecognized by the client (Coles and Bridger, 1969:p. 235). As Rice put it, 'What appears on the surface as a simple organizational problem . . . may often be found to have underlying it deep-seated and largely unrecognized emotional conflicts (Rice, 1963:p. 5).

Building on a remark made by Bridger, Lisl Klein suggests that at the start of the intervention the consultant probably has at hand the essential data needed to make a diagnosis and solve the problem. The difficulty lies in grasping the meaning of the data and how they interrelate, in seeing the wood for the trees (Klein, 1976:p. 224)[1] On the basis of several case studies in management selection Bain develops a similar idea. He suggests that the process of consultancy consists of radical reconceptualization of what is already known. He asserts that 'the presenter . . . of the problem initially defines what should be looked at as something which is outside of himself. . . . The problem . . . has a location 'out there,' in a space distant from himself. . . . As the consultancy work progresses the meaning of the problem is shown . . . not to be distant from the presenter and located 'out there' . . . but a problem which includes the presenter within its . . . ambit. . . . [T]he presenting problem . . . [is] the first of a series of . . . triangulations involving 'client,' 'problem,' and 'consultant' . . . . (Bain, 1976:p. 655–657). He concludes that the work of the action researcher 'reverses the projective process that occurs with the presenting problem,' and suggests how this may be done: 'the consultant's role can . . . serve as a projective container for the denied aspects of 'group' and 'institutional' relationships to a problem' (Bain, 1976:p. 656–657).

REFERENCES

BAIN, A. 'Presenting Problems in Social Consultancy: Three Case Histories Concerning the Selection of Managers.' *Human Relations*, 1976, 29, No. 7.

BRYANT, DON. *Work Plus: An Account of an Experiment to Improve the Quality of Worklife in the Cominco Lead Smelter in Trail, B.C.* Vancouver: British Columbia Research Council and Tavistock Institute of Human Relations, 1979.

COLES, R. B. and BRIDGER, H. 'The Consultant and His Roles.' *British Journal of Medical Psychology*, 1969, 42.

DE BOARD, ROBERT. *The Psycho-Analysis of Organizations.* London: Tavistock, 1978.

KLEIN, LISL. *A Social Scientist in Industry.* London: Croom Helm, 1976.

MENZIES, I. E. P. 'A Case Study in the Functioning of Social Systems as a Defense Against Anxiety.' *Human Relations*, 1960, 13, No. 2.

RICE, A. K. *The Enterprise and Its Environment.* London: Tavistock, 1963.

SOFER, C. *The Organization from Within.* London: Tavistock, 1961.

SUTHERLAND, J. D. and MENZIES, I. E. 'Two Industrial Projects.' *Journal of Social Issues.* 1947, 3, No. 2.

WILSON, A. T. M. 'Some Implications of Medical Practice and Social Case-Work for Action Research.' *Journal of Social Issues*, 1947, 3, No. 2.

[1] Bryant repeats the point approvingly (Bryant, 1979:p. 59).

Entering Into Relationships*

Leonard Schatzman and
Anselm L. Strauss

Despite considerable writing about field work, relatively little information is available specifically on the problem of entrée and on tactics used to effect it. . . . Yet, the matters of entrée and of establishing amicable relations are of such great importance that we need at least to review the more salient considerations that any field researcher must bear in mind. Considering that people's privacies are to be "invaded," that commitments to their work and even their very identity are likely to be called into question, it does not take much imagination to realize how tactical error, blunder, or social crudity can complicate an otherwise worthy project. . . . In a mutually voluntary and negotiated entrée, the host holds options not only to prevent entrée but to terminate relations with the researcher at almost any stage thereafter. This suggests that how one gets in and manages to stay in will shape, if not determine, what one gets out of the site and its host.

Furthermore, it suggests that entrée is a *continuous* process of establishing and developing relationships, not alone with a chief host but with a variety of less powerful persons. In relatively complex sites, particularly those with multiple leadership and jurisdictions, there are many doorways that must be negotiated; successful negotiation through the front door is not always sufficient to open other doors, though at first it may appear to do just that. In many situations, the chief host may not himself have the kind of access to his own sub-jurisdictions that a good field researcher requires; he may be hated or feared. Often, interior organizational lines lead to districts guarded by lesser chiefs who also exercise options—if not to bar physical access, then to withhold a necessary level of cooperation. Some institutions and social movements have stronger local barons than emperors; therefore, the researcher endeavors to negotiate his own way through every door. Wisdom dictates that the approach to people anywhere in the hierarchy, and negotiation with them, will not be unlike the initial one at the "front door." This includes "casing" the sub-site ahead of time—a task rendered somewhat easier than the original grande entrée, since not only will he pick up cues about sub-sites from his initial quick visit there but from conversations elsewhere that touch on particular sub-sites; if need be, he can ask judicious questions about the one he is about to visit ("tell me a little about what goes on at . . .").

* SOURCE: Leonard Schatzman and Anselm L. Strauss, *Field Research: Strategies for a Natural Sociology,* pp. 21–23. © 1973. Reprinted by permission of Prentice-Hall, Inc., Englewood Cliffs, N.J.

. . . [T]he experienced researcher recognizes that entering relatively complex human organizations is a process in which he will be engaged long after "permission" to enter has been granted. The continuity is assured on two counts: first, to the extent that anyone in the organization has autonomy and some options on cooperation, *each person,* theoretically, must be negotiated with; second, relationships that are initially established naturally do change—and not always for the better. After all, the researcher will be in the field for weeks or months; he will change as he learns more about the people and their work. His study will lead him to unanticipated perspectives and unanticipated places; therefore his actions—and identity—will also change and probably impel frequent reaffirmations of his person and purposes. On some sub-sites there may be some change of personnel, even of the chief authority there, so new exploration of purpose and renegotiation must occur. Likewise, over time, the work of the many hosts will be different—or appear so—and the hosts will be variously embarrassed, outraged, or pleased with their own performance under scrutiny. Finally, the researcher will find that his relations with some hosts will be so tangential to his developing objectives, and his visits with them so intermittent, that he will find it necessary again and again to identify himself— and probably to apologize for not observing or listening to them as much as to others. Often, the very persons who at first seek to avoid the observer's eye or ear are the ones who later feel insulted for his not valuing their persons and work.

The underlying message here is that good human relations in field research require considerable attention and intelligent regulation. They do not guarantee good results but are prerequisite to gaining and maintaining entrée ultimately into a world and sub-worlds of meaning—of nuance in thought and of subtle variations in human conduct. The field researcher needs to create situations which invite visibility and disclosure for others; otherwise, he is left to construct his sociology out of clichés, platitudes, literal performance, plus whatever meanings he can derive.

The Entry Problem in Consultation*

John C. Glidewell

The aim of this paper is to contribute to the definition of a complex problem—the problem faced by a consultant and a client when they first try to enter into a working relationship. It would be presumptuous to propose a solution to such a knotty problem. It seems more appropriate and realistic to limit this paper to defining the problem.

The paper is based upon the assumption that the entry of the consultant is a special case of a more general problem: the attachment of a new person to an existing social system.

Examples are legion. They might include the introduction into a family of a tutor for a child temporarily unable to attend school, the attachment of a social work consultant to an existing nursing staff, the assignment of a nursing consultant to a teaching staff, or the introduction of a human relations consultant to a corporation board. In each case the members of a functioning social system find that some operations are being initiated and performed by a new person. In this case, the new person, being a consultant, is presumably authoritative, and also, being new, he is relatively unpredictable. The problem is that some relationship to this new person must be developed. Some relationship must be developed so that his performance, and the responses of others to it, can be better predicted. Better prediction will make his performance more amenable to control in the interests of the goals of the system—both substantive achievement goals and affiliative human relations goals.

LIMITATIONS ON THE PROBLEM

For the purposes at hand, a special and limited meaning will be given to the phrase, "attachment to a social system." It will be used to refer to the process of development of relationships with a person who is to be only temporarily a member of the system. It will not be used to refer to the process of development of relationships with a person who is to be a permanent member of the system.[1]

* SOURCE: John C. Glidewell, "The Entry Problem in Consultation," *Journal of Social Issues,* 15 (1959), pp. 51–56. Reprinted with permission.

[1] The term "attachment to a social system" was borrowed from Jules Henry (1959) who uses it to refer to the state of being an integral part of a social system—in no way limited to temporary membership. For present purposes, however, "attachment" seems to carry the implication of a temporary arrangement as intended here. Perhaps the appropriate analogy is the military arrangement by which a person who is "attached" to an organization is only temporarily associated and entitled to only limited support from the organization.

It is clearly true that the consultant role is often being established these days as a permanent one, but this permanence involves either the development of a new role and, therefore, a basic structural change, or it involves the socialization of a new person into an existing role. Both are more fundamental processes than can be explored here.

Accordingly, this paper is limited to the exploration of the process of initiating a relationship between a client system and a temporary consultant. The consultation functions are to be performed temporarily either because the need is temporary or because the functions can be taken over—after a time—by existing roles.

CONSULTANT VERSUS CONSULTANT-TRAINER

It is important to differentiate those functions which are expected to terminate at the expiration of a short term need from those which are expected to be taken over and continued by existing roles. The first requires the application of objects, skills, ideas, or feelings which the client need never possess or control (like prescribing medication, or greasing an auto). The second requires that the client acquire possession and control of the objects, skills, ideas, or feelings, and it, therefore, implies learning (like the improvement of a golf swing, or the recognition of the proper consistency of a pancake batter). The first relationship involves a consultant role; the second, a consultant-trainer role. This paper will be concerned with both roles. The distinction should be kept in mind, however, because the role of the consultant provokes less concern about demands for change in the system than does the consultant-trainer role.

ORGANIZATIONAL ATTACHMENT AND PREDICTABILITY

It is proposed that a basic criterion of attachment to a social system is predictability. This is a special case of the general proposition that a basic criterion of the existence and nature of relationships is predictability. The statement of lawful relationships takes the form of predicting some aspect of one object or force from a knowledge of other objects or forces.

Any application of this proposition to social relations must take account of the notion that social systems develop ultimate values and immediate goals. For the members of the system, the significant predictability for social roles is the forecast of performance in relation to ultimate values and immediate goals. The kinds of relationships to be developed in the process of attachment to a social system are those which insure, not that one knows just what a member will do in a given situation, but that, whatever he does, it will contribute to ultimate values and immediate goals. If the people in the system set a great store by creativity and invention, it may be important that the exact nature of the performance be *unpredictable*—so long as its goal-orientation is assured. To illustrate, it is not too important to predict just what sort of medicine a doctor will give you when you are sick. You may, in fact, feel that if he is a really good doctor, his treatment will be so clearly unique to the time, to you and your illness, that it would be impossible to predict from facts previously known to you. It is quite important, however, to insure that the physician contributes to the ultimate value of survival (that he doesn't kill you) and to the immediate goal of relief from distress and disability.

A REDEFINITION OF THE PROBLEM

From the foregoing conceptions, limitations, and distinctions, the entry problem can be redefined as that of initiating the development of relationships to provide a basis for predicting the contribution to ultimate values and immediate goals of a set of functions having certain characteristics, namely:

> They are now needed by the system, although probably to a different degree by different members.
>
> They either are needed only temporarily or can be taken over by existing roles.
>
> They are not now available in the system.
>
> They can be performed expertly by the prospective consultant.

In summary the entry problem becomes more or less difficult, depending upon the goodness of fit between the consultant and the client system with respect to stabilities and change tendencies in terms of perception of need, assignment of values, role expectation, resource and reward allocation, and feelings about the control of dependency. Goodness of fit is intended to imply both congruence (as with values) and complementation (as with roles). The significant dimensions to be fitted can be outlined as follows:

1. Perception of need, in terms of the
   a. extent of consensus in the total system that an immediate need exists, and
   b. importance of the need as measured against the ultimate values of the total system.
2. Perception of appropriateness of role allocation by those empowered to allocate roles, in terms of the criteria that
   a. the needed resources are not available in appropriate persons within the system, and
   b. the needed resources are available in the prospective consultant.
3. Perception of the appropriateness of resource distribution by those empowered to distribute resources, in terms of the criteria that
   a. the consultant will be available to the different members on an equitable basis, and
   b. any new objects, ideas, skills, or feelings developed by the consultation process will be equitably distributed.
4. Perception of the appropriateness of reward distribution by those empowered to distribute rewards, in terms of the criteria that
   a. the consultant's fee is appropriate to the need (relative to other needs), and of the quality and quantity of service proposed, and

     b. any rewards (income to the system) accruing from the prospective need reduction will be equitably distributed among the members.

5. Perception of the appropriateness of the probable emotional interchange between the consultant and the members of the system, in terms of the criteria that

     a. the members do not become so dependent that they will not be able to work without consultative support, and

     b. the members do not become so hostile toward or frightened by the dependency involved in the consultation that the consultant cannot be constructively employed.

Each of the five dimensions carries its own dynamic for change. Need perceptions are never entirely satisfactory, and the search for the "real" needs is perpetual. Role allocation can never truly fit the individual differences among people and the ever-changing requirements of the tasks of the system. Both formal and informal role reallocation is continuous, although sometimes painfully slow. Resource distribution can never keep pace with changing needs nor reward distribution with the balance between needs and changing contributions (Parsons & Shils, 1952; Parsons, 1954). Finally, the exchange of feeling can never be all-supportive. Interdependencies always yield fears of dependency. Deprivation—even relative deprivation—yields apathy or rebellion. Evaluation yields fight and flight. Even support can yield jealousy. Any situation into which the consultant intervenes has its own dynamic for constructive changes and restraints (Lewin, 1947). The task is to find and reduce the restraining forces—liberating the growth potential of the system.

VARIATIONS IN OPTIMAL CONDITIONS FOR ENTRY

The foregoing outline of the significant conditions for entry were cast in terms of perceptions. It might be construed to mean that the optimal conditions for entry are those in which the perceptions of the consultant and those of the power centers of the system are in substantial agreement. Such a construction was not intended—and it seems unlikely that such a situation can ever be found. The entry of the consultant into the system implies more or less change in the system—due in part to success or failure in substantive problem solving and in part to the impact of the attachment of a new role to the old system of role, resource, and reward allocation. The question of optimal entry conditions involves estimates of the extent to which the consultant and the client system may hold congruent, complementary, or conflicting perceptions and change tendencies. Congruence implies almost no change; complementation, slow change; and conflict implies fast change or fast termination of the attachment. The possible combinations of conditions are tremendously large, but it seems likely that most of them have been met somewhere or other in the practice of the helping professions.

Consultation in conflict. Sometimes a consultant finds himself motivated to attach himself to a social system which disagrees with him in all significant respects: about the existence of the need, about the internal availability of resources, about the consultant's resources, about the basis for role, resource, and reward allocation, and about the feelings appropriate in reaction to the consultant's efforts.

The great tradition of the reformer carries with it the theme of consultation in conflict. The theme has had many variations, but more often than not the reforming consultant and his client system have differed most sharply in their perception of the proper locus of power. For example, Poston's work has been stimulated by a gnawing dissatisfaction with power vested in central control of material resources.

> Human values were lost in a maze of punch cards and number systems which were devoid of flesh and blood. Neighborhood life in any meaningful sense, the environment which had nurtured initiatives, civic integrity, and social responsibility, began to grow sterile. The control which men had once exercised over their own lives gradually slipped away into distant offices of a centralized and impersonal society. (Poston, 1953, p. 6.)

It was the intent of the consultant to alter the locus of power in the system, and consequently the distribution of roles, resources, and rewards. The success of the first foray of such a reform movement would appear to depend in part upon the direction of changes already under way in the system and in part upon the availability of a sub-system ready to promote the reform. Taylor's dream of a "third force" of efficiency experts independent of both labor and management lacked a power point of entry—until it sold its independence to either management or labor (Taylor, 1911). Poston (1953) seeks his power point of entry in community organization of dormant leadership. His goal is to transfer power from existing "non-democratic" organizations to the new democratic community organization.

Where resistance to consultation is involved, some consultants have been successful as methodologists who suggest and assist in the conduct of self-surveys or other interpretative appraisals by the client system. Attempts to provide interpretive consultation in conflict have produced some remarkable successes, as with the work of Jacques (1952) and the Tavistock Institute, and Lindemann (1957), Kline (1958), and their associates at Wellesley.

One can ask, quite justifiably, whether such change agents as Poston or especially Alinsky (1946) were acting in the consultant's role. There is a broad and vague area which separates the consultant group from the assault force, but, differentiated or not, both must select carefully the point in the power structure at which they enter.

Entry in the dark. As often as not a consultant is called upon to enter the system without any information about the state of affairs within the system with respect to the dimensions significant to entry. He must gather data as he enters, and he must face the possibility that the need is not seen by the most powerful member (e.g. Poston in Montana); that there is no place for the consultant role in the correct perception of role, resource, and reward allocation;

and that the typical emotional reaction to the prospect of the consultant role is one of hostility or fear or both. The entering consultant can assume that, in spite of manifest pleas for help, within the informal channels of communication in the client system, many members are committed—each to a different diagnosis, doctor, and treatment plan. Considering the amount of resistance that consultants regularly encounter, the fact that a consultant will enter in the dark is either a compliment to his courage, a comment on his conceit, or a manifestation of his masochism—or all three.

REFERENCES

ALINSKY, SAUL D. *Reveille for Radicals.* Chicago: University of Chicago Press, 1946.

HENRY, JULES. Concepts of Social Structure and Personalization. Unpublished manuscript, Washington University, St. Louis, Mo., 1959.

JACQUES, ELLIOTT. *The Changing Culture of a Factory.* New York: Dryden, 1952.

KLEIN, DONALD C., & ROSS, ANN. Kindergarten entry: a study of the role transition. In Morris Krugman (Ed.) *Orthopsychiatry and the School.* New York: American Orthopsychiatric Association, 1958.

LEWIN, KURT. Frontiers in group dynamics. *Human Relations,* 1947, *1*, 5–41.

LINDEMANN, ELIZABETH. Mental health in the class-room: The Wellesley experience. A paper presented at the annual meeting of the American Psychological Association, New York, 1957.

PARSONS, TALCOTT, & SHILS, EDWARD A. (Eds.) *Toward a General Theory of Action.* Cambridge: Harvard University Press, 1952.

PARSONS, TALCOTT (Ed.) *Essays in Sociological Theory.* Glencoe, Illinois: The Free Press, 1954.

POSTON, RICHARD W. *Small Town Renaissance.* New York: Harper, 1950.

POSTON, RICHARD W. *Democracy Is You.* New York: Harper, 1953.

TAYLOR, FREDERICK W. *The Principles of Scientific Management.* New York: Harper, 1911.

Orientation to the Client*

Roy McLennan

It follows from the psychoanalytic form of thought, the prevalent ideas of Institute action researchers about the emotional state of the client when he comes the consultant's way, and how the problem is presented, that from the start of the intervention the Tavistock action researcher attends to both overt, manifest, conscious data, and covert, latent, unconscious data, with particular reference to feelings and emotions. In the initial encounters between the consultant and members of the client organization the consultant concentrates on listening, in a more or less non-directive, client-centred fashion, in one-to-one and group interviews. On the occasion of the first meeting of the consultant and members of the prospective client system, 'whatever the agenda, the most important event which occurs is a process of mutual sizing up and testing out' (Wilson, 1947:p. 25). Miller remarks that in early interactions with client members: 'I struggle towards being a sort of tabula rasa on to which projections can be made.' The action researcher 'projects himself into the psychology of the client', says Sofer, 'and tries to empathize with him, to see the world from his point of view' (Sofer, 1961:p. 106). As best he can the consultant submerges himself in the client system in order to try to answer the question: 'What does it feel like to be a member of this organization?' (Stern and Abraham). He attempts this by listening for things members are saying and not saying (Coles and Bridger, 1969:p. 234). He looks for discrepancies in what they are saying, as well as consistencies (Stern and Abraham; Menzies Lyth; Dartington). He steadily tries not to be blinded by the conscious processes going on, but also to look at the unconscious processes (Lawrence). Menzies Lyth says: 'You're listening at a lot of different levels at once. You're listening to what people are saying and taking that for its face value and respecting that. But at the same time you're hearing what they're not saying. Or what else is built into what they're saying.' The researcher becomes conscious of unconscious processes in the members of the client system by several means in addition to the 'discrepancy' model. He is, for example, on the alert for evidence of client self-deception, vehement denial and 'protesting too much'. If one member of a client system becomes indignant with some other member's behavior, there is a good chance that he is unconsciously trying to disown an unacceptable aspect of himself. When the member takes a polarized stance on something he may be expressing a deeply entrenched aspect of his personality. There is good evidence of this

* SOURCE: Excerpt from "Feelings and Emotions in Action Research: A Tavistock Approach", paper delivered at the Management Educators' Conference, Monash University, Australia, August 1980.

if he responds to rational counter-arguments as if they were a personal attack (Miller, 1975:p. 74–83).

'The way in which the consultant is used and experienced, and also the feelings evoked in him,' says Miller, 'may provide evidence about underlying issues and feelings about them within the client system' (Miller, 1977:p. 35). More personally he remarks, 'The feelings evoked in me when working with a client are part of the data I have on what's going on between the client and me and what's going on in the client system itself.' These include the games played inside the client organization, which are also played on the action researchers. Some members of the client system may, for example, try to play off the consultants against other client system members, 'setting us up.' Clients may try to use consultants for their own internal political ends (Stern and Abraham). Jaques describes the researcher's likely reception in the heightened emotional atmosphere of the intervention: 'Outsiders or newcomers to a community will, consciously or unconsciously, become to a certain extent a focus for the discharge of the community's own internal pressures. . . . [T]he people . . . maintain a semblance of harmony by denying their suspicion of each other and instead projecting such feelings outwards upon some convenient, commonly satisfactory object . . . the newcomer. . . . [T]he social research worker is likely to have transferred on to him any unrecognized or unresolved stresses which individuals or groups in the community [organization] wish to avoid in relation to each other' (Jaques, 1951:p. 12). Several consultants make references to the scape-goating role they are frequently pushed into in relation to the client organization, a phenomenon which is not limited to the early stages of an intervention (King, 1948:p. 397; Miller and Gwynne, 1972:p. 35).

Given his role it is of course of prime importance for the consultant to be able to distinguish between 'feelings that belong to him and feelings projected into him' (Miller, 1977:p. 35), and to be in touch with his feelings if he is to be useful as an action researcher. He needs to know 'about inside worlds and outside worlds and transactions between the two' (Lawrence). He too is subject to the dynamics of the transference, projection, displacement and the like. The consultant 'should be sufficiently aware of his own emotions', says Sofer, 'to use them . . . as data, i.e. . . . known material about the situations in which he becomes involved. He should be able to 'read off' in his own reactions some of the things that are happening in the process he is examining' (Sofer, 1961:p. 137–8). Rice and Miller use a mechanical analogy and refer to the researcher using himself as a 'measuring instrument' (Rice, 1963:p. 7; Miller, 1977:p. 35) and the need 'to try to develop means of calibrating it so as to correct for some of the distortions' (Miller and Gwynne, 1972:p. 7). Rice says, 'So far as I am sure that some of the feeling arises in the situation and not as a result of idiosyncracies of my own personality, I can use myself as a measuring instru-ment—however rough and ready—to give me information about the underlying difficulties and their strength. With this information I may then be able to take action' (Rice, 1963:p. 7). He also describes how he worked with his feelings:

'If, as a consultant, I find I am becoming anxious, embarrassed, hurt, or pleased, I can ask myself why I am feeling what I am feeling and attempt to sort out what comes from within myself and what from the consultant-client relationship' (Rice, 1963:p. 6–7). Again he says, 'Often the only information I had [about a client organization] was how I was feeling' (Rice, 1963:p. 9). The action researcher needs training in order to attain clarity about what is outside him and what inside him, and to get in touch with his feelings. The traditionally preferred kind at the Institute is, as observed above, for him to undergo personal psychoanalysis (Miller and Gwynne, 1972:p. 7).

REFERENCES

COLES, R. B. and BRIDGER, H. 'The Consultant and His Roles.' *British Journal of Medical Psychology,* 1969, 42.

JAQUES, E. *The Changing Culture of a Factory.* London: Tavistock, 1951.

KING, P. M. H. 'Task Perception and Interpersonal Relations in Industrial Training: Part II.' *Human Relations,* 1948, *1,* No. 3.

MILLER, E. J. 'Demands and Problems of Face-to-Face Work with People.' In Open University, A Post-Experience Course, The Handicapped Person in the Community, Units 1–10, Block 3, Part 1, Providing Supporting Services. Milton Keynes: Open University Press, 1975.

MILLER, E. J. 'Organizational Development and Industrial Democracy: A Current Case Study' in C. L. Cooper (ed.). *Organizational Development in the UK and the USA.* London: Macmillan, 1977.

MILLER, E. J. and GWYNNE, G. V. *A Life Apart.* London: Tavistock, 1972.

RICE, A. K. *The Enterprise and Its Environment.* London: Tavistock, 1963.

RICE, A. K. *Learning for Leadership.* London: Tavistock, 1965.

SOFER, C. *The Organization from Within.* London: Tavistock, 1961.

SOFER, C. *Organizations in Theory and Practice.* London: Heinemann, 1972.

WILSON, A. T. M. 'Some Implications of Medical Practice and Social Case-Work for Action Research.' *Journal of Social Issues,* 1947, *3,* No. 2.

The Internal Consultant*

Robert R. Blake
and Jane S. Mouton

By virtue of having organization membership and sometimes over many years, internal consultants may have a deep and detailed knowledge of what actually goes on in a firm, including the hidden politics and the subtle but unstated agreements, collusions, and so on. As such, the internal consultant is in a more fully informed position regarding organization barriers to effectiveness than is likely to be possible for an external consultant. The insider can make interventions based on his or her knowledge that might not be credible if made by someone without such knowledge. Furthermore, the internal consultant has the likelihood of greater continuity of working with members of the same organization over an extended period. Under these conditions, interventions are possible on a continuing rather than on an interrupted basis.

Of the several disadvantages that are encountered by internal consultants, the most important is related to holding membership in the hierarchy. Since many, if not most, internal consultants are staff and assigned to the personnel function, it is difficult for the consultant to work effectively at ranks higher than his or her own reporting relationship. The reason is that if an internal consultant, whose membership is in the personnel function, were to challenge persons of higher rank, he or she would run the risk of arousing negative feelings and appearing insubordinate.

Linkages between Internal and External Consultants. One of the arrangements that permits organizations to benefit from both internal and external consulting is through external-internal consultant cooperation. This solution is close to an optimal basis for bringing consultation help to bear on solving real needs. Some of the advantages to be derived by organizations arranging the collaboration between external and internal consultants include the following.

The internal consultant, knowing the situation more intimately than the external consultant, can aid the external consultant to gain insight as to what goes on in the organization. Thus, the external consultant's knowledge of the organization is deepened through insight that can be made available to him or her by the internal consultant.

By virtue of his or her continuity, the internal consultant can aid the organization through implementation of agreed-upon next steps. A third basis of collaboration is that the internal consultant may see important confrontations

* SOURCE: Robert R. Blake and Jane S. Mouton, *Consultation: A Handbook for Industrial and Organization Development*, 2nd ed. ©, 1983. Addison-Wesley Publishing Company, Inc., Reading, Mass., pp. 564–565. Reprinted with permission.

that need to take place, but by virtue of his or her position in the hierarchy, it is unsound to attempt such prescriptions or confrontations. Nonetheless, the internal consultant can create the conditions under which the external consultant can implement these interventions. In other words, the external consultant can often do work in levels of the hierarchy that are off limits to the internal consultant.

Organizational Diagnosis: Six Places to Look for Trouble with or without a Theory*

Marvin R. Weisbord

No single model or conceptual scheme embraces the whole breadth and complexity of reality, even though each in turn may be useful in particular instances. This is why management remains an art, for the practitioner must go beyond the limits of theoretical knowledge if he is to be effective. (Tilles, 1963, pp. 73–81).

For several years I have been experimenting with "cognitive maps" of organizations. These are labels that would help me better describe what I saw and heard, and understand the relationships among various bits of data. I started this endeavor when I realized that though I knew many organization theories, most were either (1) too narrow to include everything I wished to understand or (2) too broadly abstract to give much guidance about what to do.

This article represents a progress report on my efforts to combine bits of data, theories, research, and hunches into a working tool that anyone can use. It is one example of a process I believe goes on among practitioners that is neither well documented nor well understood (Weisbord, 1974a). The process does not take place in a mode consistent with the protocols of social science research. It is not tied to any particular theory, nor is it subject to easy translation into research instruments. It is not intended to prove or disprove hypotheses. Rather, it represents what Vaill (1975; Friedlander & Brown, 1974) calls a "practice theory"—a synthesis of knowledge and experience into a concept that bears "some relation to public, objective theories about organizational situations, but in no sense (is) identical to them."

I think this accurately describes what I have been calling, for want of a more elegant name, the "Six-Box Model." This model (Figure 1) has helped me rapidly expand my diagnostic framework from interpersonal and group issues to the more complicated contexts in which organizations are managed. It provides six labels, under which can be sorted much of the activity, formal and informal, that takes place in organizations. The labels allow consultants to

* SOURCE: Marvin R. Weisbord, "Organizational Diagnosis: Six Places to Look for Trouble with or without a Theory," *Group and Organization Studies, 1* (December 1976), 430–447. Copyright Sage Publications, Inc. Reprinted by permission of Sage Publications, Inc.

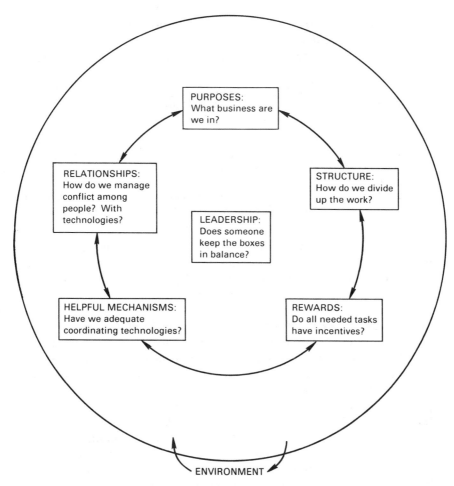

Figure 1: The Six-Box Organizational Model

apply whatever theories they know when doing a diagnosis and to discover new connections between apparently unrelated events.

We can visualize Figure 1 as a radar screen. Just as air controllers use radar to chart the course of aircraft—height, speed, distance apart, and weather—those seeking to improve an organization must observe relationships among the boxes and not focus on any particular blip.

Organizational "process" issues, for example, will show up as blips in one or more boxes, signaling the blockage of work on important organizational tasks. (Process issues relate to *how* and *whether* work gets done, rather than *what* is to be done.)

Unfortunately, such issues too often are seen as the result of someone's personality. For example, the failure of a group to confront its differences may be diagnosed as the inability of one or two people to assert themselves. Yet, if the consultant were to look closely, he might find that no one in the organization confronts, independent of the assertion skills they may have. Those who do confront may be considered deviant and may be tolerated only to the extent that they have power.

From a management standpoint, it is probably more useful to think of process issues as systemic, that is, as part of the organization's management culture. This culture can be described as:

1. "Fit" between *organization* and *environment*—the extent to which purposes and structure support high performance and ability to change with conditions; and/or
2. "Fit" between *individual* and *organization*—the extent to which people support or subvert formal mechanisms intended to carry out an organization's purposes.

The relationship between individual and organization is the basis for many important books in the organizational literature. McGregor (1960) argued that a better fit might be attained under Theory Y assumptions (people like to work, achieve, and be responsible) than Theory X assumptions (people are passive, dependent, and need to be controlled). Blake and Mouton (1964) devised elaborate change strategies (variations of "Grid" theory) based on the notion that productivity and human satisfaction need not be mutually exclusive.

Maslow (1971) struggled in his last years to reconcile employee self-actualization—personal growth and creativity—with an organization's needs for structure, order, and predictability. Argyris has written extensively on the potential incompatibilities of individuals and organizations and the threat that bureaucratic structures pose to self-esteem (Argyris, 1957).

In the last 10 years, both managers and consultants have become much more conscious of organizations as open systems in which structure and behavior are heavily influenced by environment. Lawrence and Lorsch (1967) compared high- and low-performance businesses in terms of structural requirements—based largely on rate of change in business technology and environment—and came up with a contingency theory: the way subunits of an organization are structured depends not only on their functions but on environmental factors, which results in different policies and procedures for different organizations.

Sociotechnical theorists such as Trist (1969) have tried to reconcile structured technologies and work systems with people's individual and social needs, theorizing that high performance equals an optimum balance between technology ("task") and people ("process").

Each of the possible frameworks highlights important organizational issues; each has been the basis for useful interventions in the organization development repertoire. Yet, none is an adequate tool for the management of an entire organization without an expansion of concepts.

Management needs a view simple enough, and complete enough, to improve the quality of its decisions. What follows is a description of how the Six-Box Organizational Model can be used to put into perspective *whatever*

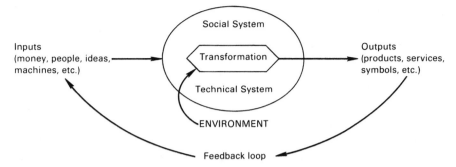

Figure 2: The Six-Box Organizational Model Using Input-Output Terms

theories and concepts a consultant already knows along with *whatever* problems present themselves in diagnosing an organization's problems.

The circle in Figure 1 describes the boundaries of an organization to be diagnosed. *Environment* means forces difficult to control from inside that demand a response—customers, government, unions, students, families, friends, etc. It is not always clear where the boundaries are or should be. Although such a system can be characterized accurately as "open," its rationality depends on partially closing off infinite choices. Deciding where the boundary lies is an act of reason wed to values, for there are no absolutes (Vickers, 1965).

The consultant may find it necessary to set boundaries arbitrarily so that a diagnosis can proceed. I do this by picking a unit name (i.e., XYZ Company, ABC Department, QUR Team) and listing groups or individuals inside the boundary by virtue of dollar commitments, contract, or formal membership. Within the boundaries, the boxes interact to create what is sometimes called an input-output system, whose function is to transform resources into goods or services. Figure 2 illustrates the Six-Box organization/environment using input-output terms. Given that organizations function or do not function depending on what is going on in and between each of the six boxes, a consultant has a basis for doing an organizational diagnosis.

FORMAL AND INFORMAL SYSTEMS

Within each box are two potential trouble sources—the formal system that exists on paper and the informal system—or what people actually do. Neither system is necessarily better, but both exist. In doing a diagnosis, it helps to identify blips in each system and to attempt to define the relationships among them.

Diagnosing the formal system requires some informed guessing, based on knowledge of what the organization *says*—in its statements, reports, charts, and speeches—about how it is organized. The guessing comes after comparing its rhetoric with its environment and making a judgment about whether everything fits—whether society will value and underwrite an organization with such a purpose and such a means of organizing itself. Much expert consultation is aimed at bringing organizational rhetoric into better harmony with the outside world.

However, in every organization there is another level of behavior— what people actually do. Diagnosing these informal systems is sometimes called 'normative" diagnosis (Clapp, 1974). It focuses on the frequency with which people take certain actions in relation to how important these actions are for organizational performance. Normative behavior usually determines whether otherwise technically excellent systems succeed or fail, because normative behavior indicates the degree to which the system as designed meets the needs of the people who have to operate it. Sometimes norms cannot be changed informally, so there is a need to study relationships *between* the two levels of analysis. By persisting in such an inquiry, a consultant discovers some of the reasons why the input-transformation-output stream is not flowing as smoothly as it could.

HOW TO COLLECT DATA

Collecting data on which to base a diagnosis can be as simple as brainstorming or as complex as a "grand design" research methodology involving hypotheses, instruments, and computer analysis. Complexity aside, there are four ways to collect data:

1. *Observation.* Watch what people do in meetings, on the job, on the phone, etc.
2. *Reading.* Follow the written record—speeches, reports, charts, graphs, etc.
3. *Interviews.* Question everyone involved with a particular project.
4. *Survey.* Use standard questionnaires or design your own. Surveys are most useful when they ask for information not readily obtainable in any other way, such as attitudes, perceptions, opinions, preferences, beliefs, etc.

All four methods of data collection can be used to isolate the two major kinds of discrepancy—between what people say (formal) and what they do (informal) and between what is (organization as it exists) and what ought to be (appropriate environmental fit). The trick is not to use any particular methods, but to sort the evidence of one's senses into some categories that encourage sensible decisions.

WHERE TO START

There are two main reasons why one might want to diagnose an organization: to find out systematically what its strengths and weaknesses are or to uncover reasons why either the producers or consumers of a particular output are dissatisfied. Because the latter reason is most often the trigger for corrective actions, I suggest starting a diagnosis by considering one major output. Tracing its relationship to the whole system will result in an understanding of the gaps in the organization between "what is" and "what ought to be."

Let us look at one output—say a single product or service—and determine how satisfied the *consumers* are and how satisfied the *producers* are. The central assumption behind this activity is that consumer acceptance, more than any other factor, determines whether an organization prospers or fades. Satisfied consumers generally indicate a good fit with the environment at one major contact point. Without satisfied consumers, producer satisfaction is likely to be unstable.

A consultant must watch for two situations in particular when diagnosing helpful mechanisms. One is the lack of any rational planning, budgeting, control, or measurement systems. In this case, no amount of interpersonal or group process work will "improve" an organization. Second, and worse, is the organization that has budgeting and controls, but no goals that the people doing the work agree are *organizationally* relevant (for them). The latter describes some universities and medical centers, for example, in which financial control systems provide an illusion of rationality that, like beauty, is only skin deep (Drucker, 1974b).

OD in such situations is not an *organization* development process at all. The best that a consultant can do is help members make more rational decisions about their own careers, thereby contributing to their personal growth. Certainly there is no interdependency to be negotiated in the absence of agreement about the ends toward which the organization is being managed (Weisbord, 1976).

The Six-Box Organization Model is a useful "early-warning system" for a consultant who is trying to decide where and whether to take corrective action. There are three levels of diagnosis that provide clues to appropriate interventions.

1. Does the organization fit its environment? If not, it cannot be developed until the fit can be rationalized and supported.
2. Is the organization structured to carry out its purposes? If not, work on structure is required before an examination of interpersonal and group processes can take on meaning other than personal growth.
3. Are the organization's norms out of phase with its intent? How much discrepancy exists between formal and informal systems? If this is the main problem (as it often is in otherwise successful businesses) most of the management and organization development interventions will apply.

Any diagnostic questions a consultant asks about any of the boxes will yield useful data. Figure 3 summarizes the important questions about both formal and informal systems. There are as many ways to use these ideas as there are managers. I have offered this practice theory as the basis for starting new teams, task forces, and committees or for helping existing teams decide what they need to do next. Others have adapted the Six-Box Model to screen prospective employers, evaluate the management literature in terms of which issues it illuminates, write job descriptions, and organize research findings. It is also a useful teaching tool in comparing various types of organizations.

Figure 3   Matrix for Survey Design or Data Analysis

	FORMAL SYSTEM (WORK TO BE DONE)	INFORMAL SYSTEM (PROCESS WORKING)
1. Purposes	Goal clarity	Goal agreement
2. Structure	Functional, program, or matrix?	How work is actually done or not done.
3. Relationships	Who should deal with whom on what? Which technologies should be used?	How well do they do it? Quality of relations? Modes of conflict management?
4. Rewards (incentives)	Explicit System What is it?	Implicit, psychic rewards. What do people *feel* about payoffs?
5. Leadership	What do top people manage? What systems in use?	How? Normative "style" of administration?
6. Helpful Mechanisms	Budget system Management information (measures?) Planning Control	What are they actually used for? How function in practice? How are systems subverted?

Note: Diagnostic questions may be asked on two levels:

1. How big a gap is there between formal and informal systems? (This speaks to the fit between individual and organization.)
2. How much discrepancy is there between "what is" and "what ought to be"? (This highlights the fit between organization and environment.)

Finally, the Six-Box Organization Model provides an easy way of testing the extent to which an intervention seems right. I have used it both to explain and to anticipate my failures and have found that more anticipating means less explaining. In my experience, all interventions that "fail" eventually do so for one of three reasons (Bowers, Franklin, & Pecorella, 1975):

1. The intervention is inappropriate to the problem or organization. (A T-group may improve relationships without surfacing serious deficiencies of purpose, structure, or technology.)
2. The intervention deals with the wrong (less salient) blip on the radar screen. (When the pressing problem is ineffective leadership, a new reward system, no matter how desirable, may not make a difference.)
3. The intervention solves the identified problem, thus heightening issues in other boxes it was *not* designed to solve. An organization can be restructured to better fit its environment without changing norms and relationships that require other interventions.

REFERENCES

ARGYRIS, C. *Personality and organization: The conflict between system and the individual.* New York: Harper & Row, 1957.

BLAKE, R. R. & MOUTON, J. S. *The managerial grid.* Houston, Tex.: Gulf Publishing, 1964.

BOWERS, D. G., FRANKLIN, J. L., & PECORELLA, P. A. Matching problems, precursors, and interventions in OD: A systemic approach. *Journal of Applied Behavioral Science,* 1975, *11*(4), 391–409.

CLAPP, N. W. Work group norms: Leverage for

organizational change, I-theory, II-application. *Organization development reading series* (No. 2). Plainfield, N.J.: Block Petrella Associates, 1974.

DRUCKER, P. F. The dimensions of management. In P. F. Drucker, *Management: Tasks, responsibilities, practices.* New York: Harper & Row, 1974.(a).

DRUCKER, P. F. Why service institutions do not perform. In P. F. Drucker, *Management: Tasks, responsibilities, practices.* New York: Harper & Row, 1974.(b).

FIEDLER, F. E. *A theory of leadership effectiveness.* New York: McGraw-Hill, 1967.

FRIEDLANDER, F., & BROWN, L. D. Organization development. *Annual Review of Psychology*, 1974, *25*, 319.

GULICK, L. Notes on the theory of organizations. In L. Gulick & L. F. Urwick (Eds.), *Papers on the science of administration.* Columbia University, Institute of Public Administration, 1937.

HERZBERG, F., MAUSNER, B., & SNYDERMAN, B. *The motivation to work.* New York: John Wiley & Sons, 1959.

KAST, F. E., & ROSENZWEIG, J. E. *Organization and management: A systems approach.* New York: McGraw-Hill, 1970.

KINGDON, D. R. *Matrix organization: Managing information technologies.* London: Tavistock, 1973.

LAWRENCE, P. R., & LORSCH, J. W. *Organization and environment.* Boston: Harvard University, Graduate School of Business Administration, 1967.

LAWRENCE, P. R., WEISBORD, M. R., & CHARNS, M. P. *Academic medical center self-study guide.* Washington, D.C.: Report of Physicians' Assistance Branch, Bureau of Health, Manpower Education, National Institute of Health, 1973.

LIKERT, R. *The human organization: Its management and value.* New York: McGraw-Hill, 1967.

MASLOW, A. H. *Motivation and personality.* New York: Harper & Row, 1954.

MASLOW, A. H. Synergy in the society and in the individual. In A. H. Maslow, *The farther reaches of human nature.* New York: Viking Press, 1971.

McGREGOR, D. *The human side of enterprise.* New York: McGraw-Hill, 1960.

MEYER, H. H. The pay-for-performance dilemma. *Organizational Dynamics*, 1975, *3*(3), 39–50.

SELZNICK, P. *Leadership in administration.* New York: Harper & Row, 1957.

STEERS, R. M., & PORTER, L. W. *The role of task goal attributes in employee performance* (Report No. TR-24). Washington, D.C.: Office of Naval Research, April 1974.

TILLES, S. The manager's job: A systems approach. *Harvard Business Review*, 1963, *41*(1), 73–81.

TRIST, E. L. On socio-technical systems. In W. G. Bennis, K. D. Benne, & R. Chin, *The planning of change* (2nd ed.). New York: Holt, Rinehart & Winston, 1969.

VAILL, P. B. Practice theories in organization development. In J. D. Adams (Ed.), *New technologies in organization development: 2.* La Jolla, Calif.: University Associates, 1975.

VICKERS, G. *The art of judgment.* New York: Basic Books, 1965.

WEISBORD, M. R. The gap between OD practice and theory—and publication. *Journal of Applied Behavioral Science*, 1974, *10*(4), 476–484.(a).

WEISBORD, M. R. A mixed model for medical centers: Changing structure and behavior. In J. Adams (Ed.), *Theory and method in organization development: An evolutionary process.* Arlington, Va.: NTL Institute for Applied Behavioral Science, 1974.(b).

WEISBORD, M. R. Why organization development hasn't worked (so far) in medical centers. *Health Care Management Review*, April 1976, 17–28.

WHYTE, W. F. & MILLER, F. B. Industrial sociology. In J. B. Gittler (Ed.), *Review of sociology: Analysis of a decade.* New York: John Wiley & Sons, 1957.

Selecting a Setting and a Method of Work*

Edgar H. Schein

The final phase of the exploratory meeting or subsequent meetings involves the selection of a setting in which to work; the specification of a time schedule and a method of work; and preliminary statements about goals to be achieved in the particular setting chosen. These decisions are crucial because, by implication, they define the immediate client system to which the consultant will relate himself. I use a number of general criteria for making such decisions.

THE SETTING

1. *The Choice of What and When to Observe Should Be Worked Out Collaboratively with the Client.* The process consultant must avoid the image of a psychologist wandering around the plant making observations about anything that strikes him as needing attention. Instead, the consultant should engage in a focused process of observation and feedback where both participant and observer have agreed to inquire into the interpersonal process for the sake of improving it.

If the consultant feels the locus of observation should shift, he must involve the people who work in this new locus and establish a similar contract with them. Since the participants are themselves the targets of the process interventions, it is essential that they be involved in the decision to try to learn. Without this kind of psychological contract there is at best no readiness to hear what the consultant might have to say, and, at worst, real resentment at being observed by an outsider.

2. *The Setting Chosen Should Be as Near the Top of the Organization or Client System as Possible.* The reasons for beginning observations at the highest possible level are two-fold: first, the higher the level, the more likely it is that basic norms, values, and goals can be observed in operation. It is the higher levels that set the tone of the organization and ultimately determine the criteria for effective organizational functioning. If the consultant does not expose himself to these levels, he cannot determine what these ultimate norms, goals, and criteria are, and if he does not become acquainted with them, he is abdicating his own ethical responsibility. Only if the consultant can personally accept the norms, goals, and criteria of the organization can he justify helping the

* SOURCE: Edgar H. Schein, *Process Consultation.* © 1969. Addison-Wesley Publishing Company, Inc., Reading, Mass., pp. 89–92. Reprinted with permission.

organization to achieve them. If the consultant feels that the organization's goals are unethical, immoral, or personally unacceptable for some other reason, he can choose to attempt to change them or terminate the relationship, but this choice should be made. The consultant should not operate in ignorance of what the established authority in the organization is trying to do.

Second, the higher the level, the greater the payoff on any changes in process which are achieved. In other words, if the consultant can help the president to learn more about organizational process and to change his behavior accordingly, this change in turn is a force on his immediate subordinates which sets a chain of influence into motion. The more general way to put this point is to say that the consultant should seek that setting or group of people which he considers to be *potentially most influential* on the rest of the organization. Usually this turns out to be the top executive group.

3. *The Setting Chosen Should Be One in Which It Is Easy to Observe Interpersonal and Group Processes.* Often this turns out to be a weekly or monthly staff meeting, or some regularly scheduled activity in which two or more of the members of the key group being observed transact business together. It is important to observe processes among the members, not just between individual members and the process consultant. For this reason, a survey or interview methodology is only a stopgap measure. Ultimately, the consultant must have access to a situation where the organization's members are dealing with each other in their usual fashion.

4. *The Setting Chosen Should Be One in Which Real Work Is Going On.* The consultant should avoid the situation where a group initially agrees to meet with him only to discuss their interpersonal relations. Such a meeting would be appropriate after a relationship had developed between the group and the consultant but would be premature before. The group cannot as yet trust the consultant enough to really have an open discussion of interpersonal relations, and the consultant does not yet have enough observational data to be able to help the group in such a discussion. Regular committee or work-group meetings are ideal, on the other hand, because the consultant not only sees the organization members in a more natural role, but learns what sort of work the members are concerned about. At later intervention stages, it is much easier to link observations to real work behavior, and it is much more likely that real changes will occur in members if they can relate process observations to work events.

METHOD OF WORK

1. *The Method of Work Chosen Should Be as Congruent as Possible with the Values Underlying Process Consultation.* Thus observation, informal interviewing, and group discussions would be congruent with:

   1. the idea that the consultant does not already have pat answers or standard "expert" solutions, and

2. the idea that the consultant should be maximally available for questioning and two-way communication.

If the consultant uses methods like questionnaires or surveys, he himself remains an unknown quantity to the respondent. As long as he remains unknown, the respondent cannot really trust him, and hence cannot really answer questions completely honestly. The method of work chosen, therefore, should make the consultant maximally visible and maximally available for interaction.

Often I choose to start a consultation project with some interviewing, but the purpose of the interview is not so much to gather data as to establish a relationship with each of the people who will later be observed. The interview is designed to *reveal myself* as much as it is designed to *learn something about the other person.* I will consider the use of questionnaires only after I am well enough known by the organization to be reasonably sure that people would trust me enough to give direct and frank answers to questions.

In summary, the choice of a setting and a method of work is highly variable. It is important that both the setting and working procedure be jointly decided between the contact client group and the consultant. Whatever decisions are made should be congruent with the general assumptions underlying P-C so that whatever changes result can be self-perpetuating.

The Organization Development Contract Revisited*

Marvin R. Weisbord [†]

In OD consulting the contract is central to success. Most contracts—employment, service, research—focus heavily on content, that is, the nature of the work to be performed, the schedule, and the money to change hands. They are seen primarily as legal documents. The OD contract is a working agreement which above all involves expectations for a certain kind of relationship.

Most contracts are negotiated through a proposal, which one party writes and the other accepts. The consulting contracts people know best might be called "expert" and "pair of hands."

1. Expert Contract—You hire me to study the problem and tell you what to do. Like a medical doctor, I diagnose and prescribe based on my skill, experience and judgment. Your role is limited to describing symptoms and taking your medicine. The main drawback to this contract is that it rarely requires that people make commitments to each other but only to the consultant. The prescribed action may be seen as too threatening or disruptive to implement.

2. Pair of Hands Contract—You hire me to solve the problem for you. You have already done the diagnosis and written your own prescription. It's up to me to carry out your wishes. (Many training contracts are framed this way—a trap for consultants who conduct a workshop only to find out that the main problem is not lack of skill or knowledge so much as lack of motivation.)

In either case the quality of the advice and/or the solution is the focus, and the *consultant* is a central figure. Whatever happens, the consultant takes most of the risk.

In OD consulting, *clients* are the central figures, and the consultant requires that the client be directly involved in every decision leading up to a diagnosis, and in framing conclusions and action steps. I contract, then, to work together *with* clients on important problems, achieving better diagnoses and better action steps than either of us could do alone. This is a form of collaboration which, if successful, helps the principal client also to achieve better working relationships with others, for example peers, boss, and subordinates. This model of collaborative consultation—a 50/50 relationship—is not widely understood

---

* Source: *Organisationsentwicklung*, no. 4 (1984), 15–26. Copyright 1984 by Marvin R. Weisbord. Used by permission.

† *Author's note:* Adapted from *The OD Practitioner*, 5 (Summer 1973), published by the OD Network U.S.A. I wrote this new version, incorporating some recent thinking, in Spring 1984 at the request of my colleague Karsten Trebesch.

in the world of business, government, or education. Done well, it leads to committed implementation of changes identified as important and to greater use of expertise and competence within the client's own organization.

For that reason, in OD contracting, more so than other kinds, the *process* by which action steps are planned is critical. Unless this negotiation is a model of the consultant's values and problem-solving behavior, the contract, when it's tested, probably won't stand up. More about testing later.

What do I mean by contract? I mean an explicit exchange of expectations, part dialogue, part written document, which clarifies for consultant and client three critical areas:

1. What each expects to get from the relationship;
2. How much time each will invest, when, and at what cost;
3. The ground rules under which the parties will operate.

WHAT EACH EXPECTS

Clients expect, and have a right to expect, change for the better in a situation that is making their lives hard. This situation, as my clients experience it, has three main components:

1. Business opportunities, which provide the main motivation for action. The most obvious are changing market conditions, mergers, new technologies, and/or the need to cut costs, improve quality, increase production.
2. People problems, i.e. one, two or more others are singled out as particular sore spots.
3. Personal dilemma, i.e. whether this job, or this career, is what I really want.

The third component always grows in direct proportion to the first two. Clients in a bind don't get much fun out of their work. They long for something simpler, better suited to their strengths, more consistent with their values. Above all, most clients long for outcomes. They want permanent "change" for the better, with no backsliding. I, on the other hand, see new outcomes as evidence the client is learning a better way of coping. From my point of view the *process*—gathering information, becoming aware of deeper meanings, making choices—is my most important product. While the client identifies difficult situations to work on, I keep in mind three levels of improvement to be achieved:

1. Solution of the immediate crisis—changing structures, policies, procedures, relationships;
2. New learning for clients about their own coping styles—how they deal with crises, how they might do it better;
3. Learning a *process* for coping better: When and how to involve others, build support, manage conflict.

The existing problem is a vehicle for learning how to manage better.

I always ask prospective clients to name what outcomes they hope to achieve by working with me. Here are some typical replies:

- "Higher motivation."
- "Want others to understand our goals better."
- "Better communications, fewer misunderstandings."
- "Better meetings—more excitement, more decisions made."
- "More interesting jobs."

Notice that each of these statements is somewhat abstract, self-evidently "good," and very hard to measure. I never accept such generalities as adequate statements of a client's expectations. Instead, I push hard on outcomes. What would you see happening that would tell you communications are improving? How will you know when goals are clearer, or morale has gone up? What will people do? Can you watch them do it? When I push at this level, I get more realistic statements:

- Deadlines will be taken seriously and met more often.
- In meetings, decisions will be made, actions agreed upon, and names and dates put on them.
- I will understand how to set up the Department A and will have commitments from others to reorganize.
- We will have a new procedure for handling customer complaints.
- We will get orders into production more quickly.

These statements are good short-run indicators of change. They are realistic expectations. Are changes like these worth the client's investment of time and money? It's important that clients be clear that they are choosing to do whatever we do together because it's worth it to them (and not because it's this year's panacea, or somebody else tried it and liked it, or because they think their problems will go away). In addition, I like to know what the client wants personally out of this. More support? More acceptance? Fame? Recognition?

I expect some things too. Clients know I work for money just as they do. However, I also indicate some of my other motives for working with them in particular projects. At the moment I'm interested in work redesign and future planning strategies. The chance to do something along these lines raises my incentive with any client. So does a client's ready acceptance of some responsibility for the situation. If clients are well-motivated to work on their problems, so am I—and I tell them so. In doing this, I am trying to say that each of us has a right to some personal benefits from our relationship, in addition to benefits the organization may derive.

STRUCTURING THE RELATIONSHIP: TIME AND MONEY

OD, like much of life, is carried forward mainly by meetings. The central decision in any contract discussion is which people should be involved and how.

Which room will we meet in, for how long, and with what objectives? There is no contract until we name people, pick dates, and set a budget. The client has a right to know how much time I will invest in interviewing, or survey sampling, or in whatever diagnostic procedure we agree on, and how long our meetings will require. If I need time in between to organize data, I estimate how much. Usually the initial contract is diagnostic, to be completed at a face-to-face meeting where the data will be examined, a common diagnosis arrived at, and next steps decided upon. Always, I work to clarify the costs, time and money, of each next step. Generally, this information will be written down.

There are some things I won't do, which I only mention if the client does. For instance, I always turn down opportunities to work weekends. On weekends my contract is with my family. *When* you work on your organization indicates how important you consider it. People get themselves into crises during the week. If they don't make time to untangle during the week, they're unlikely to get out working weekends. (I have never lost a client because of this policy.)

GROUND RULES

Ground rules speak to the process of our relationship. Sometimes I write them down, sometimes not. In any case, I work towards an understanding along these lines:

1. I supply methods, techniques, theory, etc. to help you understand and work better on your problems. You supply energy, commitment, and share responsibility for success. I do not study your problems and recommend expert solutions that I would not be prepared to help you implement.

2. Part of my job is to raise sticky issues and urge you to consider them. You have a right to say no to anything you don't want to deal with. If you feel free to say no, I'll feel free to push.

3. Tell me if I do something puzzling or irritating, and encourage me to do the same.

4. Part of my job is to make you aware of what you do, and what possible consequences your actions have for me and for the people around you. My job is also to preserve and encourage your freedom of choice about what, if anything, you should do. I also have a strong bias towards openness and accepting responsibility. Because I believe a core value of OD is to create more open systems, I turn down or terminate contracts when openness is not valued.

5. My client is the whole organization. That means I intend not to be seen as an advocate for anybody's pet ideas if they fall outside my own area of competence. However, I do advocate a participative process for problem-solving, and recognize that some people oppose my process. I accept that risk.

6. Often the information I collect and present will be anonymous. However, I don't want confidential information, meaning anything which people are unwilling for other organization members to know.

7. All data belongs to the people who supply it. I will not show it to anyone without their permission.

8. Either of us can terminate on 24 hours notice, regardless of contract length, so long as we have a face-to-face meeting first.

Contracting, like the seasons, is repetitive and continually renewable. If I have a long term contract (e.g. 4 days a month for a year) I may also have a separate contract for certain individual meetings, which I sometimes present and discuss at the outset. If I have a contract with a boss to help build a team, I need to extend it to the team members before we go to work. If I succeed with the team, and some members want to work with their teams, I need again to negotiate a new deal with the new people. Once, having worked with a team, I found the boss wanting to confront his boss. He wanted the whole team to do it with him, with me as consultant. I pointed out that that would require a temporary contract between me, him, and his boss. He set up a dinner meeting—the night before the confrontation—and his boss and I made a one-day contract which stood up very well next morning.

In short, I'm never finished contracting. Each client meeting requires that I reexamine the contract. Does it cover everybody I'm working with? Is it clear what we're doing now? And why?

Moreover, contracting—while it deals ostensibly and mainly with content issues—has a process side crucial to its success. Consider, in some detail, where and how an OD contract is made.

OD contracts usually begin with a phone call or letter. Somebody has heard about what I did somewhere else. I respond with a phone call to the writer or caller at a time when I can spend 10 minutes or more discussing what is wanted and whether or not it makes sense to meet. This initial contact is crucial to any contract. Each of us is trying—over the phone—to decide whether we like the other well enough to proceed. I try not to prejudge the conversation. I want a face-to-face meeting *if* there's a chance of getting a solid contract. Here are some questions running through my mind:

1. How open is the caller with me? How open do I feel?
2. Is the caller window-shopping, maybe calling several consultants? Sometimes prospective clients don't know what they want. Then I have a good chance to consult with them on the phone, helping them clarify what they are after and whether they could benefit by working with me.
3. Does the client already have a diagnosis? If so, what makes me the solution? Is it a workshop? A meeting? A series of meetings? Magic? Is there still a chance for a joint diagnosis?
4. Is there a budget adequate to the expectations? If the answer is no, I decide not to pursue it further.
5. Is this an issue in which I (and my firm) have a special interest? In the '70's we were especially alert for team-building and organization-wide surveys. In the '80's we find ourselves attracted by work redesign, product and service quality improvement, mergers and reorganizations. This shift in focus parallels a general shift in the OD profession towards business-related projects and away from "people problems" exclusively.
6. Would the potential project require more than one person? I do better work with a partner, and we have more flexibility in following up with the client. My interest is greater when there is room for a second consultant, from my own organization or from the client's own staff.

7. Assume a budget, and willingness on both our parts to go forward. We need a meeting. Who else should be there? Can the caller enter into a contract? If not, who is? Can that person make the meeting? Is the client open to my bringing an associate?

I end the phone call by clarifying that this will be an exploratory meeting, no commitments on either side.

FIRST MEETING

I arrive, greet my prospective client, introduce myself and associate. We have coffee, discuss the ball game, or the climate. Each of us is deciding, silently, privately, and perhaps unconsciously, how much we like the other. I have heard some salespeople say that they often know within the first 10 minutes whether they are going to make the sale. While I don't feel that certain, I *do* know fairly soon whether I could picture myself consulting with this client.

Soon we get down to business—or appear to. The content issues might include:

1. Our backgrounds—potential client needs to know enough about me to feel I can help, before putting out major problems.
2. Issues bothering client system—Are they symptomatic of other things, which are not being discussed?
3. What changes would the people I'm talking to like to see? What things would they observe happening that would tell them they are getting desired outcomes? This step in naming outcomes is important in reducing the level of fantasy about what OD consultants can do.
4. What first event would be appropriate? Nearly always, this event should be diagnostic. It should be an activity which will heighten the awareness of the people I'm meeting with about how the issues they raise are seen by others in the system—bosses, subordinates, customers, peers. In addition, I need this to find out—really find out—whether I can help. Is the system ready for a diagnosis? If so, the diagnosis will give me a much better idea of how ready people are to act, and on which issues.

If the system is ready, a budget exists, and the boss is willing to lead the effort, I may propose a workshop as a way to examine and validate the diagnostic information. Sometimes, it makes more sense to consult to a work group during their regular weekly or monthly meetings. Sometimes, a questionnaire provides a data-base for a diagnostic meeting.

Whatever the event, we need a schedule, a place to meet, and a division of labor for briefing participants, organizing materials and sending agendas in advance. Sometimes these things can be decided in the first meeting. Sometimes I agree to write a formal proposal. Always I try to close on the next step— what I will do, what the client will do, and by what date.

The above considerations focus mainly on content. However, there are several process issues surrounding this meeting which I'm continually working on too:

1. First among these is, "Would I wish to work with this person?" If not a spark of warmth or empathy, then what am I feeling? Annoyance? Frustration? Wariness? Can I find something to like, respect, or admire about the other person? We use the task at hand to help us get greater clarity about our relationship. Any time I'm uncertain about a relationship I believe my contract is in jeopardy, no matter what fine words are spoken or written on paper.
2. The client's depth of commitment is an issue for me. Does this person really want to change things? Does the client accept responsibility—at least a little bit—for the way things are? If the message is, "I want you to change them," and I say, "Okay, but how open are *you* to changing?", do I get a blank stare? My value about organizations improving themselves by learning to do things in a more open way—is obvious to me. I need to test how my client feels about that.
3. Part of client commitment is resources. Clients find time and money to do things they want to do. If either money or time seem to be sticky problems, I look for other explanations—anxiety about failure, a boss who's negative about OD, fear of opening up "destructive issues." Helping the client speak about these possibilities is valuable for both of us, whether I get the contract or not. How do it? By asking such questions as: What is the risk? What's the worst thing that could happen? How much exposure can you stand? Does this give you the control you need? I also ask what good things might happen, and whether the possible outcomes are worth the risks and costs.

The question I continually confront is: Which problems would you rather have? The ones you have now? Or the ones you will have if you try to solve the ones you have now? Often this process leads to greater commitment on both our parts to be successful.

Once in a while potential clients decide they would rather live with what they've got. I support that insight. It's better that both of us know it sooner than later. I am learning to spot conditions under which I may fail, and an uneasy contract ranks high on the list.

STRUCTURING THE RELATIONSHIP

My way of thinking about contracts is heavily influenced by Chris Argyris (1970), who specifies valid data, free choice, and commitment to act as key goals of intervention. These become real in an OD contract when the following conditions are met:

1. The contract is responsive to the client's perceived problem. It must be seen as helping people gain greater clarity, insight and control over whatever issues are bugging them. It cannot be based on my need to use any particular trick in my bag.
2. It names the people who will come together, when, for how long, and why. "Why" is generally the clients' to answer. The boss must tell people why they

are there, and I tell them what sort of working agreement I would like with them. It is not my job to tell people why they are there.

3. It involves joint diagnosis. That means some information (valid data) is collected which will heighten the clients' awareness and enlarge their freedom of choice. Sometimes this information fits some conceptual scheme, which I make explicit. Sometimes I help clients build their own scheme. The data collection must be done in a way that people who supply the data will recognize it as useful to their work together when I organize and hand it back. The more interpreting, or categorizing I do in advance, the more I deprive clients of the chance to become committed to their own diagnosis.

There is a fine line between too much and too little. If I simply hand back what the client told me, without any organization or concepts, I add very little to answering the question, "Why bother?" So I need some conclusions—only a few, and then framed as tentative and subject to change after discussion.

I state my ground rules about anonymity and/or confidentiality. If I opt for neither, this usually elicits useful conversation on how open people are likely to be, and what it means to take responsibility for your own views. (After 10 years of practicing this way, I have yet to conclude that people held back anything of important because I might attribute it to them by name.) I always specify how much time people must give, what kinds of questions will be asked, and what will become of the answers. This structuring reduces anxiety and sets up reasonable expectations.

4. I establish that part of the contract is mutual feedback. I expect clients to confront me openly on my behavior when it doesn't make sense, to question anything I do, and to point out to me words or behavior that violate their sense of what's appropriate. In return, I expect to be open with them.

It is around this clause, I think, that all contracts are tested sooner or later. In a workshop the test may come in the form of protest that the activities are irrelevant to the agenda and a waste of time. In a one-to-one consulting the test may be something I did or said that really irritated the client. It takes some risk to let me know. In opening the issue, the client is checking to see whether I'm as open as I claim to be.

I define testing the contract as an emotion-provoking exchange between me and the client in some risky situation. As a result our relationship will become more "real," more truly mutual. I think both of us have a responsibility to test the contract when either does something that affects our relationship. Once, I had a client continually express disappointment in others, and told him I was worried that one day—if not already—he was going to feel the same way about me. He assured me I would be the first to know, which, when the time came, I was. The confrontation deepened our relationship and strengthened the contract. It might have ended it, too.

I welcome ending a contract explicitly by having it tested and found wanting. Better a clean death than lingering agony. It is time to test (and maybe end) a contract when—

- the client keeps putting things off;
- agreements are made and forgotten (by either side);
- the consultant appears to have a higher emotional stake in the outcomes than the client does;
- the consultant asks for events, or activities, which intensify the feeling of crisis and pressure without much prospect for eventual relief;
- the client looks to the consultant to do things which operating managers should be doing—i.e. arranging meetings, sending out agendas, carrying messages, and getting other people to do everything the client always wanted them to do but was afraid to ask;
- I have lost interest or enthusiasm for the project (because others have lost momentum or because my own interests have changed);
- the client is doing better and no longer needs outside help;

For me, a crisp, clean ending remains desirable, but sometimes elusive. Reviewing 14 major contracts in one four-year period, I found nine ended cleanly with no "unfinished business," three ended because the boss lacked commitment to continue, and two because organizational changes left a leadership vacuum and me uncertain who the client was.

Where the boss lacked commitment, the intended follow-up meetings never took place, and I let things alone, feeling, I suppose, relatively little commitment myself. In the cases of organizational changes, it became plain the interim leadership lacked either incentive or authority to keep up the contract, and I had other fish to fry.

In the last decade I deliberately ended two long consultations involving retainer fees, in one case because I felt I was no longer helping (the client agreed) and in the other because the client seemed unable to follow through on decisions made in meetings with subordinates who in turn withdrew their support. (The client denied this was happening and asked me to continue. I refused.)

Every contract, it seems to me, has a natural life. Organizations eventually outgrow or tire of or cease needing a particular consultant, and vice versa. It's better for me and my client that we acknowledge when it's time to part.

REFERENCES

ARGYRIS, C. *Intervention Theory and Method: A Behavioral Science View.* Reading, MA: Addison-Wesley, 1970.

BLOCK, P. *Flawless Consulting.* Austin. TX: Learning Concepts, 1981.

9

IN THE MIDST OF THE PROCESS

———————◄●►————————

INTRODUCTION

The Torenton Mine is a four-part account of an intervention that proceeded over a substantial period of time, and provides thoughtful consultant introspections about its evolution. *The Torenton Mine (A)* opens with a description of the mine and the external change agent, who initially conducted a supervisory training program, an attitude survey-feedback intervention, and a consultation skills workshop. The intervention process clearly proceeded with some difficulty.

This chapter presents a further installment about the course of the Multi Company intervention, introduced in Chapter 8. *The Multi Company (B)* outlines further the project intended to help stimulate innovation in the company and redirect the company's energies. It describes the second annual company meeting, in which the consultant participated, and the organization's use of groups. Discussion may fruitfully revolve around the change agent's behavior and the kinds of organizational dynamics uncovered.

Pan Pacific briefly describes an intervention that seems to have started promisingly, then somehow becomes becalmed or stuck. The problem posed consists of elaborating an interaction process that will unstick it and get things moving.

The models and schemes begin with two contributions about the design of activities in interventions. *Structuring Activities in Interventions* is a sage piece that provides concentrated advice, from leading writers and consultants, on operating principles to be observed in designing events in the course of managing change efforts. *Models of Consulting* contrasts the "installation" model of consultancy, where a pre-existing package of some sort is simply plugged into the client organization, and the *de novo* model, where an intervention is specifically designed from scratch to suit the unique organization. The change agent's emphasis should, in principle, be on tailoring any intervention to fit the unique circumstances of the organization concerned, in the light of the range of intervention possibilities available *in situ*, and from experiences and models and schemes elsewhere.

Argyris's Model I and Model II contrasts two modes of behavior. Model I implies that managers are "culturally unable to behave participatively"; model II builds on the "learning how to learn" assumptions implicit in group dynamics training, and emphasizes such practices as seeking valid data before making decisions. These models were invoked by the change agent at work in the Torenton Mine and help cast light on that intervention.

In *The Consultant Role* a well-known Tavistock consultant speaks directly and frankly about the way he worked as a consultant during the highly successful interventions he carried out in India. This is the only systematic outline of his approach as a change agent that he ever wrote.

It Takes a Group to Understand a Group elaborates on the notion of change agents helping each other to elucidate what is going on during an intervention in a client organization, and to cope with data overload. *Working Notes* addresses an attempt by a consultant to develop a method to record and clarify, both for himself and fellow consultants, the point his thinking had reached at a particular time. Such a device may be useful to consultant teams working in large-scale interventions.

The Action Research Process follows through the cyclical, repetitive pattern emergent in action research, and outlines various ways in which different Tavistock change agents handle client data. *The Dynamics of Dependency* reports how several Tavistock consultants conceptualize and act in regard to dependency during the course of an intervention. Appropriate consultant behavior at one point in an intervention's history is unlikely to be appropriate at another.

Choosing the Depth of Organizational Intervention tackles the problem of whether or not the consultant should lead the client, if at all, and resolves it in favor of minimum leading, given the problem. This issue perhaps differentiates many essentially behavioral science–based consultants from those employing more psychoanalytically informed models, where members of the client system are conceived to be less fully conscious of the significant dynamics at work. It is beyond the purpose and scope of this book to attempt some resolution of these distinctive frames of reference.

The Torenton Mine (A)*

James F. Gavin

The Client

The body of ore now being mined at Torenton . . . was first discovered in 1967 far beneath the snow-covered peak of Antler Mountain. More than nine years later, after an investment of more than a half-billion dollars, Torenton's first ore car emerged from the tunnel precisely on schedule—a modern-day marvel of engineering and technical acumen. From the outset, Torenton was one of the safest and most efficient hard rock mines in the industry.

By 1981, nearly 1,800 employees worked at Torenton, producing more than 30,000 tons of rock each day. They came from all areas of the nation, and for most Torenton was the first mine they had ever seen. Torenton had no labor unions, and the majority of employees apparently had little desire for one. The wage and benefits policies were highly competitive for the industry and certainly better than those of other regional employers. Experienced miners regarded Torenton as something resembling a "country club," an odd association for those uninitiated to the rigors of mining. As with most mines, Torenton's work force structure became dense with engineering and technical personnel as one ascended the hierarchy.

Torenton was an operating company that belonged to a large mining corporation. As such, the corporate office dictated many of the mining policies. Staff departments often had dual reporting relationships with local and corporate management. Emerging from the tradition of mining, expertise in technical matters far exceeded the company's sophistication in managing human resources.

THE CONSULTING SYSTEM

My association with Torenton began in early 1974. At the time I had been involved in OD for eight years, but had never worked with a mining company. A graduate faculty member in an industrial/organizational psychology program, I had as resources colleagues and students. Sometimes during the course of my work I managed a temporary team of as many as 25 persons, while at other times I worked only with one or two colleagues. For the most part, the senior-level staff members of the consulting team were other faculty, while the support staff tended to consist of advanced graduate students.

* SOURCE: James F. Gavin, "Observations from a Long-Term Survey—Guided Consultation with a Mining Company," *Journal of Applied Behavioral Science*, 21 (1985), 204–220. Reprinted with permission.

THE FIRST ATTITUDE SURVEY

The OD process at Torenton began in 1973. Concerned about a turnover rate for hourly employees of more than 14% per month, the company hired a consultant to conduct an attitude survey of these employees. A sample of 20% of the work force participated in face-to-face interviews and completed written questionnaires. The consultant made a report to the management committee, which comprised all department heads and the general manager. Although the data pointed out interdepartmental conflicts and problems with vertical communication occurring above the first line of supervision, the managers concluded that the supervisors needed human relations training.

THE TRAINING PROGRAM

Following this decision, the human resources (HR) manager invited me to conduct a supervisory training program at Torenton. The original request was in the form of a "work order" to "fix the supervisors," but the managers proved flexible enough to consider an alternate proposal that called for everyone in a supervisory position to complete a two-day training program in basic human relations skills. The training relied heavily on a behavior modeling approach . . . but also included more philosophical discussions of such concepts as Theories X and Y.

For most first-line supervisors, this training represented their first exposure to management education. The written and verbal feedback was mostly positive, although as many as one-fourth of the participants commented on the implied shift in management style communicated by the program's emphases. This was one of the early signs of potential differences in client-consultant theories of action. But the most pernicious snag in the program occurred when we decided to practice certain management principles, and not just talk about them, during the management committee's training workshop. In the process of working on a group problem-solving exercise, the second most influential member walked out, seeming to end any further OD processes, and perhaps any additional behavioral science programs.

THE SECOND ATTITUDE SURVEY AND THE FIRST FEEDBACK

Even though the training session with the top team ended in disarray, the HR manager—with the consent of the general manager—invited me to prepare a proposal for a follow-up attitude survey of hourly employees. The motivation for doing this stemmed partly from the HR manager's desire to estimate the impact of the supervisory training. Moreover, the turnover rates for hourly employees remained at about 10% per month. I developed a written questionnaire from 61 face-to-face interviews, a literature review, and items from the

1973 survey. The questionnaire was administered during working hours in the summer of 1975. Before doing this, I was allowed to work underground as a miner for about one month so that I could better understand the miner's world.

In negotiating this contract, I argued for the inclusion of a feedback component to the program that would call for employees to meet in "family groups" to review the data. . . . Although implementation was problematic, feedback sessions were held with all hourly crews. The format provided employees with comprehensive survey reports for their crews and the company as a whole, and it allowed them not only to comment on company-wide issues but also to engage in action planning for change. Sessions were held during working hours in meeting rooms throughout the mine.

The managers actually had little conception of what might result when they granted permission to hold the feedback sessions. Discussions of the management philosophy possibly associated with a survey feedback program (SFP) had been held with the management committee, but their comprehension was superficial at best. This confusion became dramatically evident during a last-minute confrontation that occurred the day before the first feedback session was to take place. At this time, the general manager had to be reconvinced that employees needed to have access to the data during a feedback meeting. Also, it was not management's style (theory of action) to become involved in programs the way we expected them to. Typically, they hired a "contractor" to take on a task and report to the client following completion of the work. Because we were dealing with processes and relationships, however, our work required violations of the norms of appropriate contractor behavior.

The 1975 SFP supported a number of changes, and within a year the managers had revised some major policies and instituted new programs. For example, a highly criticized attendance policy was revised, the employee orientation program was redesigned, a credit union was established, and a preventive maintenance program was implemented. The HR manager acted as the internal change agent, providing continuity and direction both during and after the major programmatic activities.

COUNTERING APATHY WITH EVIDENCE

Even though the SFP appeared to be a major success, the top managers remained cool toward behavioral science interventions. They viewed these programs as a nuisance, part of the modern management style but unrelated to such important matters as productivity—and certainly inconsistent with the style of a "real" mine boss.

With the support of the HR manager, I launched a study to evaluate the degree of relationship between employee attitudes and job behaviors. Evidence suggested that, on the average, mining crews supervised by bosses with high ratings in consideration and participatory practices outproduced crews whose supervisors had low ratings by more than a half-million dollars in ore per year. Data on the relationship of job morale to criteria of safety and turnover also had impressive cost implications. These results were summarized in a report entitled "Attitudes Count!"

We did not attempt to imply that attitudes and supervisory style were the sole factors affecting these criteria; given our correlational research design, we had to be extremely cautious in interpreting these findings. . . . The managers seemed aware of the limits of these data, but intrigued nonetheless. Though we suggested conducting a controlled experiment, the HR manager and others felt that the essential point had been made—that is, that a *probable* relationship existed between attitudes/style and outcomes—and that further study would have only questionable value.

Reactions to the report held one major surprise. Up to this point the managers had said that attitudes were mostly irrelevant; now they switched to saying, "Of course! We all know the happy worker is a productive worker. So what's so new about this?" While the response was unenthusiastic, criticism of the survey program diminished markedly following the publication of this report.

CONSULTATION SKILLS

Because much of the follow-up work of the 1975 survey fell onto the HR staff, I suggested arranging a consultation skills workshop for this group. Through this training I hoped to enhance the effectiveness and scope of organization interventions by the HR function. A program based on Argyris's model for intervention . . . was implemented during a six-month period (1976–77). In this program the Model I and Model II theories of action were described and the staff, using role plays and actual consultations in the mine, diagnosed their models in use, discussing the appropriateness and feasibility of consultations with either model. The results were quite mixed. Some HR staff members felt disappointed, for they had wanted to improve their skills in a win-lose model of intervention. Others felt discouraged because of the apparent discrepancy between the organization's current state and the state it needed to achieve to implement Model II strategies.

The few skeptics remained unconvinced throughout the project, but other HR staff members found that Torenton's climate was more receptive to Model II approaches than they had anticipated. The management actions of the 1980s particularly reflected this. I must attribute the survival of these ideas in the midst of disbelief and disillusionment to the HR manager, who continued to foster and reward Model II approaches made by his staff.

MORE HUMAN RELATIONS TRAINING

The 1975 SFP extended well into 1976, followed by the consultation skills training and a series of reports based on the survey and productivity data. In preparation for their survey feedback sessions, supervisors had participated in training in 1974 and in 1975–76. By the end of 1977, the HR manager indicated that human relations skills needed reinforcement. I was asked to conduct another on-site training program, this time without the participation of the top managers. I was pleased with continuing the training, but also felt that the limited time allocated for it would make the effort more symbolic than functional. Our research had identified supervisory consideration, participatory practices, and the giving of feedback as critical factors with high criterion relationships. The training design was largely based on the outcomes of our action research.

The training experience was unremarkable. Yet the idea that we were continuing to emphasize supervisory behaviors of consideration, participation, and feedback seemed to convey a political message of sorts to the trainees. They interpreted the consistency of our training messages over the years to mean that this "new style" had the backing of the top managers. The irony of this interpretation was that the top managers, by authorizing the human relations program but failing to participate in it, were labeled hypocrites by the trainees, who asked such questions as, "How can they tell us that we should let our 'hands' participate when they won't even participate in the training they're sending us to, or when they don't give us a 'say' around here?"

SOME UNSOLICITED FEEDBACK

Prior to the training program, the consultants asked the management committee if they would be interested in a further appraisal of the organization based on the perceptions of the supervisors in the training session (both the 1973 and 1975 surveys had focused primarily on the hourly employees). The managers agreed, but their decision was noncommittal.

This latest survey reflected the verbal input of the training participants, who—characteristic of the mine employees—knew how to criticize but not how to praise. We entitled the report "Problems of Supervision" because of the overriding tone of the supervisors' comments. The report criticized highly the upper managers' style of operation and their attention to supervisors' concerns.

The management committee reacted vehemently to the report. The general manager accused the consultants of fabricating the results, because none of his managers had ever indicated the existence of problems so pervasive and deeply felt as the report suggested. Although we convinced him that the data came from the supervisory staff, we could not dispel the impression that we had somehow evoked only the most critical statements.

One must consider the validity of the general manager's impression. During the latest round of training our access to the top group had been restricted. We unequivocally believed that the top team members needed training. We also believed that for OD to succeed in this organization required continuous efforts to keep the management committee involved so that all of our consultations did not become the functional responsibility of one depart-ment—human resources. The survey of supervisors was directed toward increasing the managers' awareness and commitment. Were we on the project making our own feelings about the top managers apparent by the way we collected data—that is, did we bias the responses?

I find it hard to answer this with absolute certainty. We believe we did not bias the responses, and while gathering the data were actually surprised by the paucity of positive comments. We did, however, readily accept this negativism as another confirmation of the mine staff's prevailing norm of informing people only about their mistakes. Moreover, most of the information we ordinarily received in off-the-record communications criticized some dimension of orga-nizational life and thus corroborated the criticisms we heard while conducting the training survey. This seemed to highlight the nature of communications of employees to consultants, and it possibly reflected a slowly evolving definition of our roles vis-à-vis the employees.

AN ORGANIZATION-WIDE SURVEY FEEDBACK PROGRAM

Remarkably, this management group persevered: While we consultants were more and more frequently perceived as bearers of bad tidings, when the management committee approved plans for a third attitude survey it asked me to submit a proposal. My plan called for all employees in all departments to become involved in both the survey and feedback activities. After considering the rationale for an organization-wide program, the committee gave its approval.

Although I have no proof of this, I conjecture that their surprise at the results of the unsolicited survey may have heightened the managers' curiosity about "concealed" attitudes held by those in staff groups and the ranks of management. This hypothesized interest could have provoked greater support for surveying heretofore neglected segments of the organization.

By this time, Torenton had almost 1,700 employees. With all depart-ments and all levels involved in the SFP, we had to establish mechanisms for following up the feedback sessions. The management committee designated a system-wide survey committee to track major departmental and organizational problems, but once again the HR staff bore primary responsibility for ensuring long-term follow-up. Consultations and work with the survey and feedback data continued well into early 1980.

The HR staff members each facilitated an average of 25 feedback sessions. The frequent repetitions of complaints and pointed attacks on company practices took their toll on the staff. This, in combination with the staff's attempts to follow up on issues and convince various managers to implement a myriad of changes, led some HR personnel to experience emotional burnout. The managers, feeling pressured from all sides to make changes stimulated by survey and feedback data, eventually called for an end to "all this survey talk" so that employees could "get back to work."

Changes were evident at all levels of the organization, both during and following the program. In most feedback sessions, participants agreed upon local actions and provided input for wider decision making. The follow-up by the survey committee virtually assured that the commitments would be implemented, because mine managers resented being reminded by committee members to do something. Months later, departments continued to analyze survey data to obtain potential support for system-wide decisions. We action researchers made sure we knew how the survey and feedback input was used. Clearly, few people in the organization had any idea of the far-ranging impact of the program. Company communications regarding the follow-up of the SFP were typically neglected.

A PERIOD OF INTEGRATION

A hiatus in the consultations took place during 1980. During that time, information from the survey continued to serve as justification for policy changes or program design, but external consultations consisted primarily of advisory sessions with the HR manager and the implementation of some personnel research projects, such as selection research and performance appraisal development. The follow-up work from the survey did, however, include the attendance at external management programs by a large number of middle and senior managers. The orientation of these programs was quite compatible with the directions of the project's work. Also significant was the company's decision in 1980 to enact a policy providing for the annual human relations training of all supervisory personnel.

Since the completion of the survey, I had requested another tour of work underground on a mining crew. Although I undertook this action to increase my personal understanding of the mining profession, it also affected the managers' perceptions of my involvement with them and their organization. Throughout this tour of work, I could contrast my underground experiences in 1975 with the organizational realities of 1979. The improvements were dramatic, particularly in the domain of supervisor-employee relationships. A new order of management prevailed at Torenton.

REPLICATION OF THE ORGANIZATION-WIDE SURVEY
FEEDBACK PROGRAM

The survey concept had gradually become an institutionalized communications tool, for the company adopted a policy of conducting periodic employee attitude surveys and made explicit reference to them in the employees' handbook. The managers asked me to submit a proposal for an attitude survey in late 1980. Other consultants entered bids, but our expertise with Torenton weighed heavily in favor of our project staff. To a large extent, the survey made in early 1981 replicated—with some improvements—the one made in 1978.

Institutionalization had some apparent consequences. Employees were better informed not only about the process, but—more importantly—about the potential of this program. They knew its limits, and thus were less optimistic that substantial changes would result. We consultants felt concerned about our changing role in an institutionalized program, and wondered if the same impetus for change would exist in a program that was becoming increasingly routine and for which the sluggish change processes of previous SFPs seemed to produce a general lowering of expectations.

To our surprise, the increased sophistication of the employees regarding the style and philosophy of survey feedback efforts caused managers and department heads to become significantly more involved in this program. One manifestation of this increased involvement was the managers' tendency to schedule ongoing feedback meetings with their staffs following the initial survey feedback sessions. Another indication was the conceptual exploration of quality circle programs by the most influential members of the top staff.

While we were concluding our work with Torenton on the fourth survey, the downturn in the national economy began to affect the mining industry. Because of this, the managers scuttled many of the intended follow-up programs and redirected their attention to the more pressing issue of survival. Despite this, our observation of the mine during the hard times indicated that the organization had become a far more collaborative system than before.

The Multi Company (B)*

Edgar H. Schein

Unfreezing at Second Annual Meeting. The first segment of the meeting was devoted to presenting financial data, division by division, followed by small-group meetings to digest and analyze the situation and formulate proposals for reversing the business decline. What made the situation complicated was that some of the divisions, those operating in mature markets, were losing money and needed major restructuring, while other divisions were growing and making good contributions to overall profit levels.

The division managers from the problem divisions were embarrassed, apologetic, and overconfident that they could reverse the situation, while others said privately that the losing divisions could not possibly accomplish their goals, were not really committed to change, and would make only cosmetic alterations. The division managers from the profitable divisions bragged, felt complacent, and wondered when top management would do something about the "losers" who were dragging others down with them. But many people from the losing divisions said privately that even the profitable divisions—although they might look good relative to others *inside* the company—were not performing as well as they should if compared to *outside* competitors in their own industrial market segment.

During the divisional reviews and presentations, another important cultural assumption surfaced. The company had been diversifying for a number of years and was attempting to get into consumer goods via a line of toiletries and cleaning products. I was sitting next to a chemist, a member of the executive committee, when some of the consumer-oriented advertisements were shown on the screen as part of the division review. He was clearly upset by the "low" level of the message and whispered to me in an agitated tone, "Those things aren't even *products;* they don't do anything." The assumption seemed to be that a "product" had to be something useful, such as a cure for disease or a successful pesticide that reduces starvation. Managers took pride in the important and useful products that were a current source of success. Selling something only because it made money did not fit into some of their cultural assumptions about the nature of their business; and, as we will see, the fate of the consumer products division is still very much a matter of internal debate.

The *country managers*, representing subsidiary companies in the major countries of the world, who were measured on their total cross-divisional performance, acknowledged the cross-divisional issues but were actually more

* SOURCE: Abstracted from Edgar H. Schein and edited by Roy McLennan from *Organizational Culture and Leadership: A Dynamic View,* (San Francisco: Jossey-Bass, 1985), pp. 244–269. Reprinted with permission.

upset because the headquarters organization—representing such functions as research and development, finance and control, personnel, and manufacturing—had become overgrown both in corporate headquarters and in the divisional headquarters. These managers insisted that the headquarters functional staffs should be reduced, because they were an unnecessary overhead and, in many cases, an active interference in running the businesses in the countries. A high degree of centralization of research and development, manufacturing, and financial control had made sense when the company was young and small; but as it expanded and became a worldwide multinational, the small regional sales offices had gradually become large autonomous companies that managed all the functions. Country heads needed their own staffs; but these staffs then came into conflict with the corporate staffs and the division staffs, who felt that they could communicate directly with their division people in each country.

Because of the hierarchical nature of the organization, the headquarters groups asked for enormous amounts of information from the regions and frequently visited the regions. If they had worldwide responsibility for something, their way of staying in control was to be fully informed about everything at all times. Because of the lack of lateral communication, the functional staffs did not realize that their various inquiries and visits often paralyzed local operations because of the amount of time it took to answer questions, entertain visitors, get permission to act, and so on.

As the cost structure of the company came under increasing scrutiny, the country organizations were asked to reduce costs, while the headquarters organizations remained complacent, fat, and happy. The question that most worried the country managers was whether top management considered the crisis serious enough to warrant reductions in the headquarters functional staffs. If not, it must mean that this was only a fire-fighting drill, not a real crisis.

By the end of the first day of the second annual meeting, the financial data had been presented and groups had met to consider what should be done, but the feedback from the groups indicated neither a complete understanding nor a real acceptance of the problem. The planning committee met to consider what to do and decided that the other consultant could help the group recognize the seriousness of the problem if he "interrogated" the group members in the style of a Harvard case discussion and led them to the inevitable conclusion that a crisis really existed. He did this very effectively on the second day of the meeting in a two-hour session that proved conclusively to all present that the group could not sustain any profitability in the long run unless major changes were made. The result was a real sense of panic and depression. For the first time, the message had really been accepted collectively, laying the stage for the introduction of the Redirection Project.

Why did this work? I had the sense that, in a culture where senior managers function symbolically as parent figures, it is difficult for the parents to tell the children that the family may fail if they don't shape up. The children find it too easy to blame each other and the parents and to collectively avoid feeling responsible. There was too much of a tradition that senior managers (the parents) will take care of things as they always have. The anxiety of facing up to the "family problem" was too overwhelming, so a great deal of denial had been operating. The outside consultant could, in this case, take the same information but present it as a problem that the family as a whole owned and had to confront and handle as a total unit. He could be much more direct and confrontive than insiders could be with each other, and, at the same time, he could remind the total group that everyone was in this together—the executive committee as the symbolic parents along with all the children. This recognition did not reduce the resultant panic; however, it forced it out into the open, since denial was no longer possible. The group had been genuinely unfrozen.

The next problem, then, was how to deal with the panic and discouragement that were now present in the group. How could we provide some psychological safety that would permit the group to redefine the situation, to begin to feel capable of doing something constructive? The other consultant and I took a long walk to think this out and came up with the idea that now would be a good time to give some lectures on the nature of resistance to change and how to overcome it. He had been confrontive, so I should now come on as supportive and facilitative.

I hurriedly pulled together notes, made transparencies, and on the following morning gave lectures on (1) why healthy organizations need to be able to change; (2) why individuals and groups resist change; (3) how to analyze forces toward and forces resisting change; and (4) how to develop valid change targets for the coming year, in the context of the Redirection Project, with timetables, measurements of outcomes, and accountabilities. I emphasized a point that is central to change projects: that the period of change has itself to be defined as a stage to be managed, with transition managers specifically assigned (Beckhard and Harris, 1977).

These lectures had the desired effect of giving the group members a way of thinking positively, so that when they were sent back into small groups to develop priority issues for making the Redirection Project a success, they were able to go off to these meetings with a sense of realism and optimism. The general results of the small-group meetings were quite clear. They saw the need for the unprofitable divisions to shrink and restructure themselves and the need for profitable divisions to become more effective relative to the competition, but they stated clearly that neither of these could happen if the headquarters organization did not confront the excess people in the headquarters and the style of management that was emanating from the functional groups. The ideas were not new, but they were now shared and with some conviction.

Creating a Structure for the Redirection Project: The Use of Groups. The Multi managers were skillful at working in groups. Richards and the executive committee used this skill by creating a project team to organize the Redirection Project into thirty or so separate manageable tasks; they also created steering committees for each of these tasks and assigned one of the members of the executive committee to be accountable for the performance of that task group. Some of the tasks were to shrink and restructure the less profitable divisions, something that would be inherently difficult for the executive committee member who had previously been responsible for that division to confront. Too many prior loyalties and commitments would get in the way of seeing clearly what had to be done and then ensuring that it was done. To avoid putting executive committee members into such conflicts, the group reshuffled formal responsibilities and ensured that each redirection task would fall to someone who could be objective about it. This structural change in job responsibilities was a major innovation invented by the project team itself, but everyone agreed that it was a major facilitator of later project success.

The skillful use of groups both at the annual meeting and in the design of the projects struck me as paradoxical. How could a company that was so hierarchical and so concerned about individual turf be so effective in inventing groups and in operating within a group context? I do not know the facts historically, but, because the top management of the company is itself a group, and because as scientists most of the members of the company recognize the value of input from others, they not only respect group effort but have acquired skills in managing group meetings. This point was reinforced recently in a meeting where I was advising two young managers of executive training programs on the design of a one-week middle-management course. I suggested the use of one of the group survival exercises that illustrates clearly how groups can resolve some objective problems better than individuals. I was told that they used to do the exercise but that participants routinely asked why their time was being wasted, since they were already committed to the use of groups and therefore felt that the training should go straight to the skill level, where much needed to be done.

The overall steering committee for the Redirection Project created the individual component projects, the teams that would run them, the managers who would be accountable, the timetables, and the broad targets; they also invented some subtle devices to ensure action. For example, each project group was assigned one or two outside "challengers," managers not involved in the project, who were to examine critically what the group had done and was proposing to do. This provided an opportunity to test diagnoses and remedies before presenting them to top management. Each team was also given the services of an internal organizational consultant to help with the organization of the team itself, and several of the teams asked for and obtained my help on how to structure their work.

All this was communicated clearly by top management in written form, through meetings, and through trips to various parts of the company. Not only the process but the necessity for it and top management's commitment to it were highlighted in the communications. Great emphasis was given to the particular project that would reexamine the headquarters structure, functioning, and head counts and attempt to reduce the overhead by at least one third.

One might speculate that group work had such importance in Multi because it was virtually the only form of lateral communication available in the company. The sensitivities that might be operating if managers from one division offered or asked for help from another division could be overcome, with faces saved, if a task force consisting of members of both divisions adopted a process of taking turns reporting to each other on the progress of effective and ineffective interventions. The listener could then learn and get new ideas without either identifying himself as a problem or having others identify him as a target of their input. Group meetings thus preserved "face" all the way around.

It was also recognized that groups helped to build commitment to projects even though the implementation system was essentially hierarchical. If groups had discussed the issue, the hierarchy worked more smoothly—as in the Japanese system, where consensus is sought before a decision is announced. In various ways the Redirection Project was using the cultural strengths of the company and was redefining its formal procedures in order to deal with the business problem without changing the culture overtly.

Second Year: Consolidation of the Redirection Project. During my several visits following the second annual meeting, I worked on two important areas. First, I made myself available to any project group or group members who wished to discuss any aspect of how to proceed, the appointment to be made at their initiative. If I learned something that would help other projects, I would summarize it and write it up for circulation to others. I was consulted by several managers on how best to think about early retirement, how to ease people out in their home community, how to get managers to think about innovative restructuring, and so on. I soon discovered that my memos pulling good ideas together died on the desks of the people to whom I gave those memos. That was my first encounter with the cultural norm that at Multi information does not circulate laterally.

I also spent a good deal of time with the executive committee member who was responsible for this project, helping him keep his role and his leadership behavior in his project group clear and effective. Several project managers wanted help in thinking through their roles as project chairmen and solicited my reactions to proposals prior to running them by the challengers.

Second, I became more familiar with the management development inventory and planning system and began a series of meetings with the manager of this function by way of seeing how it could be improved. Bringing in and developing better and more innovative managers was seen as a high-priority longer-range implication of the Redirection Project. It was also known that the present manager of the function would retire within a year and his successor might need a consultant who had learned something about the company to help him think out his program.

Pan Pacific*

Roy McLennan

In your capacity as an experienced change agent you have carried out part of a planned intervention in a branch office of the Pan Pacific Company. You had been invited by Pan Pacific's national office to help the company develop a model branch, in terms of the use, development and satisfaction of the people working in it, teamwork and branch performance.

The Yorktown branch had been selected as the site for the intervention. After discussions with national office managers, the Yorktown manager, Don Spence, and branch employees, it had been agreed that you would begin the intervention with an interview-feedback-action planning workshop cycle involving all the branch's 15 members, as the first major attempt to surface and work on client data. As part of the intervention process it had been agreed, following your suggestion, that after the workshop the initiative in taking action would lie in the hands of the branch. The expectation held by you and national office managers was that various requests would come from the branch, as the issues surfaced in the initial intervention cycle were worked on, and the branch pursued action to improve satisfaction, teamwork and performance.

The idea of the intervention had been greeted with interest by Don Spence and his people, and their enthusiasm mounted as it proceeded and climaxed at the feedback/action planning workshop. You were impressed by the energy displayed.

It is now two months since you took part in the workshop, and the response to your call to the national office is that the Yorktown branch is not taking any substantial initiatives on any matters.

What action would you now take, if any? Would you look further into the matter? How? Would you attempt to continue the intervention in the Pan Pacific Company? Why? How?

* SOURCE: Roy McLennan, © 1981.

Structuring Activities
in Interventions*

Wendell L. French
and Cecil H. Bell, Jr.

OD interventions are structured activities of selected target groups. Some "secrets" of OD are contained in this statement, because there are "better" ways and "worse" ways to structure activities for learning and change to take place. Organization development practitioners know how to structure activities in the "better" ways through attending to the following points:

1. Structure the activity so that the relevant people are there. The relevant people are those affected by the problem or the opportunity. For example, if the goal is improved team effectiveness, have the whole team engage in the activities. If the goal is improved relations between two separate work groups, have both work groups present. If the goal is to build some linkages with some special group, say, the industrial relations people, have them there and have the linking people from the home group there. This preplanning of the group composition is a necessary feature of properly structuring the activity.

2. Structure the activity so that it is (a) problem oriented or opportunity oriented and (b) oriented to the problems and opportunities generated by the clients themselves. Solving problems and capitalizing on opportunities are involving, interesting, and enjoyable tasks for most people, whether it is due to a desire for competence or mastery (as suggested by White),[1] or a desire to achieve (as suggested by McClelland),[2] or whatever. This is especially true when the issues to be worked on have been defined by the client. There is built-in support and involvement, and there is a real payoff when clients are solving issues that they have stated have highest priority.

3. Structure the activity so that the goal is clear and the way to reach the goal is clear. Few things demotivate an individual as much as not knowing what he or she is working toward and not knowing how what the individual is doing contributes to goal attainment. Both these points are part of structuring the activity properly. (Parenthetically, the goals will be important goals for the individuals if point 2 is followed.)

4. Structure the activity so that there is a high probability of successful goal attainment. Implicit in this point is the warning that expectations of practitioners

* SOURCE: Wendell L. French and Cecil H. Bell, Jr., *Organization Development* (Englewood Cliffs, N.J.: Prentice-Hall, 1984), pp. 122–124. Reprinted by permission.

[1] R. W. WHITE, "Motivation Reconsidered: The Concept of Competence," *Psychological Review*, 66 (1959), pp. 297–334.
[2] D. C. McCLELLAND, J. W. ATKINSON, R. A. CLARK, and E. L. LOWELL, *The Achievement Motive* (New York: Appleton-Century-Crofts, 1953).

and clients should be realistic. But more than that, manageable, attainable objectives once achieved produce feelings of success, competence, and potency for the people involved. This, in turn, raises aspiration levels and feelings of self- and group-worth. The task can still be hard, complicated, taxing—but it should be attainable. And if there is failure to accomplish the goal, the reasons for this should be examined so they can be avoided in the future.

5. Structure the activity so that it contains both experience-based learning and conceptual/cognitive/theoretical–based learning. New learnings gained through experience are made a permanent part of the individual's repertoire when they are augmented (and "cemented") through conceptual material that puts the experience into a broader framework of theory and behavior. Relating the experience to conceptual models, theories, and other experiences and beliefs helps the learning to become integrated for the individual.

6. Structure the climate of the activity so that individuals are "freed up" rather than anxious or defensive. Setting the climate of interventions so that people expect "to learn together" and "to look at practices in an experimenting way so that we can select better procedures" is what we mean by climate setting.

7. Structure the activity so that the participants learn both how to solve a particular problem and "learn how to learn" at the same time. This may mean scheduling in time for reflecting on the activity and teasing out learnings that occurred; it may mean devoting as much as half the activity to one focus and half to the other.

8. Structure the activity so that individuals can learn about both *task* and *process*. The task is what the group is working on, that is, the stated agenda items. The term *process*, as used here, refers to *how* the group is working and *what else is going on* as the task is being worked on. This includes the group's processes and dynamics, individual styles of interacting and behaving, and so on. Learning to be skillful in working in both of these areas is a powerful tool. Activities structured to focus on both aspects result in learnings on both aspects.

9. Structure the activity so that individuals are engaged as whole persons, not segmented persons. This means that role demands, thoughts, beliefs, feelings, and strivings should all be called into play, not just one or two of these. Integrating disparate parts of individuals in an organizational world where differentiation in terms of roles, feelings, and thoughts is common probably enhances the individual's ability to cope and grow.

These features are integral characteristics of OD interventions and also of the practitioner's practice theory of organization development. Little attention is given to characteristics of structuring activities in the literature, but knowledge of them helps to take some of the mystery out of interventions and may also be helpful to people who are just beginning to practice OD.

Models of Consulting*

Roy McLennan

One issue about ordering the confusion in client transference and other data concerns the fine line which should allegedly be trod by the consultant between the alternative perils of what Miller and Lawrence deprecatingly call the 'installation' model of consultancy, where some existing organizational model or solution is simply installed in the client organization, and *de novo* treatment of each successive organizational problem as if it were brand new, for which there are no precedents or applicable frames of reference. If the consultant feels certain and clear about what the client is doing to him and why, and what he should do about it, especially early in an intervention, then this implies several things about his behavior as consultant. Since the social sciences are 'still relatively medieval' (Miller and Gwynne, 1972:p. 6) in terms of frameworks, models and resolutions, it shows a lack of sensitivity to the data. It also means he is carting along his preconceptions, previous solutions to apparently similar organizational problems, products of previous interventions, and cannot be really listening to the client. It probably implies, in addition, that the consultant is using his frame of reference and his role defensively, as a means of keeping himself as a person out of the relationship. The consultant who wields a theory 'can feel less involved, more detached, safer and superior on his higher plane' (Miller and Gwynne, 1972:p. 5). The desirable framework, on the other hand, is 'a set of ideas for discovering what may be realities' (Lawrence, 1980:p. 15). The consultant should bear in mind L. C. Knight's dictum: 'There is always the risk of anticipating and imposing when it is our business to discover' (quoted in Lawrence, 1980:p. 15). The operational maxim arising from these considerations are summed up in the aphorism, 'If you don't have a theory of confusion it means you're not being sensitive to the data' (Abraham).

REFERENCES

LAWRENCE, W. G. 'A Psycho-analytic Perspective for Understanding Organizational Life', in R. N. Ottaway (ed.). *OD Practices in Europe*. New York: Wiley, 1980. (typed manuscript).

MILLER, E. J., and GWYNNE, G. V. *A Life Apart*. London: Tavistock, 1972.

* SOURCE: Excerpt from "Feelings and Emotions in Action Research: A Tavistock Approach," paper delivered at the Management Educators' Conference, Monash University, Australia, August 1980.

Argyris's Model I and Model II*

Edgar H. Schein

Argyris notes that most managers and leaders whom he has observed operate from two different "theories": (a) an *espoused* theory, consisting of the goals, assumptions, and values that the person *says* guide his or her behavior; and (b) a *theory-in-use*, consisting of the implicit assumptions that actually guide overt behavior (Argyris & Schon, 1974; Argyris, 1976). Espoused theories vary widely from autocratic to participative, but when leaders are actually observed in groups, it turns out that their theories-in-use almost uniformly reflect what Argyris has called Model I. This model of behavior is built on four basic assumptions, what he terms "governing variables": (1) that one must achieve one's own goals as one sees them; (2) that one must win rather than lose; (3) that one must minimize eliciting negative feelings in relationships; and (4) that one must be rational and minimize any emotionality.

These governing variables, Argyris claims, lead to behavior which is controlling of others, which maximizes one's own safety, and which leads to minimal confrontation of any emotionally charged issues. If one is confronted by others, it leads to defensiveness. The net result is what he calls a "self-sealing" process, or single-loop learning in which one sets up the situation to confirm one's own premises, but never learns whether or not those premises themselves are valid. If one starts with the assumption that confronting people is bad because it will elicit defensive emotional behavior, one will most likely confirm this expectation and learn how to be less confrontive, rather than learning how to deal with one's own and others' defensiveness. In the end, the basic assumptions upon which the model is based will never be tested publicly, thus preventing the leader from learning potentially more effective behavior.

Argyris and Schon have studied leaders' "espoused" and "in use" theories through analysis of tape-recorded scenarios in which both overt verbal behavior and the private thoughts which accompany the overt behavior are elicited and categorized. The striking thing in these protocols is the degree to which the overt behavior is not only nonconfrontive but also in direct contrast to the person's inner feelings. Since subordinates can often sense the incongruity but are playing by the same rules, real feelings are rarely confronted, forcing both leaders and subordinates to engage in guessing at the others' feelings and then manipulating the situation to accomplish their intentions.

It is this circular process which accounts for the frequent reports that leaders can go to training programs and learn new methods such as how to be more participative, yet find that their subordinates do not respond to their new approaches. The fact is that the leader may have changed only his or her

* SOURCE: Edgar H. Schein, *Organizational Psychology*, 3rd ed., pp. 127–129, 1980. Reprinted by permission of Prentice-Hall, Inc., Englewood Cliffs, N.J.

espoused theory, not the actual, contextual behavior. If this finding is generally correct, and if Model I behavior is on the autocratic end of the leadership behavior scale, Argyris is, in effect, saying that leaders are culturally *unable* to behave participatively in any real sense of this term, even if they believe in and espouse participation as their preferred style. Participation requires a degree of openness to one's own and others' feelings, and it is precisely such openness which is difficult for leaders in organizational contexts to achieve.

Argyris proposes that organizations would be better off if leaders could learn how to behave according to Model II, which is governed by a different set of premises: (1) that action should be based on valid information; (2) that action should be based on free and informed choice; and (3) that action should be based on internal commitment to the choice and constant monitoring of efforts to implement one's choices. Here, the theory builds on the basic "learning how to learn" assumptions which underlie such group dynamics training as is exemplified in encounter groups, sensitivity training groups, and the like (Bradford, Gibb, & Benne, 1964; Schein & Bennis, 1965).

The training program Argyris proposes to help people reach Model II behavior is a direct extension of the kinds of mutual exploration and feedback common to sensitivity training groups. Trainees (administrators, company presidents, managers, and so on) must first discuss artificial scenarios from the point of view of what they would do and what their inner feelings are in order to learn how their own Model I assumptions enter into their thinking. Such training occurs in groups and is aided by professional staff members who help trainees become aware of the pervasiveness of Model I assumptions. Trainees are then invited to invent new solutions to the scenarios and to become consultants to each other on their progress in applying the collaborative, confrontive, open assumptions of Model II.

During this gradual learning process of several days, trainees begin to consider how best to experiment with the new assumptions in their real settings. The anticipation of negative responses from subordinates often rekindles the anxieties common to Model I thinking, namely, that being more confrontive will just produce more defensiveness. It is then necessary to combat this potential setback by working through these anxieties and developing a more experimental attitude toward one's own behavior. Group support is crucial at this stage because group members at least share the new set of assumptions and have learned how to be more open and confrontive with each other. Because this method permits leaders to get at their basic assumptions and to change them if needed, Argyris and Schon have termed it "double-loop learning."

REFERENCES

ARGYRIS, CHRIS, Leadership, Learning, and Changing the Status Quo. *Organizational Dynamics*, Winter 1976 29–43.

ARGYRIS, CHRIS & DONALD SCHON, *Theory in Practice: Increasing Professional Effectiveness.* San Francisco: Jossey-Bass, 1974.

BRADFORD, LEYLAND P., J. R. GIBB & KENNETH D. BENNE, (Eds) *T-Group Theory and Laboratory Method.* New York: Wiley, 1964.

SCHEIN EDGAR H., and WARREN G. BENNIS, *Personal and Organizational Change Through Group Methods.* New York: Wiley, 1965.

The Consultant Role*

A. K. Rice

THE CONSULTANT-CLIENT RELATIONSHIP

The work reported in Parts II and III was carried out within a consultant-client relationship. My job was to help my clients, so far as I was able, to solve the problems they encountered in running the various enterprises for which they were responsible. My terms of reference have been broad; starting-points have been technological, economic, sociological, political, and psychological. In practice this has meant discussion of whatever problems chief executives, managers, or workers have found most urgent and collaboration with them in trying to find some kind of solution. I was not, and am not, the only consultant employed in the enterprises I describe, and with those whose fields have impinged on, or overlapped, my own I have been able to cooperate.

The elaboration of theories about organization and the collection of data to support hypotheses have usually had the severely practical objective of attempting to clarify the difficulties that my clients and I were meeting. The book is also based on work of a similar kind with other Institute clients and on research work carried out by my colleagues and myself in the Tavistock Institute.

Sofer (1961) has discussed the therapeutic and research components in work of this kind and has outlined some regularities and principles in the field of what he has called 'social consultancy'. He has added new dimensions to, and formalized, earlier attempts to describe an approach to problem solving and data collection. He makes a sharp distinction between the collection of data and their presentation to those from whom they have been collected in such a way that they can become aware of relations between variables that have not previously been explicit. He discusses in detail the effects of the 'observer' on the field he is studying and the way in which the consultant can use these effects to enrich his perceptions of what is happening. He argues the advantages and the disadvantages of the approach. On the one hand, the data are biased and may be unique, and it is virtually impossible to obtain concrete measures for comparison or control; on the other, without identification and sympathy between the observer and those with whom he collaborates, access to data about close personal relationships is invariably limited and usually denied.

He describes the conflicts that can and do arise in the complex constellation of relationships between the client organization, the consultant, and the groups and the individuals with whom he works. In such conflicts he says: 'Whatever arrangements are made it is necessary to give absolute priority

* SOURCE: A. K. Rice, *The Enterprise and Its Environment* (London: Tavistock Publications, 1963), pp. 4–9. Reprinted by permission.

to the needs of the organization, to serve its overall interests and contribute to its primary task.' Wilson has made a similar point about research in the same field: 'Within the approach described, however, any action for research purposes alone, without regard for the needs of the client, would be regarded as a breach of the professional role of the research worker.' Sofer concludes with a description of the similarities and differences in the course run by each of three projects he carried out with widely differing kinds of enterprise—an industrial company, a technical college, and a research laboratory attached to a hospital.

It is not my purpose in this book to argue for a particular approach or to suggest that the role I took was the only one available. Most of my colleagues would accept that our own feelings of pleasure and pain, anxiety and relief, excitement and sobriety, are frequently the only measures we have available to assess what is real and what unreal in a difficult situation. The use we make of our feelings may differ. Sofer states that he avoided remarks about his clients' feelings towards him and his work 'which would have included elements not fully conscious to respondents or displaced from other real and fantasy relationships'. By contrast it will be seen that I frequently did make such comments. I used my experience of my clients' attitudes towards me and my feelings about them when I thought that, by so doing, I could illuminate the problems we were discussing.

If the members of an organization ask me to discuss some problem with them I assume that they have done so because they have not been able to find a satisfactory solution by themselves. Implicit in my being called in, therefore, is their acceptance, consciously or unconsciously, of failure—a failure to which they are likely to be very sensitive if the problem involves human relationships. Their inability to solve it may be due to its intrinsic difficulty. It may also be due, in part, to other problems, the causes of which are hidden and of which the overt problem is only a symptom. What appears on the surface as a simple organizational problem, for example, may often be found to have underlying it deep-seated and largely unrecognized emotional con-flicts—conflicts which, if brought into the open, would cause great distress and even destruction. A solution to the overt problem may therefore provide no relief; indeed it may exacerbate the underlying difficulties by removing a symptom, attention to which has provided a defence against the anxiety of having to face the real causes. In the extreme, a client may well wish to keep the overt problem alive and unsolved as a means of containing the anxiety inherent in its solution. Unconsciously, the client may demand that his consultant go into collusion with him not to find a solution. If the consultant accepts collusion he only confirms insolubility; if he tackles only the overt problem, he does nothing to help with the underlying difficulties.

So far as the client is aware, however faintly, of the symptomatic nature of the overt problem, so far will he want the underlying difficulties dealt with, and, at the same time, hope that such drastic action will be unnecessary. If by what he says or how he behaves the consultant shows that he is aware of the underlying difficulties and that he is prepared to tackle them, the client's feelings about him can be expected to range all the way from profound relief at his insight to hatred at his dashing of hopes. Usually the consultant will be regarded with a mixture of both—the relief will be mixed with a fear that the insight will not be backed by sufficient practical skill, and the hatred with a knowledge that the hopes were forlorn.

In responding to the contradictory demands made on him the consultant can behave in four ways: take up the overt problem only; deal with the overt problem but take account of what he believes to be the underlying difficulties without referring to them; take up both directly; or ignore the overt problem and take up directly only what is underlying. Which of these courses he takes will depend on his insight into the total situation; on his judgement of the real, as distinct from the expressed, needs of his client; on the relationship he has already built with his client; and on his belief in his ability to cope with whatever develops in the situation he helps to create.

If, as a consultant, I find I am becoming anxious, embarrassed, hurt, or pleased, I can ask myself why I am feeling what I am feeling and attempt to sort out what comes from within myself and what from the consultant-client relationship. So far as I am sure that some of the feeling arises in the situation and not as a result of idiosyncrasies of my own personality, I can use myself as a measuring instrument—however rough and ready—to give me information about the underlying difficulties and their strength. With this information I may then be able to take action. Even then my intervention may be inappropriate or ill-timed, or both. But I believe I have the right to intervene only when I feel sure, at the time, that what I say will be helpful. Sometimes, in the light of subsequent events, it is possible to look back and to realize that a particular intervention was helpful, or that it was not. More frequently it is impossible to relate cause and effect so precisely, and the uncertainty has to be accepted by both client and consultant.

In the accounts that follow, readers will make their own judgements about the appropriateness and timing, in terms of results, of my interventions. In practice I try to state how I am feeling and why I think I feel as I do. To some extent, such statements can provide a framework in which my clients, too, can release for discussion data that would otherwise be unavailable. If the data are essential for making adequate decisions, their release, however painful and embarrassing at the time, can be reassuring.

TERMS OF REFERENCE

When I first visited Ahmedabad I discussed my role and my terms of reference with Mr Gautam Sarabhai, Chairman of the Calico Mills, and then with his senior managers. It was agreed that I should be responsible directly and only to the chairman, and that, except in any selection procedures in which I might be involved, I would not report on any individuals working in the company. It was also agreed that any managers or workers could, if they wished, discuss with me, as individuals or as groups, their work, their roles, and their relationships, and that such discussions would be private: that is, nothing would be reported from them without full permission of the participants. I then spoke about the Institute, myself, and my proposed work to a meeting of all ranks of management, which was attended also by the president and leading members of the Textile Labour Association (the recognized trade union) and some members of the Ahmedabad Textile Industry Research Association. Thereafter it became standard practice to invite the members of the Textile Labour Association to inspect any work that involved reorganization on the mill floor.

Formally, my role has continued as it was first defined, but in my more recent work there has been the added complication that I have been working with Dr Vikram Sarabhai, Mr Gautam Sarabhai's brother, and in other companies than the Calico Mills. In the Calico Mills I have continued to report, as before, to Mr Gautam Sarabhai. In other companies I have reported to Dr Vikram Sarabhai.

Mr Gautam and Dr Vikram Sarabhai are both members of the Boards of directors of all the companies with which I worked, and many of their managers have previously reported to each of them at different times. I frequently had considerable trouble in trying to sort out whom I was advising and about what, particularly when the problems under discussion were concerned with relationships between chief executives and their subordinates. In such situations my own role was always the subject of early comment.

In practice, discussions about organization and reorganization, roles, and tasks have frequently implied comments on individuals or groups. So far as I have been able, I have tried to take up and to clarify the implications with those concerned. But I have frequently failed, either because I could not see how to take them up without disclosing information communicated privately or because I missed the implications myself. Perhaps this matters less now when I have worked with the majority of senior managers for many years; and when even those with whom I have not previously worked directly have had considerable indirect experience of my role and the way I behave in it. I have frequently felt that I was balanced precariously between two temptations: to behave executively and to take on jobs that would have been inappropriate in my role as consultant; or to accept the authority to give advice but none of the responsibility for the consequences of putting it into practice. I have often not been quite sure whose problems I was trying to solve—my clients' or my own—but by now they are not always easy to differentiate.

Some reviewers of my earlier book . . . about the Calico Mills regretted that I had not described my working methods in more detail; others generously inferred that my interviews and discussions must have been conducted with skill—an inference for which I was grateful, but which, in retrospect, I frequently found it difficult to believe.

In this account of the work with the Calico Mills and other Sarabhai concerns I have tried to give a fuller record of discussions and interviews than

I did previously, and, in the appendices, I have given examples of working notes that were written as a result of early discussions and became the basis for subsequent reorganization. I hope that the records will give some idea of the information on which I worked and of the effect of my own interventions in the discussions. Because often the only information I had was how I was feeling, I have had to describe many events in personal terms. One effect is sometimes to make it appear that changes occurred only when I was present, and that what happened when I was not there was unimportant. This I do not believe for one moment, and I hope the results will give sufficient sense of continuity. The working notes are presented as my clients received them, with all their half-formed hypotheses and their imperfections of style and grammar. They were never intended for more than strictly limited circulation to those who had participated in earlier discussions and for whom, therefore, the brevities and allusions had some meaning.

If a consultant does not care enough about his clients, they will probably not care enough about him to allow him access to the data he needs; if he cares and identifies himself with them, then his observations will, of necessity, be prejudiced and less detached than is desirable for scientific assessment. In the work reported here my own position was worse. I was in India, a long way from my home base and from the colleagues with whom I could discuss my own problems and difficulties. My clients and their families became my close friends. I have to accept that this undoubtedly prejudiced my observations even more than is usual in this kind of work. It is also possible that it permitted me to learn more than I would otherwise have learnt.

REFERENCES

SOFER, C. *The Organization from Within.* London: Tavistock, 1961.

WILSON, A. T. M. Some implications of Medical Practice and Social Case-work for Action Research. *Journal of Social Issues* 3. 2, 1947.

It Takes a Group to Understand a Group*

Roy McLennan†

In practice the Tavistock consultant works with another Institute consultant in a pair or in a group of some sort, although 'not necessarily within the frame of a particular project' (Miller, personal letter). Only very rarely, in exceptional circumstances, does he work on his own. Menzies Lyth summed up the general attitude of Institute action researchers to solo consultancy: 'It's Hell's own job working alone!' 'The important support', says Miller, 'is in the solo consultant having someone else with whom he can occasionally check out his experiences and hypotheses' (Miller, personal letter). The pairs or groups formed for particular interventions include consultants internal to the client organization, as well as Tavistock action researchers (Bryant, Dartington, Miller). Working with one or more other action researchers provides many obvious and less obvious advantages to the individual consultant. It allows him to 'recover' himself, to babble harmlessly after a heavy day in the field, providing a cathartic function. Sofer says, 'On any of his projects he [the consultant] will go through phases in which his perceptions will be blocked by his own feelings.' For this and other reasons action researchers 'find it highly advisable to work from a technical base consisting of colleagues who have shared complementary skills, culture, philosophy, objectives, and experience' (Sofer, 1961:p. 140–141). The consultancy group is a sort of refuge the individual researcher returns to, 'where I can trust my colleagues to tell me when they think I'm pissing about' (Dartington). Consultants get together and test each other's observations, deductions, inferences, hypotheses and interpretations. They review what is happening between themselves as one way of understanding what is happening in the client organization. The client state might, for example, divide the researchers into various split positions, or push them together as a single lump. Understanding the character of the emerging consultant-client relationship is very much aided and increased through the complementary and even competing observations of a colleague, as well as those of the individual researcher himself (Sofer, 1961:p. 133). Consultants can experience radical swings in one another's moods and emotions, especially in stressful and difficult interventions: they can find themselves subjected to 'pronounced oscillation of feeling.' In working

---

* SOURCE: Excerpt from "Feelings and Emotions in Action Research: A Tavistock Approach," paper delivered at the Management Educators' Conference, Monash University, Australia, August 1980.

†The title of this paper is a saying attributed to W. R. Bion.

with the Cheshire homes, for example, Miller and Gwynne found that 'One day we would be overwhelmed with sympathy and pity for the plight of the disabled, doubly persecuted by their physical handicaps and by the destructiveness of the environment in which they lived. Next day we would see the staff as victims of the insistent, selfish demands of cripples who ill deserved the money and care that were being so generously lavished upon them. Since we worked as a pair, our opposite oscillations sometimes damped one another. But if the oscillations coincided, we relied heavily on the intervention of an uninvolved colleague to restore some semblance of balance' (Miller and Gwynne, 1972:p. 7–8). In this way Rice acted as backup to them. As they also observed: 'The opportunity of working on other assignments—we are usually . . . engaged on more than one at a time—also helps to maintain a steadier perspective' (Miller and Gwynne, 1972:p. 7).

Some pairs and groups share the field work in an intervention, and tend to be referred to as 'primary' or 'engaged' consultants. Others consist of one or more field workers, who are usually of more junior status, together with a more senior, experienced colleague who does little or no field work. The latter tends to be referred to as a 'secondary' or 'detached' consultant (Miller, Stringer). The secondary or detached interventionist, the 'consultant's consultant', adopts a role much like an analyst, Stringer suggests: 'A consultancy between the engaged consultant and the detached consultant is very close to the psychoanalytic relationship', in which the engaged says, in effect, 'Let's have our one hour session to discuss how I've handled life this week' (Stringer). Primaries use secondaries for tactical purposes within the strategy of an intervention. The primary brings in his 'powerful secondary to leapfrog the issue higher in the client organization' (Stringer). The secondary is 'a big gun who can be brought in by the primary person, sometimes as a way of getting access to something or unlocking something' (Stringer). Top consultants can get the access to top managers denied to less exalted interventionists.

The different configurations, work, and tactics of primary and secondary interventionists lead to different feelings and emotions in and between them. Miller and Gwynne say, 'Discussions with colleagues not directly engaged in a project help us to identify our prejudices and . . . regain some detachment' (Miller and Gwynne, 1972:p. 7). The secondary, detached consultant has psychological distance from the field work (Dartington), often takes on a great load of depression from the primary consultant, and helps him work through it (Miller). 'Secondaries' help 'primaries' work through confusions, and help them understand and conceptualize the organizational situation they are working on. The secondary's input tends to be much more cognitive than affective. He offers a greater degree of objectivity to the primary. The advantage of the secondary is that he is 'less caught up in the immediate pressures and not caught up in the transference between the researcher and those he's working with in the field' (Dartington). The counterpart of greater objectivity is limitation of his insight into the client organization and the work of the primary (Dartington). But the secondary is not necessarily relatively free of emotional involvement in the intervention: his emotions can become mobilized as, for example, feeling indignant with the primary for colluding with members of the client system (Miller). And a different kind of transference goes on within the research team (Dartington). The secondary's input is often experienced by the primary as challenging and disruptive to his ideas (Dartington). Primary and secondary consultants in project groups often get into confused arguments which are, one said, 'hopefully creative confused arguments.'

A time process of a particular kind commonly takes place in an intervention. A kind of pressure, from a lot of ideas about the client problem, builds up among the consultants: 'At a certain point a sort of pressure builds up within the [consultancy] team, which causes them to say, 'We shall have to go away for a couple of days, lock ourselves away, and think this thing through'. There is a feeling, within the group, that somehow, 'something is about to be born. . . . In many such instances they seem to have been a highly creative couple of days' (Stringer).

Tavistock intervention teams make use of what are variously called 'working notes' (Rice, Menzies Lyth) and 'field notes' (Stringer), intended for circulation among the group working on the intervention, for the primary cognitive, task-centred purposes of clarifying, conceptualising, interpreting and formulating hypotheses about what is going on in the client system, and spreading the word around the team. The first working note was invented by Rice in 1953 as a consequence of his first two weeks as a consultant in India: 'I had been told and had seen so much that I had to reassure myself that I could make something coherent out of the overcrowding facts and impressions' (Rice, 1963:p. 282). 'I have found . . . that forcing myself to put vague ideas and mixed feelings into writing does help me clarify some of the problems I am trying to help to solve' (Rice, 1963:p. 281). The working note, he says, 'is a record of conversations between consultant and members of the client organization . . . a statement of what my clients and I think might be the next steps'; 'heavily loaded with our observations and interpretation,'; 'attempts to record where our thinking had reached at the time they were written' (Rice, 1963:p. 281). Working notes are often used by Tavistock teams as a navigational aid: 'When, as often happened, we found ourselves stuck, we could always go back to the notes to find how we had arrived at where we were, and what our starting point had been' (Rice, 1963:p. 281). They could also be used punitively, 'as evidence of the mistakes I had made years before' (Rice, 1963:p. 281). Working notes and field notes are used to put a set of ideas, a conceptual scheme into currency. Such notes, 'circulating among members of a team, are often very influential' (Stringer).

REFERENCES

MILLER, E. J., and GWYNNE, G. V. *A Life Apart.* London: Tavistock, 1972.

RICE, A. K. *The Enterprise and Its Environment.* London: Tavistock, 1963.

SOFER, C. *The Organization from Within.* London: Tavistock, 1961.

Working Notes*

A. K. Rice

A working note is not, as I use it, a report from consultant to client. It is a record of conversations between consultant and members of the client organization. Even if it contains recommendations they are a statement of what my clients and I think might be the next steps. They do not commit anyone to action. Sometimes they were produced as drafts and, after discussion and amendment, given a wider circulation. Sometimes they led to action. Sometimes they died where they were written. Occasionally they were flatteringly, but embarrassingly, used as evidence of the mistakes I had made years before. Because they were actually written by Dr Miller or myself, or by both of us, they are heavily loaded with our observations and interpretations; but in most of them Mr Gautam Sarabhai, his managers, and workers are our unacknowledged collaborators.

In effect, they are attempts to record where our thinking had reached at the time they were written. They were frequently difficult to write, seldom as concise as they should have been, and never polished. But I have found, and this may well be a personal idiosyncrasy, that forcing myself to put vague ideas and mixed feelings into writing does help me to clarify some of the problems I am trying to help to solve. My clients in Ahmedabad fortunately shared this view and were prepared to accept the inaccuracies of fact and mistakes of judgement that were inevitable. 'I should think we could get out a draft note' has usually been a sign that we have made, or think we have made, some progress. More importantly, it has been evidence that we were still working at solutions. When, as often happened, we found ourselves stuck, we could always go back to the notes to find how we had arrived at where we were, and what our starting-point had been. If, for the solution of problems not previously encountered, we had to be free to take our feet off the ground, it was reassuring to know where the ground was. Our fantasies could range more freely and sometimes we were able to discover connections between what we had previously regarded as unrelated events or independent variables.

The first note .... was written after I had been in India for only two weeks. I had been told and had seen so much that I had to reassure myself that I could make something coherent out of the overcrowding facts and impressions. I had got into the state when meeting more people and hearing more views did nothing to clarify but only confused .... because it was the

* SOURCE: A. K. Rice, *Enterprise and Its Environment* (London: Tavistock Publications, 1963), pp. 281–282.

433

first note written it set the pattern for future work. . . . There were many more on all kinds of topics from the layout of the Calico Mills to detailed examination of wage and salary structures. They also included a large number of progress reports on the experiments in the automatic and non-automatic loom sheds, accounts of which have been given in *Productivity and Social Organization.*[1]

---

[1] A. K. Rice, *Productivity and Social Organization: The Ahmedabad Experiment* (London: Tavistock, 1958).

The Action Research Process*

Roy McLennan

From the primary consultant's point of view the process of an intervention follows a cyclical pattern, starting with the feelings evoked in him by client contact, which give him clues or insights leading to cognitions, which are succeeded by working hypotheses, which are in turn fed back to the client. Feedback leads to client reactions to the hypotheses, further evocation of feelings in the consultant, fresh working hypotheses, and so on. This sketch of the action research or intervention process, however, like an old-fashioned swimsuit, conceals more than it reveals, and warrants closer inspection. Figure 1 outlines the cycles in the action research process. Lawrence asserts that the intervention cycle is first and foremost about feelings: 'I share the view of Miller and Gwynne . . . that the consultant is the research instrument because he is using his feelings. . . . Ideally, he becomes a 'container' for the feelings of the client system; a repository; a spittoon. He is available for the good and bad feelings that are held about the institution [organization] and the parties within it. . . . These are the feelings the people have about the consultant that are derived from their previous experiences of . . . influential figures in their lives. . . . The consultant also has feelings about the client. . . . Both transference and counter-transference feelings can be utilized fully to understand the . . . particular enterprise' (Lawrence, 1980:pp. 14, 19–20).

The action researcher's initial interactions with a new client bring to him an increasing sense of chaos, dissonance and ambiguity about the organizational problem he and members of the client system are confronted with (Stern and Abraham, Miller). It also brings to him anxiety, discomfort, strain and 'pain' of even severe dimensions: 'It can be disorienting and even terrifying' (Abraham), 'painful for both the consultant and the client' (Lawrence, 1980:p. 19). This chaotic, dissonant phase is conceived by Institute consultants as a major creative, innovative phase in an intervention, and hence most valuable for its successful outcome (Stern and Abraham, Miller). For this reason consultants do their best to tolerate the anxiety and pain it brings, resist premature structuring of the data, and use the opportunity to make free associations from them. In order to avoid the pain, there is always a 'temptation to take refuge in premature conceptualization' (Lawrence, 1980: p. 19). Miller deliberately tries to prolong the chaos for as long as he can, to maximize the creative opportunity. He refers to the work style he adopted when working in Mexico: 'At the end of the day I just brood, I don't think. I just let things come

* SOURCE: Excerpt from "Feelings and Emotions in Action Research: A Tavistock Approach," paper delivered at the Management Educators' Conference, Monash University, Australia, August 1980.

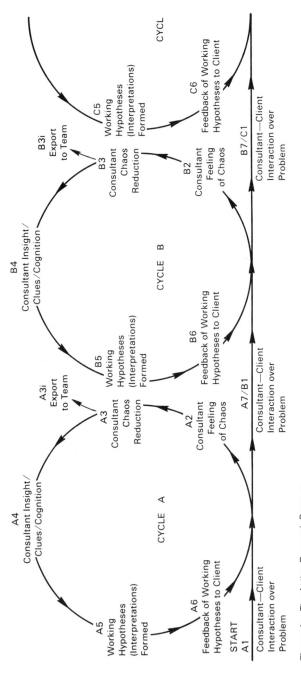

Figure 1: The Action Research Process

into my mind . . . something takes shape in my head, some hypothesis, some data. Once a formulation floats into my head then I'm able to begin to think as opposed to ruminating. I try to bring my cognitive apparatus to bear on it'[1] This ruminative, associative model conjures up a picture of a consultant with his tie off, feet up, staring at the ceiling as he sips his gin and tonic in relaxing surroundings. These images are in an important sense misleading, as they refer to the practices of a consultant who has perhaps a very high tolerance of ambiguity and who, in some circumstances, works much more on his own than others. Along with other Institute consultants Miller agrees, however, that 'It is inevitable that to some extent I must be redefining 'reality' in order to defend myself from more dissonance than I can cope with' (Miller, 1977:p. 31).

The Institute consultant resolves some of his chaos himself, and exports some to his fellow consultant or team, who in turn absorb some of it themselves, and so help him get back into some kind of cognitive balance in order to resume the intervention. At this point the researcher feels the merest flickering, glimmering sense of clarity or insight about the client data he is working on. He produces some dim cognition, conceptualization, model or frame of reference which, early in an intervention, is often of a primitive nature. The consultant uses his monitoring of what is going on in the consultant-client relationship to make working hypotheses. Consultant feedback to the client, in the form of these working hypotheses, 'the equivalent of psycho-analytic interpretations' (Miller, 1977:p. 35), is often presented in ordinary, everyday, non-technical, metaphoric, emotive, sometimes even poetic language, which encourages rich ambiguity in client and consultant perceptions, fruitful for creative leaps in innovative thinking about the client problem. Lawrence suggests that 'The working hypothesis is a sketch of the social situation' in the client organization, 'It is there to be elaborated on, or erased and replaced by another, either by the client or the consultant. . . . The use of evidence around working hypotheses allow both the client and the consultant to develop and refine their ideas as to what might be the . . . situation in the client system' (Lawrence, 1980:p. 19). Typically some hypotheses are found fruitful; some rejected by the client (but not by the consultant) because they challenge his defences (Menzies Lyth); others are abandoned because of more mundane inadequacies. Speaking in a medical idiom Jaques says, 'The timing and dosage of interpretations are a matter of clinical judgment, and present one of the greatest problems of treatment' (Jaques, 1947b:p. 65).

The practices of various consultants in using the idea of working hypotheses show individual differences. Rice offers a clear statement on his practices: 'I try to state how I am feeling and why I think I feel as I do. To some extent, such statements can provide a framework in which my clients, too, can release for discussion data that would otherwise be unavailable' (Rice, 1963:p. 7). Sofer provides a full account of his practices in offering working

---

[1] In writing this paper I tried to follow the Tavistock practice of resisting premature resolution of the dissonance I felt as I studied 'what must have been a chaotic mass of material we all poured out on you' (Menzies Lyth, personal letter).

hypotheses, and says he offered 'No interpretations of unconscious motivations or associations of ideas . . . in terms of internal psychological dynamics at the individual level. . . . (I use the term 'interpretation' here to mean the making conscious of what is unconscious in the mental functioning of an individual). . . I . . . tried to avoid making remarks to respondents at a level more personal than that of ordinary exchanges between colleagues. . . . In dealing with both individuals and groups I avoided making 'transference' interpretations, i.e. remarks about their feelings towards me and my work which would have included elements not fully conscious to respondents or displaced from other real and fantasy relationships. . . . However, I carefully observed behavior and attitudes towards me, so that I could make inferences from this that would be helpful to the work, and sometimes voiced these inferences at some later stage' (Sofer, 1961:p. 106–107). Rice says, 'The use we [Tavistock consultants] make of our feelings may differ' (Rice, 1963:p. 5), that in contrast to Sofer he frequently did make remarks about his clients' feelings towards him and his work which 'included elements not fully conscious to respondents or displaced from other real and fantasy relationships,' and that he did so without delay (Rice, 1963:p. 5). He also mentions his criteria: 'I used my experience of my clients' attitudes towards me and my feelings about them when I thought that, by so doing, I could illuminate the problems we were discussing' (Rice, 1963:p. 5). Sofer suggests that Rice went well beyond providing working hypotheses: 'Rice has been more inclined than most other . . . [Institute] consultants to make direct recommendations to his clients' (Sofer, 1972:p. 406).

After several or many cycles in the action research or intervention process the consultant develops what seems to him to be a satisfying conceptualization of the problem, and a relatively comprehensive model of it. Eventually, 'you get to a point where people no longer have anything surprising to tell you' (Abraham). This is not to suggest that the problem is necessarily solved, of course, but rather that such conceptualization is a necessary condition of problem resolution.

REFERENCES

JAQUES, E. 'Social Therapy: Technocracy or Collaboration?' *Journal of Social Issues*, 1947b, 3, No. 2.

LAWRENCE, W. G. 'A Psycho-analytic Perspective for Understanding Organizational Life', in R. N. Ottaway (ed.). *OD Practices in Europe*. New York: Wiley, 1980. (typed manuscript).

MILLER, E. J. 'Organizational Development and Industrial Democracy: A Current Case Study', in C. L. Cooper (ed.). *Organizational Development in the UK and the USA*. London: MacMillan, 1977.

RICE, A. K. *The Enterprise and Its Environment*. London: Tavistock, 1963.

SOFER, C. *The Organization from Within*. London: Tavistock, 1961.

SOFER, C. *Organizations in Theory and Practice*. London: Heinemann, 1972.

STERN, E. and ABRAHAM, F. *The Systems Group: Its Internal and External Relations*. London: Tavistock Institute of Human Relations, Document No. 2T 276, 1979.

The Dynamics of Dependency*

Roy McLennan

An intervention starts when a prospective client approaches Tavistock or a particular Institute action researcher for help with some consciously perceived problem, i.e. from the would-be client's conviction that some knowledge, skill or means exist which can cure, alleviate or even window dress that problem. The client depends on the consultant for something he does not have at the start of their relationship: client dependency on an outside agency for some or other service is the cause of the intervention. It follows that the feelings and emotions evoked by dependency in the client, on the one hand, and in the consultant, on the other, must inevitably be coped with as part and parcel of each and every intervention. For the duration of the intervention the dynamics of dependency are, therefore, in a profound sense at the heart of that intervention, and affect it for better or worse. The feelings and emotions members of the client system experience from their dependent organizational situation express, to a greater or lesser degree, 'a wish for return to the security of the womb or of early infancy' (Miller, 1979a:p. 181). The infantile emotions generated are 'closely akin to the 'basic assumption' behaviour in groups that was identified by Bion' (Miller, 1979a:p. 181). Client dependency 'serves a function in keeping at bay emotions of anger and aggression' in the client, while it can become transformed into 'fight' (Miller, 1979a:p. 182,186). At times organizations and institutions, like groups, 'Operate as if they are seeking dependency upon an omniscient and omnipotent leader, who will satisfy all the needs of every member.' (Miller, 1979a:p. 181). Miller suggests that dependency is 'intransigent' in some organizations, such as health care systems, where there often is a 'massive dependency culture' (Miller, 1979a:p. 183). And, 'although the culture of dependency and associated defensive structures are especially pervasive in 'people-processing institutions', such as hospitals, they are present in all organizations' (Miller, 1979a:p. 187).

Dependency is a set of dynamic variables, which alter in potency during the course of an intervention: 'When the consultant has shown the usefulness of his work a certain elation develops around him; he and his competence are idealized' (Sofer, 1961:p. 126). These feelings are intensified in the consultant by early indications that the consultant-client pairing is going to be successful in resolving the client's problem. Feelings of high competence, potency, even invincibility are evoked in him, 'illusions of omnipotence and omniscience' (Miller, 1979a:p. 183). Paradoxically, as indications of the usefulness of the

* SOURCE: Excerpt from "Feelings and Emotions in Action Research: A Tavistock Approach," paper delivered at the Management Educators' Conference, Monash University, Australia, August 1980.

work appear, the intervention simultaneously runs into deeper waters of intensified dependency. The action researcher becomes viewed by the client as the great man from outside who has 'all the knowledge which will solve the intractable internal problem experienced by the client' (Miller). There are many such client fantasies relating to the expert. The consultant is viewed as an 'exceptionally potent source of wisdom and enlightenment' (Dartington). Implicit religious models are applied to him: he may be viewed as the high priest of some new, wonderful and efficacious religion. Religious imagery is frequently used about him, such as 'saviour', 'crusader', and the like (Miller). The Miller-Gwynne book, *A Life Apart*, on their intervention in an institution for cripples, was itself regarded with veneration and even religious awe by members of one client system (Dartington). The consultant may also become viewed with excessive hope. In his work with the cripples Miller became perceived as 'not only going to solve the short term practical problems but even the problem of death itself' (Miller).

Figure 1 attempts to illustrate several aspects of client dependency on the consultant over the course of the intervention in graph form. In principle dependency does not follow a straight line curve, as in the PD (Pseudo Dependency) curve, but an inverted 'U' curve. This curve is illustrated by the D (Dependency) curve in Figure 1. The steepness of the curve at any point in the intervention, such as early, middle or late, remains conjectural at this time. It seems clear that different interventions will, however, exhibit different configurations, with peak dependency being skewed to either left or right, early or late in the intervention. And some interventions will no doubt exhibit curves higher up the Y (Dependency) scale than others. The position of the curve at

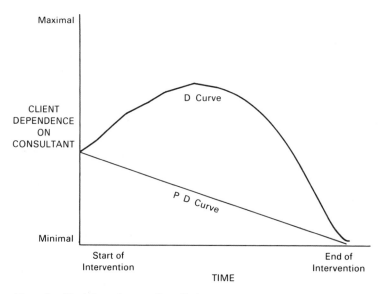

Figure 1:   Client Dependence on Consultant

the end of a successful intervention will be lower on the Y scale than at the start: successful interventions by definition do not result in increased client dependency. It seems in principle possible to thumbprint and rate the degree of effectiveness of a particular intervention in terms of the scales generated, and to compare various interventions, although to do so in any rigorous sense would of course require some way of expressing degrees of dependency in numbers.

Dependency can sometimes present itself in the form or guise of collusion between client and consultant. An intervention can run into difficulty, Wilson says, 'as the result of unrecognized collusion between 'patient' and 'doctor' in evading the real problem' (Wilson, 1947:p. 28). 'In the extreme,' Rice remarks, 'a client may well wish to keep the overt problem alive and unsolved as a means of containing the anxiety inherent in its solution. Unconsciously, the client may demand that his consultant go into collusion with him not to find a solution. If the consultant accepts collusion he only confirms insolubility' (Rice, 1963:p. 6). The consultant's work will, of course, 'have defeated its own purpose if he has acquired a vested interest in the incapacities of the organization and made himself indispensable' (Sofer, 1961:p. 130). Mutual dependency of consultant on client, and client on consultant might continue indefinitely. The distortions and dysfunctions of dependency are not restricted to consultant-client relations, but also affect consultant-consultant relationships. There is, for example, always the danger that younger, less experienced consultants will become unhealthily dependent on older, more experienced and prestigious consultants. Dartington remarks pungently that a seasoned, well-known consultant, 'can come out with any old crap, and we'll think its bloody marvellous.'

What the usual canons of action research professionalism suggest is that the consultant's task is to work through the client's dependency on him, in order to leave the client in a state of enhanced autonomy, to manage his own affairs better, at the end of the intervention. The objective of consultancy, says Miller, for example, is 'not simply the solution of a problem, whether presenting or underlying, but also an attempt to leave the client equipped with greater problem-solving competence' (Miller, 1976:p. 9). Bryant says, 'The client system is encouraged to build up its own problem-solving competence and eventually to take over from the consultant' (Bryant, 1979: p.5). To combat client dependency Sofer offered a douche of cold water: 'I often voiced my opinion after observing exaggerated dependence on me that the fate of the project depended far less on my personal contribution than on how much respondents were prepared to learn to do for themselves' (Sofer, 1961:p. 107–8). Miller declares that 'the consultant needs rigorous and continuing self-discipline to distinguish between the authority that rightly belongs to his actual competence and the fantasied powers that are imputed to him' (Miller, 1979a:p. 184–5). The researcher's colleagues can help him resist the heady tendencies.

Dependency is a *necessary* component of an intervention: it is not necessarily functional or dysfunctional to it. Whether or not the dependency which is part of a particular intervention is functional for it or not is to some extent contingent upon the sort of dependency relationship it is. Miller makes a rough distinction between 'mature' and 'immature' dependency relationships: 'In the mature relationship, I as . . . client confer my authority on a professional, whom I judge to be competent, to take care of something on my behalf. It is a form of delegation [in] which I continue to have authority to withdraw. In the immature relationship, this may still be the formal situation: but *de facto* I surrender my authority and the professional takes me over' (Miller, 1979a:p. 180–1). In Wilson's language, 'It is not uncommon for worried executives to make an offer to hand over a problem *in toto* to the outside therapist' (Wilson, 1947, p.27). It is in the immature relationship that the consultant may collude with the client to behave 'as if he is more knowledgeable and more powerful than he actually is; hence a reciprocal relationship is established which confirms the inadequacy of the one party and the superiority of the other' (Miller, 1979a:p. 180–1). Mature dependency, or researcher-client efforts to move dependency in a mature direction, constitute one of the process objectives of consultancy. And there may be a positive utilization of dependency by the researcher in progressing the intervention. This has been adumbrated by Miller, who says that one function of the consultant during an intervention is to act as 'a reliable repository' or 'receptacle for dependency' during the phase in which the organization (or subpart of it) is changing i.e. altering its defensive structure. The change has to be supported at the next higher level of the organization or system from the targeted change client. The prevailing defensive structure is dislodged to the next higher order system within which it operates: 'Individuals and groups most directly affected by the change need temporarily to deposit dependency in a leadership that encompasses both the pre-change and post-change configurations' (Miller, 1979a:p. 187–188).

REFERENCES

BRYANT, DON *Work Plus: An Account of an Experiment to Improve the Quality of Worklife in the Cominco Lead Smelter in Trail, B.C.* Vancouver: British Columbia Research Council and Tavistock Institute of Human Relations, 1979.

MILLER, E. J. 'Introductory Essay: Role Perspectives and the Understanding of Organizational Behaviour', in E. J. Miller (ed.). *Task and Organization.* New York: Wiley, 1976.

MILLER, E. J. 'Autonomy, Dependency and Organizational Change', in D. Towell and C. Harries

(eds.). *Innovation in Patient Care.* London: Croom Helm, 1979a.

MILLER, E. J. and GWYNNE, G. V. *A Life Apart.* London: Tavistock, 1972.

RICE, A. K. *The Enterprise and Its Environment.* London: Tavistock, 1963.

SOFER, C. *The Organization from Within.* London: Tavistock, 1961.

WILSON, A. T. M. 'Some Implications of Medical Practice and Social Case-Work for Action Research'. *Journal of Social Issues*, 1947, *3*, No. 2.

Choosing the Depth
of Organizational Intervention*

Roger Harrison

Since World War II there has been a great proliferation of behavioral science–based methods by which consultants seek to facilitate growth and change in individuals, groups, and organizations. The methods range from operations analysis and manipulation of the organization chart, through the use of Grid laboratories, T-groups, and nonverbal techniques. As was true in the development of clinical psychology and psychotherapy, the early stages of this developmental process tend to be accompanied by considerable competition, criticism, and argument about the relative merits of various approaches. It is my conviction that controversy over the relative goodness or badness, effectiveness or ineffectiveness, of various change strategies really accomplishes very little in the way of increased knowledge or unification of behavioral science. As long as we are arguing about what method is better than another, we tend to learn very little about how various approaches fit together or complement one another, and we certainly make more difficult and ambiguous the task of bringing these competing points of view within one over-arching system of knowledge about human processes.

As our knowledge increases, it begins to be apparent that these competing change strategies are not really different ways of doing the same thing—some more effective and some less effective—but rather that they are different ways of doing *different* things. They touch the individual, the group, or the organization in different aspects of their functioning. They require differing kinds and amounts of commitment on the part of the client for them to be successful, and they demand different varieties and levels of skills and abilities on the part of the practitioner.

I believe that there is a real need for conceptual models which differentiate intervention strategies from one another in a way which permits rational matching of strategies to organizational change problems. The purpose of this paper is to present a modest beginning which I have made toward a conceptualization of strategies, and to derive from this conceptualization some criteria for choosing appropriate methods of intervention in particular applications.

The point of view of this paper is that the depth of individual emotional involvement in the change process can be a central concept for differentiating

* SOURCE: Roger Harrison, "Choosing the Depth of Organizational Intervention," *Journal of Applied Behavioral Science,* 6, 1970, 182–202. Reprinted with permission.

change strategies. In focusing on this dimension, we are concerned with the extent to which core areas of the personality or self are the focus of the change attempt. Strategies which touch the more deep, personal, private, and central aspects of the individual or his relationships with others fall toward the deeper end of this continuum. Strategies which deal with more external aspects of the individual and which focus upon the more formal and public aspects of role behavior tend to fall toward the surface end of the depth dimension. This dimension has the advantage that it is relatively easy to rank change strategies upon it and to get fairly close consensus as to the ranking. It is a widely discussed dimension of difference which has meaning and relevance to practitioners and their clients. I hope in this paper to promote greater flexibility and rationality in choosing appropriate depths of intervention. I shall approach this task by examining the effects of interventions at various depths. I shall also explore the ways in which two important organizational processes tend to make demands and to set limits upon the depth of intervention which can produce effective change in organizational functioning. These two processes are the autonomy of organization members and their own perception of their needs for help.

Before illustrating the concept by ranking five common intervention strategies along the dimension of depth, I should like to define the dimension somewhat more precisely. We are concerned essentially with how private, individual, and hidden are the issues and processes about which the consultant attempts directly to obtain information and which he seeks to influence. If the consultant seeks information about relatively public and observable aspects of behavior and relationships and if he tries to influence directly only these relatively surface characteristics and processes, we would then categorize his intervention strategy as being closer to the surface. If, on the other hand, the consultant seeks information about very deep and private perceptions, attitudes, or feelings and if he intervenes in a way which directly affects these processes, then we would classify his intervention strategy as one of considerable depth. To illustrate the surface end of the dimension let us look first at operations research or operations analysis. This strategy is concerned with the roles and functions to be performed within the organization, generally with little regard to the individual characteristics of persons occupying the roles. The change strategy is to manipulate role relationships; in other words, to redistribute the tasks, the resources, and the relative power attached to various roles in the organization. This is essentially a process of rational analysis in which the tasks which need to be performed are determined and specified and then sliced up into role definitions for persons and groups in the organization. The operations analyst does not ordinarily need to know much about particular people. Indeed, his function is to design the organization in such a way that its successful operation does not depend too heavily upon any uniquely individual skills, abilities, values, or attitudes of persons in various roles. He may perform this function adequately without knowing in advance who the people are who will fill these slots. Persons are assumed to be moderately interchangeable, and in order to make this approach work it is necessary to design the organization so that the capacities, needs, and values of the individual which are relevant to role performance are relatively public and observable, and are possessed by a fairly large proportion of the population from which organization members are drawn. The approach is certainly one of very modest depth.

Somewhat deeper are those strategies which are based upon evaluating individual performance and attempting to manipulate it directly. Included in this approach is much of the industrial psychologist's work in selection, placement, appraisal, and counseling of employees. The intervener is concerned with what the individual is able and likely to do and achieve rather than with processes internal to the individual. Direct attempts to influence performance may be made through the application of rewards and punishments such as promotions, salary increases, or transfers within the organization. An excellent illustration of this focus on end results is the practice of management by objectives. The intervention process is focused on establishing mutually agreed-upon goals for performance between the individual and his supervisor. The practice is considered to be particularly advantageous because it permits the supervisor to avoid a focus on personal characteristics of the subordinate, particularly those deeper, more central characteristics which managers generally have difficulty in discussing with those who work under their supervision. The process is designed to limit information exchange to that which is public and observable, such as the setting of performance goals and the success or failure of the individual in attaining them.

Because of its focus on end results, rather than on the process by which those results are achieved, management by objectives must be considered less deep than the broad area of concern with work style which I shall term instrumental process analysis. We are concerned here not only with performance but with the processes by which that performance is achieved. However, we are primarily concerned with styles and processes of work rather than with the processes of interpersonal relationships which I would classify as being deeper on the basic dimension.

In instrumental process analysis we are concerned with how a person likes to organize and conduct his work and with the impact which this style of work has on others in the organization. Principally, we are concerned with how a person perceives his role, what he values and disvalues in it, and what he works hard on and what he chooses to ignore. We are also interested in the instrumental acts which the individual directs toward others: delegating authority or reserving decisions to himself, communicating or withholding information, collaborating or competing with others on work-related issues. The focus on instrumentality means that we are interested in the person primarily as a doer of work or a performer of functions related to the goals of the organization. We are interested in what facilitates or inhibits his effective task performance.

We are not interested per se in whether his relationships with others are happy or unhappy, whether they perceive him as too warm or too cold, too authoritarian or too laissez-faire, or any other of the many interpersonal relationships which arise as people associate in organizations. However, I do not mean to imply that the line between instrumental relationships and interpersonal ones is an easy one to draw in action and practice, or even that it is desirable that this be done.

DEPTH GAUGES: LEVEL OF TASKS AND FEELINGS

What I am saying is that an intervention strategy can focus on instrumentality or it can focus on interpersonal relationships, and that there are important consequences of this difference in depth of intervention.

When we intervene at the level of instrumentality, it is to change work behavior and working relationships. Frequently this involves the process of bargaining or negotiation between groups and individuals. Diagnoses are made of the satisfactions or dissatisfactions of organization members with one another's work behavior. Reciprocal adjustments, bargains, and trade-offs can then be arranged in which each party gets some modification in the behavior of the other at the cost to him of some reciprocal accommodation. Much of the intervention strategy which has been developed around Blake's concept of the Managerial Grid is at this level and involves bargaining and negotiation of role behavior as an important change process.

At the deeper level of interpersonal relationships the focus is on feelings, attitudes, and perceptions which organization members have about others. At this level we are concerned with the quality of human relationships within the organization, with warmth and coldness of members to one another, and with the experiences of acceptance and rejection, love and hate, trust and suspicion among groups and individuals. At this level the consultant probes for normally hidden feelings, attitudes, and perceptions. He works to create relationships of openness about feelings and to help members to develop mutual understanding of one another as persons. Interventions are directed toward helping organization members to be more comfortable in being authentically themselves with one another, and the degree of mutual caring and concern is expected to increase. Sensitivity training using T-groups is a basic intervention strategy at this level. T-group educators emphasize increased personalization of relationships, the development of trust and openness, and the exchange of feelings. Interventions at this level deal directly and intensively with interpersonal emotionality. This is the first intervention strategy we have examined which is at a depth where the feelings of organization members about one another as persons are a direct focus of the intervention strategy. At the other levels, such feelings certainly exist and may be expressed, but they are not a direct concern of the intervention. The transition from the task orientation of instrumental process analysis to the feeling orientation of interpersonal process analysis seems, as I shall suggest later, to be a critical one for many organization members.

The deepest level of intervention which will be considered in this paper is that of intrapersonal analysis. Here the consultant uses a variety of methods to reveal the individual's deeper attitudes, values, and conflicts regarding his own functioning, identity, and existence. The focus is generally on increasing the range of experiences which the individual can bring into awareness and cope with. The material may be dealt with at the fantasy or symbolic level, and the intervention strategies include many which are noninterpersonal and nonverbal. Some examples of this approach are the use of marathon T-group sessions, the creative risk-taking laboratory approach of Byrd (1967), and some aspects of the task group therapy approach of Clark (1966). These approaches all tend to bring into focus very deep and intense feelings about one's own identity and one's relationships with significant others.

Although I have characterized deeper interventions as dealing increasingly with the individual's affective life, I do not imply that issues at less deep levels may not be emotionally charged. Issues of role differentiation, reward distribution, ability and performance evaluation, for example, are frequently invested with strong feelings. The concept of depth is concerned more with the *accessibility* and *individuality* of attitudes, values, and perceptions than it is with their strength. This narrowing of the common usage of the term *depth* is necessary to avoid the contradictions which occur when strength and inaccessibility are confused. For instance, passionate value confrontation and bitter conflict have frequently occurred between labor and management over economic issues which are surely toward the surface end of my concept of depth.

In order to understand the importance of the concept of depth for choosing interventions in organizations, let us consider the effects upon organization members of working at different levels.

The first of the important concomitants of depth is the degree of dependence of the client on the special competence of the change agent. At the surface end of the depth dimension, the methods of intervention are easily communicated and made public. The client may reasonably expect to learn something of the change agent's skills to improve his own practice. At the deeper levels, such as interpersonal and intrapersonal process analyses, it is more difficult for the client to understand the methods of intervention. The change agent is more likely to be seen as a person of special and unusual powers not found in ordinary men. Skills of intervention and change are less frequently learned by organization members, and the change process may tend to become personalized around the change agent as leader. Programs of change which are so dependent upon personal relationships and individual expertise are difficult to institutionalize. When the change agent leaves the system, he may not only take his expertise with him but the entire change process as well.

A second aspect of the change process which varies with depth is the extent to which the benefits of an intervention are transferable to members of the organization not originally participating in the change process. At surface levels of operations analysis and performance evaluation, the effects are institutionalized in the form of procedures, policies, and practices of the organization which may have considerable permanence beyond the tenure of individuals. At the level of instrumental behavior, the continuing effects of intervention are more likely to reside in the informal norms of groups within the organization regarding such matters as delegation, communication, decision making, competition and collaboration, and conflict resolution.

At the deepest levels of intervention, the target of change is the individual's inner life; and if the intervention is successful, the permanence of individual change should be greatest. There are indeed dramatic reports of cases in which persons have changed their careers and life goals as a result of such interventions, and the persistence of such change appears to be relatively high.

One consequence, then, of the level of intervention is that with greater depth of focus the individual increasingly becomes both the target and the carrier of change. In the light of this analysis, it is not surprising to observe that deeper levels of intervention are increasingly being used at higher organizational levels and in scientific and service organizations where the contribution of the individual has greatest impact.

An important concomitant of depth is that as the level of intervention becomes deeper, the information needed to intervene effectively becomes less available. At the less personal level of operations analysis, the information is often a matter of record. At the level of performance evaluation, it is a matter of observation. On the other hand, reactions of others to a person's work style are less likely to be discussed freely, and the more personal responses to his interpersonal style are even less likely to be readily given. At the deepest levels, important information may not be available to the individual himself. Thus, as we go deeper the consultant must use more of his time and skill uncovering information which is ordinarily private and hidden. This is one reason for the greater costs of interventions at deeper levels of focus.

Another aspect of the change process which varies with the depth of intervention is the personal risk and unpredictability of outcome for the individual. At deeper levels we deal with aspects of the individual's view of himself and his relationships with others which are relatively untested by exposure to the evaluations and emotional reactions of others. If in the change process the individual's self-perceptions are strongly disconfirmed, the resulting imbalance in internal forces may produce sudden changes in behavior, attitudes, and personality integration.

Because of the private and hidden nature of the processes into which we intervene at deeper levels, it is difficult to predict the individual impact of the change process in advance. The need for clinical sensitivity and skill on the part of the practitioner thus increases, since he must be prepared to diagnose and deal with developing situations involving considerable stress upon individuals.

The foregoing analysis suggests a criterion by which to match intervention strategies to particular organizational problems. It is *to intervene at a level no deeper than that required to produce enduring solutions to the problems at hand.* This criterion derives directly from the observations above. The cost, skill demands, client dependency, and variability of outcome all increase with depth of intervention. Further, as the depth of intervention increases, the effects tend to locate more in the individual and less in the organization. The danger of losing the organization's investment in the change with the departure of the individual becomes a significant consideration.

AUTONOMY INCREASES DEPTH OF INTERVENTION

While this general criterion is simple and straightforward, its application is not. In particular, although the criterion should operate in the direction of less depth of intervention, there is a general trend in modern organizational life which tends to push the intervention level ever deeper. This trend is toward increased self-direction of organization members and increased independence of external pressures and incentives. I believe that there is a direct relationship between the autonomy of individuals and the depth of intervention needed to effect organizational change.

Before going on to discuss this relationship, I shall acknowledge freely that I cannot prove the existence of a trend toward a general increase in freedom of individuals within organizations. I intend only to assert the great importance of the degree of individual autonomy in determining the level of intervention which will be effective.

In order to understand the relationship between autonomy and depth of intervention, it is necessary to conceptualize a dimension which parallels and is implied by the depth dimension we have been discussing. This is the dimension of predictability and variability among persons in their responses to the different kinds of incentives which may be used to influence behavior in the organization. The key assumption in this analysis is that the more unpredictable and unique is the individual's response to the particular kinds of controls and incentives one can bring to bear upon him, the more one must know about that person to influence his behavior.

Most predictable and least individual is the response of the person to economic and bureaucratic controls when his needs for economic income and security are high. It is not necessary to delve very deeply into a person's inner processes in order to influence his behavior if we know that he badly needs his income and his position and if we are in a position to control nis access to these rewards. Responses to economic and bureaucratic controls tend to be relatively simple and on the surface.

Independence of Economic Incentive

If for any reason organization members become relatively uninfluence-able through the manipulation of their income and economic security, the management of performance becomes strikingly more complex; and the need for more personal information about the individual increases. Except very generally, we do not know automatically or in advance what styles of instrumental or interpersonal interaction will be responded to as negative or positive incentives by the individual. One person may appreciate close supervision and direction; another may value independence of direction. One may prefer to work alone; another may function best when he is in close communication with others. One may thrive in close, intimate, personal interaction; while others are made uncomfortable by any but cool and distant relationships with colleagues.

What I am saying is that when bureaucratic and economic incentives lose their force for whatever reason, the improvement of performance *must* involve linking organizational goals to the individual's attempts to meet his own needs for satisfying instrumental activities and interpersonal relationships. It is for this reason that I make the assertion that increases in personal autonomy dictate change interventions at deeper and more personal levels. In order to obtain the information necessary to link organizational needs to individual goals, one must probe fairly deeply into the attitudes, values, and emotions of the organization members.

If the need for deeper personal information becomes great when we intervene at the instrumental and interpersonal levels, it becomes even greater when one is dealing with organization members who are motivated less through their transactions with the environment and more in response to internal values and standards. An example is the researcher, engineer, or technical specialist whose work behavior may be influenced more by his own values and standards of creativity or professional excellence than by his relationships with others. The deepest organizational interventions at the intrapersonal level may be required in order to effect change when working with persons who are highly self-directed.

Let me summarize my position about the relationship among autonomy, influence, and level of intervention. As the individual becomes less subject to economic and bureaucratic pressures, he tends to seek more intangible rewards in the organization which come from both the instrumental and interpersonal aspects of the system. I view this as a shift from greater external to more internal control and as an increase in autonomy. Further shifts in this direction may involve increased independence of rewards and punishments mediated by others, in favor of operation in accordance with internal values and standards.

I view organizations as systems of reciprocal influence. Achievement of organization goals is facilitated when individuals can seek their own satisfactions through activity which promotes the goals of the organization. As the satisfactions which are of most value to the individual change, so must the reciprocal influence systems, if the organization goals are to continue to be met.

If the individual changes are in the direction of increased independence of external incentives, then the influence systems must change to provide opportunities for individuals to achieve more intangible, self-determined satisfactions in their work. However, people are more differentiated, complex, and unique in their intangible goals and values than in their economic needs.

In order to create systems which offer a wide variety of intangible satisfactions, much more private information about individuals is needed than is required to create and maintain systems based chiefly on economic and bureaucratic controls. For this reason, deeper interventions are called for when the system which they would attempt to change contains a high proportion of relatively autonomous individuals.

There are a number of factors promoting autonomy, all tending to free the individual from dependence upon economic and bureaucratic controls, which I have observed in my work with organizations. Whenever a number of these factors obtain, it is probably an indication that deeper levels of intervention are required to effect lasting improvements in organizational functioning. I shall simply list these indicators briefly in categories to show what kinds of things might signify to the practitioner that deeper levels of intervention may be appropriate.

The first category includes anything which makes the evaluation of individual performance difficult:

> A long time span between the individual's actions and the results by which effectiveness of performance is to be judged.
> Nonrepetitive, unique tasks which cannot be evaluated by reference to the performance of others on similar tasks.
> Specialized skills and abilities possessed by an individual which cannot be evaluated by a supervisor who does not possess the skills or knowledge himself.

The second category concerns economic conditions:

> Arrangements which secure the job tenure and/or income of the individual.
> A market permitting easy transfer from one organization to another (e.g., engineers in the United States aerospace industry).
> Unique skills and knowledge of the individual which make him difficult to replace.

The third category includes characteristics of the system or its environment which lead to independence of the parts of the organization and decentralization of authority such as:

> An organization which works on a project basis instead of producing a standard line of products.
> An organization in which subparts must be given latitude to deal rapidly and flexibly with frequent environmental change.

I should like to conclude the discussion of this criterion for depth of intervention with a brief reference to the ethics of intervention, a problem which merits considerably more thorough treatment than I can give it here.

The Ethics of Delving Deeper

There is considerable concern in the United States about invasion of privacy by behavioral scientists. I would agree that such invasion of privacy is an actual as well as fantasied concomitant of the use of organizational change strategies of greater depth. The recourse by organizations to such strategies has been widely viewed as an indication of greater organizational control over the most personal and private aspects of the lives of the members. The present analysis suggests, however, that recourse to these deeper interventions actually reflects the greater *freedom* of organization members from traditionally crude and impersonal means of organizational control. There is no reason to be concerned about man's attitudes or values or interpersonal relationships when his job performance can be controlled by brute force, by economic coercion, or by bureaucratic rules and regulations. The "invasion of privacy" becomes worth the cost, bother, and uncertainty of outcome only when the individual has achieved relative independence from control by other means. Put another way, it makes organizational sense to try to get a man to *want* to do something only if you cannot *make* him do it. And regardless of what intervention strategy is used, the individual still retains considerably greater control over his own behavior than he had when he could be manipulated more crudely. As long as we can maintain a high degree of voluntarism regarding the nature and extent of an individual's participation in the deeper organizational change strategies, these strategies can work toward adapting the organization to the individual quite as much as they work the other way around. Only when an individual's participation in one of the deeper change strategies is coerced by economic or bureaucratic pressures, do I feel that the ethics of the intervention clearly run counter to the values of a democratic society.

ROLE OF CLIENT NORMS AND VALUES IN
DETERMINING DEPTH

So far our attention to the choice of level of intervention has focused upon locating the depth at which the information exists which must be exchanged to facilitate system improvement. Unfortunately, the choice of an intervention strategy cannot practically be made with reference to this criterion alone. Even if a correct diagnosis is made of the level at which the relevant information lies, we may not be able to work effectively at the desired depth because of client norms, values, resistances, and fears.

In an attempt to develop a second criterion for depth of intervention which takes such dispositions on the part of the client into account, I have considered two approaches which represent polarized orientations to the problem. One approach is based upon analyzing and overcoming client resistance; the other is based upon discovering and joining forces with the self-articulated wants or "felt needs" of the client.

There are several ways of characterizing these approaches. To me, the simplest is to point out that when the change agent is resistance-oriented he tends to lead or influence the client to work at a depth greater than that at which the latter feels comfortable. When resistance-oriented, the change agent tends to mistrust the client's statement of his problems and of the areas where he wants help. He suspects the client's presentation of being a smoke screen or defense against admission of his "real" problems and needs. The consultant works to expose the underlying processes and concerns and to influence the client to work at a deeper level. The resistance-oriented approach grows out of the work of clinicians and psychotherapists, and it characterizes much of the work of organizational consultants who specialize in sensitivity training and deeper intervention strategies.

On the other hand, change agents may be oriented to the self-articulated needs of clients. When so oriented, the consultant tends more to follow and facilitate the client in working at whatever level the latter sets for himself. He may assist the client in defining problems and needs and in working on solutions, but he is inclined to try to anchor his work in the norms, values, and accepted standards of behavior of the organization.

I believe that there is a tendency for change agents working at the interpersonal and deeper levels to adopt a rather consistent resistance-oriented approach. Consultants so oriented seem to take a certain quixotic pride in dramatically and self-consciously violating organizational norms. Various techniques have been developed for pressuring or seducing organizations members into departing from organizational norms in the service of change. The "marathon" T-group is a case in point, where the increased irritability and fatigue of prolonged contact and lack of sleep move participants to deal with one another more emotionally, personally, and spontaneously than they would normally be willing to do.

I suspect that unless such norm-violating intervention efforts actually succeed in changing organizational norms, their effects are relatively short-lived, because the social structures and interpersonal linkages have not been created which can utilize for day-to-day problem solving the deeper information produced by the intervention. It is true that the consultant may succeed in producing information, but he is less likely to succeed in creating social structures which can continue to work in his absence. The problem is directly analogous to that of the community developer who succeeds by virtue of his personal influence in getting villagers to build a school or a community center which falls into disuse as soon as he leaves because of the lack of any integration of these achievements into the social structure and day-to-day needs and desires of the community. Community developers have had to learn through bitter failure and frustration that ignoring or subverting the standards and norms of a social system often results in temporary success followed by a reactionary increase in resistance to the influence of the change agent. On the other hand, felt needs embody those problems, issues, and difficulties which have a high conscious priority on the part of community or organization members. We can expect individuals and groups to be ready to invest time, energy, and resources in dealing with their felt needs, while they will be relatively passive or even resistant toward those who attempt to help them with externally defined needs. Community developers have found that attempts to help with felt needs are met with greater receptivity, support, and integration within the structure and life of the community than are intervention attempts which rely primarily upon the developer's value system for setting need priorities.

The emphasis of many organizational change agents on confronting and working through resistances was developed originally in the practice of individual psychoanalysis and psychotherapy, and it is also a central concept in the conduct of therapy groups and sensitivity training laboratories. In all of these situations, the change agent has a high degree of environmental control and is at least temporarily in a high status position with respect to the client. To a degree that is frequently underestimated by practitioners, we manage to create a situation in which it is more unpleasant for the client to leave than it is to stay and submit to the pressure to confront and work through resistances. I believe that the tendency is for behavioral scientists to overplay their hands when they move from the clinical and training situations where they have environmental control to the organizational consulting situation, where their control is sharply attenuated.

This attenuation derives only partially from the relative ease with which the client can terminate the relationship. Even if this most drastic step is not taken, the consultant can be tolerated, misled, and deceived in ways which are relatively difficult in the therapeutic or human relations training situations. He can also be openly defied and blocked if he runs afoul of strongly shared group norms; whereas when the consultant is dealing with a group of strangers, he can often utilize differences among the members to overcome this kind of resistance. I suspect that, in general, behavioral scientists underestimate their power in working with individuals and groups of strangers, and overestimate it when working with individuals and groups in organizations. I emphasize this point because I believe that a good many potentially fruitful and mutually satisfying consulting relationships are terminated early because of the consultant's taking the role of overcomer of resistance to change rather than that of collaborator in the client's attempts at solving his problems. It is these considerations which lead me to suggest my second criterion for the choice of organization intervention strategy: *to intervene at a level no deeper than that at which the energy and resources of the client can be committed to problem solving and to change.* These energies and resources can be mobilized through obtaining legitimation for the intervention in the norms of the organization and through devising intervention strategies which have clear relevance to consciously felt needs on the part of the organization members.

THE CONSULTANT'S DILEMMA: FELT NEEDS VERSUS DEEPER LEVELS

Unfortunately, it is doubtless true that the forces which influence the conditions we desire to change often exist at deeper levels than can be dealt with by adhering to the criterion of working within organization norms and meeting felt needs. The level at which an individual or group is willing and ready to invest energy and resources is probably always determined partly by a realistic assessment of the problems and partly by a defensive need to avoid confrontation and significant change. It is thus not likely that our two criteria for selection of intervention depth will result in the same decisions when practically applied. It is not the same to intervene at the level where behavior-determining forces are most potent as it is to work on felt needs as they are articulated by the client. This, it seems to me, is the consultant's dilemma. It always has been. We are continually faced with the choice between leading the client into areas which are threatening, unfamiliar, and dependency-provoking for him (and where our own expertise shows up to best advantage) or, on the other hand, being guided by the client's own understanding of his problems and his willingness to invest resources in particular kinds of relatively familiar and nonthreatening strategies.

When time permits, this dilemma is ideally dealt with by intervening first at a level where there is good support from the norms, power structure, and felt needs of organizational members. The consultant can then, over a period of time, develop trust, sophistication, and support within the organization to explore deeper levels at which particularly important forces may be operating. This would probably be agreed to, at least in principle, by most organizational consultants. The point at which I feel I differ from a significant number of workers in this field is that I would advocate that interventions should *always* be limited to the depth of the client's felt needs and readiness to legitimize intervention. I believe we should always avoid moving deeper at a pace which outstrips a client system's willingness to subject itself to exposure, dependency, and threat. What I am saying is that if the dominant response of organization members indicates that an intervention violates system norms regarding exposure, privacy, and confrontation, then one has intervened too deeply and should pull back to a level at which organization members are more ready to invest their own energy in the change process. This point of view is thus in opposition to that which sees negative reactions primarily as indications of resistances which are to be brought out into the open, confronted, and worked through as a central part of the intervention process. I believe that behavioral scientists acting as organizational consultants have tended to place overmuch emphasis on the overcoming of resistance to change and have underemphasized the importance of enlisting in the service of change the energies and resources which the client can consciously direct and willingly devote to problem solving.

What is advocated here is that we in general accept the client's felt needs or the problems he presents as real and that we work on them at a level at which he can serve as a competent and willing collaborator. This position is in opposition to one which sees the presenting problem as more or less a smoke screen or barrier. I am not advocating this point of view because I value the right to privacy of organization members more highly than I value their growth and development or the solution of organizational problems. (This is an issue which concerns me, but it is enormously more complex than the ones with which I am dealing in this paper.) Rather, I place first priority on collaboration with the client, because I do not think we are frequently successful consultants without it.

In my own practice I have observed that the change in client response is frequently quite striking when I move from a resistance-oriented approach to an acceptance of the client's norms and definitions of his own needs. With quite a few organizational clients in the United States, the line of legitimacy seems to lie somewhere between interventions at the instrumental level and those focused on interpersonal relationships. Members who exhibit hostility, passivity, and dependence when I initiate intervention at the interpersonal level may become dramatically more active, collaborative, and involved when I shift the focus to the instrumental level.

If I intervene directly at the level of interpersonal relationships, I can be sure that at least some members, and often the whole group, will react with anxiety, passive resistance, and low or negative commitment to the change process. Furthermore, they express their resistance in terms of norms and values regarding the appropriateness or legitimacy of dealing at this level. They say things like, "It isn't right to force people's feelings about one another out into the open"; "I don't see what this has to do with improving organizational effectiveness"; "People are being encouraged to say things which are better left unsaid."

If I then switch to a strategy which focuses on decision making, delegation of authority, information exchange, and other instrumental questions, these complaints about illegitimacy and the inappropriateness of the intervention are usually sharply reduced. This does not mean that the clients are necessarily comfortable or free from anxiety in the discussions, nor does it mean that strong feelings may not be expressed about one another's behavior. What is different is that the clients are more likely to *work with* instead of *against* me, to feel and express some sense of ownership in the change process, and to see many more possibilities for carrying it on among themselves in the absence of the consultant.

What I have found is that when I am resistance-oriented in my approach to the client, I am apt to feel rather uncomfortable in "letting sleeping dogs lie." When, on the other hand, I orient myself to the client's own assessment of his needs, I am uncomfortable when I feel I am leading or pushing the client to operate very far outside the shared norms of the organization. I have tried to indicate why I believe the latter orientation is more appropriate. I realize of course that many highly sophisticated and talented practitioners will not agree with me.

In summary, I have tried to show in this paper that the dimension of depth should be central to the conceptualization of intervention strategies. I have presented what I believe are the major consequences of intervening at greater or lesser depths, and from these consequences I have suggested two criteria for choosing the appropriate depth of intervention: first, *to intervene at a level no deeper than that required to produce enduring solutions to the problems at hand;*

and second, *to intervene at a level no deeper than that at which the energy and resources of the client can be committed to problem solving and to change.*

I have analyzed the tendency for increases in individual autonomy in organizations to push the appropriate level of intervention deeper when the first criterion is followed. Opposed to this is the countervailing influence of the second criterion to work closer to the surface in order to enlist the energy and support of organization members in the change process. Arguments have been presented for resolving this dilemma in favor of the second, more conservative, criterion. The dilemma remains, of course; the continuing tension under which the change agent works is between the desire to lead and push, or to collaborate and follow. The middle ground is never very stable, and I suspect we show our values and preferences by which criterion we choose to maximize when we are under the stress of difficult and ambiguous client-consultant relationships.

REFERENCES

BYRD, R. E. Training in a nongroup. *Journal of Humanistic Psychology,* 1967, 7, (1), 18–27.

CLARK, J. V. Task group therapy. Unpublished manuscript, University of California, Los Angeles, 1966.

10

LATER IN THE PROCESS

————◆————

INTRODUCTION

> *To explain social change we must always relate events to the order in which they occur. We must furthermore see the event as the culmination of a process or a new stage in the process.*
>
> —R. M. MacIver*

This chapter concentrates on the dynamics that occur in interventions as they mature in client organizations or have run their course. The chapter presents another episode describing the Multi Company intervention, which was introduced in Chapter 8 and developed in Chapter 9. *The Multi Company (C)* describes the consultant's efforts to help members of the organization by deciphering their corporate culture, and his work on career development for the company's top managers.[1]

The chapter also presents three further installments on the Torenton intervention, which was introduced in Chapter 9. *The Torenton Mine (B)* presents details of employee turnover, productivity, and safety records of the mine over the period of the intervention, and answers some questions about its effectiveness. *The Torenton Mine (C)* describes change processes at different points in time during the intervention and encourages constructive discussion of intervention process. *The Torenton Mine (D)* considers questions of mine management—consultant understanding and misunderstanding, and poses the intriguing question of why management stuck it out over the course of the intervention.

---

* Quoted in Barry Glassner, *Essential Interactionism* (London: Routledge & Kegan Paul, 1980), p. 8.

[1] *The Multi Company (D)*, available in the Instructor's Manual, reviews the outcomes of the intervention, the changes made, and the state of company culture at the end of the intervention.

The Apex Manufacturing Company chronicles the course of an intervention, from beginning to end, from the point of view of the external change agent. The account describes in some detail his data-gathering and feedback activities, in the context of ongoing organizational action.

This chapter is relatively heavy on empirical accounts, and light on models and schemes. *Evaluation of Results and Disengagement* discusses desirable changes in the members of client organizations, as a result of process consultation, and issues about client-consultant disengagement. *Behavior Changes in Successful Organization Development Efforts* presents the outcomes of a study that sought to pin down behavior changes in successful change efforts. From studying the views of a substantial number of leaders in the field of organizational change the authors concluded that several characteristic behavior changes are common to successful change efforts, and suggest these as useful change levers. There are, of course, many more issues about evaluating the outcomes of interventions than may be encompassed here, in a book essentially aimed at the overall education and training of change agents.

Intervention and Historical Process points out that significance or meaning in an account of an intervention "comes from looking backward." A narrative account of an intervention consists not of "what is 'remembered', but what is constructed." Knowledge about interventions is derived retrospectively: "Patterns are not detectable except after the fact." A viable, scientific approach to how best to intervene must adopt "a fundamentally retrospective perspective for at least a portion of the questions it addresses." These central considerations underlie the entire rationale for Part Three of this book.

The Multi Company (C)*

Edgar H. Schein

Planning for Third Annual Meeting. I had made it clear that one should think of change as a stage to be managed, with targets and assigned change managers. From this point of view, the third annual meeting provided a natural opportunity to review progress, check out what problems had been encountered, share successes and good innovations, replan some projects if necessary, and, most important, announce newly defined role relationships between executive committee members, division heads, and country heads.

Experience with the Redirection Project had revealed that the headquarters organization was too involved in the day-to-day operation of the local businesses. As the functions were shrunk and restructured, it also appeared desirable to redefine the corporate headquarters role as more "strategic," while the operating units would do more of the day-to-day management. This was possible because country managers were now willing and able to assume more responsibilities and because the executive committee increasingly recognized the importance of its strategic role. The whole economic crisis forced some strategic rethinking, which highlighted the role of the executive committee in formulating a new direction for Multi's future.

Third Annual Meeting: Consolidating Gains and Remotivating for Future Efforts. At the opening session of the third annual meeting, I was asked to review the progress of the Redirection Project. My review was based on interviews with a series of managers about their experiences with the project. This lecture was designed to remind the participants of change theory, to legitimize their individual experiences and frustrations by giving a wide range of examples, to illustrate how restraining forces had been dealt with by innovative managers, and to introduce to the group the concept of corporate culture as a force to be analyzed.

I had spent some time during the second year working with members of the management development group to try to decipher the assumptions that were operating, to develop a "concept" of the company culture that could be shared with managers in order to assess how it aided or hindered the Redirection Project. I learned two powerful lessons from this process and from my lecture.

First, it was very difficult for insiders to decipher their own culture without my active intervention, probing, stating hypotheses, mentioning incidents that had happened to me, citing puzzling anomalies, and so on. Together

---

* SOURCE: Abstracted from Edgar H. Schein and edited by Roy McLennan from *Organizational Culture and Leadership: A Dynamic View* (San Francisco: Jossey-Bass, 1985), pp. 244–269. Reprinted with permission.

we could reach some clarity, at least enough clarity to present a picture of the culture for discussion following the lecture.

The reaction to the lecture produced the second important insight. Many participants said that I had stated things more or less accurately, but they clearly were not pleased that I, as an outsider, had made their culture public. Some of them insisted that I had made errors of misinterpretation, and one or two executive committee members subsequently decided that I was not a useful consultant. Once I had revealed my "misunderstanding" or unwittingly revealed some feelings about aspects of their culture, I created a polarized situation. Some managers moved closer to me, while others moved further away. I concluded that, if one did not want that kind of polarization, one should help the group decipher its own culture rather than presenting one's own view of that culture in a didactic manner.

Both consultants were present throughout the meeting to serve as audience, reinforcers, and sources of new ideas. Following the general presentation on change, each of the projects was asked to give a brief review of its status, and small groups met to consider implications and make suggestions. The last part of the meeting, and from the point of view of the planning group the most difficult, concerned the problem of how to inform everyone about the new roles of the executive committee, the division heads, and the country heads.

The executive committee members planned a major change in their own role, pushing toward strategic management and toward more individualized accountability for divisions and functions, but they were not sure that the message would get across just by saying it. We therefore planned a three-step process: (1) a formal announcement of the new roles; (2) a brief lecture by me on the implications of role realignment, emphasizing the systemic character of role networks and the need for each manager to renegotiate his role downward, upward, and laterally if the new system was to work; and (3) a powerful emotional speech by the vice-chairman of the executive committee on the effect of this new alignment in streamlining the company for the future.

The third annual meeting ended on a high note, based on a sense of what had already been accomplished in one year, what accomplishments were in the works, and what improvements could be expected from the new role that the executive committee had taken for itself. The fact that the headquarters organization had begun to shrink through early retirements and had reduced some of its more bothersome control activities sent the clear message that top management was serious about its role in the Redirection Project even though the early retirement of headquarters people was an extremely painful process. The fact that people were being retired destroyed the taken-for-granted assumption that people had a guaranteed career in the company, but the highly individualized and financially generous manner in which retirements were handled reinforced another basic assumption: that the company cared very much for its people and would not hurt them if there was any way to avoid it.

Assessment During Third Year. Most of my regular visits subsequent to the third annual meeting were devoted to working with the new manager of management development. Though I continued to meet with members of the executive committee on Redirection matters, the priority shifted to helping the new head of the management development function think through his own role and reexamine how the entire process could be improved. The former manager of this function wanted to continue some project involvement following his retirement. Therefore, he and I jointly proposed a project in which his insights could be used to study the careers of the top two hundred senior managers in the company, with the purpose of identifying critical success factors or problems in those careers. The project was approved by the executive committee with the condition that I was to act as "technical supervisor" of the project, to ensure that any findings would be scientifically valid. I was reminded once again that my credibility as a consultant rested heavily on my scientific reputation and that scientific validity was the ultimate decision criterion for the company.

The study involved a detailed reconstruction of the careers and revealed surprisingly little geographical, cross-functional, and cross-divisional movement as those careers progressed. A presentation of these and other results was given to the executive committee by the former manager of management development, which led to a major discussion of how future general managers should be developed. A consensus was reached that there should be more early career rotation geographically and into and out of headquarters, but cross-functional and cross-divisional movement remained a controversial issue.

The executive committee members also realized that rotational moves, if they were to be useful, had to occur early in the career. They decided that such early movement would occur only if a very clear message went out to the entire organization. This decision led to the design of a half-day segment on management development, to be inserted into the management seminars that are periodically given to the top five hundred managers of the company.

A new policy on early rotation was mandated, and the data from the project were used to justify the new policy. Once senior management accepted a conclusion as valid, it was able to move decisively and to impose a proposed solution on the entire company. The message was communicated by having executive committee members at each seminar, but implementation was left to local management.

During this year Richards relinquished the job of chairman of the executive committee for reasons of health, providing a potential succession problem. However, the executive committee had anticipated the problem and had a new chairman and vice-chairman ready. The persons chosen for these new positions allowed the company to reaffirm its strategic posture, which, not surprisingly, reemphasized its scientific values. The succession also provided a test of the executive committee's commitment to the Redirection Project, since its launching was associated with Richards' leadership. The new chairman and vice-chairman strongly reaffirmed that commitment and thereby sent a further clear signal to the organization that the crisis was real and needed to be addressed.

By the end of the third year, the financial results were much better, and the restructuring process in the unprofitable divisions was proceeding rapidly. Each unit learned how to manage early retirements, and a measure of interdivisional cooperation was achieved in the process of placing people who were redundant in one division into other divisions. Initial attitudes were negative, and I heard many complaints from managers that even their best people were not acceptable to other divisions; but this attitude was gradually eroded because the assumption that "We don't throw people out without maximum effort to find jobs for them" eventually overrode the provincialism of the divisions. Managers who were too committed to the old strategy of running those divisions were gradually replaced with managers who were deemed to be more innovative in their approach.

Because it had fulfilled its functions, the Redirection Project was officially terminated. Relevant change projects would now be handled by the executive committee, and I was asked to be "on call" to line managers needing help. The new head of one of the previously unprofitable divisions, for example, wanted help in restoring the morale of those managers who remained after many of their colleagues were retired or farmed out to other divisions. He sensed a level of fear and apathy that made it difficult to move forward positively. In true Multi fashion, he had tried to solve this problem on his own by bringing in an *outside* training program, but it had been unsuccessful. He then requested a meeting with me to seek alternative solutions. Given the Multi culture and his own commitment, it was obvious that he should build his program internally and enlist the aid of the corporate training people, who would know how to design a program that would be culturally congruent. He had never considered using the corporate training group to help him, though he knew of it and liked some of the people in it. I found myself being the broker between two parts of the organization that could have been talking to each other directly. He did follow up, and in the subsequent year a successful in-house program was developed.

Looking Ahead. On the original issue that Richards had asked me to get involved with, the stimulation of innovation, very little change has taken place from my point of view. But the culture of Multi "works," so one cannot readily assume that some other way would be better. Rather, my job as a consultant is to help the company be more innovative within the constraints of its culture. I meet with several cross-departmental groups who are at a low level of the organization and want to share the kind of information that does not circulate freely at senior levels. As a result of these meetings, some lateral communication links are being built.

By continuing to work on management development issues, I can raise questions (as indeed many in the company are) about what kind of manager should be recruited in the future, and what kinds of job assignments and rotation system should be used to produce the manager of the future, leading to a gradual reevaluation of what is effective management in Multi.

The Torenton Mine (B)*

James F. Gavin

BEHAVIORAL INDICES

Although assessing the project's contributions to organizational effectiveness and health is difficult, I can, however, speculate as to how the intervention possibly influenced such indicators as the turnover, productivity, and safety records of the mine from 1974–81.

Turnover

Because a major rationale for conducting the first and second survey programs was Torenton's high rate of turnover, the decline in turnover from an annual rate of 117.6% (9.8% per month) in 1974 to one of 18% (1.5% per month) in 1981 suggests that the organization successfully solved the problem of employee attrition (see Figure 1). Although one might argue that economic fluctuations could provide a more parsimonious explanation for this trend, I would partially counter this by noting that even in the prosperous period of the late 1970s the attrition rates fell substantially. Other counterarguments point to organizational changes resulting directly or indirectly from the SFPs, including a major revision in the attendance policy, an expanded screening and orientation program, vastly improved transfer and promotion systems, a definable shift in supervisory style to a more participative approach, and a variety of new communications channels.

One might reasonably argue that turnover reductions could have been solely a reflection of structural change—in this case, an improved attendance policy. To address this objection, one must examine the data on absenteeism. The policy prior to the intervention gave supervisors total discretion in declaring absences excused or unexcused, and it set an upper limit of six excused absences per year. The new policies allowed supervisors little input into deciding the nature of the absence, and it permitted an employee to take off as many as 12 days per year. One might predict that this policy change would lead to an increase in absenteeism and a decline in turnover, if other factors such as supervisor relationships, work group climate, and communications remained the same. Before the change, the absenteeism rates for hourly employees were 11.1% (1974) and 9.5% (1975). The new policy took effect in January 1976, and following this absenteeism rates were 7.5% (1976), 7.3% (1977), 8.0%

* SOURCE: James F. Gavin, "Observations from a Long-Term Survey—Guided Consultation with a Mining Company," *Journal of Applied Behavioral Science*, 21 (1985), 204–220. Reprinted with permission.

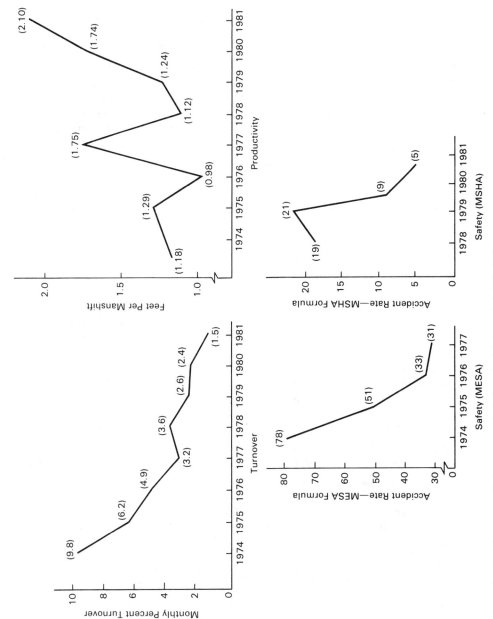

Figure 1. Monthly averages for turnover, productivity and safety for period 1974–1981.

(1978), 8.2% (1979), 8.5% (1980), and 8.2% (1981). This seems to suggest that other factors such as those mentioned above had indeed improved.

While these arguments increase the plausibility of attributing improvements to the interventions, action research as a design strategy leaves much to be desired when one attempts to corroborate a view scientifically. To increase credibility in the data, one might obtain a "control group" against which to contrast trends. Fortunately, we could obtain turnover data from another mine that produced the same ore, was located in the same region, and was owned and operated by the same corporation. This second mine differed from Torenton in that it employed about 2,500 workers (Torenton employed 1,800) and had been in operation for more than 25 years. More critically, this other mine did not have an ongoing program of behavioral science intervention. It did, of course, make "normal" efforts to improve—without the assistance of external consultants. From 1974–81, this comparison mine reduced its turnover rate from 3.7% per month to 1.6%, representing an improvement of 58%. The turnover rate at Torenton declined from 9.8% to 1.5%, an improvement of 85%. Because Torenton had a higher turnover rate in 1974, this comparison could be misleading and should be considered only as suggestive of the pace of improvement at Torenton.

Productivity

A second criterion—mining productivity—has been traditionally measured according to a complex formula of "feet per manshift." One can partially account for the erratic performance graph shown in Figure 1 by noting that a hiring boom took place in 1978 and 1979. The dip in feet per manshift in 1976 was thought to reflect the mine's changing from developmental to production mining as Torenton began producing ore for the market. In general, the trend suggests an improvement in mining effectiveness and, as most mine operators would realize, this occurred despite major additions to safety procedures that greatly slowed ore production.

A look at the comparison mine gives one a better perspective on Torenton's progress. The technology of the two mines differed only slightly, and any technological changes—such as advances in methods or tools—were relatively minor in both settings during this period. The other mine used a productivity index known as "tons per manshift." In 1974, the comparison mine had a productivity rate of 34.9. Productivity declined steadily until 1979, after which it showed some recovery, but as of 1981 productivity remained at 32.3 tons per manshift and failed to regain the 1974 level. During this period, Torenton moved from a productivity level of 1.18 feet per manshift (1974) to one of 2.10 (1981). Because of the different scales of measurement, perhaps one can only state that the data imply that Torenton gradually improved its performance during this period by more than 75%, while the comparison mine showed a slight decline.

Safety

The third criterion is safety, and the method for assessing it changed in 1977 from the MESA (Mine Enforcement Safety Administration) formula to the MSHA (Mine Safety and Health Administration) formula. Figure 1 describes a relatively continuous improvement in each graph, but inconsistencies in computational procedures do not allow a simple assertion of safety progression during the 1974–81 period. Informal judgments by Torenton's safety personnel, however, suggest this was the case.

Using the same MESA and MSHA formulas for the comparison mine, one finds that the MESA rates moved from 38 in 1974 to a high of 47 in 1976 before dropping to 29 in 1977. The MSHA rates moved from 8 in 1978 to a high of 10 in 1979 and then declined in 1981. The degree of change, using either formula, seems more marked at Torenton. According to mine officials at Torenton, however, this may have partly been an artifact of the interpretations given the MESA and MSHA formulas by the two mines when they were first presented by the government agencies.

As an alternative means of gauging the Torenton safety record, we considered industry records for this period from the appropriate mining sector—that is, metal and nonmetal mining (cf. *Statistical Abstract of the United States: 1982–1983,* 1983, p. 718). Data from 1974 to 1980 show a slight increase in the rate of nonfatal injuries per million work hours (24 to 28) as well as in the rate of nonfatal injuries per 1,000 workers (44 to 51). This seems to suggest that Torenton's trend toward fewer on-the-job injuries ran counter to the industry pattern.

The Torenton Mine (C)*

James F. Gavin

I will describe three significant change processes that occurred at Torenton during 1975, 1979, and 1982.

1975. During the initial period of our project's work at Torenton, turnover was a major organizational problem. That the organization had to bring in outside consultants with expertise in "people problems" to deal with this issue supports the argument that Torenton had not resolved its turnover problems because the managers did not know how to generate problem-relevant data. By the time we conducted the second survey in 1975, however, the human resources manager not only had a rudimentary idea as to how to develop relevant data, he also had a specific theory of action as to why employees were leaving the organization: The attendance policy gave supervisors too much discretion over the acceptability of excuses regarding absences (once employees had a certain number of unexcused absences on their records, the organization automatically terminated their employment). The 1975 survey included questions on the attendance policy, and the resulting data indirectly supported this theory. A revised program was recommended by the HR manager and implemented by the management committee. It removed all discretionary powers from the supervisors. This represented a clear case of unilateral "win-lose" strategy that the HR department seemingly used to win against the operating departments. The mine supervisors, in turn, strongly resented the loss of one of their mechanisms for controlling employees.

If one considers Argyris's points on using data to generate alternatives and develop a shared commitment to decisions, then one sees that the change process lacked these attributes. Even the validity of the data comes into question, given that the supervisors might have had other perspectives on which information one might need to evaluate the problem. To appraise this change strategy fully, one needs to know that, for one, turnover continued to decline after 1975 and that employees expressed greater satisfaction with the new policy, and, second, that as late as 1980 one could hear supervisors criticizing the "new" attendance policy—and, by implication, its advocates.

1979. The second change, although less dramatic, significantly illustrates an evolving process. Before implementing a new employee benefits program in 1979, the HR manager decided to consult employees about it. Some of the initial reformulations of this program had been based on industry studies, but the manager wanted to obtain reactions to a range of options before

* SOURCE: James F. Gavin, "Observations from a Long-Term Survey—Guided Consultation with a Mining Company," *Journal of Applied Behavioral Science*, 21 (1985), 204–220. Reprinted with permission.

deciding on a plan. In crew meetings deliberately modeled after the survey feedback sessions, the employees were invited to comment on their benefits program and on some changes advocated by the HR department. These consultations served to shape the eventual benefits package more appropriately, although the employees did not actually decide on the final ingredients.

Through this example we can again see a mixture of governing variables and action strategies. The HR manager seemed to have a greater appreciation of how to generate problem-relevant data and even of how to use the data to develop alternatives and make decisions, which conformed more closely to Argyris's conception of a valid intervention. A major disparity was apparent, however, in the effort to achieve shared commitment—that is, the HR manager made the decision unilaterally, without the formal consensus of the employees.

1982. The third change process took place in 1982, when the mine was affected by severely reduced markets for its products and had to sharply reduce the size of its work force. Traditionally in the mining industry, the almost automatic solution to this problem would be to make progressive layoffs based on seniority. Instead, the management committee approached the problem according to a process model similar to that of action research and, as I will demonstrate, employed more of a Model II action strategy. The managers held meetings with employees at all levels of the organization and conducted research on approaches used by other organizations, including those in other industries. From this process they developed alternatives, which they presented to groups of employees for discussion and reaction. Eventually, a final set of options was presented that varied depending on the individual's tenure and role in the system. Employees thereby had permission to choose from among alternatives that they had helped originate. According to several observers, this program proceeded smoothly and to the satisfaction of most employees. This approach to problem solving clearly had evolved over the years, and it represented a markedly different management philosophy than that which had existed at the outset of our consultations.

The Torenton Mine (D)*

James F. Gavin

In covering the history of consultations with Torenton, I indirectly referred to a few issues. Initially, the mine sought help with a specific problem: turnover. The mine managers also had a style—theory of action—for dealing with organizational problems. As consultants, we had our own theory of action, which directed *our* approaches to *their* problems. When the client and the consultants met to discuss methods, we talked about processes, such as communications, human relations, and feedback; the miners talked about outcomes, such as turnover, safety, and productivity. Because members of the management committee had been exposed to various behavioral science constructs, they nodded their heads appropriately as we described our approaches—attitude surveys, feedback sessions, human relations training—and, after we indicated how these methods could address their problems, gave us their approval. In one sense it may seem as if we functioned with bilateral control based on valid information. Soon, however, we realized that whatever we thought management understood about us was largely presumptuous, and, in turn, whatever they thought they understood about us was also unjustified. Simply put, our languages and theories of action were different, and only experience would inform us of our misunderstandings. . . .

When the management committee members told us that they wanted supervisors to be good listeners, to manage by participation, and to be skilled at offering constructive feedback, were they espousing a theory of action inconsistent with their ingrained behavior styles? Was this merely wishful thinking? Or did we simply have a problem of semantics? My experience with other mines, and one in particular, informs me that the popularity of behavioral science jargon in industry—and the relative innocence of the mining industry with respect to the behavioral sciences—leads to a higher risk of misunderstanding between clients in mining and OD consultants. To compound this further, the underground mining environment differs exceptionally from most other industrial settings. Certain OD methodologies may be quite problematic, even though they may appear eminently well-suited to this industry.

For example, examine the rationally based data-gathering and analysis procedures of an SFP and imagine the response to an SFP proposal made by a mining engineer who presumably values logical-rational processes and sees in this program a clearly delineated flow chart of activities. A match appears evident. Now consider the management style and skills appropriate to the

* SOURCE: James F. Gavin, "Observations from a Long-Term Survey—Guided Consultation with a Mining Company," *Journal of Applied Behavioral Science*, 21 (1985), 204–220. Reprinted with permission.

effective implementation of such a program, particularly in its feedback and follow-up phases. When a mining company has been run "successfully" for decades under a style of management that one might describe as a "benevolent autocracy," both the client and the consultant will have to face a few surprises when the program gets underway. In this light, one can appreciate why the personnel at Torenton would understand and value the SFP approach only after the third program had taken place in 1978. The dilemma consists of knowing how to generate valid information for the decision makers of the mine in the absence of actual or related process experiences.

This leads to perhaps the most intriguing question: Why did the management team at Torenton stick it out? I speculate that the managers' theory of action valued outcomes, whereas they tended to devalue—or at least deemphasize—the inner emotional world. The managers had access to daily indicators of organizational functioning, even to the point of being able to determine if a training intervention made any difference in a particular supervisor's behavior or if feedback sessions on a particular day affected productivity. They had access to an active grapevine that we know carried stories about our acceptability to employees at different levels and the positive consequences of our work. Not only did major behavioral measures indicate improvement, but the HR staff also noted reductions in the number of employee grievances filed and a lessening of daily complaints about supervisory and management actions. That some managers disliked our philosophy, our approach, or our emphasis on process was, in a sense, less relevant than the results of our consultations. With the passage of time we received growing support as younger managers who were more in tune with the behavioral sciences and the "new" management styles replaced older managers. Additionally, from about 1975 onward, upper-level managers began attending external laboratories on leadership and returned to Torenton with changed perspectives regarding the rationale for and utility of the interventions. Finally, we had an internal advocate—the HR manager—who not only helped interpret and justify our behaviors to the managers, but also reined in our enthusiasm when he felt our proposals would outstrip the organization's ability to adapt to change.

I can find no simple way to sum up this apparently successful consulting relationship or to derive a template for interventions in the mining industry. . . . Using hindsight, I can see that much of the disruptive tension of the consultations resulted from some fundamental differences regarding the objectives of the intervention . . . and that more open and ongoing discussions between the client and consultant about the orientations of our work together might have been beneficial. In saying this, of course, one must keep in mind the organizational culture of the 1970s, the nature of the client system, and the pragmatic leanings of Torenton's management. Accordingly, the safest conclusion might be that future interventions can be launched from a more solid platform because of the foundations provided by this long-term effort. Any philosophical or strategic shortcomings manifest in this case may thus guide change agents along more propitious paths.

The Apex Manufacturing Company*

Edgar H. Schein

ENTRY

Chuck Channon, a senior manager in the Apex Manufacturing Company, asked me to act as a consultant to help the company over some communication and relationship problems. Apex was a large manufacturing concern, organised into several divisions. A vice-president, Chuck managed one of the company's divisions and reported directly to the president. At our exploratory meeting, Chuck spoke openly about his concerns that the president needed help in handling certain key people, shared his worries that the chief executive and his immediate subordinates were not in good communication, and indicated that recent company history suggested the need for some stabilising force in the organisation. He indicated that there were communication problems in the top management group resulting from a recent reorganisation. Because the company expected to grow rapidly in the next several years, they felt they should work on these kinds of problems now. I asked him whether the president knew he had come to me, and what the president's feelings were about bringing in a consultant. Chuck indicated that the president as well as other key executives were all in favour of bringing someone in to work with them. All of them saw the need for some outside help.

This meeting between Chuck and me led to the decision that I should attend one of the regular meetings of the company's executive committee, its top decision making body, to meet the president and the other six senior executives, to discuss further what could and should be done. At this meeting I found a lively interest in the idea of having an outsider help the committee group and the organisation as a whole become more effective. I also found that the executive group was willing to enter into an open-ended relationship. I explained as much as I could my philosophy of process consultation, and suggested that a good way of getting further acquainted would be to set up a series of individual interviews with each member of the group. At the same time I suggested that I sit in on the weekly half-day meetings of the executive committee. The interviews could then take place after several of these meetings.

At this initial meeting with the executive group I was able to observe a

* SOURCE: Abstracted from Edgar H. Schein and edited by Roy McLennan from *Process Consultation*. © 1969. pp. 80, 83, 86–7, 91–2, 100, 104–8, 111–16, 119, 126–7, 129–30. Addison-Wesley Publishing Company, Inc., Reading, Mass. Reprinted with permission.

number of key events. For example, the president, Alex Armstrong, was very informal but very powerful. I got the impression initially (and confirmed it subsequently) that the relationship of all the group members to the president would be the critical issue, with relationships to each other being relatively less important. I also got the impression that Alex Armstrong was a very confident individual who would tolerate my presence only as long as he saw some value in it; he would have little difficulty in confronting me and terminating the relationship if my presence ceased to have value.

It was also impressive, and turned out to be indicative of a managerial style, that Alex did not feel the need to see me alone. He was satisfied from the outset to deal with me inside the executive committee group. Near the end of the initial meeting with the committee I requested a private talk with him to satisfy myself that he understood the psychological contract we were entering into. He turned out to be surprisingly uncomfortable in this one-to-one relationship, had little that he wished to impart to me, and did not show much interest in my view of the relationship. I wanted the private conversation in order to test his reaction to taking some personal feedback on his own behaviour as the consultation progressed. He said he would welcome this, and indicated little or no concern over it. As I was to learn later, this reflected a very strong sense of his own power and identity. He felt he knew himself very well, and was not a bit threatened by feedback.

Part of the initial mandate arranged with me as consultant was to help the executive group to relate to the president. In the interviews which I subsequently conducted with individual executive group members I did not have a formal interview schedule, but rather held an informal discussion with each executive around certain issues. I concentrated quite heavily on what kinds of things went well in the group member's relationship with the president; what kinds of things went poorly; how relationship problems with the president were related to job performance; in what way the member would like to see the relationship change; and so on.

MORALE IN THE DIVISIONS

There was some concern, on the part of the executive committee, that there might be a morale problem at the organisational level immediately below the vice-presidents. After getting to know the top management group through several group meetings, I suggested that it might be useful to interview and give feedback to the people at this level. Initially I was asked merely to do an interview survey and report back to the top management committee. I declined this approach because it violated process consultation assumptions: it would not involve the people who were the sources of the data in analysing their own process. I suggested instead that I conduct the interviews with the ground rule that all my conclusions would first be reported back to the interviewee group, and that I would tell top management only those items which the group felt should be reported.[1] The group would first have to sort the items and decide which things they could handle by themselves, and which should be reported up the line of authority because they were under higher management control. The real value of the feedback should accrue to the group which initially provided the data. They should become involved in examining the issues they had brought up, and consider what they themselves might do about them.

This procedure was agreed upon by the top management. One vice-president sent a memorandum to all the company's members who would be involved in the interview programme, informing them of the procedure, his commitment to it, and his hope that they would participate. I then followed up with individual appointments with each person concerned. At this initial appointment I recounted the origin of the idea, assured the interviewee that his individual responses would be entirely confidential, told him that I would summarise the data by department, and said that he would see the group report and discuss it before any feedback went to his top management boss.

In the interview I asked each person to describe his job, tell what he found to be the major pluses and minuses in it, describe what relationships he had to other groups in the organisation, and how he felt about a series of specific job factors, such as challenge, autonomy, supervision, facilities, salary, benefits and so on. I later summarised the interviews in a report in which I tried to highlight what I saw to be common problem areas. All the respondents were then invited to a group meeting at which I passed out the summary, explained that the purposes of the meeting were to examine the data, deleting or elaborating where necessary, and to determine which problem areas might be worked on by the group itself. We then went over the summary, item by item, permitting as much discussion as any given item warranted. Following the group meeting the revised summary was given to top management.

The group meeting had its greatest utility in exposing the interviewees, in a systematic way, to interpersonal and group issues. For many of them what they had thought to be private gripes turned out to be organisational problems which they could do something about. The attitude 'let top management solve all our problems' tended to be replaced with a viewpoint which differentiated between intra-group problems, inter-group problems, and those which were higher management's responsibility. The interviewees not only gained more insight into organisational psychology, but also responded positively to being involved in the process of data gathering itself. It symbolised to them top management's interest in them and concern for solving organisational problems.

Subsequently I met with each of the vice-presidents in the company whose subordinate groups I had interviewed, and gave them a list of comments which had been made about their respective managerial styles. By this time in the intervention I knew each man well, and felt that he would be able to accept the kinds of comments which were made. In each case we scheduled at least a one hour session, so we could talk in detail about any items which were unclear

---

[1] This procedure was first brought to my attention by Mr. Richard Beckhard.

and/or threatening. These discussions usually became counselling sessions, to help the individual overcome some of the negative effects which were implied in the feedback data.

FINANCIAL CONTROL

I found that the treasurer, Ralph Macalister, consistently made the operating managers in the executive committee feel uncomfortable, by presenting financial information in an unintentionally threatening way. Ralph wanted to be helpful, and he felt everyone needed the information he had to offer. But it often had the appearance of an indictment of the executive concerned: his costs were too high, his inventory control had slipped, he was too high over budget, etc. Furthermore, this information was often revealed for the first time in the executive committee meeting, so that the manager concerned had no fore-warning, and no opportunity to find out why things had gone out of line. The result was often a fruitless argument about the validity of the figures, a great deal of defensiveness on the part of the manager concerned, and irritation on the part of the president because the operating managers could not deal more effectively with the treasurer.

As I observed this process occurring repeatedly over several weeks, I decided that merely drawing attention to the pattern would not really solve it, because everyone appeared to be operating with constructive intent. What the executive group needed was an alternative way to think about the use of financial control information. I therefore wrote a memo on control systems and circulated it to executive group members. See Exhibit 1. When this came

---

Exhibit 1 Memo: Some Comments on Internal Auditing and Control Programs

---

A. *Some Ideas Why Internal Auditing Is Seen as Nonhelpful or as a Source of Tension:*

1. Auditors often feel primary loyalty to auditing group rather than company as a whole; they tend, at times, to feel themselves outside of the organization. Managers, on the other hand, feel primary loyalty to organization.

2. Auditors are typically rewarded for finding things wrong, less so for helping people get their work done. Managers, on the other hand, are rewarded for getting the job done, whether things were wrong or not.

3. Auditors tend to be (a) *perfectionists,* and (b) focused on *particular* problems in depth. Managers, on the other hand, tend to be (a) "*satisficers*" rather than maximizers (they tend to look for workable rather than perfect or ideal solutions), and (b) *generalists,* focusing on getting many imperfect things to work together toward getting a job done, rather than perfecting any one part of the job.

4. The auditor's job tempts him to *evaluate* the line operation and to propose solutions. The manager, on the other hand, wants *descriptive* (nonevaluative) feedback and to design his own solutions.

Exhibit 1 *(continued)*

B. *Some Possible Dysfunctional Consequences of Tension between Line Organization and Auditing Function:*

1. Members of the line organization tend to pay attention to doing well, primarily in those areas which the auditor measures, whether those are important to the organizational mission or not.

2. Members of the line organization put effort into hiding problems and imperfections.

3. Management tends to use information about their subordinates in an unintentionally punishing way by immediate inquiries which give subordinates the feeling of having the boss on their back even while they are already correcting the problem.

4. Members of the line organization are tempted to falsify and distort information to avoid punishment for being "found out," and to avoid having their boss "swoop down" on them.

5. *Detailed* information gathered by the auditing function tends to be passed too far up the line both in the auditing function and the line organization, making information available to people who are too far removed from the problem to know how to evaluate the information.

C. *Some Tentative Principles for the Handling of Auditing:*

1. *Line involvement:* The more the line organization is involved actively in decisions concerning (a) which areas of performance are to be audited, and (b) how the information is to be gathered and to whom it is to be given, the more helpful and effective the auditing function will be.

2. *Horizontal rather than vertical reporting:* The more the auditing information is made available, *first* to the man with the problem (horizontal reporting), then to his immediate boss only if the problem is not corrected, and then only to higher levels in either the line or the auditing group if the problem is still not corrected, the more likely it is that auditing will be effective (because line organizations will be less motivated to hide or falsify information and less likely to feel punished).

3. *Reward for helping rather than policing:* The more the managers in the auditing group reward their subordinates for being *helpful* (based on whether they are being perceived as helpful by the line) rather than being efficient in finding problem areas, the more effective will be the auditing function.*

4. *Useful feedback:* The more the auditing information is *relevant* to important operational problems, *timely* in being fed back as soon after problem discovery as possible, and *descriptive* rather than evaluative, the more useful it will be to the line organization.

---

* Auditing people tend to be undertrained in how to use audit information in a helpful way; an appropriate reward system should be bolstered by training in how to give help.

up for discussion at a later committee meeting I was in a better position to make my observations about the executive group, since a clear alternative had been presented. My feeling was that I could not have successfully presented this theory orally because of the amount of heat the issues always generated, and because the executive group members were highly active individuals who would have wanted to discuss each point separately, making it difficult to get the whole message across.

EXECUTIVE COMMITTEE DEVELOPMENT

I sat in for several months on the weekly executive committee meeting of the president and his key subordinate managers. I quickly became aware that the group was very loose in its manner of operation: people spoke when they felt like it, issues were explored fully, conflict was fairly openly confronted, and members felt free to contribute. The climate seemed constructive, but it created a major difficulty for the executive group. No matter how few items were on the agenda the group was never able to finish its work. The list of backlog items grew longer, and the frustration of group members intensified in proportion to this backlog. The committee responded by trying to work harder. They scheduled more meetings, and attempted to get more done at each meeting, but with little success. Remarks about the ineffectiveness of groups, too many meetings, and so on became more and more frequent.

My diagnosis was that the executive group was overloaded. The agenda was too large: the members tried to process too many items at any given meeting. The agenda was a mixture of operational and policy issues, without recognition by the group that such items required different allocations of time. I suggested to the group members that they seemed overloaded, and should discuss how to develop the agenda for their meetings. The suggestion was adopted after a half hour or so of shared feelings. It was then decided, with my help, to sort the agenda items into several categories, to devote some meetings entirely to operational issues, while others would be exclusively policy meetings. The operations meetings would be run more tightly in order to process these items efficiently. The policy questions would be dealt with in depth. Once the executive group had made this separation, and realised that it could function differently at different meetings, it then decided to meet once a month for an entire day. During this day they would take up one or two large questions and explore them in depth. The group accepted my suggestion to hold such discussions away from the office in a pleasant, less hectic environment.

By rearranging the agenda the group succeeded in rearranging its whole pattern of operations. This rearrangement also resulted in a redefinition of my role. The president confronted me with the statement that my continued attendance in the operational group meetings was no longer desirable from his point of view. As he put it, I was beginning to sound too much like a regular member to be of much use. He had decided that I should phase out my attendance at the operational meetings, but should plan to take a more active role in the monthly one-day policy meetings. He would set time aside for presentation of any theory I might wish to make, and for process analysis of the meeting. He had previously been reluctant to take time for process work in the earlier meeting pattern, but now welcomed it. I concurred in these decisions, and reduced my involvement in the company to the all day policy meetings of the executive group, though the initiative for inviting me remained entirely with the group.

The full day policy meetings changed the climate of the executive group dramatically. For one thing it was easier to establish close informal relationships with other members during breaks and meals. Because there was enough time people felt they could really work through their conflicts, instead of having to leave them hanging. It was my impression that as acquaintance level rose, so did the level of trust in the group. Members began to feel free to share more personal reactions with each other. This sense of freedom made everyone more relaxed and readier to let down personal barriers and report accurate information. There was less need for defensive distortion or withholding. I concluded that my intervention had tended to help the top management group move from chaotic meetings towards a more differentiated, organised pattern. In the end the group spent more time in meetings than before, but they minded it less because the meetings were more productive. The group had also learned how to manage its own agenda and how to guide its own processes.

INTERPERSONAL DIFFICULTIES

After many months of working with the president and his executive committee members, I arrived at a point where all of them saw me as a potentially useful communication link. They asked me to report to each one of them the feelings or reactions of others whenever I learned anything I felt should be passed on. At the same time they were quite open with me about each other, knowing that I might well pass on any opinions or reactions they voiced to me. They did not want me to treat everything as confidential because they trusted me and each other enough. The idea was sincerely intended. My own feeling was that serving as the carrier of this type of information was not an ideal role for me, and reflected an insufficient ability on their part to tell each other things directly. Hence I took two courses of action. First, I tried as much as possible to train each man to tell others in the group directly what he thought about an issue. At the same time I intervened directly in their process by passing on information and opinions if I felt this would aid the working situation.

A simple yet critical event illustrates what I mean. Two members of the executive committee, Pete Denton and Joe Goodman, did not always communicate freely with each other, partly because they felt some rivalry. Pete Denton had completed a study and written a report which was to be discussed by the executive group. Three days before the report was due I visited the company, and stopped in at Pete's office to discuss the report with him, and ask him how things were going. He said he was puzzled about why Joe Goodman hadn't come to him to look at some of the back-up data pertaining to Joe's company function. He very much wanted to share the data with Joe. He felt this was just another bit of evidence that Joe did not really respect him very much. An hour or so later I was working with Joe Goodman, and raised the issue of the report. Joe and his staff were very busy preparing for the meeting, but nothing was said to me about looking at the back-up data. When I asked why they had not done anything about it Joe replied that he was sure it was private, and would not be released by Pete. He wanted badly to see it, but felt sure that Pete had deliberately not offered it. I decided on the spot to report to him how Pete was feeling. Joe expressed considerable surprise. Later in the day he went to Pete, who gave him a warm welcome and turned over to him three volumes of the data. In making this intervention I had to judge carefully whether I would hurt either Pete or Joe by revealing Pete's feelings, and had decided there was little harm in intervening: the potential gains outweighed the risks.

CONFRONTIVE FEEDBACK

About one year after I became consultant to the company the executive group decided at one of the monthly all-day meetings, quite spontaneously, to try some direct confrontive feedback. Alex Armstrong announced that he thought each group member should tell the others what he felt to be their strengths and weaknesses, and asked me to help in designing a format for this discussion. I first asked the group members whether they did in fact want to attempt this type of confrontation. The response was sincerely positive, so we decided to go ahead. The format I suggested was based upon my prior observation of group members. I had noticed that whenever anyone commented on anyone else, there was a strong tendency to answer back, and to lock in on the first comment made. Hence, further feedback tended to be cut off. To deal with this problem I suggested that the group discuss one person at a time, and that a ground rule be established: that the person being described was not to comment or respond until all the members had had a chance to give all their feedback. In this way he would be forced to continue to listen. The ground rule was accepted, and I was given the role of monitoring the group to ensure that the process operated as the group intended it.

For the next several hours the group went into a very detailed and searching analysis of each member's managerial and interpersonal style, including that of the president. I encouraged them to discuss both the positives and the negatives they saw in the person. I also played a key role in forcing people to make their comments specific and concrete. I demanded examples, insisted on clarification, and generally asked the kind of question which I thought might be on the listening manager's mind as he tried to understand the feedback he was receiving. I also added my own feedback on points I had observed in that member's behaviour. At first it was not easy for the group members either to give or receive feedback, but as the day wore on they learned to become more effective.

The confrontation exercise was considered highly successful, both at the time and some months later. It deepened relationships, exposed some chronic problems which could now be worked on, and gave each member much food for thought in terms of his own self-development. It should be noted that the group chose to do this confrontive exercise spontaneously after many months of meetings organised around work topics. I am not sure they could have handled the feedback task effectively had they been urged to try sooner, even though I could see the need for this type of exercise some time before the initiative came from the group.

It was clear that with increasing experience the executive group was learning to tune in on its own internal processes, was beginning to pay more attention to these, to give more meeting time to analysis of interpersonal feelings and events, and was now able to manage its own agenda and do its own diagnoses without my presence. The group first discovered the latter from having to conduct some of its all-day meetings in my absence. Where in the past such meetings had been devoted entirely to work content, the group now found that in my absence they could discuss interpersonal process with profit. The members themselves described this change as one of 'climate.' The group felt more open and effective; members felt they could trust each other more; information was flowing more freely; less time was being wasted on oblique communications or political in-fighting.

MANAGEMENT DEVELOPMENT

During the second year of my association with the Apex company my involvement was considerably reduced, though I worked on some specific projects. The company had set up a committee to develop a management development programme, consisting of several members of the executive committee, together with some other managers. I was asked to sit in with this committee and help in the development of a programme. After a number of meetings it became clear to me that the kind of programme this committee group needed was one in which the content was not too heavily predetermined. The problems of different managers in the company were sufficiently different to require that a formula be found for discussing a whole range of problems. One of the reflections of the value change which had taken place in the executive committee managers was their recognition that they should be prime participants in any programme which they might invent. If a programme was not exciting or beneficial enough to warrant the committee's time, it could hardly be imposed on the rest of the organisation.

We developed a model which involved a series of small group meetings, at each of which the group would set its own agenda. After every third meeting or so a larger management group would be convened for a lecture and discussion period on some highly relevant topic. Once the first group (the management development committee plus others at the vice-presidential level) had completed six to eight meetings, each member of the original group would become the chairman for a group at the next lower level of the organisation. These ten or so next level groups would then meet for six to eight sessions around agenda items developed by themselves. In the meantime the lecture series would continue. After each series of meetings, at a given organisational level, the model would be reassessed and either changed or continued at the next lower level, with the previous members again becoming group chairmen.

My role in this whole enterprise was, first, to help the group invent the idea outlined above; second, to meet with the development committee group as a facilitator of the group's efforts to become productive; third, to serve as a resource on topics to be covered and lecturers to be used in the lecture series; and fourth, to appear as an occasional lecturer in the lecture series, or as a source of input at a small group meeting. As this procedure took form my involvement was gradually reduced, though I still meet with the original development committee to review the overall concept.

In recent months I have met occasionally with individual members of the development committee, and with the expanded group as a whole. My function during these meetings is to act as a sounding board, to contribute points of view which might not be represented among the members, and to help the group assess its own level of functioning. I have been able to provide the group with some perspective on its own growth as a group, because I could more easily see changes in values and skills. It has also been possible for the group to enlist my help with specific interpersonal problems. A measure of the growth of the group has been its ability to decide when and how to use my help, and to make these decisions validly, from my point of view, in terms of where I felt I could constructively help.

Evaluation of Results
and Disengagement*

Edgar H. Schein

So far in this book we have examined in some detail the thinking and activities of a process consultant. We have not concentrated on the big picture: what kinds of outcome or result does the process consultant look for over a period of time, how does he measure these outcomes, and how does he decide at some point to reduce his involvement with the client system?

These questions will not be easy to answer because the goals of P-C cannot be stated in simple measurable terms. The ultimate goal of any organization-development effort is, of course, improved organizational performance. Those organization-development efforts which involve P-C attempt to achieve this effectiveness by changing some of the *values* of the organization and by increasing the *interpersonal skills* of key managers. Performance is, in turn, related to these value changes and increases of skill. In the short run, then, the process consultant looks for evidence that certain values are changing and that certain skills are increasing. Let us look at what these values and skills are.

VALUES AND SKILLS TO BE CHANGED THROUGH PROCESS CONSULTATION

Values

The single most important value to be changed in any organization-development effort involving P-C concerns the relative attention given to task *vs.* human concerns. Most managers start with the value that the most important concerns of management are efficient task performance primarily, and human relations secondarily (or as time permits). The problem for the process consultant is to change this value—make the manager feel that human relations and the management of interpersonal and group events is at least as important as immediate task performance. The logic behind this value is that for the manager his task can only be accomplished through other people; hence effective interpersonal relations become a prime means to the end of efficient task performance. Organizations in the end are nothing more than networks

* SOURCE: Edgar H. Schein, *Process Consultation.* © 1969. Addison-Wesley Publishing Company, Inc., Reading Mass. pp. 123–126, 128–131. Reprinted with permission.

of human relationships. If these networks do not function effectively there is nothing with which to perform the tasks to be accomplished.

A *second* value which has to be changed in any OD effort involving P-C concerns the relative attention given to the content of the work and the structure of the organization *vs.* the *process* by which work is done. Managers tend to focus much more on the content of decisions, interactions, and communications. They tend to devalue the importance of "personality," of "feelings," and of "how things are done," or they attempt to dodge such process-related issues by perpetual redesign of the structure of the organization. The process consultant faces the problem of showing managers that processes in the organization follow patterns which can be studied and understood, and which have important consequences for organizational performance. Most importantly, processes can be rationally changed and adapted to increase the effectiveness of performance. Therefore, one should attempt to improve the organization through a joint consideration of the structure and of the processes of the organization.

A *third* value concerns the relative attention given to *short-run output* vs. *long-run effectiveness*. Most managers feel that every hour of every day should be occupied with activities that have an immediate output. The process consultant knows from his experience that the diagnosis of interpersonal events often involves periods of slow and calm analysis which may at first appear to be a terrible waste of time. He must change the manager's value system, so that he becomes tolerant of such periods, in the realization that the time invested in building *effective interpersonal relations* leads to much quicker and more effective *ultimate task performance*.

A *fourth* value which the process consultant must inculcate is the acceptance of the need for *perpetual diagnosis* as an alternative to insistence on *generalizations and principles* by which to operate. It is my assumption that the rate of change in the environment (and, therefore, within organizations) will increase, and that this in turn will require an increase in the organization's ability to diagnose both the environment and itself. A principle may hold up for the next six months but may be invalid within a year. The manager must accept perpetual diagnosis of process as a way of life if he is to avoid obsolescence and organizational failure. Ideally, the manager would not merely accept this value grudgingly, but would discover that perpetual diagnosis can be fun and can lead to perpetually better day-to-day task performance. I am not advocating what so many managers seem to fear—that if they do too much diagnosis they will be unable to be decisive when an occasion demands it. I am advocating that decisions be made, within the time constraints imposed by the task requirements, but that they be made in terms of a *diagnosis,* however short, rather than a *policy* or *general principle* which may no longer have any validity.

In summary, the process consultant attempts to change the manager's attitudes and values in the direction of more concern for human problems, more concern for process issues, more concern for long-run effectiveness, and more concern for the diagnostic process itself as a way of achieving organizational adaptability. By implication, one major way in which to assess the results of a P-C effort is to gauge the degree to which these values have taken hold in key managers. Such an assessment cannot be made formally or through some kind of specific measuring tool. It must be made by the consultant through observation of the activities of managers in the organization, or by the managers themselves.

Skills

As I have been repeating endlessly throughout this volume, the most important skill to be imparted to the client is the ability to diagnose and work on his own problems in the interpersonal, group, and organizational area. Initially the process consultant has more knowledge and skill than the client. As the P-C effort progresses, he should be able to observe an increase in the knowledge and skill of the various managers who have been involved. One of the best indicators of the growth of such skills is the willingness of various groups of teams to tackle process-analysis periods or agenda-review periods by themselves. How willing are they to assign an observer role, and how skillful are they in picking out key group events, in sharing feelings, in reviewing group action?

It should be clear that a willingness to engage in activities which initially have been the consultant's reflects a change in values. Even if a given manager were able to engage in more self-diagnostic processes, he might resist such an activity if none of the values cited above had changed. On the other hand, willingness reflecting a value change is not enough if there has not been a corresponding development of skill.

The assessment of the skill of the client system in diagnosing and working on its own problems must, as in the case of values, be made by observations on the part of the consultant and/or by the client system itself. It is important that managers feel confident in solving their own problems, and solving them effectively. Even if the consultant doubts that the level of skill reached is sufficient, he must be prepared to back off if members of the client system themselves feel they are able to go ahead without his help.

Process consultation is an emergent process and therefore it is difficult to put simple boundaries upon it. Similarly, it is difficult to give overall evaluations. One can look at gradual changes which occur in the culture of the client organization; one can look at the results of specific projects like an interview-feedback cycle; and one can assess the immediate impact of an intervention in a group. But one cannot measure specific indicators, however much this might be desirable. In the end, the outcome of a period of process consultation must be judged jointly by members of the client system and the consultant. Both must make a judgment of whether to continue the relationship and in what manner to continue it. If, in the judgment of either party, there should be a reduction of involvement, how is this process accomplished?

DISENGAGEMENT: REDUCING INVOLVEMENT
WITH THE CLIENT SYSTEM

The process of disengagement has, in most of my experiences, been characterized by the following features:

1. reduced involvement is a mutually agreed upon decision rather than a unilateral decision by consultant or client;
2. involvement does not generally drop to zero but may continue at a very low level;
3. the door is always open from my point of view for further work with the client if the client desires it.

Let me comment upon each of these points, and give some examples.

1. Joint Decisions. In most of my consulting relationships there has come a time when either I felt that nothing more could be accomplished and/or some members of the client system felt the need to continue on their own. To facilitate a reduction of involvement, I usually check at intervals of several months to see whether the client feels that the pattern should remain as is or should be altered. In some cases where I have felt that a sufficient amount had been accomplished, I have found that the client did not feel the same way and wanted the relationship to continue on a day-a-week basis. I have sometimes been in the situation of arguing that I remain fully involved even when the client wanted to reduce involvement, and in many cases I was able to obtain the client's concurrence.

The negotiation which surrounds a reduction of involvement is in fact a good opportunity for the consultant to diagnose the state of the client system. The kinds of arguments which are brought up in support of continuing (or terminating) provide a solid basis for determining how much value and skill change has occurred. The reader may feel that since the client is paying for services, he certainly has the right to make unilateral decisions about whether or not to continue these services. My point would be that if the consultation process has even partially achieved its goals, there should arise sufficient trust between consultant and client to enable both to make the decision on rational grounds. Here again, it is important that the consultant not be economically dependent upon any one client, or his own diagnostic ability may become biased by his need to continue to earn fees.

2. Involvement Not Zero. If the client and consultant agree on a reduced involvement, it is important that both should recognize that this does not necessarily mean a complete termination. In fact, a complete termination is not desirable because the diagnosis on which reduced involvement is based may not be accurate enough to warrant termination. A more desirable arrangement is to drop the level to perhaps a half-day every three or four weeks, or attendance only at certain kinds of special meetings, or an interview with key members of the client system once every two or three months. Through this mechanism it is possible for the client and the consultant to reassess periodically how things are going.

3. Reinvolvement Is Always Possible.

This point is closely related to the previous one, but I want to separate it to bring out a special aspect of the obligation of the process consultant. In any P-C consulting relationship with a client, I think the consultant should make it clear that the door is always open to further work once the relationship has begun. The reason for this obligation is that a good relationship with a consultant is difficult for a client to develop. Once both the consultant and the client have invested effort in building such a relationship it does not terminate psychologically even if there are prolonged periods of lack of contact. I have had the experience with a number of clients of not seeing them for many months and yet being able to tune in on the group very quickly once contact has been reestablished.

As a general rule it should be the client who reestablishes contact, but I would not advocate sticking to this rigidly. I have, after some period of no contact, called a client and asked if I could talk with him to find out what was going on. In several cases such a call was welcomed and served as the basis for some additional counseling or process observation. The consultant must be careful not to violate his role by selling himself back to the client. It must be an honest inquiry which can comfortably be turned down by the client should he desire to do so. I have been turned down often enough to know that there is nothing inherent in the situation to force an artificial contact. Rather, it sometimes helps a client who wanted help anyway to ask for it in a face-saving way.

Behavior Changes in Successful Organization Development Efforts*

Jerry I. Porras
and Susan J. Hoffer

Jerry I. Porras and Susan J. Hoffer carried out a study which sought "to identify and specify common behavior changes characteristic of successful change efforts" (p. 477). They remarked that they ". . . consider it valuable to learn whether any behavior changes are common to successful change efforts, and, if so, what those behavior changes are" (p. 478). In the words of one of the participants in their study,

> . . . this whole OD effort is to help people be more effective in their behavior with each other. Behind that behavior may be all kinds of things that need to be looked at, but immediately it is the behavior. . . . One of the challenges I throw out to groups is if when we're finished there is no behavior change, then I think you've wasted your money spending [time] here, or even having me come to talk to you . . . because what is the purpose of it all if there's no behavior change? (p. 491)

Porras and Hoffer "identified 47 leaders in the field of planned organization change, defining leaders as those who, by writing about their theoretical models, research, or interventions, had made a significant and sustained contribution to the field for at least 10 years" (p. 482). They then surveyed these top scholars and practitioners, using interviews and open-ended questions. In the interviews "the participants listed all the behaviors they thought common to their successful attempts at planned change" (p. 483). In this way ". . . data were provided by the . . . persons who have shaped and guided the field" [of OD] (p. 489). The researchers remarked that "we doubt that the sample excluded anyone generally considered to be a "pioneer" in the field of planned change" (p. 492).

* SOURCE: From Jerry I. Porras and Susan J. Hoffer, "Common Behavior Changes in Successful Organization Development Efforts," *Journal of Applied Behavioral Science*, 22 (1986), pp. 477–494. Reprinted with permission from NTL Institute.

RESULTS

The researchers concluded that "the intellectual leaders of the field do perceive behavioral changes common to the intervention efforts ..." (p. 489). The participants in the study "nearly unanimously reported behavior changes common to their interventions and showed at least moderate agreement as to what those changes were" (p. 477). They note that

> The leaders showed a reasonable amount of consensus as to the behavior categories ... the high level of agreement for the two most frequently mentioned categories, "communicating openly" and "collaborating" (mentioned by 79% and 74% of the respondents, respectively) is notable. The frequency of response rates for the other categories is lower; most are about 50%.... (pp. 489–90)

The researchers also concluded that these behaviors "... provide a focus for intervention activity and suggest potential intervention "levers" by highlighting the organizational factors promoting or inhibiting desired behavior" (p. 491). The following summary presents Porras and Hoffer's findings in detail.

COMMON BEHAVIOR CHANGES IN
SUCCESSFUL ORGANIZATION DEVELOPMENT EFFORTS
AS REPORTED BY PARTICIPANTS

Question 1: Common Behavior Changes for Individuals
at all Organizational Levels

Communicating Openly.   Sharing intentions, motives, needs, feelings, and cognitions relevant to the work situation. Giving feedback that is descriptive rather than evaluative, and specific rather than general. Asking for and accepting feedback. Listening—including paraphrasing, summarizing, restating, asking for clarification, and checking out impressions. Directly confronting differences when they arise. Acting to produce structural and normative changes that lead to increased information sharing, such as loosening implicit or explicit guidelines as to who should talk to whom, and circulating minutes of meetings.

Collaborating.   Solving problems as close to where they occur as possible. Discussing, planning, and readjusting organizational actions jointly and cooperatively. Holding more group and intergroup discussions and meetings. Involving critical outsiders to the organization in decisions that pertain to them. Making all the serious and creative decisions—particularly decisions where there are multiple stakeholders—in teams. Expanding influence skills beyond bargaining and authoritative commands to include softer means of influence such as seeding ideas, cajoling, and nudging. Moving away from "oneupmanship" and competition, and toward agreement and cooperation.

Taking Responsibility.   Figuring out for oneself what is necessary to be effective in one's job and taking initiative for getting whatever information, cooperation, services, or materials are needed from other relevant parties inside or outside of the organization. Asking for and taking responsibility and authority. Persisting in the struggle to make needed changes, especially in the face of frustration and ambiguity. Forming and offering more suggestions. Stating one's own contribution to a problematic situation rather than blaming others. Exhibiting behaviors that demonstrate movement along a continuum from monitoring one's own work to managing and prioritizing it to affecting the design of it to affecting its organizational context (e.g., policies and procedures) to affecting the goals and directions of the organization itself. Taking responsibility is also reflected in expressions of interest and excitement in the work and in *decreased* approval seeking, face saving, indifference, burnout, or "coasting."

Maintaining a Shared Vision.   Developing and communicating written statements of philosophy. Holding meetings to develop clarity of values, purpose, and the means by which the purpose will be achieved. Talking about how organization values translate into daily work behavior. Changing organizational structure, policies, and practices to reflect stated values. Having and telling a "story," a shared history that gives meaning to the organization's activities. Creating rituals and ceremonies to reestablish and remember values. Setting, discussing, and reinforcing high standards.

Solving Problems Effectively.   Defining problems from a win/win perspective, with an open-minded search for solutions that are mutually acceptable instead of pressing for one's own "right" answer. Taking problems out of a personal context and instead working on them vis a vis an agreed-upon superordinate goal. Keeping problem definition separate from solution seeking. Generating and simultaneously entertaining multiple explanations for a phenomenon. Generating and discussing multiple alternatives for resolving problems.

Respecting/Supporting.   Providing recognition for a job well done. Talking about what's going well versus what's deficient. Making use of an individual's assets versus trying to "correct" their shortcomings. Acknowledging people. Encouraging and rewarding people for taking time for themselves and their families. Equalizing status symbols. Helping; standing in for one another. Treating people equitably. Suspending judgment when things go wrong; allowing for goodness in others and not automatically attributing negative motives. An *absence* of disrespectful and nonsupportive behaviors such as racial, ethnic, and sexist jokes, "scapegoating," and stereotyping. An *absence* of discrimination based on race, sex, or ethnicity. An *absence* of aggressive or punitive behavior.

Processing/Facilitating Interactions. Stopping meetings or one-on-one discussions to examine the process when things are not going well. Assigning (and rotating) the task of observing group process. Reserving time at the end of meetings to critique what was done well/poorly, what facilitated making the decision and/or doing the task, and so on. Clarifying meeting goals and purposes. Rotating the chairperson role. Making group-facilitating rather than group-hindering interventions. Group members changing their roles in the group depending on what is needed for the group to function well. Effectively managing the process of meetings by consensually establishing relevant agendas, holding to them, and recording what is going on so people can understand and follow.

Inquiring. Taking multiple and numerous measures of the discrepancies between the organization's goals and its current state. Taking baselines and using surveys, audits, unobtrusive measures and control groups where possible to gain information about how the organization is functioning. Experimenting with changes in such a way that the outcome will allow causal inference and useful conclusions. Soliciting information from customers, regulators, and competitors. Looking for new ideas in books, articles, technical studies, speeches, and from one another. Frequently examining and questioning structure, practices, and policies to be sure they maximize achievement of the organization's goals.

Experimenting. Taking risks. Having a "bias for action" and not waiting for the perfect design or plan before trying things out. Allowing time to meet, talk, and try new behaviors. Accepting mistakes. Rewarding good tries. Having fewer restrictions on how things get done. Eliminating symbols of conformity (e.g., three-piece suits) and structures/policies that demand conformity (e.g., timeclocks). Deemphasizing action plans, milestones, and measurable objectives. Acting as umbrellas over experimental programs. Backing/sheltering risk takers, especially when they fail. Defending against intrusions from higher levels. Working with those who are experimenting to demonstrate that experimentation is valued and represents an investment in the organization's future.

Question 2: Common Behavior Changes for Managers

Generating Participation. Linking planning and implementation in terms of time and who does it. Involving people when they have the necessary expertise, when the decision must be high quality, and when implementation depends on them. Using meetings, workshops, or a consultant to solicit input from people on proposed changes. *Not* dictating the exact way to accomplish a delegated task. Structuring the work in a way that opens possibilities for self-management by the job incumbent. Providing task and job designs that provide meaningful work, real responsibility for work outcomes, and reliable knowledge of results. Relaxing traditional authoritarian forms of control (e.g., over budgets and allocations of resources and people) and allowing workers to do more. Changing behavior *away from* unilateral edicts and imposing one's will as the basis for power and toward softer influence techniques. Facilitating more than directing.

Leading by Vision.   Continually articulating the organization's purpose, goals, values, and standards and the means by which they are to be carried out operationally. Setting up feedback mechanisms to find out if the vision is being implemented. Structuring the organization and devising policies to be consistent with stated purpose, values, and goals. Reinforcing behaviors that reflect organizational values. Creating ceremonial occasions to reinforce values and goals. Scheduling their own activities to reflect commitment to values and goals. "Role-modeling" behaviors that exemplify the organization's priorities and values.

Functioning Strategically.   Talking about underlying causes, interdependencies, and long-range consequences and acting accordingly. *Not* acting based on a single-function view of the organization. Having long time horizons. Resisting giving in to short term pressures for quick results in order to allow people to learn new behaviors. Deliberately and thoughtfully planning the markets and businesses in which the organization is engaged. Fitting the organizational structure to the organization's key objectives and to the nature of its businesses and markets. Planning for the skills and knowledge required for meeting future objectives. Creating a well thought out and well understood strategic design to guide operating plans and activities.

Promoting Information Flow.   Clearly communicating the elements of the job that need to be accomplished in order to succeed (e.g., communicating standards, goals, tolerances to be worked within, and limits of authority). Being clear about feelings, needs, expectations, commitment, and loyalty issues. Establishing multiple channels for upward, sideways, and downward communication that complement the core chain of command lines (e.g., use of task forces, advisory groups, and unions). Enhancing mechanisms and influencing social norms to promote direct cross-unit communication.

Developing Others.   Teaching needed skills. Helping subordinates identify needs, interests, skills, aspirations, and talents. Rewarding desired behaviors with "strokes" or whatever rewards the manager controls. Delegating tasks based on subordinates' competencies and according to a developmental plan. *Not* doing subordinates' jobs for them. Relating subordinates to a larger context.

Giving people accurate information regarding their performance. Providing personal growth experiences for subordinates. Judging subordinates by their end outputs, not the methods used to produce them. Processing successes and failures with subordinates to help them learn. Helping subordinates take advantage of opportunities and resources offered by the organization.

Intervention and Historical Process*

Roy McLennan

The path towards adequate understanding of particular interventions seems, as has been aptly remarked about human development, a "very rough road, pitted with obstructions, interspersed with blind alleys, and dotted with seductive stopping places."[1] In his valuable paper on history and the life course, Mark Freeman draws widely on epistemological issues in the philosophy of history, in ways which illuminate several core issues about the there-and-then accounts of interventions which appear in this book and elsewhere. This note interprets and applies something of the analysis in his substantial paper to explicating the nature, status and function of accounts of interventions.

In the sense that they are writings about the past, intervention accounts are a sub-species of the general field of history. The undertaking of the researcher or consultant in writing them is thus a similar task to that faced by the professional historian. An historical approach to an intervention, Freeman remarks, "looks back over the flow of events in an attempt to understand and explain their possible connections". (1)[2] An intervention history should, implicitly or explicitly, show how things happened the way they did. The ultimate reference is of course to the data about that intervention. Writing an intervention history requires constant selection and assessment of what data to gather, what data to include, what data to exclude, and how to present them. A "multiplicity of variables [is] needed for anything approaching a thorough explication of human change". (11) And the writer's preconceptions come into play in constructing the explication. There is in this task "a disjunction between . . . detecting a sense of causality" in the interactions which occurred in the intervention, on the one hand, and the feasibility of arriving at some conclusions about contributing conditions, on the other. (8) The complexity of variables as well as the multidirectionality of their influence militates against resolving this disjunction with any ease. "The very process of 'singling out' historical connec-

* SOURCE: Adapted and edited by Roy McLennan from Mark Freeman, "History, Narrative, and Life-Span Developmental Knowledge," *Human Development*, 27 (1984), 1–19. Reprinted by permission of S. Karger AG, Basel. The kind help of Dr. Mark Freeman in preparing this note is gratefully acknowledged.

[1] KENISTON, K. "Psychological Development and Historical Change," *Journal of Interdisciplinary History*, Vol. 2, 1971, p. 337, quoted in Mark Freeman, "History, Narrative, and Life-Span Developmental Knowledge", *Human Development*, Vol. 27, 1984, p. 11.
[2] Passages in quotation marks are referenced to Freeman's article by a page number in parentheses.

tions requires examining their rational necessity within some situation or context, a sequence of related events. . . ." (8).

The intervention researcher, concerned with historical explanation, attempts to situate the events being examined within a whole pattern. Freeman declares that

> . . . the study of the life course [of an intervention] is, of necessity, not only a historical form of inquiry, but one which demands . . . acknowledgement of its narrative structure. More than a simple mapping of discrete and isolated events . . . it is, in a distinct sense, an ongoing story to be told. (3)

It is the story of "how change from beginning to 'end' takes place". (9) A "markedly linear, sequential continuity [emerges] which . . . implies a distinct 'leading to' type of determination, where successive forms are reducible to prior ones." (6) Historical narratives are "cohesive renditions of constellations of events having undergone a process of translation into a whole configuration. Significance, meaning, come from looking backward." (7) Freeman suggests that "to understand history is like following a story, where themes and patterns are retroactively detected across arrays of contingencies." (8) To the philosopher Dilthey,[3] Freeman says, "there was a certain artfulness in the sort of understanding that took place in the making of [an intervention] history, in that it represented an imaginative arrangement of discovered facts. . . ." (4). The key notion is that historical narrative "is precisely not what is 'remembered,' but what is constructed." (4) There is thus "a marked disparity between the data of immediate experience and those of recollection". (9) And "the hard and fast line between the fictional and the real is, in a sense, erased". (4)

In any intervention "Patterns are not detectable except after the fact". (5) This is the case "because of our very vantage point as observers, where the knowledge of outcomes is available, that we are able to make historical connections, derive meanings." (5) Events in their unfolding can in this way be understood—perhaps even explained—after the fact. This gives rise to "the virtually inevitable coloring of the past with the notions of the present." (4) The intervention writer's knowledge is, as R. G. Collingwood[4] put it,

> not either knowledge of the past and therefore not knowledge of the present, or else knowledge of the present and therefore not knowledge of the past; it is knowledge of the past in the present, the self-knowledge of the historian's own mind as the present revival and reliving of past experiences. (4)

Freeman considers that

> To be alive to the historical significance of events as they happen, one must know to which later events these will be related—and these are descriptions

[3] DILTHEY, W. "The Construction of the Historical World in the Human Studies" (1910), in Dilthey, *Selected Writings* (Ed. Rickman), Cambridge University Press, Cambridge, 1976.
[4] COLLINGWOOD, R. G. *The Idea of History*, Oxford University Press, Oxford, 1946, p. 175.

which the actor himself cannot give at the time of experience. . . . As F. Wyatt[5] concludes . . . 'history, qua history, does not really exist when it occurs'. It can be plotted only after the entries have already been made; then—and only then—can the variety of plausible contexts be 'tried for fit'. And, as new data enter the picture . . . this may call for a new, even more comprehensive and plausible context. . . . Particular forms of knowledge derive from retrospection, from an essentially backward look over the terrain of experience. (9)

Freeman remarks that "while the anticipated meaning of the particular configuration at hand is derived from the parts which constitute it, it is through the horizon of the configuration that the parts can acquire meaning". (12) And "data are interpreted and corrected by coherence with theory while theory . . . remains constrained (hopefully) by the data". (13) "The relation under consideration is . . . part to whole . . . this whole being, in essence . . . the central subject the narrative considers". (9)

This way of viewing intervention history implies an organismic or organic model of organization development: "The basic orientation is toward holism, structures and functions". (9) This approach allows "a genuine story to be told, a history—or development—to be written. There is . . . a unifying or synthesizing component in the organismic model by virtue of the . . . recognition of the totality which is the subject of discourse". (10) Thus

> . . . we can make sense—real sense—out of change and time through our ability to extract patterns out of events that have no necessary teleological order of their own. Thus, according to this view of narrative, generalized hypotheses are regarded . . . as guides which are suggestively . . . fertile. (10)

Freeman asks rhetorically

> *What is it . . . that permits the historian to explain? Nothing less than the process itself.*[6] The understanding and describing of what has transpired will, provided it is relatively complete and systematic, require nothing more to be deemed explanation. This does not . . . necessarily make it correct—for the problems of interpretation must inevitably enter in here—but an explanation nonetheless. (8)

There is the overarching problem of the degree of trust we may place in the intervention historian's interpretation: "the task of interpretation necessitates critical self-reflection for there to be validity, a respect for the autonomy of the text". (12) And "the validity of a particular historical interpretation . . . will not be addressed through testing or verification, but rather through critical

---

[5] WYATT, F. "The Reconstruction of the Individual and Collective Past", in White, *The Study of Lives,* Atherton Press, New York, 1964, p. 308.
[6] Editor's italics, not Freeman's.

assessment, public scrutiny", the critical assessment of a sophisticated human group. (12)

> And lest we conclude that this enterprise is doomed owing to the caprices of 'mere' opinion or ideology, there is surely some comfort in the fact that there will inevitably be a finite realm of parameters for interpretation which are capable of being agreed upon due to the (more or less) common stock of knowledge present in a given research community. . . . While no one particular approximation can be said, ultimately, to be purely objective or correct, there exists the possibility of choosing from a hierarchy of plausible alternatives. Despite the fact that there can be no 'last word', intersubjective consensus minimizes the likelihood of arbitrariness or even outright falsity in interpretation. Historial science need not be deemed hopelessly idealistic or relativistic. (3)

Freeman declares that "it is ultimately impossible to deny the interpretive nature of dealing with historical data". (6) Truth is "only to be had via criticism, as opposed to the verification frequently possible in the observational sciences". (9) "There are", he says,

> simply no detachable conclusions in history; the validity and meaning of what has transpired always refers backward to the ordering of evidence, with events deemed significant represented by the narrative order itself. (7)

The philosopher C. G. Hempel, however, "insists that historical narrative . . . embodies the very same fundamental principles as those which ground more systematic observational enquiry". (5) He

> argued that history, while its explanations were often somewhat incomplete, more like 'sketches' than full-blown scientific explications, could be conceptualized in exactly the same manner as any of the other sciences.[7] (5)

Hempel declares that

> History . . . is a form of genetic enquiry where 'each stage must be shown to "lead to" the next and thus be linked to its successor by virtue of some general principles which make the occurrence of the latter at least reasonably probable given the former'. (5)

Accounts of interventions may fruitfully be conceptualised and written from an end-of-intervention point in time, as Freeman treats here. In an attempt to apply a little of his thinking to one or two aspects of intervention accounts, of pedagogic value, the next few remarks extrapolate from his text. The written account of the life cycle of an intervention may be tied to a perspective which allows an element of looking forward in time, as well as

---

[7] HEMPEL, C. G. *Aspects of Scientific Explanation,* New York University Press, New York, 1965, p. 449.

backward. Longer intervention accounts may be presented in an historical sequence of phases. A long account may be exploded into a chain of islands, and each island of data looked back on from the 'present'—studied, analysed, discussed and 'predictions' made—before the next island is subjected to similar treatment. In this way it is possible, via an island-hopping operation, to immerse ourselves in successive segments of the past, and in a sense enable in discussion "a reproduction or reliving of the experience of the . . . subjects studied", a re-living of the past scene in the intervention. (4) Something like "reliving the past or resurrecting the past is to reproduce it with all its uncertainties" takes place in such discussions.

In this way an account of an intervention embodies not only some description and analysis about how things were during the intervention, but also imply how they might otherwise have been. With an intervention history exploded into parts, where what happened next is concealed or simply not studied at the time, we can have our cake and eat it too. We can fruitfully oscillate between not knowing what happened at the subsequent point in time, and the vantage point of finding out what actually did happen. In this way some sort of knowledge about interventions may be derived prospectively as well retrospectively. The intervention story, however, remains the synthesis of the intervention historian, constructed retrospectively.

The task at hand is not solely to understand and explain the evolution of a particular intervention, the movement of events in that intervention in its own terms, but to systematize them, to attempt to discover regularities which can inform future practice. We are dealing with presumably recurrent phenom-ena in the study of the course of interventions. There are surely continuities in the sequence of interactions, activities and events which make up an intervention. The possibility of systematization or generalization should be forthcoming. There is, Freeman suggests, the problem of "achieving a respect-able degree of predictability" in interventions. Such "Problems in predictability are more a function of the limits of knowledge than any sort of uniqueness in the structure of historical understanding and explanation". (6) A viable, scientific approach to how best to intervene must adopt "a fundamentally restrospective perspective for at least a portion of the questions it addresses—a willingness to entertain the possibilities of aposteriority." Such "Aposteriority need not be . . . unsystematic, as numerous historians have amply demonstrated". (3)

Freeman presents a neat dichotomy: "If science, in its quest for revealing what is inevitable, moves irretrievably forward, history moves back; understand-ing and explanation cannot take place until all is said and done". (9) But historical explanation is not "equivalent to prediction 'turned upside down'". (7) Human "intentionality, intention, purpose" also need to be invoked in the study of interventions. This holds true not only of the organizational actors in the intervention, but also includes the consultant or action researcher. (7) The explication of organizational change in an intervention must be "founded not only on the dialectic of influences contributing to the formation and reformation" of the organization concerned, "but the dialectic . . . of the researcher and the researched". (12)

The intervener is "enmeshed within social relations which call for a uniting of theory and practice". (17) In attempting this "There is a distinct sense in which the researcher involved in attempting to know historical subjects must 'see the world through that person's eyes'". (13) A "measure of insight . . . is simply indispensable in the human sciences". (13) In one sense empathic understanding is no more than a heuristic; behind this are rationally perceivable empirical generalizations. The "necessary immersion of the researcher in the researched precludes the possibility of establishing any final objectivity, but need not detract from the validity of the knowledge which can derive from intersubjective consensus". (1)

CONCLUSION: MANAGING ORGANIZATIONAL CHANGE, VALUES AND SCIENCE

INTRODUCTION

The scientific method in this field is to become a very careful unbiased observer.
—Edgar H. Schein*

This chapter places the practice and process of managing organizational change in a scientific context, linking these to a consideration of values, how these may be operationalized in the service of organizations and individuals, and encouraging thinking about how best to do research in this field. The few there-and-then experiences presented have a strong research flavor, and are intended to raise issues about appropriate scientific methodology and justification for such methodology.

The Rushton Quality-of-Work-Life Experiment (A) outlines a systematic attempt to carry out an experiment aimed at improving employee job satisfaction

* From "Marshall Sashkin Interviews Edgar Schein, Organizational Psychologist," *Group & Organization Studies*, p. 4 (December 1979), p. 412.

and organizational performance. Intergroup conflict developed and intensified, however, culminating in the termination of the experiment. Discussion may fruitfully examine the causes and possible prevention of the conflict. *The Rushton Quality-of-Work-Life Experiment (B)* carries the story of the experiment a little further, and provides additional information about events.

Preface to an Intervention summarizes the phases of an intervention project and the methods by which the researcher concerned conducted it. It outlines his objectives in seeking to set up an intervention in a major national newspaper. These clearly include social and scientific values, as well as organizational values.

The many short items in the models and schemes section are intended to provide a suggestive sketch of the knotty, scientific, ethical, and philosophic issues posed by attempts to manage organizational change. *Traditional Research Design* succinctly outlines standard research methods followed in many fields, and throws light on *The Rushton Quality-of-Work-Life Experiment*. *The Involved Helper*, by contrast, argues that the interventionist should, for pragmatic as well as scientific reasons, adopt a collaborative, involved posture in working with members of the client system. *Themes for Collaborative Research* suggests a set of appropriate program agendas or areas for client-consultant joint effort. Although the list is hardly new, it makes enduring sense.

It may be contended that *Qualitative Research* is the most appropriate approach and methodology for intervention research, partly because it is predicated on intimate familiarity with the subject matter, that is, the members of the organization implicated in the intervention. Such research, it is suggested, "is based upon the conviction that knowledge is promoted by a close interplay between the abstract and the concrete." *The Organizing Myth in the Social Sciences*, on the other hand, accuses most social scientists of surrounding themselves "with activities which distance themselves from their clients"; the appropriate strategy implies the reverse.

Ethnographic versus Clinical Perspective contrasts the essentially different kinds of agendas and relationships of the ethnographer and the clinician. The ethnographer seeks concrete data from organization members because he or she is interested in understanding the culture for his or her own knowledge-building purposes. The help of the clinician is, in contrast, sought by organization members, in order to help them solve some problem or embrace some opportunity.

Action Science commends the importance of bringing together and keeping together the client-centeredness of action research with a similar emphasis on theoretical contribution. The thinking bears clear links to *Preface to an Intervention*. This is the first of the final set of items in this book to explore the scientific and value position of action research. The table *Comparisons of Positivist Science and Action Research* makes telling contrasts between the two scientific traditions under the spotlight. *Action Research as a Corrective to the Deficiencies of Positivist Science* summarizes characteristics of action research that do not share the disadvantages of traditional research design.

Two Versions of Action Research distinguish what are termed "weak" and "strong" versions of that concept. The latter is clearly the one toward which the underlying rationale for the field of managing organizational change should steer, that is, the status of a paradigm. *Towards a Definition of Action Research* analyzes the meaning of the concept on the basis of an extensive survey of the literature, strongly anchored in European contributions. It concludes with a measured definition of action research.

Values and Organization Development provides a survey of value issues in managing organizational change, and concludes that it is not easy to serve organizational and human ends simultaneously. *Openendedness* suggests that "unbridled" participation invites scrutiny of the ways in which managers perform their roles: Organizational life is lived inside a glasshouse rather than behind closed doors. Constructive organizational change sets a process in motion, the outcome of which is not predetermined and, hence, frightening to some. Managers with presumably low tolerance for ambiguity find openendedness frightening. *Managing Change* remarks that "we ourselves by our decisions and actions create the future: we can be proactive, not merely adaptive."

The Rushton Quality-of-Work-Life Experiment (A)*

Melvin Blumberg
and Charles D. Pringle

In the spring of 1973, the president of Rushton Mining Company and the president of the United Mine Workers of America signed a letter of agreement to collaborate on a quality-of-work-life (QWL) experiment at Rushton Coal Mine in Pennsylvania. The experiment was designed by Trist and his colleagues . . . to improve employee skills, safety, and job satisfaction while simultaneously raising the level of performance and earnings. The change agents built this experiment on earlier work in the United Kingdom . . . and were particularly interested in exploring the consequences of autonomous work groups in American underground mining operations.

After five months of deliberations by representatives of management and the union, the firm posted job bids requesting volunteers for an autonomous work group. These miners would have direct responsibility for the production of an entire geographic "section" of the mine. The foremen of the section would abandon their traditional roles as "pushers" and develop new roles as advisors, consultants, trainers, and planners.

The autonomous work group employed an entire 27-man section, comprised of three shifts and three foremen. The group met with the research team two days a week for six weeks in an above-ground classroom where they received training in safety laws, good mining practices, job safety analysis, and group problem solving. On the remaining three days, the men mined coal in their new underground section and learned to work toward a common goal— safely maximizing production of the section rather than the shift.

This was a new emphasis. Production was traditionally recorded by shift and crews. Hence, crews often competed with each other for the best location in the section to mine. A crew would often run a machine that leaked oil badly to the end of the shift, then leave the problem for the next crew to "discover" and repair.

To encourage job switching and shared responsibility for the work, all 27 miners received the same rate of pay as the highest-skilled job classification on that section. This resulted in an increase to the top rate of $50 a day for 15 of the men.

* SOURCE: Melvin Blumberg and Charles D. Pringle, "The Rushton Quality—of—Work—Life Experiment," *Journal of Applied Behavioral Science*, 19, (1983), 410–414. Reprinted by permission.

Following the orientation period, the group met in the classroom with the research team at six-week intervals to discuss productivity, absenteeism, costs, health, and safety matters. During this time the research team developed several means for resolving intragroup conflict and enhancing intershift coordination. These included a "joint committee," comprised of one man from each shift, two local union leaders, one foreman, the mine's safety director, a training director, and two members of management; biweekly foreman meetings; higher level management meetings; and underground visits by the research team several times a week.

THE SEEDS OF CONFLICT

While intragroup coordination improved, inter-section hostility grew. At first, the other miners found the activities of the autonomous group and their association with the university research teams amusing, and humorously used such terms as "automatic miner" and "super miner" when the men of the autonomous section entered the waiting room before boarding the man-trip cars. In time, however, the good-natured banter changed to silent hostility— and eventually to open opposition—as other miners grew jealous of the privileged status of the autonomous section of the mine. Subsequent interviews with the men in the control sections suggested that they felt deprived because the research team gave them no information and little attention. Not only did the autonomous group work under generally favorable physical conditions, but it also received special training and, when requested, special tools and equipment. It had its own university researcher who spent an entire shift several times a week interviewing and observing the group's miners, sharing their danger and fatigue, and helping with training, development, and conflict resolution. It had the privilege of spending one day every six weeks out of the mine in a section conference with top management and top union officials. In addition, several of the miners attended quality-of-work-life conferences at the company's expense, enjoying rides to and from the airport in the mine president's helicopter and receiving honoraria for their presentations. Moreover, the president "treated" the autonomous section to a steak-and-lobster dinner at the conclusion of their training period.

A few of the men on the autonomous section aggravated this already-difficult situation by behaving in a haughty, arrogant manner toward other men in the mine who questioned their preferential treatment. For example, when one of the men on a control section complained of a "hard-nosed" boss who "works your tail off," the autonomous worker replied that he could tell his boss "where to get off." Another worker bragged that he had "retired" when he went into the autonomous section and planned to start bringing a sleeping bag with him into the mine so he could be more comfortable during his shift. Some evidence exists, however, that many of the autonomous workers felt stung by the criticism by their peers. In the early days of the experiment, the autonomous miners developed the habit of rubbing their hands—which were stained with coal dust—across their faces while pondering a problem. Although this seemed to be an unconscious action, it probably provided some protection against remarks from other miners that the autonomous workers did not look "dirty enough" to have worked very hard.

THE GROWTH AND SPREAD OF CONFLICT

About 10 months after the experiment began, the mine opened a new section. The men from the original autonomous section, many of whom had never attended a union meeting before, had by this time become enthusiastic proponents of "our way of working" and strongly influenced the favorable vote in the union hall that permitted the new section to be organized along autonomous lines.

When the company opened the new section, management and the researchers anticipated that experienced men would bid from other positions all over the mine to fill the vacancies. This, however, did not occur. Because of a reluctance to leave established patterns of working, a resentment toward being kept uninformed, and rising hostility toward the project, the older miners refused to place bids for jobs in the new section. New men who had been hired to fill the anticipated vacancies in other parts of the mine and who still wore the yellow hat of the inexperienced and uncertified miner obtained positions in the new autonomous section. The section thus consisted mostly of men with less than one year's experience who nevertheless drew the same or higher pay as miners with at least 40 years of experience.

Although it rapidly became one of the highest producers, the new section initially had the lowest production rate in the mine. This appeared to stem from the inexperience of the men and from the fact that they had to work with used equipment that continually broke down. Frequently, mechanics from other parts of the mine would have to help the young, inexperienced mechanics from the new section repair their equipment. The combination of high pay, inexperience, and perceived low production of the new section increased the hostility and resentment the control group members felt towards the experiment.

As the weeks progressed, the members of the control sections became increasingly vociferous in their comments. They accused autonomous miners of "riding the gravy train" and of being "spoon-fed," and called them "parasites" who were "carried" by the rest of the men in the mine. Rumors began to spread through the mine with increasing frequency and intensity. Some of the most widely circulated ones held that autonomy constituted a communist plot since everybody received the same top rate and that the company was being subsidized by the government and was "making out" at the expense of the men. An extremely damaging rumor defined the QWL project as a management subterfuge in conjunction with "pinko" college people to "bust the union."

This concept seemed especially credible since the company president had strongly resisted the unionization attempts led by "Jock" Yablonski 10 years earlier. Many of the older miners who had been involved in organizing felt greatly concerned that the project's committees, joint decision making, and universally high pay rate could cause a weaning away of the younger men from the traditional values of the United Mine Workers of America and possibly result in an independent or company union.

Although all of the men in the mine had access to general information regarding the purpose of the experiment, they could not learn about details. Effective refutation of the growing suspicions and rumors would have required the research team to spend considerable time with the control groups revealing the specifics of the experiment—and this would have disrupted the evaluation effort at an early stage.

The National Quality of Work Center, then affiliated with the Institute for Social Research of the University of Michigan, required as a condition for funding that the project be independently evaluated on a common model by a separately financed evaluation team. . . . The model used at Rushton followed the pattern referred to . . . as a split-role field experiment, which requires two different teams: a research team that designs and implements the research, and an evaluation team that observes and collects the data.

The rumors and innuendoes continued until the talk inevitably became translated into action. Five months after the formation of the new section, the union membership voted to terminate the experiment unless the other men in the mine were given a chance to work at the top rate of pay.

THE CONSEQUENCES OF CONFLICT

During the next two months, the research team feverishly interviewed and observed the men in the control groups at their jobs so that the team could perform the sociotechnical analysis required for a proposal for mine-wide autonomous working. In addition, the researchers made great efforts to explain the principles of autonomous working to all the miners and to refute the rumors that sprang up in the darkness and gloom of the underground environment. What appeared to be ridiculous speculation outside in the bright sunlight somehow seemed believable hundreds of feet underground.

This process culminated in a request by the local union for written proposals that would specify how the rest of the mine would become autonomous. The research team submitted proposals to the membership, who voted on them at a special election. The miners rejected the proposals by a vote of 79 to 75, and the experiment was terminated.

The Rushton Quality-of-Work-Life Experiment (B)*

Melvin Blumberg
and Charles D. Pringle

In the mine, researchers were not only unable to make a random assignment of subjects, but they also found it impossible to seal off the experimental group from the control groups. For example, men from both groups shared compartments in the same man-trip cars that took them into the mine, they shared the same bathhouse, they rode in car pools, and they attended union meetings in which miners discussed the experiment. Furthermore, many of the men were related by blood or marriage. The experimental sections alone employed three sets of brothers and one uncle-nephew pair who bowled and hunted together and shared produce from their gardens at Sunday dinners. Furthermore, most of the supervisors at the time were Masons, and the miners considered an invitation to a newly promoted supervisor to join the local lodge a sign that he had "arrived."

An additional complicating factor was the grapevine—the organization's informal communication network. In the mine, a worker who spends several hours alone, hundreds of feet underground, and several miles from the entrance becomes eager to converse with a fellow human being. The prime carriers of information include the following: the motormen, who take supplies to the sections over the mine's narrow gauge trolley system; the pumpers, who control water seepage; the mechanics, who travel widely in the mine to keep the equipment functioning; and the general crews, who maintain the tunnels and airways leading from the mine entrance to each section.

In the mine, men outside the experimental group would often ask informed, detailed questions of the researchers during chance encounters underground. To avoid contaminating the control group, researchers gently turned aside specific questions regarding day-to-day activities of the experiment with a smile and a vague answer. This only reinforced the men's beliefs that the researchers were hiding something from them.

This reaction may turn a no-treatment control group into a "resentful-of-no-treatment" group. In such cases, the base-line data from the control group may reflect the resentment the members feel toward being ignored by the researchers and, hence, will be misleading.

* SOURCE: Melvin Blumberg and Charles D. Pringle, The Rushton Quality—of—Work—Life Experiment, *Journal of Applied Behavioral Science*, 19, (1983), pp. 410–414. Reprinted with permission.

A less obvious indication of treatment contamination was the mysterious transference of technical innovations from the experimental sections of the mine to the nonexperimental sections of the mine. For example, in one of their meetings, the men requested that the autonomous sections receive portable telephones. These phones permitted a mechanic to tap into the mine's phone system to request parts or assistance when he located a failure in the conveyer belt that carried coal out of the mine. Without the phones, the worker had to walk perhaps a mile in a slippery, low tunnel to inform the supervisor of the nature of the problem and the projected delay for mining operations. Shortly after the arrival of the new equipment, "spare" phones began to disappear from the supply room and reappear in the control sections.

Numerous examples of this type occurred. The autonomous section foremen enjoyed extolling the accomplishments of their men to the other foremen in the locker room at the end of their shifts or at the biweekly foremen's meeting. Although the other foremen publicly disparaged the work of the autonomous miners, if one of them heard a discussion of a technique, tool, or piece of equipment that would improve safety or reduce the level of effort required by his men, he would quietly adopt it.

Preface to an Intervention*

Chris Argyris

The research reported in *Behind the Front Page* was guided by two interdependent objectives. The first, a policy-oriented objective, was to discover what must be done to create newspapers that are self-examining and self-regulating. The second, a scholarly objective, was to add to our knowledge of the processes needed to enhance organizational health and to create effective, on-going renewal activities within organizations. A few words about each seem necessary.

Creating self-examining newspapers. The press in this country has been under attack from many elements of society: the angry and the quiet, the thoughtful and the thoughtless, the old and the young, the minorities and the establishment, the left and the right. The call for change has also come from some of the more thoughtful people in journalism. . . . The credibility of the press has been shaken to the point where a national blue-ribbon task force, privately financed by the Twentieth Century Fund, has recommended that a national press council be established. . . . All this is happening at a time when the press in the United States can be shown to be among the finest and most responsible in the world.

The underlying reasons, the Twentieth Century Fund panel suggests, are that the press has grown remote and unresponsive to its constituencies; the public feels a sense of alienation and helplessness in its relationship with the press. The causes of remoteness, frustration, lack of credibility, and unresponsiveness include too much emphasis on the dramatic (emphasizing the shocking, negative, and deviant), a lack of nationwide standards for the profession, non-competitive salaries, decreased competition between newspapers . . . and control of newspapers by individuals who are forced to be profit-conscious. . . .

Although these causes are certainly important, when I first chose to study a large metropolitan newspaper I had no idea that my research would be relevant to them. I elected to study the newspaper which I shall call *The Daily Planet* for three reasons. First, my long-range interest has been in learning how healthy organizations can be designed and managed effectively. Organizational health requires continual self-examination and self-renewal. Yet, as far as I could see, the communications media had shown little interest in such activities. The *Planet*, I had been told by my informants, would be especially resistant to a behavioral science inquiry. "To put it mildly," said one informant, "they would consider your views to be nonsense."

That comment led to my second reason. I had never studied an organization that was skeptical about the value of behavioral science. All the

* SOURCE: Chris Argyris, *Behind the Front Page* (San Francisco: Jossey-Bass, 1974), pp. 9–16. Reprinted with permission.

organizations I had studied had asked to be studied, which meant that my sample was highly self-selective. If I could be admitted to an organization that was skeptical and not particularly cooperative, then I might learn more about the processes of gaining credibility where, given a behavioral scientist's bias, we are needed most. How do you get cooperation from a skeptical organization? One strategy is to speak to the top, ask for their cooperation, and be honest about your motives as well as about the possible pay-off for the clients. I did this and was invited in. That was a start. The problem of getting cooperation from that point on is the subject of most of this book.

My third reason for selecting this newspaper was my interest in the basic problem of the relationship between thought and action. I wanted to learn what impact, if any, the internal system and the quality of life within the organization had upon the perceptions, thoughts, and writing of the participants. I did not realize then how relevant this issue was for understanding the credibility gap that exists between newspapers and the public and for developing insights into the creation of self-examining systems.

The realization of the connection between my research and the possibility of self-examining newspapers came as I was reading the Twentieth Century Fund report. *The Daily Planet* was acknowledged in this report to be a newspaper with high professional standards and one not plagued with the causes of low credibility identified above. Nevertheless, this newspaper, even though an excellent one, was having credibility problems with many of its constituencies. I knew, from first-hand observations, that the causes for this credibility gap were as much internal as external. Moreover, many members of the newspaper expressed a genuine sense of helplessness about changing these internal conditions, which included the win-lose dynamics among reporters and between reporters and copywriters, management by crisis and with hypocrisy, and the conception of advocacy journalism held by many of the top young reporters. If the public feels helpless in relation to newspapers, newspapermen themselves feel the same way. "Not you or anyone else will ever change this place" was a prediction I heard often at *The Daily Planet*—and it was backed up by serious offers to bet large sums of money on it.

It is doubtful that a newspaper or any organization can develop effective self-examination processes if its personnel hold these pessimistic attitudes about change. However, unlike most organizations, newspapers are protected by law. This protection can be healthy to the extent that newspapers are able to manage themselves effectively to produce news and editorial products of the highest quality. But, as the reader will see, most of the top news and editorial officials on *The Daily Planet* eventually admitted that they were not ready to become the open system that they have said newspapers should be, and that they have argued that our societal institutions should become. One question that I hope this book raises is whether newspapers should be protected if, by their own admission and behavior, they are not capable of creating an open learning system within their own boundaries.

The genuine autonomy of newspapers therefore may depend ultimately upon their being able to manage themselves. But, in order to accomplish this objective, newspapers will have to find ways to reduce the repetitive, compulsive processes of their internal systems. A system that behaves compulsively in ways that its members acknowledge are ineffective creates the conditions for organizational neurosis and invites outside intervention and control.

The self-sealing, non-learning processes that lead to organizational dry-rot and inhibit self-examination are not unique to this newspaper or to all newspapers. These processes of decay are so prevalent in all our organizations that a law of organizational entropy has been proposed. . . . And an outside regulatory agency, such as a national press council, would probably develop the same processes of deterioration just as many other regulatory commissions and courts have become rigid and ineffective.

Acquiring knowledge about organizational health. My second primary objective is to add to our knowledge about the factors that determine organizational health and about the kind of interventions that can effectively enhance organizational health. Specifically, the objectives are (1) to understand the inner workings of the upper managerial and editorial activities of a newspaper so as (2) to be able to explain why events occur as they do, (3) to be able to predict, under specified conditions, what will happen, and (4) to help the participants redesign their system to become more effective. The objectives are listed in order of increasing difficulty. The easiest task for the action researcher is to describe and understand; the most difficult one is to describe and understand in such a way as to make new things happen.

The same is true for the participants. Publishers, top editors, and for that matter managers and administrators in any organization must understand the inner workings of their systems in order to be able to predict behavior and alter it wherever and whenever necessary. As the analysis here shows, the participants find that understanding human behavior in their organization is difficult; that making valid predictions about it is even more difficult; and that altering it seems nearly impossible. There is, therefore, a high degree of compatibility between the interests of a researcher committed to understanding complex systems and the interests of administrators responsible for managing these complex systems.

Several differences between the researcher and the administrator, however, are important if for no other reason than that they affect what is included in this book. The researcher conducts research and develops models or theoretical frameworks to explain his findings in such a way that they may apply to other organizations which may have similar problems. Thus the intention, in this research, is to produce some knowledge that may help to understand other newspapers. . . .

In addition, my objective is to be of help to other communications-producing organizations. Indeed, I hope that some of the findings, such as the existence of a star system of reporters and columnists, may be of help to executives in many fields, ranging from radio and television to university administration. A university president, for example, is faced with a faculty which contains a few stars. The stars provide the attraction for graduate students and other faculty members, but the rest of the faculty members do the bulk of the teaching and are largely responsible for the everyday effectiveness of the university. How can an organization be designed that rewards both groups justly and simultaneously minimizes the jealousies and fears that usually go along with differentiations that place people in first- and second-class status? The hope is to bridge the two worlds with a minimum of falling out between them.

The phases of research. The *Daily Planet* was studied in depth and over a long period of time. The study began with interviews and observations of the top forty news, editorial, and business personnel. This phase lasted approximately one year. I was free to observe and tape-record any naturally occurring meeting between two or more people. During the diagnostic phase, I was never excluded from any meeting that I chose to attend. Interviewing and observing for a year made it possible for me to sample meetings, problems, and issues over a long period of time and under many different conditions. (I varied my visits to the newspaper so that I systematically covered all the days of the week.)

On the basis of these data (and others described in the first two chapters) I prepared a diagnosis of the internal workings of the *Planet*. The diagnosis showed that the credibility problems of the paper were related to its internal system, which in turn caused top people to have credibility problems with each other.

The next phase was a series of interventions, which lasted for two years. They provided additional longitudinal information about the internal system of the newspaper. More important, they were designed to become a test of the potential for self-examination of the newspaper. In other words, the objective of the second phase was to try to solve problems which the participants agreed (after studying the diagnosis) were critical for self-regulation and self-renewal *and* which up to that point had seemed to them unsolvable.

For the intervention to become a legitimate test of the potential for self-examination and self-renewal, the intervention processes had to be so designed and executed that their success or failure could be traced explicitly to the participants. Under these conditions, a "failure" of progress could become a valid indicator of the lack of capacity for self-renewal within the system.

It was also important to show that I did not intervene in ways that unilaterally, made success or failure more or less probable. This does not mean that I was a passive observer. I was very active, continually suggesting strategies and courses of action which, if carried out, could become genuine tests for the members of their own capacities to learn and change. However, I believe the data also show that I worked patiently and actively to encourage the participants to reject my suggestions whenever they could not accept them fully as their own. The participants could reject their own ideas, or mine, even after they had translated them into objectives to be accomplished.

This is a case study, therefore, with some qualities not frequently found in case studies. The organization (1) was studied with multi-research methods,

(2) over a three-year period, where not only (3) was a diagnosis developed but (4) it was fed back to begin a process of intervention within the system, which led to (5) the creation of statistically rare events which in turn (6) provided learning for the participants (about their system and themselves) and which (7) became tests for the capacity for self-examination and self-renewal within the system.

The organization of the book. A tension exists between the several themes of this book which may frustrate some readers, especially those whose main interest is to learn about newspapers and how they can examine themselves. First, this is a study that focuses on the internal processes by which one newspaper maintains itself as a system. Second, it is also a study of an attempt to change parts of that system. Finally, these two studies are intended to shed light on the problem of self-examination within a newspaper.

One way to make sense of these three themes is to view the diagnosis of the internal workings of the system as helping us to discover what forces inhibit or facilitate self-examination. The intervention activity may be viewed as an attempt to change the system. Therefore, if the intervention strategy is designed to enhance self-examination, it becomes a living test of the capacity of the organization to change itself. In order to be such a test, the intervention strategy cannot be based on the typical management-consulting philosophy, which usually dictates that the experts diagnose and manage the change. The intervention program must be designed and executed so that every step becomes a test of the ability of the client organization to learn how to become self-examining. Such a theory of intervention has already been developed . . . and it was in this study. Therefore the focus on newspaper self-examination cannot be developed without first presenting the diagnosis and making explicit the steps and processes of intervention.

Traditional Research Design*

Melvin Blumberg
and Charles D. Pringle

Argyris maintains that traditional or "rigorous" research designs assume that organizations are closed systems.[1] Under this assumption, research is deliberately undertaken to satisfy the researchers' needs and to provide maximum control over the subjects' behavior. Conditions are specifically defined and controlled so that the researcher can vary one or more variables and observe the resultant change in other variables, while minimizing the extent to which the subjects can contaminate the experiment.

These principles of rigorous research seem strikingly similar to the principles of classical organization design, in which the manager designs the task as simply and clearly as possible so as to minimize employee discretion, provides little or even erroneous information regarding the context of the task, and defines the reward for participation. In sum, traditional research design creates "a world for the subject in which [her or] his behavior is defined, controlled, evaluated, manipulated, and reported to a degree that is comparable to the behavior of workers in the most mechanized assembly-line conditions" (Argyris, 1968, p. 186).

* SOURCE: Melvin Blumberg and Charles D. Pringle, "Traditional Research Design," *Journal of Applied Behavioral Science*, 19 (1983), p. 419. Reprinted with permission.

[1] Argyris, C. Some unintended consequences of rigorous research. *Psychological Bulletin*, 1968, *70*, 185–197.

The Involved Helper*

Chris Argyris

I . . . maintain that research ought to have meaning and that the subjects are not *subjects;* they are *clients.* We should treat them as clients for two reasons. One is pragmatic: It increases the probability that we will be permitted to do the study. The second reason is the subject of my latest book,[1] the inherent problems with rigorous research. If you're seen as a researcher who is helping, you obtain data and results that are different from those you obtain when you are seen as an objective, detached scientist. Both approaches produce results and both may produce distortion, so one is not obviously better. However, you have a higher probability of identifying and accounting for such distortions if you are an involved helper, if people constantly confront you, asking what you are doing, and if they don't see you as detached. In the bank study, where I first used this approach, I initially studied fifty employees. Frankly, I was there because they were nice to me. They let me in the bank because Bakke asked them to. He probably told them, "This fellow has tried to get into so many organizations, and they have all rejected him." The president of the bank was a Yale graduate, so he said, "All right, I'll let him in." First I wrote a technical report, which was published in a scholarly journal, and then I wrote a nontechnical report. The president was pleased with it, and he gave the Labor Management Center funds so that I could study the entire bank. I accepted with the provision that I could reinterview some of the people in the first study, because now I was coming in, not as a disinterested, detached scientist, but as a paid consultant, whose data might have some influence on the lives of the employees. The people I reinterviewed told me significantly different things the second time. I called about twenty-five of them to a meeting and said, "Hey, folks, when I was a disinterested observer, you told me this, but as a researcher with the probability of having some impact on your lives, I was told these things. Now tell me which are true?" They helped me to decipher their answers and showed me that sometimes when I was a disinterested observer, they lied to me. They had said, in effect, "There's no need to try to go through all the details; it doesn't make any difference." Sometimes when I was a consultant—an involved researcher—they also lied to me, but I could not have discovered this if I hadn't brought them into a room and confronted them directly. I asked how I could increase the probability of being confronted by the people whom I had studied, and we decided that I should *avoid* separating consulting from

* SOURCE: Marshall Sashkin, "Chris Argyris, Action Scientist," *Group and Organization Studies,* 6 (1981), 414–416. Reprinted by permission of Sage Publications, Inc.
[1] C. Argyris, *Inner Contradictions of Rigorous Research* (New York: Academic Press, 1980).

research or learning from research. The clients ought to be learning; and if they're learning, then they're going to feel more free to say, "Wait a minute, how useful is this? How helpful is this?" That kind of confrontation increases the probability of finding errors and distortions and also gives us more valid data.

Themes for Collaborative Research*

Eric Trist

The identification of themes for collaborative research programs cannot be made in the abstract. They can only be reached by understanding the meaning of field experiences in concrete social science engagement. Some years ago members of the Human Resources Centre of the Tavistock Institute held an off-site conference to review their work in organizational development. They wished to obtain a better understanding of its thematic content. This chapter will conclude with a summary of the findings. They are offered as an example of the kind of assessment that research groups may need to make in order to improve their programmatic engagement with the social field.

The first step was to identify program areas. These represented domains of action research in which there was increasing preoccupation among client organizations and persisting scientific interest among staff members. Four program areas were identified. Together they composed a frame of reference within which to take research initiatives and to appreciate client approaches. They were:

Creation of Nonalienated Work Relationships. Earlier sociotechnical studies had shown that human needs, satisfactions, and interests could be met in the work situation without sacrificing economic goals. Attempts to increase economic efficiency need not lead to alienation. Organizations and jobs had to be designed so that alienation could be replaced by satisfying involvement.

Study of Life Careers and Changing Character of Work. There had been a noticeable shift in the concern of many organizations toward the long-term planning of careers that seek to optimize the development and release of human resources. There was a need to consider the strategies of the individual as he faced the crises of the life cycle and the changing position of work roles in the life space.

Building of Institutions in Complex and Uncertain Environments. Reanalysis of experience with a number of large organizations had suggested that many of their common problems arose from the need to cope with environments of increasing complexity and uncertainty. The study of what is involved in building institutions better able to meet this turbulence had been hampered by assumptions of the machine theory of organization. Work would now be centered on problems of management philosophy and company objectives. It would seek to identify the values the organizations needed to pursue if they were to cope

* SOURCE: Eric Trist, "Action Research and Adaptive Planning," in *Experimenting with Organizational Life: The Action Research Approach,* ed. A. W. Clark (New York: Plenum Press, 1976), pp. 55–57. Reprinted with permission.

with their environments. These findings would then need to be built into organizational practice.

Diffusion of Social Science Knowledge in User Organizations. This area was concerned with discovering general principles that govern the acceptance and diffusion of change. The problem was to increase the use that non-social scientists make of the insights and skills of social scientists. There was experience of the complexities and unpredictable outcomes that followed attempts to diffuse the understanding gained from field studies in Norway, Eire, and the U.K. This indicated the urgent need to develop greater understanding of the diffusion process. Recent work suggested that task-oriented group relations training seemed appropriate to the diffusion of a greater understanding of organizational values, objectives, structures, and processes.

To realize the program, long-term collaborative relationships covering work in all four areas should be established, preferably with science-based enterprises. These enterprises should be of sufficient stature to command respect and set an example to others. Trade unions as well as managements should participate. The enterprises should agree to work together in arranging workshops and seminars.

Projects should be funded, not only by clients, but also by independent bodies. This would give public sanction to innovations and enhance the chances of their diffusion.

British studies would need to be complemented by studies in other countries. This would enable cross-cultural comparisons to be made. It would also exploit favorable environmental conditions that may exist in one country but not in another.

The Human Resources Centre should commit itself to the program as a mission shared by all its members. Its resources, however, would need to be augmented by the exchange of personnel with other research organizations. Attention should be paid to widening the number of disciplines represented. In addition, fieldwork opportunities should be provided for postgraduate students; the training function should be accepted by client organizations.

Qualitative Research*

Iain Mangham

The research methodology appropriate to . . . a perspective upon human action is, of course, not that of positivism with its emphasis upon the average and, all too often, its heavy reliance on statistical inference about concepts which have an indefinite relation to the empirical world. Positivism, at least in the form I am criticizing, has tended to stand off from its potential subject matter; conversely, an appropriate research methodology, *qualitative research*, manifests a close association with human action. An empirical science is not to be brought into being by endless debate and disputation about concepts with the weakest of empirical referents; it is constructed out of the interplay of data and speculation that generates the concepts and at the same time *grounds* them in a context of empirical materials. Blumer (1969) puts it with his usual clarity:

> Most of the improper use of the concept in science comes when the concept is set apart from the world of experience, when it is divided from the perception from which it has arisen and with which it ordinarily ties. Detached from the experience which brought it into existence, it is almost certain to become indefinite and metaphysical. I have always admired a famous statement of Kant which really defines the character of the concept and indicates its limitations. Kant said brilliantly: "Perception without conception is blind; conception without perception is empty". (Herbert Blumer, *Symbolic Interactionism: Perspective and Method,* © 1969. By permission of Prentice-Hall, Inc., Englewood Cliffs, New Jersey.)

The way to avoid emptiness and to stimulate groundedness is to be intimately familiar with one's subject matter—to have a detailed and dense awareness of a particular set of social actors over a period of time and to seek to understand how it is that they go about defining and acting in their particular social world; to participate with them while observing or, as a second best, to spend a considerable amount of time talking to them in a relatively unstructured form about their perceptions and their actions.

In this respect many organization development practitioners may be surprised to find that, like Molière's character who discovered he had been talking prose all of his life, they have been practising qualitative research all of their lives. Participation, immersion, and deep familiarity with a particular set of social actors in specific circumstances, however, while a necessary condition,

* SOURCE: Iain Mangham, *Interactions and Interventions in Organizations* (Chichester, England: John Wiley, 1978), pp. 15–17. Reproduced by permission of John Wiley and Sons Ltd.

is not a sufficient one for the development of a research tradition. Qualitative research, if it is to develop, needs to go beyond the case study, beyond the mere collection of data and the accumulation of experiences. A qualitative research programme needs to be able to link the specific with the general and to delineate the particular in terms of its universal, transcendent, and analytic aspects. To do this, working from the observed situation or from the perceptions of those involved in that situation, the qualitative researcher should be able to draw out a number of inferences which have wider application and to present these inferences at an appropriate level of abstraction. The best work in this developing tradition presents both concepts and the concrete instances which embody or illustrate them. Within the field of organizational development the work of Dalton (1970) on the processes of organizational change and of Argyris (1970) on intervention come down to the kind of qualitative approaches I have in mind. Such examples, however, are as yet rare in the literature. Much of what is claimed as research consists of (1) little more than the forcing of new data into pre-established categories or existing theoretical frameworks, (2) abstract ramblings about concepts such as values divorced from any empirical referent, or (3) detailed accounts of particular interventions with little or no attempts at generalization. Qualitative research is based upon the conviction that knowledge is most effectively promoted by a close interplay between the abstract and the concrete. Too much abstraction carries with it the danger of empty speculation, too much concreteness the possibility of blind floundering in a morass of data. Qualitative research seeks to redress or to avoid some of the problems of positivism while at the same time not denying the rigour essential to the development and accumulation of ideas. In Reason's (1976) terms it is *holistic* in the sense that its practitioners seek to immerse themselves in the stream of experience and understand it as a totality rather than as a series of separate, manipulatable variables. The would-be qualitative researcher begins by discovering what it is that his coparticipants are doing, feeling, thinking, and experiencing; the actual experience as it occurs is the starting point, from which "buzzing, blooming confusion" the researcher seeks to draw out and articulate the concepts which capture the experience. Such an approach raises all sorts of issues about researcher/client relationships about which it is not appropriate to speculate here, but it does, in its very proximity to its material and its reluctance to impose concepts upon it, represent a significant alternative to the more familiar positivistic approaches.

Social interactionism provides the basis of a theoretical perspective for those engaged in organization development; qualitative research gives a perspective on the nature of the appropriate method for generating knowledge in the area. The two approaches are both complementary and congruent. The activist image of human conduct that suffuses much of social interactionism, the central position it accords to the individual social actor, fits well with emphasis of qualitative research upon the understanding of the concrete experience of individuals as they participate in social situations.

REFERENCES

ARGYRIS, C. (1970), *Intervention Theory and Method,* Addison-Wesley, Reading, Mass.

BLUMER, H. (1969), *Symbolic Interactionism,* Prentice-Hall, Englewood Cliffs, N.J.

DALTON, G. W. (1970), in Negandhi and Schwitter (eds.), *Influence and Organizational Change in Or-ganization Behaviour Models,* Comparative Administration Research Institute, Kent, Ohio.

REASON, P. (1976), Notes on Holistic Research Processes and Social System Change, Working Paper, Centre for the Study of Organizational Change and Development, University of Bath.

The Organizing Myth
in the Social Sciences*

W. Gordon Lawrence

In this dissociation of the knowable from the unknowable the social sciences have had their part to play. Indeed, the salient methodologies of the social sciences in a sense have legitimated the myth of the split between the individual and society. Practitioners of the social sciences, for the most part, have failed to use their imaginative capabilities. Subjectivity has been pushed out of scientific discourse. It may well be that this is because practitioners have been concerned about their own purity and have avoided situations and methodologies which might endanger their 'professionalism'. The danger for the social anthropologist has always been that he 'goes native' and ceases to be a 'professional'. More generally, the stance of some social scientists has been to maintain an I–It, instrumental, pseudo-professional relationship with their world of 'respondents'.

A useful way of thinking about the social sciences and which points to why social science practitioners may be failing to use their imagination has been advanced by John O'Neill who suggests that sociology is best thought of as a 'skin' trade. In this context, sociology is not unlike the skin trades such as haircutting or dentistry which, like the professions of priest or medical doctor, are concerned with the sacredness and profanity which surrounds the human body. Because of the ambivalence felt about this, skin trade practitioners literally have to surround themselves with activities which distance themselves from their clients. Metaphorical skin trade practitioners, such as social scientists, are also caught in the same ambivalence. Hence the movement to objectify the subject of research; to convert the person into a collection of variables, for example. As O'Neill puts it:

> Much of the sociological apparatus functions, I suggest, to support a ritual of decontamination between the scientist and his subject. It is essential he view his subject only with professional eyes and that he resist the look in the eyes of the sick, the poor, and the aimless who turn his questions back on him. In this way the erotic symbiosis of talk is reduced to the interview schedule or attitude survey in which the client comes clean before the professional *voyeur*. (O'Neill, 1972)

My argument is that the social sciences ought to be a skin trade exploring the boundaries that are problematic—psychic, social, and political

* Source: W. Gordon Lawrence ed., *Exploring Individual and Organizational Boundaries: A Tavistock Open Systems Approach* (Chichester, England: John Wiley, 1979), pp. 239–241. Reprinted by permission of John Wiley and Sons Ltd.

skins—because disorder is not to be kept at bay but entertained, understood, and worked with as a route to new forms of being which would include the political relatedness of the individual to society. Some research methodologies, however, because they protect the scientist from uncertainty, preclude this kind of knowing.

What Martin Buber has called the I–It relationship is often the organizing myth of the social sciences. The I–It relationship of the social scientist to his subject is often seen as being a proper scientific stance. But this is the inevitable outcome of the separation of the observer from the observed and rests on the presuppositions that there exists outside any one individual man a 'kingdom of order' in the sense that it is outside his will and desire. Hence, truth means the discovery of that preestablished order. The second presupposition is that man's 'cognitive apparatus does not materially affect the observation of this preestablished order' (Hampden-Turner, 1973). On these presuppositions are based social science methodologies such as behaviourism, functionalism, and operational research.

The question is whether the social sciences are to provide neatly ordered accounts of reality or whether the accounts are to reflect the complexity and the latent disorder. The behavioural sciences, for example, as Eugene Schwartz indicates, are a good instance of a particular formulation of the purpose of the social sciences:

> The thrust of the behavioural sciences is to stamp out disorder because the sciences cannot deal with it; to create activities that are conducive to control and hence to prediction; to make the complex simple because otherwise it cannot be comprehended. More serious is that science declared it a *sine qua non* that it must be objective by eliminating all subjective values and judgements, although, as has been shown earlier, subjective judgements were the bases of the axioms upon which science itself was built. Science, it is claimed, is thus neither good nor bad, but neutral. But if science is ahuman in its neutrality by banishing all human qualities, is it not but a short step to become inhuman? (Schwartz, 1971)

All of these strictures can be applied to many social science practitioners. My major point is that such a conception of social science is not adequate for working with the complexity of reality. This is not an argument against measurement *per se* as, clearly, certain features of reality can be quantified. The issue is whether the quantification is an avoidance of complexity or not. For example, the social scientist, in trying to understand what takes place in groups of people, attempts to reduce human group life to variables and their correlations. Not only is the choice of variables frequently faulty—chosen, often, because of their measurability—but also such an approach only interprets the outward facts of the situation. The basis of the behaviour of the participants—that is, what they hold in their minds about the situation and themselves in relation to that situation—is not taken into account.

The kind of difficulty this gets us into has been identified by a colleague, Peter Barham, in an earlier paper on group relations training (Barham and

Lawrence, 1974). He referred to Poulantzas, the political scientist, who wrote of the difficulty: 'in comprehending social classes and the State as objective structures and their relation as an objective system of regular connections, a structure and a system whose agents, "men", are in the words of Marx "bearers" of it—*träger*' (Poulantzas, 1969). Poulantzas went on to speak of the impression thus given that:

> social classes of 'groups' are in some way reducible to inter-personal relations, and the State is reducible to inter-personal relations of the diverse 'groups' that constitute the State apparatus, and finally that the relations between social classes and the State itself as reducible to inter-personal relations of 'individuals' composing social groups and 'individuals' composing the State apparatus. (Poulantzas, 1969)

At this juncture I merely want to hold on to the view that this kind of impression is an inevitable outcome of the split between the knowable and unknowable community; the dissociation of objectivity from subjectivity; the division between modes of knowing. The healing of these splits, it is commonly believed, can only be brought about through 'solving' interpersonal relations; the mechanics of relating. The subjective society carried inside the individual is disregarded. But I am beginning to believe that it is the society 'in the mind', the internalized experiences, the introjected and projected experiences of that object we call 'society', that need to be identified. My hunch is that if the necessary language could be created to explore these experiences of the fatal split between what is perceived to be knowable and unknowable we would be some way towards making available for inspection the not so conscious social processes which I have been indicating, albeit in terms of a social cartoon.

REFERENCES

BARHAM, P., and LAWRENCE, W. G. (1974) 'Some notes on Tavistock working conferences'. *Group Analysis*, VII, no. 2.

HAMPDEN-TURNER, C. M. (1973) 'Radical man and the hidden moralities of social science'. *Interpersonal Development*, 2, no. 4.

O'NEILL, J. (1972) *Sociology as a Skin Trade*. New York: Harper Torchbooks. Poulantzas, N. (1969) 'Capitalism and the State'. *New Left Review*, No. 58. Schawartz, E. (1971) *Overskill*. New York: Ballantine Books.

Ethnographic Versus Clinical Perspective*

Edgar H. Schein

In reviewing my own "data base," the sources of my own knowledge about organizational culture, I have found it necessary to distinguish the perspective of the *ethnographer* from that of the *clinician*. The ethnographer obtains concrete data in order to understand the culture he is interested in, presumably for intellectual and scientific reasons. Though the ethnographer must be faithful to the observed and experienced data, he brings to the situation a set of concepts or models that motivated the research in the first place. The group members studied are often willing to participate but usually have no particular stake in the intellectual issues that may have motivated the study.

In contrast, a "clinical perspective" is one where the group members are clients who have their own interests as the prime motivator for the involvement of the "outsider," often labeled "consultant" or "therapist" in this context. In the typical ethnographic situation, the researcher must obtain the cooperation of the subjects; in the clinical situation, the client must get the cooperation of the helper/consultant. The psychological contract between client and helper is completely different from that between researcher and subject, leading to a different kind of relationship between them, the revelation of different kinds of data, and the use of different criteria for when enough has been "understood" to terminate the inquiry.

Clients call in helpers when they are frustrated, anxious, unhappy, threatened, or thwarted; when their rational, logical approaches to things do not work. Inevitably, then, the clinical view brings one to the topic of the "irrational" in organizations. I have found and hope to show in this book that one of the simplest ways of understanding the seemingly irrational is to relate such phenomena to culture, because culture often explains things that otherwise seem mysterious, silly, or "irrational."

Consultants also bring with them their models and concepts for obtaining and analyzing information, but the function of those models is to provide insight into how the client can be *helped*. In order to provide help, the consultant must "understand" at some level. Some theories, in fact, argue that only by attempting to change a system (that is, giving help) does one demonstrate any real level of understanding (Lewin, 1952; Schein, 1980). For me this criterion has always been the relevant one for "validating" my understanding, even though that understanding often is incomplete, since the clinical relationship

* SOURCE: Edgar H. Schein, *Organizational Culture and Leadership: A Dynamic View* (San Francisco: Jossey-Bass, 1985), pp. 21–22. Reprinted with permission.

does not automatically license the helper to inquire into areas the client may not wish to pursue or considers irrelevant. On the other hand, the level of understanding is likely to be deeper and more dynamic.

The point of spelling all this out now is to let the reader know that my data base is a clinical one, not an ethnographic one. I have not been a participant-observer in organizations other than the ones I had membership in, but in being a consultant I have spent long periods of time in client organizations. I believe that this clinical perspective provides a useful counterpoint to the pure ethnographic perspective, because the clinician learns things that are different from what an ethnographer learns. Clients are motivated to reveal certain things when they are paying for help that may not come out if they are only "willing" to be studied.

So this kind of inquiry leads, I believe, to a "deeper" analysis of culture as a phenomenon—deeper in the sense of its impact on individual members of the organization. This perspective also leads inevitably to a more dynamic view of how things work, how culture begins, evolves, changes, and sometimes disintegrates. And . . . This perspective throws into high relief what leaders and other change agents can or cannot do to change culture deliberately.

REFERENCES

LEWIN, K. "Group Decision and Social Change." In G. E. Swanson, T. N. Newcomb and E. L. Hartley (Eds.), *Readings in Social Psychology*. (Rev. ed.) New York: Holt, Rinehart & Winston, 1952.

SCHEIN, E. H. *Organizational Psychology*. (3rd Ed.) Englewood Cliffs, N.J.: Prentice-Hall, 1980.

Action Science*

Chris Argyris

The intellectual beginnings of intervention and action science can be traced to Kurt Lewin's early concepts of action research. In his work during the Second World War, Lewin's action research was characterized by six features: it was problem-driven, it was client-centered, it challenged the status quo and was simultaneously concerned with producing empirically disconfirmable propositions that could be systematically interrelated into a theory designed to be usable in everyday life (Lewin, 1946; Marrow, 1969).

As action research became more popular, Lewin's plea to keep these six features together went unheeded. Practice-oriented scholars became so client-centered that they failed to question how clients themselves defined their problems and they ignored the building and testing of propositions and theories embedded in their own practice. On the theoretical side, these scholars conducted research that met normal science criteria in its rigor and precision but which became disconnected from and distanced from everyday life (Argyris, 1980).

A similar trend away from combining these six features can be found in a number of academic disciplines with an interest in the usefulness of knowledge. For example, operations research (OR) was begun by scholars who put aside their interest in basic science research to help England solve critical practical problems during the Second World War. As Stansfield[1] and Waddington (1973) attest, this early work was continuously problem-driven and client-monitored. Little thought was given to separating basic from applied knowledge, and in the war years there was no time to wait until the "basic" knowledge added up to provide answers. As scholars worked on OR issues, they uncovered exciting intellectual problems, the understanding of which would contribute to basic knowledge. But the OR field also expanded rapidly, and soon the same split between scholars and practitioners was repeated in this field. The scholars built models disconnected from practice while the practitioners contributed little to theory. More recently, leading OR scholars have begun to question this split and to ask for a return to the original pattern (Boothroyd, 1978; Wagner, 1971).

*SOURCE: Chris Argyris, "Action Science and Intervention," *Journal of Applied Behavioral Science,* 19 (1983), pp. 115–117. With permission of JAI Press, Inc., Greenwich, Conn.

[1] Stansfield, R. G. *To expect no more exactness than the situation permits.* Society for Applied Anthropology, Conference on Rethinking Applied Anthropology, Edinburgh, Scotland, April 1981. Pp. 1–5.

Action science represents an attempt to restore to primacy the six features of Lewin's early action research. Action scientists assume that learning is the first and overarching objective for the researcher, the clients, and the system in which they are embedded. The second major objective is that any knowledge produced should be formulated into empirically disconfirmable propositions that in turn will be organized into a theory.

In order to achieve these objectives, we must take into account the way individuals and systems learn and the way research is conducted and theory is created. An examination of the literature shows a wide array of ideas, often contradictory, about human learning, systems learning, and effective research methods.

To make choices, as well as to guide our research, the following action-science strategy was developed. First, we defined the kinds of learning on which we intended to focus. Second, we developed models of human nature and social systems that told us what each requires to learn. Third, we developed a methodology for action science and intervention that did not violate these requirements, yet which satisfied tough criteria for knowledge usefulness and validity.

REFERENCES

ARGYRIS, C. *Inner contradictions of rigorous research.* New York: Academic Press, 1980.

BOOTHROYD, H. *Articulate intervention.* London: Taylor & Francis, 1978.

LEWIN, K. Action research and minority problems. *Journal of Social Issues,* 1946, 2(4), 34–46.

MARROW, A. J. *The practical theorist: The life and work of Kurt Lewin.* New York: Basic Books, 1969.

WADDINGTON, C. H. *OR in World War II.* London: Paul Elek, 1973.

WAGNER, H. M. The ABC's of OR. *Operations Research,* 1971, *19,* 1259–1281.

Comparisons of Positivist Science and Action Research*

Gerald I. Susman
and Roger D. Evered

POINTS OF COMPARISON	POSITIVIST SCIENCE	ACTION RESEARCH
Value position	Methods are value neutral	Methods develop social systems and release human potential
Time perspective	Observation of the present	Observation of the present plus interpretation of the present from knowledge of the past, conceptualization of more desirable futures
Relationship with units	Detached spectator, client system members are objects to study	Client system members are self-reflective subjects with whom to collaborate
Treatment of units studied	Cases are of interest only as representatives of populations	Cases can be sufficient sources of knowledge
Language for describing units	Denotative, observational	Connotative, metaphorical
Bases for assuming existence of units	Exist independently of human beings	Human artifacts for human purposes
Epistemological aims	Prediction of events from propositions arranged hierarchically	Development of guides for taking actions that produce desired outcomes
Strategy for growth of knowledge	Induction and deduction	Conjecturing, creating settings for learning and modeling of behavior
Criteria for confirmation	Logical consistency, prediction and control	Evaluating whether actions produce intended consequences
Basis for generalization	Broad, universal, and free of context	Narrow, situational, and bound by context

* SOURCE: Gerald I. Susman and Roger D. Evered, "An Assessment of the Scientific Merits of Action Research," *Administrative Science Quarterly*, 23 (December 1978), p. 600. Reprinted with permission.

Action Research as a Corrective to the Deficiencies of Positivist Science*

Gerald I. Susman
and Roger D. Evered

Six characteristics of action research provide a corrective to the deficiencies of positivist science we discussed earlier. These characteristics are representative of the methods and objectives of key developers and practitioners of action research (A.R.).

A.R. is future oriented. In dealing with the practical concerns of people, A.R. is oriented toward creating a more desirable future for them. Human beings are therefore recognized as purposeful systems (Ackoff and Emery, 1972) the actions of which are guided by goals, objectives, and ideals. In being future-oriented, A.R. has close affinities to the planning process, so that planning research may be potentially useful in informing A.R. and vice versa.

A.R. is collaborative. Interdependence between researcher and the client system is an essential feature of action research, and the direction of the research process will be partly a function of the needs and competencies of the two. On the one hand, A.R., as Cherns, Clark, and Jenkins (1976: 33) state, "challenges the position of the social scientist as privileged observer, analyst, and critic." On the other hand, it prevents him from taking the role of disinterested observer and obliges him to clarify and represent his own ethics and values so that they, along with those of the client system, can serve as guidelines against which to assess jointly planned actions.

A.R. implies system development. The action research process encourages the development of the capacity of a system to facilitate, maintain, and regulate the cyclical process of diagnosing, action planning, action taking, evaluating, and specifying learning. The aim in action research is to build appropriate structures, to build the necessary system and competencies, and to modify the relationship of the system to its relevant environment. The focus is on generating the necessary communication and problem-solving procedures. The infrastructure of the system, which the action research generates, is the key instrument for (1) alleviating the immediate problematic situation, and (2) generating new knowledge about system processes.

* SOURCE: Gerald I. Susman and Roger D. Evered, "An Assessment of the Scientific Merits of Action Research," *Administrative Science Quarterly,* 23 (December 1978), pp. 589–590, 594. Reprinted with permission.

A.R. generates theory grounded in action. In action research, theory provides a guide for what should be considered in the diagnosis of an organization as well as for generating possible courses of action to deal with the problems of members of the organization. This is the case for psychoanalytic theory, Lewinian field theory, and general systems theory (see Susman, 1976). Furthermore, A.R. contributes to the development of theory by taking actions guided by theory and evaluating their consequences for the problems members of organizations face. Theory may then be supported or revised on the basis of the evaluation.

A.R. is agnostic. The action researcher recognizes that his or her theories and prescriptions for action are themselves the product of previously taken action and, therefore, are subject to reexamination and reformulation upon entering every new research situation. The action researcher also recognizes that the objectives, the problem, and the method of the research must be generated from the process itself and that the consequences of selected actions cannot be fully known ahead of time.

A.R. is situational. The action researcher knows that many of the relationships between people, events, and things are a function of the situation as relevant actors currently define it. Such relationships are not often invariant (Blumer, 1956) of free of their context, but can change as the definition of the situation changes. Appropriate action is based not on knowledge of the replications of previously observed relationships between actions and outcomes. It is based on knowing how particular actors define their present situations or on achieving consensus on defining situations so that planned actions will produce their intended outcomes.

. . . . [W]e propose that action research can be legitimated as science by locating its foundation in philosophical viewpoints which differ from those used to legitimate positivist science. We also propose alternative criteria of science and alternative methods as appropriate for action research. Finally, we consider what action research can contribute to the growth of knowledge.

REFERENCES

ACKOFF, RUSSELL, and F. E. EMERY. 1972. On Purposeful Systems. Chicago: Aldine-Atherton.

CHERNS, A. B., P. A. CLARK, and W. I. JENKINS. 1976. "Action research and the development of the social sciences." In Alfred W. Clark (ed.), Experimenting with Organizational Life: The Action Research Approach: 33–42. New York: Plenum.

SUSMAN, GERALD I. 1976. Autonomy at Work: A Sociotechnical Analysis of Participative Management. New York: Praeger.

BLUMER, HERBERT. "Sociological Analysis and the 'Variable'," *American Sociological Review*, Vol XXII, 1957, pp. 47–59.

Two Versions of Action Research*

Michael Peters and Viviane Robinson

Our review of contemporary writers suggests that, as in Lewin's own writings, two versions of action research exist. While most commentators see it as a research methodology or strategy, three authors have sought to develop an underlying conception of social science, emphasizing the emancipatory potential of social research and the central importance of the participants' beliefs, values, and intentions. The former weak version and the latter strong version share the following minimal requirements:

1. They both share the involvement-in-change characteristics—i.e., they are problem-focused and directed toward the improvement of some existing social practice.
2. They share the organic process characteristics—i.e., research consists of a series of systematic cyclical or iterative stages of fact finding, reflection and planning, strategic action, and evaluation.
3. They share the collaborative characteristic—i.e., research is carried on as a joint, cooperative endeavor among the participants.

The weak version, which satisfies these three minimal conditions of action research, is not incompatible with other forms of social research. It provides a problem-solving methodology that one may use within a variety of social science perspectives, and it does not necessarily entail a commitment to a particular form of explanation of human action or to a particular philosophy of social science. With the weak version, collaboration will typically take place between an independent "expert" and a client group who wishes to improve an existing practice, and the degree of collaboration will be something less than total.

Following the work of Lewin, and that of the three contemporary action researchers who have addressed themselves to questions that go beyond considerations of methodology, we suggest that the strong version of action research requires a commitment to an underlying philosophy of social science—one consistent with a particular interpretation of the three minimal conditions indicated above.

Given the central importance that exponents of the strong version attach to the actors' values, beliefs, purposes, and intentions, these researchers will reject both the traditional separation of the "knower" from the objects of

* SOURCE: Michael Peters and Viviane Robinson, "The Origins and Status of Action Research," *Journal of Applied Behavioral Science,* 20 (1984), pp. 120–122. Reprinted with permission.

knowledge and the associated thesis of neutrality that underlies "objectivist" or positivist research programs. Accordingly, they will tend to construe the collaborative relationship in terms that preclude the independent role of the "expert" observer and will focus on the equal participation of group members in all aspects of the research process, from initial problem formulation to the implementation of strategies. Furthermore, exponents of the strong version will favor a constructivist/interactionist epistemology that emphasizes a dynamic and mutually determining relationship between the knowing subject and the object known. Such an epistemology stresses that our understanding of the world is both *social* and *constitutive*, that social actors who have created their own histories can also reflect upon themselves and their situation and transform or change their reality. To this extent one can consider the strong version emancipatory.

Many stock arguments in the philosophy of science support the notion of a constructivist/interactionist epistemology. Hanson (1958), Kuhn (1962), and Popper (1968), among others, have seriously questioned the positivist belief in an epistemologically privileged observation language, arguing that all observation is preceded and influenced by theoretical beliefs and expectations. Furthermore, such social theorists as Taylor (1971) and MacIntyre (1971) have criticized the categorical distinction between the objective (the observable) and the subjective (the unobservable) maintained by social scientists, pointing out the artificiality of the distinction between social reality and the language used to describe it. Bernstein (1979) notes:

> This very ideal of the theorist as disinterested observer is bound up with closely related categorical distinctions: the distinction between theory and practice, where "practice" is understood as the technical application of theoretical knowledge; the distinction between empirical and normative theory, where the former is directed toward the description and explanation of what *is*, while the latter deals with the clarification and justification of what *ought to be;* the distinction between descriptive and prescriptive discourse; and the distinction between fact and value. (p. 173)

The strong version of action research stands opposed to these traditional categorical distinctions underlying mainstream social science. This version maintains that theory and practice develop together in a series of evolutionary steps designed to lead to improvements in practice during the life of the research project. It proceeds from a normative base and recognizes that the actors' shared values, expectations, and beliefs—i.e., the whole realm of intersubjective "meanings"—actually constitute what counts as social reality. Here the distinction between what *is* and what *ought to be*, between the descriptive and the prescriptive elements, does not easily hold up; the world cannot be neatly divided into facts and values.

While agreement exists over the necessity of "interpretive understanding" as a feature peculiar to a knowledge of social reality, and thus also of the action research perspective, we find an apparent conflict between Argyris

(1980)—who follows Lewin—and Kemmis (1981) and Elliot (1978) over the type of explanation appropriate for explaining human actions. A debate over resolution of the causes versus reasons is crucial to the future development of the strong version, although some grounds exist for believing that the two types of explanation are not necessarily incompatible (Davidson, 1963).

Action research in either the weak or strong version clearly does not currently enjoy the status of a paradigm in the social sciences, even though a small number of writers have spoken of it as such. Paradigms, in Kuhn's (1962, 1970) sense, are shared by the members of a scientific community. Despite some common methodological procedures for addressing social concerns, action researchers do not yet form such a group. Talk of membership in the same scientific community implies something more than a shared problem and a common methodology. It implies at least a certain self-consciousness by practitioners of their common membership, indicated by such things as professional journals and associations, a textbook tradition, and the like. At present, action researchers clearly fail to comprise a scientific community on the basis of this sort of sociological criteria.

We do not say that action research does not hold the potential for paradigmatic status. To explore and develop such potential, however, action researchers must form a professional community in which the exchange of views, in true dialogue fashion, may lead to a better conceptualization of the approach.

REFERENCES

ARGYRIS, C. *Inner contradictions of rigorous research.* New York: Academic Press, 1980.

BERNSTEIN, R. *The restructuring of social and political theory.* London: Methuen, 1979.

DAVIDSON, D. Actions, reasons and causes. *Journal of Philosophy*, 1963, *60*, 685–700.

ELLIOT, J. What is action research in schools? *Journal of Curriculum Studies*, 1978, *10*, 355–357.

HANSON, N. *Patterns of discovery.* Cambridge: Cambridge University Press, 1958.

KEMMIS, S. Research approaches and methods: Action research. In D. Anderson & C. Blakers (Eds.), *Transition from school: An exploration of research and policy.* Canberra: Australian National University Press, 1981.

KUHN, T. *The structure of scientific revolutions.* Chicago: University of Chicago Press, 1962.

KUHN, T. Reflections on my critics. In I. Lakatos & A. Musgrove (Eds.), *Criticism and the growth of knowledge.* London: Cambridge University Press, 1970.

MACINTYRE, A. *Against the self-images of the age.* New York: Schocken Books, 1971.

POPPER, K. *The logic of scientific discovery.* London: Hutchinson, 1968.

TAYLOR, C. Interpretation and the sciences of man. *Review of Metaphysics*, 1971, *25*, 3–51.

Towards a Definition of Action Research: A Note and Bibliography*

Margarete Hult and Sven-Åke Lennung

I. BACKGROUND

The relationship between research and application has always been of focal interest. Social science continually produces findings and increased knowledge. It is by no means certain that this knowledge is fed back and used. The re-awakened interest in action research could be seen as one way of coping with this difficulty. Lately, practitioners as well as researchers with increasing frequency have claimed to be using 'an action research approach'. The actual meaning of 'action research', however, does not always seem to be clearly defined.

A survey of the literature—listed in the bibliography—has revealed not only a variety of definitions and emphases but also rather distinct traditions.[1] It is also evident that different meanings have been attributed to the concept over the years. The notions proposed by Lewin[2] and Curle[3] would today more properly be labelled 'field experiments'.

The following analysis is based mainly on writings within the organization tradition.

In order to produce a valid definition, available descriptions of action research were examined and broken down into their constitutive elements. The

* SOURCE: Margarete Hult and Sven-Åke Lennung, "Towards a Definition of Action Research: A Note and Bibliography," *Journal of Management Studies*, 17, 2, (1980), 241–250.

[1] There is, for example, a school tradition, see Clifford, G. J., 'A History of the Impact of Research on Teaching', in Travers, M. W. (Ed.), *Second Handbook of Research on Teaching*, Chicago: Rand McNally, 1973, pp. 1–46 (see especially pp. 21–2); a community development tradition, see Lippitt, R., *Training in Community Relations*, New York: Harper and Row, 1951; an organization tradition, see Foster, M., 'An Introduction to the Theory and Practice of Action Research in Work Organizations', *Human Relations*, Vol. 25, No. 6, 1972, pp. 529–56 and Clark, A. W. (Ed.), *Experimenting with Organizational Life: the Action Research Approach*, New York and London: Plenum, 1976.

[2] Lewin, K., 'Frontiers in Group Dynamics, II. Channels of Group Life, Social Planning and Social Action', *Human Relations*, Vol. 1, No. 2, 1947b, pp. 143–54.

[3] Curle, A., 'A Theoretical Approach to Action Research', *Human Relations*, Vol. 2, 1949, pp. 269–80.

subsequent analysis aimed at uncovering the 'least common denominators' which included the variant elements and aspects mentioned in the literature. These were summarized and integrated into a new comprehensive definition.

In the following section this new definition will be introduced gradually with a short discussion of each core element.

2. DEFINITION

Action research simultaneously assists in practical problem-solving and expands scientific knowledge . . .

> Action research aims to contribute both to the practical concerns of people in an immediate problematic situation and to the goals of social science . . .[4]
> Thus action research must possess an aspect of direct involvement in organizational change, and simultaneously it must provide an increase in knowledge.[5]

The quotations above illustrate the view, favoured in most discussions, namely, that in action research problem-solving and knowledge expansion are pursued simultaneously. This view is not universally held. All writers in our review do emphasize, however, the problem-solving aspect. An action research project emerges from and has to contribute to the solution of existing practical problems. It never emanates from theory alone.

This emphasis on practice bears a danger that the scientific interest may be reduced to a mere means towards improved problem-solving.

> . . . this type of inquiry is undertaken by practitioners in order to guide and correct their present and future decisions and actions . . . Action research is undertaken on the hypothesis that the research approach to the solution of practical problems will result in better decisions and actions than will result if major dependence is placed upon intuition and subjective recall of evidence about consequences.[6]

The use of scientific method solely as a problem-solving procedure is not in accordance with our proposed definition. Action research must aim at action *and* research.

. . . as well as enhances the competence of the respective actors . . .

The specific nature of the skills and competences that can be learned and developed within an action research project vary slightly for the different

---

[4] Rapoport, R. N., 'Three Dilemmas in Action Research', *Human Relations*, Vol. 23, No. 6, 1970b, pp. 499–513, p. 499.

[5] Clark, P., *Action Research and Organizational Change*, London: Harper and Row, 1972, p. 23.

[6] Corey, S., 'Action Research by Teachers and the Population Sampling Problem', *Journal of Educational Psychology*, Vol. 43, 1952, pp. 331–8, p. 331.

parties involved. The claim is that an action research project is very deliberately designed to also serve as a learning process.[7]

Action research is an integrated concept with its own distinct meaning. It is not merely a summation: 'Action cum research'. The assumption is that projects can be *simultaneously* beneficial for problem-solving, theory expansion and competence enhancement. And this is based on the fact that a good research strategy by definition involves a rational, systematic analysis of a phenomenon (a 'problem'), and secures information, hypotheses and action-suggestions from all parties involved, as well as evaluates the actions taken towards solution of the problem. The project environment therefore provides a learning situation in which participants learn from the actual investigation *per se* and from its theoretical implications but, also, from the process of a collaborative problem-solving strategy.

. . . being performed collaboratively . . .

An overpowering requirement is the demand for a collaborative activity. The action researcher and the client are mutually dependent on each other's skills, experiences and competences to achieve problem-solving, knowledge expansion and learning. The success of a project is assumed to be sufficiently desirable to all parties involved.[8] This requirement of a cooperative social situation does not exclude a rational division of labour based on distinct individual competences. Neither must all parties engage in all elements of goal realization. It is only rational, therefore, that the task of editing research reports to the scientific community is left with the action researcher—unless the mastery of such skills are deemed to be of importance for the client.

Ideally, every action should simultaneously contribute to problem-solving, knowledge-expansion and competence-enhancement. This cannot always be so, as, for practical reasons there have to be instances when one must be more concerned with one of these objectives for a certain amount of time. It is essential, however, that no intervention counteracts any of these goals in any serious respect. As a consequence, the 'art' of action research is a continuous creative solution of dilemmas due to the fact that at least three interests are pursued at the same time.[9]

The changes resulting from this process should also be undertaken in close collaboration between the parties involved. They together share the responsibility for the outcome of the project. Some writers[10] even claim that the whole action research project must be carried out by persons within the client system, keeping external sources on a strict consultancy basis. Cunning-

---

[7] As discussed, for example, by Corey, S., *Action Research to Improve School Practices,* New York: Bureau of Publications, Teachers' College, Columbia University, 1953, pp. 107–25.

[8] See, for example, Foster, M., op. cit., pp. 542ff.

[9] See, for example, Rapoport, R. N., op. cit.

[10] See, for example, Cunningham, B., 'Action Research: Towards a Procedural Model', *Human Relations,* Vol. 29, No. 3, 1976, pp. 215–38, p. 216.

ham's view does not correspond with the opinion expressed in this paper—we acknowledge the practicality in divisions of labour, as long as such a division does not counteract problem-solving or relevant competence-enhancement.

. . . in an immediate situation . . .

> Action research is a type of applied social research differing from other varieties in the immediacy of the researcher's involvement in the action process.[11]

In traditional investigations a study is carried out *on* a social system, a report is delivered and, at best, acted upon and evaluated. The action researcher performs these activities *within* the system and follows the process of the social system under study. He also takes part in the implementation of findings from the project. Consequently, an action research project is not completed until the changes resulting from the study have been carried out.

. . . using data feedback in a cyclical process . . .

The action research procedure requires the use of participative methods for data collection, analysis and diagnosis. The data are fed back to those who originated it in a way aiming at understanding the functioning of the system.[12]

Some writers particularly emphasize the diffusion as an important part of the action research strategy.

> In action research the creation and use of a diffusion channel is an essential part of the research. Utilization is built into the research design.[13]

> It avoids the danger that findings will not be applied or that they will be applied only after a long delay.[14]

The interpretation and analysis of these data will be undertaken in collaboration between the action researcher and the client. The action researcher contributes methods, a pre-understanding of the problem as well as intervention skills. The client contributes his understanding of the specific situation and its idiosyncracies. The choice of techniques and methods is contingent upon the nature of the problem. Any valid and reliable method for diagnosis, model-building, deduction, data collection, data analysis and evaluation may be used.

> . . . its practitioners may use the full range of research designs and methods of inquiry with confidence and rigour.[15]

[11] Rapoport, R. N., op. cit., p. 499.

[12] Heller, F., 'Group Feedback Analysis as a Change Agent', *Human Relations*, Vol. 23, No. 4, 1970, pp. 319–33; Clark, P. A., op. cit.

[13] Cherns, A. B., 'Social Research and its Diffusion', *Human Relations*, Vol. 22, No. 3, 1969, pp. 209–18, p. 215.

[14] Clark, A. W., op. cit., p. 2.

[15] Ibid., p. 1.

Action research, therefore, is not distinguished by choice of method, but rather by the way these methods are employed.

The knowledge gained often results in a redefinition of the situation and of the problem. This, in turn, demands new action planning, if the outcome is to be followed up, fed back and evaluated. Action research thus is a cyclical process of problem definition, action planning, implementation, data feedback and evaluation.

The scientific interest in a problem procures a rational analysis, a systematic fact-finding and hypothesis-testing, leading to a clearer definition and understanding of a problem. This procedure leads to more goal-directed solution-attempts ('actions'), the results of which are evaluated and understood in the light of the previous analysis.

. . . aiming at an increased understanding of the totality of a given social situation . . .

In action research a deliberate attempt is made not to divorce phenomena from the environment which give them meaning.[16] This is contrary to conventional research where it is customary to single out one or two factors, the effects of which are studied and described, assuming all other factors being equal.

Consequently, the researcher using an action research approach will be studying interconnections, interdependencies and the dynamics of a total functioning system rather than isolated factors. One reason is that social phenomena always occur in combination and in contexts—situational as well as historical. Another advantage—compatible with the problem-solving interest—is that a 'good enough' picture of a totality is more useful than detailed knowledge about abstract factors devoid of their contexts.

. . . primarily applicable for the understanding of change processes in social systems . . .

Many writers point out that only phenomena which are amenable to change can be approached by the action research method.

> The process by which a researcher seeks to study social change by deliberately contributing to the introduction of a planned change in the process of the social system under study.[17]

There is also agreement in the literature on the fact that action research is concerned with social systems. The action research method is particularly suited for the study of the process of change, but facts and insights regarding social structures may also be secured. Examples of topics studied are improvement of school practice,[18] attempts to provide more housing and jobs in a small

---

[16] Hodgkinson, H. L., 'Action Research—a Critique', *Journal of Educational Sociology,* Vol. 31, 1957, pp. 137–53, p. 137.

[17] Henley, J., 'Planned Organizational Change in Public Administration: Towards an Advanced Industrial Society?' *British Sociological Association,* (mimeo), 1975a.

[18] Corey, S., 1953, op. cit.

isolated community,[19] codetermination in decision-making in hospitals,[20] and industrial democracy.[21]

The specific nature of the change effort (the 'action') is to be decided by the project team. It may be '. . . any professional intervention from a social or behavioural science perspective in the ongoing processes of a socially structured entity'.[22] Examples of actions are organizational re-design, changes in wage systems or administrative procedures, *etc.* One possibility is to use the research programme itself as the agent of change. Sanford[23] develops this point and consequently prefers the term 'research-action'. His own report provides an illustrative example of findings and changes produced in such a way. Brown[24] argues a similar case.

. . . undertaken within a mutually acceptable ethical framework

This aspect has received scant interest in the literature. Writers who explicitly discuss ethical issues usually emphasize the importance of participation by those primarily affected by the planned change. In our opinion, however, it is not quite clear whether this aspect should be treated exclusively as an ethical issue. Sometimes participation and collaboration is equally a question of method and strategy.

Some writers also discuss the objectives of the client system itself. Emery[25] and Rapoport,[26] in commendable discussions of several ethical issues, mention the problems posed by working with organizations which produce products like weapons or tobacco. Otherwise, there seems to be a tacit agreement that the action researcher shares no responsibility for the goals of the client system.

A related issue deals with whose interests are served in an action research project. In the Scandinavian tradition a distinction between 'functional-technocratic' and 'culture-radical-progressive'[27] is often upheld. The 'technocratic' projects aim at ameliorating the functioning of a system, while the 'progressive' projects are characterized by a solidarity with underprivileged groups. This tradition can be traced back to Lewin and recent examples of

[19] Aubert, V., 'Action Research', in *Social Politics and Social Research,* Oslo: Universitetsforlaget, 1970, pp. 105–50.

[20] Revans, R., 'I Thought They Were Supposed To Be Doing That', The Hospital Centre, London, 1972.

[21] Thorsrud, E., 'A Strategy for Research and Social Change in Industry: A Report on the Industrial Democracy Project in Norway' (mimeo), 1969.

[22] Seashore,

[23] Sanford, N., 'Whatever Happened to Action Research?', *Journal of Social Issues,* Vol. 25, No. 1, 1970, pp. 3–23.

[24] Brown, L. D., '"Research Action": Organizational Feedback, Understanding, and Change', *Journal of Applied Behavioral Science,* Vol. 8, 1972, pp. 697–711.

[25] Emery, F. E., 'Professional Responsibility of Social Scientists', in Clark, A. W., 1976, op. cit., pp. 11–18.

[26] Rapoport, R. N., op. cit., pp. 503–5.

[27] Langsted, 'Action Research', *Teori og Praksis,* Vol. 1, 1973, pp. 7–35.

such research are found in Bülow, Fricke and Windisch[28] and in Axelsen and Finset.[29]

In our view, a minimal ethical requirement for an action researcher is to state clearly the value premises of his work. One example of negligence in this respect is provided by Greenbaum, Rogovsky and Shalit[30] in a paper on the use of social science techniques in a combat unit. That paper does contain a section labelled 'ethical issues'. The problems of confidentiality and of working with commanders—not soldiers—are discussed under this heading. No reference is made to the fact that their model is developed to facilitate the wounding and killing of fellow human beings.

SUMMARY

In summary:

Action research simultaneously assists in practical problem-solving and expands scientific knowledge, as well as enhances the competencies of the respective actors, being performed collaboratively in an immediate situation using data feedback in a cyclical process aiming at an increased understanding of a given social situation, primarily applicable for the understanding of change processes in social systems and undertaken within a mutually acceptable ethical framework.

REFERENCES

(translation of non-English titles within brackets)

ABRAHAMSSON, B. and SWEDNER, H., 'Organisation och forskning' ['Organization and Research'], Lund: Department of Sociology (mimeo), 1976.

AUBERT, V., 'Aksionsforskning, [Action research], in *Sosialpolitikken og samfunnsforskningen*, [*Social Politics and Social Research*], Oslo: Universitetsforlaget, 1970, pp. 105–50.

AXELSEN, T. and FINSET, A. (Eds.), *Aksjonsforskning: Teori og Praksis* [*Action Research: Theory and Practice*], Trondhjem: Cappelen, 1973.

BECKHARD, R., *Organization Development: Strategies and Models*, Reading, Mass.: Addison-Wesley, 1969.

BENNE, K. D., BRADFORD, L. P. and LIPPITT, R. 'The Laboratory Method', in Bradford, L. P., Gibb, J.

R. and Benne, R. (Eds.), *T-Group Theory and Laboratory Method*, New York: Wiley, 1964, pp. 15–44.

BENNIS, W. G., BENNE, K. D. and CHIN, R., *The Planning of Change*, 2nd ed., New York: Holt, Rinehart and Winston, 1969.

BENNIS, W. G., BENNE, K. D., CHIN, R. and COREY, K. E., *The Planning of Change*, 3rd ed., New York: Holt, Rinehart and Winston, 1976.

BERG, H., *Att förändra*, [*To Change*], Stockholm: The Swedish Council for Personnel Administration, 1976.

BLUM, F. H., 'Action Research—A Scientific Approach', *Philosophy of Science*, Vol. 22, 1955, pp. 1–7.

---

[28] Bülow, M., Fricke, H. P., and Windisch, A., 'Socialization of Guest-Workers' Children', in Haag, F., Krüger, H., Schwärzel, W. and Wildt, J. (Eds.), *Action Research. Research Strategies, Research Fields and Research Plans*, München: Juventa Verlag, 1972, pp. 227–43.

[29] Axelsen, T. and Finset, A. (Eds.), *Action Research: Theory and Practice*, Trondhjem: Cappelen, 1973.

[30] Greenbaum, C. W., Rogovsky, I. and Shalit, B., 'The Military Psychologist During Wartime: A Model, Based on Action Research and Crisis Intervention, *Journal of Applied Behavioral Science*, Vol. 13, No. 1, 1977, pp. 7–21.

BROCK-UTNE, B., *Monsterplanprosjektet—et Aksjons-forsknings-Prosjekt* [*The Curriculum Project—an Action Research Project*], Reports (1–) from Sosialpedagogiske Studium, Department of Education, University of Oslo, 1977.

BROWN, L. D., '"Research Action": Organizational Feedback, Understanding, and Change', *Journal of Applied Behavioral Science*, Vol. 8, 1972, pp. 697–711.

BURGOYNE, J. G., 'An Action Research Experiment in the Evaluation of a Management Development Course', *Journal of Management Studies*, Vol. 10, No. 1, 1973, pp. 8–14.

BÜLOW, M., FRICKE, H. P. and WINDISCH, A., 'Sozialisation von Gastarbeiterkindern,' ['Socialization of Guest-Workers' Children], in Haag, F., Krüger, H., Schwärzel, W. and Wildt, J. (Eds.), *Aktionsforschung. Forschungsstrategien, Forschungsfelder und Forschungsplane,* [*Action Research, Research Strategies, Research Fields and Research Plans*], München: Juventa Verlag, 1972, pp. 227–243.

CHEIN, I., COOK, S. and HARDING, J., 'The Field of Action Research', *The American Psychologist*, Vol. 3, 1948, pp. 43–50.

CHERNS, A. B., 'Social Research and its Diffusion', *Human Relations*, Vol. 22, No. 3, 1969, pp. 209–18.

CHERNS, A. B., 'Behavioural Science Engagements: Taxonomy and Dynamics, *Human Relations*, Vol. 29, No. 10, 1976, pp. 905–10.

CHESLER, M. and FLANDERS, M., 'Resistance to Research and Research Utilization: The Death and Life of a Feedback Attempt', *Journal of Applied Behavioral Science*, Vol. 3, 1967, pp. 469–87.

CLARK, A. W. (Ed.), *Experimenting with Organizational Life: The Action Research Approach,* New York: Plenum, 1976.

CLARK, A. W., 'Sanction: A Critical Element in Action Research,' *Journal of Applied Behavioral Science*, Vol. 8, 1972, pp. 713–31.

CLARK, P. A., *Action Research and Organizational Change,* London: Harper and Row, 1972.

CLARK, P. A., 'Action Research: A Personal View of Some Key Problems', paper presented at *Association for Teachers of Management's Conference on Action Research* in Chelmsford, England, May 1975.

CLIFFORD, G. J., 'A History of the Impact of Research on Teaching', in Travers, M. W. (Ed.), *Second Handbook of Research Teaching,* Chicago: Rand McNally, 1973, pp. 1–46.

COOPER, R. and FOSTER, M., 'Sociotechnical Systems', *American Psychologist*, Vol. 26, 1971, pp. 467–74.

COREY, S., 'Action Research by Teachers and the Population Sampling Problem', *Journal of Educational Psychology*, Vol. 43, 1952, pp. 331–8.

COREY, S., *Action Research to Improve School Practices,* New York: Bureau of Publications, Teachers College, Columbia University, 1953.

CUNNINGHAM, B., 'Action Research: Toward a Procedural Model', *Human Relations,* Vol. 29, 1976, pp. 215–38.

CURLE, A., 'A Theoretical Approach to Action Research', *Human Relations,* Vol. 2, 1949, pp. 269–80.

DAHLSTRÖM, E., 'Aktionsforskning' ['Action Research'], in Jungen, B. (Ed.), *Rapport om Surte,* [*Report about Surte*], Göteborg: Centrum för tvärvetenskapliga studier, 1976, pp. 10–6.

DOCHERTY, P., 'Organisationsutveckling för ökat medinflytande i tjänstemannaföretag: forskarrollen i ett aktionsforskningsprojekt', ['Organization Development for Increased Co-Determination in a White Collar Organization: The Researcher Role in an Action Research Project'], Stockholm: *Report from the Swedish Council for Personnel Administration,* Nr. 008876, 1970.

EICHNER, K. and SCHMIDT, P., 'Aktionsforschung—Eine Neue Methode?' ['Action Research—A New Method?'], *Soziale Welt*, Vol. 25, 1974, pp. 145–68.

ELDEN, M., 'Sharing the Research Work', Trondheim, Norway: Institute for Industrial Social Research (mimeo), 1977.

EMERY, F. E., 'Professional Responsibility of Social Scientists', in Clark, A. W. (Ed.), *Experimenting with Organizational Life,* New York and London: Plenum, 1976, pp. 11–8.

ENERSTVEDT, R. T., *Vetenskap Som Pedagogik,* [*Science as Pedagogy*], Stockholm: Prisma, 1971.

FERGUSON, C., 'Concerning the Nature of Human Systems and the Consultant's Role', *Journal of Applied Behavioral Science*, Vol. 4, 1968, pp. 179–226.

FIEDLER, P. A. and HÖRMANN, G. (Eds.), *Aktionsforschung in Psychologie und Pädagogik,* [*Action Research in Psychology and Education*], Darmstatt: Steinkopff, 1978.

FOSHAY, A. W., 'Action Research on Children's Social Values', *Educational Leadership*, Vol. 12, 1955, pp. 249–50.

FOSTER, M., 'An Introduction to the Theory and Practice of Action Research in Work Organizations', *Human Relations,* Vol. 25, 1972, pp. 529–56.

FRENCH, W., 'Organization Development: Objectives, Assumptions and Strategies', in Margulies, N. and Raia, A. P., *Organization Development: Values, Processes and Technology,* London: McGraw-Hill, 1972, pp. 31–49.

FRENCH, W. L. and BELL, C. H., *Organization Development: Behavioral Science Interventions for Organization Improvement,* Englewood Cliffs, N.J.: Prentice Hall, 1973.

GREINER, L., 'Patterns of Organization Change', *Harvard Business Review*, Vol. 45, No. 3, 1967, pp. 119–30.

GREENBAUM, C. W., ROGOVSKY, I. and SHALIT,

B., 'The Military Psychologist during Wartime: A Model based on Action Research and Crisis Intervention,' *Journal of Applied Behavioral Science*, Vol. 13, 1977, pp. 7–21.

GRÜNBAUM, L., 'Aktionsforskningens Muligheder som en Samfundsaendrende Praksis' [Possibilities for Action Research as Practice for Societal Change'], in Haslebo, G., Holbøll, P., Høyrup, S., Madsen, F. H. and Nesjum, B. (Eds.), *Magt og Påvirkning i Systemer*, [*Power and Influence in Systems*], Copenhagen: Reitzel, 1973, pp. 99–116.

GUSTAVSEN, B., 'Aktionsforskning,' ['Action research'], *Rapporter*, Nr. 13, Stockholms Universitet, Psykologiska Institutionen, 1976.

HALSEY, A. H. (Ed.), *Educational Priority*, 1, London: H.M.S.O., 1972.

HAVELOCK, R. G., *Planning for Innovation through Dissemination and Utilization of Knowledge*, Ann Arbor: Institute for Social Research, University of Michigan, 1969.

HEINZET, T., MÜLLER, E., STICKELMANN, B. and ZINNECKER, J., *Handlungsforschung im pädagogischen Feld* [*Action Research in Pedagogical Field*], München: Juventa Verlag, 1975.

HELLBLOM, L., 'Anteckningar om Aktionsforskning', [Notes on Action Research'], *Psykologi: Teori och Praktik*, Vol. I, 1975, pp. 9–15.

HELLER, F., 'Group Feedback Analysis as a Change Agent', *Human Relations*, Vol. 23, No. 4, 1970, pp. 319–33.

HENLEY, J., 'Planned Organizational Change in Public Administration: Towards an Advanced Industrial Society?' *British Sociological Association*, (mimeo), 1975a.

HENLEY, J., *Strategies for Research in Organizations: The Case of Action Research*, Unpublished doctoral dissertation, London School of Economics, 1975b.

HJORT, H., 'Om att Förstå det Allmänna Genom det Särskilda', [On Understanding the General through the Particular], in Holter, H., Gjersten, A., Ve Henriksen, H. and Hiort, H., *Familjen Klassambället*, [*The Family in Class Society*], Stockholm: Aldus, 1976, pp. 219–58.

HODGKINSON, H. L., 'Action Research—a Critique', *Journal of Educational Sociology*, Vol. 31, 1957, pp. 137–53.

HULT, M., *Aktionsforskning*, [*Action Research*], Stockholm: Swedish Employers' Confederation, Training and Education Unit, 1978.

JENKS, S. R., 'An Action Research Approach to Organizational Change', *Journal of Applied Behavioral Science*, Vol. 6, 1970, pp. 131–50.

LANGSTED, 'Aktionsforskning', ['Action Research'], *Teori og Praksis*, Vol. I, 1973, pp. 7–35.

LEES, R. and SMITH G. (Eds.), *Action Research in Community Development*, London: Routledge and Kegan Paul, 1975.

LEWIN, K., 'Frontiers in Group Dynamics I. Concept, Method and Reality in Social Sciences: Social Equilibria and Social Change', *Human Relations*, Vol. 1, 1974a, pp. 5–41.

LEWIN, K., 'Frontiers in Group Dynamics II. Channels of Group Life, Social Planning and Social Action', *Human Relations*, Vol. I, 1947b, pp. 143–54.

LIPPITT, R., *Training in Community Relations*, New York: Harper and Row, 1951.

LØCHEN, Y., *Sociologens Dilemma*, [*The Sociologist's Dilemma*], Oslo: Gyldendal, 1972.

MARGULIES, N. and RAIA, A. P., *Organizational Development: Values, Process and Technology*, New York: McGraw-Hill, 1972.

MARRIS, P. and REIN, M., *Dilemmas of Social Reform*, London: Routledge and Kegan Paul, 1967.

MILES, R., 'Organization Development', in *IRRA Annual*, London, 1974, pp. 165–91.

MITCHELL, G. D., *A Dictionary of Sociology*, London: Routledge and Kegan Paul, 1968.

RAPOPORT, R. N., *Community as a Doctor*, London: Tavistock, 1967.

RAPOPORT, R. N., *Mid-Career Development*, London: Tavistock, 1970a.

RAPOPORT, R. N., "Three Dilemmas in Action Research', *Human Relations*, Vol. 23, No. 6, 1970b, pp. 499–513.

REVANS, R., *Developing Effective Managers*, London: Longman, 1971.

REVANS, R., 'I Thought They Were Supposed To Be Doing That', The Hospital Centre, London, 1972.

SANFORD, N., 'Whatever Happened to Action Research?' *Journal of Social Issues*, Vol. 26, 1970, pp. 3–23.

SHEPARD, H., 'An Action Research Model', in *An Action Research Programme for Organizational Improvement*, Ann Arbor: Foundation for Research on Human Behavior, 1960, pp. 33–4.

SHUMSKY, A., 'Cooperation in Action Research: A Rationale', *Journal of Educational Sociology*, Vol. 30, 1956, pp. 180–5.

SHUMSKY, A., 'Learning about Learning from Action Research', in 1959 *Yearbook of the Association for Supervision and Curriculum Development*, NEA: Learning and the Teacher, 1959.

SILVERMAN, D., *The Theory of Organisations*, London: Heinemann, 1970.

SPENCER, J. (with TUXFORD, J. and DENNIS, N.), *Stress and Release in an Urban Estate. A Study in Action Research*, London: Tavistock, 1964.

STEELE, F. I., 'Consultants and Detectives', *Journal of Applied Behavioral Science*, Vol. 5, 1969, pp. 187–202.

THORSRUD, E., 'A Strategy for Research and Social Change in Industry: A Report on the Industrial Democracy Project in Norway', (mimeo), 1969.

THORSRUD, E., 'Policy-Making as a Learning Process—Work Note on Social Science Policy', Work Research Institutes Oslo, (draft paper), 1970.

THURLEY, K. E., 'The Research Process in Work Role Studies', in Graves, D. (Ed.), *Management Research: A Cross-Cultural Perspective,* Amsterdam: Elsevier, 1973a.

THURLEY, K., 'Evaluating Action Research', paper presented at *European Institute for Advanced Studies in Management and London Graduate School of Business Studies Conference* on 'Evaluating Action Research', 1973b.

THURLEY, K. and WIRDENIUS, H. *Supervision: A Reappraisal,* London: Heinemann, 1973.

TRANKELL, A., 'Undersökning rörande möjligheterna att underlätta de skolpliktiga zigernarnas skolgång i Stockholm' ['Investigation into the Possibilities of Facilitating School-Attendance in Stockholm for the School-aged Gyspsies], *Report from the Department of Education,* Stockholm, Nr. 4, 1967.

TRIST, E., 'Engaging with Large-Scale Systems: Some Concepts and Methods based on Experience gained in Field Projects at the Tavistock Institute', paper contributed to the *McGregor Conference on Organization Development,* Endicott House, 1973.

VANSINA, L. S., 'Beyond Organization Development?' in Warr, P. B. (Ed.), *Personal Goals and Work Design,* London: Wiley, 1976.

WHYTE, W. and HAMILTON, E., *Action Research for Management,* Homewood, Ill.: Irwin-Dorsey, 1964.

WILSON, A. T. M., 'Some Implications of Medical Practice and Social Case-Work for Action Research', *Journal of Social Issues,* Vol. 3, 1947, pp. 11–28.

Values and Organization Development*

Clayton P. Alderfer

Human values have always played a key role in organization development. A strong force motivating the emergence of this field has been the desire to "humanize" organizations, that is, to enable organizations to be more responsive to the human concerns of members. Along with the pursuit of humane values, OD has also been advocated as a set of technologies for improving the effectiveness of organizations. In the earliest days of OD there was less reason to question whether these two classes of values conflicted with each other because the scope of OD applications was much narrower than it is today. Although there were variations among OD theorists and practitioners in terms of relative emphasis on these two classes of values, most people in the field believed that they could pursue both with minimal conflict. As the field has grown, however, increasing numbers of questions have been raised about just how easy it is to pursue both kinds of values with approximately equal vigor. OD has always been a field that emphasized self-scrutiny by its members. Today there is a substantial and significant debate about the value implications of much of OD work among thinkers in the field. The literature on value implications has arisen from practitioners who question themselves in public and from systematic research efforts to determine how practitioners are thinking and acting.

Friedlander (4) attempted a philosophical inquiry into the underlying values of OD. He found that three philosophical systems—rationalism, pragmatism, and existentialism—each played a significant part in determining the basic values of OD. Rationalism stresses the importance of logic, consistency, and determinism. It calls for better empirical and conceptual research. In contrast, pragmatism presses for improvement in the immediate situation. Learning is accomplished by experiments which bring forth improved practice. While rationalism and pragmatism tended to have lengthy time perspectives, linking the past and future, existentialism emphasized the present. This position focused on the here-and-now and valued a person's own immediate, subjective experience. Friedlander (4) sees the contemporary value conflicts within OD as arising from the three philosophical positions.

Evidence for the value dilemmas confronting practitioners in the field arises from both existential and rational research traditions. Tichy (9, 11)

* SOURCE: Clayton P. Alderfer, "Organization Development," *Annual Review of Psychology,* 28 (1977), pp. 198–200. Reprinted by permission of Clayton P. Alderfer.

reported personal interviews with Harrison and Pages. Both practitioner-researchers recounted severe value conflicts in their professional lives. Harrison said that he frequently found himself in conflict between the organization's need for more effective and efficient use of its resources and the individuals' needs for personal growth and development. Pages indicated that he had stopped working for organizations, preferring to help individuals destroy the organization forms in which they were imprisoned. Tichy (10) also reported the results of a survey comparing several types of change agents, including OD practitioners. Organization development change agents as a group were found to be incongruent with respect to their values and actions. In terms of values, they said that they wanted to promote individual freedom and power equilization in society, but in terms of behavior they said that they actually worked to improve productivity and problem-solving ability. In a later study Tichy (8), reported that the diagnostic orientation of OD practitioners was consistent with their value-practice discrepancies. OD practitioners were most likely to examine the culture and formal structure of the systems they worked with and to expect changes in problem-solving effectiveness to follow from changes in culture and formal structure.

While the basic work of OD consultants takes place inside social organizations, the systems themselves exist within turbulent external environments. It is becoming increasingly clear to many thoughtful observers that failure to take account of the value conflicts outside the system as well as inside can result in OD being used to dehumanize social processes rather than to humanize them. Singer & Wooton (7) drew some striking and disturbing parallels between the internally democratic and structurally imaginative organization strategies used by Albert Speer to build the Nazi war machinery and the approaches of many OD practitioners. Nord (5) severely criticized the OD field for failing to recognize the political and economic institutions in which modern organizations exist. He argued that OD has been largely unsuccessful in developing more humane organizations because the theory and values of the field have failed to take account of the potency of the larger political-economic institutions. Bennis (1, 2) made a complementary point arguing from a different perspective. As a major OD theorist who changed roles from academic-consultant to administrative practitioner, Bennis (2) initially raised questions about the relevance of OD methods for the needs of top level administrators in a public service bureaucracy when he changed roles. With so much time spent on external relationships, Bennis (1) felt he could not afford the luxury of team building with top level associates. A year later, however, he was reporting the benefits of OD intervention within his own group, despite the impact of external relations and the very large number of internal conflicting constituencies within the university (1).

At the crux of the value disputes within OD is the problem of power. OD professionals must struggle with whether their professional competence (power) is being used to advance humane values and with whether they can harness enough power to bring about desirable change in human organizations.

Pettigrew (6) has confronted the issues directly, noting that for a long time the subject has been omitted from consideration by OD theorists. He argues that the internal consultant inevitably deals with political processes if change is to occur. The consultant's major choice is whether to be proactive or reactive in the use of power, and Pettigrew (6) clearly favors the proactive position. In his analysis of OD in transition, Burke (3) has noted that the growing amount of knowledge in the field has allowed and encouraged many practitioners to base more of their interventions on authoritative expertise as well as on the traditional nondirective methods.

Questions of values in the practice of organizational change have always been present. But one must say that as the field has grown and diversified the issues have become more complex. Vansina (12) has cautioned against the excessive simplicity of assuming that task accomplishment and other human values can be integrated easily by the adoption of a particular managerial style. Rather practitioners must be alert to the difficult choices between conflicting values, to the danger of their colluding with inhumane objectives, and to the inevitability of their participation in conflicts about the proper use of social power.

REFERENCES

1. BENNIS, W. 1974. Conversation with Warren Bennis. *Organ. Dyn.* Winter: 50–66
2. BENNIS, W. 1973. An OD expert in the cat bird's seat. *J. Higher Educ.* 44:389–98
3. BURKE, W. W. 1976. Organization development in transition. *J. Appl. Behav. Sci.* 12:22–43
4. FRIEDLANDER, F. 1976. OD researches adolescence: an exploration of its underlying values. *J. Appl. Behav. Sci.* 12:7–21
5. NORD, W. R. 1974. The failure of current applied behavioral science: A Marxian perspective. *J. Appl. Behav. Sci.* 10:557–78
6. PETTIGREW, A. M. 1975. Towards a political theory of organizational intervention. *Hum. Relat.* 28:191–208
7. SINGER, E. A., WOOTON, L. M. 1976. The triumph and failure of Albert Speer's administrative genius. *J. Appl. Behav. Sci.* 12:79–103
8. TICHY, N. 1975. How different types of change agents diagnose organizations. *Hum. Relat.* 28
9. TICHY, N. 1973. An interview with Roger Harrison. *J. Appl. Behav. Sci.* 9:701–29
10. TICHY, N. 1974. Agents of planned social change: congruence of values, cognitions, and actions. *Admin. Sci. Q.* 19:164–82
11. TICHY, N. 1974. An interview with Max Pages. *J. Appl. Behav. Sci.* 10:8–26
12. VANSINA, L. S. 1975. Beyond organizational development. In *Personal Goals and Work Design*, ed. P. T. Warr. New York: Wiley

Open-Endedness*

Eric J. Miller

Perhaps a better heading for this closing section would be 'Interim Comments', since what has been reported is very much work in progress. And the direction of the 'progress' is unknown.

That open-endedness, however, is to me one of the most crucial features of this approach. In our role as consultants, we can give people an opportunity to extend their personal and conceptual understanding of relations between individuals, between groups and between systems. We can help them to reflect on what they are doing as they apply this understanding in their work-roles and relationships. We can draw their attention to assumptions they are making and to choices they may not have recognized, and in this way they can acquire greater consciousness of the organization as a system and of their own actual and potential contributions to the shaping of that organization. We can offer them greater scope for managing themselves in their roles. But what we cannot do is to predetermine what use they will make of these opportunities. Perhaps one of our more important functions, as they set about their task of managing themselves, is simply to be available.

Open-endedness is often found frightening by managers (and also by some OD consultants) who therefore often seem to impose limits on the development of participative processes: thus far and no further. Part of managers' fear, I think, is that their competence will come under close scrutiny; part, too, is that if the managerial role and authority are called into question, this poses a threat to all the trappings of 'management'—the assumption of power, status, privileges, the sense of self-importance, and so on. Such fears are not without foundation. Unbridled participation certainly does invite scrutiny of the ways in which roles are performed. But what tends to get forgotten is that appraisal of superiors by subordinates does not originate with participation. Judgments are constantly being made; and corresponding patterns of behaviour are developed as a means of exploiting weaknesses or expressing contempt. Sometimes these take the form of adjustments to the work-role itself; sometimes the union role is used as the vehicle. Participative mechanisms, therefore, do not provoke appraisal of superiors as a new phenomenon; they are much more likely to sanction the overt expression of views that have hitherto been covert.

Notwithstanding the immense gulf between the affluent industrial

* SOURCE: Eric J. Miller, "Organizational Development and Industrial Democracy: A Current Case-Study," in *Organizational Development in the UK and USA: A Joint Evaluation*, ed. Carry L. Cooper (London: Macmillan, 1977), pp. 57–58. Reprinted by permission of Macmillan.

worker in western society and the Third-World peasant living in squalor and poverty, the industrial worker in his relationship to his work-place has something in common with the underdeveloped or the handicapped, in that within his work-role as such he is frequently in a dependent and relatively impotent position. To be sure, he may invent devices to cope with his situation, but they do not basically alter the typical posture of inferiority and subordination. He often has to rely on union membership to redress the balance. Hence . . . the union becomes the vehicle for expressing the fight that in the work relation has to be suppressed.

Managing Change*

Eric J. Miller

Ten years ago, a colleague and I concluded a book with these words: 'Long-term solutions to the problem of maintaining adaptiveness to change cannot ... depend on manipulative techniques. On the contrary, they must depend on helping the individual to develop greater maturity in controlling the boundary between his own inner world and the realities of his external environment.'[1] This theme and the values implied in it have continued to be dominant in my own work and thinking, and also for a number of colleagues in the Tavistock Institute and Clinic and associates outside. If I were rewriting that paragraph now, I would want to reword it in a couple of places. The phrase 'adaptiveness to change' might imply that change in an extraneous—almost superhuman—process and that all we ordinary mortals can do is to make less or more satisfactory adjustments to it; hence I would prefer now to speak of 'management of change', so as to imply that we ourselves by our decisions and actions create the future: we can be proactive, not merely adaptive. Secondly, 'controlling the boundary . . .' could sound negative, as if the impulses and fantasies of the inner world should be inhibited; whereas my concern is with making the most fruitful use of one's internal resources: some are appropriately held out of one situation and brought forward in another. Consequently, 'understanding and managing the boundary . . .' might be a better formulation. But these are clarifications and refinements: I remain committed to the essence of the earlier statement.

* SOURCE: Eric J. Miller, "Organizational Development and Industrial Democracy: A Current Case-Study," in *Organizational Development in the UK and USA: A Joint Evaluation*, ed. Carry L. Cooper (London: Macmillan, 1977), p. 33. Reprinted by permission of Macmillan.

[1] E. J. Miller and A. K. Rice, *Systems of Organization*, London: Tavistock, 1967, p. 269.